P9-DCM-892

ARGUMENTS AND DOCTRINES

By the same author

MARTIN BUBER
THE NATURAL AND THE SUPERNATURAL JEW
THE CARPENTER YEARS
THE MYTH OF THE JUDEO-CHRISTIAN TRADITION

Editor of

THE ANATOMY OF FAITH: THEOLOGICAL
ESSAYS OF MILTON STEINBERG
HUMANISTIC EDUCATION AND WESTERN CIVILIZATION

ARGUMENTS
AND
DOCTRINES

A READER OF
JEWISH THINKING
IN THE AFTERMATH
OF THE
HOLOCAUST

Selected with introductory essays by
ARTHUR A. COHEN

THE JEWISH PUBLICATION
SOCIETY OF AMERICA
5730 Philadelphia 1970
by arrangement with
HARPER & ROW, PUBLISHERS

ARGUMENTS AND DOCTRINES: A READER OF JEWISH THINKING IN THE
AFTERMATH OF THE HOLOCAUST

Copyright © *1970* by Arthur A. Cohen.

*All rights reserved. Printed in the United States of America. No part of this book
may be used or reproduced in any manner whatsoever without written permission except in the case of brief quotations embodied in critical articles and reviews. For information address Harper & Row, Publishers, Inc., 49 East 33rd
Street, New York, N.Y. 10016. Published simultaneously in Canada by Fitzhenry
& Whiteside Limited, Toronto.*

FIRST EDITION

LIBRARY OF CONGRESS CATALOG CARD NUMBER: 78–83589

FOR E. L. C. AND W. D. R.

CONTENTS

vii

Contents

PART FOUR
The Expectation and the Trust

ix

ACKNOWLEDGMENTS

Grateful acknowledgment is made for permission to reprint the following:

Harold Rosenberg, "Does the Jew Exist?" Reprinted from *Commentary,* by permission. Copyright © 1949 by the American Jewish Committee.

Hannah Arendt, "The Jew as Pariah," *Reconstructionist,* March 20, 1959, and April 3, 1959. Reprinted with the permission of the *Reconstructionist.*

Leslie Fiedler, "Simone Weil: Prophet Out of Israel." Reprinted from *Commentary,* by permission. Copyright © 1951 by the American Jewish Committee. Also by permission of the author.

Hans Meyerhof, "Contra Simone Weil." Reprinted from *Commentary,* by permission. Copyright © 1957 by the American Jewish Committee.

Nahum N. Glatzer, "Franz Kafka and the Tree of Knowledge." Reprinted from *Between East and West,* edited by Alexander Altmann, East and West Library, 1958, pp. 48–58. Reprinted with the permission of the author.

Will Herberg, "From Marxism to Judaism." Reprinted from *Commentary,* by permission. Copyright © 1947 by the American Jewish Committee.

J. L. Talmon, "Uniqueness and Universality of Jewish History." Reprinted from *Commentary*, by permission. Copyright © 1957 by the American Jewish Committee.

Erich Ungar, "Modern Judaism's Need for Philosophy." Reprinted from *Commentary*, by permission. Copyright © 1957 by the American Jewish Committee.

Lou H. Silberman, "Prophets and Philosophers," The Goldenson Lecture, Hebrew Union College Press, 1958. Reprinted with the permission of the author.

Arthur A. Cohen, "The Philosopher and the Jew," *Judaism*, Fall, 1962. Reprinted with the permission of the author.

Steven S. Schwarzschild, "To Recast Rationalism," *Judaism*, Summer, 1962. Reprinted, with slight revisions, with the permission of the author.

Monford Harris, "Interim Theology," *Judaism*, Fall, 1958. Reprinted with the permission of the author.

S. H. Bergman, "God and Man in Modern Jewish Thought," *Judaism*, Spring, 1957. Reprinted with the permission of the author.

Emil Fackenheim, "Self-Realization and the Search for God," *Judaism*, October, 1952. Reprinted with the permission of the author.

Emil Fackenheim, "Jewish Existence and the Living God," *Commentary* Magazine, August, 1959. Reprinted with the permission of the author.

Will Herberg, "The 'Chosenness' of Israel," *Midstream*, Autumn, 1955. Reprinted by permission of the author.

David Baumgardt, "Man's Morals and God's Will." Reprinted from *Commentary*, by permission. Copyright © 1950 by the American Jewish Committee.

Gershom Scholem, "Tradition and Commentary as Religious Categories," *Judaism*, Winter, 1966. Reprinted with the permission of Schocken Books, Inc., from a forthcoming volume to be published by Schocken Books, by Gershom G. Sholem. Copyright © 1969 by Schocken Books, Inc.

Acknowledgments

Baruch Kurzweil, "Job and the Possibility of Biblical Tragedy," *Iyyun*, October, 1961. Reprinted with the permission of *Iyyun* and the author. Translated from the Hebrew by David S. Segal.

Irving Kristol, "God and the Psychoanalysts." Reprinted from *Commentary*, by permission. Copyright © 1949 by the American Jewish Committee.

Ben Halpern, "Apologia Contra Rabbines," *Midstream*, Spring, 1956. Reprinted by permission of the author.

Ernst Simon, "Are We Israelis Still Jews?" Reprinted from *Commentary*, by permission. Copyright © 1953 by the American Jewish Committee.

Jacob Taubes, "The Issue Between Judaism and Christianity." Reprinted from *Commentary*, by permission. Copyright © 1953 by the American Jewish Committee.

Aharon Lictenstein, "Religion and State: The Case for Interaction," *Judaism*, Fall, 1966. Reprinted with the permission of the author.

Hans J. Schoeps, "How Live by Jewish Law Today?" Reprinted from *Commentary*, by permission. Copyright © 1953 by the American Jewish Committee.

Yehezkel Kaufmann, "The Pangs of Redemption" (*Hevlei Geulah*), *Exile and Alienage*, (*Golah v' Nechar*), Dvir Publishing Co., Tel Aviv, 1930, pp. 455–477. Published in translation with the permission of Dvir Publishing Co. Translated from the Hebrew by David S. Segal.

Erich Isaac, "Judaism and the Nations," *Judaism*, Fall, 1964. Reprinted with the permission of the author.

Steven S. Schwarzschild, "Personal Messiah" *Judaism*, Spring, 1956. Reprinted with the permission of the author.

INTRODUCTION

Most anthologies are constructed around a theme, but lack an attitude. This is no necessary defect, since an anthology is usually the documentation of the theme, presenting a conspectus of the movement, tradition, or idea to which it is devoted. The problems posed by this anthology required that the typical anthological principle of organization be altered, for there is no single Jewish religious thinking in the decades following the Holocaust and hence it would be unreliable to offer an anthology which concealed the persona of the anthologist. The anthologist usually sets forth the qualifications of his own interest, introducing the matrix of ideas, interpreting the general significance of the selections, validating his inclusions and exclusions, and then leaves the reader free to make up his own mind.

This anthology is inescapably more daring. In the period prior to the Second World War, the Judaism of crisis was more simplistic. The issues which engaged even the greatest of Jewish religious thinkers—and it was the period of the most significant intellectual productivity since the Jewish Middle Ages—was that of a Judaism polarized by Christianity (and anti-Semitism) and secular assimilation (and anti-Semitism). The common psychological denominator of the thought of Baeck, Cohen, Rosenzweig, Buber, and the numerous secondary satellites of Germany, Czechoslovakia, and Austria was Jewish *ressentiment,* Jews in alienation from historical

Judaism. The mechanism of alienation was always set in motion against a background of lethargy and anger aggravated by the social and intellectual anti-Semitism of European culture. The initial task of the prewar Jewish thinkers was to validate the Jewish enterprise, to make a denationalized, cosmopolitan, culturally productive elite into an authentic community. Regardless of the differences in method which the theologians we have mentioned employed, their first concern was to demonstrate that a viable Jewish existence was meaningful, that it contained the requisite ingredients which justified the attention of otherwise indifferent, but intellectually creative, Jews. Indeed, for Rosenzweig and Buber, the relation between the creative God and the vitalities of the person constituted a central ontological preoccupation of their thinking, but involved a no less rhetorical appeal. There was no question, however, but that prewar European Jewish thinking recognized that religious Judaism, classical Judaism, the Judaism of Bible and tradition had to be smuggled back into the armamentarium of the Jew. They were concerned to make Judaism relevant to a Jew who no longer believed that either the Jew or Judaism had a significant future or could endure one if it had.

The war and its aftermath, while augmenting certain confusions, dissolved others. Although individual Jews may now opt to disappear (the realm of free choice having been widened by the era of toleration inaugurated by the bad conscience of the postwar West), the State of Israel has made it clear that Jews as a whole will not disappear (or at least will not disappear as six million fellow Jews disappeared). One consequence of this continuum from the freedom of the individual Jew to the destiny of the Jewish community is that Jewish religion has become inescapably personalist in character. The Jew is no longer held together in the Diaspora by the Law imposed or the authoritarianism of the community, for the normative Jewish community—both secular and religious—is in Israel. The Jewish communities of the Diaspora, particularly in America, are personalist and fideist, and not generally *halakhic*. Jews return to the Synagogue less to affirm their solidarity against an inhospitable environment (for the environment is no longer inhospitable), nor do they return because they accept the givenness of the law and the Teaching and have resolved, in some mysterious *teshuvah*, to repent and to do. What seems ever more apparent is that the return of the third generation of American Jews to the Synagogue is motivated by an uninstructed quest for life meaning and the conviction that the Synagogue possesses or should posses a body of relevant insight and instruction. They do not return to pray, but to listen, not to do *mitzvot*, but to learn of them. It is a more speculative, and hence more tentative, serious, uncommitted, and intense preoccupation than the earlier generations of American Jewry, when Jews were traditional because their parents were, or Reform because their parents were assimilated, or secularist and antireligious because their heritage was Socialist, culturalist, Yiddishist, or Zionist. The old alliances have broken down, and the old reasons for coming into the religious community or staying away have disappeared.

The new Jewish religious community is resurgent because all the reasons for escape have disappeared. In place of anguish and embarrassment, there is a renascent pride. Whether that pride is founded upon ethnocentrism, or the admiration of a powerful and militant Israel *redivivus,* or the brandishing of the sword of guilt and anger over a culpable non-Jewish world, no matter, for the fact remains that the Jews who survived the Holocaust or lived through the era of the Holocaust have learned a decisive human category: human beings died because they were thought to represent an alien meaning, because they, in fact, did represent a believed meaning, and because they transmitted the value of that meaning. Instead of Judaism's being a principle of cohesion and communality, it is for those Jews come lately to learn in the Synagogue a source of meaning.

Viktor Frankl, the Viennese psychoanalyst whose reflections on his years in the concentration camps, *From Death Camp to Existentialism,* set forth the rudiments of his doctrine of logotherapy, makes as the central principle of his psychotherapy the search for meaning. Meaning is indispensable to life, and the sense of meaninglessness kills. If anything, Judaism as a religion of life is the search for meaning. Sometimes the meanings seem opprobrious and irrational; sometimes they are brutally realistic and unsentimental about the human condition; often they are astringently rational or magnificently rich with feeling, but always the meanings are ordered to an end. The end of Judaism is that man and nature be raised up to the God who formed them.

The search for meanings in Judaism, Jewish existence, and the Jewish People is the intention of this anthology. But since the task is ongoing and the issues alive, all the essays in this volume are themselves in passage. They are not closed either by authority or scholarship to question. They are open precisely because they open up the realities of Jewish existence. I have felt free, therefore, to comment upon each of them, to gloss them by suggesting my caveats or my endorsements, to make of them a personal document for myself and by implication for the reader. These essays are selected, not because they are necessarily the best or the only statement of the point of view they reflect, but because they are deeply felt and strongly argued, because they are suggestive and allusive, because they form a continuum from the beginning to the end, from the analytical-skeptical essay of Harold Rosenberg with which the volume opens to the Messianic enthusiasm of Steven Schwarzschild with which it closes. Many Jewish writers of note and importance are omitted either because quite frankly I did not know an essay which was appropriate or because the position they represented seemed too closely tied to an institutional alliance. Thus what is offered is a tension, an argument, a dialectic of unfolding in which all the essays have become part of me and I have given myself into each of the essays. It is a selection which is personal, but not subjective, since the reasons for adopting the essay and locating it where it stands in the volume are explicated and defined. If you will, as anthologist, I have gone on record. This anthology is one to be argued with and argued from, to be used as a medium of platform or argumentation; not as a last word, but as an instrument of teaching and learning; and certainly not as a statement of *the* doctrine to be taught or learned.

Arthur A. Cohen
November 29, 1968

PART ONE

THE FOREGROUND OF JEWISH EXISTENCE

INTRODUCTION TO

DOES THE JEW EXIST?

Harold Rosenberg

The hypostatic Jew does not exist. To fabricate the Jew is possible: to construct fictions which distil his essence is a continuous preoccupation of the Western tradition. The Biblical tradition hardly spoke of Jews, although it cared profoundly for the People of Israel, that motley collective which had obligations and duties, affections and disaffections from its assumptive Lord and King. Jews were never a problem to themselves. They were a perplexity to God and his prophets, but never a problem. The Jews have only been a problem to non-Jews. Unfortunately millennia of Gentile discomfort with the Jew (and any discomfort exacerbated by continuous abrasion becomes a suppurating boil) has produced a tragic mirror reaction.

The distortions and mythologies of anti-Semitism, already familiar to the pre-Christian ancient world, were endlessly elaborated and refined by centuries of Christian anger at Jewish intransigence before what is believed to have been the historical fulfillment and spiritual redemption of the Jewish People in Jesus Christ. No need to rehearse this further; it has been done countless times in countless books (the hollow chest resounds to the thump of *mea culpas*). At the same time, however, that Christianity institutionalized the teaching of anti-Semitism (supplying it with an ideological foundation as well as juridical mechanism of effectuation), the Jew remained quite as insouciant as before. Although the Rabbis of the Talmud were fully aware that the Jews had become a problem

3

(they had always been, but not as Jews, only as theologoumenon) to the non-Jews and that proselytizers and lapsed converts had become a painful aggravation to them, Jews were not yet problems to themselves. The erosion of identity takes time. A people as solidly integral as were the People of Israel do not undergo the crisis of identity immediately. The epidermis of the psyche needs to be pierced and bruised for centuries before the pain affects its deepest recesses. That has been accomplished, most profoundly, most effectively, most totally in the modern era. The Jew is now psychically habituated to anti-Semitism; moreover, he is psychically habituated to his own anti-Semitism.

It is to the monstrosity of Jewish anti-Semitism that Jean-Paul Sartre in fact directed his *Réflexions sur la Question Juive* (1946: translated as *Anti-Semite and Jew,* Schocken Books, 1948). Ostensibly Sartre's essay is an existential-phenomenological inquiry into the mechanism of anti-Semitism—the modes of the psyche which define and systematize the irrational energies and passions of anti-Semitism. It would appear that Sartre is defending the Jew against his enemies by submitting the intellectual and emotional life of the anti-Semite to the devastation of public exposure. This is only a half-truth, for Sartre is resolutely ambivalent. On the one hand he refutes the inauthenticity of the anti-Semite, his refusal to recognize that he manipulates the Jew in order to mask his own inadequacies. And yet equally and consistently the Jew who does not succumb to the strictures of Sartre's inverted theology of Jewish "nothingness" is equally inauthentic. The Jew who enters the culture of the West and forms it is inauthentic to his situation as much as the Jew who is Zionist, religious, ethnically rooted.

Harold Rosenberg's essay, in analysis of and riposte to Sartre, is particularly relevant to this post-Holocaust era for Rosenberg has to my mind brilliantly identified the unarticulated presupposition of Sartre's ambivalence. Sartre, philosophic descendant of the phenomenologist Edmund Husserl (another inauthentic Jew, presumably), can penetrate a human situation only if it has been stripped bare of cloudy presuppositions, bracketed off from historical, psychological, environmental conditions which impose structure and thereby prejudice the lucid consciousness which Sartre regards as the metaphysical precondition to authenticity. And, clearly enough, the only moment in modern Jewish history in which the Jew was forced to choose himself, independently of the subtle valences and

4

pressures of society, was when the Jew was in the concentration camp. Where there is no exit, *there* is the beginning of choice. When all doors are shut and man is left in the darkness of his own solitariness—*then* he can choose. It is a grotesque doctrine which makes wisdom out of criminal bestiality, but then even engaged philosophers take their models where they find them. Clearly Sartre is not interested in the Jew; he is interested in exemplifications of doctrine and the construct of the divested Jew, stripped bare of all presuppositions, imprisoned in hell. The Jew is become an archetype. Rosenberg says it all. It need not be elaborated by me other than to underscore its significance for us now.

The double merit of Harold Rosenberg's critique is that he is himself Jewish intellectual, intellectual and Jew, engaged as Jewish man, deracinated as Jew, precisely all those commitments and distances which are for Sartre the condition of the inauthentic Jew. What echoes from his analysis is not simply a genuine warmth and affection for the Jewish People, but a recognition that in our time the Jew has endured beyond the People, that the Jewish man, the individual, solitary, passionately engaged Jew can no longer rely on the People, the History, the Ancestry to protect him. He stands alone, as an individual, and makes his way in the world—authentic, inauthentic, but ineffaceably a Jew among Jews, a Jew among the millions of mankind.

DOES THE JEW EXIST?

Sartre's Morality Play about Anti-Semitism

HAROLD ROSENBERG

Eternity changes him into himself.
Mallarmé

In considering Sartre's conception of the Jew and his relation to anti-Semitism we must not forget that *Reflections on the Jewish Question* was written immediately after the downfall of the Nazis. It was a moment of intense confusion as to the meaning of the terrible events that had just taken place and of uncertainty as to the attitudes and groupings that would now emerge in liberated France. The Occupation had enlivened the current of anti-Semitism among Frenchmen of all classes. With the return of those Jews who had escaped the German hangman everyone was most anxious that this "question" should not once more stir up hidden rancors. Thus, as Sartre tells us, in the midst of the general greeting of returned prisoners and deportees not a word about the Jews, for fear of irritating the Anti-Semites. This testimony is supported by André Spire's account, in his preface to *Bilan Juif,* of the difficulties experienced in finding a publisher in Paris by those who wished to speak of what had happened. "There has been too much hate," they were told. "Let's have a love story."

Under such circumstances for Sartre to have challenged the anti-Semite as a menace to Frenchmen, to have called upon Gentiles to organize in a war on anti-Semitism, and to have welcomed the French Jews into the French nation was an act of generosity, of feeling, courage, and good sense. With different shadings of collaborationists and supporters of the Resistance bitterly eyeing one another, no opportunist or politician calculating the advantages to be derived from attracting segments of public opinion would have *isolated* the question of anti-Semitism. Yet here was the ultimate poison of the mind from which many social contaminations had flowed and could still be expected to flow. The Dreyfus Affair had permanently established the role of anti-Semitism in all conspiracies against the French people. Precisely because it might have been bad politics at this instant to launch an assault against the slanderers and murderers of Jews, it was sound patriotism and a gesture of human solidarity.

So as an *act* performed in a given circumstance we ought wholly to applaud Sartre's *Réflexions sur la Question Juive*. With its three characters—the vicious leering psychopathic anti-Semite, the "inauthentic" Jew vainly trying to escape in disguise, and the "authentic" Jew proudly turning upon his tormentors—one can consider the work in its original appearance as a kind of twentieth-century morality play sent to do service at a political battle front. Anyone coming upon it should have been stirred to greater effort against the enemy and against the traitor in himself.

Reading Sartre's essay in America at the present moment is, however, a somewhat different matter. Not that the battle against anti-Semitism is over, of course. But Sartre's study cannot play the same part in it at this date and in this country. Hence we are not tempted to ask, "Is it useful?" rather than, "Is it true?" Although still attracted by the magnanimity of Sartre's act, we can scutinize dispassionately his image both of the Jew and of the anti-Semite.

For Sartre the Jew exists. The Jewishness of the Jew is not merely, as with the democratic thinkers, a few ethnic, religious, and physical traits added to a *man*. In dissociating himself from liberal rationalism and its abstract man, Sartre asserts the reality of the Jewish identity as a "concrete synthesis" created by history. There is, in short, THE JEW, not only men and women who happen to be Jewish. With this conclusion, "unscientific" as it may appear, it is necessary, I believe, to agree. In fact, the best passage for me in Sartre's essay is his criticism of the democratic defender of the Jew, for whom all men are essentially alike, for whom the Jew can belong to human society only to the extent that he suppresses himself as a Jew, and for whom the assertion by Jews of Jewish difference is a sign of stubbornness, backwardness, or ill will. The liberal-scientific concept of the human being, and the demands for uniformity that go with it, somehow seemed sounder while plans for a universal society were on the order of the day. We would have been willing to lose ourselves as we were for the sake of the men we might have become.

The dream of eliminating all inherited differences among peoples has proven, however, to be Utopian, and not only not possible but not even desirable as a program. Has not democratic universalism meant in practice not a society of man but the absorption of small nations and minorities into large ones, even if with full equality and freedom? Theoretically, the democrat is for the assimilation of all nations into man in general; actually, man turns out to be the American, the Englishman, the Frenchman, the Russian. As soon as concrete questions of the language, the mores, the style of the future One World are raised, the difficulties involved in universalism become visible. Sartre is justified in beginning with these difficulties, with the concrete historical "syntheses" represented by nations, peoples, cultures. The Jewish question centers on the fact of Jewish difference.

Yet Sartre's recognition of the Jewish fact does not take him beyond the democratic conception of the big nation assimilating minorities. For in the end he, too, wishes to dissolve the Jewish collective identity into its abstract particles, that is, into men made more human by ceasing to be Jews. He wants the French Jew to become a Frenchman, as the democrats do. Sartre differs from the democrats only in falling short of the idealism of their theory of man which seeks the ultimate homegeneity of human beings. Though he comes out for socialism he does not say a word about dissolving the French identity. For Sartre it is enough that *the Jews* should be assimilated.

This exceptionalism he maintains on the grounds of the peculiar nature of the Jewish identity, that the Jews "have no history" and are but the wretched creatures of anti-Semitism. We shall take up this characterization shortly. Here let us note that Sartre offers us much less than the liberals. For it makes sense that the Jews should assimilate into *man* (though it makes sense only as a theroy) . But why, especially for a Socialist, should the Jew look forward to becoming a *Frenchman?* Even if, as Sartre says, "bit by bit and by the very course of history." The Frenchman himself, from the Socialist point of view, should look forward to becoming something else, through, to use Sartre's term, "choosing himself" as a European or as a socialist.

After all, the democrat is really not unaware that the Jews exist. He simply does not believe that they *have* to exist as Jews. He believes that by changing their situation, by creating a situation common to all men, the Jews, together with all peoples, will shed their particularities "bit by bit." Sartre, like the liberal, anticipates that with social improvement both the Jew and the anti-Semite will be eliminated, but he does not anticipate that the Frenchman will be eliminated. Thus what Sartre calls "concrete liberalism" is nothing else than liberalism that has discarded its abstract theory of man and embraced its nationalist reality, the Frenchman, the American, the Englishman, though with an ideology of good will. It leads Sartre to a nationalist socialism in which the democratic ideal of a free, equitable, and united community is conceived as realizable within the confines of the old national state. But in such a socialism, at least as much as among the liberals criticized by Sartre, the Jew as Jew is felt to be an obstacle inherited from the past—as we see among certain British Socialists—and the sooner he liquidates himself into the larger "whole" the better.

It seems to Sartre that all Jews wish to disappear into the nations in which they live and would do so were they not prevented by anti-Semitism: "the authentic Jew . . . is not opposed to assimilation." No doubt many Jews agree that if there were no anti-Semitism there would be no Jews. They reason as follows: Political freedom and social opportunities for the Jews have gone hand in hand with enlightenment; enlightenment has brought assimilation. The flight from Judaism has been stopped only by persecution and discrimination. Hence it is a "law" of history that the perfection of liberty and enlightenment will see the end of the Jews. If that were the case, Sartre, regardless of the validity of his arguments, would have gotten to the heart of the matter.

The fault in this reasoning is that it links the process of assimilation with one aspect of the situation in the free Western countries during the past one hundred fifty years—their liberalism—but not with its other aspects—their racial and national prejudice. The conditions under which minorities like the Jews have tended to merge into the cultures around them have not been those of complete freedom and equality but of partial liberty and limited equality. Even in the most liberal democracies, where the greatest

9

opportunities for merging have been available, prejudice against "aliens" has never ceased to exist. To overcome handicaps, Poles, Irishmen, Italians, Ukrainians, Jews have desired in various countries to lose their identifying marks. The drive to assimilation, in short, represents reaction to pressures exercised by a more powerful culture at least as much as it does to liberty and enlightenment.

Jewish assimilation of the past century belongs to transitional conditions of partial freedom and partial enlightenment. No "law" of assimilation can be deduced from this experience. We have no historical proof that in a completely free world the Jews, or any other minority, would choose to dissolve itself. We have equal grounds to assume that in such a world every group, regional or cultural, would find no opposition between its interest in itself and its past and its interest in the rest of mankind. Just as the individual would remain interested in himself, his history, and his development and not feel forced to "assimilate" his uniqueness into an overpowering environment. The assimilationism of Jews in France thus provides no basis for Sartre's thesis that the Jew wants to get rid of his Jewishness.

The Jew exists, says Sartre, but he exists in a mirror. "It is the anti-Semite who creates the Jew." The entire life of the Jew, his innermost sentiment of self as well as his relations to other men, is made of the substance of the anti-Semite's glare. In himself and for himself the Jew is nothing: he is "one whom other men consider a Jew."

To establish this anti-Semitic "being" of the Jew, Sartre relies on the theory that a man "cannot be distinguished from his situation." If we look at the situation of the Jew we see only the anti-Semite and the victim of his peculiar hatred. For the Jew today, Sartre insists, can point to no historical identity save that springing from anti-Semitism.

Let us analyze this method of defining the Jew. "If I wish to know *who* the Jew is," says Sartre, "I must first inquire into the situation surrounding him, since he is a being in a situation" (his italics). This could imply that human identity can be deduced from "environment." To know a Flemish miner I would study his work and conditions and the landscape in which he lives, etc.; the same for a Parisian novelist. But such an approach, defining human reality by external factors, would be frankly mechanistic, and Sartre rejects mechanism. For him the individual and his situation "form a synthetic whole" not in the sense of deriving the man from the situation but in that the man is a *free actor* within it. To know the situation means for Sartre also to know the "being" in it, whether one's own or another's. To know "who the Jew is," we have been told, we have to inquire into his situation, but to know his situation we have to inquire who the Jew is.

Sartre breaks out of this circle by adopting in practice the externality which he rejects in theory, just as he adopts the conclusion of liberalism whose philosophy of man he criticizes. His Jew, though he "makes himself" by his choices, has his being given by his environment, defined as the immovable scrutiny of the anti-Semite. But Sartre's externality is more limited than that of the materialists. Besides anti-Semitism the latter would include in the situation of the Jew various developments of modern history: the Industrial Revolution, the breakup of the old communities, the decline of church and family, the establishment of cosmopolitan cultures. They would recognize that to the extent that the modern Jew is the product of other men, the democrat too has "created" him by *his* glance. Sartre refers to such factors only as explanations for various unpleasant "Jewish traits." The self of the Jew he defines *demoniacally* as formed by anti-Semitism, which to Sartre is a free, autonomous, uncaused, disembodied, and measureless spirit of evil.

If the situation is to reveal the "who" of the man in it, its dimensions must extend to his beginnings. For instance, the situation of Oedipus at the opening of Sophocles' tragedy does not tell us who Oedipus is. Here the situation, which includes the present and a limited portion of the past but stops short of Oedipus' origins, *conceals* the identity of the hero. If, following Sartre, I were "to inquire into the situation surrounding him," I should learn that King Oedipus is the son of Polybus and that he is now "choosing" with respect to the plague in Thebes. This knowledge of the situation would cause me to be mistaken as to Oedipus' identity, as it would prevent Oedipus from "choosing himself." My ignorance could not be overcome until the situation, which now proves Oedipus to be another, had been changed into one that reveals the content of the moment when Oedipus came into the world. *In brief, a man is not always knowable through his situation.* The situation will form a genuine "synthetic whole" with the individual in it only when the fact *originating his identity*—that Oedipus is the son of Laius and Jocasta—becomes a visible part of it.

The situation of the Jew does not reveal who the Jew is except when it becomes a situation that discloses his link with Abraham, Moses, and David, from whom the Jewish identity sprang. Such a revealing situation has come into being during the various movements to regain the Land of the Fathers, whether by prayer or politics. In these moments—and with the Orthodox Jew the "moment" has lasted for two thousand years, since his constant prayer is a continuing act directed toward redeeming the Land—the Jew and his situation are indeed one.

Sartre fails to consider the Jew and his situation in relation to his beginnings. He splits his "being" in time and in place. "It is the Christians," he says, "who have created the Jew." The opposite is, of course, the case: the Jews created Christianity. But Sartre has cut the Jews off from their past; he even thinks it possible to speak of the Jews while "limiting my description to the Jews in France." If, nevertheless, the Jew's historical feet still protrude from under the blanket of the situation with which Sartre has "surrounded" him, Sartre has misunderstood fundamentally the problem of identity. It is surely not enough simply to state that the Jews of the Exile are in a different predicament from those who "at a remote time in the past [possessed] a religious and historical community that was called Israel." The position in the world of King Oedipus of Thebes differed entirely from that of the infant exposed on the mountain—yet he was the same individual. To show that the origin of the Jew lies not in Abraham but in the anti-Semite, Sartre would have to indicate *at what point* the Jew of former times ceased to exist and a different Jew was born out of anti-Semitism. It was not when they were driven out by the Romans, for Sartre himself asserts that the Christian created the Jew "by putting a stop to his assimilation"—in other words, that the act of the Christians was a negative one and that even in the Diaspora the original Jews existed.

Thus Sartre's argument that the Jews of the Exile are disconnected from the Jews of antiquity rests entirely on external considerations; they no longer live in the same place, perform the same rites, possess the same institutions. But the continuity of the modern Jew with the Jews of the Old Testament is established by those acts that arise from his internal cohesion with his ultimate beginnings, in which his future is contained as possible destiny—the acts of turning toward the Promised Land in his crises. And these acts, not

12

deducible from his surroundings, *make* the Jew's situation and reveal who the Jew is.

Having mistaken the Jew's identity, Sartre cannot comprehend *his* history, *his* creative accomplishments, *his* possibilities. Measureing the Jews by general standards of ethnic uniformity, sovereignty, and church-going, he finds that the Jews are not a people or a race (or that belonging to this "race" means "a hooked nose, protruding ears, thick lips"), not a nation, not a religion. From this he concludes that "the sole tie that binds them is the hostility and disdain of the societies that surround them." The Jews, says Sartre, "have no history . . . twenty centuries of dispersion and political impotence forbids its [the Jewish community's] having a *historic past*" (his italics).

What is the conception of history that excludes the Jews from possessing a historic past? Sartre refers to Hegel's idea that "a community is historical to the degree that it remembers its past." Obviously, *remembering* is not something that can be "forbidden" by "dispersion and political impotence." What can be forbidden is that this remembered past should be "historical" in the nationalist sense of civil rebellions and wars. That this is precisely what Sartre means by a historic past becomes plain when he adds to Hegel's dictum, "the Jewish community is the least historical of all, for it keeps a memory of nothing but a long martyrdom, that is, of a long passivity." The Jews, of course, remember many things besides martyrdom, and even in that relation they may recall not passivity but resistance; for instance, the dialectical battles of the rabbis against the overwhelming power of the medieval Church. But they were not able to resort to arms, and on this score alone can Sartre deny them a history.

Only if warfare is the essence of the historical is the memory of the Jew during the past two thousand years without historical quality. Is not this period of Exile, with its hopes, coherent with earlier exiles, previous redemptions? The entire story of the Jew—*including the movements toward assimilation that form part of it from the beginning*—has an inner meaning and a structure that would seem to make it history *par excellence.* To such an extent is the Jew identified by the story he remembers, that political and social institutions, linguistic and somatic characteristics, even religious beliefs and practices appear superficial to the common autobiography: these may change, through the uniqueness of his tale the Jew remains himself. In fact, history is the burden under which the Jew all but breaks.

The common story of the Jews and not "the hostility and disdain" of others is the principle of their togetherness. That each member of a group has the same story to tell, which is the story of all as well as the story of the teller, is the basis of collective identities, whether it be the story of the miraculous founding of a cult or of the exploitation and struggles of the proletariat. This story alive in the individual may not make itself manifest in his behavior except in peculiar circumstances, perhaps even to his surprise, for no man acts "historically" all the time. The Jews have shown that without being a race, a nation, or a religion, it is possible for people to remain together in a net of memory and expectation.

It is because of his presumed lack of history that the French Jew is to become a good Frenchman. "We have only to welcome him without reserve; our history will be his history, or at least his son's." The motive is no doubt laudable. But to say that the Jew has no history in comparison with the French *worker*—for to Sartre only a socialist France will truly absorb the Jews—is to create a nationalist confusion with respect to the history of both the Jews and of France.

Each community has a common story, beginning in an event—a revolution, a conquest, a miracle, the founding of a city—which gave birth to its identity, creating it, so to speak, out of nothingness. The Jews differ from other peoples, both ancient and modern, in that every Jew, regardless of class or even of blood origin, is included equally in the entire common account. Whether he begins with himself as a French Jew, an American, a Pole, a Turk, or as worker, scholar or millionaire, the Jew who extends his story backwards in time reaches the same substance of events converging into the Old Testament and its lucid geography of his childhood. The survival of the Jews may well be attributable to this "democratic" participation in the Jewish past which appears in the earliest Biblical situations and which was immeasurably strengthened by the prophets. The peasants and the urban proletariat of Greece and Rome were not, and could not remain, the vessels of ancient Greek or Roman history, which was created above them and to their exclusion by aristocrats and heroes. With the decline of their élites those historic identities disappeared. Each Jew, however, possessing from the first the equal status of a member of a clan, could call himself by the primary name of Son of Abraham and preserve the whole in his single existence. In this respect the history of the Jews resembles that of a religion, in which all believers have the same status, more than it does the history of nations. The vision that sees the Jews as "a nation of priests and a holy people" stresses this totality equivalent to the religious. Yet Jewish history is the history of a people, not of a cult, since the participation is not metaphysical but in an actual past.

It is likely that there are Jews in France who feel that they have no history, except a history of persecution. But if such sentiments exist among Jews they give no support to Sartre's "no-history" thesis, since he is not attempting to derive his definition of the Jew from what the Jews feel about themselves but from their situation. Besides, not all Jews even in post-Vichy France regard Jewish history as a prison sentence that is not yet over. The various contributors to *Bilan Juif,* referred to above, are witnesses that very lively and positive conceptions of the Jewish past exist in France today.

Jewish history belongs to all Jews; most Frenchmen possess only a portion of theirs—at least, so a Socialist should insist. This implies no advantage—perhaps the less history the better. At any rate, French history as the history of the worker goes back only to 1789. At that point another France appears, in the story of which he has no part. The French worker cannot hear the story of aristocratic France, its court, its clergy, its great men, without recognizing his own anonymity in it. From the Revolution backwards he has lost his identity—he does not embody the France of feudalism. He cannot say as Roosevelt did: "Let us not forget that we are all descendants from revolutionaries and poor immigrants." The ultra-nationalist and anti-Semite attempts to bridge the subjective gap between the two Frances, of before and after 1789. Even putting aside Marx's contention that "the workers have no fatherland," Sartre should be concerned as a Socialist with denying history to the French workingman or with limiting it to the France of the Revolution. Instead, it is of the French Jews that he makes the unfounded and brutal observation: "These are Frenchmen who have no part in the history of France."

To reinforce his notion that anti-Semitism provides the exclusive content of Jewishness, Sartre claims that the Jews "cannot take pride in any collective work that is specifically Jewish." If he means a national style of architecture or of painting, he is undoubtedly correct. If he means a Jewish post-office system or a Jewish army, he *was* correct. There is, of course, a fairly large literature that is "specifically Jewish," and the world is becoming increasingly aware of Jewish philosophical and mystical thinking throughout the centuries. Sartre is either ignorant of, or indifferent to, this. I shall, therefore, mention one collective work of which he must be aware— I mean the Jewish creation of a unique type of human being, the "Jewish intellectual," who springs from the tradition of *talmid hacham*, the lifelong student. For two thousand years the main energies of Jewish communities in various parts of the world have gone into the mass production of intellectuals. From among these have emerged several noble traditional figures: the pure-minded judge, the scholarly man of affairs, the poverty-loving saint. I estimate this enterprise of the Jews to be as civilized and "historical" as the catching of herring to which the Dutch devoted themselves in their great period, or the processing of cotton by the British. True, the Jewish output of intellectuals was not a "planned" project and often resulted in surpluses. This occurs in any one-crop or one-product economy, and peanut growers or pottery makers then experience a crisis. When the Jews began to "export" their major commodity in the nineteenth century, they found themselves competing against "home products." While this is, of course, not all there is to modern anti-Semitism, its peculiarly odious form of "protectionism" attests to "the collective work that is specifically Jewish."

The unique "culture heroes" created by Jewish communities continue to live in the imagination and memories of individual Jews. They play their part in that "mystical and prelogical feeling of kinship" among Jews which to Sartre is but a reaction to a common history of humiliation. If the Western Jew is, as Sartre claims, a "haunted man" (the term is rather melodramatic), whose life is doubled by self-disguise and self-scrutiny, it is not by the opaque eye of the anti-Semite that he has been haunted but by the sweetness and metaphysical security of his sages and by the sense of treachery and degradation that overcomes him when he decides to renounce such grandfathers.

The Jew, Sartre maintains, having no original existence, has his identity to create. He will "make" himself by his choices in his present anti-Semitic situation. The Jew can either consciously become what this situation demands that he be and, "accepting it in pride and humiliation," attain "authenticity." Or he can strive, futilely, to evade his situation and make himself "inauthentic."

In that it seems to offer us a clear choice in dealing with anti-Semitism—to stand our ground come what may, or waste our lives in fruitless ruses of disguise and escape—Sartre's formulation has a tonic quality. The lens of the anti-Semite is permanently trained upon us, it will not allow us to be anything but Jews. We cannot dare to pretend that it is not there; we must decide how we shall behave under this scrutiny.

Were "authentic" and "inauthentic" simply different ways of confronting anti-Semitism, we could have no objection. But Sartre *is not offering a choice in action.* In fact, he feels that the Jew can do little about anti-Semitism, and in general "his situation is such that everything he does turns against him." What is left to the Jew is the choice of *being* "authentic," that is, of accepting himself as the creature of anti-Semitism and nothing else. Let this be clear—not choosing to *do* but choosing to *be*. Nor is it to be Orthodox or a Zionist or openly a Jew in any specific manner. It means ceasing voluntarily to be a man: "the authentic Jew *makes himself a Jew* in the face of all and against all" (his italics). He proudly becomes what the anti-Semite says he is, for "he knows himself and wills himself into history as a historic and damned creature." Not only does he accept the hatred and disgust of his neighbors; he makes himself what they hate and despise.

Naturally, most Jews reject this choice. Some write philosophical works like Bergson, novels like Proust, create mathematical theories like Einstein—in a word, they behave as if they were men in a world, not reflections in the glass of anti-Semitism. According to Sartre, such gestures of belonging to the human race render them "inauthentic." They amount to falsifying their natures and "being ashamed of their own kind." These Jews develop the characteristics of people who are permanently in flight from the truth and from themselves. Sartre's inauthentic Jew is a quivering, self-conscious creature, anxiously hiding his inescapable Jewishness or masochistically embracing it as degradation. This Jew is a rationalist without intuitions or spontaneity; he is tactless, acquisitive, denies his very body, etc. Sartre is careful to tell us that it is only the "inauthentic" Jew that he has thus portrayed. But it turns out that this painful and, in large part, repulsive figure is none other than *the* Jew, because very few people are authentic and those that are contribute

17

nothing to Sartre's image, since, as he tells us, the authentic man "escapes description."

In short, on the basis of his authentic-inauthentic conception, Sartre has consciously permitted himself to accept the anti-Semite's stereotype of the Jew. His disagreement with anti-Semitism reduces itself to arguing that these Jewish traits which he enumerates are not so bad; besides, not the Jew himself but the anti-Semite is responsible for the Jew and his character. Though about this responsibility for the Jew he is not altogether certain, since it seems to him that it was "by taking advantage of certain aspects of the conduct of inauthentic Jews that the anti-Semite has forged his general mythology of the Jew." If this is the case, the behavior of Jews, of most Jews, provides the material for the anti-Semitic caricature.

The fallacy in Sartre's notion of "authentic" and "inauthentic," which results in such profound distortions, may be traced to his erroneous conception of a "situation." "Authenticity," Sartre tells us, "consists in having a true and lucid consciousness of the situation, in assuming the responsibilities and risks involved, in accepting it in pride and humiliation, sometimes in horror and hate." Can one have a "true and lucid consciousness" of his situation? Only if "situation" is defined in terms of external relations. I can be conscious that I am an American, a Jew, a husband, a father. But to Sartre, one's self is part of the situation. Therefore, to know my situation I must know myself. I must have solved the Socratic problem. But if we Jews strove to arrive at such a consciousness of our situation and of ourselves we should surely develop that "almost continuously reflective attitude" which for Sartre is "the first trait" of the inauthentic Jew. If like Socrates, Pascal, Hamlet, Kierkegaard, we really attempted to reach a "true and lucid consciousness" of ourselves, we should not attain to authenticity at all but merely demonstrate to Sartre that we are inauthentic Jews.

Here again Sartre, attempting to leap from instrumentalism to subjectivity, falls into an abyss. The choice between being authentic or inauthentic has to do not with any specific historical or social condition in which one may find oneself but with one's metaphysical situation, with the fact of being alive as a unique individual. In the particular situation we cannot *choose* ourselves, since our action in it is the means by which we *discover* ourselves. Could Oedipus, while still unconscious of his origin, have chosen himself and achieved authenticity by "assuming the risks and responsibilities" of his situation as king, father, husband? The distinction between choosing to be oneself and choosing not to be oneself was made by Kierkegaard. But to Kierkegaard, both to choose to be oneself and to choose not to be oneself are *forms of despair,* not of authenticity and inauthenticity. The Jew who wills to make himself nothing-but-a-Jew (and, according to Sartre, as a Jew nothing) does not thereby become more authentic than the Jew who wills not to be a Jew. Both have taken the way of despair, since they have willed to transform themselves from what they are, as given, into what they conceive the situation to demand them to be. They are guilty of the Sartrian fallacy of imagining that they have a total knowledge of the situation and can, therefore, like God, create the "being" in it.

There *is* a situation in which a man's choices appear to "make" him entirely, instead of altering what was given by his origin and his past: the concentration-camp situation. Sartre's categories of authentic and inauthentic apply to the concentration-camp victim. He has been deprived of his identity; his entire past has been wiped out; he was born again "in horror and hate" upon the closing of the gate. Starting in nothingness, he will make himself by his choices in his situation, of which he can have a "true and lucid consciousness," since its limits and those of his existence in it are visible from moment to moment. The prisoner, the pure human Nobody, is restricted to authentic and inauthentic, an adjective without a noun.

This concentration-camp vision of beginning one's life anew within a situation imposed by others is primary in Sartre's metaphysics. It has a traumatic fixity in him; it also inspires him. I suspect it came upon him with the force of a religious conversion during the Occupation. It is *the* Sartrian situation, decorated with a "no-exit" sign, and inhabited not by "concrete syntheses" but by the watched and the watchers, the prisoners and the guards.

Sartre's Jew is a personification of the man in the camp, and it is as a concentration-camp drama that his study of the Jew hangs together. First appears the anti-Semite, murderous lord of a "total" world.[1] Even when he does not kill outright, his ultimate intent is

---

[1]. For all his viciousness and "mediocrity," Sartre's anti-Semite is more human than his Jew. True, the anti-Semite is "inauthentic," in that instead of a true consciousness of his situation he interprets his miseries as caused by Jewish malevolence. Yet he is a man of passionate conviction and has the glamor and

to slay. His victim, the Jew, like the concentration-camp prisoner, has no history because he was cut off from it; he is nothing but what his guards have made of him. His life is a choice between trying to hide this fact from himself through philosophizing or dreaming or making plans like other men—or consciously confronting the situation and the existence that the camp has imposed upon him. It is peculiar to Sartre's philosophy that the latter choice means to recover one's humanity and one's "freedom" in the very degradation which he accepts. But free or not, the Jew will not alter his fate by becoming "authentic"; his situation "is such that everything he does turns against him." Nor will authenticity establish for him any connection with the "outside" world of humanity: his choice must be "in the face of all and against all." For the point is that there is no Jew on this side of the walls where human beings dwell. The sole Jewish fact is the camp of the anti-Semite. Under the circumstances the Jew would have but one goal—to get out. He would assimilate to anything, for outside are human beings—and what imprisoned nothing does not dream of becoming *any* human being? But assimilation, escape, is not possible. First the camp has to be removed by the acts of the good men outside (all Gentiles) .

Such is the image behind Sartre's *Reflections*. When Sartre says "Jew" he means someone else, the prisoner. For instance, the Jew to

---

initiative of one who has made "a total choice of himself and the meaning of the world"—while the Jew, no matter what he does, thinks, or feels, is degraded and impotent.

Concentrating on his sentimental image of the "passionate" anti-Semite, Sartre fails to consider a type much more menacing historically: the anti-Semitic conspirator. This anti-Semite may be quite lacking in the "passion" and the concept of the world of the anti-Semite in Sartre's portrait (Sartre might have called him the "authentic" anti-Semite, since he is conscious of his situation, and of the uses of anti-Semitism in it) . In a given historical situation this cold manipulator of anti-Semitism may prove far more deadly than Sartre's "Manichean" and folklorist. Robert Pick's observation (*Commentary*, September 1948) that the fatal point in the development of anti-Semitism occurs when it receives encouragement from above seems to touch the essence of the problem. The Jew is truly endangered when different forms of anti-Semitism come together and achieve the power to act. Sartre is unaware of this turning point, since for him the Jew is always a marked man. Thus he fails to distinguish between the regime of the yellow star and the normal environment of the Jew in Western democracies. "The Nazi ordinances," he says, "only carried to its extreme a situation to which we had formerly accommodated ourselves very well." But the very life of the Jew depends on distinguishing sharply between a situation in which he will be killed if he arouses someone's hostility and one in which his enemy can only try to injure him through prejudice or disdain.

him, like the camp inmate, feels solidarity only with those who have suffered the same experience—no fraternity is possible with outsiders. Were he not carried away by his fantasy, could Sartre have made the following dreadful statement? "In effect the Jew is to another Jew the only man to whom he can say 'we.'" If this were true the most destructive accusations of the anti-Semite would be justified. Unable to enter into community with non-Jews for whatever reason, the Jew would deserve to be shunned. A Jew in a trade union whose "we" was weaker than his brother's; a Jew on a baseball team, a Jew in a political party or a military squad, with his "we" restricted to the other Jews in it, would deserve to be kicked out, at least. This person without a positive historical tie to his fellow Jews would yet be fused to them in rejecting humanity—one almost detects here the leer of the Elders of Zion munching their conspiratorial matzot.

But we need not be shocked because Sartre is not really talking about the Jew at all but about his favorite theme, the concentration-camp situation and the man in it, a man hopelessly cut off from the world and subjected to the behavior of his enemies. We see this most clearly in Sartre's discussion of Bergson. The world thinks of Bergson as a philosopher of intuition. Benda, a Jew, attacked Bergson as the demiurge of modern irrationalism and the type of the "musical Jew" who scorns rationality. But Jews, say the anti-Semites, are incapable of intuition; they are all just clever rationalists. Yes, Sartre agrees, the anti-Semites have made rationalists of the Jews. Since Bergson is a Jew his "system is a rationalism that has undergone a change of name." (Not a bad characterization of Sartre's existentialism, by the way.) "For my part, I see it as the supreme defense of the persecuted." Spinoza and Husserl, too, are rationalists in spite of themselves. Bergson, among other inauthentic Jews, thought as he did, and what he did, because he was defending himself against a "true and lucid consciousness" of his Jewish situation. His philosophy is an inutile attempt to say "we" with all mankind when he could only really say "we" with Jews. Bergson's entire intellectual life—which Valéry hailed during the Occupation as the quintessence of French thought, in contrast to the system-building of the German philosophers—this entire life is to Sartre but a symbolic activity designed to conceal from Bergson himself the impermeable fact of his Jewishness. Jews are incapable of metaphysics—"metaphysics is the special privilege of the 'Aryan' governing classes"—they can only defend themselves. At this point the existentialist philosophy of freedom, dominated by its terrible dream, has dropped far below the deepest cellars of psychological and historical determinism. Even the most rigid Freudian sees the source of a writer's involuntary fictiveness in some private fact that may be changed through consciousness; while the most mechanical Marxist regards an individual's thought as compelled by the broad movement of world history. For Sartre, Bergson is moved neither by himself nor by the world. He is locked into a middle area, the Jewish situation. And yet he is moved absolutely, for that is what he *is*. "Whatever he does, his course is set for him. . . . He cannot choose not to be a Jew."

Here are some other characteristics of the inauthentic Jew. He is uneasy, but his uneasiness is social rather than metaphysical (in the camp anguish comes not from God or the universe but from society). He is not a surrealist, for he does not believe in destructiveness (destruction has chosen him as its victim). He feels himself forever surrounded by others; no Jew can "perceive the loneliness of each man in a silent universe" (in the camp one never has the chance to be alone). Let Sartre poll Paris today to see how many Frenchmen are secure, metaphysical, surrealist, and in love with solitude. The irony is, however, that Sartre himself, precisely because the concentration camp is central to his thought, is outstandingly anxious, rationalistic, lacking in the metaphysical sense, opposed to surrealism and "disengaged" poetry, and conceives every situation as a purely social one. (I am not suggesting that he is secretly a Jew.)

Those "Jewish traits" collected by Sartre which are not directly deducible from the concentration-camp situation belong to the modern city man, Gentile or Jew, as he appears in the perspective of nostalgia. For instance, Sartre comments about the Jews that "they do not feel toward their bodies that tranquil sentiment of property which characterizes most 'Aryans.' For these latter the body is a fruit of French soil." One recalls what D. H. Lawrence had to say about the "tranquil" physicalness of the "Aryans." Sartre's remarks are in the tradition of twentieth-century ideologists of "aristocracy." Like them he ascribes to the Jew, regardless of class or locality, the personality of the big-city bourgeois ("he prefers this form of property [commodities] to all others . . . because it is universal") seen in contrast with the sentimentalized peasant. This identification of the Jew and the cosmopolitan plays an enormous role in modern anti-Semitism.

In sum, Sartre's inauthentic Jew is a fiction justified neither by philosophy, history, nor direct observation. Not that there are no Jews who have psychological qualities mentioned by Sartre. Jews in the United States may recognize them as typical of the assimilationist who nervously tries to "lose himself in the Christian world." And they will approve Sartre's moral enjoinder to this harassed man: Be a Jew, be yourself, whatever the cost. But in the midst of our approval let us remember that we cannot agree with Sartre (and with the assimilationist) that the Jew is nothing but anti-Semite bait. This is a distortion common to Gentile friends of the Jew. To them the Jew is one who against his will is kept from being a "man like everybody else" by the anti-Semite, who includes every *goy* who has not made anti-anti-Semitism his vocation. We have had several recent examples of such humanitarian exuberance. But here in America, where Jews are not the only "foreigners," nor the only target of racialism, it should be clear that being singled out by an enemy is not the cause of our difference from others, is not what makes us Jews.

In opposition to Sartre's compendium of Jewish nothingness, Jewish imprisonment in his situation, and Jewish traits we may assert the following: Since the Jew possesses a unique identity which springs from his origin and his story, it is possible for him to be any kind of man—rationalist, irrationalist, heroic, cowardly, Zionist or good European—and still be a Jew. The Jew exists but there are no Jewish traits. The Jew who chooses to flee his Jewishness does not thereby turn into something other than a man, any more than does an Italian who decides to become an American. Whatever it is, the desire to assimilate is not "inauthentic"; one may choose to suppress the past in oneself or to surpass it. Today, all collective identities, Jewish and non-Jewish, are undergoing deep changes and no longer exist in individuals as firmly and persuasively as they once did.

INTRODUCTION TO

THE JEW AS PARIAH

Hannah Arendt

The interpretation of the Jews as a "pariah people," first proposed by the great German sociologist Max Weber in his essay, "Class, Status, Party" (*From Max Weber: Essays in Sociology,* translated by H. H. Gerth and C. Wright Mills, Oxford University Press, 1946, pp. 188–90) and elaborated toward the end of his life in his extended sociological inquiry into the origins and foundation of Jewish institutions, *Ancient Judaism* (translated by H. H. Gerth and Don Martindale, The Free Press, 1962) provides Hannah Arendt with the essential interpretive category for her discussion of a "hidden tradition" in Judaism. The hidden tradition is not that Jews constitute a pariah people, but that they have developed, ever since the Enlightenment and the Emancipation, various devices of resisting, transcending, and ultimately ransoming themselves from the constrictions imposed by pariah status.

Hannah Arendt accepts the truth of Weber's sociological description of the Jews as a pariah people. In fact, it seems to me that Weber's *Ancient Judaism* failed to demonstrate his insight. His analysis of the social structure of Hebrew society does persuade one that our ancestors, meticulous in their concern for ritual obedience and consequent ritual purity and separation, often obliged other enclaves in their midst to stand aside from full participation in its polity because they were either inadequately converted or like the Amalekites were immemorial (almot essential and symbolic) enemies of Israel. The Jews, from their inception and throughout the

24

course of their life upon their own land, were not pariahs. To interpret, as Weber does, the institutions and rituals of ancient Judaism as providing the social structures of pariahship well in advance of the dispersion and the Diaspora which enforced pariahship upon the Jews is to argue by *petitio principii*. The conclusion is at best a restatement of the premise. The pariah is a pariah is a pariah. Not enough. *Ancient Judaism* is a profoundly insightful work, respectful of Jewish history and tradition, admiring of the Jewish achievement which Weber places alongside classic Hellenism, Roman Law, and the organization of the Catholic Church, and Protestantism as progenitor and cosharer in the genius of the West, but Weber's understanding of Jewish religious and intellectual history is, to my mind, defective.

Hannah Arendt seems to me more right-headed in her employment of Weber's innovative notion. The Jews *became* a pariah people. They did not begin as one. A guest nation, for that is what Weber meant by pariah, certainly defines the experience of the Jews among the nations. Of course, Exile is not a sociological category nor is *Galut* a substantive historical condition. They are both metahistorical categories, describing a vertical connection between the People and its self-exiled God and a horizontal tension between the rootedness of neighboring peoples and the precariousness of its own existence among them. There is little doubt that the Jews assented to the judgment of the nations upon their difference. Surely a people is different which not only affirms of itself the honor of divine election, but is willing as well to assume the onus of that honor. Such a people (whose polity is religiously defined and whose understanding of politics is both as Utopian and realist as was that of classic Judaism) cannot help but concern itself with separateness (to insure the uncontaminated perseverance of the cult) and purity (to preserve the ethnic continuity of the people). Separateness and purity can be maintained when the people enjoy the power to conserve the social institutions which support them. Remove such a people from its historic place, destroy its instruments of cohesion, mix it among other nations, and consummate uprootedness by persecution and murder, and it is no wonder that such a people acquires the neurasthenic disorders of a sufferance society. Where Weber rarely amends sociological description with psychological glossalia, Hannah Arendt's illuminating discussion of the techniques of flight from pariahship developed by Heinrich Heine,

Bernard Lazare, Charlie Chaplin (who, though not a Jew, nevertheless suggests through the Tramp those devices of earthy impudence and suspicion which give an exit to the entrapment of the Western Jew), and Franz Kafka, depends upon the forcing of psychological postures into political and ideological positions. She has made the notion of the Jews as a pariah people an investigative and diagnostic instrument.

THE JEW AS PARIAH

A Hidden Tradition

HANNAH ARENDT

When it comes to claiming its own in the field of European arts and letters, the attitude of the Jewish people may best be described as one of reckless magnanimity. With a grand gesture and without a murmur of protest it has calmly allowed the credit for its great writers and artists to go to other peoples, itself receiving in return (in punctiliously regular payments) the doubtful privilege of being acclaimed father of every notorious swindler and mountebank. True enough, there has been a tendency in recent years to compile long lists of European worthies who might conceivably claim Jewish descent, but such lists are more in the nature of mass-graves for the forgotten than of enduring monuments to the remembered and cherished. Useful as they may be for purposes of propaganda (offensive as well as defensive), they have not succeeded in reclaiming for the Jews any single writer of note unless he happen to have written specifically in Hebrew or Yiddish. Those who really did most for the spiritual dignity of their people, who were great enough to transcend the bounds of nationality and to weave the strands of their Jewish genius into the general texture of European life, have been given short shrift and perfunctory recognition. With the growing tendency to conceive of the Jewish people as a series of separate territorial units and to resolve its history into so many regional chronicles and parochial records, its great figures have been left perforce to the tender mercies of assimilationist propagandists—to be exploited only in order to bolster selfish interests or furnish alleged illustrations of dubious ideologies.

27

No one fares worse from this process than those bold spirits who tried to make of the emancipation of the Jews that which it really should have been—an admission of Jews as *Jews* to the ranks of humanity, rather than a permit to ape the Gentiles or an opportunity to play the parvenu. Realizing only too well that they did not enjoy political freedom nor full admission to the life of nations, but that, instead, they had been separated from their own people and lost contact with the simple natural life of the common man, these men yet achieved liberty and popularity by the sheer force of imagination. As individuals they started an emancipation of their own, of their own hearts and brains. Such a conception was, of course, a gross misconstruction of what emancipation had been intended to be; but it was also a vision, and out of the impassioned intensity with which it was evinced and expressed it provided the fostering soil on which Jewish creative genius could grow and contribute its products to the general spiritual life of the Western world.

AMBIGUITY OF EMANCIPATION

That the status of the Jews in Europe has been not only that of an oppressed people but also of what Max Weber has called a "pariah people" is a fact most clearly appreciated by those who have had practical experience of just how ambiguous is the freedom which emancipation has ensured, and how treacherous the promise of equality which assimilation has held out. In their own position as social outcasts such men reflect the political status of their entire people. It is, therefore, not surprising that out of their personal experience Jewish poets, writers and artists should have been able to evolve the concept of the pariah as a human type—a concept of supreme importance for the evaluation of mankind in our day and one which has exerted upon the Gentile world an influence in strange contrast to the spiritual and political ineffectiveness which has been the fate of these men among their own brethren. Indeed, the concept of the pariah has become traditional, even though the tradition be but tacit and latent, and its continuance automatic and unconscious. Nor need we wonder why: for over a hundred years the same basic conditions have obtained and evoked the same basic reaction.

However slender the basis out of which the concept was created and out of which it was progressively developed, it has nevertheless loomed larger in the thinking of assimilated Jews than might be inferred from standard Jewish histories. It has endured, in fact, from Solomon Maimon in the eighteenth century to Franz Kafka in the early twentieth. But out of the variety of forms which it has assumed we shall here select four, in each of which it expresses an alternative portrayal of the Jewish people. Our first type will be Heinrich Heine's *schlemihl* and "lord of dreams" (*Traumweltherrscher*); our second, Bernard Lazare's "conscious pariah"; our third, Charlie Chaplin's grotesque portrayal of the suspect;[1] and our fourth, Franz Kafka's poetic vision of the fate of the man of goodwill. Between these four types there is a significant connection—a link which in fact unites all genuine concepts and sound ideas when once they achieve historical actuality.

HEINRICH HEINE: THE SCHLEMIHL AND LORD OF DREAMS

In his poem, *Princess Sabbath,* the first of his *Hebrew Melodies,* Heinrich Heine depicts for us the national background from which he sprang and which inspired his verses. He portrays his people as a fairy prince turned by witchcraft into a dog. A figure of ridicule throughout the week, every Friday night he suddenly regains his mortal shape, and freed from the preoccupation of his canine existence (*von huendischen Gedanken*), goes forth like a prince to welcome the sabbath bride and to greet her with the traditional hymeneal, *Lekha Dodi*.[2]

This poem, we are informed by Heine, was especially composed for the purpose by the people's poet—the poet who, by a stroke of fortune, escapes the gruelling weekly transformation of his people and who continually leads the sabbathlike existence which is to Heine the only positive mark of Jewish life.

Poets are characterized in greater detail in Part IV of the poem, where Heine speaks of Yehudah Halevi. They are said to be descended from "Herr Schlemihl ben Zurishaddai"—a name taken from Shelumiel ben Zurishaddai mentioned in the biblical Book of Numbers as the leader of the tribe of Simeon. Heine relates his name to the word *schlemihl* by the humorous supposition that by

---

1. Chaplin has recently declared that he is of Irish and Gypsy descent, but he has been selected for discussion because, even if not himself a Jew, he has epitomized in an artistic form a character born of the Jewish pariah mentality.

2. *Lekha Dodi:* "Come, my beloved, to meet the bride; Let us greet the sabbathtide"—a Hebrew song chanted in the synagogue on Friday night.

standing too close to his brother chieftain Zimri he got himself killed accidentally when the latter was beheaded by the priest Phinehas for dallying with a Midianite woman (cf. Numbers, 25:6–15.). But if they may claim Shelumiel as their ancestor, they must also claim Phinehas—the ruthless Phinehas whose

> . . . spear is with us,
> And above our heads unpausing
> We can hear its fatal whizzing
> And the noblest hearts it pierces.

History preserves to us no "deeds heroic" of those "noblest hearts." All we know is that—they were *schlemihls*.

Innocence is the hall-mark of the *schlemihl*. But it is of such innocence that a people's poets—its "lords of dreams"—are born. No heroes they and no stalwarts, they are content to seek their protection in the special tutelage of an ancient Greek deity. For did not Apollo, that "inerrable godhead of delight," proclaim himself once for all the lord of *schlemihls* on the day when—as the legend has it—he pursued the beauteous Daphne only to receive for his pains a crown of laurels? To be sure, times have changed since then, and the transformation of the ancient Olympian has been described by Heine himself in his poem *The God Apollo*. This tale tells of a nun who falls in love with that great divinity and gives herself up to the search for him who can play the lyre so beautifully and charm hearts so wondrously. In the end, however, after wandering far and wide, she discovers that the Apollo of her dreams exists in the world of reality as Rabbi Faibusch (a Yiddish distortion of Phoebus), cantor in a synagogue at Amsterdam, holder of the humblest office among the humblest of peoples. Nor this alone; the father is a *mohel* (ritual circumciser), and the mother peddles sour pickles and assortments of odd trousers; while the son is a good-for-nothing who makes the rounds of the annual fairs playing the clown and singing the Psalms of David to the accompaniment of a bevy of "Muses" consisting of nine buxom wrenches from the Amsterdam casino.

PORTRAIT OF THE JEWISH PEOPLE

Heine's portrayal of the Jewish people and of himself as their poet-king is, of course, poles apart from the conception entertained by the privileged wealthy Jews of the upper classes. Instead, in its gay, insouciant impudence it is characteristic of the common people. For the pariah, excluded from formal society and with no desire to be embraced within it, turns naturally to that which entertains and delights the common people. Sharing their social ostracism, he also shares their joys and sorrows, their pleasures, and their tribulations. He turns, in fact, from the world of men and the fashion thereof to the open and unrestricted bounty of the earth. And this is precisely what Heine did. Stupid and undiscerning critics have called it materialism or atheism, but the truth is that there is only so much of the heathen in it that it seems irreconcilable with certain interpretations of the Christian doctrine of original sin and its consequent sense of perpetual guilt. It is, indeed, no more than that simple *joie de vivre* which one finds everywhere in children and in the common people—that passion which makes them revel in tales and romances, which finds its supreme literary expression in the ballad and which gives to the short love song its essentially popular character. Stemming as it does from the basic affinity of the pariah to the people, it is something which neither literary criticism nor anti-Semitism could ever abolish. Though they dubbed its author "unknown," the Nazis could not eliminate the *Lorelei* from the repertoire of German song.

It is but natural that the pariah, who receives so little from the world of men that even fame (which the world has been known to bestow on even the most abandoned of her children) is accounted to him a mere sign of *schlemihldom,* should look with an air of innocent amusement, and smile to himself at the spectacle of human beings trying to compete with the divine realities of nature. The bare fact that the sun shines on all alike affords him daily proof that all men are essentially equal. In the presence of such universal things as the sun, music, trees, and children—things which Rahel Varnhagen called "the true realities" just because they are cherished most by those who have no place in the political and social world—the petty dispensations of men which create and maintain inequality must needs appear ridiculous. Confronted with the natural order of things, in which all is equally good, the fabricated order of society, with its manifold classes and ranks, must needs appear a comic, hopeless attempt of creation to throw down the gauntlet to its creator. It is no longer the outcast pariah who appears the *schlemihl,* but those who live in the ordered ranks of society and who have exchanged the generous gifts of nature for the idols of social privilege and prejudice. Especially is this true of the parvenu who was not even born to the system, but chose it of his own free will, and who is called upon to pay the cost meticulously and exactly, whereas others can take things in their stride. But no less are they *schlemihls* who enjoy power and high station. It needs but a poet to compare their vaunted grandeur with the real majesty of the sun, shining on king and beggarman alike, in order to demonstrate that all their pomp and circumstance is but sounding brass and a tinkling cymbal. All of these truths are old as the hills. We know them from the songs of oppressed and despised peoples who—so long as man does not aspire to halt the course of the sun—will always seek refuge in nature, hoping that beside nature all the devices of men will reveal themselves as ephemeral trifles.

It is from this shifting of the accent, from this vehement protest on the part of the Pariah, from this attitude of denying the reality of the social order and of confronting it, instead, with a higher reality, that Heine's spirit of mockery really stems. It is this, too, which makes his scorn so pointed. Because he gauges things so consistently by the criterion of what is really and manifestly natural, he is able at once to detect the weak spot in his opponent's armor, the vulnerable point in any particular stupidity which he happens to be exposing. And it is this aloofness of the pariah from all the works of man that Heine regards as the essence of freedom. It is this aloofness that accounts for the divine laughter and the absence of bitterness in his verses. He was the first Jew to whom freedom meant more than mere "liberation from the house of bondage" and in whom it was combined, in equal measure, with the traditional Jewish passion for justice. To Heine, freedom had little to do with liberation from a just or unjust yoke. A man is born free, and he can lose his freedom only by selling himself into bondage. In line with this idea, both in his political poems and in his prose writings Heine vents his anger not only on tyrants but equally on those who put up with them.

The concept of *natural* freedom (conceived, be it noted, by an outcast able to live beyond the struggle between bondage and tyranny) turns both slaves and tyrants into equally unnatural and, therefore, ludicrous figures of fun. The poet's cheerful insouciance could hardly be expected from the very respectable citizen, caught as he was in the toils of practical affairs and himself partly responsible for the order of things. Even Heine, when confronted with the only social reality from which his pariah existence had not detached him—the rich Jews of his family—loses his serenity and becomes bitter and sarcastic.

To be sure, when measured by the standard of political realities, Heine's attitude of amused indifference seems remote and unreal. When one comes down to earth, one has to admit that laughter does not kill and that neither slaves nor tyrants are extinguished by mere amusement. From this standpoint, however, the pariah is always remote and unreal; whether as *schlemihl* or as "lord of dreams" he stands outside the real world and attacks it from without. Indeed, the Jewish tendency towards Utopianism—a propensity most clearly in evidence in the very countries of emancipation—stems, in the last analysis, from just this lack of social roots. The only thing which saved Heine from succumbing to it, and which made him transform the political nonexistence and unreality of the pariah into the effective basis of a world of art, was his creativity. Because he sought nothing more than to hold up a mirror to the political world, he was able to avoid becoming a doctrinaire and to keep his passion for freedom unhampered by fetters of dogma. Similarly, because he viewed life through a long-range telescope, and not through the prism of an ideology, he was able to see further and clearer than others, and takes his place today among the shrewdest political observers of his time.

By fearlessness and divine impudence Heine finally achieved that for which his coreligionists had vainly striven with fear and trembling, now furtively and now ostentatiously, now by preening and vaunting, and now by obsequious sycophancy. Heine is the only German Jew who could truthfully describe himself as both a German and a Jew. He is the only outstanding example of a really happy assimilation in the entire history of that process. By seeing Phoebus Apollo in Rabbi Faibusch, by boldly introducing Yiddish expressions into the German language, he in fact put into practice that true blending of cultures of which others merely talked. One has only to remember how zealously assimilated Jews avoid the mention of a Hebrew word before Gentiles, how strenuously they pretend not to understand it if they hear one, to appreciate the full measure of Heine's accomplishment when he wrote, as pure German verse, lines like the following, praising a distinctively Jewish dish:

> Schalet, ray of light immortal
> Schalet, daughter of Elysium!

> So had Schiller's song resounded,
> Had he ever tasted Schalet.

In these words, Heine places the fare of Princess Sabbath on the table of the gods, beside nectar and ambrosia.

While the privileged wealthy Jews appealed to the sublimities of the Hebrew prophets in order to prove that they were indeed the descendants of an especially exalted people, or else—like Disraeli—sought to validate their people by endowing it with some extraordinary, mystic power, Heine dispensed with all such rarefied devices and turned to the homespun Judaism of everyday life, to that which really lay in the heart and on the lips of the average Jew; and through the medium of the German language he gave it a place in general European culture. Indeed, it was the very introduction of these homely Jewish notes that helped to make Heine's works so essentially popular and human.

WORLD-CITIZENSHIP

Heine is perhaps the first German prose writer really to embody the heritage of Lessing. In a manner least expected, he confirmed the queer notion so widely entertained by the early Prussian liberals that once the Jew was emancipated he would become more human, more free and less prejudiced than other men. That this notion involved a gross exaggeration is obvious. In its political implications, too, it was so lacking in elementary understanding as to appeal only to those Jews who imagined—as do so many today—that Jews could exist as "pure human beings" outside the range of peoples and nations. Heine was not decieved by this nonsense of "world-citizenship." He knew that separate peoples are needed to focus the genius of poets and artists; and he had no time for academic pipe dreams. Just because he refused to give up his allegiance to a people of pariahs and *schlemihls*, just because he remained consistently attached to them, he takes his place among the most uncompromising of Europe's fighters for freedom—of which, alas, Germany has produced so few. Of all the poets of his time Heine was the one with the most character. And just because German bourgeois society had none of its own, and feared the explosive force of his, it concocted the slanderous legend of his characterlessness. Those who spread this legend, and who hoped thereby to dismiss Heine from serious consideration, included many Jewish

34

journalists. They were averse to adopting the line he had suggested; they did not want to become Germans and Jews in one, because they feared that they would thereby lose their positions in the social order of German Jewry. For Heine's attitude, if only as a poet, was that by achieving emancipation the Jewish people had achieved a genuine freedom. He simply ignored the condition which had characterized emancipation everywhere in Europe—namely, that the Jew might only become a man when he ceassed to be a Jew. Because he held this position he was able to do what so few of his contemporaries could—to speak the language of a free man and sing the songs of a natural one.

BERNARD LAZARE: THE CONSCIOUS PARIAH

If it was Heine's achievement to recognize in the figure of the *schlemihl* the essential kinship of the pariah to the poet—both alike excluded from society and never quite at home in this world—and to illustrate by this analogy the position of the Jew in the world of European culture, it was the merits of Bernard Lazare to translate the same basic fact into terms of political significance. Living in the France of the Dreyfus Affair, Lazare could appreciate at first hand the pariah quality of Jewish existence. But he knew where the solution lay: in contrast to his unemancipated brethren who accept their pariah status automatically and unconsciously, the emancipated Jew must awake to an awareness of his position and, conscious of it, become a rebel against it—the champion of an oppressed people. His fight for freedom is part and parcel of that which all the downtrodden of Europe must needs wage to achieve national and social liberation.

In this heroic effort to bring the Jewish question openly into the arena of politics Lazare was to discover certain specific, Jewish factors which Heine had overlooked and could afford to ignore. If Heine could content himself with the bare observation that "Israel is ill-served, with false friends guarding her doors from without and Folly and Dread keeping watch within," Lazare took pains to investigate the political implications of this connection between Jewish folly and Gentile duplicity. As the root of the mischief he recognized that "spurious doctrine" (*doctrine bâtarde*) of assimilation, which would have the Jews "abandon all their characteristics, individual and moral alike, and give up distinguishing themselves only by an outward mark of the flesh which served but to expose them to the hatred of other faiths." He saw that what was necessary was to rouse the Jewish pariah to a fight against the Jewish parvenu. There was no other way to save him from the latter's own fate—inevitable destruction. Not only, he contended, has the pariah nothing but suffering to expect from the domination of the parvenu, but it is he who is destined sooner or later to pay the price of the whole wretched system. "I want no longer," he says in a telling passage, "to have against me not only the wealthy of my people, who exploit me and sell me, but also the rich and poor of other peoples who oppress and torture me in the name of my rich." And in these words he puts his finger squarely on that phenomenon of Jewish life which the historian Jost had so aptly characterized as "double slavery"—dependence, on the one hand, upon the hostile elements of his environment and, on the other, on his own "highly placed brethren" who are somehow in league with them. Lazare was the first Jew to perceive the connection between these two elements, both equally disastrous to the pariah. His experience of French politics had taught him that whenever the enemy seeks control, he makes a point of using some oppressed element of the population as his lackeys and henchmen, rewarding them with special privileges, as a kind of sop. It was thus that he construed the mechanism which made the rich Jews seek protection behind the notorious general Jewish poverty, to which they referred whenever their own position was jeopardized. This, he divined, was the real basis of their precarious relationship with their poorer brethren—on whom they would be able, at any time it suited them, to turn their backs.

As soon as the pariah enters the arena of politics, and translates his status into political terms, he becomes perforce a rebel. Lazare's idea was, therefore, that the Jew should come out openly as the representative of the pariah, "since it is the duty of every human being to resist oppression." He demanded, that is, that the pariah relinquish once for all the prerogative of the *schlemihl*, cut loose from the world of fancy and illusion, renounce the comfortable protection of nature, and come to grips with the world of men and women. In other words, he wanted him to feel that he was himself responsible for what society had done to him. He wanted him to stop seeking release in an attitude of superior indifference or in lofty and rarefied cogitation about the nature of man per se. However much the Jewish pariah might be, from the historical viewpoint, the product of an unjust dispensation ("look what you have

made of the people, ye Christians and ye princes of the Jews"),
politically speaking, every pariah who refused to be a rebel was
partly responsible for his own position and therewith for the blot
on mankind which it represented. From such shame there was no
escape, either in art or in nature. For in so far as a man is more
than a mere creature of nature, more than a mere product of Divine
creativity, in so far will he be called to account for the things which
men do to men in the world which they themselves condition.

Superficially, it might appear as though Lazare failed because of
the organized opposition of the rich, privileged Jews, the nabobs
and philanthropists whose leadership he had ventured to challenge
and whose lust for power he had dared to denounce. Were this the
case, it would be but the beginning of a tradition which might have
outlived his own premature death and determined, if not the fate,
at least the effective volition of the Jewish people. But it was not
the case; and Lazare himself knew—to his own sorrow—the real
cause of his failure. The decisive factor was not the parvenu;
neither was it the existence of a ruling caste which—whatever com-
plexion it might choose to assume—was still very much the same as
that of any other people. Immeasurably more serious and decisive
was the fact that the pariah simply refused to become a rebel. True
to type, he preferred to "play the revolutionary in the society of
others, but not in his own," or else to assume the role of *schnorrer*
feeding on the crumbs from the rich man's table, like an ancient
Roman commoner ready to be fobbed off with the merest trifle that
the patrician might toss at him. In either case, he mortgaged himself
to the parvenu, protecting the latter's position and in turn protected
by him.

However bitterly they may have attacked him, it was not the
hostility of the Jewish nabobs that ruined Lazare. It was the fact
that when he tried to stop the pariah from being a *schlemihl,* when
he sought to give him a political significance, he encountered only
the *schnorrer.* And once the pariah becomes a *schnorrer,* he is worth
nothing, not because he is poor and begs, but because he begs from
those whom he ought to fight, and because he appraises his poverty
by the standards of those who have caused it. Once he adopts the
role of *schnorrer,* the pariah becomes automatically one of the props
which hold up a social order from which he is himself excluded. For
just as *he* cannot live without his benefactors, so *they* cannot live
without him. Indeed, it is just by this system of organized charity

and almsgiving that the parvenus of the Jewish people have contrived to secure control over it, to determine its destinies and set its standards. The parvenu who fears lest he become a pariah, and the pariah who aspires to become a parvenu, are brothers under the skin and appropriately aware of their kinship. Small wonder, in face of this fact that of all Lazare's efforts—unique as they were—to forge the peculiar situation of his people into a vital and significant political factor, nothing now remains. Even his memory has faded.

While lack of political sense and persistence in the obsolete system of making charity the basis of national unity have prevented the Jewish people from taking a positive part in the political life of our day, these very qualities, translated into dramatic forms, have inspired one of the most singular products of modern art—the films of Charlie Chaplin. In Chaplin the most unpopular people in the world inspired what was long the most popular of contemporary figures—not because he was a modern Merry Andrew, but because he represented the revival of a quality long thought to have been killed by a century of class conflict, namely, the entrancing charm of the little people.

CHARLIE CHAPLIN: THE SUSPECT

In his very first film, Chaplin portrayed the chronic plight of the little man who is incessantly harried and hectored by the guardians of law and order—the representatives of society. To be sure, he too is a *schlemihl,* but not of the old visionary type, not a secret fairy prince, a protégé of Phoebus' Apollo. Chaplin's world is of the earth earthy, grotesquely caricatured if you will, but nevertheless hard and real. It is a world from which neither nature nor art can provide escape and against whose slings and arrows the only armor is one's own wits or the kindness and humanity of casual acquaintances.

In the eyes of society, the type which Chaplin portrays is always fundamentally suspect. He may be at odds with the world in a thousand and one ways, and his conflicts with it may assume a manifold variety of forms, but always and everywhere he is under suspicion, so that it is no good arguing rights or wrongs. Long before the refugee was to become, in the guise of the "stateless," the living symbol of the pariah, long before men and women were to be forced in their thousands to depend for their bare existence on their own wits or the chance kindness of others, Chaplin's own childhood had taught him two things. On the one hand, it had taught him the time-honored Jewish fear of the "cop"—that seeming incarnation of a hostile world; but on the other, it had taught him the time-honored Jewish truth that, other things being equal, the human ingenuity of a David can sometimes outmatch the animal strength of a Goliath.

Standing outside the pale, suspected by all the world, the pariah —as Chaplin portrays him—could not fail to arouse the sympathies of the common people, who recognized in him the image of what society had done to them. Small wonder, then, that Chaplin became the idol of the masses. If they laughed at the way he was forever falling in love at first sight, they realized at the same time that the kind of love he evinced was their kind of love—however rare it may be.

Chaplin's suspect is linked to Heine's *schlemihl* by the common element of innocence. What might have appeared incredible and untenable if presented as a matter of causistic discussion, as the theme of high-flown talk about the persecution of the guiltless, etc., becomes, in Chaplin's treatment, both warm and convincing. Chaplin's heroes are not paragons of virtue, but little men with a thousand and one little failings, forever clashing with the law. The only point that is made is that the punishment does not always fit the crime, and that for the man who is in any case suspect there is no relation between the offense he commits and the price he pays. He is always being "nabbed" for things he never did, yet somehow he can always slip through the toils of the law, where other men would be caught in them. The innocence of the suspect which Chaplin so consistently portrays in his films is, however, no more a mere trait of character, as in Heine's *schlemihl;* rather it is an expression of the dangerous incompatibility of general laws with individual misdeeds. Although in itself tragic, this incompatibility reveals its comic aspects in the case of the suspect, where it becomes patent. There is obviously no connection at all between what Chaplin does or does not do and the punishment which overtakes him. Because he is suspect, he is called upon to bear the brunt of much that he has not done. Yet at the same time, because he is beyond the pale, unhampered by the trammels of society, he is able to get away with a great deal. Out of this ambivalent situation springs an attitude both of fear and of impudence, fear of the law as if it were an inexorable natural force, and familiar, ironic impudence in the face of its minions. One can cheerfully cock a snoot at them, because one has learned to duck them, as men duck a shower by creeping into holes or under a shelter. And the smaller one is, the easier it becomes. Basically, the impudence of Chaplin's suspect is of the same kind as charms us so much in Heine's *schlemihl;* but no longer is it carefree and unperturbed, no longer the divine effrontery of the poet who consorts with heavenly things and can therefore afford to thumb noses at earthly society. On the contrary, it is a worried, careworn impudence—the kind so familiar to generations of Jews—the effrontery of the poor "little Yid" who does not recognize the class order of the world because he sees it in neither order nor justice for himself.

It was in this "little Yid," poor in worldly goods but rich in human experience, that the little man of all peoples most clearly discerned his own image. After all, had he not too to grapple with the problem of circumventing a law which, in its sublime indifference, forbade "rich and poor to sleep under bridges or steal bread"? For a long time he could laugh good-humoredly at himself—laugh at his misfortunes and his comic, sly methods of escape. But then came unemployment, and the thing was not funny any more. He knew he had been caught by a fate which no amount of cunning and smartness could evade. Then came the change. Chaplin's popularity began rapidly to wane, not because of any mounting anti-Semitism, but because his underlying humanity had lost its meaning. Men had stopped seeking release in laughter; the little man had decided to be a big one. Today it is not Chaplin, but Superman.

FRANZ KAFKA: THE MAN OF GOODWILL

Both Heine's *schlemihl* and Lazare's "conscious pariah" were conceived essentially as Jews, while even Chaplin's suspect betrays what are clearly Jewish traits. Quite different, however, is the case of the last and most recent typification of the pariah—that represented in the work of Franz Kafka. He appears on two occasions, once in the poet's earliest story, "Description of a Fight," and again in one of his latest novels entitled *The Castle.*

"Description of a Fight" is concerned, in a general way, with the problem of social interrelations, and advances the thesis that within

40

the confines of society the effects of genuine or even friendly relations are invariably adverse. Society, we are told, is composed of "nobodies"—"I did wrong to nobody, nobody did wrong to me; but nobody will help me, nothing but nobodies"—and has therefore no real existence. Nevertheless, even the pariah, who is excluded from it, cannot account himself lucky, since society keeps up the pretense that it is somebody and he nobody, that it is "real" and he "unreal." His conflict with it has therefore nothing to do with the question whether society treats him properly or not; the point at issue is simply whether it or he has real existence. And the greatest injury which society can and does inflict on him is to make him doubt the reality and validity of his own existence, to reduce him in his own eyes to a status of nonentity.

ESCAPE

The reality of his existence thus assailed, the pariah of the nineteenth century had found escape in two ways, but neither could any longer commend itself to Kafka. The first way led to a society of pariahs, of people in the same situation and—so far as their opposition to society was concerned—of the same outlook. But to take this way was to end in utter detachment from reality—in a bohemian divorce from the actual world. The second way, chosen by many of the better Jews whom society had ostracized, led to an overwhelming preoccupation with the world of beauty, be it the world of nature in which all men were equal beneath an eternal sun, or the realm of art where everyone was welcome who could appreciate eternal genius. Nature and art had, in fact, long been regarded as departments of life which were proof against social or political assault; and the pariah therefore retreated to them as to worlds where he might dwell unmolested.

But it is just this method of escape, this retreat into nature and art, against which Kafka directs his shafts in "Description of a Fight." To his twentieth-century sense of reality, Nature had lost its invulnerable superiority over man since man would not "leave it in peace." He denied, too, the living actuality of monuments which were merely inherited from the dead and abandoned to everybody— that same everybody whom contemporary society would call a "nobody." In his view, the beauties of art and nature when used as an escape-mechanism by those to whom its right had been refused were merely products of society. It does no good, he says, to keep thinking of them; in time they die and lose their strength. For Kafka only those things are real whose strength is not impaired but confirmed by thinking. Neither the freedom of the *schlemihl* and poet nor the innocence of the suspect nor the escape into nature and art, but thinking is the new weapon—the only one with which, in Kafka's opinion, the pariah is endowed at birth in his vital struggle against society.

It is, indeed, the use of this contemplative faculty as an instrument of self-preservation that characterizes Kafka's conception of the pariah. Kafka's heroes face society with an attitude of outspoken aggression, poles apart from the ironic condescension and superiority of Heine's "lord of dreams" or the innocent cunning of Chaplin's perpetually harassed little man. The traditional traits of the Jewish pariah, the touching innocence and the enlivening *schlemihldom*, have alike no place in the picture. *The Castle*, the one novel in which Kafka discusses the Jewish problem, is the only one in which the hero is plainly a Jew; yet even there what characterizes him as such is not any typically Jewish trait, but the fact that he is involved in situations and perplexities distinctive of Jewish life.

DILEMMA OF ASSIMILATION

K. (as the hero is called) is a stranger who can never be brought into line because he belongs neither to the common people nor to its rulers. ("You are not of the Castle and you are not of the village, you are nothing at all.") To be sure, it had something to do with the rulers that he ever came to the village in the first place, but he had no legal title to remain there. In the eyes of the minor bureaucratic officials his very existence was due merely to a bureaucratic "error," while his status as a citizen was a paper one, buried "in piles of documents forever rising and crashing" around him. He is charged continually with being superfluous, "unwanted and in everyone's way," with having, as a stranger, to depend on other people's bounty and with being tolerated only by reason of a mysterious act of grace.

K. himself is of the opinion that everything depends on his becoming "indistinguishable," and "that as soon as possible." He admits that the rulers will assuredly obstruct the process. What he seeks, namely, complete assimilation, is something which they are not prepared to recognize—even as an aspiration. In a letter from the castle he is told distinctly that he will have to make up his mind "whether he prefers to become a village worker with a distinctive but merely apparent connection with the Castle or an ostensible village worker whose real occupation is determined through the medium of Barnabas (the court messenger)."

No better analogy could have been found to illustrate the entire dilemma of the modern would-be assimilationist Jew. He, too, is faced with the same alternative, whether to belong ostensibly to the people, but really to the rulers—as their creature and tool—or utterly and forever to renounce their protection and seek his fortune with the masses. "Official" Jewry has preferred always to cling to the rulers, and its representatives are always only "ostensible villagers." But it is with the other sort of Jew that Kafka is concerned and whose fate he portrays. This is the Jew who chooses the alternative way—the way of goodwill, who construes the conventional parlance of assimilation literally. What Kafka depicts is the real drama of assimilation, not its distorted counterpart. He speaks for the average small-time Jew who really wants no more than his rights as a human being: home, work, family and citizenship. He is portrayed as if he were alone on earth, the only Jew in the whole wide world—completely, desolately alone. Here, too, Kafka paints a picture true to reality and to the basic human problem which assimilation involves, if taken seriously. For insofar as the Jew seeks to become "indistinguishable" from his Gentile neighbors he has to believe as if he were indeed utterly alone; he has to part company, once and for all, with all who are like him. The hero of Kafka's novel does, in fact, what the whole world wants the Jew to do. His lonely isolation merely reflects the constantly reiterated opinion that if only there were nothing but individual Jews, if only the Jews would not persist in banding together, assimilation would become a fairly simple process. Kafka makes his hero follow this "ideal" course in order to show clearly how the experiment in fact works out. To make a thorough success of it, it is, of course, necessary also that a man should renounce all distinctive Jewish traits. In Kafka's treatment, however, this renunciation assumes a significance for the whole problem of mankind, and not merely for the Jewish questions. K., in his effort to become "indistinguishable," is interested only in universals, in things which are common to all mankind. His desires are directed only towards those things to which all men have a natural right. He is, in a word, the typical man of goodwill. He demands no more than that which constitutes every man's right, and he will be satisfied with no less. His entire ambition is to have "a home, a position, real work to do," to marry and "to become a member of the community." Because, as a stranger, he is not permitted to enjoy these obvious prerequisites of human existence, he cannot afford to be ambitious. He alone, he thinks (at least at the beginning of the story), must fight for the minimum—for simple human rights, as if it were something which embraced the sum total of all possible demands. And just because he seeks nothing more than his minimum human rights, he cannot consent to obtain his demands—as might otherwise have been possible—in the form of "an act of favor from the Castle." He must perforce stand on his "rights."

As soon as the villagers discover that the stranger who has chanced to come into their midst really enjoys the protection of the Castle, their original mood of contemptuous indifference turns to one of respectful hostility. From then on their one desire is to cast him back upon the Castle as soon as possible; they want no truck with the "upper crust." And when K. refuses, on the grounds that he wants to be free, when he explains that he would rather be a simple but genuine villager than an ostensible one really living under the protection of the Castle, their attitude changes in turn to one of suspicion mingled with anxiety—an attitude which, for all his efforts, haunts him continually. The villagers feel uneasy not because he is a stranger, but because he refuses to accept favors. They try constantly to persuade him that his attitude is "dumb," that he lacks acquaintance with conditions as they are. They tell him all kinds of tales concerning the relations of the Castle to the villagers, and seek thereby to impart to him something of that knowledge of the world which he so obviosuly lacks. But all they succeed in doing is to show him, to his increasing alarm, that such things as human instinct, human rights and plain normal life—things which he himself had taken for granted as the indisputed property of all normal human beings—had as little existence for the villagers as for the stranger.

What K. experienced in his efforts to become indistinguishable from the villagers is told in a series of grim and ghastly tales, all of these redolent of human perversity and the slow attrition of human instincts. There is the tale of the innkeeper's wife who had had the "honor" as a girl, to be the short-lived mistress of some underling at the Castle, and who so far never forgot it as to turn her marriage into the merest sham. Then there is K.'s own young fiancée who had had the same experience but who, though she was able to forget it long enough to fall genuinely in love with him, could still not endure indefinitely a simple life without "high connections" and who absconded in the end with the aid of the "assistants"—two minor officials of the Castle. Last but not least, there is the weird, uncanny story of the Barnabases living under a curse, treated as lepers till they feel themselves such, merely because one of their pretty daughters once dared to reject the indecent advances of an important courtier. The plain villagers, controlled to the last detail by the ruling class, and slaves even in their thoughts to the whims of their all-powerful officials, had long since come to realize that to be in the right or to be in the wrong was for them a matter of pure "fate" which they could not alter. It is not, as K. naively assumes, the sender of an obscene letter that is exposed, but the recipient who becomes branded and tainted. This is what the villagers mean when they speak of their "fate." In K.'s view, "it's unjust and monstrous, but you're the only one in the village of that opinion."

It is the story of the Barnabases that finally makes K. see conditions as they really are. At long last he comes to understand that the realization of his designs, the achievement of basic human rights—the right to work, the right to be useful, the right to found a home and become a member of society—are in no way dependent on complete assimilation to one's *milieu,* on being "indistinguishable." The normal existence which he desires has become something exceptional, no longer to be realized by simple, natural methods. Everything natural and normal in life has been wrested out of men's hands by the prevalent regime of the village, to become a present endowed from without or, as Kafka puts it, from "above." Whether as fate, as blessing or as curse, it is something dark and mysterious, something which a man receives but does not create, and which he can therefore observe but never fathom. Accordingly K.'s aspiration, far from being commonplace and obvious is, in fact, exceptional and magnificent. So long as the village remains under the control of the Castle, its inhabitants can be nothing but the passive victims of their respective "fates"; there is no place in it for any man of goodwill who wishes to determine his own existence. The simplest inquiry into right and wrong is regarded as querulous disputation; the character of the regime, the power of the Castle, are things which may not be questioned. So, when K., thoroughly indignant and outraged, bursts out with the words, "So that's what the officials are like," the whole village trembles as if some vital secret, if not indeed the whole pattern of its life, had been suddenly betrayed.

Even when he loses the innocence of the pariah, K. does not give up the fight. But unlike the hero of Kafka's last novel, *Amerika,* he does not start dreaming of a new world and he does not end in a great "Nature Theatre" where "everyone is welcome," where "there is a place for everyone" in accordance with his talents, his bent and his will. On the contrary, K.'s idea seems to be that much could be accomplished, if only one simple man could achieve living his own life like a normal human being. Accordingly, he remains in the village and tries, in spite of everything, to establish himself under existent conditions. Only for a single brief moment does the old Jewish ideal stir his heart, and he dreams of the lofty freedom of the pariah —the "lord of dreams." But "nothing more senseless," he observes, "nothing more hopeless than this freedom, this waiting, this inviolability." All these things have no purpose and take no account of men's desire to achieve something in the here below, if it be only the sensible direction of their lives. Hence, in the end, he reconciles himself readily to the "tyranny of the teacher," takes on "the wreched post" of a school janitor and "does his utmost to get an interview with Klamm"—in a word, he takes his share in the misery and distress of the villagers.

On the face of it, all is fruitless, since K. can and will not divorce himself from the distinction between right and wrong and since he refuses to regard his normal human rights as privileges bestowed by the "powers that be." Because of this, the stories which he hears from the villagers fail to rouse in him that sense of haunting fear with which they take pains to invest them and which endows them with that strange poetic quality so common in the folk-tales of enslaved peoples. And since he cannot share this feeling he can never really be one of them. How baseless a feeling it is, how groundless the fear which seems by some magic to possess the entire village, is clear from the fact that nothing whatever materializes of all the dreadful fate which the villagers predict for K. himself. Nothing more serious happens to him, in fact, than that the authorities at the Castle, using a thousand and one excuses, keep holding up his application for legal title of residence.

The whole struggle remains undecided, and K. dies a perfectly natural death; he gets exhausted. What he strove to achieve was beyond the strength of any one man. But though his purpose remained unaccomplished, his life was far from being a complete failure. The very fight he had put up to obtain the few basic things which society owes to men, had opened the eyes of the villagers, or at least of some of them. His story, his behavior, had taught them both that human rights are worth fighting for and that the rule of the Castle is not divine law and, consequently, can be attacked. He had made them see, as they put it, that "men who suffered our kind of experiences, who are beset by our kind of fear . . . who tremble at every knock at the door, cannot see things straight." And they added: "How lucky are we that you came to us!"

EPILOGUE

In an epilogue to the novel Max Brod relates with what enthusiasm Kafka once repeated to him the story of how Flaubert, returning from a visit to a simple, happy family of many children had exclaimed spontaneously: *ils sont dans le vrai* ("Those folk are right"). A true human life cannot be led by people who feel themselves detached from the basic and simple laws of humanity nor by those who elect to live in a vacuum, even if they be led to do so by persecution. Men's lives must be "normal," not exceptional.

It was the perception of this truth that made Kafka a Zionist. In Zionism he saw a means of abolishing the "abnormal" position of the Jews, an instrument whereby they might become "a people like other peoples." Perhaps the last of Europe's great poets, he could scarcely have wished to become a nationalist. Indeed, his whole genius, his whole expression of the modern spirit, lay precisely in the fact that what he sought was to be a human being, a normal member of human society. It was not his fault that this society had ceased to be human, and that, trapped within its meshes, those of its members who were really men of goodwill were forced to function within it as something exceptional and abnormal—saints or madmen. If Western Jewry of the nineteenth century had taken assimilation seriously, had really tried to resolve the anomaly of the Jewish people and the problem of the Jewish individual by becoming "indistinguishable" from their neighbors, if they had made equality with others their ultimate objective, they would only have found in the end that they were faced with inequality and that society was slowly but surely disintegrating into a vast complex of inhuman crosscurrents. They would have found, in short, the same kind of situation as Kafka portrayed in dealing with the relations of the stranger to the established patterns of village life.

THE ALTERNATIVES

So long as the Jews of Western Europe were pariahs only in a social sense they could find salvation, to a large extent, by becoming parvenus. Insecure as their position may have been, they could nevertheless achieve a *modus vivendi* by combining what Ahad Haam described as "inner slavery" with "outward freedom." Moreover those who deemed the price too high could still remain mere pariahs, calmly enjoying the freedom and untouchability of outcasts. Excluded from the world of political realities, they could still retreat into their quiet corners there to preserve the illusion of liberty and unchallenged humanity. The life of the pariah, though shorn of political significance, was by no means senseless.

But today it is. Today the bottom has dropped out of the old ideology. The pariah Jew and the parvenu Jew are in the same boat, rowing desperately in the same angry sea. Both are branded with the same mark; both alike are outlaws. Today the truth has come home: there is no protection in heaven or earth against bare murder, and a man can be driven at any moment from the streets and broad places once open to all. At long last, it has become clear that the "senseless freedom" of the individual merely paves the way for the senseless suffering of his entire people.

Social isolation is no longer possible. You cannot stand aloof from society, whether as a *schlemihl* or as a lord of dreams. The old escape-mechanisms have broken down, and a man can no longer come to terms with a world in which the Jew cannot be a human being either as a parvenu using his elbows or as a pariah voluntarily spurning its gifts. Both the realism of the one and the idealism of the other are today utopian.

There is, however, a third course—the one that Kafka suggests, in which a man may forego all claims to individual freedom and inviolability and modestly content himself with trying to lead a simple, decent life. But—as Kafka himself points out—this is impossible within the framework of contemporary society. For while the individual might still be allowed to make a career, he is no longer strong enough to fulfill the basic demands of human life. The man of goodwill is driven today into isolation like the Jew-stranger in the castle. He gets lost—or dies from exhaustion. For only within the framework of a people can a man live as a man among men, without exhausting himself. And only when a people lives and functions in consort with other peoples can it contribute to the establishment upon earth of a commonly conditioned and commonly controlled humanity.

INTRODUCTION TO

SIMONE WEIL, PROPHET OUT OF ISRAEL

Leslie A. Fiedler

and

CONTRA SIMONE WEIL

Hans Meyerhoff

Why Simone Weil? Why more attention to one self-hating Jew than to any of the tens of thousands of other equally distinguished (or undistinguished) self-hating Jews of our time or of any other? One sufficient, but not necessary, reason is that no Jew is without some grain of self-hatred, some lowering of the eyes in embarrassment, some cheek reddening, some annoyance at the unexpected, unprepared recognition (secretly acknowledged) that his life must be shared with all those others—those German Jews or those East European Jews, or those Zionists, or those *nouveaux riches* or those poor and vulgar, whatever, however, some order of interior discontent which is an unhealed, an unhealable wound.

Leslie Fiedler recognizes Simone Weil's self-hatred as one aspect of her intellectual condition, and though he interprets it generously, to her benefit, if not to ours, what is of moment to me (including Fiedler's encomium to her and Hans Meyerhoff's equally astute debunking) is that her life is almost archetypal. At a moment when the Jewish people were being destroyed for being Jews, Simone Weil—loathing her Jewish origins and the Jewish literature of ecstatic covenant, exile, and suffering—was herself passing through the identical Jewish experience, though she could not acknowledge it, though she lacked every instrument of interpreting to herself that her own willful assumption of pain and suffering had much in common with the saints and sages of Israel. But even this is unimportant to us, except in so far as we may read

50

her books as individuals in search of enlightenment, rather than as Jews seeking familiars and similitudes. Leslie Fiedler's moving, sympathetic, even affectionate evocation of Simone Weil is an essay in the understanding of one type of secular intellectual of Jewish origin, who wanders so far in search of a way of returning home that home becomes impossible, transitory, meaningless. What remains for her is to penetrate into the aridities of the soul and to pray that one flower of compassion or love may be permitted to grow on the pitiless and rocky soil she meticulously prepared.

Hans Meyerhoff's fitting counterpoint to Fiedler's essay is an examination of one radical consequence of Simone Weil's self-hatred, her Marcionism, her refusal to acknowledge any continuity —historical, metaphysical, religious—between the Creator God of the Hebrew Bible and the Redeemer God of the New Testament. Meyerhoff shows that from such a Gnostic doctrine one might ask how it could be hoped that the Living God, indeed any God who would embrace life in our time, could endure. It is no wonder, Meyerhoff might have written, for God to be written off with obloquy, proclaimed dead, if indeed the alternatives—as Weil saw them—are so radical and hopeless: perfection and pure love or complete wretchedness and total despair. With such an *entweder-oder,* who could imagine that God would not become silent, would not become abscondite, would not, as some novelty thinkers suggest, "die"?

Meyerhoff's critique of Simon Weil's ignorance of Judaism (beautifully elaborated in Martin Buber's address, "The Silent Question," which treats of Weil and Bergson [*At The Turning,* Farrar, Straus, and Young, New York, 1952, pp. 29–44]) raises what is a crucial issue in the post-Holocaust history of Judaism—a human fury against a species of divine betrayal of historic man and a partisan, outraged flight into self-torment, punitive narcissism, and love rendered hopeless by the despair of ever finding it.

51

SIMONE WEIL,
PROPHET OUT OF ISRAEL

A Saint of the Absurd

LESLIE A. FIEDLER

"Cast aside all beliefs that serve to fill up emptiness or sweeten what is bitter: the belief in immortality; the belief that good somehow comes of sin, *etiam peccata;* the belief in the providential ordering of events—in short, all the 'consolations' that we ordinarily seek in religion.

"Ineluctable necessity, misery, distress, the crushing weight of poverty and of work that drains the spirit, cruelty, torture, violent death, constraint, terror, sickness—all these are God's love!"

When, in 1941, Simone Weil, the author of these extraordinary words, first met Gustave Thibon, the man who was to preserve them for us,[1] the scene promised to be a comic one, a series of burlesque misunderstandings. M. Thibon was a lay Catholic philosopher of peasant origin who preferred not to be called a theologian, though he had written several remarkable books developing a theory of the sublimation of erotic love to divine charity through the family. Simone Weil, a letter from a common friend had already informed him, was "a young Jewess, a militant left-winger, with a higher degree in philosophy," who wanted to try living close to the soil. Jew, radical, intellectual, back to the land!—she seemed a living cliché, so precise an epitome of all he considered the fashionable sham of a whole generation that M. Thibon feared for his reserves of patience and courtesy.

---

1. In a collection of aphorisms called *La Pésanteur et la Grâce* ("Down-drag and Grace") , published by Plon in 1948 and edited after the death of Simone Weil by M. Thibon (*Gravity and Grace,* published by Putnam, New York) .

It would end badly he knew; for although—he naively assures us—he was "untainted, thank God, by any *a priori* anti-Semitism," he had known enough Jews to be convinced that the Jewish temperament was not only alien to his own, but quite unsuited to communal living, though much attracted to such attempts. As for Marxists and *agrégées de philosophie* on the land. . . . The first interview turned out to be quite as ridiculous as he had expected. Simone Weil, nervous, aware of her superficial unattractiveness and compelled to exaggerate it, talked at him endlessly in a maddening monotone, a brutal assault of talk that made it impossible to settle any practical problems, and left him physically exhausted.

Eventually, M. Thibon lost, in his love for her astonishing purity, his sense of the atmosphere of high comedy created by Simone Weil's inability to be charming on the human level, to be even "human" in any of the lower senses of the word; but the glimpse of her absurdity preserved in his memoir seems a vital clue not provided in other accounts of her life. Her pitiless pursuit of the absolute, her violence in rescuing religious belief from the "pious," are perhaps more important to remember in the end; but in the beginning one must dare to know her as a comic character, anti-heroic, a *shlemazl* and a *nar*.

Simone Weil was born in Paris in 1909 of fairly comfortable people, her father a doctor, and both of her parents the sort of un-Jewish Jews capable of bringing her up without even a vestigial sense of any tradition alien to her Frenchness. At the École Normale Supérieure, she became a disciple of the philosopher Alain, a rationalist, a Platonist, an unconventional moralist—and a radical. Already she had begun to define herself in terms of the stock comic characters of the bourgeoisie: the female intellectual, the Jew who does not admit to being a Jew, the schoolteacher as small-town radical—and though young she was obviously marked even then for the extreme comic role of our civilization: the old maid.

Though she participated in left-wing demonstrations and marched on picket lines, the authorities refused to take her seriously enough to fire her. When a school inspector threatened the revocation of her teaching license, she replied that she had always foreseen such revocation as the crown of her career. But the license was not revoked; another crown awaited her, the crown of an antiheroic heroism beyond the melodramatic dream of martyrdom of the young radical. (Much later, to be sure, she was refused a post under the Vichy regime, but this was for nothing she *specifically* was or had done; it was just as another Jew, almost anonymous, that she was rejected; and she did not even know how to admit that she was a Jew.)

Cheated of revocation, she decided to take a leave of absence to go to work in the Renault plant, a banal decision and fundamentally silly, the illusion of the Vassar girl of all lands that in a brief excursion into a factory she can get to know the life whose essential quality is its endlessness. For Simone Weil the outcome was more than usually distressing; not only did she suffer, not as a worker, but as an *agrégée de philosophie* desiring to suffer like a worker—but, ill to begin with, she was attacked by pleurisy and had to quit. In the disgust she learned to feel over her machine, she found a reward, but it was not the easy identification with the workers she had sought.

Regaining some measure of strength, she enlisted with the Loyalists in Spain (vowing all the while never to learn to use the gun she was given) and was hurt, not in combat, but in a trivial accident. Her grandest gestures were fated to end bathetically. Concerned with the possibilities of combining participation and nonviolence, pondering the eternal, she forgot the "real" world of missteps and boiling water. Burned and badly cared for, she was rescued from a field hospital by her parents, whose baffled but stubborn love was always coming between her and the denouement of agony to which she aspired.

During the Second World War, desiring to participate again, she worked out a scheme for being parachuted into occupied France to bring to the wounded members of the Resistance—not medical care, for she lacked even the simplest skills of healing, but her mere presence as a woman! What the military authorities made of this offer we can only guess; we know that they told her that her characteristically Jewish features might compromise her associates— but she had not even been remembering that she had a body, much less one that might bear the typical marks of a people in whose existence she did not believe.

She had no common sense, no sense of humor, no discretion— only an immense, naive seriousness and a contempt for reality. Encouraged by an imaginary gleam of response in the eye of a young peasant girl, she had once embarked on a series of lectures on the Upanishads that left her poor victim utterly bewildered, though too polite to stop her torrent of erudition. She was, in short, a bore—yet another role in the comic repertory. Capable of being only one thing to all men, and despising all strategies or etiquettes of discourse, she risked not only the snicker and the raised eyebrow, but often betrayal or serious political reprisals.

The only case of which I have read when her disregard for the limitations of other people did not produce an absurd anticlimax occurred in Italy, when she revealed to a stranger, in whom she sensed a growing weakness of resolve, the fact that she had fought in Spain. This impulsive decision to temper the shaky soul by temptation did not end in the denouncement which one might have expected; the stranger, though poor, resisted the rewards offered informers and said nothing. Perhaps, after all, this scene, too, remained in character; for to have found a Judas would have thrust her into the role of the betrayed, made of her the hero, and the hero to her seemed the mere ersatz of the prophet or saint, the man who dies publicly for ultimate victory rather than in silence for failure's sake.

Even on the verge of her death in England, a semisuicide at the age of thirty-four (she had refused, although weak and sick, to eat more than the rations allowed at that time in occupied France), she was baffled in her quest for absolute suffering by special attentions, being removed against her will to the comparative peace of the countryside.

Her eternally frustrated asceticism is a special modern instance: foiled by loving parents and kindly friends, even by impersonal hospital attendants in a world where the choice of the hairshirt is thought ridiculous or "pathological"—or even a hoax. For most of her life she had, however, one invulnerable advantage over her frustrators, being ceaselessly tormented by headaches (that ill, she called it, "which attacks me at the meeting place of body and soul") that grew greater or lesser but never left her, and which had grown so severe in her early adolescence that for a long time she was at the very point of suicide. Later there were added the ravages of pleurisy, whose marks she bore until her death.

But her illness never seemed to her a sufficiently willed *askesis;* in factory life, in manual labor on the soil (she chose always the most difficult tasks and demanded of herself the same speed and competence as the most experienced workers, insisted on sleeping in the most miserable of quarters), she sought additional mortifications.

What "everybody" longed for she ridiculously spurned. She had refused to leave Paris during the war until it had been declared an open city, and when life had become impossible for her parents in France and she had agreed to emigrate for their sake, she even succeeded in hating the United States to which they had fled. Its material comforts she found as humiliating and harmful to her vocation as the "spiritual" comforts of conventional religion.

Instead she plotted an underground return to France, or even emigration to the Soviet Union, whose politics she despised and where she could doubtless not have lived in freedom for a month. Among the Communists in France she had been known as a Trotskyite and had once been threatened with physical violence for delivering an anti-Stalinist report at a trade union convention. But the Russians were just then retreating before the German attack, and she felt obliged to "add a counterweight," to restore a proper balance; for with the defeated, she felt, was whatever could be found, in this world, of justice, "that fugitive from the camps of the victorious." One can barely imagine her in that improbable context, the pure Comedian, with the gun that would doubtless have blown off her fingers if she had attempted to fire it, flanked by the assured killers of "fascist beasts."

One thinks finally of Don Quixote, of Melville's Pierre, of the tragic buffoons who can never keep our time because they are set by the eternal chronometer—of the Holy Fool, whose wisdom is an unforeseen power of what we call stupidity, the ridiculous raised to the level of the ultimate, divine, absurd.

It is necessary to insist upon Simone Weil's religious vocation and her dedication to the absurd, because in this country she is likely to be known, if at all, mainly through the translations of her writings that appeared in Dwight MacDonald's defunct magazine, *Politics*.[2] The emphasis of these articles is largely social; and in the context of a periodical with an outlook more purely "political," less mystical, complicated, and ambiguous than her own, they tend, I think, to misrepresent her. Such a piece as "Factory Work," for instance, with its final plea for the humanization of machine work,

---

2. "Reflections on War," February 1945; "The Iliad: or The Poem of Force," November 1945; "Words and War," March 1946; "Factory Work," December 1946. (Some of these essays, in different translations, appear in *Selected Essays 1934–43* [translated by Richard Rees, New York, Oxford University Press, 1962] and *Intimations of Christianity* [translated by Elisabeth Chase Geissbuhler, Boston, Beacon Press, 1957].

strikes one as naive and more than a little trite (its conclusions, taken alone, might be echoed enthusiastically by any personnel men trained in the Harvard Business School) until reread in the light of the concluding aphorisms in *Gravity and Grace*. "Why has no worker or peasant mystic written on the use of the disgust that arises from manual labor. . . . Disgust in all its forms is one of those most precious miseries granted to man as a ladder by which he may ascend. . . . No earthy finality separates the workers from God. Only they are in this situation . . . revolution is the opium of the people. . . ." Simone Weil has no sociology, properly speaking, certainly not in the final stages of her thought.

Unlike true political or social thinkers, she is never concerned with the *solution* to war or poverty, but always with their *use*. She fears more than anything the proffered hope, Utopian or "practical," which diverts the attention of the workers toward the future, toward consolation; the politics of redemption is, like any false religion, an opiate. It is true that Simone Weil's earliest writings, in the organ of the French Teachers Union or *La Révolution Prolétarienne*, a syndicalist journal, were political in the narrower sense she later eschewed; and that she felt obliged at one point to make a full-dress criticism of Marxism; but the culmination of her thought is metapolitical. Politics and sociology were for her what rhetoric and women were for Augustine or exegesis of the Torah for Paul— that through which she moved to a final conversion, and consequently that which may have controlled the metaphors, but not the meaning, of her final belief.

Political activity was always a temptation for Simone Weil. Charity urged her to embrace causes that she knew in advance were imperfect, even radically wrong. Her absolute contempt for politics, paradoxically enough, made it possible for her to turn to compromises (her proposed journey to help the Russians, her joining with the Gaullists) that a quasi-absolutist radical would have found impossible. She never deceived herself, however; she knew that those causes which defeat made tolerable would in victory show the face of the Great Beast that lurked behind all political action. The hope of the City of God, as opposed to the fact of the Leviathan, was a hope only, never achievable in this world of necessity and force.

The articles in *Politics* are by no means without value; read in the light of their limitations, they provide a sense of Simone Weil's generosity, her passionate awareness of all human suffering, and the tension between involvement and withdrawal that characterizes her life. But only "The Iliad: or The Poem of Force" reveals her larger views and final values with any clarity. It is by far her best-known work and, together with two essays thus far untranslated into English ("*L'agonie d'une civilisation*" and "*L'inspiration occitanienne*," both in *Cahiers du Sud,* August 1942), furnishes the best indication of her total viewpoint outside Gustave Thibon's collection.

The language of the essay on the *Iliad* is especially remarkable, though Simone Weil affected to despise style (and it has been astonishingly well translated by Mary McCarthy, with the sort of warmth and lucidity seldom found together). In a single, gradual crescendo, it builds from its very first sentence until just before its close to a splendid height of pathos. Transported without a sense of display or melodrama to that peak of feeling, one wonders how one has got there, and cannot wait to return to the Homeric poem to see if the pathos has been legitimately deduced. It has not—not quite, I am afraid. The reading is a tour de force, but what we are presented with is an expurgated poem, the *Iliad* as a Christian epic— devoid of that celebration of honor, the boys' vision of *gloire* that nowadays half intrigues, half exasperates us, and lacking the personal story, the individualized tragedy of Achilles and his wrath— an epic in which all that for Simone Weil is foreground was for Homer mere background. And yet—as a partial reading and for its own sake, this version is not without delight and wisdom.

Here is the poem, as Simone Weil reads it. "The true hero, the true subject, the center of the *Iliad* is force. Force employed by man, force that enslaves man, force before which man's flesh shrinks away. In this work, at all times, the human spirit is shown as modified by its relations with force, as swept away, blinded, by the very force it imagined it could handle, as deformed by the weight of the force it submits to."

The rest of the essay specifies this generalization, showing it in the context of the Homeric poem, the degradation of the conquered as corpse and slave, and of the conqueror as the prey of *hybris* and *nemesis*. Against the degradation, the down-drag of force, only love can survive, and the victories of love are few and transitory. A note in the pamphlet edition of this essay prepared by *Politics* suggests that it may intend an "indirect commentary" on the fall of France

—but it is more than that, almost a commentary on the fall of man, certainly one on the failure of politics, which is to say, war. "The purest and loveliest of mirrors," Simone Weil calls the *Iliad*—a mirror for politicians.

Politics is, after all, force; in intent the discreet control of force, but in fact the inevitable failure of that control. "A moderate use of force," Simone Weil says ruefully at one point, "which alone would enable man to escape being enmeshed in its machinery, would require superhuman virtue, which is as rare as dignity in weakness." That "superhuman virtue" she will later identify with grace, but at this point in her life she is unwilling to name it. She does not hesitate, however, to identify force, removing it from the sphere of the social to the metaphysical, by translating it first into necessity and then into matter, until the struggle is seen finally in Manichaean terms as the cosmic conflict of love and matter.

It is scripture that Simone Weil has been seeking at the walls of Troy and not a mere poem, and so she selects and distorts. The impersonal bitterness of Homer in the face of necessity (his gusto is ignored), his equity which refuses to distinguish between Trojan and Greek, she interprets as the spirit which culminates in the New Testament: the cry of despair from the cross and universal charity. The *Iliad* is Simone Weil's Pentateuch, with Plato her Prophets and the tragedies of Aeschylus and Sophocles her Hagiographa. It is from these roots that she sees the Christian Gospels spring, for in her theory the Old Testament of the Hebrews is an evil book, justifying the Leviathan.

But to understand these views fully, we must turn to *Gravity and Grace*, remembering that the Greeks of Simone Weil are not the sunny, assured pagans of the handbooks on the classics, but the inventors of holy despair.

"Agony," Simone Weil has said, "is the supreme 'dark night' which even the perfect need to attain absolute purity; and to attain that end, it has to be bitter agony." This is a difficult doctrine in all times and places, and it is especially alien and abhorrent in present-day America where anguish is regarded as vaguely un-American, something to be grown out of, or analyzed away, even expunged by censorship; and where certainly we do not look to our churches to preach the uses of affliction. It is consolation, "peace of mind," "peace of soul," that our religions offer on the competitive market place; the means are different, the pew versus the analyst's couch or the newest best seller, but the product promised is always the same: adjustment, the opposite of agony.

There is scarcely a Christian church that dares remind its faithful that the final words of Jesus were words of despair, "My God, my God, why hast thou forsaken me!" But to Simone Weil that cry is more precious than the Beatitudes. "The extreme greatness of Christianity lies in its not seeking a supernatural remedy for suffering, but a supernatural use of suffering," she has said, and we remember that this was once, with perhaps more right, the boast of Judaism, before we swapped Job for Joshua Loth Liebman and the Prophets for "community service." Indeed, Simone Weil insists, his ability to suffer gives to man a superiority over God that would have been a cosmic scandal except for the "incarnation."

Of all the false comforts which the "believer" interposes between himself and the acceptance of agony that alone can purify him, none is more vicious than the hope of "immortality," understood as an assurance that the ego will go on and on in an infinite orgy of self-ness. To Simone Weil the ego is the enemy of Love, the screen between us and God, which we must "de-create" in the contemplation of misery and death, permitting God once more to become the Everything from which he withdrew in the act of creation. This more-than-suicide is the love which we must return for that affliction which is God's love for us, the awareness, at the bottom of all misfortune, of his absence, which is all of him that we can know as long as we are trapped in the ego. Misery frees us from the downward pull, the *pésanteur*, of false comforts and permits Grace to raise us out of ourselves. "Misery forces us to recognize as real, what we would not even have believed possible."

In our time the "atheist" is nearer reality than the kind of "believer" to whom the church is an illusory escape from terror. At least the atheist is unhappy! Nonbelief may be a spiritual purification, doing for those outside the church what the exercises of the mystics must do for those within.

"Between two men who have no experience of God, he who denies him is perhaps closer to him."

"A case of contradictories, both of them true. There is a God. There is no God. Where is the problem? I am quite sure that there is a God in the sense that I am sure my love is no illusion. I am quite sure that there is no God, in the sense that I am sure that there is nothing which resembles what I can conceive when I say that word. . . ."

The last quotation exemplifies Simone Weil's essential method of speculation, her dialetic which gives to a casual reader the sense of inconsistency: God is everything and he is nothing; "revolution is the opium of the people" but revolutionary activity can discipline one to a true contempt for the social. "Method of investigation—" she has jotted down in a note to herself, "as soon as one has arrived at any position, try to find in what sense the contrary is true."

But there is a kind of knowledge certain beyond the possibilities of speculation. Notice that she has said above in the aphorism about who is closer to God, "between two men *who have no experience of him.*" Such experience she believed to be possible to those who have passed through the "dark night of the soul," either by way of the mystical exercise or through the secular purgation of political activity and agonized nonbelief. Certainly, she was convinced that there had come to her such a direct, experiential knowledge of God—perhaps several times, though we have been given a description of only one such encounter.[3]

Just after her year as a factory worker had ended in total exhaustion and sickness, she was possessed by the sense of having become to the deepest level of her being a "slave," beyond any temptation to hope, and too weary for self-pity. There was left only agony and love. The name of God she neither dared nor knew how to think, but, she has written, "In a moment of intense physical suffering, when I was forcing myself to feel love, but without daring to give a name to that love, I felt, without being in any way prepared for it (for I have never read the mystical writers) a presence more personal, more certain, more real than that of a human being, though inaccessible to the senses and the imagination. . . ."

The immediate occasion of the experience is odd enough to notice. It is a touching case and strangely typical of the contemporary intellectual, compelled to seek underground in literature the uses and satisfactions of ritual, which he is inclined to despise without knowing. Simone Weil was saying to herself a piece of George Herbert. "I thought I was merely reciting a poem," she writes, "and I was saying a prayer":

---

3. In a letter to Joé Bousquet, printed in *Cahiers du Sud*, No. 984 (1947).

Love bade me welcome: yet my soul drew back,
    Guiltie of lust and sinne.
But quick-ey'd Love, observing me grow slack
    From my first entrance in,
Drew nearer to me, sweetly questioning,
    If I lack'd any thing.

A guest, I answer'd, worthy to be here:
    Love said, You shall be he.
I the unkinde, ungratefull? Ah my deare,
    I cannot look on thee.
Love took my hand, and smiling did reply,
    Who made the eyes but I?
Truth Lord, but I have marr'd them: let my shame
    Go where it doth deserve.
And know you not, sayes Love, who bore the blame?
    My deare, then I will serve.
You must sit down, sayes Love, and taste my meat:
    So I did sit and eat.

This poem is essential to an understanding of Simone Weil's thought. Its final lines sum up her sense (deeply felt but only tentatively expressed) that there is a love in whose light our deepest intuitions are revealed as partial glimpses of paradoxes more wonderful than any we dare conceive. This is the Grace, the upward attraction that all the time secretly combats the downward tug of an earthly gravity everywhere only too apparent; and knowing it, we know that our misery is our joy, that God is our slave in so far as we have become slaves for his sake. Not all misery and abjectness is per se a way to this revelation, but properly used and cherished it can become such a way.

Simone Weil knew that there is a last trap even for those who deny illusory happiness, an ersatz of holy suffering and sacred self-contempt—mere masochism and neurotic self-hatred. For every virtue there is a corresponding disease, and equivalent to the most splendid virtues the grossest sicknesses of the spirit. The end of the lower self-hatred is suicide, the destruction in despair of the possibilities of more ultimate suffering; the end of the higher self-hatred is "de-creation," the burning away in misery of all in us except that which responds to love. For those who can conceive of no "self" beyond that which is the captive of *pésanteur* and the flesh, it may be difficult to see the difference between the self-hatred of Simone Weil (or such chastisers of the flesh as Gautama Buddha or Moshe Leib of Sasov) and that of a pathological suicide like Otto Weininger. The understanding of such matters depends on what one makes the final ground of explanation; whether from the "psychological" point of view, one regards the striking resemblances between certain neurotic and mystical states as evidence that the latter are frauds; or whether from a religious standpoint, one takes such resemblances as evidence that everywhere the spirit tries to achieve certain relations with the divine that are continually baffled and parodied by a mocking counterforce.

Even from a pragmatic point of view, a self-conscious and principled self-hatred can be understood to have a mithridatic value, harmlessly purging away tendencies which, unrecognized and undeclared, might cause great psychic harm. And certainly self-hatred can be viewed as an *askesis* by way of which we may be delivered of enervating self-pity, and the even more dangerous impulse to project outward onto the Other that which we secretly despise in ourselves. To turn our malice inward away from the guilt-evoked lay figures of Jew, anti-Semite, homosexual, intellectual, or bourgeois, will lead us at least to do less harm to men if not prepare us to see the living God. Such a course is beset by the temptation to despair, and some may founder there; but beyond lies a more ultimate love than we can ever know this side of despair. Here is the ultimate *rite de passage*, the night-journey, the descent into Hell— from which we must not be deterred by the example of those who have not found the strength to emerge, or who, falling in love with the infernal, have chosen to remain.

In Herbert's poem, Simone Weil found her initial assurance of the reality beyond darkness, and the central metaphor of the poem stayed with her always.

"The great sorrow of man, which begins in childhood and lasts until death," she wrote much later, "is that looking and eating are two separate operations. Eternal beatitude is a state in which looking and eating are a single act." And her life itself works out strange variations of longing and repulsion on the theme: her death through fasting, her refusal to "eat" in the Catholic ritual act of Communion the God she had "seen" in ecstasy.

Simone Weil never became a communicating Catholic, though from that moment forward she desired desperately to be able to enter the Church. Like the great prophets of Israel, she required a vital priestly orthodoxy against which to define her revolt; and it was the Church of Rome that she chose to play the Deuteronomist to her Jeremiah. That she could not turn to Judaism is her tragedy and ours.

Of Judaism as a faith she knew nothing; neither she nor her parents nor two of her grandparents had ever seen the inside of a *shul*, and no voice was raised to attract her in an Israel narrowing on one side into mechanical orthodoxy and broadening on the other into secularism, Zionism, and sociology. To have considered herself a Jew would have seemed to her a betrayal of enlightened ethnology; her actual tradition she felt to be "Christian, French, and Greek." Indeed, what vague sense of an obligation to Jewry survived in her was expressed in revulsion, a passionate anti-Semitism that upsets for once her cherished method of honoring contradictories. She will admit no favorable interpretation of the mission of the Jews:

"Israel. All from Abraham on inclusively (except for a few prophets) is filthy and monstrous, as if on purpose. As if to point out with absolute clarity: Note well! here is evil! A people chosen for blindness, chosen to be the executioners of Christ.

"The curse of Israel weighs heavily on Christianity. The atrocities, the Inquisition, the liquidation of heretics and infidels, this was Israel. Capitalism was (and to a certain degree still is) Israel. Totalitarianism, especially among the worst enemies of Israel, is Israel."

"Anti-Israelism" or even, perhaps, "anti-Judaism" would most accurately describe the doctrines of Simone Weil in this regard, since it was the *beliefs* of the Jews that she especially despised; and yet she herself succumbs to the racism she attributes to them and their mortal enemies: "a *people* chosen etc." In her opposition to Hitler she would never admit the presence of any identification with the Jews; quite the contrary, she accused Hitler always of fighting the battle of Israel, seeking only to revive under another name and for his own benefit the God of Israel, "earthly, cruel, and exclusive." Sometimes, indeed, she insisted that Jehovah and Hitler were Gods in the same sense and on the same plane.

She had recast the whole history of the Jews in terms reminiscent of Houston Chamberlain, so that only her distrust of force seems sometimes to mark off her position from that of the persecuting anti-Semites. "God made purely temporal promises to Moses and Joshua at a time when Egypt was groping toward the eternal salvation of the soul. Having refused the Egyptian revelation, the Hebrews got the God they deserved: a corporeal and collective God who spoke to no one up to the Exile. . . . No wonder that a nation of fugitive slaves, conquerors of a land of milk and honey cultivated by civilizations whose labors they did not share but which they destroyed in a series of massacres, no wonder such a people was able to give scarcely anything good to the world. . . ."

Most of the writers on Simone Weil have chosen to slight this distressing aspect of her thought; but it is, alas, no peripheral vagary but rather an obsessive theme to which she recurs at the unlikeliest moments, even—as we have seen—in her piece on the *Iliad*. Typical in so many ways of the generation whose allegiances and revolts she turns improbably to the service of God, she must express, too, its deepest shame. Antibourgeois, radical, attracted to nonviolence yet a participant in the Spanish civil war—she must also be a Jew and an anti-Semite, the anti-Semitic Jew, both sides of our most desperate cleavage in a single body. It is not inappropriate that the one contemporary writer she mentions with favor is Arthur Koestler.

It is easy enough to say at this point, with some of our defenders of an embattled secularism, that any Christian religious revival necessarily entails the exacerbation of anti-Semitism. But the immediate tradition to which Simone Weil belongs, the tradition of Léon Bloy and Charles Péguy, was before her violently philo-Semitic. Bloy, who scandalized the good Christians of his day by his fury and absolutism (he ran hurrahing through the streets when a church bazaar, with a few score of the conventionally pious, burned to the ground), doubly scandalized them by his defense of the Jews. "Each day in Communion I eat a Jew," he had cried out to his challengers, "and I depend on a bunch of Yids for my eternal salvation!" Involved in his attempt to redeem Christianity is the shame and guilt brought into focus by the Dreyfus Affair and the consequent resolve to make it clear beyond doubt that anti-Semitism is a function not of a living Church but only of a dying one. From Bloy the tradition passed to Péguy and reached a climax in the attempt of Jacques Maritain to define a post-Christian mission of the Jews, and in his vision of Israel under persecution coming to resemble more and more the figure of Jesus. "The chastisement of our peace was upon him. . . ."

In the teeth of this tradition, Simone Weil denied to the Jews *any* mission, pre-Christian or post-Christian, except the negative one of embodying a species of evil, the idolatrous worship of what Plato had called the "great beast." As ancient Rome represented the "great beast" in its materialistic, atheist form, Israel represented it in its pseudospiritual form, the idolatry of the social as an ersatz of religion. It is not as the "excluded" that she hated the Jews, but as the eminently successful, the inventors of nationalism; she could not include them, as had Bloy and Péguy, with the insulted and injured.

To Péguy and Bloy the Jews had been the Others, immune to the self-contempt these Christians preached as the beginning of wisdom; to Simone Weil, whatever she publicly asserted, the Jews were herself, her own. And upon them fell that pious hatred—oddly blended of the Gospel saying that "a man's foes shall be they of his own household" and the socialist teaching that one's own bourgeoisie was the worst enemy—which in her predecessors had been directed against the "good Christian." What makes this reaction finally illegitimate in Simone Weil is her terrible refusal to *live* her Jewishness, the quality which to everyone else seemed the very essence of her being. Her hatred of Israel could have been redeemed only by her accepting its pathos as her own.

Against such an acceptance she defended herself by ignorance. Knowing nothing of Jewish mystical thought, she was able to remain undisturbed by the resemblances between her own doctrine and the traditions of Judaism. Though she knows the falsifications of anti-Semitic historians, she displays no real knowledge even of the Old Testament, much less of any of the later religious writers of the Jews. Immensely learned in Greek, and willing to devote much time to learning Sanskrit, she was apparently never even tempted to learn Hebrew.

"There can be no personal contact between man and God," she wrote. "Except through a mediator, the presence of God to man can only be collective, national. Israel simultaneously chose a national God and refused the mediator; though it may from time to time have tended toward a true monotheism, it always relapsed, and it *had* to relapse, to the tribal God." That in Israel, too, the problem of an absolutely transcendent God who can yet be apprehended personally was wrestled with in terms of the theory of *sephiroth*, she does not know. It is the dogma of Incarnation which possessed her imagination, and not the theory of Emanation; so that, exposed to the mystical experience, she cries out that Christ has taken her, unaware of even the name of the Shechina. The blame is not entirely hers; the frantic retreat from mysticism, the embracing of rationalism as a sufficient faith had made Israel inhospitable to the impassioned believer in her country in her time; and she, who might have been a prophet in Israel, sat on the doorstep of an alien church.

Though she entered no church completely and finally, it was the Roman Catholic Church of which she quoted again and again ". . . and the gates of hell shall not prevail against it." She is even reputed to have helped convert others to that faith. "You are like the church bell," a monk, who was one of her dearest friends, once told her, "which calls others into the church, but itself must remain outside." At one point, just before her departure from France, she was on the verge of becoming a communicant, but at the last minute withdrew because the Roman Church was—too Jewish!

In identifying the God of Love of the Gospels with the Lord of Hosts of the Law, she believed, Catholicism had failed to purify itself of the abomination of Israel. Reviving an ancient heresy of the Gnostics, Simone Weil maintained the absolute discontinuity of the Old Testament and the New. Undisturbed by the mosaic of quotations from the Prophets and Psalms which determine the very pattern of the life of Jesus, and ignoring the source of the injunction, "Thou shalt love thy neighbor as thyself," in Leviticus, she insisted that the Gospels were a work of the Greek genius, the culmination not of the Hebrew Scriptures, but of a tradition beginning with Homer and running on through the great tragedians and the philosophy of Plato (Aristotle she distrusted as a kind of Greek Jew). She could never forgive the Church for believing in the Jews as a chosen people, rather than the Greeks or the Hindus— or even the Egyptians!

And yet, finally, there is a sense in which without violence this anti-Semite can be claimed as a Jewish thinker. She escapes all orthodoxy, to be sure, but it is perhaps as a Jewish heretic rather than a Christian one that she can best be understood. The slogan whose absence from the mouths of contemporary Christians she decried, the lament, *"Eli, Eli, lama sabachthani,"* Simone Weil could have heard on the lips of the Jews, who have never wholly forgotten the uses of despair. The regard for agony and suffering, the belief in the experience of alienation as a supreme proof of God's love, the unwillingness to yield up terror to consolation—

these are qualities never entirely absent among the people she contemned.

Man's absolute exile from God, the nonpresence and nonintervention of the *deus absconditus,* upon which Simone Weil so uncompromisingly insisted, can be found in the terrible dogmas of Lurianic Cabalism, and in that astonishing metaphor of the Zohar: the figure of *tsimtsum* or the withdrawal of God on himself, which conceives of our being as possible only in the interstices of the universe where God has willed his own nonbeing.

The refusal to speculate on immortality for fear of giving a lying reassurance to the lowest cravings of the ego, and of losing the absolute savor of death that can alone purify belief—this Simone Weil has in common with the main tradition of the Old Testament. And though she will not yield to the logic of her position and deny the possibility of a savior in time, she feels that Christianity, by moving the Redemption back out of a never attained futurity, has betrayed us to history and the heresy of progress. "The notion of history as a guided continuity is Christian. It seems to me that there are few ideas more utterly false."

The denial of impending redemption protects one from the temptation to demand in the kingdom of this world what is valuable only in the Kingdom of Heaven, as for instance absolute chastity, about which Simone Weil is silent, or absolute nonviolence, with which she is greatly concerned. Her limited and reasonable pacifism, though not exclusively Jewish, would be more at home in the tradition of Johanan ben Zakkai than in some of the absolutist Christian traditions, Scriptural or Tolstoyan. And that is why she can answer with more certainty than Gandhi: "Nonviolence is not good unless it is efficacious. So with the question of the young man to Gandhi about his sister. The answer should have been: use force, in so far as you are not able to defend her with as much possibility of *success* by nonviolent means."

It is finally the note of zeal, the willingness to scream, to be ridiculous, to offend the standards of decorum and good taste, that makes Simone Weil, like Christianity in general, less Greek than Jew. The stone-cold doctrine of "nothing in excess" denies true fervor and true humility alike. The notion that the lukewarm shall be spewed out of the mouth of the living God comes, after all, from the Hebrews and not from her beloved Greeks, to whom any passionate commitment seemed a betrayal of reason, or a disease.

We have traced a common tradition backward from Simone Weil to Léon Bloy, but the ultimate source of that tradition is the prophet Hosea, the holy fool who married the harlot he had bought in the market place and called his son "Ye-are-not-my-people!" The absurdity, the absolutism, the incandescence of the prophets survive in Simone Weil, and for all her blemishes, their terrible purity.

That she insists on measuring us all, as she measures herself, by that ultimate standard of purity, embarrasses us. Before her assumption that we are worthy of being weighed in such a scale, what are we to say? "It's a lucky thing for all of us," a friend of Simone Weil's once told her, "that you are not God!" And that, perhaps, will do as a final word.

CONTRA SIMONE WEIL

"The Voices of Demons for the Silence of God"

HANS MEYERHOFF

The significant facts of Simone Weil's life have grown into something like a legend. Born in 1909, she was the child of well-off, assimilated French Jews. The biographical sources—found chiefly in the reminiscences of Gustave Thibon, an intimate friend and Simone Weil's literary executor[1]—do not say much about her parents, but a brother who became a brilliant mathematician seems to have played a crucial role in her life. She believed that she would never be able to equal his intellectual genius, and this feeling seems to have produced two severe emotional crises in her adolescence and to have deepened the sense of inferiority and personal worthlessness from which she suffered all her life.

Yet her own intellectual powers were remarkable. She showed extraordinary gifts at school and won the respect of such teachers as the philosophers Le Senne and Alain. Combining exceptional learning with passionate religious temperament, she was capable of startling intellectual insights. She became a scholar and teacher of philosophy, mathematics, and Greek, and by the age of twenty she began publishing articles. But she frequently interrupted teaching and research for action. She threw herself into politics—communist, syndicalist, and anarchist; and for a year she worked in a factory. When the Nazis occupied France she sought refuge at M. Thibon's farm and worked in the fields.

---

1. M. Thibon and Father Perrin, another friend, have published a book about her life and thought: *Simone Weil telle que nous l'avons connue.*

Her death was the climax of an extremely ascetic, self-denying life. It was almost a suicide. Although she had contracted tuberculosis, she refused, while in England—to which she returned after a short stay in the United States—to eat more than the hunger rations of the people in occupied France. Throughout her life she showed a complete disregard—even contempt—for physical needs and comforts, and suffered constantly from pains and ailments, particularly from violent chronic headaches. These physical sufferings coincided with intense spiritual torments. Drawn ever closer to Catholicism, she occupied herself increasingly with theology, and came to feel herself completely a Christian; yet she refused baptism. The writings for which she is best known were all published posthumously. *Gravity and Grace,* with an introduction by M. Thibon, and *Waiting for God* are records of her religious quest and spiritual struggle. *The Need for Roots,* with an introduction by T. S. Eliot, is a religio-political tract written for the Gaullist movement and intended as a contribution to postwar planning.

Her brief life, the Stoic endurance of her sufferings, the long dark night of her soul, her asceticism, her mysticism and radicalism, her passionate, uncompromising pursuit of spiritual illumination, and the dramatic circumstances of her death—these aspects of Simone Weil's life and personality have helped shape the image of a religious hero—almost a saint. In the words of a recent English critic (E. W. F. Tomlin), she was "one more and perhaps the greatest 'pilgrim of the absolute' in our time." And her friend Thibon, while acknowledging that she was a difficult, perplexing, and often exasperating person, testifies that "in no human being have I come across such familiarity with religious mysteries; never have I felt the word *supernatural* more charged with reality than when in contact with her."

Now the private *Notebooks of Simone Weil*[2] (from which her earlier publications were excerpted) have been published in their entirety. They throw a new and sharper light upon an aspect of her thought and personality that has been rather neglected so far, and which has a special significance for the Jewish reader. I mean her extreme religious anti-Semitism. "Her anti-Semitism," M. Thibon writes, "was so violent that the continuity established by the Church between the Old and New Testament was one of the chief

---

2. Putnam, 2 vols., 1958.

obstacles to her becoming a Catholic. She was fond," he continues, "of saying that Hitler hunted on the same ground as the Jews and only persecuted them in order to resuscitate under another name and to his own advantage their tribal god, terrestrial, cruel, and exclusive." T. S. Eliot observed that it was Simone Weil's "rejection of Israel that made her a very heterodox Christian," and that, in this respect, she fell "into something very like the Marcionite heresy."

Marcion was a Christian theologian of the first half of the second century whose thought belongs to the religious phenomenon known as Gnosticism. When he failed to gain acceptance for his ideas among the Christians of Rome, Marcion founded his own church, for which he supplied a radical theology in a work called *Antitheses*. Gnosticism and Marcion celebrate a bizarre revival in the writings of Simone Weil; and it is this aspect of her work to which I wish to address myself particularly.

Gnosticism takes its name from the Greek word for knowledge. But *gnosis* meant knowledge in a special sense—a higher, mysterious, esoteric kind of knowledge primarily designed to obtain personal salvation. In Gnosticism, speculative philosophy was fused with religious revelation; or incarnations and mystic rites, allegories and numerologies, dogmas of faith and superstitions were integrated into a systematic body of ideas purporting to represent knowledge about man and the universe. The final product was usually an eclectic, syncretistic mixture drawing upon a great variety of intellectual and religious sources.

Gnosticism was a typical product of Helenism. Gnostic movements and sects arising in Persia, Greece, Rome, Egypt, Syria, and elsewhere mingled with each other in the great cultural and ideological melting pot of Hellenism. Gnostic influences may also be found in Jewish history: for example, in the revolt of the Maccabees against Hellenistic culture, and in the impressive eclectic philosophical synthesis concocted by Philo of Alexandria. Cabbalistic thought and literature represent a late flowering of Gnostic mysticism in Jewish life.

Gnosticism derives its chief historical significance, however, from its impact upon Christianity. Seeing it as a threat to the entire creed, the early Fathers of the Church carried on an unremitting theological struggle against Gnosticism. The Gnostics, too, were theologians, but their theology differed from that of the Church

Fathers in that they were much more radical and indiscriminate in bringing Gnostic ideas, Oriental mystery religions, and allegorical fantasies into the body of Christian dogma. This far-reaching fusion of Christianity with pagan religious symbolism was opposed by the bishops and Fathers of the early Church. Gnosticism was declared a heresy and, after long and bitter controversies, was finally overcome by Augustine, who put down Manicheanism, the last potent Gnostic uprising against the Church.

Most Gnostic thinkers, including Marcion, combined their synthesis of Christianity and Hellenism with a radical attack upon the religious tradition of Judaism. It is this aspect of Gnosticism which comes to life again in the writings of Simone Weil.

The early history of the Church is haunted by a dilemma which must have had a special poignancy for Jewish converts. How should they reconcile the old faith of their fathers with the new gospel of the Son of God? Beginning with Paul, the foremost Jewish convert to Christianity, two attitudes may be distinguished in this matter. The attitude which won out in the doctrinal struggle is embodied in the official Catholic dogma that the teachings of the Old Testament are restored and preserved in the new faith. The God of Genesis, i.e., the God of Israel, is the Creator of the world; he is the Father of mankind, and Jesus is his only begotten son. Moreover, Jesus came to fulfill, not to abolish, the old law of Moses; the Messianic voices of the Hebrew prophets proclaimed, and thus vindicated, him as savior. This position was reaffirmed in 1933, when Pope Pius XI, in answer to the new Christian paganism and the persecution of the Jews in Germany, proclaimed that "spiritually we are all Semites."

The other attitude was to reject and repudiate the authority of the Old Testament, which is what the Gnostics did. Paul himself had resolved the personal and religious dilemma posed by his conversion by hammering out a set of doctrinal antitheses—between the flesh and the spirit, between the old Law and the new Gospel, between the old God of anger and the new God of love, between salvation by works and salvation by faith, between the despair over the sickness unto death and the hope of life everlasting in Jesus.

Pauline theology did not lead to an outright repudiation of the Old Testament, but it did constitute a severe attack upon it; and it was chiefly under the influence of Paul's teachings that Gnostic thinkers moved toward a radical break with the Jewish origins of

Christianity—partly in order to accommodate Christianity more easily to non-Jewish religious cults and ideas, partly in order to establish the uniqueness of the new soteriological faith in Jesus. The common element in the Gnostic trend was the belief that the essence of the new faith lay in its break with the world of man's fall depicted in the Old Testament, and by its triumph over the God of Israel who had created this world of sin, suffering, and death. Thus the view developed, as Adolf Harnack wrote, that "the believers in Christ were the only true community of God . . . and that the Jewish Church, persevering in its stubborn unbelief, was the synagogue of Satan."

Marcion—who, unlike St. Paul, was a Gentile—developed these views to an extreme. The ideas contained in his *Antitheses* throw into sharp relief the significant features of the Gnostic revolt ("antithesis") against the Old Testament.

The Christian gospels reveal a God of love, mercy, and compassion; the God of the Old Testament is jealous, cruel, and revengeful; hence they cannot be the same. Since Jesus proclaimed redemption through faith and love, he cannot be the son of the malign, cruel God of the Old Testament; hence he is the son of the new "unknown" God whom Paul hailed in the market place of Athens. This is confirmed by Jesus himself, who declared war on the Pharisees and constantly broke the old Law in words and deeds; hence he repudiated the old God behind this Law and asserted that new wine should not be poured into old vessels. The Old Testament is the record of man's history in the state of fall, sin, despair, and death; it is, in fact, the reign of Satan on earth. This history has come to an end with Jesus who redeemed mankind and destroyed the power of the old evil God. Hence the new faith and its sacred scriptures must be purged of all Jewish influences (which Marcion set out to do) lest it be distorted and contaminated by them. Textual revisions, finally, were used to defend doctrinal differences. Thus Marcion distinguished between the spirit of Christ that dwelled everlastingly with God, and the man Jesus who was born and died on this earth; he also repudiated, as did other Gnostics, the dogma of the resurrection in the flesh, and the early Christian faith in the return of Jesus and the establishment of his kingdom on earth.

These Gnostic ideas, as we have said, were defeated in the struggle for official supremacy within the Church, but they have lived on as undercurrents in the history of Christian theology and heresy. Simone Weil's religious struggle represents, as it were, a violent "return of the repressed." It seems almost as if the Jew faced with the crisis of conversion to Christianity relives a historical drama. He must come to terms with his religious heritage, and perhaps can do so in only one of two ways: either he must feel that the Apostolic Church represents the natural fulfillment and fruition of the religious seeds contained in the Jewish faith (this seems to have been the solution adopted by contemporary converts like Alfred Stern and Edith Stein) or he must radically and violently repudiate that faith. This was what Simone Weil did.[3]

What makes her case so dramatic is that she launched her Gnostic revolt against the Jewish *religion* at a time when the Jewish *people* were suffering the worst agonies and tortures they have ever undergone within the Christian world. Staking her whole life on the hope and faith of salvation in Jesus, she was driven to indict the religion of her own people in the language of their worst enemies and persecutors.

Reading this indictment one sympathizes with the writer who protested against the review of *The Notebooks* which appeared in the *New York Times* on December 16, 1956. The reviewer called Simone Weil "Jewish, supremely and proudly so," praised "everything" she wrote as "new-minted, pure gold," and hailed her as "one of the greatest minds of our time." It is odd how such reviews make their appearance, but it is perhaps more disturbing to see how Simone Weil is presented to the public as *nothing but* a spiritual hero—a woman endowed with a restless, brilliant mind, who wrote about Homer, Plato, politics, mythology, and mathematics, a woman who explored the mysteries of divine love and transformed herself into a "pilgrim of the absolute." This transfiguration of Simone Weil has now become the conventional public portrait. Perhaps she was all these things, but she was more: she was also blind, cruel, and almost delusional, and she indulged in orgies of self-laceration. Did she draw up the terrible indictment of the

---

3. The case of actual or potential converts must be distinguished from individuals who leave the Jewish faith, or are excluded from it, without joining another "faith." Thus Spinoza does not belong in this group. His rational or mystical pantheism was as anti-Christian as it was anti-Jewish, and he was just as bitterly attacked, after the publication of his *Politico-Theological Tractatus,* by Christian theologians as by rabbis before his excommunication.

religion of her people in order to inflict yet deeper wounds upon herself, and did she believe this new agony would make her more pleasing in the eyes of the new God?

In her discussion of the *Iliad*, Simone Weil perceived, and partly admired, a supernatural quality and magnificence behind the inhuman, wasteful violence which she assumed to be the main theme of Homer's epic. But the bloodshed, violence, and brutality she reads of in the Old Testament inspired in her only horror. "Moses —starts off with a murder—Joshua—then a host of 'Judges' (murders, betrayals)—Samuel—Saul—David—Solomon—Kings of Judah and Israel. . . ." For Simone Weil the history of the ancient Hebrews is a unique record of murders and massacres. "Practically the only thing the Hebrews did was to exterminate." She duly notes "Abraham's cruelty towards Hagar and Ishmael"; the "horrible crime" committed by Jacob's children against the Hivites; "Joseph's atrocious conduct towards the Egyptians"; she counts the number of deaths caused by battle, plague, and earthquakes; and she dwells with horror and disgust upon the "deceitful," "barbarous" actions enjoined in Deuteronomy 20:10–18: and "thou shalt utterly destroy them, the Hittites, the Amorites, the Canaanites, the Perrizites, the Hivites and the Jebusites"—as if the Greeks she so admired had not sacked and ravaged Troy. Or, more importantly, as if these dark and stark injunctions of the Old Testament did not have a meaning in the natural evolution of the Jewish faith and people beyond their overt cruelty. For Simone Weil there was but one conclusion: Israel was an "artificial people, held together by a terrible violence." "What about the human sacrifices made to Baal?" Her answer: "The extermination of whole peoples is something far more appalling." Thus "everything [in the Old Testament] is of a polluted and atrocious character . . . beginning with Abraham, right down through all his descendants . . . as though to indicate perfectly clearly: Beware! That way lies evil."

Israel's "pollution" lies in its immorality and materialism. Here the record, according to Simone Weil, is, if anything, worse than that of the atrocities. The books of the Old Testament reek of carnal lust, incest, prostitution, defilement, drunkenness, deceit, theft, and fraud. There are but a few among the patriarchs who escape this charge. "Abraham defiles himself" and "hands his wife over to Pharaoh out of cowardice." Thus "the history of Israel begins with a prostitution. It is Israel's original impurity." And the original impurity was multiplied on a grand scale: Isaac "repeats Abraham's sin of cowardice. He allows himself to be deceived by Jacob, blinded by gluttony and foolishness. . . ." Jacob, in turn, "obtains the rights of the first-born by a cruel form of blackmail, and his father's blessings by lies and fraud. At Bethel he practices blackmail on God. He swindles Laban about the cattle. . . . Reuben (his eldest son) cohabits with his father's concubine. . . . Judah lies with his son's widow taking her to be a prostitute." There is nothing overlooked in Simone Weil's violent outbursts of moral indignation—not even the "excessive prosperity of the children of Israel in Egypt."

This is not the first time (nor will it be the last) that such accusations have been made against Israel, and against Israel alone —as if the civilizations of Greece, India, Egypt, and other peoples, among all those in whom Simone Weil discovers sparks of divine incarnation, did not reveal the same primitive morality of nature. Or, more importantly, as if we were not here (as elsewhere) dealing with stories, myths, and memories which recapture the dramatic origins of and transitions toward the so-called civilized morality which she applies in judging them. For Simone Weil there is but one conclusion: "The Hebrews, having rejected the Egyptian revelation, got the God they deserved—a carnal and collective God, who never spoke to anyone's soul, up to the time of exile." They were "too carnal-minded for any other God but Jehovah."

Hence Jehovah is Satan in disguise; and the religious mission of Israel is, at best, a warning that "this way lies evil," at worst, a terrible fraud and deceit. The only good thing that can be said for Israel is that it "represents an attempt at a supernatural form of social life," that "it succeeded in producing the best example of its kind"; but that "the result shows the sort of divine revelation of which the Great Beast [this is Simone Weil's way of designating the world of nature and man] is capable." Both Israel and ancient Rome are incarnations of the Great Beast. And the Famous Law of the Old Testament "was a sort of curse, as St. Paul says."

Thus, in the Pauline-Gnostic tradition, no good, let alone salvation, can come from the Law, or from this attempt to infuse social life with a supernatural or divine spirit. "Israel's spirituality was exclusively collective," and to ascribe any divine mission to the Jewish people is a mockery in view of their carnal and cruel nature. They were "*chosen* in order to be rendered blind, to be the executioner of Christ." (Perhaps Simone Weil, too, remembered taunts heard in childhood that she belonged to the people of "Christ-killers.") Rome and Israel "are perhaps the only two people to be ignorant of incarnation," and "it is for this reason that everything in Israel is contaminated with sin, because there is nothing pure without a participation in the incarnate divinity."

This passionate Gnostic denial of any trace of divinity or spirituality in the sacred Scriptures of Israel caused Simone Weil considerable trouble. After all, the Old Testament did preach an undeniably pure monotheism and did contain many specific injunctions against idolatry, and it was equally undeniable that the prophets, at least, displayed a "Messianic mentality." But, alas, this mentality "blinded them to the truth of the Messiah." It is pathetic to see how Simone Weil twists and distorts the Old Testament to make it all appear as pure deficit on her balance sheet. "The belief in a one and only God," of course, is incompatible—at least, for non-Christians—with religious dogmas like the Trinity or with faith in a divine mediator. But for Simone Weil, this striving for a pure monotheism was precisely "the cause" of what she called the "moral blindness" or the "tribal collectivism" of Israel. "There cannot be any contact as from one person to another between man and God except through the person of the Mediator. Apart from him, the only way in which God can be present to man is in a collective, a national way." The divine spirit without mediation turns into the "demoniacal." Hence, paradoxical as it may sound, their opposition to idolatry was the greatest misfortune of the Jewish people. In the first place, this opposition made an *eidolon*—and not a holy people—out of Israel itself: "no statue used to be created for Jehovah; but Israel is the stature of Jehovah"; and, in the second place, it caused Israel's doom: "The Jews were not allowed to be 'idolaters,' because otherwise they would not have killed Christ. If some ancient Hebrews were to come amongst us, the images of Christ crucified, the worship of the Virgin, and above all the Eucharist, God's real presence in a piece of matter, would be regarded by them as being that very thing which they were accustomed to name idolatry." The refusal to submit to this idolatry, then, constitutes Israel's religious failure; for the problem of "monotheism" can be "solved" only, as in Christianity, "through the Incarnation, and . . . the Virgin and Saints."

The specific accusations rise to a veritable paroxysm of religious anti-Semitism in the terrible summing up of the indictment: "It is not surprising that a people composed of fugitive slaves, or rather of the children of fugitive slaves, led forth to take possession by a series of massacres of a land whose soft climate and natural fertility gave it a paradise-like quality, and which had been organized on a flourishing basis by civilizations in whose labors they had taken no part, and which they proceeded to destroy—that such a people was unable to produce anything very good. . . . To speak of 'God as educator' in connection with this people is a heinous sort of joke. Is it surprising that there should be so much evil in a civilization—our own—which is corrupted at its roots, in its very inspiration, by this atrocious lie? The curse of Israel weighs upon Christendom. The atrocities, the extermination of heretics and of unbelievers—all this was Israel. Capitalism was Israel. . . . Totalitarianism is Israel (more particularly so among the latter's worst enemies)." There is only one poison in the modern world—"the notion of progress"—which is "specifically Christian." "The other poisons mixed up with the truth of Christianity are of Jewish origin" and must be purged, as Marcion before her believed, from the body of Christian faith and dogma. "Jehovah, the Church of the Middle Ages, H[itler]—all these are earthly Gods"—in short, incarnations of Satan.

Reading this terrible outburst, one is moved to hope that Simone Weil attained in death what she did not attain in life: the peace that passeth understanding, and that she did not take the voices of demons for the silence of God. But these are matters on which we cannot cast any light. We can ask a more modest question and wonder, on a human plane, what sources may have contributed to this revival of Gnosticism, to this individual recapitulation of a historical crisis.[4] Why could Simone Weil believe in a God of love and grace only through converting the God of the Jewish people into an incarnation of Satan? *The Notebooks* reveal that she inflicted this deep wound upon herself and committed this slander upon her own people as a last desperate measure of defense against total despair. The Christian faith (into which she was never baptized) was her last hope among the ruins of existence. For Simone Weil's "reading of reality"—as she called the struggle raging in her soul—yielded a pattern of alienation from the world, man, and God.

---

4. The case of Simone Weil is not unique. Similar Gnostic revivals, with implications of a religious anti-Semitism, may be found in A. J. Toynbee's *Study of History*, and in other historical and psychological writings of our time.

"The world is uninhabitable"; and everything in it is evil. "That is why we have to flee to the next." The natural order of things, according to her, was subject to an inexorable, meaningless necessity—the force of "gravity," and gravity produced nothing but suffering and pain, disgust and despair. It is Kafka's world: "Our life is nothing but impossibility, absurdity. . . . Contradiction is our wretchedness; and the feeling of our wretchedness is the feeling of our reality. . . . That's why we must love it." It is the world of Ivan Karamazov: there is no reason, "absolutely none," by which the intellect can answer Ivan's doubt and despair at all the senseless and unjustifiable evil in this world—or, "one only": that it is an inscrutable, unintelligible manifestation of "supernatural love; that it is God's will. And for this last reason I would just as readily accept a world which was only evil and whose consequences could only be evil as a child's tear."

The world as it is, then, is utter darkness, and to think that a God could illuminate or "sanctify" it, in the language of Jewish tradition, blasphemes the faith that Simone Weil sought to embrace. Such Gnosticism voices an anguished protest and revolt against the sufferings of the human race throughout history, and against the hypocrisy by which it has often tried to cover over its misery. But when dark despair saps the marrow of the self, such a revolt is condemned to remain a pathetic, futile, impotent gesture that delivers human fate all the more completely into the hands of the mysterious, incomprehensible powers responsible for the suffering and the evil endured by mankind.

It is the estimate of man and of his powers vis-à-vis the world and God that decides the quality and direction of the Gnostic revolt. In Simone Weil, the curse of "gravity" or heaviness laid upon the world produced a painful excess of self-mortification. "Everything which is in me, without exception, is absolutely valueless. . . . Everything which I appropriate to myself becomes immediately valueless. *Ouden eimi:* I am nothing." *The Notebooks* develop ingenious variations on this theme: "I have to love to be nothing. How horrible it would be if I were something. I have to love my nothingness, love to be nothingness." Or, in the moments of greatest despair: "Leprosy—that is me. All that I am is leprosy. The 'I' as such is leprosy."

The Need for Roots—Simone Weil's political testament—to the contrary notwithstanding, these attitudes toward the world and the self do not create genuine possibilities in the sphere of social action. Simone Weil, as we have seen, participated in social movements and political affairs, but "what she cared about," as T. S. Eliot put it, "was human souls"—more specifically the salvation of human souls, not social blueprints or political manifestoes. For "the social is irremediably the domain of the devil." "Man is a social animal, and the social element represents evil. . . . It follows that life cannot be anything else but a spiritual laceration." Simone Weil's social ethics was as simple and severe as her personal ethics: unconditional surrender to the inscrutable will of God. "Even if one could be like unto God, it would be preferable to be a handful of mud that is obedient to God."

That the spirit of God may prevail, the body must die. Simone Weil lived to die unto the body. Most of the Gnostic sects, too, subscribed to an extreme asceticism and other-worldliness. Spiritual existence, especially for the elect, was incompatible with the desires of the flesh. The Marcionites, it is said, required married people to submit to divorce in order to be eligible for baptism. Somewhat analogously, Simone Weil believed that the church was even too lax in its taboo against all sexual intercourse not serving the purpose of procreation. According to her, one should "utterly renounce" the sexual act as such, and then "resort to it on the few occasions in the course of a lifetime" that were unavoidable lest the race become extinct. "In this way there would scarcely be any difference between the father of a family and a monk, so far as chastity is concerned." A casual remark like this is worth pondering in order to appreciate the kind of revulsion Simone Weil must have felt when reading the early books of the Old Testament—or when contemplating her own sexuality.

A reading of reality like Simone Weil's is prelude to a religion of absurdity. Like Kierkegaard, the solitary Danish thinker of the nineteenth century who has come to mean so much to the distraught minds of our time, Simone Weil leaped into faith on the wings of the absurd. "Extreme justice combined with the appearance of extreme injustice . . ."; "God both One and three . . ."; "Christ both God and man . . ."; "The Host both earthly matter and body of God . . ."—these are some of the religious paradoxes over which Simone Weil brooded and suffered. But, as we have seen, human existence itself is absurd: "Contradiction is our wretchedness; and the feeling of our wretchedness is the feeling of our reality." Crushed by contradictions, she made "contradiction" the criterion of faith. "Contradiction is our path toward God because we are creatures, and because creation is itself a contradiction." Or: "Contradiction experienced right to the very depths of the being means spiritual laceration, it means the Cross." The two realms of being, nature and the spirit, body and soul, the world and God, loomed in her mind as absolutely incommensurable and irreconcilable. True to the Gnostic tradition, Simone Weil tried to overcome the terrible strain between these two dimensions, which she could not reconcile by human powers, by an appeal to mysterious, supernatural powers of mediation. She searched frantically for signs of mediation, and discovered mediating incarnations everywhere: in the religion of the Chaldeans and of the Egyptians, in the Upanishads and the Bhagavad-Gita, in Greek mythology, poetry, and drama, in Plato, Homer, and the Orphic mysteries, in Norse mythology, in Taoism and Zen Buddhism, in music and in mathematics —everywhere, she believed, there were signs and indications which anticipated man's final delivery from sin and death in the incarnation of Jesus as the Christ: everywhere—except in Israel and Rome.

Perhaps it is not so difficult to see now why Israel remained the great offense and stumbling block in this desperate pursuit of personal salvation. And perhaps the terrible curse Simone Weil laid upon the religion of her own people is a blessing in disguise. For what makes her shrink back in horror from "the goodly tents of Jacob and the tabernacles of Israel" upon which Balaam bestowed a reluctant blessing? What else but the purity of its monotheism gradually cleansed of all traces of magic and idolatrous imagery; the simple faith that the ordinary life of man, the intractable Adam, the mighty Leviathan, the great Earth Mother, the flesh, society, and nature, might be infused with a spirit of civilized humanity, or, in religious language, might be hallowed and sanctified; the prophetic faith that peace, love, and justice might transform man into a being pleasing in the sight of God; the human faith that the divine word is a gift to man in this life, not a promise of blessedness beyond; that the *Shechinah* is imprisoned in this world, not enthroned in the next; hence, the stubborn faith that this world is unredeemed; and perhaps the most creative of all ideas of religion, that which is born of the tension between the faith that the world is not redeemed and the resolve that it be redeemed by man's works and love. I don't know what the learned rabbis say, but speaking for myself, I find these "offenses" to be Israel's great and lasting contribution and the basis for my own private belief that it is worth being a Jew in a Christian world.

Simone Weil chose to condemn these "offenses" in the name of divine love and grace at a time when the prophetic faith of Israel was being gassed out of existence. She was not satisfied with such simple roots of faith as Israel's, but it is at least an open question whether she herself was not more uprooted—by *her* faith, which left her dangling in the No Man's Land of theological obscurantism—than the people to whom she offered *The Need for Roots*. Since she ultimately despaired of man, she could not believe that there might be a *human* life beyond despair. And thus her struggle for a new faith, powerful, passionate, and poignant as it is, is ultimately the expression of a desperate nihilism. The last message of hope is that of *The Grand Inquisitor:* magic, mystery, and authority. And perhaps this is the message that will prevail in our time.

Why did the God of Israel become the incarnation of Satan? Why did Simone Weil choose to condemn only the Jewish people? As we have seen, she discovered divine incarnations among a great many peoples of the ancient world—even though their historical and religious records (not to speak of that of the Christian peoples) were likewise filled with lust, incest, rape, cruelty, violence, and murder. Why the exception in the case of Israel? Why the one terrible curse amid the many generous blessings? And why did she even misread the text of the Hebrew Bible in order to make the curse stick? Thus, Jacob's wrestling with the angel is seen as another instance of "Israel's original impurity." What offends her so deeply in this story is the fact that Jacob is not destroyed by the angel, but seems to emerge victoriously from the struggle. Hence her accusing question: "Isn't it the greatest possible calamity, when you are wrestling with God, not to be beaten?" It is indeed—when the encounter between the human and the divine cannot be envisaged in any other terms but those of unconditional submission, obedience, and impotence on the part of man. The Biblical tale is much more subtle, however, than Simone Weil could perceive. Jacob does not emerge simply as the victor; or his alleged victory has quite a different meaning. The episode ends with these words: "And Jacob asked him, and said, Tell me . . . thy name. And he said, Wherefore is it that thou dost ask after my name? And he blessed him there" (Genesis 32:29) . In other words, Jacob receives a blessing from, but not the "name" of, the angel; or the power of the blessing does not derive from Jacob's gaining possession of the *magic* name of the God. The characteristic religious significance of this incident[5]—the conflict of magic and monotheism—escapes her altogether, just as she is completely blind to the Hebrew Scriptures' depiction of the slow, painful transformation of tribal hordes into a holy people making a covenant with God.

It is difficult to think, against the background of contemporary history, that such blind spots are due only to a Gnostic theology; or to avoid the suspicion that personal factors must have contributed to this revival of Gnosticism. *The Notebooks* reveal despair and self-hatred *in extremis;* they cry out in anguish over the absence of perfection and love in this world. Perhaps the faith of her fathers assumed such monstrous shape in the mind of Simone Weil because she demanded from them—her fathers and her people—a degree of perfection and a purity of love which are inhuman. Because they were not pure and perfect, her incapacity to love them as they were—or her incapacity to be loved as she was—turned into hatred and despair. Because her people were tainted with the flaws of our common mortality, she despaired at ever erasing these flaws in herself. And thus she came to curse those she may have loved most—and herself for the failure of perfection and love in their lives and hers. Perhaps this helps to explain the wild Gnostic "antitheses" that took shape in her mind: either absolute perfection and pure love or complete wretchedness and total despair—either all or nothing.

"What does it matter that there should never be joy in me, since there is perpetually perfect joy in God." What does it matter, indeed, if the lovelessness of one's own existence is ultimately the only condition for believing in the infinite love of God. "The attentive contemplation of misery, without compensation and consolation, drives us into the supernatural, and then we cannot do otherwise than love the source of it." We cannot do otherwise, because the only proof of God's perfection "is that we love him" precisely because of the misery he has inflicted upon us. The deepest roots of such a theology, all verbal protestations and overt actions to the contrary notwithstanding, are nourished by contempt, hatred,

---

5. A similar story is told when Rachel "steals" her father's "images"—for Simone Weil simply another clear case of thievery among the Jews.

and cruelty toward man. "Contempt of human misery is the only source of supernatural felicity." Where did she find these bitter words in the sayings of Jesus? Perhaps she had to be so cruel and unforgiving to those she loved because she could not forgive herself for the contempt and cruelty in her own love. And thus she exalted to the level of supernatural grace what she could not resolve on the level of human gravity. Faith is the last refuge from despair at the failure of life: "Relentless necessity, misery, distress, the crushing burden of poverty and the exhausting labour, cruelty, torture, violent death, constraint, terror, disease—all this is but the divine love. It is God who out of love withdraws from us so that we can love him."

Thus God withdraws from a world that is doomed; he becomes the "absent God," *Deus absconditus*—because of the total absence of love and hope on earth. "Life," according to Simone Weil, was but "an ersatz form of salvation." Perhaps the salvation she sought was but an ersatz form of life.

INTRODUCTION TO

FRANZ KAFKA AND THE TREE OF KNOWLEDGE

Nahum N. Glatzer

Franz Kafka is no Simone Weil; however, he creates for settled Jews much the same anxiety that Simone Weil does, for none of Kafka's formulations can be unambiguously identified as Jewish. He is as much a perplexity of fidelity as Weil is a conundrum of alienage, which is not to say that there are not profound elements of alienation and self-hatred in Kafka as there are Jewish figurations in Weil. In other words, when Jews play their special game—the game of who's Jewish and how—it's hard to be sure of Franz Kafka. He's Jewish but not specially so, for he is Central European, German-speaking and -writing, urban, bourgeois, university educated, familiar with European literature, non-Hebrew oriented, Jewishly disaffected, and yet full of affection and longing for the closed world of Yiddish culture, a Zionist sympathizer, and above all a profound interpreter of the Bible.

What one comes to understand of the alienation and loyalty of Kafka (his pariah sensibility) to Jewish experience and tradition is that it has become radically individual and utterly autonomous—the Laws come no longer to a people but to a soul stripped bare "without grace, without forgiveness, without purpose" (as Hans Joachim Schoeps describes the Kafka man in his essay, "The Tragedy of Faithlessness," in *The Kafka Problem,* edited by Angel Flores, New Directions, 1946, p. 287)—and yet a soul which is nonetheless the only vehicle in the modern world to bear the message of salvation and the news of damnation. Kafka, like Weil,

86

is an archetypal narcissist: where for Weil the self obliterates itself in order to be elevated, the Kafka self stands against God for permission to endure, to be justified, and to be saved. Kafka prepares the saeculum for its immolation, trains the secular spirit to be courageous before an unrelenting heaven. But at the same time that the nameless man of the twentieth century is taught the price of eating of the Tree of Knowledge, Kafka holds out the promise of the Tree of Life, the source of contemplation, silence, solitude, waiting, and patience.

Nahum N. Glatzer's essay is a gathering of sources, an interpretive essay which organizes the strands of the Kafka meditation and indicates a way out, a way out not for the reader but for its creator. Kafka had no interest in communicating a message to us, but only of writing to God (writing he once observed was "a form of prayer"), exposing his own sense of the distance which separated himself from God, from the Law, and from salvation. Glatzer makes us aware of how profound a paradigm of our own situation Kafka really was.

FRANZ KAFKA AND THE
TREE OF KNOWLEDGE

NAHUM N. GLATZER

Who is Joseph K in *The Trial,* K in *The Castle,* who are the other heroes in Kafka's stories? Various suggestions have been advanced by Kafka commentators—alienated man, modern escapist, neurotic man, homeless Jew, man of negative faith, and others. It would be unjust to press for a uniform answer. Diverse and manifold levels of meaning have to be assumed in reading the work of a great writer. The following attempt to find a clue to some of Kafka's stories in his own nonfiction should be taken as but one out of many attempts at interpretation.

I

In a short parenthetical sentence (many of his crucial utterances are hidden in parentheses) Kafka remarked: "Sometimes I believe I understand the Fall as no one else." This statement must be regarded with careful attention. The fact that it is addressed to his friend Milena Jesenská adds to the weight of the statement; it was to Milena that Kafka confided some of his innermost concerns.

In the group of aphorisms which Kafka excerpted from his Notebooks (and which Max Brod published years ago under the title *Reflections on Sin, Suffering, Hope and the True Way*) there appears the motif of the Fall. But only the recent publication of the full text of the Notebooks[1] reveals the extent of Kafka's preoccupa-

---

1. Included in the volume published by Schocken under the title *Dearest Father* (New York, 1954) and by Secker and Warburg under the title *Wedding*

tion with the Fall story in the third chapter of Genesis and the ever-increasing importance it played in his thinking. The Notebooks record Kafka's reflections in the years 1917 and 1918, i.e., shortly after completing *The Trial* (in 1915) and before writing *The Castle* in 1921. The writing of *The Great Wall of China* falls in the period covered by the Notebooks. The reader can hardly escape the notion that both in the novels and in the Notebooks Kafka deals with the same human phenomenon. The cause of man's predicament as Kafka presents it in the Notebooks may in a measure help to understand his heroes' encounters in the novels.

II

Kafka understands man's peculiar condition as resulting from the fact that he has eaten from the Tree of Knowledge but was prevented from eating from the Tree of Life. Thus he has become a person, has gained the power of thinking, a sharpened consciousness, an awareness of what is good and what is evil, but he has forfeited eternal life, the state of undisturbed happiness. Knowledge implies a certainty of life's finiteness. Such a life appears unbearable, another form of life unattainable; thus the wish to die (in Genesis: the punishment of death) is a first sign of nascent knowledge (35).[2] The original closeness between God and man has come to an end; now "the Fall separates us from him, the Tree of Life separates him from us" (85). Unconsciously in harmony with ancient Hebrew traditions, Kafka was aware of the paradox that Life assumed its supreme meaning only after man had acquired Knowledge (or, in the words of the Aggadah, that the Tree of Life was hidden within the Tree of Knowledge) so that knowledge is "both a step leading to eternal life and an obstacle in the way." Man in his desire for boundless life, a desire that originates in his knowledge, will have to destroy the obstacle which is himself, the knowing man (88). The sin of the first man of which the Genesis story speaks is applied by Kafka both to the eating from the Tree of Knowledge and to the not yet having eaten from the Tree of Life.

Preparations in the Country (London, 1954). The translations are by Ernst Kaiser and Eithne Wilkins. Both this rendition and the translations of the Aphorisms by Willa and Edwin Muir in *The Great Wall of China* (Schocken, New York, 1946) have been consulted and drawn on, in part, in this essay.

2. The numerals refer to identical pages in *Dearest Father* and *Wedding Preparations*.

"The state in which we find ourself is sinful" (43). No wonder that when the night of subconscious existence wanes, man, awakening to full consciousness, finds himself under indictment.

From this involved interpretation of the complex nature of knowledge Kafka moves to a simpler plane in referring to the expulsion motif. Following the Genesis story he states that the expulsion from Paradise was to prevent man (Kafka employs throughout the personal pronoun, we, us) from eating of the Tree of Life (43). The expulsion was the mildest of possible punishments; a worse vengeance of the divine would have been the destruction of the Paradise; the most terrible step would have been "the cutting off of eternal life and leaving everything else as it is" (88). It is significant to Kafka that in the text of the story the curse was restricted to man and did not befall the garden of Eden. Had man not been expelled, something more unfortunate would have happened: Paradise would have had to be destroyed. But now, though man's destiny changed, the destiny of the Garden to serve man was not altered (85). Man, who not only gained knowledge but "had become knowledge of the divine" (86), lives in the consciousness that Paradise and the Tree of Life, though beyond reach of man, still retain their meaningful place in the scheme of things.

The possession of knowledge turns man into an exile; exiled from the realm of the Tree of Life, man is destined to know but is not allowed to live; *cogito ergo non sum*. Life is but a primordial memory, a longing never to be fulfilled.

However, mere knowledge of good and evil can never satisfy man; man will endeavour to *act* in accordance with this knowledge. The next step in Kafka's thinking is decisive: The power to translate knowledge into action was not granted to man (43f.). Man will forever strive to act but the range of his action will never correspond to the scope of his knowledge. Faced with the futility of his attempts which may ultimately break him, man would prefer to annul his knowledge in order to escape the dilemma. Thus annulment of knowledge, so man hopes, might bring him rest and peace. Or: Man will wish to accept knowledge as a distant goal to be reached later in time. A vain hope indeed; to man who has eaten from the Tree of Knowledge conscious awareness of good and evil is not his future but his immediate actuality (44).

Thus man exists in a double tension: the one between knowledge and life, the other between knowledge and deed. Both result from man's rebellion against the paradisical world, the world of a dream-harmony between God and him who was to become man, the eternal world of quiet, instinctual happiness. Man became man by his rebellion, by his impatience with his original state (34). The knowledge he gained by his revolt estranged him from the world that remained in the power of the lord of the Garden. The world became the place "where we went astray," it is "the fact of our being astray" (90).

An indication of man's not belonging is the loss of his name. Most of Kafka's heroes (or, rather, the manifestations of the one hero of Kafka, man) have no names or go mainly by initials. "I am twenty-three years old but I have no name yet" ("Gespräch mit dem Betrunkenen"). The exile, the lonely stranger, is not being addressed; there is no communion between him and the world outside and no name is, therefore, needed. The Genesis story emphasizes Adam's ability to give names to living beings around him—before he gained knowledge and lost life. The Fall brought about a radical change in man's position. Now, the awareness of the "I" makes the discovery of the "Thou" a difficult task; the name is without meaning so long as the two exist without a relationship.

The memory of the original domicile lives on; exile accentuates the consciousness of the lost home. Could he forget his home he would no longer be a stranger. The remembrance of the Tree of Life constitutes a disturbing antithesis to the—never fully realized—existence under the sign of knowledge. Man, to use Kafka's simile, is attached to a chain that allows him movement on earth but prevents his leaving its narrow confines and ascending to heaven; at the same time, belonging not only to earth but also to heaven, he is attached to a similarly calculated heavenly chain that prevents his attempts to go down to earth (41). Man is torn between the two realms.

What establishes a bond between this world of ours and the realm of the positive is suffering; in fact, suffering is the only link between the two (90). The Genesis story speaks of suffering as entering human existence as the consequence ("punishment") of knowledge; both Adam and Eve suffer in their most genuine activities: he in working for his daily bread, she in childbirth. Both try through these activities for which they suffer to penetrate into the realm of—no longer naïvely attainable—life.

III

Kafka, who as no other Western writer had penetrated into one of the most meaningful stories of the East, must have considered the question how the Book which he called a sanctum (80) resolved the problem that it placed at its beginning. There are indications—though no proof—that indeed he so did. The inquiry into the Fall in Kafka's Notebooks is followed by a discussion of Abraham, and references to the Tower of Babel, to Moses, Mount Sinai and the Law are scattered throughout the whole of Kafka's work.

In the Biblical story, man's estrangement from God and his exile from the Tree of Life (one brief Notebook entry of Kafka reads: "Tree of Life—Lord of Life") was not to last forever. True, the road to the Garden is guarded and there is no return. But the Lord called knowing man back into his presence to accord him that which from now on would take the place of the fruit of the Tree of Life. On Mount Sinai God again addressed himself to man and revealed the Law, which is called a Tree of Life. Knowledge had implied the awareness of death and the fear of death. But now man may choose life again. Death is not being abolished but it will no longer threaten to make life meaningless. Knowledge is not being annulled but it will no longer isolate man; imbued with "life," "knowledge" will be a source of communication rather than a demonic power. The order which the Law will bring into life will seemingly restrict the independence of knowing man; in reality it will establish inroads for the divine in the community of man and in the human heart. The laws will be visible signs of the covenant between God and man whom the Fall had turned into antagonists. The relationship between man and God on the mythological level had come to an end; now, the relationship is being renewed on the level of revelation.

Kafka understood well the function of the Law. In his conversations with Gustav Janouch,[3] Kafka said that the Jewish people never sank to "the level of an anonymous and therefore soulless mass," "never has been nameless" as long as it held fast "to the fulfilment of the Law." Only "through a fall from the Law which gives it form" mankind becomes "a gray, formless, and therefore nameless mass." Then, what could be "life" is "leveled out into

---

3. Gustav Janouch, *Conversations with Kafka* (translated by Gorouwy-Rees), New York, 1953.

mere existence. . . . But that is not the world of the Bible and
Jewry." The people of the Bible Kafka calls "an association of
individuals by means of a Law." Modern masses, on the other hand,
"resist every form of association; they split apart by reason of their
own lawlessness. . . . Mankind has lost its home." The relationship
between "law" and "eternal life" is seen by Kafka when he assigns
to the poet the task of "leading the isolated and mortal into eternal
life, the accidental into conformity to law."

If Kafka, to whom writing, as he expressed himself, was "a form
of prayer," approached the task which he assigned to the writer, he
did it in a radically negative manner. The central motif of his
novels is not to lead homeless, nameless, lawless humanity to law.
Rather, his novels present man, the exile from Paradise, who tries to
gain Life but who is not able to take the road to Sinai and to accept
the new form in which Life is being offered to him. Knowing man
knows that the distance between him and the Lord of Life can no
longer be bridged; that if God wished to speak to man again his
voice would not reach him.

"Many people prowl round Mount Sinai. Their speech is blurred,
either they are garrulous or they shout or they are taciturn" (312).
Kafka calls Moses "a judge, a stern judge." The laws may lead to
judgment; they do not create form, do not accord a name to the
anonymous individual. In *The Great Wall of China* there is a
reference to the schools where "superficial culture mounts sky-high
round a few precepts that have been drilled into people's minds for
centuries, precepts which, though they have lost nothing of their
eternal truth, remain eternally invisible in this fog of confusion."
In the Notebooks, Kafka relates the image of the messengers of the
king racing through the world and, since there are no kings, shout-
ing to each other their meaningless and obsolete messages (30).

In *The Problem of Our Laws* Kafka speaks of the remote nobility
that keeps secret the ancient laws; the people are ruled by the law
which one does not know; the nobles scrupulously administer the
law, but they themselves stand above the laws. That the laws exist is
an old tradition, and it may be that they do not exist at all. Those
who believe that they do exist, are inclined to hate themselves
"because we have not yet shown ourselves worthy of being entrusted
with the laws." In spite of these complications nobody would dare
to repudiate the belief in the laws and the nobility. "We live on
this razor's edge."

IV

Thus man who has eaten from the Tree of Knowledge may spend his existence on earth in distrust, uncertainty, doubt as to whether the Law—the form-giving, community-building, name-according force—will show him the way to the Lord of Life. The Lord himself does exist, though in an endless distance from man; the original, primordial nearness between him and man is being treasured in deep memory, however indistinct and indefinite. The Castle does exist; its lord had issued a call to the Land Surveyor to do his work and is expecting him. Here ends the extent of K's, the Land Surveyor's, knowledge. The villagers who live in childlike naïveté are not troubled by the reality of the Castle. K, who had come to answer the call, remains isolated from both Castle and village; his knowledge estranges him from the simple village folk that do not know; he cannot translate this knowledge into life, because real, meaningful, eternal life is in the Castle and beyond the reach of knowing man. The expanse—so small, so vast—between Castle and village is filled with the hierarchy of officials, an organization of intermediaries. They seem to connect, to correlate, to co-ordinate—to personify the function of the law; in reality they only accentuate the distance. The Genesis story relates man's acquisition of knowledge as a yielding to temptation. It is not without significance that Kafka called his preliminary sketch of *The Castle,* "Temptation in the Village."

In *The Trial* (which lasts one year—a symbolic unit of life) Joseph K soon realizes the abysmal paradox in the world of law. There is an authority that holds him guilty and that issued an order concerning him. But no judge will confront him, no lawbook will be available to advise him. The more the accused will try to advance his cause, the more uncertain will he become about his situation. He faces an overwhelming machinery engaged in reducing to shreds his most precious possession: his conscious personality. The parable "Before the Law"—one of the greatest parables in literature—points to the basic tragedy of man who has eaten from the Tree of Knowledge but cannot reach the Tree of Life: He stands before the door to the Law (which in the parable stands for the promise of life, of fulfillment, of the goal) prevented from entrance by the keeper of the door. (The entrance to the Garden is guarded by the cherubim "to keep the way to the Tree of Life.")

94

After spending the rest of his life ardently contemplating all the moves of the doorkeeper, the man asks: "Everyone strives to attain the Law, how does it happen that in all these years no one else has come to seek admittance?" To this final question of the dying man the doorkeeper answers: "No one but you could gain admittance through this door, since this door was intended only for you. I am now going to shut it."

The strangely paradoxical story puzzles all Kafka interpreters. However, the clue to its understanding may lie in the fact that all thoughts of the man in the text of this parable and of the "commentators" that follow are directed not toward the real issue, which is the law, but are concentrated upon the doorkeeper. The doorkeeper fulfills the function of the officials of the Castle and the bureaucracy of the Trial. All of them stand between knowing man and Life, Law, the Lord. Kafka has said it: The possession of knowledge implies the urge to act, but the strength to act was not given to man. He acts too much and, thus, wrongly. Thus: Going out to search for Life (and his search will become a ceaseless activity) he will encounter the intricate and senseless clerkship; in his search for Law he will not hear the voice coming down the mountain that cannot be ascended but will face the lowest agents of a law machine and—a doorkeeper.

Woman, who in Paradise was instrumental in gaining knowledge, will be used in an attempt to break through the maze of obstacles in the way to life. "Woman . . . is the representative of life" (98). But Leni, Frieda, Olga, Fräulein Bürstner will only seemingly be of help. They will come in sight as little redeemers but ultimately blur the vision of the goal.

Connections, manipulations, reasonings and calculations, feverish activities will be futile. The world of blind machines is but a mirrored reflection of man's machinations. The question of life remains unanswered; the expelled one remains in exile. "Man with his knowledge of good and evil is but a helpless atom in a world which has no such knowledge" (B. Russell).

V

Is there no way open out of the impasse of knowing man as depicted in Kafka's tragic stories? There is indeed a note of hope in Kafka's writings, a pointing out of what appears to him the only possible direction.

All human error is impatience, he says (34) ; impatience was the cause of the expulsion from Paradise; the return to Paradise—contact with life—is prevented by the same impatience (34). If there is hope it can only come from patience, from quiet waiting, from a withdrawal into the realm of creative inactivity that must precede all deed, from the stillness of soul that precedes the breaking forth of will, from the calmness of the spirit in which intuitive life is born. In this realm there is no desire, striving and scheming, no struggle for success and achievement, no display of power *versus* power; man goes back to the sources of his being—before knowledge and life—and chooses life.

Seeking is of no avail; but there is salvation in not-seeking: "He who seeks will not find; he who seeks not—will be found" (80). Happiness can be realized by "believing in the indestructible element in oneself and not striving towards it" (41). Poets have dreams; life, real life, as Kafka said to Janouch, is but "a reflection of the dreams of poets." An advice to Janouch: "Do not excite yourself. Be calm. Quietness is indeed a sign of strength. . . . Calmness and quietness make one free—even on the scaffold." From the outside one will victoriously impress theories upon the world and "then fall straight into the ditch one has dug, but only from the inside will one keep oneself and the world quiet and true" (67). *The Great Wall of China* includes the parable of the Emperor "who has sent a message to you . . . to you alone"; the messenger who set out to deliver the message will never reach you; too vast is the distance between the Palace and your door. The Palace itself is an endless expanse of buildings, chambers, stairs and courts; never, never will the message come to you; "but you sit at your window when evening falls and dream it to yourself." Or, in the incomparable words of the Notebooks: "You do not need to leave your room. Remain sitting at your table and listen. Do not even listen, simply wait. Do not even wait, be quite still and alone. The world will freely offer itself to you to be unmasked; it has no choice, it will roll into ecstasy at your feet" (48). This is the happiness of being found that comes to him who seeks not. Such promise of happiness "resembles the hope of eternal life," says Kafka in his Diaries.

This *vita contemplativa,* creative passivity, is the true home to which the exiled may return. "Both contemplation and activity have the appearance of truth; but only the activity that emanates from contemplation, or better, that which returns to it again, is truth" (97). In advancing this answer to the central human question, Kafka refers back to the symbolism of the two trees in the Garden.

The Tree of Knowledge represents the truth of activity [*die Wahrheit des Tätigen*], the Tree of Life stands for nondoing, not seeking, waiting—the truth of the quietude [*die Wahrheit des Ruhenden*]. The first truth we acquired in reality, the second is ours only by intuition. This discrepancy is man's fate and is sad to realize. A positive aspect, however, is that the first truth refers to a moment of time, the second to eternity; thus the first truth vanishes in the light of the second (91).

Kafka, who let his fictional characters—mediocre creatures—struggle in the sphere of impatient, impersonal, routinized, aimless activity, has transcended this sphere in his nonfiction notations. Here, to quote Kafka in his *Letters to Milena,* "there is something of the air which one has breathed in Paradise before the Fall." Kafka, standing between East and West in his belief that he understood the meaning of the Paradise story as no one else, seems indeed to have gained the freedom to behold the Tree of Life which is hidden within the Tree of Knowledge.

FROM MARXISM TO JUDAISM

Will Herberg

The ways of resistance traversed by Kafka and Weil—ways which however much they separate and divide are comparable in their styles of articulation and by what they reveal of the person passing judgment upon the institutions of their times—reflect their resolution to say no to authority. However much Weil hankered to find a way of squaring her conscience with a Catholic theology which misrepresented the teaching of the Church and Kafka tried to accommodate his sensibility to the sinuous ways of the Law (taken here not so much as Torah, but the Divine Presence in its aspect of justice), both were thinkers whose personal way was always in opposition to any form of public power, force, authority.

Quite as much is Will Herberg's seminal essay, "From Marxism to Judaism," a confessional tracing of his own path from a false absolute and an idolatrous authoritarianism to a giving of faith to the true and living God. It is no wonder that when Herberg's essay appeared in January 1947, to be followed in 1951 by *Judaism and Modern Man* (undoubtedly one of the few genuine, synthetic works of Jewish theology written against the background of the American experience), he was warmly embraced (not, to be sure, by the institutional paladins of Jewish life, for they rarely embrace anyone or any teaching not edified by their particular instruction) by a large sector of American-Jewish postwar college students and young adults. Herberg's experience, recounted with great simplicity and precision, describes his commitment as a young man to Marxism and the Communist party, his efforts to absolutize the partial Messianism implicit in the Marxist vision of history, his inability to define within the confines of Marxist scientism an ethical "system" which was authentically humanist—that is, capable of embracing, not only the tension of exploited and exploiters, proletariat and capitalist, but the whole complexity of individual life, its psychological idealism and self-deception, its darkness of purpose and motive, and its luminous capacity for mercy and compassion. Marxism's ethic of power had for Herberg no other justification by faith than in "the redemptive power of history operating through the Dialectic."

The break in the Marxist circuitry of argument and doctrine Herberg acknowledges to have taken place *ab initio* in "subconscious processes" which had been going on for some time before becoming precipitant, but he recognizes that the entente of Hitler and the Soviet Union in 1939 was the decisive moment, for it became clear then that freedom had succumbed to despotism while still calling itself freedom, that humane values had been subverted in the interest of expediency, that the individual was really superfluous in the collective mass. Marxist religion had exploded itself.

Having described the nature of his commitment to Marxist doctrine and the course of its collapse, Herberg goes on to set forth the basic theological *docta* which he elicited and substantiated from the sources of Judaism. One intellectual doctrine goes and another is born; one absolute decapitated, another enthroned. He ends by calling for "a great theological reconstruction in the spirit of a neoorthodoxy distant alike from sterile fundamentalism and secularized modernism."

What has always attracted me to Herberg's mind is precisely his unflinching and courageous confessional posture—a confessional posture which is individualist, radical, open to the complexities of the human heart, its polarities, contradictions, deceits, receptive to every current of teaching, any source of insight, any guide to the truth.

Buber, Rosenzweig, Baeck, Cohen were not indifferent to the currents operative in non-Jewish theologies; they recognized that Judaism, whatever the eternity of its People, is not an eternal teaching, unless the teaching is directed and formed for the People. *Am Yisrael* is a theological doctrine and as such the People as a hypostatic essence cannot perish as long as one mind, even God's,

preserves the image of its essence. That it can perish and disappear
—like the Ten Lost Tribes—is an historical possibility, although
it can endure as an intellectual essence. But what is the point of
living as an idea in God's mind? None at all. It doesn't satisfy
anyone and hence the difficulty of making the notion of eternity
or eternal memory vivid and meaningful. Only if the teaching,
the holy instruction, is appropriate to the Teacher and the Taught
is there a meaningful communication. There can be no question
that the substance of the Teaching—honoring the decretals of the
Teacher and the painful susceptibilities and temptations of the
Taught—is the task of this generation and of generations to come.

FROM MARXISM TO JUDAISM

Jewish Belief as a Dynamic of Social Action

WILL HERBERG

Until nine or ten years ago, I was a thoroughgoing Marxist. I had spent most of my life in the radical movement, and Marxism was to me more than a mere strategy of political action, more than a program of economic and social reconstruction, more even than a comprehensive theory of history and society. Marxism was to me, and to others like me, a religion, an ethic, and a theology: a vast, all-embracing doctrine of man and the universe, a passionate faith endowing life with meaning, vindicating the aims of the movement, idealizing its activities, and guaranteeing its ultimate triumph. In the certainty of this faith, we felt we could stand against the world.

It was a faith committed to freedom, justice, and brotherhood as ultimate ideals and supreme values. But it was also a faith that staked everything on the dogma of Progress, that is, on the unlimited redemptive power of history. Through its own inherent energies, the materialist Dialectic of history would sooner or later solve every problem, fulfill every possibility, and eliminate every evil of human life, leading mankind through terrific struggles to a final perfection of uncoerced harmony amidst peace, plenty, and untroubled happiness.

The motive power of this redemptive process of history the Marxist metaphysic found in economics. Man's essence was economic, the root of his frustrations and miseries was economic, and his salvation would be economic as well. "Economic development" was the invincible power that in the last analysis determined everything, and in the final outcome would bring the processes of history to consummation and fulfillment: it was the invisible god of the Marxist faith.

But this invisible god operated through visible instrumentalities, through economic classes. The proletariat was the savior of humanity, and the class struggle the engine of salvation. From this conception emerged a system of ethics that I found increasingly untenable. Marxism, it is true, did not admit to possessing an ethical system; it prided itself on its "scientific" character, and scornfully rejected all moral imperatives. But in fact it followed an extreme moral relativism, according to which good and evil were constituted by a shifting class interest.

Whatever served the "interest of the proletariat" was good; whatever ran counter to it was evil. Everything, literally everything, was permitted if only it promoted the "proletarian class struggle." But the proletariat could attain self-consciousness only in its "vanguard party," so that in the end the interest of the proletariat really amounted to the interest of the party. Party interest—power for the party and its leaders—thus became the ultimate, indeed the only criterion of right and wrong.

This ethic of power was very conveniently justified by faith in the redemptive power of history operating through the Dialectic. The Dialectic prescribed the course of world history and to Marx, as to Hegel, *Weltgeschichte* was *Weltgericht*. Only world history could decide who was really right and since world history was bound to decide in our favor, everything we might do to promote the success of our cause—that is, of our party—was justified in advance. Ultimately, the only true moral agent was power, for only power could claim a hearing before the bar of world history.

Such was the faith by which we lived and fought. And so long as this faith remained unchallenged from within, no attacks from without could shake it. Doubts were ignored or else drowned in action.

But reality could not be forever withstood. I do not know what is the secret mechanism by which subconscious processes which have been going on for years are suddenly precipitated into consciousness under the impact of some great event. In my case, it was the course of the Russian Revolution and the development of events in Europe, culminating in the triumph of Hitler, that had this effect. Put to the test, the Marxist faith failed. It proved itself incapable of explaining the facts or sustaining the values that gave meaning to life, the very values it had itself enshrined as its own ultimate goals. It could not meet the challenge of totalitarianism because it was itself infected with the same disease. By the logic of its own development, the ideal of unlimited freedom had become the reality of unlimited despotism. The individual personality, instead of being liberated for self-fulfillment, as Marx and Lenin had promised, was being engulfed in a total collectivism that left no room whatever for personal autonomy. Sacrificial dedication to the welfare of humanity had given way to narrow, ruthless, self-defeating power politics.

It was this latter point perhaps that told most. The disastrous corrosions and corruptions of the Marxist movement in politics seemed to me clearly a reflection of its lack, or rather of its rejection, of an ethic transcending the relativities of power and class interest, and the lack of an adequate ethic to be the result of a radically false religion.

Not that I felt myself any the less firmly committed to the great ideals of freedom and social justice. My discovery was that I could no longer find basis and support for these ideals in the materialistic religion of Marxism. On the contrary, it seemed to me that in its philosophy and ethics Marxism went far toward destroying the very objectives it was presumably out to achieve. I felt intensely the need for a faith that would better square with my ideal, which in tenor, doctrine, and spirit could give impulse and direction to the radical reconstruction of society which I so deeply desired.

For this Marxist religion itself, it now became clear to me, was in part illusion, and in part idolatry; in part a delusive Utopianism promising heaven on earth in our time, and in part a totalitarian worship of collective man; in part a naive faith in the finality of economics, and in part a sinister fetishism of technology and material production; in part a sentimental optimism as to the goodness of human nature, and in part a hard-boiled, amoral cult of power at any price. There could be no question to my mind that as religion, Marxism had proved itself bankrupt.

With Marxism went the entire naturalistic outlook as it affects the nature and destiny of man. I began to see that though man is undeniably part of nature and remains embedded within it, he quite as undeniably transcends it by virtue of his spirit, by virtue of his reason, his imagination, and his moral freedom. I began to see new meaning in the poignant words of Bertrand Russell, himself an uncompromising naturalist, describing man's paradoxical status in nature:

> A strange mystery it is that nature, omnipotent but blind, has brought forth at last a child, subject still to her power but gifted with sight, with knowledge of good and evil, with the capacity of judging all the works of his unthinking mother. . . . Man is yet free, during his brief years, to examine, to criticize, to know, and in imagination, to create. To him alone, in the world with which he is acquainted, this freedom belongs, and in this lies his superiority to the resistless forces that control his outer life.

These were the words of a great naturalist philosopher, but naturalism had so far not succeeded in explaining or building on this paradox. And so naturalism seemed to me bound in the end to fail to satisfy any one who demanded something better than the narrow and paltry conception of human life and destiny it offered.

The conclusion I reached as the final outcome of the long and painful process of reorientation was that neither man nor his fate could be understood in terms of an outlook that limited itself to the two-dimensional plane of nature and history, that the ultimate meaning of human life was to be found in a dimension transcending both and yet relevant to both—in a dimension that, in the most genuine sense of the term, was *supernatural*.

To suggest the process by which I and perhaps others found our way out of Marxist materialism and power-worship, I will paraphrase the words used recently in derision by a well-known writer, himself an unreconstructed Marxist, to describe an experience in some ways very like my own. In trying to discover what went wrong with economics—he says—they (that is, people like me) came to politics; but politics revealed that it was tainted and so they strove to cure the taint of politics with ethics; but ethics alone could not withstand the taint either, and so they went on finally to religion.

These are scoffing words, but they are not without their truth. I found in religion what I sought: and that was not an escape from social responsibility, but a more secure spiritual groundwork for a mature and effective social radicalism. The calamitous schism that had so long divided socialism from religion seemed to me to be at last coming to an end: in the profound insights and spiritual resources of religion, socialism would find a philosophy and a dynamic far superior to the shallow materialism that had led it so woefully astray. In short, I came to the conclusion that by abandoning the Marxist metaphysic in favor of a positive religious affirmation, I was becoming a better socialist and, if I may venture the paradox, even a better Marxist, taking Marxism in terms of its best insights and ultimate ideals. For the great contributions of Marxism were, it seemed to me, in the fields of economic understanding, social thought, and political action. And these could best be conserved, I now saw, within the framework, not of a shallow materialism, but of a profound religion that would give full recognition to the transcendent aspects of man's nature and destiny.

In my particular case, finding my way to religion meant finding my way to Judaism. Was this a return or in reality a first encounter? I cannot tell. But I can tell, I think, what it was that I discovered in essential Judaism that came to me as a revelation in my perplexities. If I now describe it in entirely intellectualistic terms, I hope it will not be concluded that I ignore or deny the devotional, mystical, and ritual elements that are so vital to any true religious experience. I limit myself to the intellectual, one might say theological, aspect because that has been foremost in my thinking and has had greater meaning for me in the solution of my own perplexities.

I. GOD AND MAN

The very heart of Judaism, it seems to me, is its magnificent conception of the Deity. It is a conception at once profound and paradoxical: a God transcendent, yet working in life and history, infinite yet personal, a God of power, justice, and mercy, but above all a holy God. The worship of a holy God who transcends all relativities of nature and history, as Reinhold Niebuhr has pointed out, saves the soul from taking satisfaction in any partial performance, curbs self-righteousness, and instills a most wholesome humility which gives man no rest in any achievement, no matter how high, while a still higher level of achievement is possible. The worship of a holy and transcendent God who yet manifests himself in history saves us alike from the shallow positivism that leaves nature and history and life all without ultimate meaning, from a pantheism that in the end amounts to an idolatrous worship of the world, and from a sterile other-worldliness that breaks all connection between religion and life. The worship of a holy and transcendent God who is the one God of the universe, besides whom there is no other, saves us, finally, from the many debasing idolatries that are bedeviling mankind today.

The scriptural doctrine of God, as I read it, is also a doctrine of man. For man is created "in the image of God": that is his glory but also his inescapable responsibility. The Biblical doctrine seems to me to hinge upon a dramatic tension both in the nature of man and in his relations with God. On the one hand (Psalms 8:5), man is "but little lower than the angels"; on the other (Genesis 8:21), "the inclination of man's heart is evil from his childhood." In this I see no contradiction, but rather a profound insight into the para-doxical, the ambivalent nature of man. It is an insight that does justice both to his grandeur and to his misery, both to his capacity to transcend self in righteousness, reason, and loving-kindness and to the inescapable limits of self-transcendence because of the irre-ducible egotism of his nature.

The scriptural conception of man thus refuses to countenance either the fatuous optimism of the Rousseauistic doctrine of the natural goodness of man or the dismal pessimism of the ultra-Calvinist doctrine of his utter depravity. It is at once more realistic and more complex, for it sees both sides in their coexistence and conflict, in their state of eternal struggle out of which is generated that tragic sense of life which is the mark of every high religion. But it is a sense of tragedy that is never final, for with God all things are possible.

The same dialectic tension that converts the human soul into the field of a battle never won, yet always within reach of victory, is to be found in another form in the relations between God and man. "Everything is in the power of Heaven except the fear of Heaven," the Sages tell us. "God in his providence determines beforehand what a man shall be and what shall befall him but not whether he shall be righteous or wicked." We need not take even this partial determinism too literally to see the profound significance of the uncompromising insistence on man's freedom of will. Evil is the result not of the forces of nature or of the promptings of the flesh: that is a Greek-Oriental notion which has had a most unfortunate effect upon our popular moral outlook. Both nature and the flesh are good in themselves, for did not God create both and find them good? Evil is rooted in man's spiritual freedom and consists in the wrong use of that freedom, in sinful disobedience to God.

I find this conception, which as far as I know is unique to

Judaism and the religions that derive from it, the only adequate foundation for a significant moral life. It does justice alike to man's creaturely subjection to the mortal law as the law of God and to his self-determination as a free moral agent. It combines freedom and responsibility in a synthesis that no philosophy has been able to transcend.

II. MAN AND SOCIETY

If there is one strain that has run through Judaism from the earliest codes to the present day, it is the passion for social justice. No modern attack upon economic exploitation can equal in earnestness and power the denunciations of the Prophets against those who "grind down the faces of the poor." No modern warning against the evils of authoritarianism is so arresting as the words of Samuel rebuking the people of Israel for desiring to subject themselves to the yoke of kingship.

But even more important, it seems to me, is the fact that the scriptural doctrine relating man to God provides the only really adequate groundwork for the ideals of freedom and equality, as well as the only fully realistic justification of democracy in political and economic life.

At the bottom, the affirmation of the freedom of the individual person can be grounded in nothing less ultimate than the belief that he is created in the image of God and is, therefore, a being in comparison with whom all of the nonhuman world is as nothing in worth. It is the belief in the eminent dignity of the human personality—in other words, in the infinite value of the individual human soul. This has received its modern formulation in the Kantian teaching that every man is an end in himself, and is not to be used as a mere means or tool for some external purpose. In the same way, the affirmation of human equality cannot be grounded in empirical fact; it can be grounded in nothing less ultimate than the belief in the Fatherhood of God and the Brotherhood of Man. For men are equal not in power or wisdom or beauty or goodness, but in their spiritual essence, in the infinite worth of their individual souls, in their relation to God. It is this equal relation to God, it seems to me, that alone can serve as the ultimate criterion of human relations. True understanding of this principle—of the value and significance of human personality—came to the world for the first time with the Prophetic insistence on the spiritual autonomy and moral responsibility of the individual person.

The scriptural insight into the ambivalent nature of man makes for a clear and realistic view of power and government. Power of man over man is intrinsically evil, for it involves the subjection of some men to others, the violation of their God-given personal autonomy, *and by that much their enslavement.* Power, moreover, has its own logic of expansion and corruption: it corrupts the wielder as well as those upon whom it is wielded, feeding the pride and arrogance of the one, and instilling a slavish spirit of sub- serviency in the other. Yet power is necessary, because man's "incli- nation to evil"—that is, his egotism and self-centeredness—makes coercion at some point necessary in order to protect society from the centrifugal forces of individual and group self-interest. The recog- nition of power as an inescapable necessity, and yet as a corrupting influence, endows social life with the same sense of tension and pathos that we have noted in the spiritual life of the individual. The moral law, which is embattled in every human soul, is also imperiled, and at least partially thwarted, in every transaction in the world.

It is out of this keen sense of the perils of power, so strinkingly absent in traditional Marxism, that democracy grows. For democ- racy is at bottom an institutional system for the control of power in the interests of freedom and social welfare. It is predicated on the conviction that no man possesses sufficient imagination, wisdom, or virtue to make him a safe repository of the interests of others—that no man is good enough or wise enough to be entrusted with absolute power over his fellow men. This is a principle that applies not only to politics but to economics as well, where it serves as the starting point of democratic socialism, as well as of all other programs of economic reform in the interest of social justice. Democracy is, in effect, a dynamic reconciliation on the social level of man's grandeur and misery, of his eminent dignity as a person and his perennial inclination to sinfulness as manifested in the egoistic self-assertion of power.

Judaism, as I see it, is the sworn foe of the totalitarian state in its claim to absolute control over the individual and all his activities. Unconditional obedience to a universal and transcendent God precludes the possibility of total and absolute subjection to any earthly power. Earthly powers making such claims are usurpers and pretenders to the prerogatives of Deity. They are to be resisted to the bitter end. "For unto Me are the children of Israel slaves," says the Talmud; "they are not slaves unto slaves."

The profound insights of scriptural religion reveal a logic of social action that escapes the pitfalls alike of power-mad cynicism, secular Utopianism, and other-worldly quietism. As against the cynicism that recognizes no rule but power, Judaism vindicates the validity and relevance of the moral law, however impossible it may be to live up to it fully in any given situation. As against other-worldly quietism, it raises the witness of the Prophets and the duty to one's neighbor. As against the secular Utopianism, whether liberal or Marxist, which hopes to achieve perfection within history, it stresses the inescapable relativities of this world and places the grand consummation to come at the *end* of time rather than within it.

It is here that the uncompromising monotheism, the abhorrence of idolatry that distinguish Judaism are, to my thinking, so relevant. The modern world is full of the most obscene idolatries—idolatries of race, of class, of society, of the state, of dictators, of science, even of ideologies. It is most vital to emphasize, as Judaism does, that faith cannot be placed, finally and unreservedly, in any person, institution, or order of this world. To do so would be not only to invite inevitable disillusionment; what is worse, it would be to destroy even the partial good embodied in the person, institution, or order thus idolatrously worshipped. By attempting to exalt a relative into an absolute good, we can but convert it into a total evil. Faith and worship can rest finally and unreservedly only in the transcendent, the ultimate, the absolute, in the one true God; all other faith must be partial, tentative, and provisional at best.

The insights into the nature and destiny of man revealed in scriptural religion supply a dynamic as well as a logic of moral action. For it discloses how the ideal standards of the moral law, though impossible of achievement amidst the intractable forces in man and society, are yet directly pertinent to life in their function as transcendent principles of aspiration, judgment, and action. It is this tension between the immediate relevance, and yet ultimate impossibility of the absolute imperatives of the moral law, that generates the dynamic of moral action in social as well as in individual life.

III. ISRAEL AND THE WORLD

On this question, I speak with great reluctance and hesitancy, for who can penetrate the mystery of Israel? A sociologist of our time, Carl Mayer, has given it as his verdict that:

> The Jewish problem is ultimately inexplicable. . . . . It can be stated, described, and analyzed in so far as its external manifestations are concerned, but it cannot be explained. . . . The Jewish problem in its fundamental aspects appears to be of such a character as to transcend human understanding, and thus essentially belongs to a sphere which is open only to faith. . . .

Judaism is embodied and incarnated in a people which is not a race or a nation or even a religious group in the usual sense of the term. "The Jewish people," says the sociologist I have just quoted, "represent a sociologically *unique* phenomenon and defy all attempts at general definition." The mystery of Israel is one that escapes all categories of nature and society.

This, it is my conviction, is true of Israel, its history, and its scriptures. The history of Israel is not simply the history of an ethnic or cultural or religious group, but in truth a providential history that reveals God's ways with men in a sense in which the history of no other people does. The holy books produced by the Jews are not simply part of the sacred writings of the people of the world: they are the word of God in a way in which the holy books of no other people are. In what way I could not define, but that they are so I cannot but believe.

What I have been saying amounts to an affirmation of the age-old doctrine that Israel is a chosen people. As I read Scripture and history, Israel was chosen both for a mission and for suffering; indeed, the two are probably two sides of the same thing. I believe that Israel was chosen to be a "light unto the nations," to bring the highest reaches of the moral law to the peoples of the world. The Exile and Dispersion came not as punishment of Israel but as an opportunity to spread the word of God to the four corners of the earth. But the mission thus entrusted to Israel creates a tension between Israel and the world: Israel remains *in* the world but is not entirely *of* it. "Like an activating ferment . . . [Judaism] gives the world no peace. It bars slumber. It teaches the world to be discontented and restless as long as the world has not God. It stimulates the movement of history." Thus speaks the Christian philosopher Jacques Maritain. For the sake of this, Israel must undergo persecution, humiliation, agonies of pain and death. Bringing God to the world, Israel must suffer the hatred and resentment of the world against God and his law. Israel as the Chosen People is Israel the Suffering Servant of the Lord, of whom it is written in the words of Isaiah: "He is despised and rejected of men; a man of sorrows and acquainted with grief."

The message of Israel is universal. The Jews, it has been acutely pointed out, are "an ethic group with a universal religious faith which transcends the values of a single people but which they are forced to use as an instrument of survival in an alien world." This is the irony of Jewish existence: devotion to a universal faith marks off the Jews as a "peculiar" people, a "chosen people," and only too often, an "accursed" people! Where this will end, when this will end, is a mystery within the greater mystery of Israel.

These are the things I must think of when I think of my faith as a Jew. And I must add that I am among those who see fundamental spiritual kinship rather than opposition between Judaism and at least the more Hebraic forms of Christianity. Indeed, I find that many of what I conceive to be crucial Jewish insights are illumined rather than obscured when viewed in the light of the development they have undergone in Christian doctrine. I, therefore, believe that whatever significant differences there may be between Judaism and Christianity considered as total systems, there is real and vital meaning in the idea of a Judeo-Christian religious tradition basically distinct from all other religions of the world.

Thinking about religion, so I have found, is no easy way of arriving at simple solutions. It is not a refuge from reality but a challenge to realistic thinking. It means an endless grappling with problems that are never fully solved. In the course of my reorientation, I have encountered perplexities that I was not even aware of before. What is the ultimate meaning of the ritual observances so central to the Jewish tradition? How are we to distinguish their transient historical from their eternal religious aspect? Or the existing Jewish community, how is it related to, yet distinguished from, the spiritual community of Israel? And what are the implications of the universality of Judaism? At various times in its history, Judaism was an expansive force. Will it ever become such again, or is its expansive role at an end since the rise of Christianity and Islam?

Some of these questions will undoubtedly be answered by time, experience, and increased understanding on my part. But other problems will surely arise in their place. Nor is any answer ever likely to be final or conclusive, for in question of such ultimacy, it seems to me, inquiry must end in an irreducible mystery at the heart of things.

For all my uncertainties, however, there is one remark, or rather plea, I would venture to make. It is an appeal for a renewal of Jewish theology. I have lately been reading Dr. Solomon Zeitlin's book *Disciples of the Wise*, which professes to detail the social and religious opinions of American rabbis, as expressed in answers to a questionnaire. One cannot but be gratified at the advanced views on social and economic questions of the Rabbis. But it would be difficult to feel the same gratification at the general state of their theological views. According to Dr. Zeitlin, the group of nearly 250 rabbis "as a whole, as well as the several wings, is divided between the acceptance of the concept of salvation as (a) achievement of an integrated personality, and (b) participation in efforts for social progress." Thus religion is conceived either as a kind of inexpert psychotherapy or else as an auxiliary social reform agency. In one case as in the other, it seems entirely secondary, and as such, can claim no significant place in modern life. Have we really come to the pass where such profound and tradition-laden words as salvation can mean nothing more; where (to take another example from the study) sin is conceived exclusively in such shallow external terms as "harm to neighbors, friends and business associates; harm to society; support of accepted institutions which are socially harmful"; or where (to take still another example) prayer is interpreted entirely in subjectivistic and sociological terms? I cannot believe it. For this would mean that Judaism has been reduced to nothing more than routine observances and a somewhat emotionalized social ethic. Surely Judaism has not yet come to this pass. What we are witnessing, I think, is the gradual corrosion of faith by the naturalistic and secularist temper of the time. It is a corrosion that can and must be arrested and undone by a vital theology, cast in contemporary terms.

Throughout the world, even in America, there is a widespread hunger for metaphysics, engendered by disillusionment with the shallow formulas and plausible half-truths of positivism. Throughout the world, there is a renewed concern with theology, amounting to a renaissance. Catholicism has its neo-Thomism. Protestantism has its new and vital neo-orthodoxy associated, in various forms, with the names of Karl Barth, Emil Brunner, and Reinhold Niebuhr. What Judaism needs today, in my sincere opinion, is a great theological reconstruction in the spirit of a neo-orthodoxy distant alike from sterile fundamentalism and secularized modernism. I earnestly hope that we will not have much longer to wait for this great and high undertaking to get under way.

INTRODUCTION TO

UNIQUENESS AND UNIVERSALITY OF
JEWISH HISTORY

J. L. Talmon

Professor Talmon's meditation on the uniqueness and universality of Jewish history is unpredictably permeated by the sense of providence. The doctrine of providence has always created theological difficulties; its utility has, however, continued to outweigh its perplexities and never more persuasively than when it is applied to the fortuities of Jewish history. Talmon is a brilliant and imaginative historian who recognizes, as he says, that "no historian . . . can be a complete rationalist." Every historian, confronted by the formidable and frequently unassimilable particularities of events, is required to arrest their dynamism in the imagination, if only to be able to describe them as they occurred. Barring even the temptation to judge history, to define its entelechy, or adduce the meaning of particularly startling or decisive events entails, as Talmon admits, a poetic, philosophic, or even mystic turn of mind. The gatherer of facts must give way to the theoretician of their order and significance, for without some position respecting their order and significance, the enterprise of gathering is made useless.

Talmon is most thoughtful in describing the change that has taken place in the focus and concentration of Jewish historiography. Whereas in the past it was possible to intuit and seize the prevailing currents and dispositions of the Jewish intellect and sensibility, incapsulated, sustained, and transmitted as they were by small, autonomous, and closely knit communities, this condition no longer obtains. The Jew is no longer available from within and the Jewish historian of today must rather seek connections between the Jew and his encounter with the Gentile world and general history. This is not to say that the Jew was not always a counterpoint and surd of general history, but in writing of the Jew it was not necessary to account for general history while accounting for the specifics of Jewish historical forms. Today it is necessary. The mystery of Jewish existence is no longer to be found in its survival through separateness, but in its survival amid mixture, conglomeration, and dispersion through all the communities and cultures of the inhabited world.

It is perhaps for the reason of Talmon's sense of the changing method of Jewish historiography that he has been so strenuous in his opposition to Arnold Toynbee's negation of the Jewish factor in civilization (cf. as well the fascinating exchange between Toynbee and Talmon on the Israel-Arab War of June 1967 in *Encounter,* October 1967, and *Congress Bi-Weekly,* November 6, 1967). Toynbee's annoyance that the Jews have endured, that they did not wither away as did the syncretistic religions of the Near East which he admired, is an example to Talmon of methodological Procrusteanism which, over and above Toynbee's dislike for the Jewish mind, for Jewish ethnocentrism or Jewish nationalism, makes it impossible for him to understand the poetics of Jewish survival.

It is not clear whether Talmon is an orthodox or a secularist. It doesn't much matter except in so far as his own view of personal salvation is concerned (and that is irrelevant to the needs of public discourse). What does matter is that regardless of his personal beliefs and practices, he understands the majesty and mystery of Jewish existence and is concerned with making that majesty and mystery historically relevant not only to Jews but to universal history.

UNIQUENESS AND UNIVERSALITY
OF JEWISH HISTORY

A Mid-Century Revaluation

J. L. TALMON

The epoch-making changes that have taken place in recent Jewish history have caused more than one Jewish historian to re-examine the basic assumptions of earlier writers. Not only does the extirpation of Jewish civilization in Eastern and Central Europe mark a decisive shift in the distribution of the Jewish population of the world, it appears to negate Simon Dubnow's view that the essence of Jewish history lies in the urge for full Jewish self-expression through autonomous institutions.

The Western Jewries that lived most of their lives within non-Jewish patterns seemed to the Dubnovist school a pale reflection and dry limb of the real Jewish existence of Eastern Europe. Today these Jewries may have come to represent a primary datum, a culminating point, rather than a peripheral and secondary manifestation of Jewish life. And in view of the decline of Jewish cohesion and unity that has taken place in both the democratic West and the Communist East, under circumstances of real or merely formal civil equality, it would seem doubtful whether the historian will be entitled to apply the same terms of reference to the Diaspora history of the future as he did to Jewish history in the still not too distant past—terms like "the community of a special fate," "identifiable modes of Jewish self-expression," "a corporate Jewish contribution or ingredient."

The emergence of Israel has vindicated the Messianic-nationalist vision and laid for the first time in two thousand years the foundations for a wholly integrated Jewish life. The fact, however, that the majority of Jews, though powerfully affected by the resurrection of Jewish statehood, show every intention of continuing to live outside Israel is bound to bring about a revision of that strenuously dynamic conception, wholly dominated by the category of "becoming," which treated all of Diaspora history as one long preparation for the Zionist consummation, and hardly acknowledged the force of the inertia of mere "being" here and now.

The main question the future historian must resolve for himself is this: Is it right to consider the problem of Jewish nationhood in Israel, and the problem of the Jews living in the Diaspora among other nations, as one subject?

There are people in the Western dispersion who, afraid of being accused of a dual loyalty, claim that the State of Israel is to them just another little state, the only difference being that most of its inhabitants profess, at least nominally, the Jewish religion. There are some cocksure Israelis who proclaim that the sovereign State of Israel, a country like any other, stands in no special relation to Jews outside its borders. But even if there were no religious or cultural ties between Israel and the Diaspora, this attitude would still be completely at variance with reality. It is just not true that Israel and the Diaspora are becoming so dissociated in the consciousness of Jews and Gentiles as to do away with the deeply ingrained habit of associating all Jews everywhere in a common responsibility. Should one of those calamities with which Jewish history is punctuated overtake the Western Diaspora, above all American Jewry, the State of Israel would be shaken to its foundations. On the other hand, should the Jewish state be engulfed by a catastrophe, the legal status and economic position of Jews elsewhere might not be affected at once, but the blow to their self-confidence, the loss of the vicarious prestige which Israel had bestowed upon them in the eyes of the world, and the general disenchantment would be too great to be sustained for long.

Nor can Israel claim that as "an independent state like any other" she has placed herself beyond the reach of those special laws to which the unique Jewish destiny has been subject for so long. The ultimatum addressed in the fall of 1956 by Marshal Bulganin to Ben Gurion was an eloquent comment on the fact that the handicaps besetting Israel have a dimension additional to and different from the limitations under which other small states live in our days. In a note to Libya, Sudan, or Haiti, the Soviet leader would never have hinted so darkly yet so directly about their very right to exist as states. The Jewish right to Israel is not taken for granted. One is reminded of the famous words of General Bonaparte about monarchical Europe's nonrecognition of the French Republic—"France is like the sun, she needs no one's recognition, she is there in blinding splendor." But Israel needs recognition as no other political entity in a world where the existence of a state is, under international law, proven solely by the fact of its recognition by other states.

Thus, at a deeper level, Israel is still involved in the problematic ambiguity attaching to Jewish existence everywhere and at all times. Abnormality, insecurity, ambiguity, absence of full and unequivocal matter-of-factness and recognition continue to haunt her existence; the refusal of the Arab states to recognize Israel seems a parallel to the European-Christian treatment of Jews as latecomers and aliens. The bitter disillusionment of Israelis with the recent policies of the United States was not a little offset by President Eisenhower's emphatic statement that since 1948 he had never contemplated that Israeli-Arab problems could be dealt with without accepting Israel as a historic fact and as a country whose problems were like those of any other.

JEWISH FATE AND TOTALITARIAN MESSIANISM

Jews of the liberal persuasion were less shaken in their convictions by the Jewish catastrophe under Hitler, in spite of its enormity, than Jews sympathetic to communism have been by Soviet anti-Semitism. After all, the Dreyfus Affair and the persistence of discrimination amid conditions of legal equality had accustomed Jews to the limitations of their situation even under the most liberal of regimes. It was Communist Messianism that inherited in our time the fervent hopes of the early Jewish liberals that a general cure for the evils of mankind would do away with every vestige of the peculiar Jewish predicament.

Many a non-Communist was prepared to overlook the fact that totalitarian Messianism, in so far as it asserted an exclusive doctrine embracing every aspect of human life and social existence, was an uncongenial setting for Jews, who are nothing if not nonconformists. Even those to whom the unity of the Jewish people was an article of faith were willing to accept the separation of the Soviet

Jews from the rest of world Jewry on the grounds that, as a church militant surrounded by the city of the devil, the USSR could not permit any part of her population to maintain contact with an international community that had a kind of foreign policy of its own. These "tolerant" Jews knew, of course, that Jewish life shrivels when it is deprived of free channels of communication for ideas, aid, sympathy, and a general sense of kinship, and that it can prosper only in an open society. But the atrophy of Jewish life did not seem to them too high a price to pay for truly equal status.

Events have given the lie to the claim that a Communist regime would do away with the disposition of the non-Jewish world to bracket all Jews in a joint responsibility and guilt by association. The Moscow "doctors' plot," the execution of Jewish writers and artists and other manifestations of official and social anti-Semitism in the Soviet world are, like all other evils, now blamed by the Communists on Stalin or Beria. But this is to evade the fundamental issue.

It used to be confidently said that the triumph of socialism would not only eliminate all the conditions making for social and racial conflict, but that it would inaugurate the reign of fully scientific and deterministic laws of social development under which human arbitrariness and individual or group perversity would be ruled out. If such terrific effectiveness is now ascribed to the personal scientific determinism of the Communist system and to open the door to all those psychological and other influences which remain conditioned, but are rarely negated, by social and economic factors. And it is, indeed, these influences which constitute the core of what has been called the Jewish problem.

Those historians whom faith in dialectical materialism or left-wing sympathies had led to ascribe all anomalies of Jewish existence to its peculiar socioeconomic structure, and, therefore, to hope that these would be conjured away in a classless society, may well now come to see that the top-heavy socioeconomic structure of the Jews was ultimately itself an outcome of their initially exceptional character. The Jews were different and were regarded as such, and, therefore, went—and were driven—into special occupations. In a sense, the experience of the Communist countries goes to confirm a "law" of Jewish history: a new society, regime, or economic system welcomes Jews as pioneers, but thrusts them out unceremoniously as soon as the "natives" are ready to take over the Jewish functions.

This was the case in the early days of urban colonization in Europe, in the first stages of laissez-faire capitalism, and the same development appears to have taken place in Russia since the October Revolution.

Under the most dissimilar historical circumstances, the Jewish fate remains very much the same. At the end of the Second World War the Soviet troops were bound to appear as saviors to Jewish survivors emerging from the forests, bunkers, and caves of Eastern Europe. The Jews had every reason to co-operate with the new regimes, and could offer them cadres of trained personnel and even leadership. But then came the Stalinist drive against "cosmopolitanism," against Jewish intellectuals and Jews in general; and today the resurgence of the Poles, the Hungarians, and others under Soviet Russian domination hit Jews from the other side in so far as they were regarded as collaborators of Stalinism. In brief, fate seems always to prove more potent than any human resolve to change things by imposing new, man-willed and man-guided laws.

The historian need not be ashamed to use so heavily charged a word as "fate." The fate of a nation, like that of a person, may be the working out of the traumas of early childhood, the outcome of some basic and decisive experience. The Jewish psyche received a traumatic twist when the Jewish belief in chosenness sustained the terrible shock of national disaster and exile. This made most Jews impervious to the assimilating influences of Hellenism and Rome. And they could hardly be absorbed by the amorphous barbarians in whose midst they found themselves in the early Middle Ages. Not only were they the bearers of a higher and more ancient civilization, by then they were burdened with the charge that they had killed Jesus. Their status as never wholly assimilable strangers in the midst of the European nations was thus determined for centuries to come, and there is little evidence as yet that in the New World, where all are strangers and newcomers, the Jew has ceased to be regarded as more alien and more different than all other newcomers.

CONTENT AND SCOPE OF JEWISH HISTORY

What will be the subject matter of the Jewish historian of the Diaspora of the future, when Jewish life will have lost its old cohesion and the individual Jew will be living most of his life within non-Jewish patterns; when religious observance will often have been reduced to a minimum or ceased altogether, and Jewish learning will have assumed the character of a philological and antiquarian interest; and when communal activities will not amount to more than care for synagogue and cemetery, charity balls, and youth clubs?

How shall we pick out the slender threads which weave themselves into a Jewish collective pattern distinct from the so much more salient non-Jewish patterns? How shall we detect, in the behavior and actions of seemingly unconnected individuals, features significantly Jewish? To what extent shall we be justified in pronouncing these a Jewish contribution or ingredient?

We are here confronted with that supreme difficulty which Chaim Weizmann used to call Jewish "ghostliness." The world is scarcely large enough to contain the Jews and they are said to possess all the wealth of the earth, and yet when you strain every nerve to fix them in a definition they elude you like a mirage. It seems impossible to lay a finger on anything tangible and measurable in the Jew's Jewishness; yet an ailing, all-devouring self-consciousness comes like a film between him and the world. Not taken into account when things are normal and prosperous, he is seen as ubiquitous, all-powerful, sinister when there is blame to be apportioned. I believe the links holding Jews together—in the words of Edmund Burke—to be as invisible as air and as strong as the heaviest chains, and the Jewish ingredient to be as imperceptible to the senses yet as effective in results as vital energy itself. Such things, however, are too subtle for the historian's customary crude techniques and his far from subtle instruments.

Jewish impulses and reactions, attitudes and sensitiveness, Jewish modes of feeling and patterns of behavior call for the intuition of the artist, and indeed can only be intimated by symbols, conjured up by poetic incantation, and communicated by the art of the novelist. In brief, the Jew is part of a collective destiny, even when he does not know it or is unwilling to share in it. To consider as Jews only persons who explicitly affirm their Judaism by positive participation in Jewish activities would be tantamount to approving the statement made in the 1920's by a German Jewish Social Democratic leader: he maintained that he was no Jew because he had sent a letter of resignation to the Berlin Jewish community—

upon which he was asked by a Gentile British friend whether he thought that Jews were a club. Even when they live their entire life in a non-Jewish milieu and have little contact among themselves, Jews still bear within them the imprint of a centuries-old community whose members were regarded by themselves, and by the outside world, as responsible for one another: a community that lived apart, within a hermetically closed framework of laws and regulations, climatic conditions, and economic pursuits, and that was imbued with an intense self-consciousness because it believed in its own special destiny on the one hand, and was discriminated against and persecuted on the other.

Nevertheless, the Jewish historian would be quite mistaken to direct his attention to every single Jew, even one who had never had any ties with Judaism, on the assumption that all the activities and associations engaged in by every person of Jewish extraction came within the purview of Jewish history. Nor should encouragement be given to the presentation of Jewish history as a collection of biographies of persons of Jewish ancestry who made good in the world. History addresses itself to social patterns; the individual—whatever the ultimate uniqueness of every human being—is significant as a representative type. In the absence of an all-embracing Jewish life of the kind that existed in Eastern Europe, the historian's attempt to isolate specifically "Jewish" associations and activities such as attendance at services, charity campaigns, intercession on behalf of suffering brethren abroad, absorption of immigrants, and even Jewish scholarship (of mainly philological or antiquarian character) will prove depressingly unrewarding and jejune.

When the elusive yet extremely potent Jewish patterns of thought, feeling, and behavior that have crystallized around an extremely tenacious nucleus of race and religion no longer receive—outside Israel—integrated and limpid expression in autonomous and closely knit communities, the nature of these patterns will perhaps best be brought into relief by constant confrontation with general, non-Jewish patterns, and by turning our attention upon the encounter between Jew and Gentile. The earlier historians were naturally inclined to pursue their quest for meaning in Jewish history from within. The future historian of the Jews may prefer to operate from the vantage point of general history. The older historians were impressed by the uniqueness of the history of a people dwelling apart. The newer ones are likely to be struck by the paradox that it is precisely in the uniqueness of a clannish, marginal community dispersed around the world that the secret of the universal significance of Jewish history lies.

JEWISH HISTORY AS A PART OF UNIVERSAL HISTORY

An attempt to sort out the elements of an interpretation of Jewish history from the point of view of world history must nowadays take cognizance of two facts. One is of far-reaching significance: the shift of balance which has been taking place between the West and the nonwhite civilizations. The other is of a more topical and probably ephemeral nature: the treatment of the Jews in Arnold Toynbee's *Study of History,* the most ambitious world-historical synthesis so far undertaken in the twentieth century. The two facts are, in my opinion, closely connected.

I believe that the lack of respect and the air of irritation, if not downright hostility, which mark Professor Toynbee's approach to Jewish history are on a par with his violent reaction against Europe-centrism, and that both are derived from a deep sense of guilt toward the colonial peoples and a corresponding collapse of European self-confidence. What a distance divides Toynbee from Macaulay, who was so cheerfully sure that "a single shelf of a good European library was worth the whole native literature of India and Arabia," and to whom the peoples of the East were simply candidates for admission to Western civilization!

In Western Christian civilization's vision of history, the Jew occupied a vital or at least a unique place. To the multitudes of eastern and southeastern Asia, Jews are an unknown, incomprehensible, and *negligible* factor. The Jew in the West might be persecuted, reviled, despised, expelled, and massacred, but he was indissolubly connected with the central event in the history of Christendom. He constituted a terrific problem. He embodied a great mystery. Immense effectiveness was ascribed to him, for good or evil. He appeared to be a factor of significance out of all proportion to his numbers.

The Jews have a long, terrible, and blood-stained account with the Christian West. I venture to suggest, however, that the rise of non-European powers is already beginning to make the record look somewhat different and less straightforward than was the case even in the recent past. For one thing, no Jewish historian, whatever his evaluation of the various factors involved in the restoration of

Jewish statehood, can ignore the fact that Zionism would never have had a chance of success if centuries of Christian teaching and worship, liturgy, and legend had not conditioned the Western nations to respond almost instinctively to the words "Zion" and "Israel," and thus to see in the Zionist ideal, not a romantic chimera or an imperialistic design to wrest a country from its actual inhabitants, but the consummation of an eternal promise and hope. The Far Eastern civilizations, however, show no trace of Jewish associations. Their record is clean of anti-Semitism—but it is also empty of Jews.

TOYNBEE AND THE JEWS

The whole centuries-long relationship of the West to the East is made to appear by Toynbee as one of sustained aggression, motivated by insatiable avarice, against essentially contemplative and pacific civilizations. Church militant, European nationalism and racialism, modern imperialism, acquisitive capitalism, and—in some of its aspects—revolutionary Communism are only phases and versions as it were of the sin of self-centered pride and arrogance. Far from having its cause in intellectual or spiritual superiority, the victory of the West over the Eastern and other non-European peoples, Toynbee believes, is due to one single factor—technological mastery. The Western absorption in techniques is evidence that Western man was much less anxious to know the truth than he was eager to turn discoveries and inventions into instruments of self-aggrandizement and dominion. The Chinese fathomed some of the mysteries of science long before the Europeans, but remained indifferent to the possibilities of science's utilitarian application.

The sin of pride has always carried its own punishment with it. *Hubris* prepares its own undoing. Greed expanding and conquering generates irreconcilable social cleavages and antagonisms within the victorious society, and bitter resentment among the conquered. The internal proletariat, alienated from the body politic, feels a common resentment with the external proletariat of the enslaved nations. Together they evolve a system of values—a new religion—to match and oppose the values of the conquerors and to act as a sublimating compensation for the enjoyments from which they are debarred. Dominant society, which has waxed fat and sluggish and succumbed to the malaise of the satiated, is pervaded by the new religion and simultaneously destroyed by the combined blows administered from within by the internal proletariat, and from without by the external proletariat. Western civilization—with Communism corroding it from within and closing in on it from the outside—having now reached this stage, it can be saved only by a new universal religion based on a synthesis of the four great creeds—Christianity, Islam, Buddhism, and Hinduism. Such a universal religion, Toynbee holds, will redeem it from the cancer of aggressive egotism by enabling it to achieve blissful reconciliation with the eternal order of things.

Toynbee appears to trace the original sin of the West, self-idolatry, back to the "arrogant" Judaic idea of a Chosen Poeple. Hebrew society was according to him only a parochial, marginal community within a much wider Syriac civilization. Judaic religion evolved in the encounter between the Syriac exiles in Babylon and the proletariat of Mesopotamia, just as Christianity arose out of the meeting between the Jews oppressed by Rome and the proletariat of Hellenistic-Roman society.

That the tribal god Yahveh, and not any one of his so much more powerful rivals within "Syriac civilization," came to be accepted as the One God of the Universe is attributed by Toynbee to the all-devouring jealousy of Yahveh, who would not brook other gods and incited his believers to destroy all idols and images.

Obsessed by its tribal exclusiveness, Judaism failed to seize the chance, offered it by incipient Christianity, of becoming a universal religion, and instead rose against Rome in a nationalist uprising. When the Jewish revolt was crushed, Judaism's role was played out. The subsequent two thousand years of Jewish history represented the meaningless perdurance of a fossil. The Jews' only response to the challenge of exile and persecution, Toynbee says, was to maintain a hermetically closed, highly intricate ritualistic framework, and to accumulate great financial power.

At the end of this long period of fossilized existence, Zionism marked another outburst of tribal arrogance. Yielding to the essentially Western passion for archaization, the Jews, instead of keeping their hopes fixed on miraculous Divine deliverance, launched an attack on the Arab inhabitants of Palestine, succeeded in expelling them, and set up a tiny statelet of their own which in its crude aggressiveness combined all the disagreeable features of a military garrison and the Wild West.

Imbibed by the Christian West, the Judaic spirit acted as a

potent evil factor in the history of Western civilization. The intolerant militant exclusiveness of the Church—a primary Judaic legacy—was in due course transformed into the self-idolatry of parochial nationalisms like the English and the French. Taught by the example of Joshua's extermination of the pagan Canaanites, Puritan settlers felt no qualms about annihilating the Red Indians. Believing themselves to be the heirs of the Jews to whom the earth had been promised as an inheritance, European imperialist nations went out to conquer and enslave the non-European races. Having turned their backs on the One God, they abandoned themselves completely to Mammon: all their energies were applied to perfecting the means of accumulating wealth and reaching the highest degree of rational utilitarian efficiency. In brief, the West underwent—in the words of Toynbee—a process of "Judaization."

At the other end of the scale, socialism and Communism were nothing but a version of the Judaic apocalypse, except that the final consummation was again looked for, not in the intervention of the Almighty, but as the result of social cataclysm and a violent uprising of men.

So much for Toynbee's definition of the Jewish ingredient in Western civilization. How will the Jewish historian, coming from general history, define it?

There is every justification, it seems to me, for the view that finds a distinctive Jewish ingredient at the very core of Western civilization. This is the measure of the paradox: an essentially marginal group said to be the most clannish of all communities, the Jews have in their tribal seclusion in Palestine as well as in their worldwide dispersion, as spirit and as flesh and blood, played a powerful part in making a collection of tribes, communities, and countries into a civilization. Needless to add, they were not alone in the field, and their influence has not been invariably beneficial.

I shall not labor the obvious: that Judaism was the parent of Christianity, and that, therefore, almost the whole of Jewish history till Jesus, and on into the first centuries of Christianity—the period in which the latter received its shape either within the Jewish community or in the course of debate with Rabbinic Judaism, and spread through the Jewish communities along the shores of the Mediterranean—constitutes a vital chapter in world history. One can well imagine a future Israeli historian undertaking to write the history of Western Christian civilization as the story of the Judaic kernel in its encounter with Greek philosophy and art, the mystery religions of the Orient, the institutions and laws of the Roman Empire, the Germanic traditions, the facts of European economy, etc., etc.

THE IDEA OF THE CHOSEN PEOPLE IN WESTERN CIVILIZATION

I shall take up only the one idea which Professor Toynbee thinks to be the most distinctive and effective Jewish ingredient in world history—the idea of a Chosen People. I agree as to its paramount importance. But my reasons for thinking that Western civilization (and consequently universal history) would not have been the same without it are altogether different from his.

To Dr. Toynbee, the whole concept of chosenness signifies mere tribal exclusiveness and a conceited claim to racial superiority. He omits the attributes of "a holy nation," "a people of priests." I believe that the uniqueness of ancient Judaism did not consist so much in the monotheistic conception, traces of which we can find among neighboring peoples, or in moral precepts whose similitudes we can find in Greek philosophy and the teachings of the Stoa—it consisted in the idea of a whole people's recognizing, as its sovereign, God alone. The laws under which it lives are not dictated by a ruler, are not derived from the will of the people, are not a utilitarian contrivance. Hence what Matthew Arnold called the Hebraic passion for right acting, as distinct from the Greek passion for right seeing and thinking in order to know, experience, and dominate the world around.

Here we have the secret of the victory of parochial Yahveh over Helios, the god of the sun, and all the other pagan deities, and indeed over Hellenistic philosophies like the Stoa. The uniqueness of Judaism did not lie, as Toynbee says, in the devouring jealousy of Yahveh, but in the total and one-sided absorption of a whole people—not a sect of the chosen or a monastic order—in the service of an impersonal idea. The teachings of other Near Eastern religions were more tolerant, more open to sweetness and light—and left very many things outside their scope. This is why they failed to revolutionize history. The Hellenistic systems are incomparable in their broad humanity, but they were addressed to and absorbed by individuals as counsels of personal perfection. Not conclusions of close discursive reasoning, but the living model and the all-absorbing passion proved so effective in the Jewish case. From that point of view, Toynbee's attempt to dilute the sharp identity of the Judaic source by pointing to a wider Syriac context of ideas and beliefs is hardly relevant.

What distinguishes mature Christian civilization from other civilizations is to be sought not so much in particular tenets of Christianity, to which parallels of some kind may be found in other religions, but in the fundamentally and peculiarly Western relationship between church and state. There was no example of it in antiquity, and none to my knowledge in Islam or the Eastern Asiatic civilizations. And this ingredient is substantially Jewish. The church means in this respect the universality of believers, "the people of priests," and not merely the hierarchy. The members of the ecclesia are actuated by a consciousness that, as a "holy nation" and a "people of priests," they belong not to the earthly state alone, but to a community of transcendental laws and aims.

The permanent tension between church and state, as long as neither proved able to absorb the other, is to my mind the source of the essentially Western obsession with the problem of the legitimacy of power. It is not enough that the law is promulgated by the authority which is recognized to have power to legislate. King, parliament, the sovereign people, even pope and council, must all the time exhibit their credentials in the face of divine or natural law. Natural law is, of course, of Hellenistic and Roman provenance. Yet it is fair to say that without its being amalgamated with divine law, it would have failed to become the great formative influence that it did.

One should not underestimate the other factors which have shaped Western ideas of state, law, and legitimacy, such as the Germanic traditions, feudalism, the guild system, the changes in methods of production. Yet I believe with Lord Acton that none of these was so effective as the tension between church and state, which was the greatest and most important vehicle of ideas and controversies and which, as it were, enveloped all the others and set the tone. When political theorists of the West spoke of Oriental despotism, what they meant was that the Orient did not know the problem of the legitimacy of power. Power to them was a datum, a fact of nature, an elemental, amoral force to be taken for granted like sunshine and rain, storm and plague. It need not always be tyrannical and malign, it might be as benign as one could wish. But it is given, it is there, and we have to bow to it.

Now it is the tension between church and state, based on the idea of a chosen holy people, that gave the history of European nations its highly dynamic quality in comparison with the early stagnation of the non-European civilizations. Thanks to the Judaic concept the Papacy never could, and perhaps never really wished to, reduce the body of lay believers to mere receivers of grace through the instrumentality of sacramental mystery and miracle. The task of realizing the Kingdom of God was never restricted to the *ecclesia docens*. It always continued to rest with the *whole* body of believers. Hence the sense of dignity and awful responsibility of a Christian nation. It could not accept easily an evil king any more than a corrupt pope. For Christianity could never quite be reduced to a matter of personal ascetic discipline and unworldly holiness, and it could not divest itself of all responsibility for this world on the ground that its kingdom was wholly of another. It was thus bound to feel the permanent challenge to realize its high calling here and now. If this be true of the Catholic Church at all times, it is especially true of Calvinism and the Puritans in Britain and America.

There is, I submit with Dr. Toynbee, a direct line from the Church Militant permeated with the Judaic idea of a holy nation of priests, to modern nationalism with its ideology of a chosen people. We are only too painfully aware in the twentieth century of the terrible ravages wrought by nationalism run wild. Yet it would be wrong for the historian to forget that in the first half of the nineteenth century, the national idea in the mouth of a Mazzini, and indeed even of a Fichte, not to speak of the Polish Mickiewicz, was a prophetic clarion call for spiritual regeneration. Far from proclaiming tribal war on neighbors thought inferior, it imposed a special mission, a particularly strenuous obligation on one's own nation within the scheme of mankind's endeavor toward higher things and universal freedom. It is indeed most strange to read today Fichte's boast that the German nation, the *Urvolk* of Europe, would not demean itself by joining the general bloody scramble for territories and colonies, and would take no part in the squalid game of political and mercantilist rivalry. The only truly original nation in Europe, since all others had their thoughts and feelings shaped by an acquired language—whether Latin or German—the Germans were destined to maintain, with brows furrowed and spirits keyed to the highest pitch of concentration, a special communion with eternal values.

Everyone is familiar with the religious, Messianic overtones of Mazzini's philosophy of nationalism, with such slogans as "God and the people," "nationality is a mission," "nation means sacrifice"; with Mazzini's conception of patriotism as a counterpart to selfish utilitarianism and moral self-indulgence; with his vision of a federation of free peoples, each with its own mission, under the inspiring guidance of Roma Terza—Rome of the people—the first Rome having been that of the emperors and the second that of the popes. Mickiewicz, like Mazzini, consciously drew on Biblical ideas and imagery in describing Poland as the suffering Remnant of Israel, destined to atone for the sins of other nations and redeem them through her self-sacrifice.

SELF-SURRENDER AND SELF-ASSERTION

Professor Toynbee wrings his hands over the horrors wrought by modern nationalism and its evil offspring imperialism, seeing in them nothing but irredeemable evil, pride, and *hubris,* which stand in such crass contrast to the broad, quietist tolerance of the Eastern religions and civilizations.

It seems to me that in his prostration before the East and self-flagellation as a Westerner, Dr. Toynbee has missed a truth of awful import, a mystery of tragic grandeur—the ambivalence with which the whole of the Western achievement is charged from the start. It is an infinitely tragic fact that great good is somehow always mixed up with terrible evil, that the worst seems always to be the degeneration of the best, that some Hegelian *List der Vernunft,* a trick of Universal Reason, complicates in a sardonic manner the yearning for self-surrender with the craving for self-assertion.

Professor Toynbee is filled with reverence for those Eastern civilizations whose religions are a syncretistic synthesis of various, often heterogeneous, strands, and are ultimately the concern of the individual only, and whose churches know no intolerant militancy. He is attracted by those vast conglomerations of men who are not primarily political animals at all, and whose passion for power is held back by a highly developed capacity for contemplative communion with the invisible world and the attainment of that peace which passeth understanding—a peace for which we all strain in vain, and of which only very few in our midst ever catch a glimpse.

Nearer home Dr. Toynbee selects the Ottoman Empire for special commendation. That was a system in which racial, linguistic, and religious communities lived as *millets* side by side on a completely nonpolitical basis. He is not worried by the fact that the Turkey of the sultans was a byword for despotism, corruption, and bribery, that even the Ullema, the supreme Moslem court of experts in Islam, was most of the time unable to restrain the cruel vagaries of personal despotism; that under such a regime there could be no individual rights and no corporate consciousness or self-respect; that only a palace plot or the assassin's dagger, and at a lower level bribery and flattery, could avert the pure arbitrariness of brute power; and that consequently complete stagnation overcame all cultural endeavor and spiritual vitality under the Ottoman Turks. In the vast empires where there is no political life and no popular passion, the individual may at times attain a very high degree of personal, unworldly perfection. But it is at the cost of the vitality and the moral advancement of the body social.

It is a curious thing that a man so sensitive to any sign of arrogance and pride, and who over acres of self-analysis recording his visitations makes such tremendous efforts to be humble, should at the same time be so fascinated—as Dr. Toynbee is—by colossal dimensions, the mighty barbarian conquerors wading in blood up to their knees, building sky-high pyramids of the skulls of their slaughtered foes. England and France, on the other hand, Professor Toynbee again and again calls parochial, puffed-up little countries.

The finest flowering of culture never occurred on the vast expanses of steppe and desert but in tiny, overcrowded, noisy, and proud communities such as Athens, Jerusalem, Alexandria, Florence, and Amsterdam. Why damn vitality by calling it arrogance? The truth of the matter is that an ambitious undertaking like Toynbee's to embrace all ages and all civilizations in one system, with the help of tidy schemata, sweeping generalizations, and quantitative measurements, can afford little room for the understanding of the unique phenomenon, the local idiom, and the particular concatenation of data and circumstances; little room for the exquisite miniature; and nothing of that feeling for the specific situation, limpid and throbbing with real life, which comes from long meditation and loving immersion in it.

THE JEWISH INGREDIENT IN INDUSTRIAL CIVILIZATION

In the last two centuries Western history has indeed become universal history. The non-European civilizations, sunk in languor or atrophy, have had their fate shaped by the expansion of Western capitalism, which turned the whole world into one economic and cultural unit. In our own day the essentially European ideologies of nationalism, democracy, and Communism—not the organic growth and inner dialectic of their own heritage—stimulated the Asiatic and African peoples to assert themselves and seek self-determination.

I agree with Dr. Toynbee that in the forging of the various instruments for the unification of the world by the West—or if one prefers, by Western imperialism—the Jewish ingredient played the role of a powerful catalyst. Jews as living men, and not merely the Jewish spiritual legacy, moved onto the center of the stage of world history in the nineteenth and twentieth centuries. One need not belittle the part Jews played in maintaining international trade almost alone in the early Middle Ages, in interpreting and transmitting for Christian scholarship the classical wisdom preserved in Arab translations, and as a lever in early urban colonization. Whether you call them rapacious usurers or bankers—as one calls the more respectable because richer Christian Medicis and Fuggers, Lombards, and Templars—whether the Jews went into business from their own choice or because all other avenues were closed to them, they kept up through centuries a rudimentary credit system in Europe.

Nevertheless, I hold the somewhat chilling view that the history of most European countries, with the exception perhaps of Spain, Poland, and Holland, would not have differed very significantly had there been no Jews—but only the Judaic heritage—in Europe between the end of the Crusades and the eighteenth century. Indeed, for most of that time they had been expelled from a number of the European countries. The living ghetto commanded too little respect to influence directly a society so highly stratified as European society was for centuries.

Only in the last hundred and fifty years was it again given to Jews to affect the structural framework of universal history.

I believe it legitimate for the universal historian to call the age ushered in by the French and industrial revolutions the "era of industrial civilization based on contract." This formulation takes account of the two most salient features of the period—industrialism and democratic growth. Furthermore, it implies that capitalism and the various forms of socialism and Communism are only two poles of the same development, and not phenomena on different planes. The formulation postulates a type of spiritual-cultural superstructure evolved from the essentially universal and cosmopolitan character of industrial civilization. The main point to be borne in mind is the transformation of a society based on status and on more or less rigid patterns into a society based on contract— in other words on individual and social mobility. This meant an entirely new situation for Jews, and one of unlimited possibilities.

Nuanced thinking and formulation are required here in order not to overstate our case. None of the early inventors of the Industrial Revolution was a Jew, and there were to my knowledge hardly any identifiable Jews among the early captains of industry. Werner Sombart's attempt—in imitation of Max Weber's connecting of the Puritans with the rise of capitalism—to make the Jews of the seventeenth century bearers of early capitalism has long been discredited. Yet it is true that in the building of the sinews of the modern international capitalist economy, the part of the Jews, especially on the Continent, was that of pioneers and catalysts *par excellence*. International credit, banking and exchange, joint-stock companies, telegraphic news agencies, railway networks, chain stores, methods of mass production and mass marketing, the media of mass entertainment, experimentation in new techniques—in brief, the lifelines of a universal economy—were in very many cases laid down and set working by Jews, who thus played, in the words of Joseph Addison, the part of "pegs and nails" in the world economy.

The abstract, rational nexus holding together concrete, disparate detail was grasped more quickly by people with a long training in intellectual speculation. Not place-bound, the emancipated and detribalized Jew was unhampered by routine and conservative attachments, and his international connections helped him to forge the hinges of new artificial frameworks. It is in the nature of a marginal community, especially one living in metropolitan centers to acquire the refined sensitivity of an exposed nerve and to be the first to detect the trend and shape of things to come. Hence the disposition and the courage to experiment. Emancipated formally, but not really or fully admitted as equals, lacking the prestige of lineage and long establishment, while eager for a place in the sun, and restless and ill at ease as people in ambiguous situations are, the Jews threw all their pent-up energies into the two avenues of power open to them: economic activity and intellectual prowess.

Centuries of disciplined living and sober calculation prevented ambition from dissipating itself in a haphazard, chaotic manner. Vitality turned into a strictly rational instrument of power designed to obtain maximum results at the lowest cost.

REVOLUTIONARY MESSIANISM

As for the Jewish ingredient in revolutionary Messianism, the other pole of industrial civilization, I have come to the conclusion on somewhat closer study that it was to a large extent the Jewish Messianic vision of history that made the Industrial Revolution appear, not merely as another crisis and another bad spell, but as an apocalyptic hour leading to some preordained final denouement. It was the Jewish Messianic tradition that was responsible for the fact that the social protest of the victims of the Industrial Revolution did not take the form of another desperate, elemental *jacquerie*, but became part of the preparation for a Day of Judgment, after which justice and peace would reign supreme and history really begin as it were with all conflicts and contradictions resolved.

The earliest prophet of socialist transformation in nineteenth-century Europe, Saint-Simon, was quite explicitly linked with the Jewish Messianic expectation. Jews were the leading spirits in his fascinating and influential school, and they emphatically voiced the conviction that they were carrying on the perennial Messianic mission of Judaism. Their future city of universal harmony was to be guided by technicians and bankers who were at the same time artists and priests, and was to rest on a universal religion of humanity, *Nouveau Christianisme,* with the old division into state and church, matter and spirit, theory and practice done away with for ever. It is most significant that Jewish Saint-Simonist, the Rodriguezes, Pereiras, d'Eichthals, should have in the course of time become the architects of France's industrial and financial revolution and of much of Europe's banking and industry.

The deeply ingrained experience of history as the unfolding of a pattern of judgment and deliverance makes it almost impossible for the Jew to take history for granted as an eternal meaningless cycle. Time must have a stop. History must have a denouement. At the same time his lack of roots in a concrete tradition, with its instinctive certainties and the comfort of smooth, almost automatic procedures, combines with the absence of experience of practical government to turn many a Jew into a doctrinaire and impatient addict of schemes of social redemption. When he is of a prophetic temperament, as in the case of a Karl Marx, a torrent of relentless denunciation issues forth. A terrific, fiery oversimplification reduces everything—human laziness and thoughtlessness, the weakness of the flesh and the heterogeneity of impulse, peculiarity of tradition and complexity of situation—to greed, falsehood, and hypocrisy, a kingdom of the Devil that will be overthrown in the imminent future by a kingdom of God. Suspended between heaven and earth, rejected and excluded, tormented by the humiliations, complexities, and ambiguities of his situation, many a young Jew threw himself with the deepest yearning and passion into the arms of the religion of revolution.

We all know the inhumanities practiced by capitalism at the height of its imperialistic expansion, and the perverse denial of traditional morality and of man's freedom and dignity which accompanies the attempt to satisfy the Messianic longing for salvation by a totalitarian system. This erosion of ideals has no particular relevance to Judaism as such, for it is rooted in the tragic condition itself of man, in the essential ambivalence of things human and social—as the Christian would say, in original sin. It is at the same time not to be denied that the fact of a surplus of intensity among Jews, such as is peculiar to a marginal minority in constant need to justify its separateness by self-assertion, has its own polar ambivalence: besides idealistic self-dedication to causes and things of the mind, there is a particularly harsh, shrill, and unscrupulous style of Jewish self-seeking.

COSMOPOLITAN CULTURE

We come now to the Jewish ingredient in the universal or cosmopolitan culture characteristic of an industrial civilization based on contract instead of status, and sustained by media of mass communication.

It is one of the commonplaces of Jewish apologists to emphasize that Jews have enriched the life and culture of every country in which they have lived. Yet, as I have said, I do not believe that the culture of England, France, Italy, or even of pre-nineteenth-century Germany would have been significantly different if there had been no Jews in those countries. Modern universal civilization is, however, unthinkable without Marx, Freud, or Einstein, who have molded the consciousness of modern mankind.

Isaiah Berlin has given an acute explanation of the contrast between the superb achievements of Jews in the sciences and music, and their rather inferior showing in literature. Jewish writers have excelled in biography and the biographical novel (André Maurois and Stefan Zweig). They have written in highly stimulating fashion on the complexities and dilemmas of the contemporary human situation (Arthur Koestler, Arthur Miller, and Ilya Ehrenburg). In this they were helped by their psychological acumen, which their race acquired from its agelong need to understand and adjust to others, as well as by their being at the very nerve center of metropolitan life and at the same time detached and oversensitive. Yet, while being often stirring and provocative, their writings in no sense represent great literature. It is not enough to be able to penetrate, even lovingly, the inner springs and hidden recesses of men and societies. Vigor and intimacy come to the novel from subtle, almost unconscious and automatic associations, which are not acquired with the algebraic language of science but are imperceptibly experienced within a concrete, long-established tradition. This is why Yiddish literature has such vigor as well as warmth.

The literature produced by Jewish writers in non-Jewish languages in centers like old Vienna—where Jews as producers as well as consumers often formed a nucleus of the most cosmopolitan vanguard—served despite its lack of greatness as a barometer and stimulant of universal significance.

On the political level, the passionate patriotism of a Benjamin Disraeli, a Walter Rathenau, a Léon Blum had perhaps greater intensity and depth than the devotion of an ordinary British, German, or French statesman to his country. It was conditioned by an agonized yearning for something romantically idealized which was not a simple datum to be taken for granted. This kind of Jewish patriotism betrayed a deeper and more articulate understanding of the national tradition and its peculiarities than could the patriotism of a "normal" leader, for whom the national tradition was a matter of spontaneous reflexes. And the patriotism of Jews was always more universal (or more imperial, as in the case of Disraeli) in its awareness.

Far from lending support to any doctrine of race in the biological sense, our argument has been concerned, throughout its latter part, with a spiritual legacy and the facts of history and social psychology on the one side, and the individualistic mobility of industrial civilization on the other.

Indeed, the fate of Jews under Hitler may in this respect be seen as a focal point of twentieth-century history—and not merely because of the enormity of the crime and sufferings inflicted on them with the help of scientific long-term planning and execution, and not only because the mass violation of the sanctity of human life was not calculated to stop with the Jews but was bound to undermine the most vital foundations of our civilization and initiate general race slaughter. Hitler's racialism signified an attempt to reverse the main trend of modern Western civilization, and to return from individualistic contract to deterministic patterns of race, caste, and tribe through a denial of the unity of mankind. It is no accident that Nazism found it necessary to reinterpret the whole of history as a permanent life-and-death struggle between Nordic Aryanism and the Jewish spirit, attributing to Jews a significance and effectiveness which the most extreme Jewish chauvinist would not dream of claiming.

ISRAEL AND THE DIASPORA

Some of my readers may have begun to feel a certain surprise that there has been relatively little reference so far to Israel in this survey. Our theme has been Jewish history from the point of view of universal history. Although the Palestine problem has been one of the focal points of international politics, and albeit that little country of such strange destinies is once more a center of world attention, it is still too early to say whether the return of Jews to Zion (which coincides with the general retreat of Europe from Asia: an extraordinary fact, highly charged with symbolism) will mean more than the establishment of another little state among the dozens of new states which have come into existence in the twentieth century.

In Professor Toynbee's violent condemnation, Zionism figures as an integral part of Western imperialistic rapacity. The music of Messianic hope kept alive for two thousand years; the saga-like quality of the return to Zion; the historic perspectives and vistas opened by that event; the awful tragedy that the restoration of Jews to Israel had to be effected through a terrible conflict with the Arab world—all this fails to strike a chord. We have instead Dr. Toynbee's nonsense about Jews taking over the Western "heresy of archaization"; his tasteless, sermonizing censure of Jews for not trusting in God's miraculous deliverance, and for demeaning themselves with such unworthy things as a state, a flag, an army, and postage stamps; a selective method of presenting facts which amounts to untruth—as, for instance, the failure to mention the decision of the United Nations, as representative of world conscience, on partition, or to refer by a single word to the invasion of Palestine by five Arab armies. We then get the horrifying comparison of the treatment of the Arab population by the Jews with the extermination of six million Jews by Hitler, and finally the crowning sanctimonious blasphemy: the prophecy that on the Day of Judgment the crime of the Jews shall be judged graver than that of the Nazis.

There are one or two pointers to be borne in mind by the universal historian meditating on the future of Jews within the scheme of world history. There seems to be something almost providential in the way in which the two new centers, Israel and the United States, were as it were prepared just on the eve of the catastrophe which put an end to European Jewry's history of some fifteen hundred to two thousand years. There is also a striking analogy between the present relations between Israel and the Anglo-Saxon Jewish communities, especially American Jewry, and the relations that obtained at the time of the Second Temple between Jewish Palestine and the Mediterranean Jewish communities of the Roman Empire on one side, and the Jewish conglomeration in Mesopotamia on the other. It is a fact of very great importance that English has come to be the language of the majority of the Jewish people.

The problems that faced the Palestine-Mediterranean axis were very similar to those of the Israel-Anglo-Saxon axis today, including all those needs which had to be met by an annual United Jewish Appeal, the problems of assimilation, mixed loyalties, and so forth. The encounter of Judaism and Hellenism, and the synthesis of the two in the Alexandria of Philo, paved the way for the triumph of Christianity. Is it too fanciful to suggest that the New York of today may be destined to play the part of a Jewish Alexandria of the twentieth century? There is much food for speculation in the fact that tiny Israel, on the troubled eastern shore of the Mediterranean, has a kind of counterpart in what is the most vital country in the world today, and the one which seems destined to set the tone in the years to come.

If it was given to the Jews to make some mark on world history, it was not because God, as someone has said, was kind to the Jews in scattering them among the nations, but because they had fashioned their real contribution—the Judaic heritage—in their own country, and were dispersed only after they had been molded into a unique phenomenon. . . .

No historian, I believe, can be a complete rationalist. He must be something of a poet, he must have a little of the philosopher, and he must be touched just a bit by some kind of mysticism. The sorting out of evidence, the detective's skill in ferreting out inaccuracy and inconsistency, are of little help when the historian strikes against the hard residue of mystery and enigma, the ultimate causes and the great problems of human life.

The Jewish historian becomes a kind of martyr in his permanent and anguished intimacy with the mystery of Jewish martyrdom and survival. Whether he be orthodox in belief or has discarded all religious practice, he cannot help but be sustained by a faith which can neither be proved nor disproved.

I believe that notwithstanding all the vexations and entanglements caused by emergency and inescapable necessity—all so reminiscent incidentally of the times of Ezra and Nehemiah—Israel will one day be spiritually significant and, in conjunction with the Jewish Diaspora, spiritually effective in the world.

History would somehow make no sense otherwise.

PART TWO

THE RENEWAL OF THEOLOGY

INTRODUCTION TO

MODERN JUDAISM'S NEED FOR PHILOSOPHY

Erich Unger

"The Jews are an intellectual people," Erich Unger writes with asseverative confidence, but if so, he goes on, why "have they not been able to create a pregnant reinterpretation of their inherited system of life and thought?" This is a challenging question, and it continues to remain unanswered. It is, moreover, a question more and more desperately in need of answering, for failure to attend to it reflects less the patent fact that "pregnant reinterpretations" are wanting than an unwillingness to examine the historical situation of the modern Jew (the post-Holocaust Jew in particular) and to recognize the increasing precariousness of his religious position.

There are admittedly modern apologias, but apologetics does not supply answers. It may be said—and is often said—that Jews have no need of philosophy for Torah and Talmud Torah afford the object and method of sufficient inquiry. But this ignores the obvious fact (which in other contexts would not be ignored) that from Isaac Israeli and Saadia Gaon to Hasdai ibn Crescas and Levi ben Gerson an enormous literature of philosophic inquiry had been accumulated whose express purpose was to impart to Judaism the perspective of totality—a system of knowledge encompassing divine and metaphysical science as well as many of the practical disciplines of ethics, poetics, and politics. What the medieval Jews lacked in power they possessed in conviction, for they—no less than the medieval Christian or Muslim—believed that religion constituted a polity and that theology was the capstone of an order of knowledge that was universal and true. It is not enough to redirect modern Jewish inquirers to medieval sources for their answers, for the impetus to intellection is constant and various and the vitality of a tradition is to be found in both the generosity and resiliency with which it encourages and sustains difficult, imaginative, and frequently novel questions.

The routinization of medieval Jewish philosophy into the intellectual life of orthodox tradition demonstrates less that orthodoxy is capacious than that the philosophic inquiry has become stunted, that the old is still compelled to service the contemporary, that the present situation does not evoke new thinking. "No religion has since the Middle Ages concerned itself less with philosophy than Judaism. None has fallen more deeply into the error of divorcing religion from philosophy than the official trustees of the Jewish heritage." Professor Unger goes on to acknowledge that indeed there have been numerous Jewish philosophers in the modern period (and he cites those from Mendelssohn and Krochmal to Hermann Cohen, Buber, and Rosenzweig) but he notes the interesting fact that among his eleven thinkers, only two have been rabbis. By and large the laity have been left the task of thought. Presumably to the rabbis has been given the custodial care of the tradition. But this is a fateful dichotomy, for where the layman may enjoy the freedom of intellectual distance from the liturgical and halakhic life of the community and, as a result, introduce more invention and novelty into his formulations, the rabbis are obliged to make apologetics do the work of speculative thought, preoccupied as they are with the demands and issues of practical communal immediacy.

If Judaism, Unger argues, wishes to appear alive and healthy, its index of spiritual power is not to be measured by uniformity of thought, for such uniformity, such rehearsal of canonic doctrine, such apologetic formularization is more symptomatic of precisely the decay and obsolescence it wishes to avoid. The task of Jewish philosophy is not to have snap answers to any and all questions, for it is in fact the power of new questions that snap answers are not available, and it is precisely the vitality one seeks that there are thinkers—lay and hopefully rabbinic—for whom the challenge of unconventional questions is, not a source of abashment and fear, but an inspiriting of quest.

It has been my argument for many years that the tactics of survival are merely tactics, that Judaism cannot rely either upon the human grief that followed the Holocaust or upon the human pride that attended the rebirth of Israel for its endurance in the modern world. The modern world has far greater talent than did the Inquisition and the Medieval Church to do Judaism in; for one thing, life in the modern world is vastly more easy for the Jew than life in medieval Burgos, York, or the Rhineland. It is no less true that secular ideologies and philosophies have afforded contemporary man masks of doctrine which appear whole and encompassing. If Judaism believes them to be insufficient, its own task is to define the alternative. The definition of alternative is not only one of affirming faith indifferent to philosophy, but adumbrating faith through philosophy. It is not a new medievalism that is sought, only a legitimation of the philosophic inquiry under the terms and conditions of modern life.

Erich Unger, who died shortly after this essay was published in 1957, had made the effort in his work which he urges upon the new Jewish philosophers, for his own philosophic work, notably *Politik und Metaphysik, Gegen die Dichtung,* and *Wirklichkeit, Mythos, Erkenntnis* were all permeated by a Jewish sense of the ethical task. In "Modern Judaism's Need for Philosophy" he has written profoundly, succinctly, and authoritatively a moral justification of modern Jewish philosophizing.

MODERN JUDAISM'S
NEED FOR PHILOSOPHY

A Question of Vitality

ERICH UNGER

Philosophy has at some time or another made its appearance in all the great religions of the world. Why? Because the problem of God and the world can be approached by way of philosophy, too; because at some points both ways converge and merge; and because the dovetailing of the philosophical and the religious view of the divine becomes so important at times that upon this interaction may depend the vigor and very life of a religion.

There is a widespread view that the importance of philosophy is necessarily restricted to the small number of those who study it, and that it is, therefore, of no consequence to the overwhelming majority of mankind. On the other hand, the language of religion, its images and doctrines, are easily assimilated by all, and the words of the prophets are in a certain way grasped by the masses. Even where there is a union of religion and philosophy, however, we may find that a barrier has been interposed which prevents normal understanding and communication between the few who lead and the majority of men. What good is such a union when its result and its significance cannot be communicated to those for whom the religion exists?

History, it is held, has shown time and again that religion can stand on its own feet. Religion has often been taught without taking into account the sphere where religion and philosophy border on one another, or where they actually merge.

But there are times when "mere" religion—that is, religion which repudiates, or is incapable of undergoing a certain transformation through, philosophy—becomes divorced thereby from the spirit of the day and loses its relevance and vigor. This tends to happen when spiritual forces other than those of religion are emerging in the world. These take possession of the souls of the masses as well as the souls of their spiritual leaders, and the fate of religion then depends on whether or not the spiritual leaders can stand up to such nonreligious forces.

For the survival of religion requires that it unite with and assimilate the indestructible and life-giving forces that arise outside its domain. If such assimilation and harmony become impossible— perhaps because of the particular content of the dogmas that are inseparable from the religion in question—then religion declines. At this juncture the true accord of religion with the other authentic spiritual forces of the given time is dependent on religion's receptiveness to philosophy.

But how can the masses, from whom the refinements of philosophical reflection are indeed remote, know whether their religion is able to withstand the onslaught of free philosophical inquiry? Strangely enough, they do know. They can sense it without having the least comprehension of the battle of opposing ideas that is being fought over their heads. They can see it in their own sphere: from religious pronouncements or from the religious conduct that is being demanded of them; by all this they are able to judge whether their religious leaders can emerge from controversy with the other intellectual powers of the world with their fundamental beliefs untarnished. They themselves may be unable to penetrate the maze of knowledge, but they can sense whether their teachers are possessors of the truth.

We must pass over the interesting question of how values and ideas whose appreciation presupposes deep and subtle intellectual study can in some form or another reach and affect the untutored minds of the majority. Between the small group of creative individuals and the broad mass of mankind, there are to be found many intermediate spheres which, bordering on one another, interpret and transmit questions and answers between the many and the few. The true content of the discussion between religion and philosophy cannot be communicated to the many, but they can nevertheless perceive whether this is because of their own lack of knowledge, or whether it derives from the attempt to hide a defeat and consequent retreat on the part of religion.

One is almost tempted to say that the majority of men sense all this just as the man in the street is aware of medical and technical discoveries without understanding them at all—i.e., by their success. Religious pronouncements, religious institutions, and religious norms of conduct show clearly enough in the long run whether or not they are the real remedies for the evils of the age.

No religion has since the Middle Ages concerned itself less with philosophy than Judaism. None has fallen more deeply into the error of divorcing religion from philosophy than the official trustees of the Jewish heritage. In general, rabbis have not ventured into discussions of the relation of Judaism to free philosophical thought. No one will dispute that Moses Mendelssohn Nachman Krochmal, Lazarus Bendavid, Solomon Formstecher, Samson Raphael Hirsch, Salamo Ludwig Steinheim, Moritz Lazarus, Hermann Cohen, Ahad Ha'am, Martin Buber, and Franz Rosenzweig are the most representative names in the recent history of Judaic thought. Yet one finds only two rabbis among them. One sees that it has been mostly "laymen" who have sought, in one way or another, to reformulate the content of Judaism. The indifference of most of the appointed leaders of Judaism to a philosophical refounding of the Jewish interpretation of the world, and the rapidly growing indifference of Jews at large to the religion "of their fathers" in the same period, are certainly not unconnected. At the same time something else, of a peculiar nature, has been happening.

Was it only the Jewish spirit, or was it perhaps the spirit of Judaism itself, that in this same period broke out of the strictly religious sphere and blossomed forth in a wealth of significant, but secular, contributions to the intellectual life of mankind—contributions on the part of Jews such as had not been seen in any previous period of recent time? The earliest and perhaps the most important phenomenon in this respect is the philosophy of Spinoza. But Karl Marx, Emile Durkheim, Henri Bergson, and numerous others belong essentially to the same category.

The ready explanation of this sudden overflow of ideas and concepts—which can only be classified as Jewish biographically, and not in substance, is usually given in the slogan "Emancipation." It is not surprising, it is said, that the Jews, from the moment they were admitted to the cultural life of Europe, should have participated so eagerly in it. This appears so self-evident that one tends to overlook, rather naively, that it is only half the story. For the Jews would never have thrown themselves with such unbridled passion into the spiritual world of the European nations—from which the impulse of their genius had taught them to remain aloof for two thousand years—if Judaism had not ceased to afford room for a spiritual creativeness that would not be denied realization.

But what Spinoza and Bergson had to do outside religion in the seventeenth and nineteenth centuries, Saadia and Maimonides were able to do within it in the eleventh and thirteenth. Is this, then, only the result of a natural tendency of the spirit to outgrow the limits of religion? Or is it, perhaps, a sign that what men understood by religion in 1900 was of incredibly diminished scope compared with what had been understood by religion in the year 1000, let alone in earlier times?

It is not difficult to trace the process of atrophy of Jewish culture and show how, one after the other, all the provinces of intellectual activity—politics, law, economics, philosophy, science, art—were abandoned to the surrounding world, until only the domain of religion remained as a purely Jewish phenomenon. It is very important to note that this process of shrinkage was characterized by the gradual disappearance of a quite distinct idea: the idea of the universal significance of Judaism, the idea that Judaism would be able to fulfill a world function in an imminent future. Because Judaism had lost its world perspective—because it could no longer instill the feeling that to be concerned with Judaism was to be concerned with nothing less than the whole world—no scope was left for the productivity of its people. For this reason Judaism began to lose adherents.

A chosen people is of necessity a world phenomenon—but so is science. At one time the Jews had sincerely believed that they possessed the *true* view of the world. Therefore, it did not matter that the other nations had the power. Such power, one could be sure, was only transitory; in the Messianic view such power had to follow the path of truth. But more lately it has been the other nations that have had, not only the power, but *also* a free access to true knowledge, or at least to the avenues of approach to it. Since Moses Maimonides's *Guide for the Perplexed,* no Jewish theologian had made an intellectual effort on a high plane to harmonize Judaism with scientific truth; the profound conviction that this could be done had been lost not so much because the unattainability of truth was assumed in advance, but rather because the gulf between the religious and the nonreligious ideas of reality had become so wide that it could no longer be bridged.

The decay of the Jewish religion that resulted from the atrophy of the many-branched culture of medieval Judaism and the subsequent diversion of Jewish intellectual energy into non-Jewish culture; and, concomitantly, the desertion by the Jewish masses of a religion no longer nurtured by such energy: all this was the consequence of the ever-growing feeling that truth, the world, and reality lay now with "the others."

Has the great discussion between Judaism and the free thought of the world ever been resumed since the time of Maimonides, or since the fifteenth century? Did the theologians of Judaism take up the fight, placing themselves in that great line of thinkers which began with Saadia but stopped with Crescas? (Was it then already settled that Judaism had nothing more to contribute to the controversy than ancient moral truths known, and more than known, to the opponent, and whose significance they stressed over and over again and persistently proclaimed, because mankind persisted in ignoring them?) No such discussion has been resumed. That would have meant the rebirth of a philosophy of Judaism of a scope and intensity equal to that possessed by the philosophy of Judaism which the Middle Ages produced. This, modern rabbinic thought has not been able to achieve, nor even tried to achieve.

One can well understand why Jewish spiritual leaders should have avoided philosophy when one bears in mind the risk to their religious ideas such an approach involved. They feared that a frank discussion of the divergence of their religious ideas from the trends of free philosophical thought might do more to reduce the vigor of traditional Rabbinic Judaism than leaving everything unsaid and unsettled would. The second possibility, that of transforming Judaism so that it would be attuned to a spiritual environment different from that in which Rabbinic Judaism originated, was just as unattractive to the guardians of tradition. They saw the threat of dissolution in every change.

It has been said that the idea of God which Moses ben Maimon had was very different from that of Moses the Levite. It should have been added that this very difference contributed more to the preservation of the first Moses' idea than has the apparent identity with it of the traditional idea of the divine in which Orthodox Judaism persists. Everything living preserves itself by transformation, and when it loses the faculty for that, it perishes.

The timorous think that transformation may result in loss of identity. Rash reformers of Judaism, whose grasp of their heritage was not sufficiently firm or profound, and who were eager to sacrifice the allegedly irrational in Judaism to their own notion of rationality, have shown the fear of change to be justified inasmuch as their reforms tended to reduce Judaism to a collection of stale commonplaces in which nothing was disturbing because nothing was great or unique. Admittedly, it is difficult to know in advance whether a re-vision—the word taken in its literal sense—of a spiritual heritage will result in decay or in renascence. But the development of a sense of discrimination was, in this respect, both a religious and an intellectual duty. An attitude which, consciously or unconsciously, strove to evade the issue, or decided that it would be better not to expose Jewish tradition to the attacks of free philosophical thought, did not speak for inner security, did not speak for an undivided mind on the part of those who embodied this tradition. Nor did it speak for their own confidence in their cause.

The limited vitality and the lack of philosophical minds in Judaism for almost three centuries, the absence of a significant philosophical effort on behalf of Jewish religion in modern times—these become still more conspicuous if one modifies one's criticism of Rabbinism by extending it—as one must do—to the Jewish people as a whole. For the distinction between clergy and laity has by no means the same significance in Judaism as it has in other religions, and one may, therefore, ascribe the responsibility for the decline of Judaism to the Jewish clergy only in a limited sense. The responsibility is really that of the Jewish community as a whole.

In view of this small difference between clergy and laity, the lack of productivity in the domain of a Jewish philosophy of religion becomes even more striking. Think of all the philosophical attention devoted by non-Jewish lay thinkers to religion in general, and to Christianity in particular. Not only has every one of the great philosophers, from Spinoza to the present, made a contribution to the sphere of religion—that is to say, not only were general philosophies of religion developed by Herbert of Cherbury, Pascal, Leibniz, Locke, Berkeley, Toland, Maine de Biran, Kant, Fichte, Schelling, Hegel, Martineau, William James, *et al.*—but the non-Jewish world can also show a list, hardly any shorter, of strictly theological thinkers who have acted as spokesmen for Christianity and its dogma. Among these were minds of outstanding originality: Friedrich Schleiermacher, Cardinal Newman, Karl Barth, Barnes, Tennant, and numerous others. And the task these spokesmen for Christianity undertook was a considerably larger one than that involved in a rationalization of Judaism.

It is indeed an astonishing fact that almost all those in the first group of non-Jewish philosophers understood religion almost exclusively as pure monotheism and, in trying to harmonize religion with the results and demands of scientific knowledge, hardly attempted to justify the orthodox "dogma" of Christianity. One should give a great deal of thought and attention to the fact that all these thinkers, whether they knew it or not, argued in a direction that would have suited the theology of Judaism better than that of Christianity. They spoke, simply, of God, and the overwhelming majority of them omitted Christology altogether—i.e., any discussion of the dogma of a Man God. Christianity in this version is, to quote Seth Pringle Pattison (*Studies in the Philosophy of Religion*), "the religion of the greater prophets but only realized more inwardly," and there is no need of a Man God to inform us more authentically of the character of God.

And even among the theologically concerned philosophers of the second group there is—albeit with a few definite and certainly outstanding exceptions—a clear tendency to turn away from the literal interpretation of the tenets of Christianity, and an explicit inclination to press the meaning of these doctrines toward a religion of reason.

The polemical direction of all the work in which Christian writers like Schleiermacher, Tennant, and others have philosophized about religion has completely shifted since the era of fundamental religious discussion. Criticism is now hardly ever aimed against any specific religious system, but almost always against irreligiousness in general. This leads far more frequently to the laying of an intellectual foundation for a belief in God in general than to a belief in the Christian God. At the same time one must admit that even the intellectual inaccessibility of the content of Christian belief—which, for so many centuries, divided the domain of the human mind into faith and knowledge—never really paralyzed Christian philosophizing. Christian theology has only recently evolved new and vigorous conceptions under which the mysteries are accepted, and which are less designed to think the unthinkable than to protect the holy central points of the system of faith from the irrepressible intellect. It is to this category that such great movements as Neo-Thomism in Catholicism and Dialectic Theology in Protestantism belong.

Can Judaism show anything comparable to this productivity in the domain of Christian thought? One cannot answer this question more succinctly than Isaak Husik has done; in his survey of Jewish religious philosophy he entitles the section dealing with the post-medieval period: "No Modern Movement." It is of no use to fall back on the argument of the disproportion in numbers between Jews and Christians; a glance at any cultural sphere other than the religious one refutes it. The Jews are an intellectual people. Why, since they were not inhibited by an unacceptable and irrational dogmatism in their religion, have they not been able to create a pregnant reinterpretation of their inherited system of life and thought? Such a restatement, even if it never reached the wider field of general human thought and knowledge, would at least have given the Jewish community a new security and creativity.

It is often held that the decay of Jewish learning is what is responsible for the alienation of an ever increasing number of intellectuals and others from Judaism. Those whom the idea as such of a nation has no power to bind to their people, the argument runs, succumb inevitably to the powerful gravitation of a non-Jewish order of life and thought; in these circumstances, every consciously Jewish attitude will be discarded unless it is supported by a certain spiritual content and intention which we may call Jewish. This content, it is said, can actually be found. It lies in the immense literary heritage of Judaism; therefore, we should enjoin our youth to "go forth and study." The times of true loyalty to Judaism were the times of profoundest familiarity with its spiritual values. Re-establish this familiarity, and the loyalty will follow—or at least be strengthened.

There is undoubtedly some truth to this argument. When a person willingly acquires knowledge, instead of having it forced on him, he cherishes it. The advice to go forth and study is good, but it is too simple, and it is premature. The reasons for the alienation from Judaism are not to be sought in the decay of the knowledge of things Jewish. For no rejuvenation of the spirit issues out of learning, knowlege, education, and study as such. The decay of learning and knowledge follows rather from a prior inner reorientation; and this reorientation concerns far more fundamental questions than are involved in the sphere of mere Jewish learning. The idea of God as it was specifically understood by Judaism, the idea from which the impulse to know and to learn originated, is not discussed, but presupposed, in Jewish learning. It was the change in this idea of God which led to the subsequent decline in the study of what were supposed to be God's commands. Learning cannot give life to an idea of God when the course of spiritual history has reached a point where that idea, precisely because of its association with what was learned for its sake, grows faint and is replaced by other conceptions of the Deity.

But awareness of God and of the complex of ideas about his nature—which is the heart of Judaism—can inspirit the old learning and even call new learning forth; every change here determines the growth or the atrophy, the content and the method, of a culture of Jewish teaching and learning. Therefore one cannot begin straightway with Jewish learning, or at least one cannot expect a renascence from such a beginning, unless a far more fundamental inner clarification has prepared the way. Such clarification cannot come, however, from the people. It must be performed in the minds of those who are able to penetrate to the central idea of the Jewish world system. It implies a grasp of the profoundest reality on which Judaism rests, the idea of God's nature and of what Buber has termed "the direction of God." Not until one knows oneself what to think about the ultimate reality can one answer other questions with certainty and confidence; and only then can one translate the answer for those who need to have it stated more simply.

But here two fallacies must be guarded against. The first holds that "feeling" is enough, that, indeed, divine reality is only accessible to feeling. This is a fallacy because the faculty of the mind that grasps reality is not feeling but cognition. Feeling can herald and signal the proximity of reality. Feeling is a psychical accompaniment of the real, which is itself transmitted otherwise—through the senses and through the intellect. Without cognition, reality cannot be truly grasped and retained. It eludes the inquiring mind, and as one's grasp on reality fails, the certainty likewise fades as to whether what one had sensed through feeling was at all real. And with the loss of certainty there disappears the impulse or the motive to learn something about the sphere—in this case, the religious one—whose reality has become uncertain. If, then, religious experience and the reality of its object are not confirmed by cognitive thought, religion cannot feed and constantly renew the flow of common ideas that shape history.

What is more, "feeling" alone cannot stand up to the world of non-Jewish thought; "feeling" alone cannot answer: "Why do you Jews do that?" "Why do you Jews believe this?" The less "mystical" the mental climate of a period, the heavier becomes the burden which the inability to answer such questions places on the Jewish mind. And as often as not, a Jewishness that cannot face up to the inquiries of free "alien" thinking is soon enough abandoned. It is vital to Judaism to have the answers—answers for Jews and for others.

At this juncture the second of the two fallacies to which we referred is likely to bemuse the Jewish teacher: the illusion that a perfect command of Jewish knowledge, as it is given to Jewish learning —a mastery of the *Wissenschaft des Judentums*—guarantees his competence to discover all the answers. But "all the answers" means answering more than just those questions one wishes to be asked; the choice of questions cannot be suited to what the teacher knows, suited, that is, to the literary heritage of Judaism. He is duty bound to admit questions the answers to which cannot be fetched, at least right off, from the storehouse of this literary heritage. He has to work out the answers for himself. In every age, he has to set out anew to search for a knowledge that should, theoretically, be valid for all times.

For the quest for truth is not the concern of the Jewish people alone. No delving into Talmud and Midrash will help the teacher answer someone who is looking for, or has discovered, an idea of the Divine different from that which is presupposed in the literature of Judaism. If it were true that all doubts and questions about Judaism could be resolved by the savant fully possessed of all the treasures of Jewish tradition, then the philosophers Saadia, Maimonides, Jehudah Halevi, and Ibn Gabirol need not have gone to the trouble that they did. Their contribution to Jewish tradition was not merely to add more traditional material. They made it their task to *relate* the spirit of the traditional material, which was certainly alive in most Jewish scholars of their times, to the spirit of a civilization *outside* Judaism of which the scholars had at best but a shadowy idea. Entering into the spirit of that "alien," or at least more comprehensive, world, the great philosophers of the Jewish religion looked back on the venerable structure of historical Judaism and saw bathed in a bright new light traits and aspects which had remained hidden to those who moved only within the structure itself.

But, one might argue, now that the relation of Jewish to "general" ideas has been established by the great medieval Jewish philosophers, and their work has itself become part and parcel of the traditional material, now, surely, Jewish learning is in a position to answer any and every question about Judaism. Not so, because the discussion is never ending.

In any historical period, the sum of Jewish traditional knowledge never embraces everything that that epoch will ask of Judaism. The unlooked for, unanticipated questions are just the most decisive ones for the men born into that time as Jews. On the authority and capacity of Judaism to answer these questions depends the Jewish readiness to "learn." To the man who lives and breathes in the ambience of modern science and art, of contemporary technology, and social and political realities, the answers of Maimonides and of Ibn Gabirol seem exiguous and remote; even though, like all great thinking, they contain indestructible truth, they would need to be reformulated and related to what has happened since, to what has now become our common world. This relation is not discovered by a theological interpretation (hermeneutics) which manipulates vague metaphorical language and assures us that a scriptural text still significantly or strikingly "applies." And surely there are newer, different things to be said besides what the great initiators of Jewish philosophy have set forth.

A Jewish philosophy is nothing but an organ of perpetual renewal. To Judaism, in its journey through the ages, in its contact with ever new aspects and strata of mankind, in its passage through new mental spheres that are apparently or really alien to it, renewal is as indispensable as it is to an organism that must respond to the changing impact of time and environment. It is the means whereby its essential identity is preserved. To achieve this the spirit of the external world, the world outside traditional Judaism, must be grasped entire, in the fullness of its meaning.

Clearly, Judaism's relation to the general mental environment need not be the explicit theme of a Jewish philosophy; that is to say, Jewish philosophy need not necessarily take some "outside" mental product as its starting point. It may give a philosophical interpretation of the meaning of Judaism in its own language, without alien mediation. For there are two kinds of Jewish philosophical ideas. The first kind is explicit in traditional Jewish literature; easily isolated, it readily lends itself to philosophical formulation—as, for example, the doctrine that God has no form. This kind of idea demands no reference to non-Jewish thought; it stands in the same implicit relation to the non-Jewish mental world as the prohibition of images does to the image cult of the Gentiles. It is not the Jewish-Gentile dialogue that matters here, but the formulation of concepts within Judaism.

The other kind of Jewish philosophical idea, however, has a content that becomes apparent only as Judaism makes contact with alien thought. It was clearly impossible to perceive that certain principles of social philosophy were implied in the Hebraic Law *before* the doctrine of socialism had made its appearance in the world. Or again, the Biblical assumptions about divine power and providence, on the one hand, and about human freedom and responsibility, on the other, could not be expressed in philosophical terms *before* philosophers began to speculate about freedom and predestination. Philosophical problems of this kind are only implicitly or potentially present in Jewish Scripture; in dealing with them, Jewish philosophy evolves by relating itself to the cultural world outside Judaism.

The first kind of Jewish idea, the generally valid, the universal—the philosophical idea, in short—is already given in the texts of Judaism. But the general validity of the second kind of Jewish idea has to be worked out and sustained in terms of, and in contact with, a different world of thought. Here the reference to trends outside historical Judaism does matter, and the very idea of Judaism itself is developed through dialogue with these. However, this does not mean that Jewish thought must be strictly divided in two. Living Jewish philosophy is bound to exhibit both sorts of ideas to some degree, taking its orientation from Jewish as well as from "alien" thought. But the distinction gains importance in an age like ours, when the presence of a civilization that is actually or apparently outside Judaism may well be overpowering.

If the preservation of the Jewish people into the twentieth century is, indeed, due, in the last analysis, to a spiritual source of strength, to an effective order of life and thought; and if, further, the effectiveness of this order depends on its not appearing, even to the untraditionally minded, to be in decay or obsolescence, then the continued existence of the majority of Jewry as Jews is still bound up with the question of Jewish religious thought. As we have already indicated, the reason for the stagnation of Jewish religious thought is to be found in the ever narrowing meaning of religion, while at the same time a transformed religious impulse sought active and wide-ranging expression in the secular sphere. The survival of Judaism may well depend on how it copes with this impulse, on how well it is able to assimilate this impulse.

PROPHETS AND PHILOSOPHERS

Lou H. Silberman

The present essay, delivered as a public lecture at the Hebrew Union College in 1958 (The Samuel H. Goldenson Lectures), suffers from the predicament of public lectures before very public audiences: it cannot dare to promise all, for its medium and its language are limited by its publicity, while it is obliged to be portentous and significant. It is an unenviable predicament, the more so for its subject is the central issue of religious thinking: the relation of prophecy to philosophy, of revelation to reason.

What is particularly ingratiating about Lou Silberman's essay is that it is passionate and its passion does not in any way diminish, as does the passion of many other earnest thinkers, the power of its argumentation. Like Unger's essay earlier, Dr. Silberman raises the critical issue of contemporary Jewish religious intellectuality. Citing Leo Strauss's essay on Spinoza's *Tractatus,* he underscores the effort of philosophy to come to terms with prophecy, for, as he crisply puts it, "to seek to understand is to philosophize," and a philosophy of prophecy is as much appropriate to the prophet seeking to interpret himself (Jeremiah's "Thou, O God, hast enthralled me, and I am enthralled") as it is to us who wish to appropriate the prophet's teaching, that is, revelation, to our own situation.

Up until Spinoza, the philosopher was required to philosophize about the content of revelation because his life was founded upon its decretals and judgments. Revelation was not the issue in any formal sense for Saadia Gaon or Maimonides. How revelation got from God to man was the real issue—how the active intellect unfolded, how the prophet was the wisest of men, and how the wisest of men (the philosopher) was the prophet. When revelation, however, was undercut, when the philosopher no longer justified his vocation to philosophize by appeal to the authority of revelation, the structure collapsed.

The waning of Jewish philosophizing in this age of unbelief is far less incredible than it might seem from Erich Unger's analysis. The warrant to philosophy until the end of the Middle Ages was the authority of revelation. Revelation was the single source from which, not only philosophy, but ethics and politics derived. When the conduct of man was no longer dependent upon that hieratic chain of command which ran down from Godhead to prophet and saint, to king and courtier, to nation, laws, and institutions, it became possible for independent sciences and arts, founded upon special principles and disciplines, to emerge.

Lou Silberman is right however to insist that no philosophizing about Jewish existence can be accredited unless it takes account of—no, comes to grips with—the primacy of the prophet. The Jew claimed, not only that God spoke—delivering tablets whole into the hands of man—but that he spoke *through men*. If the prophet is to be taken seriously he cannot be psychologized away, he cannot be romanticized nor for that matter raised so high upon the pedestal of our admiration that he can no longer be seen. He is part of Jewish *realia* and as such he, and his words, the substance of revelation, are part of Jewish existence. Correctly then, Silberman regards the efforts of such thinkers as Baeck, Buber, Rosenzweig, and Heschel to construct a teaching which permits the prophets to speak directly to us. Theirs is not the task of rationalizing the prophet, but of supplying a clarification of the standpoint from which prophecy speaks, the terrifying subjectivity, the extremity of the personal, unique self, and the objectivity which any science demands. The philosopher must mediate between prophecy and science.

PROPHETS AND PHILOSOPHERS

The Scandal of Prophecy

LOU H. SILBERMAN

The point of departure for this inquiry is the postscript of a letter
written by a distinguished British theologian who is at the same
time personally and deeply involved in the current day-to-day
political life of the British Isles. He wrote: "My puzzle: as a minister of religion I used (with what terror of heart) to say 'thus saith
the Lord'; as politician (with a light heart) I say 'I think.' But the
true prophet giving his political message could say *'Koh 'amar
'Adonai.'* Have you light on that?" Fortunately, he did not ask for an
answer to his question, but only some light on it. Thus can I avoid
the sin and danger of presumption, speaking to the matter without
the necessity of pontificating or absolutizing. I mean to take the
puzzlement seriously, in the serious meaning of that word, for its
real intent is, of course, what do we mean when we say prophet?
what is prophecy?

The justification for such an inquiry, or rather for indicating that
there is need for the inquiry, is quite the same as that offered by
Leo Strauss at the beginning of his essay "How to Study Spinoza's
Theologico-Political Treatise." There he wrote, "A glance at the
present scene is sufficient to show one that the issue [belief in
revelation] which, until a short while ago was generally believed to
have been settled by Spinoza's nineteenth-century successors once
and for all, and thus to be obsolete, is again approaching the center
of attention." He goes on to say, however, "The issue raised by the
conflicting claims of philosophy and revelation is discussed in our

161

time at a decidedly lower level than was customary in former ages."[1] Indeed, one may add, most philosophers refuse to take revelation seriously, while confessional theologians find in philosophy the flower and fruit of sinful pride. For both, prophecy, as another way of defining revelation, is a scandal. For the latter, it is the stumbling block on which proud human reason falls; for the former, an offense to reason which must be thrust down and demolished again and again.

But do these antagonists have the last word? May not Emil Fackenheim's suggestion point toward a more creative situation? "If man's concern with the divine is perennial, and if it is at least in part rational, then what is needed in our time is renewal and rejuvenation."[2]

Beyond, however, the warrant of our own needs, we recognize an enduring tradition which, if it does not offer us a made-to-order answer for our puzzlement, at least makes clear that our striving is not necessarily foolish or blasphemous. In a sense the attempt to understand prophecy is coexistent with the phenomenon (a necessary weasel word) itself. To seek to understand is to philosophize, that is, to bring reason to bear upon the object at hand. The crescendo of Amos's argument from effect to cause in chapter III, while indeed "no mere general disquisition on this oft-discussed philosophic question," as Dr. Morgenstern has pointed out,[3] is a justification of the prophet's words by indicating the naturalness of prophecy, of its understandability side by side with other understandable events. Even Jeremiah's agonizing,

"Thou, O God, hast enthralled me, and I am enthralled," echoes his understanding of the situation of prophet and prophecy; an understanding not to be thought of as part of a system yet, nonetheless, a philosophy of prophecy in a real although rudimentary sense.

It would be unwise to belabor this point and thus prove more than can be demonstrated. Philosophy as a discipline belongs to a realm of experience and thought at a distance from the Bible, but so saying does not exclude from its pages philosophy as a seeking-to-understand.

1. *Persecution and the Art of Writing* (Glencoe: The Free Press, 1952), pp. 142–43.
2. "Schelling's Philosophy of Religion," *University of Toronto Quarterly,* XXII, No. 1 (Oct. 1952), 17.
3. *Amos Studies* (Cincinnati: Hebrew Union College Press, 1941), pp. 15–16.

The same is true of the rabbinic world. The imposition of philosophic abstraction is not only an ever-present danger but constantly distorts meanings even in the hands of those whose devotion to the tradition is unquestioned. Yet even among those so cavalierly lumped together as "the Rabbis," the attempt to understand prophecy was not absent. The very discussion of the requisites for the prophetic gift, both personal: "The Holy One, blessed be He, causes His Divine presence to rest only upon him who is strong, wealthy, wise and meek"; and communal: "There is one amongst you who is worthy that the Shekinah should rest on him as it did on Moses, but this generation did not merit it," points clearly to the fact that in part, at least, prophecy was comprehensible by reason. It could to some degree be understood.[4]

What was tentative and anticipatory in the Bible and rabbinic writings, became one of the great themes of medieval thought. Human reason, daughter of Olympian Zeus, found shelter in the tents of the children of Shem. Philosophy not merely as understanding but as discipline and system soon was at home in Islam and Israel. So widely and so imperiously did philosophy hold sway and so far-reaching were its demands that Abu'l Ala could write: "Moslems, Jews, Christians and Magians, they are all walking in error and darkness. There are only two kinds of people left in the world. The one group is intelligent, but lacking in faith. The other has faith but is lacking in intelligence." To which Saadia Gaon sadly echoed, "I saw in my time many of the believers clinging to unsound doctrine and mistaken beliefs, while many of those who deny the faith boast of their unbelief and despise men of truth. . . ."[5]

It was to the support of sound doctrine (*Emunot*) that Saadia brought rational demonstration (*De'ot*). They were, he held, not adversaries but sisters whose misunderstandings and falling-out were engendered by the human will, impatient and frail. Indeed, said Saadia, reason confirms not only the content of revelation but revelation itself. Even the rational laws *halakhot sikhliot* as contrasted with the *shim'iot* (those matters on which reason has no judgment) point to the necessity of revelation. Not only does revelation fill in the details that are beyond the scope of reason—which deals only with the general—but it is made necessary by the

---

4. b. Ned. 38a; b. Sanh. 11a.
5. Saadia Gaon, *The Book of Doctrines and Beliefs,* ed. A. Altmann (Oxford: East and West Library, 1946) , pp. 11, 29.

very nature of the Creator. Revelation exhibits God's grace, for it enables man to serve Him even before reason has discovered the true pattern of human behaviour. Further, Saadia suggests, revelation provides the means by which God may bestow upon man that reward which is deserved through obedience.[6] Actually the question of revelation and prophecy as such is not central to Saadia's thought but is clearly ancillary to his discussion of the divine nature, and serves particularly as justification for God's justice.[7] In this sense prophecy in *Em'unot v' Deot* seems to be a dialectic necessity rather than an obdurate fact. Its reality is less palpable than the historical concreteness it possesses, for example, in Jehudah Halevi's thought.

Here, indeed, one faces the paradox that the medieval theologian who may be called the most confessional, the most antagonistic to the claims of rationalistic philosophy, provides a most elaborate interpretation of the phenomenon of prophecy. Far from insisting upon revelation and prophecy as mysteries beyond the approach of understanding, Halevi argues their naturalness and comprehensibility in terms of what may be called philosophic biology. Basing himself squarely upon medieval biological concepts, Halevi challenges the philosophers to explain the actuality of religion. Against the claims of philosophy as adumbrated at the very beginning of the *Kuzari* that "the highest grade of humanity (the prophet) is attained by the perfection of our spiritual powers and that, therefore, philosophical training brings us to it," Halevi retorts witheringly through the king of the Khazars. ". . . one might expect the gift of prophecy to be quite common among philosophers, considering their deeds, their knowledge, their researches after truth, their exertions and their close connection with things spiritual; one might expect that wonders, miracles, and extraordinary things would be reported of them. Yet we find that true visions are granted to persons who do not devote themselves to study or purification of their soul. This proves that between Divine power and the soul are secret relations which are not identical with those thou mentionest, O Philosopher!"[8]

---

6. *Ibid.*, pp. 94 *et seq.*; pp. 103 *et seq.*

7. Julius Guttmann, *Die Philosophie des Judentums* (Muenchen: Ernst Reinhardt, 1933), p. 80; see also, H. A. Wolfson, "Hallevi and Maimonides on Prophecy," *JQR*, n. s., XXXII (1941–42), 345.

8. Jehudah Halevi, *Kuzari: The Book of Proof and Argument*, ed. I. Heine-

But this rejection of the claims of rationalistic philosophy is not meant to suggest that prophecy cannot be understood. It is the direct relation of God to a natural species, the *homo religiosus*. It is made possible by a native endowment, the form of the species *ha'inyan ha-elohi* which enables man, when God so wills, to "see" those "temporary visible manifestations created by God during the process of His communication with men." This openness to divine influence possessed by one species only, stands at the summit of creation. It is, to use David Neumark's phrase, "the fifth kingdom of being." It is, however, only the ultimate expression of the divine activity at every level of being. ". . . Even the highest life is still life, indeed life in intensified form and subject to the same laws as all other life . . ." "Thus belief in the reality of the facts of religion in no way requires of us a 'sacrificium intellectus'; the miracle that came to light in its lowest form of development in plant life becomes more and more apparent as it passes through the animal to the human and thence to the prophetic life; but the domination in the highest spheres of the same laws as were seen to govern in the lower realms of life is consistent with the analogical schools of thought and is corroborated by the testimony of history."[9]

The actual appearance or nonappearance of prophecy can be explained—from the human side—in biological terms. It is a recessive characteristic whose manifestation requires both proper environment—the land of Israel—and proper nurture—not philosophic contemplation, but observance of Israel's religious duties. Thus prophecy is, for Halevi, susceptible of rational understanding, although it is not reason's offspring. Its actuality is demonstrated by the intersection of history and biology. The former exhibits it; the latter explains its appearance.[10]

It is in Maimonides, however, that the philosophic attempt to understand prophecy reaches its most subtle climax. Both Diesendruck and Strauss argue that it is a central theme in the Moreh Nebukhim; and more, that it is not, as some have claimed, a mere "inadequate presentation of a long-held theory." The broad sweep and the closely argued details of this Maimonidean prophetology as

mann (Oxford: East and West Library, 1947) , pp. 13, 30; see also Wolfson, *op. cit.*, p. 345–53; and Strauss, *op. cit.*, p. 141.

9. Wolfson, *op. cit.*, XXXIII, 357–58, 368; David Neumark, *Jehudah Halevi's Philosophy* (Cincinnati: Hebrew Union College Press, 1908) , pp. 36 *et seq.*; *Kuzari*, pp. 14–15.

10. *Kuzari*, pp. 64–72.

elaborated with varying emphases and interpretations by the scholars just mentioned, and quite beyond the areas of sharp disagreement between them, provides an intellectual joy that is not always the reward for submitting to scholars' demands.[11] Nonetheless, it is not to a delineation of the theory of prophecy that we turn our attention but to Maimonides' insistence that revelation itself calls man to philosophize and the reciprocal insistence that philosophy provides revelation's certainty. Strauss puts this succinctly: "Revelation itself summons those men suitable for the task to philosophize. The divine law itself commands philosophizing. Free philosophizing based on this authorization, takes all that is as its object. Revelation as the Law given by God through a prophet becomes the object of philosophy in prophetology." And further and most crucially: "Were revelation *merely* a miraculous act of God it would be entirely beyond man's comprehension. Revelation is, then, understandable only in so far as God's act occurs by means of intermediaries, taking place in creation, in created *nature*. In order *fully* to be understandable it must be plainly a *natural* fact. The means used by God in the act of revelation is the prophet, i.e., an unusual and superior human being, but, nonetheless, a *human being*. Philosophical understanding of revelation, philosophical confirmation of revelation is thus the elucidation of prophecy from the *nature of man.*"[12]

As long as the reality of prophecy, of revelation, was the situation in which he stood, the philosopher was free or perhaps even more, was required to philosophize. The philosophers in an age of belief, says Strauss, "justified their philosophy before the forum of the Law; they derived from the Law's authorization to philosophize, the duty to do so." But their world was torn asunder. Spinoza, among others, ground away at the foundations of revelation and brought its structure down in ruins.[13]

The attack was twofold. On the one hand, the documents taken as the objective statement, the content and form of revelation, were subjected to such critical literary analysis that the claims made on

---

11. Z. Diesendruck, "Maimonides' Lehre von der Prophetie," *Jewish Studies in Memory of Israel Abrahams* (New York: Press of the Jewish Institute of Religion, 1927), p. 74; L. Strauss, *Philosophie und Gesetz* (Berlin: Schocken Verlag, 1935), p. 87.

12. *Ibid.* pp. 76–77, 89, 90.

13. *Ibid.*, p. 122; Guttmann, *op. cit.*, pp. 296–300.

their behalf could not be upheld with any real intellectual assurance. On the other hand, the very idea of revelation as argued by the medieval philosophers, the very *philosophische Begruendung des Gesetzes,* was attacked by the new philosophical positions emerging in the seventeenth and eighteenth centuries. In the face of the attack, the scholastic system of Jewish philosophy collapsed, with no new synthesis to take its place. Guttmann comments concerning Jewish participation in the European philosophic enterprise from the eighteenth century onward: "The predominant part of this philosophical endeavor had no connection with Judaism as such. . . . The sphere of Jewish existence encompassed the religious in the narrow and particularist sense from which all other spiritual concerns and with them philosophy were excluded."[14] Moses Mendelssohn's philosophy of reason clearly moves along lines laid out by European thought, and revelation is saved by him at the expense of its universal meaning. For Mendelssohn, religion, true religion, is the same everywhere and for all men. It cannot be dependent upon an act of revelation. Judaism is, therefore, not revealed religion but revealed law. The Bible is for him somewhat as for Spinoza a political document governing the life of the Jewish community; at most its laws "allude to or are undergirded by the eternal truths of reason or they recall and stimulate thought about such." As Guttmann puts it: "Thus the two worlds in which Mendelssohn lived are joined together. Through faith he belonged to the universal religion of reason; through observance of the ceremonial laws, to the Jewish community." That they were no more than juxtaposed, despite Mendelssohn's endeavor to bring them together in theory as well as act, seems a tragic truth lived out in his own family.[15]

From this point onward, for the most part, the entire meaning of revelation and prophecy underwent a radical revision. As Fackenheim says: "Religion is no longer understood as the attempt of man to relate himself to a God outside himself. It is a self-transformation of finite into infinite spirit. . . ."[16] Thus in the thought of Solomon Formstecher, historical revelation is the coming to self-consciousness in man of the ideal of his spiritual life. "At first as in prophecy man's spirit does not realize that it has its content within and so assumes

14. Strauss, *Persecution,* pp. 194–95; Guttmann, *op. cit.,* p. 302.
15. Guttmann, *op. cit.,* pp. 313, 317; Eric Werner, "New Light on the Family of Felix Mendelssohn," *HUCA* XXVI (1955) .
16. *Op. cit.,* p. 3.

LOU H. SILBERMAN

that it comes from without, that it is something objectively given. But at last, after passing through intermediary stages in which truth is transmuted from the stage of objectivity to that of subjectivity, the spirit recognizes that it is in itself the bearer of truth, that the objective fixing of prophetic revelation is but a preliminary stage in the movement toward subjectivity." Thus for Formstecher, "revelation is but an hypostasis of the immanent processes of knowledge, to be recognized by mature self-knowledge as the product of the human spirit."[17]

But Formstecher and with him Samuel Hirsch raised solitary voices on behalf of a philosophic justification of Judaism as the true disclosure of the movement of the spirit. The only other writer who took the task seriously, although diametrically opposed to their formulations, Solomon Ludwig Steinheim, was rewarded for his insistence on revelation as a "divine communication made to mankind in a once and for all event at a particular time" with the epithet "free-thinker" in the Jewish Encyclopedia.[18]

For the nineteenth century it was a self-evident fact rooted in a union of Kantian philosophy and historical evolutionism that *Das Wesen des Judentums* was the purest and most complete formulation in history of the universal truth of the ethical faith of reason. This self-congratulatory assumption made "any further philosophical analysis and justification of Judaism unnecessary."[19] Jewish history took philosophy's place and demonstrated over and over again to its own satisfaction that this assertion was true. That this required radical judgment on many elements of the Jewish past was inevitable, but the task was faced boldly and such embarrassing movements as Kabbalah and Hasidism were treated clinically, although at times passionately, as aberrations and pathological formations whose existence impeded but did not hinder the course of rationality.[20] Even the fading away of certainty about the exact nature of the religion of reason has not shaken this self-assurance.

17. Guttmann, *op. cit.*, p. 324; Albert Lewkowitz, *Das Judentum und die geistigen Stromungen des 19. Jahrhunderts* (Breslau: Marcus Verlag, 1935), pp. 407, 416.

18. S. L. Steinheim, *Die Offenbarung nach dem Lehrbegriffe des Synagoge*, III (Leipzig: Leiner, 1863), 319; Guttmann, *op. cit.*, p. 338; *J. E.*, *s. v.* Steinheim, XI, 544a.

19. Guttmann, *op. cit.*, pp. 317–18.

20. See, for example, Graetz's discussion of Kabbalah and Hasidism throughout his *History of the Jews*.

That it is possible to assert the complete congruence of Judaism with any and every philosophical or nonphilosophical or antiphilosophical position is a basic postulate of contemporary Jewish discussion. It needs only to be proclaimed and provided with a few well-chosen proof texts to sweep the field and win the day.

It was to the remedy and repair of this ultimately self-denying situation that Hermann Cohen, dominant spirit of the Marburg neo-Kantian school, devoted his continuing effort, culminating in his posthumous work *Religion der Vernunft aus den Quellen des Judentums*. Here are no bland assumptions, no fatuous claims, but rigorous and demanding analysis. The lofty structure of a reformed and revitalized Kantian epistemology is offered as the dwelling place of prophetic Judaism. It is not necessary for our purpose to attempt a description of this vast and soul-stirring enterprise; what is required is the recognition in and through it that one cannot be satisfied with mere words, but needs, desperately needs, meaning. Whether or not one accepts as his meaning the crucial sentence: "This eternal (law) which is reason's basis for its own content is called revelation by the Jew,"[21] is in our context immaterial. What is of concern is Cohen's undeviating perception that such a word has a meaning, which meaning is determined by its larger context. Thus one finds within this work the continual and unflagging attempt to demonstrate what, indeed, such meanings are. Prophecy as the proclamation and working out of the meaning of correlation between God and man, as these terms are understood philosophically, conveys to him who is willing to take the matter seriously, a real content. If in the end the effort failed, it was not out of philosophic incompetence nor religious indifference. Cohen took his task to heart; indeed, he went far beyond the demands of his system and sought a place and a meaning for religion within it. What actually happened was that in the end faith conquered philosophy, but not without philosophy's earnest challenge. Thus we are not liberated from our task but thrust back into the midst of the problem.

The conclusion to be drawn from this noble attempt which began with reason alone and unaided is that revelation and prophecy are more than the heroic strategems of the human spirit to personalize

---

21. (2nd ed.; Frankfurt a.M.: J. Kaufmann Verlag, 1929), p. 97. "Dieses Ewige, als die Grundlage der Vernunft fuer allen Inhalt der Vernunft, nennt der Jude Offenbarung."

the abstract system of rational thought. They are ineluctable facts to be dealt with and understood. They are the challenge to Jewish philosophy. They are part of the given of our situation. We do not come to them as conclusions; we begin with them as of the stuff of our existence, our Jewish existence.

We can, of course, avoid such a conclusion by accepting for such words as these what Professor Cronbach calls dramatistic rather than cognitive meanings. In all candor, however, one wonders how satisfactory this solution really is. Does not the very dramatistic value of prophet or revelation lie in the recollection, be it ever so faint, of a cognitive meaning? More than this, one discovers in the most consistent transvaluation of the entire cognitive body of tradition into dramatistic terms, that of Mordecai Kaplan, not only a residue of cognitive meaning which is the effective dynamic of his system, but a real although diffuse and inconsistent metaphysic. As pragmatic instrumentalism has learned over the years, ontology continues to assert itself even after banishment from the vocabulary.

Thus the question cannot be avoided: what do we mean when we speak of prophets and prophecy? Is it at all possible to give these words any substance within our contemporary universe of discourse? Are we permitted no more than a descriptive approach to a past phenomenon that is to be taken as a more or less primitive stage in the assumed unfolding of man's religious consciousness? Are the men behind the words yet read as conveying potent meaning for us to be thought of in and of themselves as self-deluded, or psychotics with auditory or visual hallucinations? Quite frankly we cannot have our cake and eat it. Either we take seriously as the basis of our discussion the prophets' self-understanding, as for example A. J. Heschel has set it forth, or we might as well close the book at once and move on to weightier matters. Heschel wrote: "The consciousness of the prophets that they were inspired by God is the foundation of their vocation. The very right to engage in prophetic activity, the claim of authority for their words, begins with the fact of being-given-ness (*Eingebung*). Their words claim neither respect nor value on the basis of their aesthetic or logical qualities, or even because of their in-dwelling content but only because of their transcendent origin. It is this point of origin they proclaim over and over again in many ways: they are not bringing to the people the formulation of their own consciousness . . . but that which has been given. The vigorous and emphatic certainty that their messages are not inventions . . . but communications . . . as well as their condemnation of the deceit and error of the false prophets . . . constrains us to regard the form of their proclamation—'God has spoken to me' as unequivocal explanation of the source of that which is given to them."[22]

This fact, which may be for them ultimate, is for the philosopher primary. It is the point from which, not toward which, he moves. His task, as we have seen, is to discover a total frame of reference in which this fact finds its place. For Halevi the very hierarchy of nature and the immediate and continuing act of God in creation made prophecy understandable. For Maimonides it was the influence of the Active Intellect upon the imagination and the contemplation by reason of the imagery thus produced which justified the prophet's assertion. The task of any Jewish philosopher cannot, then, but include the search for such understanding as a primary concern. Prophecy belongs to the structure of Israel's experience. The attempt must be made to understand it, not explain it away.

Within contemporary Jewish thought this beginning with the fact, this existence within the community of revelation, in contrast to nineteenth-century formulations, has assumed an ever more central position. The statements of those who have addressed and are addressing our present day community with true seriousness are written from within what Leo Baeck in the subtitle of his concluding work *Dieses Volk,* called *Juedische Existenz.*[23] This is not to suggest that such thinkers as Baeck, Buber, Rosenzweig, Heschel and others belong together as a school or as a movement. Despite the tendency to throw some of them together for the purpose of derogation, it ought to be clear that these are independent attempts to understand the revelation under which they stand and which thus unites them. What is important is the recognition that these thinkers take revelation and prophecy with utmost seriousness and attempt to do what the great medieval thinkers did, construct a total statement which will enable us to understand, to comprehend what these words may mean in contemporary rational discourse. The following words of Rosenzweig make the implications of this task clear and present: ". . . [philosophy] must cling to her new point of departure, to the subjective, extremely personal unique

22. *Die Prophetie* (Krakow: 1936), p. 7.
23. *Dieses Volk: Juedische Existenz* (Frankfurt a.M.: Europaeische Verlagsanstalt, 1955).

self, absorbed in itself and the standpoint of self, and still attain to the objectivity of science. Where is the bridge to connect extreme subjectivity, one might even say, deaf and blind subjectivity, with the luminous clearness of infinite objectivity? The answer must anticipate developments and, even so, stop halfway, stop at mere suggestion. The theological conception of revelation must provide the bridge from the most subjective to the most objective. Man, as the recipient of revelation, as one who experiences the content of faith, contains both within himself. And whether the new philosophy admits it or not, such a man is the only thinker fit to deal with it. . . ."[24]

Within the compass of this exposition, all that can be done is to indicate the reality of the problem and the directions from which the answers appear to be coming. Prophetology as the focus of the question of man's dealings with God is the crucial and demanding challenge to Jewish religious thought today.

But in so projecting the task, we need to remember that the absolutizing of whatever structure we may erect must be ruled out from the very start. The scandal of prophecy must ever and again reassert itself lest *our* understanding become *the* explanation, and as explanation thrust the fact aside. It is to this danger that Gabriel Marcel addresses himself, although he speaks in terms of his own Christian tradition and to another point: "It seems certain to me . . . that if we consider the evolution of moral thought, Christianity has tended to attenuate this paradox progressively, to withdraw the scandalous from its character." If this, then, be our danger as well, we will find hope in his continuing words. "It is no less certain that periodically spiritual upheavals have appeared, violently to reopen the breach that attempts had been directed toward closing; and to denounce the work of smoothing over, indulged in more or less consciously by the doctors of the previous age."[25]

The shattering no less than the building belongs to our striving. Though we tend "to withdraw the scandalous" the scandal will not be gainsaid. Buber's valedictory for his opponent Hermann Cohen puts the matter with poignant beauty: "Cohen did not consciously

24. N. Glatzer, *Franz Rosenzweig: His Life and Thought* (New York: Farrar, Straus & Young, 1953) , pp. 208–9.
25. *Le declin de la Sagesse* (Paris: Plon, 1954) , p. 109. I am indebted to my colleague James Sellers for bringing this passage to my attention and allowing me to quote it in his translation.

choose between the God of the philosophers and the God of Abraham, rather believing to the last he could succeed in identifying the two. Yet his inmost heart, that force from which, too, thought derives its vitality, had chosen and decided for him. The identification had failed, of necessity had to fail. For the idea of God, that masterpiece of man's construction, is only the image of images, the most lofty of all the images by which man recognizes the imageless God. It is essentially repugnant to man to recognize this fact and remain satisfied. For when man learns to love God, he senses an actuality which rises above the idea. Even if he makes the philosopher's great effort to sustain the object of his love as an object of his philosophic thought, the love itself bears witness to the existence of the Beloved."[26]

And so, too, for us with prophecy. One is always driven to go beyond his understanding.

Sailors use the phrase "the loom of the land" to indicate the sense of the shore's presence even when it lies beyond their vision, even enshrouded in the dark of night. We, too, who have in our day experienced the shattering of the system, sense the loom of prophecy's vast reality below the horizon of our lives. Yet neither the hard unyielding fact nor its understanding is clear within our spirit's sight. All one dares, crying the landfall, is to attempt in fog and gloom neither to run aground on shoal or reef nor doubting, turn and sail away, but sounding with reason's lead and line, come at last unto the land.

---

26. *Israel and the World* (New York: Schocken, 1948), p. 65.

THE PHILOSOPHER AND THE JEW

Arthur A. Cohen

The preoccupation has not altered. Quite the contrary, it has been strengthened. The polarization of philosopher and Jew, which this lecture given at the University of Wisconsin at Milwaukee in 1962 describes, continues with little likelihood of abatement. In a real sense, the reading of Erich Unger's essay, offered at the beginning of this section and referred to elsewhere, was the starting point for this inquiry. How can the Jew—standing within the precincts of the Biblical tradition—renew communication with the philosopher? I presumed that the inquiry was serious and that the consequences of a renewal of communication between Jew and philosopher were profound. The essay is its own explication; there is no need for me to gloss it.

THE PHILOSOPHER AND THE JEW

ARTHUR A. COHEN

The juxtaposition of Hebrew studies to philosophy betrays a regrettable imprecision and imbalance. It is hopeless to establish even the most casual community between them as long as this imbalance remains uncorrected. Philosophy, whatever the variety of its styles and tendencies, may be defined as the reasoned pursuit of wisdom. But what are Hebrew studies? The very awkwardness of the phrase discloses a psychological bias which must at least be offset, if not remedied, before we can proceed. For where philosophy by its nature is an intellectual activity whose end and reason is the apprehension of truth, "Hebrew studies" is utterly neutral. Narrowly construed, Hebrew studies compass all disciplines of the mind which have been created in the Hebrew language—everything from the Bible to a political allocution of David Ben-Gurion may become valid objects of study. We could make this ridiculous, but why do so? Evidently the intent of the phrase is disingenuous, however much it reveals an artificial formalization of the Hebrew temperament which would make it intellectually acceptable to the presumed neutrality of the academician. And therein lies the problem.

A Jewish scholar (not merely a scholar of Jewish "subjects") could not speak of Hebrew studies, for even the most detached of Jewish scholars cannot approach the substance of historical Jewish thought with the inquisitive condescension with which even the best of humanist and Renaissance Christian scholars, for example, sought to acquire a knowledge of Hebrew idiom, language, and literature. A

Jewish scholar, notwithstanding the personal complexities of the Jewish psyche, cannot be neutral toward Jewish thought and culture. He may be exasperated by the stubborn intellectuality of the Jewish mind, by its unyielding preoccupation with the small detail, by its proud and often arrogant disinterest in the achievements of the non-Jewish world. He may be exhilarated and charmed by its beautiful innocence, by its daring imagination, its intrepidity and courage—or moved to joy by the sublimity of its vision and sense of destiny—but he can never be neutral. The Jew would never speak of Hebrew studies, although he *can* speak of philosophy. The philosopher, on the other hand, can speak of Hebrew studies, but only if he has already concluded that they are irrelevant to his enterprise. Hebrew studies is but an omnibus concept which assembles the impressive variety of works of the Jewish mind without precise determination of their subject matter, their method, and their end. We cannot accept such a term for it would justify the philosopher in his indifference to the Jewish mind.

For the Jew and the philosopher to speak with one another, for the Jew to have discourse with the philosopher and the philosopher to give attention to the Jew, it must be presumed that they share something in common. If they share nothing in common it is wholly useless to establish their community and if they share everything there would be no problem. The problem arises, therefore, from the presumption that the Jewish thinker and the philosopher are sufficiently distinct in their respective inquiries as to be discriminable one from the other and sufficiently like in enterprise as to be formally introduced.

That civil discourse—even apologetic discourse—should be a problem in our century is ample testimony to the alteration of both the Jewish mind and philosophy. It is undoubtedly true to say that most Jewish thinkers (that is, those whose major intellectual preoccupation is the mastery of classic Hebrew literature) are wholly indifferent to philosophy, and most philosophers (those whose primary passion is the apprehension of empirically verified truth) are wholly indifferent to Judaism. What, then, can a Talmudist say to a logical analyst (a predominant exemplar of the contemporary moment)? If the Talmudist is, indeed, faithful he must consider the logical analyst to be not only wasting time but consuming a precious and holy life in the service of triviality. (Though the Talmudist would recognize the value of precision in language, he would claim that such precision is not the same as truth, and to secure the meaning of a simple proposition is insufficient achievement for a contemplative life.) And the logical analyst can only look upon the Talmudist as one who takes irrelevant and often meaningless propositions and builds them into an imposing but, nonetheless, meaningless structure.

Surely, then, if we do not simplify too egregiously, the pious Talmudist and the radical analyst of language have little or nothing to communicate to one another. But such a conclusion would be to take the *de facto* condition of present history—the inability of particular people to speak meaningfully to one another in this historical moment—as sufficient reason for terminating our inquiry. This would be unjustified. The task is not to relate doctrinal extremes, but to see if we can cut beneath the suppositions of their enterprise to those preoccupations which enable not only Talmudist to carry on limited discourse with logical analyst but enables Talmudist to speak with the Reform Jewish theologian and logical analyst to speak with existentialist. If we can locate the form of the question which establishes the community of the believing mind, however it is activated, and the speculative mind, however its commitments and disposition, we may, perhaps, discover the common term which enables both communities of the mind to converse with one another.

The extremities of the present hour have their precedent in the past. Logical analysis and pious Talmudism are not radical excrescences which have been cast like so many broken clocks or statues upon a desert or silent piazza as in a surrealist canvas by Salvador Dali or Giorgio De Chirico. They are formations of history, echoes and responses to the dreams and disenchantments of earlier moments. Indeed, it may be said that the temperament which enables the Talmudist to survive unencumbered by the modern world and the analyst to pursue his logical parsing of our grammar, equally untouched by the modern world, are specific denials of something in the history of the West which occurred once, which promised much, which delivered little, which was wasted and spoiled, and is now unconsciously despised by the quiet Talmudist and the aggressive analyst.

The Jewish mind and philosophy did once speak to each other. Let us recount, ever so briefly, the modes and sources of their conversation. In the *Letter of Aristeas,* written by a Jew immersed in the Hellenistic world of the late Maccabean age, King Ptolemy Philadelphus is caused to ask all manner of questions of the Jewish Sages whom he has assembled to translate the Bible into Greek.

Although the details of their answers may differ, the Sages echo one common sentiment, that God is the source of all that they know and all that they do. Thereupon, Aristeas describes the scene which ensued: "With loud voice the king greeted them all and spoke kindly to them, and all those who were present expressed their approval, especially the philosophers, for they [the Sages] were far superior to the philosophers both in conduct and in argument, since they always made God the starting point."[1]

What is striking about this passage, notwithstanding the obvious predisposition of its author, is the fact that the philosophers, not alone unequal to the Sages, are gratified to have discovered the Sages. We may presume that the sentiment expressed here is accurate, for it is echoed by Philo and the Church Fathers. Unlike the present moment, the philosophers of that day were anxious to be availed of truth—whatever its source and origin. Moreover, they believed that the possession of the truth had the consequence of saving a man from ignorant bondage to fate and restoring him to a world of light, clarity, and knowledge. The ancient was redeemed by truth, and the achievement of wisdom was a modality of redemption. No wonder that the ancients should discover the Bible, endeavor to translate it, and, in an enthusiastic embrace of its teaching, seek to make its hoary and unfathomable antiquity the putative source of their own wisdom.

Pagan philosophy was not indifferent to the problem of divinity, although it had less compelling and urgent reason than did the Hebrew for making the gods the inspiration of the philosophic enterprise. The speculative tradition in Greece developed laterally to the spread of cultic polytheism; religion was the popular philosophy of the Greek, incorporating as mysteries what the philosopher conceived of as problems. The Greek was devout, but his religion was not profound; his paganism was all-pervasive but, nonetheless, superficial. To endure a world populated and ruled by divinities, subdued by fate, dominated by an irrational outcropping of autonomous powers, the Greek philosophized. The task of philosophy was to achieve that order of wisdom which would enable man to

---

1. *Aristeas*, 235; Wolfson, *Philo*, Vol. 1, p. 27; *JE*, Vol. II, "Letter to Aristeas."

penetrate the seeming unreason of his universe to its essential rationality, to transcend it, and to order his passions and conduct in obedience to his understanding of the laws of nature.

The Greek, and later the Hellenistic world which he created, was—notwithstanding the specificity of his gods—hospitable to the gods of other people. The rule of the gods was an instrumentality of civic order and piety; while philosophy, less a regional and national institution, became the arbitrating discipline of the educated and the ruling class. Philosophy supervened upon religion, defining a community of intellect which united in common enterprise cities and states whose polities and religions might nevertheless differ radically. Philosophy was thus a source of unity for the ancient world. It is no wonder that a new religion, founded upon a book which purported to narrate the origin and destiny of the world under the dominion of a single God, should have proved to be both a challenge and a reproach to philosophy.

For religion to approach the intellectual Hellene, it had to make pretense to philosophic teaching. By the first century of the Common Era, the popular paganisms out of which Greek philosophy grew had splintered into apocalyptic enthusiasms, leaving behind the well-established philosophic schools—Stoic, Skeptic, Neo-Platonist, Aristotelian—which still displayed pious respect to the gods coupled with dubiety regarding their relevance to the search for knowledge and truth. Hebrew Scripture introduced into the speculations of the Hellenistic world a novelty: the insistence that, not only was God one, the source and ruler of man's destiny, but that He had revealed to a specific people the ideal law by which human affairs might be governed. The Hellene, trained to move from Plato's *Republic* to the study of his *Laws*, from Aristotle's *Metaphysics* to his *Ethics* and *Politics*, was intrigued by the claim that a one and only God had communicated the manner in which human society might best be ordered to its own and His service. Hebrew Scripture seemed to combine, as had no other ancient religious doctrine, a solution to the problem of *episteme* (ἐπιστήμη) and *arete* (ἀρετή), knowledge and virtue, for the God of the Hebrews proclaimed that Him alone should all men know and obey, for He is truth, instruction, and the way of virtue. Less than seeking to reconcile Scripture and Greek philosophy for the benefit of Scripture, Philo of Alexandria undertook the reconciliation of Scripture and Greek philosophy for the benefit of philosophy.

The philosopher, secure in the knowledge of nature, was, nevertheless, unable to effect a meaningful relation between his religious myth and his philosophic doctrine. As his philosophy became more sharply defined, his religion became increasingly remote and ineffectual. Either he chose to acknowledge the gods who are inferior to the Idea of the Good (which is no god) as in Plato, or else he loved a God who by definition could not love him as in Aristotle, or he surrendered to a universal harmony "made up," as Marcus Aurelius observed, "of all things, and one God immanent in all things, and one Substance, and one Law, one Reason common to all intelligent creatures, and one Truth" in which, nevertheless, submission is submission before necessity itself. However the Greek managed the philosophic enterprise, he dealt always with some object—whether Idea, Form, Substance, Nature—before which human freedom and destiny was sheer impossibility.

Etienne Gilson, the distinguished Thomist philosopher, is quite correct in observing that to the Greek philosopher the simple counter of Hebrew faith in a self-proclaiming and, note well, a self-naming God produced not only a religious revolution but a philosophic revolution as well. Moses asked God for His name in order that he might identify Him to his people, and God answered, *Ehyeh asher ehyeh*, "I shall be what I shall be" (or as it is otherwise translated by Gilson, "I am who I am," or by theologians of history such as myself, "I shall be there when I elect to be there"). Whatever translation we employ, clearly a definition of God is given which carries within it the germ of crucial metaphysical questions: the nature and being of God, the futurity and transitive character of God's relation to history, the indefiniteness of God's locus in any given *here* and *now*. The religious answer of Scripture provides a new basis upon which philosophy undertook to interpret the nature and origin of the universe, for, where the Greek spoke of *some thing* from which all is derived either by imitation or emanation, the Hebrew spoke of *some one*, some person who reveals his activity as creator of the universe.

Could the answer of the Hebrew become more than a religious statement, meaningful only to the mind disposed to believe? Is it true, as we have come to affirm in our day, that the philosopher who is accessible to faith is perforce a philosopher without science, a philosopher closed to the palpable contrariety of empirical evidence. Is the philosophy which begins with Philo—that is, the philosophy which founds itself upon Scripture—a masquerade, an antiphilosophy, a species of unreason parading the habiliments of reason? Or is it not possible that the metaphysical enterprise, as it was pursued, has undergone sufficiently radical alteration that its use of reason is deemed to be a no longer acceptable use of reason, that its metaphysical passion is but a distortion of metaphysics, or put affirmatively, that the modern use of reason and the understanding of metaphysics which obtains in academic philosophy is so radically different from theirs as to effect its disparagement without its proper estimation?

Much as it is popular among the intellectual legatees of Descartes and Locke to affirm a historical discontinuity which eliminates from the proper history of philosophy that era of speculation which commences with Philo and ends with Spinoza (as Harry Wolfson has defined it), or, as a Christian might affirm, which begins with St. Augustine's reading of the *Enneads* of Plotinus and ends with Descartes, we should deny such a view. Nature may abhor its vacuums, but history equally abhors its discontinuities. There is no question but that the Greek developed a species of philosophic method and argument which was quite suitable as long as it contented itself with the definition of nature. However, the moment it was confronted with the task of affirming the actuality and the existence of things, it had recourse to Biblical intuition. Reason is rather more comfortable in the presence of things whose natures and laws it can define and submit to the iron casting of concepts; but it is timid and apprehensive in a world of existences, because to exist is an act, and not a thing. The Biblical intuition enabled Greek philosophy to be turned to the service of problems which it could not itself raise, and, in the hands of those instructed by the decretals of Revelation, to define and solve problems which it had not the capacity to state. Although Maimonides and Thomas Aquinas (considered as philosophers) were not students of Moses but of Aristotle, it may be said that, without the recollection of Moses' intercourse with God, their own ability to conceive of Him as that perfect identity of essence and existence which permits a universe of things to be seen in their essential *and* existential dimensions would have been impossible. As Gilson has observed: "A World where 'to be' is the act *part excellence,* the act of all acts, is also a world wherein, for each and every thing, existence is the original energy whence flows all that which deserves the name of being. Such an existential world can be accounted for by no other cause than a supremely existential God. The strange thing is that, historically speaking, things seem to have worked the other way around. Philosophers have not inferred the supreme existentiality of God from any previous knowledge of the existential nature of things; on the contrary, the self-revelation of the existentiality of God has helped philosophers toward the realization of the existential nature of things."

This insight, sharp and demanding as it is framed, may conceal much of the modern dissatisfaction with both philosophy and metaphysics and more particularly the alienation of philosophy from metaphysics in general and Hebrew studies in particular. The Hellenistic tradition of philosophy, informed by Scripture, rediscovered the existential dimension of nature, the factuality of being, the independence, indeed, isolation of objects from the formal matrix of nature in which they have their being. The existence of God, the ground of all existence, was made known by Moses to the West, and it was this disclosure—vouchsafed by God to Moses—which enabled the medieval philosopher to attempt the explanation of the natural world. The God of the medieval was a God who was not only *being itself* (*ens*) but the source of all created being and therefore that reality who exists preeminently (*esse*). God is the perfect identity of existence and essence. Although normally intelligence ascends, as does the argument of Aristotelian metaphysics, from the definition of essence to the judgment of existence, the metaphysical order of reality instituted by the juncture of philosophy and Scripture descends from an apprehension of God as pure actuality to the actuality of the world. The God of Aristotle was the pure act of self-contemplating thought; but pure act in the order of knowing is not pure act in the order of being. Because the God of Aristotle was not "the living God," the God who *is,* it was inconceivable that from such a God the existence of the world could be derived.

It may well be said that the metaphysics of the medievals was sheer arbitrariness; but wherein is its arbitrariness to be found? It is not to be found solely in its method, for its method is but an adaptation of modes of argument which both it and modern philosophy derive from the Greeks. This is not to say that the devices of argument by inductive and deductive syllogism are not open to endless abuse, nor is it to deny that argument by Platonic analogy often leads, unless patiently and honestly constructed, to vulgar sophisms. The techniques of logic being undoubtedly open to improvement, it is folly to invest the analytic devices of Aristotelian logic with more reverence than is justified by the results which they yield. The thinker upon the nature and actuality of God need not be impervious to the scrutiny of the technical logician nor unsusceptible to the improvements of symbolic logic where these enable him to state with greater concision and abstractness the problems to whose solution he is devoted. I am not aware, therefore, of any necessary reason for the metaphysician to abandon the innovations of logic; nor need the metaphysician isolate himself from the findings of science or the precise observation of nature, for the contemplation of actuality in all the forms of its disjunction and created separation will only yield greater clarity and definition in the statement of his principles. Where, then, is the objection of the modern philosopher to the medieval metaphysician? It lies, I should imagine, in the fact that the medieval chose (1) to learn from Scripture about God and to refine his understanding of God within theology, and (2) to build upon the foundations of Scripture (that is theology) an understanding of the relation of God and nature which could be adequately defended by reason.

The medieval is thus accursed for being at the same time both theologian and metaphysician, however much he might keep both activities sharply separated (for it should always be remembered that although there is neither Christian philosophy nor Jewish philosophy, there were philosophies founded upon the structure of teaching which belief first affirmed *surpassed* the understanding and for which it later sought to build a foundation *in* the understanding). In short, then, where contemporary philosophy is established upon the independence of philosophy from God, the medieval affirmed—and for him and for us it was a major discovery—that the conjunction of God and philosophy enabled the person of God to become explicit in theology and the rational *telos* and intentionality of philosophy to become explicit in metaphysics.

At the present moment, however, theology has surrendered all claim upon rational metaphysics, and philosophy has discharged itself of all relation to theology. Theologies either consume themselves in the effort to achieve rationality at the expense of historical doctrine, thereby sundering their connection with the historical function of reason in theology, or else they return to an order of subjectivity in which the unity of existence and essence is ruptured for the sake of the unrationalized concreteness of individual existence. Either radical rationalism masked as existential criticism demythologizes or existential corelation, formulated with the strictness of rational argument, presses beyond all traditional theological affirmations. In both cases, whether it be Rudolf Bultmann or Paul Tillich, the connection between theology and metaphysics (seen from the standpoint of theology) is ended. Similarly, in this age of specialization where metaphysics has become the folly of the theologian, philosophy has been returned to a form of pure rationalism which we cannot help but feel conceals an unexpressed existential agony. The logical analyst and post-Russellian positivist seem to be saying in their small and resolute enterprise: "Behold how little there really is which we can confidently affirm! We are left with but sentences and those not particularly complex nor abstract. The most that we can do which may be of use and service is to demonstrate to all of you moralists, metaphysicians, and theologians that you speak nonsense—establishing relations which cannot be empirically explicated, which cannot be properly stated, which cannot be proved. If you are content then with your imprecisions, your helpless adumbrations of inexpressible truths, go right ahead, but don't bother coming to us for consolation."

The logical analysts are not quite as free, however, of the metaphysical dilemma as they might wish. There are a number of logical analysts who have begun to wonder whether their enterprise is not in fact a dead end. Those who have returned to the gnomic world of Ludwig Wittgenstein do their analytic work in public and their private metaphysics in notebooks similar, but not less mysterious and involuted, than those of Wittgenstein. But even for Wittgenstein the philosophic enterprise was precisely *in its concern:* it was the asking of difficult questions and the hope for sublime answers. Wittgenstein might well have been intolerant of bad metaphysics, but this would by definition not make him closed to the metaphysical inquiry as such. If one examines his revolutionary *Blue and Brown Books,* one finds that Wittgenstein is not nearly as indifferent to historical philosophy as he is made to seem; rather he is annoyed, bitterly annoyed, by what he calls the characteristic metaphysical posture which is "to express an unclarity about the grammar of words in the form of a scientific question" (p. 35). What he is really protesting against is a portentous stuffness which imitates such typical metaphysical propositions as "What is the object of thought?" or "Does perception accurately record the external world?" His objection—a sensible one—is that simple language is constructed in such a fashion as to bear a load for which it was not intended; the physics of experience is forced to transport an abstract baggage for which it is unequal. Now, indeed, Wittgenstein may insist that this is a scientific objection to metaphysical language, but is it really? May it not be construed as an almost existential protest against a language which does not realize that it, too, is fashioned by the history of human experience, that metaphysical language is also historical, that it is limited precisely by the fact that the meanings of words change and the uses of our language alter in response to the new information which history constantly carries with us into the present?

It may well be, therefore, that the protest of the logical analyst, his negation of the timeless, metaphysical statement is more a furious teeth-gnashing against our human proclivity to state as eternal truth that which is always locked in the ruthless embrace of time. The logical analyst is a nasty protester, but a useful one, for he gives some pause to those who still believe that metaphysical truth rises not only transcendent to, but independent of, historical reality.

The existentialist does not do precisely what the metaphysician does, and for that reason the logical analyst is both less vicious about the existentialist and also takes him less seriously. The existentialist, unlike the metaphysician, does not pretend to the construction of scientific propositions. He forgoes them in principle on the ground that to conjoin existential and essential propositions is to perjure the former and waste one's time with the latter, for essence is always time-bound, being distilled out of the novelty and experience of existence. The analyst can tolerate such radical simplism, for the existentialist—if he really holds his course—can say precious little about existence, if he cannot use the language of the abstract noun which is in truth the language of essence. The existentialist is thus left—and one will find this predicament (however chastened by other considerations) throughout my own speculative writing—with the infantile habit of pointing to the realities he wishes to identify, because he cannot locate the proper language in which to state them specifically.

It is at this juncture that we may restore some connection

between the fragmented condition of the philosopher and the informed belief of historical Jewish (indeed religious) thinking. We do not imagine that we will reconcile them; however, our task is not to reconcile but to establish the grounds of common discourse. What we have discerned is that there is a tradition of Hebrew thinking, set forth in the Bible, which speaks of God in the rich terms of concretion—which says God is not general but specific; God is not the All but the "this" and the "that" of everything; that God is not nature or history but the source and destiny of nature and history. Thus the God of the Bible and the God of rabbinic theology (however much He may be a supernal Person unlike all persons of our acquaintance) is nevertheless a particular Person and for that reason a concrete Existence who includes everything and excludes nothing, who is simple precisely because He is all-embracing. Upon this tradition of Biblical concreteness, metaphysics built an imposing structure fashioned of the formal brick and mortar of Greek philosophy and the commonplace straw of Biblical realism. The simple became abstract, and the concrete become concept. The primal language of the Bible become the rational posturing of the scientific.

It is understandable, therefore, that a massive effort should have been made from the seventeenth century onward to restore a connection between man and the visible world, to restore the connection between perception, language, and nature. This protest against scholastic rationalism in turn became an apotheosis of autonomous reason—reason, moreover, which recommenced where Greek philosophy had left off, renewing the experience of nature which the Greek had first defined and relinquishing the sense of history which the Greek had never known and which the Bible had discovered. The nineteenth century was a long indulgence of human fatuity, a pleasure and delight in the sufficiency of reason to achieve everything, including the redemption of man and history. To this fatuity the existentialists replied by evangelizing man's return to the concrete, and the logical analysts—skeptical creatures that they are—replied by demonstrating that the high-blown metaphysics of the nineteenth century was often sheer nonsense.

Is it not conceivable, therefore, that the existentialist and positivist (the former, espousers of the historical concrete; the latter, describers of a "communicating" language) may renew communication with Biblical faith, which is a faith in the concrete and historical Person of God? Indeed, they would form a bizarre and nervous seminar, but I should imagine that once they had gotten over their fears of tub-thumping from the believers, the existentialists' mournful countenances, and the hard-nosed skepticism of the analysts, they might find the following in common: an agreement upon the primacy of history in the formation of all language; an agreement upon the bearing which historical particularity has upon the concreteness of language; an agreement to explore the meanings which simple propositions—whether they be propositions of belief or the contingent propositions of the existentialists—have for those who hold them (and it is crucial here to recognize that any meaning in a proposition is its truth). The meaning of the statement that "this is a lectern" is its truth; the meaning of the proposition "God is One" is *its* truth: the confirmation of the first proposition no less involves a theory of the external world than does the latter, although the grounds of evidence for the one may satisfy more people more quickly than the grounds of evidence for the latter. It will be easier to establish what the word "lectern" means than what the word "God" means, and because it is easier to explicate the former, more people will take the first statement to be true (without serious thought) than will take the latter to be true.

Our philosophers and Jewish theologians may gather together to explicate their concepts, that is, to elicit from the concepts the meanings which they assign to them. At the very worst this will have the benefit of eliminating much thinking which is palpably mysterious or obscurantist. But once we pass from the level of simple explication, that is, explication which does not require that the philosopher denounce the clearly stated propositions of the theologian as being nevertheless false, it is possible to move into that gray area where not exploration but genuine conversation, that is, the sharing of speech, takes place.

Speech is much more than the sequential utterance of sounds and words. Speech is the talking of one subject to another; it is the communion of persons. I presume that the only reason why anyone philosophizes or anyone studies Hebrew literature is because they seek there a form of wisdom which enables them to live. Any seeking presupposes the value of that which is sought—whether one seeks a lost jewel or a truth. There is a marvelous misplaced wisdom in the Platonic doctrine of recollection, in the understanding of philosophy as the pursuit of recall. Similarly, the Jews record a legend that when a child is born he possesses all wisdom, but at birth an angel touches his lips and he forgets everything but the knowledge that he must begin to seek what is now forgotten. Both traditions recognize that the pursuit of wisdom is a "drawing out of oneself" under the impulse of experience. The encounters of man with man and man with nature serve to trigger the self into inquiry, into the asking of "whys" and "wherefores." But once the asking begins, once the inquiry is inaugurated, it never ceases, for each new moment and each new event becomes the fresh occasion for man to refine the investigation, to texture it with new subtlety and insight. It is at such moments that philosophers acquire pupils and saints beget disciples, for not the pupil finds the master nor the disciple the holy man, but each finds the need to speak out to another, to teach and to give example. The philosopher and the religious thinker partake of speech in order to understand themselves the better, to lose the particularity and enclosure of their own universe in order to acquire a connection with a larger universe. At such moments the speech of the philosopher and the religious teacher become part of history, shaping a new historical moment to which their speech is now a formative breath. And it is only in their giving of themselves to history—or more precisely in their recognition that they are of history and their speech is historical—that they realize a truth which unites them to the condition of all men.

What joins the Biblical theologian, the existentialist, and the logical analyst is that they are all caretakers of language and creatures of history. They may never agree—that is we may never have, and God save us from having a single Jewish philosophy—but we may well have the immensely fruitful encounter of philosopher and Jew, an encounter in which the tension and alienage of time and history and language may be explored in common.

INTRODUCTION TO

TO RECAST RATIONALISM

Steven S. Schwarzschild

Beginning from the postulation that Martin Buber and Franz Rosenzweig give the fullest expression to the "post-idealist" philosophic temper of Jewish thought, Schwarzschild proceeds to raise the question which their reaction against idealism poses, but does not resolve. If the idealist metaphysics (which finds its culmination in Kant and the post-Kantians) depends for its truth upon *general* conceptions of the nature of God, world, and man, where is the truth of the particular man to be located? Buber and Rosenzweig rebelled against the abstract, to their view, dehumanizing caste of the idealist theory of knowledge. Knowledge of the universe did not hang in the air like a cloud. Knowledge is always the knowledge of a single man, seeing the world through a particular vision, ordered by feelings, concerns, preoccupations which are radically individual, unique, unrepeatable. At the same time, however, that the thinker is bound by the limits of his existence, he is obliged to speak to others about common concerns in a language which is formed by rules of sequence and logic. The individual thinker must reach out, despite himself, to scientific objectivity. But, as Schwarzschild shrewdly observes, "thinkers do not reason any longer, they narrate. . . ."

Schwarzschild proposes that we turn back the insights of Buber and Rosenzweig to their common source in Hermann Cohen, and from the sources of Cohen's canon of rationalism to supply a corrective to Jewish existentialism. It is not clear how this is to be accomplished. Schwarzschild has merely sketched the possibility and the means, but rushes on to harvest the crop. Indeed, the crop is bountiful—for nothing could be more desirable than that we might have within Judaism an order of teaching which could embrace conceptual metaphysics and mystic doctrine at the same time—but the problem is that the one and same metaphysician must also accommodate his own mysticism; the metaphysician must affirm what reason can know unaided, but provide latitude for what reason can interpret only upon the foundations of revelation.

TO RECAST RATIONALISM

STEVEN S. SCHWARZSCHILD

The most influential thinkers in contemporary Jewish philosophical theology are unquestionably Martin Buber and Franz Rosenzweig. Both give expression to the "post-idealistic temper" of our age. Both start out with certain "data," *Gegebenheiten,* of human experience. Thus Buber begins his fundamental work *I and Thou* with the famous words: "To man the world is twofold"—and then proceeds to offer what might be called a phenomenology of human relations, describing the I-Thou and the I-It relationships. Rosenzweig starts out with the reality of death but quickly arrives at the stipulation of the three elements of reality—God, man, and the world. From these respective experienced bases both then proceed to construct their theoretical systems. As they go along they always continue to analyze real life rather than to manipulate terms, concepts, or definitions.

This practical approach to the tasks of philosophy accounts to a considerable extent for their persuasiveness with modern man. In the writings of Buber and Rosenzweig he recognizes his own situations and feelings and, therefore, trusts their extrapolations and conclusions. It is philosophy in a key very different from that of the classic rationalists, who begin their considerations in such theoretical phrases as Spinoza's: "By that which is self-caused I mean that of which the essence involves existence . . ."; or Kant's: "In whatever way and by whatever means cognition is related to objects, the instrument by means of which it is immediately related to them and the goal toward which thought as a tool always aims is intuition."

Indeed, it was precisely in rebellion against this kind of preoccupation with ideas at the expense of human existence, an attitude which
the post-idealists identify with Hegel, that Kierkegaard and the
contemporary religious as well as atheistic thinkers began their new
philosophic search.

But this is also the ultimate weakness of such a stance. Suppose
one has not had the experience which Buber and Rosenzweig
simply assert? For this reason, perhaps, there is so little, if any,
discussion between the so-called existentialists on the one hand and
the naturalists and positivists of all stripes on the other: they do not
inhabit the same universe of experience. All the peremptory statements in the world, such as the one Hugo Bergman recently made
again, that "all great men of faith, in effect, testify in similar words
that God can be found and faith be achieved by every person,"[1]
will not convince an honest person who must simply stick to his
admission that, as for him, he has not found it to be so.

There is, furthermore, a fundamental philosophical objection to
be raised against this method, apart from the practical one just
mentioned. What criterion is to be used in determining what the
basic types of human experience are from which all thought must
presumably start out? And who is to make such a determination?
No one has, for example, answered Nathan Rotenstreich's perfectly
valid question[2] of why Rosenzweig picks just God, man, and the
world to be the three constituent elements of reality and why not
others, or at least additional elements. And as regards Buber,
M. Maisels' book, *Thought and Truth*[3] powerfully illustrates the
danger of such dogmatism. He starts out with precisely the basic
direction which Buber makes but, unlike Buber, does not manage
to keep the two orientations to life connected with one another
and, therefore, his universe breaks completely into two thoroughly
dichotomous parts; lack of original rational derivation leads to the
destruction of the unity of reality. Indeed, much of contemporary
"existentialist" and religious philosophy is afflicted with this kind of
dogmatism. Thinkers do not reason any longer; they narrate, much
as did Rosenzweig, who insisted that modern philosophy must be
autobiographical, and as has Rabbi J. B. Soloveitchik, who recently

---

1. *Faith and Reason*, Washington, 1961, p. 22.
2. "The Basis of Franz Rosenzweig's Philosophy," *Al Franz Rosenzweig—Bimlot 25 Shanah Lif'tirato*, Jerusalem, 5716, pp. 83 ff.
3. New York, 1956.

began a lecture by saying that he would merely tell about his own personal experiences and the listener could either accept them or not. This leads to a paralysis of reason and to an individualized atomization of truth. We must, therefore, again ask Solomon Maimon's question: *quid juris?* How do we get to the facts, to the data? And we must resume the Cartesian search for a universally acceptable basis of rational thinking.

I suggest that we can find our way out of this dead end by going back to Hermann Cohen. Cohen was the last great rationalist in Jewish philosophy. Cohen was also the teacher of both Rosenzweig and Buber. Of Rosenzweig this is known, for he himself eagerly proclaimed it. Of Buber it is not generally known, for the first great and well-known encounter between them was one in which they stood not in a relationship of teacher and disciple but of antagonists on the question of Zionism. But it is, nonetheless, true. In the *Religion der Vernunft* the following passage occurs:

> By the side of the I arises, different from the It, the He. Is this He nought but another occurrence of the I which would, therefore, already be implied in the I? Language itself guards against this error: before we get to He we come to Thou. But is the Thou only another occurrence of the I, or does the Thou require a separate discovery even after I have become aware of my I? Perhaps it is the other way around—that only the Thou, the discovery of the Thou, can bring about my awareness of my I, the ethical cognition of my I. . . .[4]

Need more be said?

In contemporary Jewish theology the great breakthrough from rationalistic, idealistic thinking to "the new thinking" is supposed to have taken place when, according to Rosenzweig's interpretation of Cohen in his "Introduction" to the latter's *Juedische Schriften,* Cohen advanced a new concept of the correlation (in his posthumously published *Religion der Vernunft*), which Rosenzweig claimed left the charmed circle of idealism behind and penetrated into ontology. Most subsequent students have followed this interpretation. Guttmann never did,[5] and in an essay, *"Hermann Cohens Bergriff der Korrelation,"* Alexander Altmann documents the untenability of Rosenzweig's thesis. Cohen, in fact, never did break out of "the system"—though it is, of course, true that his last writings taught a concept of religion considerably deeper than had

---

4. *Religion der Vernunft*, Frankfurt am Main, 1929, p. 17, cf. also pp. 22 ff.
5. *Philosophie des Judentums,* pp. 360 ff.

previously been the case. The great breakthrough actually occurred when Rosenzweig argued with Cohen[6] that the recognition of truth begins with "irrational realities" rather than without any preconceptions, with the "nothing" of the "philosophy of origin." We have seen where this deviation led. We must go back to Cohen's "nothing" so that reason and human discourse may begin again.

I am not, of course, suggesting that we revert to Cohen's liberalism, optimism, or even to his own definition of rationalism. This is neither possible nor desirable. We must, indeed, go forward to a more wholehearted resubmission to the historical realities of Jewish history and established law and doctrine, and to the theological realities of God and Revelation. This we have learned from Buber and Rosenzweig, and from our experience. But this must be done on the basis and with the means of Cohen's rational canons. It can, I believe be done.

I have in the past suggested where the *Ansatzpunkt* for such an extension of Cohen beyond himself lies, even as Cohen extended Kant beyond himself; and again Guttmann[7] supplies the stimulus:

> The further question arises, which can be fully answered only after Cohen's concept of reality will have been completely clarified, whether this function does not go beyond the character and capability of a God defined as an ideal—whether God must not be conceived as a highest reality (in the ontological sense) in order to be able, as the determining power, to guarantee the realization of the ethical ideal in the processes of nature.[8]

The same can be said of Cohen's concept of the Messiah. If it should turn out, as I believe it will, that God and the Messiah must be understood in "realistic" terms in order to satisfy Cohen's own rationalistic demands upon these concepts, then we shall have broken through the solipsism of idealism; but we shall have done it not by abandoning the rationalistic footing of scientific, critical philosophy but by pursuing this very philosophy to its own logical conclusions. Thus a rationalistically corrected doctrine of Jewish "existentialism" may be formulated.

Such a recast rationalism will also make it possible to explore

---

6. *Stern der Erloesung,* I, pp. 27–31.
7. "The Personal Messiah—Toward the Restoration of a Discarded Doctrine," *Judaism,* vol. 5, no, 2, p. 127; "The Democratic Socialism of Hermann Cohen," *HUCA,* vol. XXVII, pp. 436 ff.
8. Guttmann, *op. cit.,* p. 351.

anew and fully the complete range of the historic Jewish search for truth. It is well-known, indeed notoriously so, how rabidly and vitriolically the rationalists of the nineteenth century, for example Heinrich Graetz (but also Maimon, Krochmal, and Cohen), rejected what they called the obscurantism and superstition of the Kabbalah. But as we observe the intellectual situation today, such a neat and simple-minded differentiation between "rationalism" and "mysticism" is utterly outmoded. We can and must find truth in Kant and the Baal Shem Tov at the same time. And this is not as inconsistent or eclectic as it would have seemed a generation ago. From Buber and Rosenzweig we work our way backward to Hasidism and from Hasidism to Kabbalah and forward to Lubavitch and Rabbi Aharon Rote and from them to Roman Catholic mystics like Thomas Merton and even Hindu mysticism; at the same time we work our way back from Buber and Rosenzweig to Hermann Cohen and Kant and forward even to Jamesian pragmatism.[9]

The notion that everything from Kant to Kabbalah and from Cohen to Merton should be relevant to a proper understanding of rationalism must initially appear absurd; but it is not really absurd. Study a compendium of Kabbalah, like the *Shelah Ha-kodesh*, and it is inconceivable how anyone not thoroughly versed in scholastic Platonism and neo-Aristotelianism, and, therefore, in Plato and Aristotle, can even begin to appreciate it. Rabbi Isaiah Hurwitz and Hermann Cohen both descend from the same parents, the Bible and Plato. But then, what in Western philosophy, religion, and culture does not?

There is, on the other hand, I believe, a very clear criterion for distinguishing rational, *i.e.*, meaningful discourse from the irrational

---

9. Cf. Ernst Simon's most helpful and illuminating study, "James, Fechner and Jung on Religious Experience and Divine Education," *Judaism*, vol. 3, no. 3, where he says: "In my view, he [Thieberger, in his introduction to the Hebrew translation of *The Varieties of Religious Experience*] could have gone much further by showing the lines that run from James to Buber and to Rosenzweig," and then goes on to cite a Jamesian passage about the I and Thou which also brings us right back to H. Cohen. The intimate connection is not limited to the field of psychology; it also exists in the field of logic and ethics, even in epistemology. For Cohen the idea is the hypothesis; the hypothesis is to be derived from science and jurisprudence; and the validity of the idea, or hypothesis, is always measured by its effectiveness in helping toward the realization of the (ethical) purpose which it enshrines. For the idealist Cohen, therefore, the value of the idea is not very different, basically, from what it is to the pragmatist Dewey.

(as different from the outworn distinction between rationalism and mysticism) —and this criterion is whether any form of thought may be subsumed under the principle "truth is reality, and reality is truth," or under the opposite principle that "truth is above reality —truth is an Ought, not an Is." The outstanding philosophical exemplars of the latter are, of course, Judaism on the one hand, which awaits the Messiah and teaches that "God is the place of the world; the world is not the place of God"; and Kant-Cohen, on the other, who have demonstrated that even the cognition of reality is an ethical imperative. The outstanding exemplars of the former are Spinoza, who exclaimed *deus sive natura,* and Hegel, of whom Cohen wrote: "Perhaps nothing has contributed so much to making philosophy contemptible in the prerevolutionary age than the reactionary motto of Hegel: 'The real is reasonable, and the reasonable is real.' "[10] Thus, to identify the truth with the real—God with nature—inevitably leads to theoretical mysticism in the pejorative sense of the word, to moral and political reaction, and to religious atheism, for it deprives nature of its pedestrian, scientific character, ethics of its need for progress, and religion of its supernatural anchorage.

On the broader Jewish philosophical front, three tasks, it would seem, thus confront us: (1) a deepening of contemporary *existenz*-philosophy by retracing its development from its rationalistic sources; (2) a renewed exploration of—and strengthening of loyalty to—all of the classic and legitimate texts of Jewish revelation, from the outermost "left" boundary of scientific rationalism to the outermost "right" boundary of unreconstructed mysticism; and (3) a strengthened and aggressive reconquest of all forms of pantheism, to re-establish the Most High God whose seal is truth.

---

10. F. A. Lange, *Geschichte des Materialismus,* 7th ed., p. 463.

INTERIM THEOLOGY

Monford Harris

More of us would wish to agree with the thesis of Monford Harris' essay than are able to do so. Jewish theology is seen by Harris as being, in its consummation, self-liquidating. Jewish theology is interim theology because it must be a theology of between-being, the condition of being distant and even estranged from the classical realities of Jewish existence and the condition of renewed presence, reconsecrated standing upon Jewish ground; theology in such a view is a conduit, a medium of passage from the event past and recalled and the life lived in the presence of recall. Theology does not pose the questions of God to man: it is not apodictic, nor is it even the communication of direction. Using the distinction of Chaim Tchernowitz in his *Toledot Halacha* (History of the Law), Harris distinguishes between the divine instruction within the patriarchal narratives which spell out specific ways and directions (*halichot*) and the elevation of these ways and directions into normative *regula* for the Jewish people (*halachot*). The Law is a crystallization, a condensation of the living exigencies of choice and decision into formulations and directives. Jewish existence is challenged then to recall, to remember the way of the Patriarchs that it might live. Theology is then become what perhaps it was for Sören Kierkegaard, the appropriation of the lives of the teaching saints as our contemporaries and masters. Theology is no more nor less than the language of translating numinal antiquity into numinal present, the focusing of what was thought to be past upon the eternal present. Theology is in such a view the ontologizing of the historical, the making of history into eternity. There is certainly warrant for these attitudes towards theology. Both Rosenzweig and Buber have erred in my view by making the historical into the eternal, severing the vital contact of the numinal Israel from the terrestrial Diaspora, as though, on the map of the ancient world, Israel and its history were always shaded in the royal purple of sovereignty or the red of martyrdom while the remainder of the pagan *oikumene* were neutral white or gray. It is never so. The world, if it is layered with meanings and shades of meaning, is variously colored, and Israel is as penetrated by the world as it is integrally self-definited, unique, and sufficiently respondent to God, its creator and inspiriter. Harris, it strikes me, is correct in seeing the predicament as one of the most serious confronting modern Jewry. But, at the same time that one grants this, one is obliged to a kind of realistic charity: it may well be crucial that Jews live the teaching, practice the *mitzvot* that they have recovered—no question of this—but the work of thought is not consummated in the twinkling of an eye. The essays of Unger, Silberman, Cohen, and Schwarzschild which have preceded this important statement by Harris suggest some of the considerable difficulties which affect theology itself, the theological project which anticipates the living renewal. Even though Judaism is, as Harris observes, marked by an "endemic pragmatism," it cannot confuse the end of Jewish thinking—that Jews shall do what they hear—with the task of thought itself. In a time when all men believe the mark of the saint is the fullness of his acts, but at a time when few men believe and equally few act, it is a mistake to denigrate thought merely because its role is prior, precedent, and preliminary to action. We must beware, in prudence, of liquidating theology before we have one.

INTERIM THEOLOGY

MONFORD HARRIS

A Jewish theology is in a sense a contradiction in terms for a genuine Jewish theology is its own gravedigger. What I mean by this is not the truth that theology must ultimately keep silent before the Living God, who is beyond any final formulations of theology, but that Jewish theology, if it is true to its Jewish sources, must ultimately cancel itself out.

For the fundamental fact of Jewish theology, the central point of reflection for the Jewish thinker, *qua* Jewish thinker, is Jewish existence. The existence in this world of Jewish existence and how each Jew is to link his private existence to Jewish existence sets into motion a *Jewish* theological enterprise.

There are certain themes of theological thinking in Western civilization which are so fundamental that whether or not they occur in traditional form they may be called classical. One of these is the problem of the nature of Man. This has always been and in the nature of the case always will be fundamental for Christian thought. There is also no doubt of the fact that throughout classical Jewish literature there is *implicit* a notion of Man's nature. But none of the great classical Jewish texts or medieval Jewish books are explicitly and systematically interested in describing or analyzing Man's nature.[1] The crude and untrue quip that the church "invented" the idea of Man as sinner so that it could convince people

---

1. Cf. M. Kadushin, *Organic Thinking*, New York, 1938, p. 267. Rabbi Max Ticktin kindly recalled this reference for me.

that they needed salvation and thereby the church became a powerful institution does contain a certain truth, namely: unredeemed man must first be made aware of his miserable state before he can be redeemed. This is, of course, part of the genuine outlook of Christianity. Christianity's theological endeavor must always analyze for Man his nature so as to show him his actual misery. It is only then that Man can attain his grandeur.

Jewish thought, however, has never devoted itself in any explicit way to the nature of Man.[2] Classical Judaism does have in itself the notion of the double *yetzer,* but Jewish thought has not developed in any sustained and systematic way an outlook on the fundamental nature of Man. It has kept its thoughts on the subject muted. Man, alone and single, has not been a primary subject for discussion. It is unthinkable for even a modern Jewish thinker, as *Jewish* thinker, to write a book entitled (like R. Niebuhr's major work) *The Nature and Destiny of Man.*

Neither has there been any systematic attempt in classical Jewish sources to deal with the problem of revelation. In Christianity revelation has been perhaps the fundamental problem if we consider the question of incarnation under this rubric. Why and how did God become man? Much serious theologizing was done on such questions as Homoousianism (that the son is of the *same* substance as the Father) and Homoiousianism (of *like* substance). These terms may sound esoteric and irrelevant to us, but the problems they represent are in a way serious problems for Christian theology even today. The relationship of revelation and reason, or, the divine foolishness of Calvary to the human wisdom of Athens, has also been a cardinal problem of Christian theologizing.

Nothing like the first problem of God becoming man can even present itself in Judaism. But there is an issue in Judaism that one might have expected to see treated in as sustained a fashion as Christianity treated incarnation. This issue is, obviously, the revelation at Sinai. In Exodus 19:20 we are told that "the Lord came down at Mount Sinai." This is a serious statement and the Biblical

---

2. David Hoffmann showed that *ADAM* the basic Hebrew word for man eventually gets to mean a Hebrew man. Cf. his famous commentary on Leviticus (Leviticus 1:2, p. 80 of the Hebrew translation, Jerusalem, 1953). Rabbi Maurice Pekarsky pointed out to me in private conversation that the very title of the legal compendium "Chaye Adam" is one of the many instances in Jewish thought where Man means a Jewish man.

writer, whether we call him Moshe, or Redactor, or *Rabenu* (to use Franz Rosenzweig's synthesis of Biblical criticism and Torah) was not writing loosely. Yet in all of Jewish tradition there has been no systematic analysis of how God came down on Mount Sinai. One might have thought this statement which was taken seriously would have received some analysis.

And the problem of revelation/reason is also neglected. It is true that thinkers such as Saadia and Maimonides deal with this problem, and many others too numerous to mention devote themselves to finding a solution. This is one of the major issues for Jewish thinkers during the Middle Ages. Yet this does not contradict our observation that Jewish thought never really came to grips with the problem of revelation/reason. For the first five centuries of the Common Era—five centuries of sustained Christian thought on this problem—the Jewish mind (which also did not slumber) ignored this question. The Babylonian Talmud (and the other material in its wake) is a highly reasoned work. Yet none of these rabbinic minds ever worked on this problem. If in the aggadic literature there are hints that they thought about the relationship of revelation to reason, they certainly did not consider it important enough to devote even a chapter in all of their immense literary corpus to this question. It might be said that they never raised the problem of revelation versus reason because they solved it at the very beginning, since the hermeneutic rules that they employed they considered to be granted them through revelation. But the fact remains that it was their human reasoning powers that had to apply the "revealed logic."[3] Nevertheless, no one worked on this problem in any systematic way (comparable to a halachic discussion) in all the literature of the Talmudic period. Even the philosophers (or the theologians, depending on one's estimate of the respective functions and use of terms) such as Saadia and Maimonides who discuss revelation and reason do so only in solving the conflicts with reason in what we call the narrative portions of the Bible. But Saadia and Maimonides never raise the issue in the crucial area of Pharisaic thought: the Halacha.

It can rightly be said that the first five centuries of the Common Era form the classical period of both Jewish and Christian "expounding" of their "Bibles." The classical Christian endeavor

---

3. Cf. Baba Metziah 59b.

during this period was theological; the classical Jewish was (phari-saic) halachic. And this difference is not accidental. Controlling this difference is something crucial.[4]

No major halachic exegete or pharisee was a convert to Judaism. Some were descendants of converts, but even these were very few. The Pharisees did not come to Jewishness from the outside; they were born Jews. But the overwhelming majority of the Christian thinkers of the first five centuries were not born into "Christian nations," but were converts to Christianity. This rather obvious difference has many important ramifications, but it points to some-thing at the root of our question.

The Christian thinker of these first five centuries was by virtue of his experience *necessarily a theologian,* for his becoming Christian necessitated squaring in some way or other (depending on the individual) his former assumptions as a pagan thinker with his "new birth" as a Christian. This is the situation which gives birth to theology: *The pagan mind still has its problem that the bap-tized heart knows not of.* And so the pagan mind must formulate answers to bring both heart and mind into consonance (though in some respects it is doubtful that this is ever solved).

Jewish thought, however, was devoted to the halacha. The Jew had in the world only the four ells of halacha, and the major emphasis of systematic thought in classical Judaism was the halacha. Outside of these four cubits many things were going on, but for Jewish thought the most important subject was existence within this comparatively small area. The task of the halachic thinker was not to unite a new heart with an old mentality (such as the Christian thinker had to do) but to keep mining the four ells long ago staked out, or, to put it another way, as new situations arise how are we to live our Jewishness?

Now halacha has, of course, some crucial religious presupposi-tions. But the main Jewish systematic activity was not the theologi-cal analysis of the presuppositions but working the halacha itself. It is true that there is the aggadah. No one can justifiably maintain that the aggadah is simply musings of minds tired from halachic labors or stories to entertain children. But even if one were to question Nachmanides' reservation about the aggadah (which was

---

4. I treat here an issue, on a historical level, which is ultimately "metahis-torical."

stated under the duress of the Barcelona debate) and even if one were to assert that the aggadah was of great importance, it is certainly true that aggadah was not systematic theology and was not the decisive area of the rabbinic mind.

In the light of this analysis it would seem that theological writing in the classical sense of the term is foreign to Judaism.

It is not the misery of man, nor the paradox of reason/revelation that is the dynamic for Jewish thought. It is Jewish existence that sets into motion a Jewish "theology."

At the watershed of the twentieth century, Jewish existence finds itself in a different situation than it did at the beginning of the period of emancipation. Self-hatred is not as common a phenomenon as it was at one time. Simone Weil's self-hatred seems archaic, a case of nineteenth-century atavism but not symptomatic of a general *malaise*. Whether because of the existence of a Jewish state or because of the reaction to Hitler, or because of the specific sociological pattern of American life, or these factors in combination, young Jews are *not* forsaking their Jewishness.[5] It is here that a Jewish theology or "Jewishology"—if we can be forgiven a crude neologism— can play a genuine Jewish role. With the fact of Jewishness neither forgotten nor forsaken, a Jewish theology—to reverse the Midrash's description of the angel presiding at birth—can give the fillip of recall, the shock of recognition of what Jewishness really is. This shock treatment for Jews is the function of a twentieth-century Jewish theology. What is the situation today in which a Jewish theology must speak, for an authentic Jewish theology always speaks in terms of specific historic situations?

The most important and universally rampant question in the Jewish community today, whether its segments are in America or in the State of Israel, is not the question of God's Oneness and Uniqueness but the question of Jewry's oneness and uniqueness. Religious Jews, nonreligious Jews, antireligious Jews, all share this concern. Even the American Council for Judaism, by the very passion of its protests, reveals its entanglement.

In the Middle Ages the various Jewries did not know the problem of relationship to one another. Only in the last ten years have we known this.

Jews have always been interested in one another. Ben Baboi in

---

5. Cf. W. Herberg, *Protestant, Catholic, Jew*, New York, 1955, chap. VIII.

the ninth century wrote a compendium describing the differences in customs between Palestinian and Babylonian Jewries. Spanish Jewry was, for various reasons, interested in the Khazar Jews. Benjamin of Tudela and Petahya of Regensburg wrote travel diaries recording information about different Jewish communities. But none of these writers, and many more examples could be given, was concerned about the communities growing apart. Yet these writers and travelers were astute and sensitive enough to see deep differences. For them there was no problem.

Only today is this problem felt and only in reference to the State of Israel. We have not been concerned about Indian Jewry, for example; nor has Indian Jewry been concerned about us.

We are concerned today specifically about Diaspora and Israeli Jewry because the State of Israel presents the possibility of a basic "normalization" of a segment of Jewry. No other Jewry in the last two thousand years has found itself in this situation. Both inside and outside the State, Jews are concerned lest this normalization bring a segment of Jewry to live a life like unto the nations. Israeli Jewry also knows this concern. Both feel the common concern yet there are tensions between these two communities because each approaches this common concern from its own specific situation. American Jewry, to take the most blatant (in more ways than one) example of Diaspora Jewry, nurtures its guilt, envious of Israeli Jewry's "fulfillment." Mixed with genuine concern lest Israelis become like unto the nations is American Jewry's desire to be at one with the nations, to make America its promised land. In turn the people of the State of Israel, in spite of the vaunted normalization, are concerned about the problem of becoming like unto the nations.

Because of these tensions, our uniqueness and our desire for normalization, we talk about "bridges of understanding," "what can we offer one another," et cetera. This was unknown in the Middle Ages. Even the tensions between Polish and Lithuanian Jewry, for example, were peripheral in the sense that they were due to ordinary human pride and distrust of differences. Polish and Lithuanian Jewry were never concerned about cultural bridges and drifting apart. They were committed to the notion that they were one people. The famous Kaddish of Reb Levi Isaac of Berditschev implicitly affirms this. Shneur Zalman of Ladi, founder of Habad, and caught in many battles, was convinced that in every Jew there was implanted a love for all Israel, a love inherited from the Patriarchs.

But today we have a new problem, a segment of catholic Israel traveling a new road. This is a new situation.

A Jewish theology for our time must speak in a new way for the situation is new, but it speaks about the old themes. A Jewish theology must start with the question: what does it mean to be a Jew?

We must be clear in our minds that this is not at all similar to the Christian theological problem: how does one *become* a Christian? Jewish theology is not Christian theology minus Jesus so as to be addressable to Jews. Jewish theology is fundamentally different because it talks of a fundamentally different kind of fact: a different kind of existence. Christian theology is concerned with conversion, rebirth, becoming. Jewish theology is involved with recall, returning, being. To Christianity no one can come except he be as a "little child," i.e., reborn. To Judaism only the convert, fairly rare, is described as newborn. The central problem of Christianity is how to be something *new*, how to be reborn, how to become a Christian. This accounts for the agony and travail at the heart of authentic Christianity. The stigmata, to take an admittedly extreme example, reveal much about Christianity. This groaning is the pain and travail of rebirth.

We have intentionally referred to the stigmata for they bring us to Francis of Assisi. No stigmatics are known before the thirteenth century; Francis was the first of a long line. In spite of the self-abnegation and mystical exercises practiced by Jews in the Middle Ages, it is worth noting that the travail and agony objectivized in the stigmata are never found among Jewish mystics. It has been said that Judah the Pious, the thirteenth-century focal point for the Hassidai Ashkenaz, was a kind of Jewish Francis of Assisi. There are, it is true, some superficial parallels between the two men. But a closer look shows a profound difference, and it is this which is a basic difference between Judaism and Christianity.

The initial story about each life is the significant clue for the dynamic of the total life; and each life itself illuminates each tradition.

It is recorded[6] that Francis of Assisi was a wayward, young man,

---

6. *The Life of St. Francis* by St. Bonaventura, London and New York, 1941 (Everyman's Edition), p. 313.

living a life of intemperance and extravagance. An illness caused him to reflect. He decided to dedicate himself to God. The father, interested in Francis' carrying on the family name and business, interfered with the decision. Francis was forced to break with his father, going so far as to cast off the clothes provided by his father, saying: "Hitherto I have called you my father on earth; henceforth I desire to say only, 'Our Father Who Art in Heaven.' " So Francis broke with his father, his past.

Judah the Pious[7] also was a wayward young man. His father was not wealthy so Judah did not have the possibility of living extravagantly. But he is pictured as spending his time in play. A young student of his father's comments on this. The father offers to give Judah instruction in Torah, et cetera. Judah accepts, and when the session begins an effulgence fills the synagogue.

Common to both biographies is the early waywardness of each hero. But that is all. Francis breaks with his father so as to *become* a genuine Christian. Judah *returns* to his father; that is, he returns to what he always was. Here there is no struggle, no renunciation, no break with the father. Here there is reconciliation. Seven centuries separate Judah the Pious from the twentieth-century Jew, and profound differences exist between the two communities yet the dynamic is the same. A Jewish theology is one of recall. The immediate task of a Jewish theology is not the exploration of dogma or a formulation of dogmatics. The immediate problem, intensified by the specific situation, is a renewed understanding of the covenantal people. The primary goal of an authentic Jewish twentieth-century theology is the revitalization of the awareness of our uniqueness.

It is only after this has been done or at least attempted that we can come to grips with the Torah. This is not to say that Torah is anthropocentric, but it does take seriously the Biblical assumption of two major personalities, God and the people of Israel. Both make the Torah what it is. And so it is only after first understanding the data immediately before our eyes—our life as a corporate personality—that we can hope to understand what is implied by revelation.

This brings us to the problem that we cannot evade: the question of halacha. There have been serious attempts in our day to formu-

---

7. Moses Gaster, *Maaseh Book*, Philadelphia, 1934, vol. II, p. 336

late a Jewish Biblical theology; but in spite of the claim that these were genuine Biblical theologies, they have turned out to be pretentious. For these Biblical theologies have avoided the immense corpus of Biblical laws. A Christian Biblical theology can do this. For the "old" testament is seen by Christianity through the eyes of the "new." But through what eyes does a Jew view Torah? He has two legitimate possibilities: the normative rabbinic tradition, or the collective experience of the people down the ages. It may be that these two possibilities ultimately converge and it may be argued that they remain separate. In any case, each position necessitates an acceptance of an halachic centered existence. The only other alternatives for viewing the halacha is the Christian claim, which it is presumed the modern Jewish Biblical theologians reject, or general nineteenth- and twentieth-century humanistic assumptions which the modern Jewish Biblical theologians glory in rejecting as an idolatry.

An honest Biblically centered theology for Jews must be halachic. And this opens up a vast territory for exploration. All the fumbling attempts in the community today indicate this deep awareness on our part, if only unconscious, that halacha is an integral part of an authentic Jewish theology.

There have been many attempts to formulate a "philosophy" of halacha.[8] This had not been a major concern of Jewish thought but at most a minor footnote to halachic efforts. But in our times this has to be at least a prolegomenon to living the halacha. For after we re-explore and, thereby, rediscover what our Jewishness is, we must live it. There is this endemic pragmatism about our tradition, from the days of the people's response at Sinai, where "action" spoke prior to "understanding," which demands application of all theoretical insight to living. Alongside the corroding of applied halacha from our lives in the twentieth century there has been some quiet but significant formulations which indicate the possibility of an approach for our time.

Bialik in a very suggestive essay, *Halacha and Aggadah*, tried to show that these two are interrelated. Professor Chaim Tchernowitz in his major study, *Toledot HaHalacha*, which does not attempt to be more than just a history, did explore in passing an idea which a

---

8. I. Heinemann in his *Taamei Ha Mitzvot*, Jerusalem, 1949, has brought together all the relevant material.

Jewish theology could use with great advantage. Tchernowitz observed, very circumspectly, it must be noted, that the specific laws of the Biblical halacha in most cases have their parallels in specific events of the patriarchal narratives. And Tchernowitz summed up with an important generalization[9] that which was direction (*halichot*) originally for the Patriarchs became directive (*halachot*) for the sons.

This is a bold formulation which, so far as I know, has no parallel though Tchernowitz argued that this is implicit in the rabbinic notion that the Patriarchs observed the entire law. But this idea that the practices of the fathers became the way of the sons can help a twentieth-century Jewish theology move from covenantal recall to covenantal living.

Jewish theology, then, is an interim theology. It is not a continuous challenge to mankind, to the old Adam. But it addresses itself to the children of Abraham, to the Jew. And it speaks only when Jews have forgotten the meaning of their existence or why and how to live this existence. This theological enterprise must view itself with a rather skeptical eye; it must see itself as a product of sickness rather than as the queen of Jewish knowledge. For Jewish knowledge must pass beyond a Jewish theology and become knowledge in the original sense of the Hebrew term. When this happens, the covenantal people are happily rid of theology; for so often in our time has theology been a barrier between us and life.

---

9. *Toledot HaHalacha,* vol. I, part 1, N.Y., 1934, pp. 201 ff.

GOD AND MAN IN MODERN THOUGHT

S. H. Bergman

S. H. Bergman, philosopher at the Hebrew University, himself a Jewish religious thinker, has posed throughout his life the question he addresses in this essay. The task of this essay is not to resolve the difficulty, but to place it within the context of the history of Western philosophy. Bergman adumbrates the seriousness of the problem by citing Judah Magnes' gloss on the question of Levi Yitzhak of Berdichev: "Do I suffer for Thy sake, O Lord?" It will be remembered that the opening phrase of the Berdichever plea is a disclaimer of his desire to understand the ways of God. God is for the Berdichever incomprehensible; moreover, even if he were comprehensible, it is irrelevant to the requirements of man that he be understood by him. The "problem" of man and God, the *noesis* of man and the being of God are of no interest to him who has staked his life on God. What matters is not *who* God is, but *that* he is, for it is upon the existence of God, not his nature, that man depends, and the concern of man is not that he know God but that God takes cognizance of him, justifies his agony, and affirms its truth for his own sake. Bergman's use of Magnes' citation shifts the focus of the Berdichever's question, transforms it from the question of a single man querying his suffering, to the question of the whole Jewish people asking out of the darkness that the light come which casts out darkness. Magnes does not ask like Levi Yitzhak: "Do I suffer for Thy sake?" but rather "Does man suffer for Thy sake?" The question is no longer soul before soul, but creature before creator, all creatures before one creator.

What one can see from Bergman's inquiry—its shape and unfolding—is that the questions of the knowledge of God and the relations between man and God arise from the prior problem of evil. Would man have inquired of God's nature had the world been perfectly good? That is the point, is it not, of the story of Adam and Eve in Paradise. Would man know to query God's nature were man always in that transfigured serenity of the Garden? He would not know of his finitude; he would not know of his incapacity, his stupidity, his grossness; he would not have done evil and having done evil would not have sought to explore its depths. Theodicy is then prior to theological epistemology. The reality of evil precedes the knowledge of God, and it is from the knowledge of God that the issue of theodicy is then raised again as a philosophic problem. How can a God, who is the perfection of all qualities conceivable by men (and thus Good), allow evil to flourish in the world? Isaiah's answer that God creates evil as well (a profound assertion, I think) carries the argument half the way, for Isaiah does not regard the task of man as that of understanding God's ways, but rather of being obedient to them (Isaiah has problems, but they are challenging problems).

"When we seek for instruction and guidance on this special problem of the relation between God and man from the great classical philosophers of recent centuries, we are," Bergman observes, "on the whole, left disappointed and empty-handed." The resume of the teachings of the philosophers from Descartes and the occasionalists through Leibnitz, Kant, and Fichte which Bergman pursues in this essay points in the direction of the increasing autonomization of man. God *as* a philosophic problem is insoluble. He is the conundrum which is beyond the purview of reason. That is to say, reason can describe God's trajectory and in doing so can serve his reality, but when it seeks to make God an object of intellectual inquiry, it is reason which must triumph, it is God who must bow. When God ceases to be a reality whom one believes and becomes a problem which reason must solve, the solutions of reason become predictable: God is left, as Hans Ehrenberg observed, as Honorary Chairman of Nature and Morality.

GOD AND MAN IN
MODERN THOUGHT

Man as the Heir of God

S. H. BERGMAN

In the midst of the years of the overwhelming Jewish disaster, Judah Leon Magnes, the Hebrew University's founder and first president, spoke at the annual opening of studies. In his speech, he quoted the following statement ascribed to Rabbi Levi Yitzhak of Berdichev: "I do not ask, Lord of the World, to reveal to me the secrets of Thy ways—I could not comprehend them. I do not ask to know *why* I suffer, but only this: Do I suffer for *Thy* sake?" Dr. Magnes concluded his talk with a question whose awesome tone still resounds in my ears: "Teach us only this: Does man suffer for *Thy* sake, O Lord?"

The question was put by a religious man, who, having certain rights of his own, is permitted to formulate his query in this way. The philosopher, however, does not have these rights or this language. He has to approach his problems coldly and objectively, and make that sacrifice of emotion of which Hermann Cohen spoke when he confronted his philosophy with the demands of his warm Jewish feelings. The philosopher inquires about the meaning of Reb Levi Yitzhak's and Magnes' question. How are we to look upon the position of man before God in order to make the question of whether man suffers for the sake of God meaningful? Do we not have here an indication of man's intolerable pride and arrogance? It is written: "What is man that Thou art mindful of him? And the son of man that Thou visitest him? For Thou hast made him little lower than the angels and hast crowned him with glory and honor."

These verses from the Book of Psalms (8:4, 5) contain the whole problem with which the philosopher is here occupied: the insignificance of man on the one hand and his closeness to God on the other. How are these two extremes to be united, this absolute dependence of man on his Maker and the sovereignty of man as a creature gifted with reason, that reason which is our highest criterion of value? At the end of the novel *Dr. Faustus,* Thomas Mann speaks of the "cultural idea in which reverence for the deities of the depths blends with the civilized cult of Olympic reason and clarity, to make for a unity in uprightness. . . ." Is such a blend or merger possible? Is a covenant between man and God possible? And how can it be made so?

When we seek for instruction and guidance on this special problem of the relation between God and man, from the great classical philosophers of recent centuries, we are, on the whole, left disappointed and empty-handed.

One would have expected Descartes to see the problem in all its acuteness, since he was on the one hand an extreme rationalist, for whom reason, human reason, was the supreme criterion, and, on the other hand, he took pains under all circumstances, to uphold the omnipotence of God. In 1630, Descartes wrote to Mersenne in the following vein: Just as God created everything, He also created all the eternal truths. He is the creator of the essences of things just as He is the creator of the reality of things. God created reality by His decision like an absolute monarch. This is so even for the law of contradiction. We have not the right to say that God can not make one and two not to equal three, or that He could not make a mountain exist without a valley.

Obviously, this doctrine, that truth is the product of God's wilful decision, undermines the basis of reason. Because what value is there in the "evidence" by which man recognizes the validity of truth when truth is nothing but the wilful decision of God, endorsing it by His will or abolishing it by His will? The occasionalist philosophers who came after Descartes answered the question by saying: "Once God commanded, but ever since He always obeys His own original decision." This, however, is no solution, merely a consolation and a promise, that in our reliance on this "obedience" of God, we can also trust the truth, and the instrument, that is human "evidence," through which truth is given to us. Odd how this ambivalence of Descartes' position, this standing with one foot on the wilful irrationality of Divine decision, and with the other foot on the rationality of man in the absorption of "evidence," did not worry Descartes more. Tacitly, Descartes decided in favor of reason, and Pascal was quite justified in saying of him: "I cannot forgive Descartes; he would have been very pleased had he been able, in all his philosophy, to avoid giving the Creator a part here in this world; but he could not help allowing God a tap on the world with a finger in order to set it in motion. And having done so, he had no more need for the Creator."

In Descartes' thinking, the problem of the relation between God and man is evaded and with it the question of the status of man in the world. This, too, is curious, for Descartes did touch on this difficult and decisive problem. In his system, man is the great and unique exception in the world, in whom there takes place that wondrous and incomprehensible meeting between the two secondary substances, body and soul. Animals, according to Descartes, are merely bodies, mechanisms. But man is soul as well as body, the two substances which, according to him, have no contact with each other yet meet together in man and constitute a perplexing unity. Man is, therefore, the exceptional being in the universe. Descartes, then, sees this, but he fails to see any particular philosophic problem in man's position in the cosmos and in his special relation to the Creator of the world.

Those who came after Descartes were even more undiscerning of the problem of man. For Spinoza, man was only a mode, just as the triangle was a mode. The acosmic God of Spinoza absorbed the world, and man together with the world. There is no question of a special place for man, even though we often encounter in Spinoza expressions like "There is nothing more useful to man than man." Such statements might be interpreted as a hint of some special position held by man, but the hint remains isolated and fragmentary.

Similarly, one does not encounter the problem of man either in the occasionalists nor in the English philosophers of the eighteenth century. In the works of Leibnitz, it is true, man occupies a special and honorable place in the scheme of the monads, being the lowest monad in the "ladder of the spirits," that is, of those monads who are conscious of themselves, and are thus citizens of the "City of

God." In this manner, Leibnitz accepts the medieval outlook of man as a creature who stands as intermediate between the beasts and the angels. "When our soul discovers the sciences by which God determined everything according to weight, measure, and number, it thereby imitates within its own small compass and its own microcosm wherein it is granted to work, that which God does in the macrocosm."[1] Man, therefore, is God in miniature, but here, too, Leibnitz does not see any special problem in the relation of God to man. The relation of man to God and the questions he proceeds to ask remain the conventional ones of the existence of God and the immortality of the soul. The problem of the special metaphysical position of man in the cosmos is not raised.

Nevertheless, even though the metaphysical problem of man as man was not yet discovered by the philosophers of the first centuries of the modern era, the position of man as man in the world was radically altered. And it might even be said that the very fact that man did not occupy himself with the problem of himself, did much to further the process of changing the nature of man at that time. The man of this new era was absorbed in the conquest of the globe on which he dwelt. Philosophy—and first and foremost, the philosophy of Descartes—paved the way for this conquest. In consequence of his phenomenal success in the subjugation of material forces, man's confidence in himself and in his reasoning faculties was incalculably reinforced. This new self-confidence of Western man found fervid expression in the philosophy of Kant. With a boldness that should earn our wholehearted admiration, the philosophy of Kant transfers the center of gravity of the world to reason, to the subject; that is to say, to man. Though Kant actually called his new philosophy a "Copernican Revolution," he actually achieved the inverse effect. Copernicus made the earth, which had previously been the center of the universe, a mere tiny planet revolving around the sun. In Kant's "Copernican Revolution," man became the center of the universe.

To be sure, Kant was far from denying the existence of God. On the contrary, the concept of God was granted a specific and well-defined place in his system. Nevertheless, Kant continually emphasizes that God is not the basis of his system, merely its final consummation and its peak. Kant argued that, in his historic age,

---

1. *Principles of Nature and Grace*, par. 14.

when esteem of the inquiring mind had reached its height, we can neither prove the existence of God with our reason, nor may we legitimately employ the concept of God in order to explain nature. Least of all is the concept required as a basis for a theory of morals.

In both these realms, the subject, man, forms the basis of his own being. True, man is not the creator of his world. Human reason is receptive, it absorbs, it needs the material handed to it by the senses; and man is passive in regard to this sensual material. He is thereby revealed as finite. Nevertheless, the ordering of things, the construction of the passively received material into an ordered world, this is an act of man. In this manner, even though man is not a creator of nature in so far as the contents of its phenomena are concerned, he is still its creator in so far as rational forms, which hold the sensual content and organize it as a unity, are concerned. But in spite of his finitude, man, by virtue of his transcendental mind, has these forms, which make possible an ordering of the world of phenomena and the building up of a science of nature. In order to know the external world man must construct it first, and the transcendental forms of the world, the world in which man lives, are made by man.

Man, the subject, therefore precedes the things he makes. Kant's position here is the very opposite of Thomas Aquinas, who in this matter expresses the classical view of philosophy. Relying on the linguistic similarity of "mind" and "measure" in Latin, *mens, mensura: "nomen mentis a mensurando est sumptum,"* Thomas Aquinas states: "Clearly, the natural things from which our mind derives science serve as a measure for our mind, but for the natural things the measure is the divine mind which created them. Consequently, the divine mind is a measure and is not to be measured; the natural things are both measure and measured; while our own mind is measured by, but is not the measure of, the natural things; it can only measure the *artificial* things it 'creates.' "[2]

Thus, according to Thomas, the spontaneity of man is narrowed down to his own creations, and he is devoid of spontaneity or creative force in so far as nature is concerned. Kant overthrew this order: it is not things which determine the reason of man, but reason which determines the things by virtue of its creative action

2. Thomas Aquinas, *De Virtute*, cf. Vincenz Rüfner: *"Homo Secundus Deus," Philosophisches Jahrbuch.* vol. 63, 1955, p. 264.

in giving the world its basic forms. This creative action of man, of course, is only applicable to the world of phenomena in which we live, and not to the things in themselves. Still, even in the realm of the things-in-themselves, man is creator, since he begins by his free will a new chain of cause and effect. This is a mighty addition to the creative power of man, even if we have to admit that we, whose knowledge is limited to phenomena, do not know *how* this new chain of causality comes about. We do not know how man is made a creator in the realm of the things-in-themselves; nevertheless, by virtue of our freedom, we do know that this is done, even if we do not know how it is done.

In Kant's system, then, the place of man is central; although his moral world outlook did require the concept of God, it was in order to consummate it, and not in order to act as its foundation. Only with this concept of God is it possible to bridge the gap between the two realms, that of the theoretical realm of nature subject to natural laws and the practical realm of the freedom of man. Only with the aid of this concept can natural law and moral law be brought under a common higher unity. At the same time, the objective reality of God cannot be proven by us by any theoretical proof, although it also cannot be disproven. Of course, we most assuredly do not need God to act as basis for a theory of morals, just as there is no need of God for a foundation of natural science. Yet the concept of God belongs to the theory of morals though its function there is secondary. God has to make happiness in the world conform with morality. The moral man has the right to be happy, but one cannot say that this will be fulfilled in the world unless one presupposes some higher intelligence which is the cause of nature and at the same time is the principle of the "moral world." The "moral world" is to be considered the future world in such a way that *there* the moral act will receive its compensation and the immoral act its punishment. This, then, is the place for the idea of a God, one who apportions returns for our deeds according to our moral deserts. Furthermore, only on this condition will the ideas of morality function as motives for the acting man. Without this hypothesis of good for the righteous and evil for the wicked, Kant says, "the sublime ideas of morality would only be a praiseworthy matter of common consent but not necessarily motive forces for giving direction and for carrying into operation." Kant calls this conformity of happiness with practical morality the "highest good." And the "highest good" in this sense is guaranteed by God. It might be added that the origin of Kant's notion of God is the ideal of happiness which is so characteristic of the eighteenth century, the century of enlightenment. In another intellectual climate, for example, in that of Kierkegaard, who sharply rejected the ideal of happiness, there would have been no place for those considerations which prompted Kant—and after him Hermann Cohen in his Marburg period—to postulate the existence of God.

The concept, "God," is a postulate of the moral reason. But according to the theoretical reason, we have no idea whatever of God. He is nothing but "a regulating principle of reason, directing it to see all the relations in the world *as though* they were derived from necessary cause." Further, we think the world *"as if* the world, its existence and internal determination, flowed from divine intelligence." And when I say that one has to see the world as though it were the work of divine intelligence and will, I am merely stating that "just as the clock, the boat, the regiment are related to the watchmaker, the shipbuilder, the commander, so is the world of our senses related to the unknown."

All of these quotations, to which many more could be added, show that the function of the concept of God in Kant's system is definitely secondary. In a rather cruel, though not untrue statement, Hans Ehrenberg once commented (in his work on Fichte) on this "Moral Deism" of Kant and Fichte with the following words: "The cosmological Deism of Newton ejected God from the visible world, and provided Him with a refuge in creation as a prime mover or as a legislator of the laws of nature; God was thus made 'Honorary Chairman' of nature. Similarly, Moral Deism does the same thing; it appoints God Honorary Chairman of Morality." Of course, Kant insists that this concept constitutes the peak of the system, still, the entire weight of the structure of the system rests on man. The great innovation of his philosophy was his theory of mankind and the metaphysical dignity of humanity. We will hardly err then, if we say that with Kant, the idea of mankind absorbed all the love, the faith, and the hope that men had been accustomed to direct to God. In Kant's work, man is an in-between creature, or an ambivalent creature, half animal and half angel, and as such he becomes the ultimate goal of nature. The intent here is not, of course, the individual man, but humanity as a single whole. Mankind is distinguished by the attribute of holiness. The superiority of man over the animal is highly emphasized; it consists of his moral freedom and of his reason. True, man is made of "warped wood," but he has a potential for the good and for the progress of the species. Therefore, too, he is weak in his instinctive equipment in comparison with the beast. As Kant wrote, "Nature desired that man should create everything that exceeds the stark mechanical needs of his animal existence by his own efforts entirely and that he should not attain any happiness or perfection whatever except that which he obtains by his own reason, without instinct." Man possesses a character which he creates for himself and by himself. Fundamentally and naturally, he is an animal who can be reasonable (*animal rationabile*); his potential and his capacity are that he should make himself a reasoning animal (*animal rationale*).

Man is a citizen of two worlds, partly he is "phenomenon" and partly he is "noumenon," "intelligible character," personality in the fullest sense, *"persona."* As personality, he is the bearer of moral reason, the "priceless" (the German expression *preis* here can be interpreted in two ways, "beyond all price" and as "beyond all praise"). As animal, even as rational animal, man has a definite price, an external price which is determined, as with the beasts, by his utility; and everything that has a price can be exchanged for something else of equal price. But man as personality has an absolute, an internal price, which is dignity (*Würde*); and this can no longer be evaluated as a means to other ends, but as an end in itself. Every human being, being an end in himself, has no exchange value, and that is his dignity. This feeling of individual human dignity supplies the Kantian philosophy with its enormous moral and revolutionary force, and is the source of that fervor with which Kant said, "Do not be slaves to other men. . . . Do not let others trample your rights underfoot" (*The Metaphysics of Morals*). Man is the highest creation and the final goal of nature, and nothing on earth can compete with him.

In addition, we must note the special category of mankind as a whole, in Kant's thought. Man is a creature whose qualities and talents can develop in their perfection only within the framework of the race as an entirety, within the historic development. If there are spiritual creatures higher than man, such as angels, we can surmise that they are distinguished from man in that each angel fulfills his destiny in its entirety. Not so with man. Only the race of mankind can hope to fulfill the destiny appointed for man, not the individual man. The individual man ages and dies before he reaches perfection. "When the most penetrating mind stands on the threshold of the greatest discoveries that can be expected of him by virtue of his keenness and experience, then old age pounces on him. He becomes dull and is obligated to let the next generation continue and add its contribution to the progress of culture."

Only mankind as a whole reaches the final goal. Thereby the human race as a whole assumes a special metaphysical position. Mankind should be respected and admired, and in this way it serves as a criterion for the individual. The individual measures himself by the ideal toward which mankind is progressing. And one has the right to demand that everyone show respect to the humanity dwelling in each individual. Even if the individual is corrupt and spoiled, the human in him, that mankind whom he nevertheless represents, should necessarily be holy to him. It is an object worthy of the highest admiration.

To sum up: the problem of "God and Man" distinguished Kant's thought from that of his predecessors and opened up vistas of a new philosophy. True, within the system he acknowledged the importance of the idea of God, and he spoke with emphasis of "God" as a "necessary and quite useful hypothesis" (*eine notwendige und dienliche Annahme*), yet it was strictly a hypothesis. All his love, enthusiasm, and respect were directed to man and humanity. Prayer to God, for Kant, was nothing but "madness arising from superstition," and "the making of fetishes," whereas mankind was surrounded by a halo as something splendidly sacred. Man inherited the place of God, if not explicitly, since the system did give God a place in it, then implicitly by virtue of the feeling or attitude that animated the whole system.

That which was more a matter of general attitude or mood than explicit theory in Kant, became with German idealism a definite doctrine. With Promethean boldness, Fichte snatched the title of "absolute" from God—*aseitas*, that which is underived being—and granted it to man, who is viewed as the absolute Ego. Where, ask Fichte, and Schelling (in his early writings), are we to seek the unconditional which is the condition for all existence? Everything, every object is conditioned, they respond, and make use of a play of words: *Ding*, which is thing and *Bedingt*, which is conditioned. Where shall we look for that which under no circumstances can be considered a thing? And the answer was: in the absolute Ego. I exist and not by virtue of anything else, for then I myself would be a thing, but rather I exist by virtue of myself. "I am because I am!" In his book, *On the Ego as the Philosophic Principle*, Schelling formulates Fichte's theory thus: "I am! My 'ego' includes a being prior to every thought and every representation. It exists as it is thought and it is thought because it exists; it exists, only to the extent, and it is thought only to the extent, that it thinks itself. It exists because it, itself, thinks itself and it thinks itself by itself because it exists. It creates itself by its thought, with absolute causality. I am because I am!" "This," so Schelling concludes, "seizes everyone suddenly. The Ego exists, therefore, only by virtue of itself, and it is given as that which is unconditioned."

Kant still made the clear distinction between the *a priori* form of our world, whose origin is in the self, and between the *a posteriori* material which is given to man. Though we do not know whence this *a posteriori* material is given, and we, therefore, speak only of the "thing-in-itself." In this way, according to Kant, the world, within which mankind lives, is dependent on a different world which we do not know. But Fichte eradicates this limitation of Kant. The world is entirely the immanent world of the Ego. As Fichte writes to Jacoby: "In Kant there is still a multiplicity of given experience—God knows how and whence it is given; but I hold, in dry and simple terms, that even this multiplicity is created by us, by a creative force of our own."

Thus the "Ego" becomes the creator of its world, and the entire world is immersed within the Ego. "The ball of consciousness"—as Hans Ehrenberg formulated it—"is closed to the outside."[3]

But this very world of objects is only the expression for those obstacles which the pure "Ego" throws out for itself as hindrances in its path in order to confirm itself and corroborate itself by overcoming these obstacles. The things in the world do no more than express the relation between our particular and fixed finitude and the infinite toward which we strive. In his *Theory of Science* in the year 1794, Fichte writes: If scientific theory were asked what the qualities of things were, it would only be able to answer: things are such as we are required to make them. Nature is nothing but the "opposition which we have set up against the absolute force of the free life of the Ego, an opposition which was created by absolute

---

3. Hans Ehrenberg: *Fichte*, 1923.

thought in order to uncover and reveal the power of the Ego, which in itself would not be visible." According to Fichte's well-known saying, the world is nothing but the "material of our obligation. . . ."

Clearly, in this system there was no place for God, in the traditional sense of the word. Fichte says: "The philosopher has no God, and it is inconceivable that he should have one. God cannot be an object, for then he would be conditioned by the Ego, like all objects." "According to the point of view of Fichte's theory of science" says Windelband, "God cannot be considered as being, as something that exists, because then Divinity would not be primary but conditioned, since every reality, according to Fichte, is merely the product of an act of the Ego. But Fichte, as is the customary habit of philosophers, gave the name Divinity to his own highest metaphysical concept, which, with him, was the action of the pure Ego, or the absolute function of the moral world order. For Fichte, then, Divinity is the absolute moral ideal which is never, of course, actual, but which, nevertheless, carries within itself the reason for all actuality."

That which Fichte called our faith in God is based on consciousness of this moral ideal which tells us that as human beings each one of us is required to be pure self, the unconditional, except that in actuality, we have not fulfilled this imperative and we are only the empirical self. Our real human essence contains a contradiction: each of us is an empirical-individual self, limited by his surroundings, by the objects amongst which he lives, but his limited Ego contains within itself the concsiousness that it is destined to burst all these bounds, to eradicate from the world its character as object, as conditioned *Ding,* and to be an unlimited, an absolute Ego. God, whom Fichte also calls the moral world order, or the order which exists between that which we are in actuality and that which we are bidden to be. Divinity thus becomes a reality existing for the sake of a goal, for the task with which we are charged. However, this goal cannot ever be reached, for its attainment, the actualization of the pure Ego, would wipe out the process of the world which exists only by virtue of the fact that we do not attain that which we are bidden to attain.

This was a unique turning point in philosophic speculation, an about-face in which Fichte derived existence from the imperative, and the limited Ego from the absolute Ego. This absolute Ego does not exist, but is merely required of us. This goal, toward which we strive, is projected by religious faith heavenward, so to speak, and in this way the traditional image of God, as religions know it, is formed. But Fichte's religion of philosophic idealism frees itself from this heavenward projection and suffices with saying: God is the infinite goal toward which we are forever striving.

In the fifth lecture of his book, *Instruction for a Life of Happiness,* Fichte phrases this viewpoint of God as the infinite goal in memorable fashion. "The Divine, in its first, its primordial form, enters into you as life, as your life which you are required to live and which you shall live. God is revealed in that which sacred man does, in what man lives and loves. He no longer appears in the shadow. He is no longer wrapped in obscurity, but shows himself in man's own immediate and strong life. And as for that question: What is God? That question, to which we can give no response so long as we cling to a shadowy idea of God, is now capable of being answered. God is that which the man who is devoted to Him and who is inspired by Him *does.* Do you want to see God as He is in Himself, face to face? Do not seek Him beyond the clouds. He can be found in every place where *you* are. Look upon the life of His devotees, and you will see Him; devote yourself to God and you will find Him in your heart." In the same book in the sixth lecture he writes: "The awareness of the absolute unity between human existence and the existence of the Divine is the deepest awareness that it is given to man to attain."

In this matter of the relation between man and God, we can therefore sum up the theory of Fichte and the young Schelling as follows: It cannot be said that God *is.* God comes into being, and He comes into being more and more. Mankind is God on-the-way toward this final coming into Being. And the very nonexistence of God in reality, this very task which is imposed on us is what gives the individual Ego the strength to be, for its being then becomes a being toward a goal. This meaning of God and man, of man as God coming into being and God as the goal of man, gives Fichte's philosophy its great pathos. As illustration, I should like to quote Fichte's conclusion of his lecture in *The Vocation of the Scholar.* He had said that all men fundamentally strive toward the same goal, toward perfection, each from his own vantage point. But this goal will not be reached so long as man will not cease to be man and will not be God. At the same time, each and every person can approach this goal, and this approach is made by men mutually influencing one another. And, says Fichte, it would be difficult to see how any of us could be so perfect that he should not be able to obtain a further degree of perfection through some other person in some manner or other. In this way, all men co-operate. Fichte continues: "Honored sirs, I know few ideas that are more sublime than this idea of the general mutual action of the whole of humanity in itself, this idea of life and infinite striving, this energetic competition of give and take. This is the most noble thing that men can achieve, when innumerable wheels interlock and the motive force for them all is freedom and a beautiful harmony is created by the mutual interaction. Each and every person can say to the other: Be whoever you are, if only your countenance is human, then you are a member of this great community. Numberless intermediate links transfer my action, yet no matter what their multiplicity I act upon you and you act on me. No man who bears the mark of reason on his face, no matter how coarse these marks may be, exists for me in vain. But I do not know you, and you do not know me? Nevertheless, just as we have a common vocation to be good and to be more and more good, so, most certainly, will there come a time, even though it be in millions or billions of years—and what are years?— there will come a time and I will sweep you, too, within the periphery of my actions and I will do you good, too, just as you will do good to me and your heart will be attached to my heart by the most beautiful contact of mutual and free give and take."

This philosophic hymn of Johann Gottlieb Fichte on the holiness of man and human society strikingly indicates how the idea of man absorbed into itself the religious enthusiasm that had formerly been directed to God. It is no cause for wonder that soon the natural yearnings of man for ceremony and religious rites, whose Divine object had been excised, were now directed to a humanity which had become the new object of worship. One generation after Kant, Comte made humanity, the "Great Being" (*Le Grand Etre*) into an object for a new worship. Humanism became a religion.

In conclusion, we may take an example from Jewish life. In 1911, at the very beginning of the twentieth century, Rabbi Charles Fleischer, who had emigrated in his youth to the United States and had been ordained at the Hebrew Union College in Cincinnati in 1893, left his reform congregation in Boston and founded the religious movement "The Commoners." This movement claimed that

Judaism and Christianity were not suitable religions for American democracy. In their stead, there had to come an American-Humanistic religion. The church of this religion sang patriotic songs instead of religious hymns, and the sermon consisted of a talk on social and political problems completely divorced from religion. Instead of prayer came "Aspiration" in which man strove toward the Holy Spirit in himself. For if the Holy Spirit lives within man why need he pray to a God who is outside the world? Charles Fleischer, the leader of the movement, wrote "Man" and "He" in capital letters as befits the name of God. He said quite plainly, "Let us stand with all our hearts in reverence before the universe and let us devote ourselves to the greatness and the glory of man. We believe that *man is God*."[4]

4. Arthur Main, "Charles Fleischer's Religion of Democracy," *Commentary*, 1954.

INTRODUCTION TO

SELF-REALIZATION AND THE SEARCH FOR GOD

Emil L. Fackenheim

Obviously both humanism and supernaturalism are to be understood in the broadest possible sense (and the most broad sense of a word is very often the most precise and meaningful of its available employments), for the humanism Emil L. Fackenheim criticizes is neither the humanism of the Renaissance nor that of the American Humanist Association; and the supernaturalism he defends cannot be confused with any narrow unreflective orthodoxy or anti-intellectualist bibliolatry.

Humanism (or naturalism), as understood by Fackenheim, is the reduction of the objective complexity of the world of nature and things to the posited absoluteness of the self and its faculties of understanding. It is a passable doctrine and one which occupies a critical position in the history of Western philosophy. It has its origins, however, in a legitimate human concern for self-fulfillment. Since man does not elect to be meaningless, the palpable fatuity, confusion, contradiction of his world is either regarded as a failure to understand the object-world and its implicit harmony or as a confusion within the self from which the incompleteness of evil and the unnaturalness of defect are to be removed by right understanding. Man strives for self-integration and the criterion for the measurement of self-integration is relative health and the expungement of the unhealthy. Such a humanist enterprise sounds frighteningly athletic, but Fackenheim's description of the pursuit of health is no parody of the American gospel of self-perfection and improvement. It is a *real* teaching which underlies much of the practical morality of philosophic idealism and its consequent embodiment in secularized religion or secular religions. God either disappears (for there is no need, as classical religion thought there was, for a relationship between relative man and supernatural God to define integration) or he is transformed from reality into idea (which is, in effect, to say that man finds his self-perfection in and through the postulations of his own mind). Fackenheim's devastating critique of the deceptive securities of humanist-naturalist faith is particularly apt to the theologizing of the modern pulpit, for when in doubt of the persuasiveness of declarative, expository theology, too many of our pulpit theologians have recourse to a kind of theological Couéism in which perfection and integration are no longer even a requirement of intellectual postulation but of sheer willing to self-improvement.

The defense of supernaturalism which Fackenheim undertakes in the second part of this essay might be thought to be weaker than his critique of humanism. Many thinkers are better at the task of destruction. But this is not the case with Fackenheim, neither in this essay nor for that matter in more than a score of those he has written over the past decade and a half. Quite the contrary. He doesn't blush at the complexity he argues upon us. There is no such thing as integration through self-realization. There is no ground for imagining that man is a creature who can perfect himself *by himself*, relying upon his own resources, unaided. To seek unification despite the contradictions inherent within him either leads man to the fruitless endeavor of apotheosis or the despairing recoil into bestiality. Only with and over against God, as companion of the way and critic of our confoundings, can man be brought to deal with the contradictions of his nature. But the God of such a tension is no human idea, no irrational extension of personality in strife and striving, but a reality who gives himself to us that he may be believed by us.

SELF-REALIZATION AND THE SEARCH FOR GOD

A Critique of Modern Humanism and a Defense of Jewish Supernaturalism

EMIL L. FACKENHEIM

> *Therefore shall a man first take upon himself the yoke of the Kingdom of Heaven, and then take upon himself the yoke of the commandments.*
> —M. Berakot 2.2

I

Man will at all times seek ultimate integration. It is intolerable to him that his life as a whole should not have a unity through which he can assess meaning to all its aspects.

It is significant that the criterion governing most modern attempts at such a synthesis can be expressed by the term "self-realization." Idealists and romanticists mean by this term the realization of an ideal self slumbering within every person; pragmatists and naturalists refer rather to the whole realm of human living, physical as well as spiritual. They agree that to give ultimate meaning to his life man must turn on himself, arousing those powers in himself which represent his highest opportunity.

Underlying this view is the faith that what is contradictory and evil in human nature is merely a lack of something; that it is "unreal" or "unnatural"; and that the individual can master it and aspire to perfection by realizing what is positive, his "real" or "natural" self. Thus, "self-realization" means to the idealist the realization or approximation of an envisaged ideal self. And it is taken for granted, first, that the individual is able to form the right conception of his ideal self, and, second, that to realize or approximate it is a task which is obstructed by no basic obstacle. In the naturalist frame of reference, the prime criterion of self-realization is health. Evil is "the unnatural," which health automatically eliminates. Health produces social harmony because it balances pleasure and duty—a healthy egoism and a healthy altruism; it produces inner harmony because the healthy man concentrates on such of his problems as are solvable, ignoring those which are not. Health also gives freedom to the individual's creative powers while providing harmless outlets for his destructive urges—and creativity is fullness of life. Harmony eliminates evil; creativity eliminates emptiness.

Religion also is interpreted in terms of self-realization. The fact that many modern definitions of religion do not even include God indicates what has happened: religion has been transformed from a total integration of life through relation to a supernatural God into total integration through self-realization. The convictions leading to this transformation are again the same: all meaning that the individual can find in his life is inherent in his own nature; and any meaning that he cannot find in himself is both unattainable and practically irrelevant, therefore properly to be ignored.

Other interpretations of religion do include God. But, again, in many of these, He appears as an *idea* only, His *existence* being acknowledged with embarrassment if acknowledged at all. Afterlife, salvation, eternal judgment are here meaningless words; nature and history are interpreted in terms of science. An existing God, if affirmed at all, is at best permitted to retain the function of a First Cause, required perhaps for cosmological interpretation but of little if any significance for the life of the individual. *Ideas* of God, however, are here regarded as of utmost importance for the individual's life. For the kind of idea he has of God will determine his scale of values and, thus, indirectly, the kind of life he is motivated to live. Individual life, as well as human history, can become

> a battle for the pure idea of God and man, which is not to end until the principle of divine holiness has done away with every form of life that tends to degrade and disunite mankind, and until Israel's Only One has become the unifying power and the highest ideal of all humanity.[1]

Here man undoubtedly creates God in his own image, ideas of God deriving not from an existing God who reveals himself, but

---

1. Kaufmann Kohler, *Jewish Theology* (New York, 1918), p. 15.

from human conception and evaluation. Again, the actual faith behind this religion is a faith in the "true" or "real" self which enables man both to form adequate ideas of God and to live without basic difficulty in *imitatio Dei*.

What becomes of prayer when God is understood as an idea only? Where every trace of even unconscious belief in the being of God is lost, prayer is no longer an appeal to the Other for help and guidance; it is an activity designed to arouse and inspire the better, the true self. The individual no longer seeks help from God, but from himself.

Whatever may be the lasting value of this ideal of self-realization or the partial truth in it, as a principle of ultimate integration it is totally inadequate. The reason for its inadequacy is the error of the faith on which it is based. If an ultimate self, harmonious, perfect, and unambiguous, were realizable, "self-realization" could perhaps serve as the principle of ultimate integration. A man's ideals might not, then, be absolute, but they would be the best he could know or be expected to know. As to his realization of the ideals, he might be far from complacent; but he could be confident at least that the degree of perfection he would achieve would depend only on his knowledge of the ideals and on the energy he was ready to devote to their realization. He would definitely not need the guidance or mercy of an existing God. His unconcern with his own ultimate destiny could be understood as the heroic attitude of a good soldier who is concerned to do his duty, but gives no thought to his own fate.

But this kind of self-confidence and heroic self-sufficiency rest on a tragic illusion. There is no such thing as a single, unambiguous, perfect self, the source and end of ultimate integration. On the contrary, the more deeply the individual searches his soul, the more clearly does he come to understand the irreducible tensions which lie in his nature. Biological necessity and spiritual freedom are not merely mutually irreducible, which would still make possible a division of authority, as it were, between these two parts of human nature; they are also inextricably intertwined. Face these tensions in their sharpness and profundity, and you at once recognize that the one potential self is an illusion; you can no longer discover the unambiguous self you can and ought to be—and to give it adjectives such as "ideal," "creative," "natural," or "healthy," is no help at all.

The unprejudiced man soon senses that there is something wrong with self-realization as the principle of ultimate integration. If he attempts self-realization in the naturalist terms of health, he himself transcends this attempt sufficiently to feel that health does not exhaust his ultimate obligation. Health, with all its happy implications, seems to be merely what makes him fit to face that obligation. At times, it even seems necessary to sacrifice health in the service of ultimate responsibility. Health comes to seem something like an ultimate criterion only when sickness renders him unable to be genuinely responsible.[2] If he attempts self-realization in idealist terms, setting up an ideal and striving to reach it, he transcends this attempt sufficiently to marvel at his presumptuousness. Knowing his ideal to stem from himself, he suspects it of being tainted with hidden self-interest, and even while striving to reach that ideal, he knows his effort to be vitiated by motives which are anything but pure. Nor can he ever free himself entirely from the fetters of this impurity because every effort designed to achieve that effect has its own admixture of impure motives.

That these misgivings are not empty scruples, the twentieth century illustrates with abundant clarity. It demonstrates the fact that destructiveness is not merely something "unnatural," the product of sickness, and it demonstrates that an idealistic attitude is not in itself a sufficient guarantee of moral goodness. "Normal" men beyond suspicion of sickness, morbidity, and frustration "express themselves" in war, destruction, and wholesale murder. "Idealistic" youths serve evil tyrants in noble devotion, committing nameless crimes out of a sincere sense of duty, and sacrificing their lives to the kingdom of evil. This is the stark fact: when health becomes the ultimate law, the "blond beast" is set free for breaking the fetters of morality; when the spirit is its own unqualified measure, Satan, the perverted spirit, is free also, transforming a mere urge for security into a metaphysical lust for power, a mere desire for survival and perpetuation into a mystic yearning for eternal glory gained through terror and destruction.

To recoil from these criminal manifestations is not to free oneself of the roots of the evil. Who does not know the ruthlessness and

---

2. Psychologists may argue that all men are sick. But if this is true to an extent rendering all human responsibility relative, then men can neither heal themselves nor each other, and no one can lay down standards of health and sickness.

hardness of heart that sometimes go with health, or the difficulty of controlling the destructive urges stemming from vitality? And as for man's spiritual life, what of envy masquerading as righteousness, cruelty as justice, selfishness called freedom, avarice called equality? Happily, in most cases, such perversions only partly corrupt the ideal into which they enter; but, tragically, the perversion is only partly conscious, and only partly corrigible. The individual who understands this situation and still has the courage to attempt the realization of a pure and ideal self will do so in profound humility. But this humility, too, if conceived in terms of self-realization, becomes tainted with self-righteousness.

Ultimate integration is inaccessible through self-realization: it is equally inaccessible through religion defined in terms of self-realization. As a historical and psychological phenomenon, religion may, and perhaps even must, be defined in terms of self-realization; but as a way of life claiming to be a *valid* synthesis, it cannot be defined in these terms. Characteristically, liberalism sees no need to distinguish radically between religion considered from the standpoint of history or psychology, and religion considered from the standpoint of its validity. For its whole faith rests on the hypothesis of one normative self, progressively revealed in personal and human history. But once this illusion is destroyed, a religion defined in terms of self-realization is revealed as pure nihilism.

The weakness inherent in a religion defined in terms of self-realization cannot be overcome by merely choosing another aspect or activity of the self as the source of certainty. In Schleiermacher's celebrated definition, religion is held to be "a feeling of unqualified dependence."[3] But "feeling," too, is a kind of self-realization, and a religion defined in such terms suffers from the same weakness. Thus, if "feeling of unqualified dependence" refers to such feelings as are actual, religion will include sacrificial devotion to dictators and charlatans, and blind obedience to nation or race exalted as the manifestation of the Absolute.[4] If, on the other hand, we mean by this "feeling" an emotion men *ought* to have, we either set up arbitrarily someone's actual feeling as absolute standard, or we seek

---

3. F. D. E. Schleiermacher, *Dogmatik,* §36; cf. also *Ueber die Religion* (Leipzig, 1880) , p. 75; *Psychologie* (Berlin, 1862) , p. 461.

4. That Schleiermacher actually came close to such a position is shown by Reinhold Niebuhr, *The Nature and Destiny of Man,* vol. 1 (New York, 1945) , pp. 86 ff.

this standard through the conception of an ideal feeling. But then religion—the actual feeling of unqualified dependence—becomes secondary to the philosophy defining that ideal feeling, and dependent on its fate. Religion is no longer the ultimate source of total integration.

No religion, of course, can dispense with ideas man forms of God. What we are discussing here is the view that holds God to be an idea *only,* or else to be known and relevant only as such. Such God-ideas serve here as an ultimate principle of integration by making an absolute claim on man's allegiance. Now, it is plain that God-ideas have undergone a vast development in the history of civilization, and the claim of the liberal era that this development has the form of inevitable progress toward one fixed aim can hardly be sustained. On what basis, then, does a man give *absolute* allegiance to an idea which is relative to his civilization and to the caprices of his own nature? But let us suppose we could assume that the God-idea is steadily progressing toward absolute purity. If we believe that our God-idea is not altogether pure yet, by what standards do we know how high we have risen in the scale of purity? And by what right do we give *absolute* allegiance to an idea whose degree of relativity we do not know? If, on the other hand, we claim to have reached the final degree of purity in our idea of God, will not a later age smile at our presumptuousness? And again, by what standards do we measure its finality?

But the main objection to the religion of self-realization, however, is not relativism; quite possibly an adequate philosophy of religion could overcome it. Let us assume, therefore, that we could conceive a God-idea sufficiently free from relative admixture to claim our absolute allegiance. This God, who is an idea only, can perhaps persuade and inspire; but He surely cannot succor, love, and forgive. To speak of the succor, love, and forgiveness of a God who is an idea only is to employ a misleading metaphor. There are, of course, those who find their lives totally integrated through divine commandment and inspiration, and who calmly do without succor and forgiveness. But these are people who are caught in the idealist illusion about their nature and power which we have already analyzed. To know of the inextricable togetherness of freedom and bondage which is our state, is to know that no total unity comes from a Good-idea "enthroned on high," but unable to "look down low" (Ps. 113:5–6). While the Absolute Ideal may perhaps inspire to imitation, it at the same time paralyzes because of its very absoluteness. A God, then, who is an idea only, or relevant only as such, still fails to integrate our lives; and *this* failure is more critical than any we have yet considered. Indeed, it is the crucial failure of the religion of self-realization.

If life is to find total integration, we must seek it in a Reality transcending our contradictory self and the ideals and standards relative to it.

II

Though he may perceive the futility of attempting ultimate integration through self-realization, modern man feels that somehow he cannot escape that futility. Religious tradition once believed that it had found access to a Reality transcending the relativity of the self through divine *revelation* or else through *rational proof* of God's existence. Modern man seems to find both these paths closed to him.

Modern man has no reason to doubt the sincerity of those who have taken their own experience or the experience of others to be divine revelation. But his own intellectual conscience compels him to interpret "revelation" in terms of "experience-of-revelation." To him the authority of revelation depends on the authority of human experience.[5] This is still a form of self-realization, afflicted with all the weakness inherent in it. Thus, modern man feels himself confronted with the dilemma between a flight to a supernatural revealed authority which he can no longer accept, on the one hand, and a flight to an authoritativeness of human experience as little acceptable to him, on the other. Morally, this seems to be a dilemma between the sins of intellectual dishonesty and spiritual pride.

Nor does modern man find himself any better off when he tries to establish God's existence by rational proof. He may presuppose that

---

5. We are here concerned only with the naive, uncritical acceptance of revelation and its critical dissolution into humanism. We are, of course, very far from holding that revelation must ultimately be interpreted in terms of experience-of-revelation, and that humanism, rather than supernaturalism, has the last word. Cf. the uthor's article, "Can There Be Judaism Without Revelation?" (*Commentary*, December 1951) , and also his "Schelling's Philosophy of Religion" (*University of Toronto Quarterly*, October 1952) . Schelling was the first, and perhaps the most profound, modern philosopher to be led to supernaturalism by an internal criticism of the idealistic philosophy of experience.

his reason is equipped for the task and that, though it is part of mere relative man, its axioms and laws are those which govern ultimate reality. If so, he presupposes rather than proves the existence of a God who gave him reason so that he might know Him. This kind of faith appears to be implied in the traditional proofs of God. If modern man refuses to make that *a priori* assumption, the certainty of God becomes dependent on the capricious and relative "certainties" acquired by a relative reason; for by these God is to be proven. Such a God is never really certain; he is always a mere hypothesis, living in dependence on precarious certainties. Nor is he really God. It has often been pointed out that a God who is proved without being presupposed in this proof is both too "far" and too "near" to be God: he is too "far" because there is something nearer and more certain by which he is proved; he is too "near" because man's finite reason can pass judgment on him. Again man is faced with a dilemma. To ascertain God's existence by rational proof he must presuppose either a God who fashioned his reason, or the capacity of his reason to prove a God whom he has not fashioned. To attempt rational proof of God in awareness of this situation seems either self-deception or outright insolence.

III

An iron logic, it seems, has led man from a synthesis found in God, to a synthesis found in an autonomous self, to the surrender of all aspiration toward ultimate standards and ultimate meaning. A self revealed as caught in relativity cannot be the source of ultimate integration, nor does it seem able to recover any access to an absolute God. But we should be reluctant to accept this development as inexorable. This would be to dismiss lightly and *in toto* what seemed unquestionable reality to so many religious generations. We must, then, probe a little more deeply into man's ultimate situation. To make this difficult task somewhat easier, let us first try to understand the meaning of God and of life with God as reflected in Biblical and rabbinic tradition. For modernity has unconsciously tended to misinterpret these, in accordance with its own very different ideas.[6]

---

6. In these paragraphs, I do not, of course, attempt to give a complete picture of Biblical and rabbinic views on the subject. Our task here is rather to select such aspects as will clarify the perspective in which Biblical and rabbinic views must be understood. For thorough interpretations, see G. F. Moore, *Judaism,*

The Biblical and rabbinic tradition is pervaded by the conviction that it is impossible to doubt or deny the existence of God.

The modern mind will at once attribute this conviction to philosophical naïveté and the inabilty to deal critically with evidence. But this notion hardly goes beyond the surface. It is true, of course, that the evidence presented for divine revelation is not examined as critically as it might be. Nature is too simply taken as evidence of a God who guides it. History is too naively assumed to prove divine retribution. The certainty stemming from personal experience is not subjected to adequate criticism. But, this kind of naive acceptance of evidence is only incidental to the certainty of the existence of God. For it is realized that the evidence frequently fails. Nature harbors evil as well as good. Human nature appears afflicted with shortcomings such as cannot be attributed to man's own fault. History, above all, shows conditions which impel a Jeremiah to contend: "Wherefore doth the way of the wicked prosper? Wherefore are all they secure that deal very treacherously?" (Jer. 12:1), and a rabbi must admit: "It is not in our power to explain either the prosperity of the wicked or the afflictions of the righteous."[7] "Times of wrath" occur, when "all people cry and weep, but their voice is not heard, even though they decree fast-days, roll themselves in dust, cover themselves with sackcloth and shed tears."[8] And often man finds no evidence in his heart of the presence of God.

But while the evidence can become doubtful, God cannot. If nature reveals evil, then God "form[s] light and create[s] darkness, make[s] peace and create[s] evil" (Isa. 45:7). The fact that men cannot see divine purpose evidenced in history merely proves that: "My thoughts are not your thoughts, neither are My ways your ways" (Isa. 55:8). If inner experience is dead, it is because God "hides His face" (Ps. 13:2; 44:35; 69:18), "stands off" (Ps. 10:1), "forgets" (Ps. 13:2), "forsakes" (Ps. 22:2), or "sleeps" (Ps. 44:24); but the failure of inner evidence never suggests that God does not exist. Even the great skeptic of the Bible, Kohelet, who regards life as a

vol. 1 (Cambridge, 1927), pp. 357 ff.; also S. Schechter, *Some Aspects of Rabbinic Theology* (London, 1909), pp. 21 ff.

7. M. Abot 4.19. We follow the interpretation of J. Hertz, *Pirke Aboth* (New York, 1945), p. 77. The sentiment here expressed is, of course, unusual in rabbinic theology.

8. Tosefta Derek Eretz, Perek Haminim, 31 (*The Treatise Derek Eretz,* ed. by M. Higger [New York, 1935], text pp. 293 ff., translation pp. 110 ff.).

whole as vanity, concludes from this conviction: "This is the end of the matter, all having been heard: fear God, and keep His commandments; for this is the whole man" (Eccl. 12:13). No objective evidence to the contrary, and no feeling of being deserted, can affect the certainty of God. As Job puts it: "Though He slay me, yet will I trust in Him" (Job 13:15).

We cannot fairly dismiss this absolute and fact-denying certainty of God as the mental habit of a religious civilization. How then can we understand it? We shall be totally unable to do so unless we rid ourselves of the modern prejudice that all religious life is an evolution of religious *feelings* or *ideas*. In accordance with this prejudice, man forms notions of God with the assistance of external and internal evidence, and the more he becomes conscious of this activity of his, the more thoroughly does he arrive at a state of objective detachment in which he judges the merits of the God-idea, and weighs the evidence for the existence of God. However, when in Jewish tradition God's existence is nowhere doubted nor made dependent on evidence, this is not because man is here at too primitive a level to have reached the stage of objective and critical detachment; it is because of a profound certainty that such a detachment is impossible. *God's existence is man's existential a priori.*

> Whither shall I go from Thy spirit?
> Or whither shall I flee from Thy presence?
> If I ascend up into heaven, Thou art there;
> If I make my bed in the netherworld, behold, Thou art there.
> If I take the wings of the morning,
> And dwell in the uttermost parts of the sea;
> Even there would Thy hand lead me,
> And Thy right hand would hold me (Ps. 139:7–10).[9]

This is not a rather primitive and unscientific statement of a universal God-idea. From a God-idea one could "flee" at least to the extent of viewing it in an attitude of objective detachment. The God of the Bible is not an ultimate object; He is *the* Subject, each man's living, personal God. Any attempt to subject God's existence to critical judgment is, therefore, held to be insolence, because it means to judge the Judge. To deny His existence is more than insolence: it is "folly" (Ps. 14:1; 53:2), since it is the rejection by

---

9. For Biblical literature, cf. especially the Book of Jonah; for rabbinic literature, passages quoted by Newman-Spitzer, *The Talmudic Anthology* (New York, 1945), pp. 163 ff.

man of his own "light and salvation" (Ps. 27:1) ; it is rebellion, since it is the attempt to replace God's authority by man's (Ps. 10:4; also Ezek. 28:9). The denial of God is self-destruction or rebellion; it is never merely an erroneous objective statement. In his ultimate relation to Reality, man must be *participant;* he cannot remain *spectator.*

Attempts to describe the nature of this God in Biblical and rabbinic tradition must be understood as part of this fundamental situation. The avowed task here is not to describe consistently and adequately an infinite God as He is in Himself, a task that could be undertaken only by an objective spectator. The task is to describe the living relation between this infinite God and finite man, and to do so as an inevitable participant.

God is infinite and yet directly related to each finite person. This is the inexplicable, yet indubitable, basic fact about God. He is "enthroned on high and looketh down low" (Ps. 113:5–6). He is both "far and near":

> God is far, for is He not in the heaven of heavens? And yet He is near . . . for a man enters a synagogue, and stands behind a pillar, and prays in a whisper, and God hears his prayer, and so it is with all His creatures. He is as near to His creatures as the ear to the mouth.[10]

The direct relation between the infinite God and the finite human person is by its very nature paradoxical. If this relation were one-sided, it would destroy itself; for then the infinite God would devour the finite person's freedom and his very identity. It is a mutual relation. "Everything is in the hands of Heaven except the fear of Heaven,"[11] is the word of a rabbi to whom human freedom is real yet limited by Divine Presence. But if this relation is a mutual one, then paradoxically the free actions and reactions of finite men make a difference to the infinite God. Biblical and rabbinic tradition express the reality of this paradoxical relation in a well-nigh infinite variety of metaphors. These metaphors, which are mostly anthropomorphisms, cannot be regarded as "impure" philosophical notions; they are *symbolic* terms designed to describe a relation which cannot be grasped in any terms other than symbolic. Occasionally the rabbis are fully conscious of this, espe-

---

10. J. Berak, ix.l, 13a, line 17. In this and many other subsequent quotations, I have followed the translation of Montefiore and Loewe, *A Rabbinic Anthology* (London, 1938).

11. B. Berak. 33b.

cially when in their stress on human responsibility they even make
the omnipotent God dependent on impotent man.

> *Ye are My witnesses, saith the Lord, and I am God* (Isa. 43:12). That
> is, when ye are My witnesses, I am God, and when ye are not My wit-
> nesses, I am, as it were, not God.[12]
> When the Israelites do God's will, they add to the power of God on
> high. When the Israelites do not do God's will, they, as it were, weaken
> the great power of God.[13]

The paradox in these statements is fully intended, and the term
"as it were" has the full rank of a technical term in rabbinic
theology, indicating the symbolic character of the statement it
qualifies.[14]

God's nature, as revealed in His relation to man, reflects the
paradox inherent in this relation. In rabbinic theology, the concepts of divine *justice* and divine *mercy* are striking in their
prominence.[15] Philosophically, absolute justice and absolute mercy
are mutually exclusive; but in rabbinic theology, they remain
mutually irreducible. God's mercy, to the exclusion of His justice,
would wipe out the difference between the righteous and the
wicked. His justice, without His mercy, would destroy all men; and
even if it be conceived that God tempers His justice to finite man,
"demanding according to man's power," infinite divine retribution
would still be totally incommensurable with finite human sin.

The Lord made heaven and earth. This may be compared to a
king who had some empty glasses. Said the king: "If I pour hot
water into them, they will burst; if cold, they will contract and
snap." What then did the king do? He mixed hot and cold water
and poured it into them, and so they remained unbroken. Even so,
said the Holy One, blessed be He: "If I create the world on the
basis of mercy alone, its sins will be great; on the basis of justice

---

12. Midr. Ps. on Ps. 123:1.

13. Lam. R. I, 33, on Lam. 1:6.

14. This is expressed with particular clarity in this passage: "R. Simeon b.
Yohai said: . . . 'Only when Israel does God's will is His heavenly palace secure.'
. . . Nevertheless, R. Simeon b. Yohai also quoted, 'This is my Lord and I will
praise Him' (Ex. 15:2), and he said: 'When I praise Him, He is glorified, and
when I do not praise Him, He is, *as it were*, glorified in himself'" (Sifre Deut.,
Berakah, 346, 144a).

15. It is, of course, well known that the rabbis interpreted the biblical *Elohim*
as referring to the divine attribute of justice, and *YHWH* to that of mercy; cf.,
e.g., Pesikta (ed. Buber), 164a.

alone, the world cannot exist. Hence I will create it on the basis of justice and mercy, and may it then stand."[16]

This togetherness of justice and mercy is not a harmonious compromise. In a mutual limitation through compromise, both justice and mercy would lose their meaning. Thus R. Akiba insists on the absolute and unqualified justice of God's judgment,[17] and in the Midrash God is made to say: "All I do, I do in justice. If I sought to pass beyond justice, but once, the world could not endure."[18]

Consequently, men are warned not to make light of their responsibility before the bar of divine justice:

He who says, God is indulgent, his life shall be outlawed.[19]

If the evil inclination says to you, "Sin, and God will forgive you," believe it not.[20]

But on the other hand, divine mercy is likewise absolute and unqualified. For whatever their relative merits, before God all men need mercy absolutely. Even Moses and David asked that their sins be forgiven, by reason not of their merits, but of God's grace.[21] Nor did they pray thus only because of their humility. "All men need grace, including Abraham, for whose sake grace came plenteously into the world."[22]

The Midrash expresses the principle of mercy: "He said, 'I owe no creature anything, but I give to them gratuitously.' "[23]

Justice and mercy coexist:

"If we have merit, and if we possess good deeds, He gives us of what is ours; if not, then He acts charitably and lovingly toward us from what is His."[24]

---

16. Gen. R. XII, 15. Cf., among numerous similar passages, the following: "Abraham said unto God, 'If thou desirest to maintain the world, strict justice is impossible; and if thou desirest strict justice, the world cannot be maintained. . . . Thou desirest the world and thou desirest justice. Take one or the other. Unless thou art a little indulgent, the world cannot endure' " (Gen. R. XXXIX, 6) ; cf. also Lev. R. X, 1.

17. Tanhuma (ed. Buber) , Wayera, 49a.

18. Tanhuma (ed. Buber) , Mishpatim, 41b.

19. B. Baba K. 50a; cf. also J. Shek. v. 2, 48d, line 35.

20. B. Hag. 16a.

21. Sifre Deut., Waethanan, 26, 70b. The whole of Israel is represented as making the same request (Midr. Ps. on Ps. 71:2) .

22. Gen. R., Hayye Sarah, LX, 2.

23. Tanhuma B., Deut., Waethanan, 5a.

24. Midr. Ps. on Ps. 72:1.

But do not then both justice and mercy become meaningless? They may become so in philosophical theory, but not in the religious life. The ultimate unity of mercy and justice in God is, indeed, an ineffable mystery.[25] Man not only can but must live in the double certainty of his responsibility before the bar of divine justice and of his security in divine mercy. For radically speaking, man can, and cannot, do the will of God. In so far as he can do His will, it is only by reason of God's help;[26] yet in so far as he cannot do it, his contrition is a spontaneous and acceptable offering.[27] Man must pray, not only for forgiveness of sins already committed, but also for divine help against future temptations.[28] Yet a man who acts has full freedom, and no sin is preordained.[29]

The sins of the past, of which no man is free, do not destroy the freedom of present and future. For man is at all times free to repent, whatever the sins of the past.[30] In contrast with the gates of prayer which, tragically, are often closed, the gates of repentance are always open.[31] But again, even for the ability to repent man must pray for divine assistance.[32]

Thus the religious life is a tension between two certainties: re-

---

25. This is indicated in Midr. Ps. on Ps. 72:1.

26. Cf., e.g., Deut. R., Nitztzabim, VIII, 6: "The law and all the implements by which it is carried out have been given, namely, modesty, beneficence, uprightness, and reward."

27. Cf., e.g., Pes. K. 158b: "If a mortal man uses broken vessels, it is a disgrace, but with God it is otherwise, for all His servants are broken vessels, as it is said, 'The Lord is nigh unto the brokenhearted and the contrite in spirit he will save' (Ps. 34:18)."

28. Cf. Raba's prayer: "O Lord! Before I was formed, I was without worth; and even now, having been formed, I am as if I had not been formed. Dust I am in my life; how much more at my death! Behold, I am before Thee a vessel of shame and disgrace. May it be Thy will, O Lord my God, that I do not sin; but the sins which I have already committed before Thee, wash them away with Thy great mercy, but not through tribulations and diseases" (B. Berak. 17a); cf. also B. Yoma 87b.

29. In Lev. R. Metzora, XVIII, 1, God is represented as demanding of man that he return his soul to God in the same state of purity in which it was given to him.

30. "If your sins are as nigh as heaven, even unto the seventh heaven, and even unto the throne of glory, and you repent, I will receive you" (Pes. R. 185a); cf. also Pes. K. 163b; Midr. Ps. on Ps. 120:7.

31. Lam. R., III, 60, on Lam. 3:43.

32. Cf. J. Berak. vi. 2, 7d, line 46: "May it be Thy will, O Lord our God and God of our fathers, that Thou put it into our hearts to perform a perfect repentance before Thee. . . ."

sponsibility before God, and safety in Him. There is no *a priori* limitation to either of these.

The Israelites say to God, "Lord of the world, thou knowest how hard is the strength of the evil inclination." God says, "Remove it a little in this world, and I will rid you of it altogether in the world-to-come."[33]

How much is "a little"? That cannot be known. That is why man must both tremble and rejoice: he trembles because, before the throne of divine justice, what he does is nothing compared with what he ought to do; he rejoices because, nevertheless, it is something, and because through the mercy of God it is everything. Therefore it has been said: "Love and fear God; tremble and rejoice when you perform the commandments."[34]

IV

Guided by the insights of Biblical and rabbinic tradition, we may penetrate the problem of man's ultimate integration sufficiently to grasp this basic fact: the way in which modern man has arrived at the situation we have tried to describe is not, as he has habitually assumed, necessary and unequestionable; on the contrary, it is rather founded on subjective and dubious assumptions. Modern man has dogmatically assumed the same approach in his search for ultimate integration as he has adopted in his scientific inquiries—an attitude of objective, critical detachment.

This attitude is quite proper in the case of scientific inquiry, because scientific inquiry deals with the realm of *objects*. We know objects by detaching ourselves from involvement in them, and by simultaneously subjecting them to our critical judgment. The exercise of autonomous judgment is possible because man is, in principle, able to view the world as object. It is necessary because he requires objectivity to plan both his biological and his moral life.

However, if modern man claims objective detachment and the autonomy of his critical judgment to be basic to the problem of his ultimate integration, he commits a plain fallacy. For man's *existence* cannot become an object for him, neither can he assume toward it an attitude of objectivity, detachment, and autonomy. While he thinks in "detachment," he is in fact involved in ex-

---

33. Num. R., Behaaloteka, XV, 16.
34. Ab. R.N. (vers. I) , XLI, 67a.

istence. Thus, an attitude of objective detachment and objective judgment toward the problem of ultimate integration is a form of self-deception, due to our inability to free ourselves from the habits we form in relation to the world of objects. Or it is a hidden dogma, a subjective decision taken in relation to his own existence. In the very act of assuming an attitude of detachment, and of subjecting it to his autonomous judgment, man is already deciding to be his own judge and the master of his own life. Little wonder that the results at which he arrives on this basis confirm the hidden initial dogma.

In the same manner, we must consider the question of God's existence. If there is a God, and if He is *God*, He embraces man's existence with such totality as to make objective detachment altogether impossible. If a man can pass judgment on God and His existence, it is not God on whom he passes judgment. A God who can be an *object* is not God. Because a God who is subjected to man's objective judgment is not God, *God can neither be proven nor disproven*. If God is God, He is not an object, but *the* Subject. He is man's absolute existential *a priori*.

Insight into the impossibility of assuming an attitude of detachment and autonomous judgment would, in itself, lead merely to an infinite suspension of judgment. But if man becomes fully aware of his position, he realizes, too, that he must go further. For he cannot remain neutral here. Thought can be suspended, but not existence. Suspension of judgment itself is here an impermissible judgment. Man exists by compulsion; he is, therefore, compelled to make a *decision*. For to refuse to make a decision is also to decide.

Thus, because man cannot detach himself from his existence, he is compelled to meet it with decision. And if he is in search of ultimate integration, he must seek it in ultimate decision. Ultimate decision must be made in the perspective constituting his existence: the togetherness of, and conflict between, dependence and transcendence, and the inherent necessity to integrate these into ultimate unity.

What, basically, are the choices possible in this situation?

Man can make an effort to recover the blissful pagan ignorance which he has lost. He can tell himself that his transcendence is reducible to his dependence or his dependence to his transcendence; that his responsibility is merely the function of his needs, or that it can easily rule them. But as we have seen, history sooner or later shocks man out of such ignorance or self-deception.

Man can face his conflict but belittle the need for its ultimate integration. He may claim to be satisfied with transforming his one problem into many problems, and with solving these merely pragmatically. But he transcends the relativity of his life sufficiently to remain profoundly disturbed by a wholly relative existence.

Man can face his conflict and accept it as inexorable fate, realizing that ultimate integration cannot come through himself, and deciding to live in that knowledge. This is tragic existence. For if he lives his unreconciled conflict absolutely, his vitality and his search for happiness become tragic futility, his responsibility and sacrifice become tragic quixotism.

Man can, and in this situation often will, rise in rebellion. Aware of the inexorability of the conflict, he may yet strive to transcend it and to become his own measure. But this is the counsel of despair; it makes man say: "I shall persist in utter metaphysical defiance, infinitely lonely, supported only by my moral insight. I shall offer absolute resistance to the ultimate principle and shall despise it."[35]

Were man's weakness only biological, he might well take this heroic attitude. He might despise pain, unhappiness, and death because of the autonomy of his moral insight. But his weakness is not only biological; it is also spiritual, because it is spiritually that he is sinful. Therefore, this attempt at self-redemption amounts to rebellion, and is tragically futile.

But man can make yet another decision, the decision of faith. He can submit to God as his existential *a priori;* he can accept the "yoke of the Kingdom of Heaven."

V

The decision of faith differs from other decisions as radically as these do from objective detachment. Decision stems from the insight that existence is inescapable. The decision of faith stems from the insight that God is inescapable. Man surrenders his neutrality in the realization that he cannot be neutral; he surrenders authority over his existence in the realization that he cannot be his own authority. In the state of existential decision, he knows that he cannot refute God; in the decision of faith, he knows that he cannot reject or escape Him. He knows that whatever he decides, he is

---

35. One of Dostoevsky's formulations of the nihilistic point of view, quoted by E. Frank, *Philosophical Understanding and Religious Faith* (New York, 1945), p. 38.

under the authority of God: Nebuchadnezzar does the will of God
as fully as do Moses or David. Indeed, the very agony in which man
tries to reject God, testifies to Him. And in rebellion, man harms
not God, but himself.

We must understand clearly the specific nature of the decision of
faith. A modern writer properly warns: "If we believe in . . . a
. . . God not because He is the truth, but assume His truth only
because we believe in Him, then there are as many gods and as
many truths and values as there are beliefs."[36]

If the decision of faith is on the same level as other possible
decisions, man makes God's sovereignty or even His existence
depend on his belief in, or acceptance of, Him. This is the final
heresy. The distinctive nature of the decision of faith is that it is at
the same time no decision at all, because in accepting God's sovereignty man realizes that he accepts that to which he is subject
regardless of his decision.

We are here at the crucial point in man's religious situation.
Before he makes the decision of faith, he is free not to make it. He
may thereby lose all hope of ultimate integration; he may live a life
of self-contradiction; he may arrive at self-destruction: all the same,
he is free not to accept the "yoke of the Kingdom of Heaven." *After*
the decision of faith, there is no freedom to reject God; there is
merely freedom to rebel against Him. But in rebellion as well as in
submission, man now testifies to God. Even the nonbeliever testifies
to Him, through his tragic ignorance.

Here, then, we have the fundamental tension in the religious life:
the decision of faith in which man expresses the irrelevance of all
his deciding to the sovereignty of God is, nevertheless, the greatest
of all decisions. Total submission to God is not only the ultimate in
humility; it is also the extreme in self-confidence: "Everything is in
the hands of Heaven except the fear of Heaven."[37] If God exists,
He is the *absolute existential a priori;* yet man dares to leap from a
position in which he is free not to accept Him to total acceptance of
His sovereignty. Whence this momentous audacity?

Man finds the grounds for both his humility and his self-confidence in himself. He is in a state of dependence; yet he transcends it
in that he knows it. It is because he knows of his sin that he cannot
escape his obligation. Sin would not be sin if man could not know

36. *Ibid.*, p. 42.
37. B. Berak. 33b.

of it. Knowing it, he must face the responsibility to combat it. What is man's ultimate attitude to be? If humility leads him to surrender his obligation, he escapes from what he knows to be his responsibility. If awareness of his responsibility leads him to battle his weakness entirely by himself, he becomes involved in sinful pride.

From this contradictory situation the decision of faith derives both its audacity and its humility, which become an ineffable unity. Realizing the audacity implied in the decision of faith, man knows that to let his humility destroy *this* audacity is to escape from his responsibility. If there is a God, He does not wipe out man's responsibility; He makes it inescapable. He is each man's own personal God—"near," not "far."

But, all the same, man could not venture the decision of faith were it not for the fact that this daring is at the same time no daring at all, and that, therefore, man's supreme self-confidence is at the same time his supreme humility. For if there is a God, man's total dependence on Him includes both his dependence and his transcendence, both his acceptance and his rejection of Him. Man's faith, his own *decision,* is then at the same time *given.* Revelation, which becomes revelation only through man's decision to accept it as such, is then at the same time absolutely given, because God's sovereignty includes man's decision. For if there is a God, He is the sovereign of each man's personal destiny—"near," not "far."

The decision of faith, then, is the only decision which man can make without qualification. To accept the yoke of the Kingdom of Heaven is the only ultimate integration man can realize, because here it is not he alone who realizes it. But this ultimate integration does not imply an infallible security. On the contrary, because it transcends all evidence, proofs, and refutations, faith is the greatest of all risks. Even the ancients, who felt so secure in their faith, sensed this. "Even though He slay me, yet will I trust in Him," are the words of Job. The Mishnah says: " 'Thou shalt love the Lord thy God with . . . all thy soul' (Deut. 6:5),—that is to say, even if He takes thy soul from thee."[38]

Modern man knows that the risk is vastly greater even than this. For he understands what the ancients in their faith were not always conscious of: the position of man before the decision of faith. In a paradoxical paraphrase of the passage of the Mishnah, modern man

---

38. M. Berak. 9.5.

might tell himself: " 'Thou shalt love the Lord thy God with . . . all thy soul'—that is to say: thou shalt love absolutely Him of whom thou hast certainty only by reason of thy love. And thou shalt rejoice in this thy unique opportunity for absolute love."

VI

"A man must first take upon himself the yoke of the Kingdom of Heaven, and then take upon himself the yoke of the command-ments."[39] To accept direct and absolute responsibility is to the man facing God—the decision of faith having been made—not only a possibility, but a necessity.

Before God, man becomes free. For at last, he is redeemed from his tragic dilemma. No longer must he accept his responsibility with an implicit claim to moral autonomy—obvious presumptuousness, in the light of his confused insight and sinful actions—or live in an action-paralyzing humility which betrays his responsibility. To accept total responsibility is now no longer an act vitiated by hidden pride or self-assertion: it is a glorification of God. For it is God who "gave the Law," and along with it "all the implements by which it is carried out."[40] It is His grace which makes Him "demand according to *our* power"[41]—a power which stems from Him. The self-confidence required for the assumption of responsibility is here identical with total humility. Of course, there is still, as there always is, danger of self-perversion through sinful pride; but man may risk this danger now for the sake of God.

Man's *decision for* responsibility is here redeemed from its in-herent enigma; his *life in* responsibility is freed from the stifling influence of human failure. Environment, which often reveals indi-viduals and their consciences as products rather than agents, be-devils their sense of responsibility. Tantalizing evidence of so-called inexorable waves of the future saps the strength of conscience. But such spells have no power over the man who lives before God. For he knows that, fundamentally, he finds his law not in looking forward, but in looking upward. And he knows: "It is not given in thy hand to complete the work, but thou art not free to desist from it."[42]

---

39. M. Berak. 2.2.
40. Deut. R., Nitztzabim, VIII, 6.
41. Num. R., Pinehas, XXI, 22.
42. M. Abot. 2:21.

Even more dangerous to life in responsibility is the failure of the individual himself. Nothing ordinarily threatens a man's sense of responsibility more than the seeming inevitability of failure and defeat. But upon the individual living before God the effect is very different. For the tension between ideal responsibility and actual sinfulness becomes a source of ever-renewed spiritual energy, drawn from the certainty that through the mercy of God the discrepancy is not after all catastrophic.

To the man who lives before God the *possibility* of taking upon himself the "yoke of the commandments" is a *necessity*. God is man's own, personal God: he cannot elude or escape Him; he is personally responsible to Him; he cannot evade the directness of this claim by seeking shelter in "circumstances"—at least in principle he is always responsible. Nor can he escape it through referring to his own past habits: the doors of repentance are always open.

But how can man know the commandments of God so that he may do them? What is it that he is to do? The man who lives under the "yoke of the Kingdom of Heaven" need never be in a state of total ignorance. His knowledge of himself before God involves solid principles of social conduct. If men are directly responsible, then they possess a dignity requiring that they never treat one another "as means only."[43] If God makes men responsible, this requirement is the law of God.

But man can never hope to possess the law of God in a set of general norms to which he need only subordinate his individuality. Even in the realm of social conduct, the need for its application involves a leap from the security of the general norm into hazardous individual decision. And the individual's responsibility before God is not confined to the realm of social conduct. How then is man to gain knowledge? Is he to determine the law of God in his heart? Is not "the heart . . . deceitful above all things, and exceedingly weak" (Jer. 17:9) ? In this conflict man turns to God, calling upon Him to be his God *here and now,* even as he himself must be His servant here and now. His general fate and freedom are given to him by God in His "farness"; he now calls upon God's "nearness" to give him specific guidance. "Give me understanding that I may keep Thy law" (Ps. 119:34) . "Teach me Thy statutes" (Ps. 119:26) .

---

43. Cf. Immanuel Kant's celebrated dictum.

Sometimes, his plea is answered. Sometimes, he can say: "Thy word is a lamp unto my feet, and a light unto my path" (Ps. 119:105). But sometimes, too, he learns the law of God only in his affliction, and at other times no answer comes at all. For God hides His face and answers not.

This is tragic affliction: man's life as a whole is in God's hands, but he does not know its meaning here and now; he has accepted the "yoke of the commandments," but he is not told the unique laws which pertain to his unique situation. Yet even this affliction need not be catastrophic. If God is not "near," He is at least "far." Where God fails to speak, man both can and must dare attempt to fathom His law. He *must* do so because of his responsibility before God's judgment. He *can* do so because of the ultimate security of all he does and plans in God's mercy.

VII

"Do His will as if it were thy will, and He will do thy will as if it were His will."[44] Man cannot ultimately make himself the measure of his life. "Self-realization" cannot be his standard of ultimate integration; rather must he surrender his self to the "yoke of the Kingdom of God" and to the "yoke of His commandments." But strangely, he who thus loses his self gains it; he who surrenders the aim of self-realization to God arrives at the fullness of self-realization.

To accept the law of God is to accept the limitations of human existence. For this law is given to *men;* it is given neither to angels, who have no natural urges, nor to animals, who do not possess the direct responsibility of freedom. Therefore, to accept the law of God is neither to mortify vitality nor to stupefy moral responsibility; it is to find redemptive reconciliation between the joy of living and the burden of responsibility.

Once, when he had caught a glimpse of the radical contradictions inherent in his condition, man's vitality was paralyzed. The joy of his every breath was withered by an inescapable sense of guilt. For while he enjoyed even a single breath of life, he knew that others were crying to heaven in mortal pain. To give his joy precarious survival, he had to try to escape from his moral self. But now it is different. Having surrendered to God's commandment his self-asser-

---

44. M. Abot. 2.4.

tive joy of living, he receives it back as a gift from God. Accepting humbly God's law to men, he accepts as part of it the life of nature. What was before egoistic self-assertion set up against duty is now glorification of God through acceptance of the human lot. At least in principle, man's vital and moral selves have found reconciliation.

In the last analysis, to attempt ultimate integration through self-realization is to attempt to escape human nature. In seeking unity in himself in spite of the contradictions inherent within him, man cannot but strive to become either an angel or a beast. Both of these attempts end in a hopeless loss of self. Man finds his self only when he surrenders himself to God, because thus only does he come to accept the contradictions of his state. He no longer runs away from, but lives, his human existence. He can live thus, and do so serenely, because of his confidence that ultimately all contradictions rest in the mercy and justice of God.

Man continues to live in pain and anguish. He continues to be troubled by the question of where the expression of his vitality begins to conflict with his moral responsibility. But after his humble and serene acceptance of his human lot as a whole, this question is no longer paralyzing, this conflict no longer catastrophic. And even his pain and anguish are now a praise of God.[45]

---

45. M. Berak. 9.5.

JEWISH EXISTENCE AND THE LIVING GOD

Emil L. Fackenheim

The perduration of the Jew is a mystery to others and surely to the Jew. If the survival of the Jew has baffled the Church Fathers and traditional Christian theologians, that is no mystery, for Christian doctrine, early in its history, required that Israel wither and the Jewish people be assimilated by the mystical body of the Church. But that the Jewish people should have endured its secular history, outlived its persecutors, survived coherently and meaningfully despite the onslaughts of Western history is inconceivable on merely natural grounds. Pascal wondered at this and recognized as did many other thinkers that the survival of the Jew is a divine fact, a corrective to the apocalyptic enthusiasts of the Church who would have had Israel and its people perish as part of the divine economy of Christendom and an instruction to the nations, in that this people though enjoying similarities to the nations was dissimilar from them in having as its sovereign and king a God who was as well sovereign and king over all men.

The survival of the Jew in so far as the Jew, not the Gentile, is concerned cannot be accounted for by any psychology of defensive response to tyranny and murderous persecution, nor by the fact that Jews love their tradition or feel for each other, nor by any biogenetic postulations of mysterious blood-feeling. None of these possibilities nor any others more exalted and intellectualist suffice, for of other peoples who have not endured it may be said that they were persecuted and perished and that they loved their culture, their history, and their nation and have long since disappeared. In raising the question of Jewish survival as a primary question of Jewish religious existence, Emil Fackenheim points the way toward a primary starting point for theological inquiry. Jewish existence is a historical fact and may be regarded simply as an absurd sport of history. But that leaves us nowhere. We will have gained nothing by our endurance nor would we have lost anything had we capitulated. What must be understood, therefore, in any discussion of Jewish existence and survival is the grand vision of origins and ends which overarch the Jewish people. It is not that the Jews are better or superior (for chosenness as Fackenheim implies and as Will Herberg will make clear in his essay on "The 'Chosenness' of Israel and the Jews of Today"), but rather that they are in the grasp of an abnormal obligation: the commitment to the God who brought them into being and to the experience of whom their life testifies. The covenant between God and the Jews was not made, Fackenheim underscores, with individuals but between God and the people. In fact, only in the experience of sealing the covenant did God create the people. The people have no choice but to endure. Individuals may elect to leave or to rejoin, but the people as such have no right to perish. Of course Fackenheim presupposes throughout this essay the essential point: that God exists, that God reveals, that God has purposes. The individual is free—more free than ever before in this post-Holocaust time—to deny that God exists, reveals, or purposes fulfillment. He can deny him, however much he cannot refute him; but the people cannot deny him ever, for their reality is his. Individual Jews may not exist nor survive, but *Am Yisrael hai olam.*

JEWISH EXISTENCE
AND THE LIVING GOD

The Religious Duty of Survival

EMIL L. FACKENHEIM

The modern Jew is an enigma to himself. When he reflects on his existence as a Jew, he cannot but be filled with wonder. Other individuals and peoples may wonder how they have come to be what they are; the Jew must wonder why he should exist at all. For if there are laws of historical change, the Jew should, according to these laws, have disappeared long ago. Was there ever another people which continued to exist, under like circumstances, through the centuries? The answer is that there was not. Other people require the bond of a common land, or a common language, or a common culture in order to continue in existence. The Jew, for long centuries, has had none of these. Consequently, self-appointed experts in the laws of historical change have been ever quick to predict his impending disappearance. But thus far at least these prophecies have always been confounded. The Jew still exists—a source of wonder both to others and himself.

How is one to account for the continued existence of the Jew? Certainly not in terms of persecution or discrimination. It is true that such forms of hostility may unite their victims, creating in them a group will to survive. They may cling defiantly to the very trait which singles them out for penalty. But they may also do the very opposite, that is, try to get rid of the fatal trait. In the case of the Jew, unlike that of the Negro, this is not impossible. Furthermore, persecution, while frequent, has by no means been constant in Jewish history. There were long periods in which the Jew was invited to participate in the life that surrounded him; and he never showed any lack of eagerness to accept this invitation. The conclusion, then, is clear: it is impossible to account for Jewish survival in such negative terms as persecution or discrimination.

Nor do we fare much better with such positive terms as "love of tradition" or "loyalty feelings to the group." To be sure, tradition had a strong hold on the Western Jew until the beginning of the nineteenth century, and on his East European brother until the beginning of the twentieth. But this tradition was, for the most part, not static, fossilized, inert; it was fluid. Also, it was frequently exposed to the threat of disintegration. Yet it did not disintegrate; rather, it preserved itself. Why should Jewish tradition have preserved itself rather than disintegrated? To ask this question is to ask the question of Jewish survival all over again. In short, "love of tradition" does not explain Jewish survival; it is an aspect of the very thing in question.

Precisely the same is true of loyalty feelings to the group. No doubt such feelings are, in some periods of history, a powerful force for cohesion and survival. But in the case of the Jew the question is why there should have been such feelings at all among a people which had, for long centuries neither shared a common land, nor a common language, nor a common external destiny. In the case of Jewish survival, then, "national feeling" or "group loyalty" are not explanations, but again part of the very thing to be explained.

But perhaps collective feelings can exist and survive independently of the experiences which nourish them? Perhaps there are entities such as a "racial will" which are passed on through the blood? We need not waste our time on such fictions. For they exist only in the minds of the demagogues and charlatans of our century.

It becomes abundantly clear, then, that to account for Jewish survival is possible only in terms of the Jewish faith. All the other supposed causes of Jewish survival, such as tradition or feelings of group loyalty, can themselves be explained only in terms of the Jewish faith. It is because of the Jewish faith that the Jew still exists—as we have said, a source of wonder both to others and himself.

This fact places the Jew of our time in a unique position. Like everyone else in the world of today, he is prey to religious doubt. Like everyone else, he is unsure whether, and if so to what extent, he can accept the faith which was handed down to him. But unlike everyone else, he must admit that it is because of that faith that he exists at all.

In current usage, the term "faith" all too often signifies a mere milk-and-water assent to abstract "tenets" and "principles" which are, as a rule, nice, innocuous, and uncontroversial. This is not the kind of faith which can move mountains, or which could be responsible for Jewish survival. The term "faith," when applied to the Jewish past, signifies total commitment. And the commitment was either to an all-consuming experience in the present, or else to memories of such experiences which had taken place in the past.

Whatever one may think of the Biblical account of Jewish origins —whether one takes it to be literally true or merely mythological— two facts are beyond doubt: first, even if the Biblical account is merely mythological, there is an element in it which is true; second, countless generations of Jews accepted it as true. The first fact concerns the faith of the Biblical, the second that of the post-Biblical Jew. The first fact serves to explain how the Jewish people was born; the second, why it survived. The Jew of today must contemplate both these facts: if not in order to learn what, as a Jew, he ought to be, at least in order to understand what, as a Jew, he is.

II

It is possible to doubt that Abraham, or even Moses, ever existed. One may advance the hypothesis that Israel never stood at Mount Sinai, and that, consequently, the unique divine revelation by which Israel supposedly was constituted never took place. But it is not possible to doubt that the Biblical account of Jewish origins, however mythological, reflects something which did take place. What took place was a succession of overwhelming religious experiences. The presence of the Nameless was felt in experiences which were themselves nameless.

As such, these experiences were not specifically Jewish. To experience the presence of the Nameless is the core, not merely of Jewish, but of all religious life. What distinguishes forms of religious life is the way in which the Nameless, and the nameless experience, are interpreted.

There are, to be sure, some varieties of mysticism in which all interpretation is rejected. The Nameless, and the nameless experience, both remain nameless. They remain, consequently, utterly divorced from all that is familiar and named. And all existence becomes a striving for an end which, if achieved, transcends all understanding and all utterance.

This, however, is the exception rather than the rule in the religious life of man. The rule is that the Nameless, and the nameless experience, at once relate themselves to something familiar and nameable. In virtue of this relation, they are themselves given names. Thus a religion comes into being.

In the primeval Hebrew experience, there was such an immediate relating of the Nameless to something familiar. But the familiar in this case was not, as it was so often, a part of nature or nature as a whole; nor did the nameless experience utter itself, in this case, in nature-symbols and thus give rise to a form of life which consists in ritualistic imitation of the rhythms of nature. In the primeval Hebrew experience, any attempt at a direct relating of the Nameless to nature was explicitly repudiated. The familiar and nameable which here received religious significance was not nature but human action.

But the nameless experience was not action. It had to interpret itself as a *call* to action. And this call could not be a call unless it was "heard." Nor could there be a "hearing" unless there was a "speaking." The Nameless interpreted itself as a "speaking," and the nameless experience as "hearing." What was heard was a commandment and a promise: the call to action, and the consequences which followed if the call was heeded. Thus in the primeval Hebrew experience, the presence of the Nameless manifested itself in the form of a divine human covenant.

It must be noted, however, that this experience was not, or at least not primarily, an individual experience. It was a collective experience. It, therefore, manifested itself, not in a covenant between the Nameless and individuals, but between the Nameless and a people. Indeed, only in this experience did this people *become* a people. This is the secret of the birth of Israel.

It is sometimes said that the Jewish faith has been, since its inception, one of "ethical monotheism." This assertion is true in one sense, but not in another. If by "monotheism" is meant the belief in one universal God, the One God of the universe and mankind, it is more than doubtful that the early Hebrews were monotheists. And if "ethical" refers to codes of conduct universally human in application, it is more than doubtful that their beliefs were ethical. Its God was One, not in being the only God there was, but in demanding a commitment so total as to dwarf all else. And He was ethical in that He challenged to action, and in that this challenge was absolute. Compared to the absoluteness of this challenge its content was, for the time being, secondary in importance; and distinctions such as that between "ethical" and "ritualistic" were not made until a later age.

These facts ought to occasion no surprise. Religions begin with committing experiences, not with universal ideas; and where there is no commitment, religions do not begin at all. But if the commitment is radical, it is only a question of time before it becomes universalized. In the Hebrew experience, the only important God became, in due course, the only existing God; and His all-important commandments, commandments addressed and applicable to all men. This development completed itself in the Hebrew prophets.

The prophets universalized the primeval Hebrew experience, but they did not dissipate it into uncommitting generalities. The primeval experience persisted. The Nameless had become the God of all men: but he was still immediately challenging, here and now. His commandments had become, at least in part, universally valid, but they had not become abstract "principles." They were addressed by the Nameless, not to "mankind," but to each man. This is why the prophetic God, while universal, could remain in covenant with the people of Israel. He was the God, not of the abstraction "mankind," but of every nation.

There are those in the modern world to whom a religion is the "higher" and "more enlightened" the more it expresses itself in abstractions. The prophets would have been in vigorous disagreement. To them, the use of such terms as "mankind" and "deity" would have indicated, not enlightenment, but a flight from commitment and the divine challenge. The prophetic God, in becoming universal, had not ceased to challenge; nor did He challenge abstractions such as "mankind" which not even a God can challenge. Rather, He now challenged Ethiopians and Philistines as well as Israelites. But the business of a prophet in Israel could hardly be to fathom the challenge addressed to Ethiopians and Philistines.

It was in the experience of the Nameless, then, that the people of Israel was born. This was possible because of three factors: first, this experience interpreted itself as challenge to action; secondly, being a collective experience, it challenged the group; thirdly, it was an experience so profound as to persist even after its universal implications had become manifest.

III

But primeval experiences do not last forever. Presumably they take place, even in primeval times, only intermittently, although this fact is easily concealed from later observers by the clouds of myth. In Jewish history, as in the history of most religions, "revelation" came to be a term referring mainly to events lying in the past. The question, therefore, arises as to why the Jewish people was preserved, when the collective experience of the Nameless had become what, at first sight, was a dead past recorded in dead documents.

The answer is that neither the past nor the documents were dead. The past lived on, legislating to present and future; and the document which recorded it became the Bible, that is, the Book par excellence. Jewish thinking centered on its exegesis; Jewish living geared itself to its commandments and promises; Jewish experience interpreted itself as derived from the primeval experiences recorded in the Book. From the Biblical to the modern era, the Jews remained a people by virtue of the Book.

But is such a survival of the past, and of its record, proof that both are alive? It may well seem that, if the Book ruled the Jewish spirit for almost two thousand years, it was not because the former was alive, but because the latter was dead; and that Jewish life, during these long centuries, was composed of the monotonous practice of sterile commandments, and of a forlorn hope in a long-lost promise. How can a religious life be anything but barren which springs, not from the immediate experience of the Nameless, but from slavish submission to the authority of a codified book? But except for rare periods of religious decline, the Jew's loyalty to the Book was not one of slavish obedience. Rather, the Book without kindled the soul within. In rethinking its thoughts, the Jew thought his own. In imagining its experiences, he relived them. In obeying its commandments, he made them into a way of life. The past did not kill the present; instead, reviving itself in the present, it gave life to the present.

The question arises how such an extraordinary relation to the past was possible. Why was the present, during these long centuries, so rarely at odds with the past? Why did it not claim its own autonomous rights against the past? How could religious experience forever regard itself as subordinate to the great religious experiences of the past? There are many partial answers to these crucial questions, but the decisive answer lies in one element of the Jewish faith—the Messianic element.

The Messianic faith is, of course, Biblical in origin. It was the prophets who first spoke of an End of Days in which God alone would rule and all would be fulfilled. Moreover, this faith was implicit in the primeval experience itself. For once the experience of the Nameless had interpreted itself as challenge and promise, it was only a question of time, and religious profundity, until a new religious dimension had to come into view: that of a future in which all that was to be done by either God or man would be fulfilled.

But so long as the primeval experience persisted in Jewish life, an explicit Messianic faith was, so to speak, not needed. Religious immediacy could have lived without it. It was when the past, and its record, took the place of the primeval experience that the Messianic faith moved into the very center of Jewish religious life. Had it not done so, no mere hankering after the past could have saved Jewish life from spiritual—and physical—extinction. The past could live on in the present only because both present and past were for the sake of the future. And the Jewish people could live on, when He who is nameless was not present, only because the memory of His presence transfigured itself into the hope of His ultimate and all-consummating return.

Our account of Jewish life during these centuries is thus subject to emendation. Jewish thinking was a rethinking of past thought, but it was *thinking* only because it was directed toward a future consummation. Jewish imagination was a reliving, but it was *living* only because it anticipated the End. Finally, and perhaps most significantly, Jewish obedience to past commandments constituted a way of life, which was possible only because it regarded itself as preparing, and waiting, for Messianic fulfillment. In short, Jewish existence experienced itself as being between Revelation and Redemption. Revelation had been the call for human, and the promise of divine, action: Redemption would be the consummation of all action.

Still, it may seem that the Messianic hope leaves the fact of Jewish survival unexplained. Did this hope not concern the future of a united mankind? Should it not have led those who held it, instead of to group survival, to voluntary self-dissolution—thus anticipating the End? The mystery deepens if one considers that the Jews were, at that time, dispersed among other nations—nations which, for the most part, shared their monotheistic beliefs. Could it be that the hope of the post-Biblical Jew was, after all, not the universal prophetic hope; could it be that, having lost all universal-istic fervor, it had become nothing more than a national hope? This, however, is to confuse empty abstractions with religious realities. The truth is the reverse. Had their hope been nothing more than a national hope, the Jews of the Diaspora would have been forced many times to abandon it. It was precisely because it was more than national that they could retain it. Hence, although it may seem paradoxical, it is, nevertheless, true that it was precisely because of their Messianic sense of kinship with all the nations that the Jews did not lose their identity among the nations; whereas, had they lost that sense of kinship, they would have disappeared among the nations.

Not much reflection is needed to remove the paradox from these assertions. How could a small people live, for any length of time, amid mighty nations and rich culture without abandoning a merely national hope as both immoral and absurd? Immoral because a moral God could hardly confine His attention to one small and insignificant people; absurd because all the evidence seemed to point, instead, to the fact that this people had been overlooked by history. Clearly, in the centuries of the dispersion, only the most narrow and unthinking could have insisted on Jewish survival on the basis of a solely national hope. But it was the most thoughtful and broadminded who did, in fact, insist on Jewish survival. And this was possible only because their insistence sprang from a hope for something more than national survival. Their hope concerned the relation between the Nameless and all men.

Why, then, did this hope on behalf of mankind not lead to voluntary self-dissolution in mankind? Simply because "mankind" did not exist. There were only actual nations, and some of these did not regard the world as in need of redemption, whereas others believed that it had already arrived. For the Jew to dissolve into either would have meant to him, not to hasten the End, but to betray his post.

We conclude that the Jew of the Diaspora survived because he was able to rise to prayers such as this, uttered by a Hasidic rabbi in an age of fear and hate: "O Lord, send speedily the Messiah, to redeem Thy people Israel! Or, if this be against Thy will, send him to redeem the nations!"

IV

The question now arises as to whether the Jew of today can share the faith of his ancestors, or whether he must consider himself merely as its unwilling product. Can being a Jew today mean an acceptance of a religious commitment similar to, if not identical with, the commitment of his ancestors? Or is being a Jew, today, a mere accident of birth?

No doubt, individual Jews have asked this question throughout the ages. It became universal, however, only when the Jew entered into the modern world. Then it became inescapable. This was because the modern world cast increasing doubt on the central part both of the Biblical and the post-Biblical Jewish faith—that is, on the living God. The Biblical Jew had experienced His presence, and the post-Biblical Jew had hoped for it; but man in the modern world had come to suspect that all supposed experiences of divine presence were just so many illusions.

This attitude sprang from the modern ideal of scientific and moral enlightenment. Did not a rational universe preclude the possibility of irrational divine incursions into it? And did not a rational way of life consist in reliance, not on revelation and promises of divine aid, but on the unaided power of human reason? Ever since the Age of Enlightenment, it has seemed to the modern-minded—and who is not modern-minded, at least to a degree?—that the denial of the living God was an essential aspect of man's scientific and moral self-emancipation. If man was to be fully free in his world, God had to be expelled from it.

We use the word "expelled" advisedly. The ideal of enlightenment did not compel one to deny that a God existed, but it did seem to compel one to deny that He could be present here and now. The living God had to become a mere "Deity," a "Cosmic Principle"—remote, indifferent, and mute. Time was when the prophet Elijah contrasted the idols which could not speak with the living God who could. Ever since the Age of Enlightenment, it has seemed to the modern-minded that God could speak as little as the idols. The religion of the modern-minded came to reflect this conviction. Far from centering on the experience or expectation of a present God, it on the contrary presupposed His necessary absence. It became the mere subscription to "ideals," "principles," "tenets," and, in North America, "platforms." Would anyone think of God as a mere ideal who was prepared, so to speak, to meet Him in person?

On entering the modern world, the Jew had no reason to be suspicious of the ideal of enlightenment which ruled it. On the contrary, he had every reason to embrace it with enthusiasm. Who was to be enthusiastic about it if not the Jew, who had just emerged from the confines of the medieval ghetto? Who was to approve of the ideal of universal emancipation if not the Jew, who stood in special need of emancipation? But despite this wholehearted approval which the Jew very naturally manifested, he soon discovered something of which he was not sure he could approve. The modern expulsion of God from the human world made Jewish existence problematic. The "Jewish problem" appeared on the scene. And it was a problem without solution.

For the premodern Jew this problem did not exist. He was faced with no serious difficulties of self-interpretation. He believed himself to have once met the living God, and to be committed to this meeting until the Messianic hope would be fulfilled. But what if God did not live, that is, relate Himself to persons and peoples? What if He was a mere cosmic entity dwelling in infinite and impartial remoteness? Or perhaps did not exist at all? What if all the supposed experiences of divine presence had been so many illusions? The moment the living God became questionable Jewish existence became questionable. The Jew had to embark on the weary business of self-definition. This business was weary because no definition would fit.

Was Jewishness a matter of "religion"? Was one a Jew because one subscribed to the "tenets" of ethical monotheism? But while Judaism consisted of ethical monotheism, it could not with impunity be regarded as consisting of mere tenets; and Jewishness could not consist of subscription to them. For there were those who subscribed to ethical monotheism without being Jews, and those who were Jews without subscribing to ethical monotheism. The inescapable fact was that one was born a Jew, and that one was not born subscribing to tenets and principles. The definition omitted the fact that the Jews were a people.

This omission was by no means an accident. A living God could address Himself to a people, but an abstract and lifeless "Deity" could not, for it could not address itself at all. In the case of such a Deity, the best one could do was somehow affirm it. But such affirmations could have no connection with the origin of those who made them. In short, if the living God had to give way to an abstract Deity, the "tenets" of Judaism and the Jewish people fell apart.

But perhaps an alternative definition could heal this defect. Was Judaism not the "culture" of the Jewish people, the product of its "religious genius"? Could Jewishness not be defined in terms of the people which had produced the culture?

But this definition too had a fatal flaw. Perhaps this flaw was not apparent, or did not even exist, for the detached observer. But the Jew was not a detached observer; he was a participant. As such, he had to ask himself a crucial question which the definition could not answer. The question was: why ought he to remain a Jew?

So long as the Jew believed in a living God, the question answered itself. To remain a Jew was his duty under the divine-Jewish covenant. But what if God did not live? What if He could not enter into covenants? What if Judaism was not a diving-human encounter, but merely the product of "Jewish genius"? Jewish survival had then to be either an end in itself, or else a means to presumed future "contributions" of "Jewish genius" to the "world." But either view smacked of a chauvinism which no morally sensitive Jew was ever able to swallow. Hence the less forthright accepted the duty to Jewish survival as a mere pious fiction, while the more forthright frankly abandoned it. Jewish survival was merely a right, not a duty; whether or not one chose to remain a Jew was a matter of taste. But if this latter view found general acceptance, how long would the Jews of the Diaspora continue to exist? And how long would the Jews of the State of Israel continue to be Jews? On the other hand, how many Jews are really prepared to advocate, and work toward, Jewish self-dissolution, and to dismiss three thousand years of Jewish existence as a tragicomic mistake? If a single generalization may safely be made about the contemporary Jew, it is that he still regards Jewish survival as a duty, to be performed whether he likes it or not. He may not have the slightest idea why it should be a duty; he may even consciously reject this duty. Still, he feels it in his bones.

After two hundred years of fruitless probing, the conclusion ought to be obvious. The "Jewish problem," as a problem of self-definition, is insoluble. Jewish existence cannot be understood without reference to a living God. And the Jew of today who persists in regarding Jewish survival as a duty, either persists in something unintelligible, or else he postulates, however unconsciously, the possibility of a return to faith in a living God.

V

But the possibility of such a return must surely be dismissed by the modern-minded without a moment's thought! Can one believe, in this day and age, in a God who reveals Himself? Has this belief not been refuted, once and for all? And must not those who persist in it be dismissed as mere victims of wishful, or fearful, thinking? In the twentieth century, faith in a living God may well appear to be a mere relic of bygone ages, and Jewish self-dedication to Jewish survival, a mere part of it.

But the modern world never did refute the belief in a living God. It merely rejected it. One cannot refute the irrefutable; although— if the irrefutable is also unprovable—one is always free to decide that it does not exist.

To be sure, modern thought refuted many traditional beliefs; and some of these were once associated with the belief in a living God. In an age of natural science and critical history, it is hardly possible to believe in miraculously split seas or documents dictated by God. But to reject revealed documents is not necessarily to reject revelation. And to be suspicious of miracles is not necessarily to reduce all religious experience to projections of the unconscious mind. One does well, indeed, to suspect that much that passes for religious experience is inauthentic, and that it is, not a meeting with the Nameless, but the mere solitary disport of the mind with its own conceits. But to regard all religious experience as such—and hence to dismiss it as merely pseudoreligious—is a procedure dictated, not by scientific evidence, but by intellectual prejudice. Or rather, it is to make, under the guise of a scientific judgment, a religious choice. And the choice is against the living God.

Time was when those who made this choice were imbued with the spirit of Prometheus. Like that figure of ancient myth, they wanted total control of their world for the sake of spreading liberty and light. In the world of today, there are still some left who are imbued with the Promethean spirit, but their number is no longer large. Some of those who have decided against the living God are engaged in spreading, not liberty and light, but terror and utter darkness. Others have made that choice only to shiver in loneliness and despair. And others again—and these are the vast majority, at least in the Western world—have lost the assurance of their choice. They are no longer sure whether they have really made the Promethean choice; they are unsure even of what it is. Religiously, they are in a state of turmoil.

But perhaps this turmoil is contemporary man's most authentic religious expression. It would appear to be, at any rate, something unique in the entire religious history of man. The contemporary kind of religious turmoil may have existed, in previous ages, among individuals. But never before did it shake a whole age.

All ages prior to the modern were religious ages. They may have disagreed as to the interpretation to be given to the presence of the Nameless, but they agreed that the Nameless *could* be present. In sharp contrast, the modern age—at least in its most typically modern expressions—has been antireligious in spirit. Either by denying its existence or by expelling it into the distance of irrelevance, it denies that the Nameless can be present. What both the premodern and the modern ages have in common is that they make their respective religious choices without giving serious attention to the alternative; that is, they choose dogmatically. They make their choice without full awareness that it *is* a choice. Man today is bereft of such dogmatic certainties. Possibly for the first time in human history, he is brought face to face with the most radical of all religious questions. Like man at all times, he must face up to this question. But unlike men at other times, he is compelled to recognize that it *is* a question. Unlike the former, he cannot fail to recognize that the question can be answered only by a decision, and that the decision *is* a decision. And he suffers the turmoil of this recognition. The question is: is human existence closed or open to the Divine? Can the Nameless be present, or are all supposed experiences of such a presence mere illusions? Does God live, or is man inexorably alone?

It is all too human to shrink from great choices. One is tempted to pretend that there is no choice to be made, and to drift in indecision. Or perhaps one will escape from the choice by making it glibly, only to discover later that one has not made it at all. Such flights from choice are readily understandable, because to face up to the choice is to endure turmoil—the turmoil of the conflicting possibilities. One cannot make a genuine choice without first enduring this turmoil, and one must endure it until the time is ripe—for choice, and for action.

If this is true of all great decisions, it is true, above all, of the great religious decision placed before contemporary man. Is choosing for or against the living God a mere matter of scientific hypotheses? Or is it a matter of choosing the path of least resistance? Or of discovering, with the help of reputable psychologists, the most comfortable road to peace of mind? Is it not a choice in which one either commits his whole being or else does not commit himself at all? If this is the case, it is no wonder, then, that man in the present age seems bent on shrinking from this choice. Instead he pretends that there is no decision to be made; and he reinforces this pretense by all kinds of activity, inside and outside church and synagogue, which distract his attention from it. Or, assuming an air of glib resolution, he issues manifestoes which announce that the decision is made, and he reinforces these by repeating them at regular intervals. But the great religious choice placed before contemporary man cannot be evaded indefinitely; nor can its turmoil be circumvented by the proclamation of manifestoes, no matter how often this ritual takes place. The restless flight from the decision must yield to the quiet endurance of its turmoil. Only he who endures the tension of the conflicting possibilities can really know what the decision is about; only he can know when the time is ripe for it to be made. But what will the decision be? And when will the time be ripe for it to be made? This cannot be known in advance.

VI

The Jew of today is a man of today; he is confronted with the religious question of today; the question is whether or not the Nameless can be present to us. But he is also confronted with the Jewish question of today: whether—and if so why—Jewish survival is a duty. The remarkable thing is that he cannot authentically face up to the religious question without at the same time facing up to the Jewish question.

The Jew of today cannot authentically face up to the religious choice simply as an individual. To do so is, in effect, to evade, if not his Jewishness, then at least the question posed by his Jewishness.

And the question demands a religious answer. Hence to evade it is, for the Jew, to evade part of the religious question itself, and thus to fall into inauthenticity. The Jew cannot face up to the religious question "simply as an individual." Whether he likes it or not, he must face up to it as a Jew. To do so is to recognize that the duty to Jewish survival is, for the Jew, part of what is at stake in the religious choice. Man of today must endure the ancient question of whether or not the Nameless can be present. As part and parcel of that question for him, the Jew of today must endure the hardly less ancient question of whether or not Jewish survival is a duty. The religious turmoil is, for him, at the same time a Jewish turmoil. And Jewish religious life today consists in the endurance of this double turmoil.

When the time is ripe for decision, the Jew may well decide that the ancient duty to Jewish survival must be abandoned. Should this be the eventual choice, then the Jewish people, as it has existed for three thousand years, will cease to be. Jewishness will become a mere right, to be made use of only by those with a taste for it. Jews of the State of Israel will become Israelis, and Jews elsewhere will either become members of a denomination like other denominations or else a minority doomed to eventual extinction.

But the Jew may also, in the end, decide to reaffirm the ancient duty of Jewish survival. This will be possible only if the Jew has remembered, and accepted as authentic, the ancient encounter of his people with the living God. He will then accept himself as part of a people constituted by an encounter with the Nameless, and still extant as a people only because it continues to be committed to that encounter. He will have accepted himself as a Jew because he will have accepted the time-honored Jewish obligation: to prepare and wait for the End in which all that is to be done by either man or God will be fulfilled.

THE "CHOSENNESS" OF ISRAEL
AND THE JEW OF TODAY

Will Herberg

It is not the choice of the Jew that he is chosen. It is the choice of God. The formulation is embarrassing, ever so slightly demeaning (particularly at this moment when rational, ever free-thinking Jews reject notions of an exterior, compelling, obligatory divinity working havoc upon their volitional self-identity), seemingly racist, a source of historical confusion and difficulty. Will Herberg is right (as he has often been right) in recognizing that the concept of the "chosenness" of Israel is one of the most perplexing and disagreeable, and nevertheless decisive and meaningful, concepts of Jewish existence.

Skipping for the moment the excellent interpretation of the concept of chosenness which Herberg develops in this essay, running it through the arguments of its opponents and the defenses which Jewish fideists make for its centrality, I should like to explore at least one dimension of the problem of chosenness which may not have received the attention it deserves, but which finally, in its proper context, justifies its ominous importance and relates it to the preceding essay by Emil L. Fackenheim, "Jewish Existence and the Living God."

The individual man, formed as he is by history and environment, achieves an identity which defines his relations to the world. An identity is not given. It is true that characteristics which are assimilated by the unconscious to the totality of selfhood are without appeal or alteration, and some of these may be decisive in the formation of character, e.g., color to the Negro, physical frailty to the child of the athletic parent, or, for that matter, cultural, national, ethnic origins which place an otherwise well-formed individual under the burden of poverty, or familial instability, or the aggressive hostility of those to whom the origins are threatening or disagreeable. It is true, however, that by and large the individual regards his destiny as his own. Fatalism more often than not is an acquired doctrine, wrought out of pain and frustration. More normally a man regards his life as his own to shape. He begins with the unscrutinized assumption of freedom. It is he who can choose his destiny. No other can choose it for him.

The election of Israel and the devolution of that election upon the individual Jew cannot help but be regarded by many Jews as a psychological violation. Not by those Jews to whom election is given in the natal environment as a condition of existence along with wealth or poverty, national origin, cultural inheritance, and religious instruction, but surely to those Jews—otherwise removed or distant from an intense Jewish (or otherwise firmly articulated) identity—to be chosen by God, and to be visited with the iniquities of the world (Amos 3:2), is an insupportable burden. The people Israel may accept the choice, as the people Israel accept the fact of God's involvement in their survival, but the individual Jew, in his destemper of a partial or ill-formed Jewish identity, can only regard it with anger and hostility. And how much more so after the Holocaust, how much more so does the choice without option, the absolute choice that commands as it elects, abrade sensibility at this time of God's putative hiding. Those who remind us of God's "indifference" to Israel at the time of her greatest trial in history, her second Sinai, as Elie Wiesel has called the Holocaust, must surely wonder that the election of Israel is a curse, not blessing. The wound of election is collateral to its balsam. There is no way out of this. The collectivity if Israel may accept the choice, for the fact of being chosen is built into the reality of its existence and to deny the chosenness is to deny the historicity of God's action (it is not to deny a metaphysical pre-eminence to God, to God as idea, will, force, agency, but it is to deny the reality of the God who acts in history). The individual Jew must, however, choose to be chosen. God chooses the people and by implication chooses each Jew. Each single Jew of every generation was virtually present at Sinai but only as part of the collectivity of Israel. The incorporation of that choice, the making vivid of that election, is part of the individual's decision to believe, to submit himself to the divine choice, to be chosen and hence to choose.

THE "CHOSENNESS" OF ISRAEL
AND THE JEW OF TODAY

WILL HERBERG

In all the vast and complex heritage of Jewish belief, that element, which, according to Solomon Schechter, was so pervasive that it hardly needed to be explicitly formulated, has for many Jews of today become the most difficult to accept, perhaps even to understand. The overwhelming majority of American Jews, like the overwhelming majority of other Americans, "believe in God," and take this belief to be the essence of their religion. But that God has in some sense singled them out for His service and made of them a "chosen people," this they find strange and incomprehensible. The "chosenness" of Israel, once the Jew's fundamental conviction about himself and his place in the world, has to all appearance become meaningless, if not actually unintelligible, to the great mass of American Jews of our time.

And yet, despite appearances, it is my feeling that this belief is very far from being as obsolete and meaningless as so many present day Jews think it is. On the contrary, recent events, as well as a good deal of current Jewish self-analysis, would seem to have given it a reality and relevance it did not appear to possess in the days before Hitler and Stalin. It is my conviction, in other words, that if the modern Jew will only bring himself to face the fact of his Jewishness in the context of contemporary life, he will rediscover the meaning and power of the ancient doctrine of "chosenness."

I

Recent history teaches a strange lesson, which we modern Jews had lost sight of in the bright age of liberal cosmopolitanism. Roger Shinn, in a notable study, makes this lesson explicit in an illuminating comment: "Hitler found in the Jews *(by their very existence)*, and in faithful Christians *(by their religious protests)*, a reminder of the universalism . . . he could not tolerate" (emphasis added). What Dr. Shinn is saying here is something which we all must acknowledge once we really face the facts, that somehow the Jew, *simply by being a Jew,* constituted an offense and a challenge to Nazi totalitarianism in its time, as he does to Communist totalitarianism today. The Christian, so recent history teaches us, can make his peace with the totalitarian powers by apostasy, by ceasing to be a Christian; only the Christian who remains "faithful" and makes a "religious protest," as Dr. Shinn puts it, is a real threat to the totalitarian despot. And very much the same is true of the secular humanist; he, too, can abandon his humanistic creed and make his peace with the regime. But the Jew? Strangely enough, it is not what the Jew happens to believe or affirm that makes him so intolerable to the totalitarian; it is his *Jewishness,* his *being a Jew.* And of his Jewishness, of his being a Jew, he cannot rid himself, do what he may.

If we look a little closer, we discern some logic in this insensate totalitarian hatred of the Jew. Totalitarianism is essentially the absorption of all human life by the state. The meaning of human existence is felt by totalitarianism to be completely comprehended in the national community, of which the state is the embodiment. That is why totalitarianism is inherently chauvinistic, and why chauvinism always harbors a totalitarian potential. The very idea of a dimension of human existence that transcends the social and political, and passes beyond the limits of society and state, is something that cannot be tolerated in a system whose maxim is "everything in and through the state, nothing outside the state," and whose claim is to the totality of life. In such a society, it is possible, as I have suggested, for the Christian or the secular humanist to save himself and make his peace with the regime by abandoning his Christian witness or his humanistic ideals, by surrendering whatever may challenge the self-enclosed ultimacy of the totalitarian state. But the Jew somehow has this challenge built into his being, because built into his being is a transnational, transcultural, transpolitical dimension that makes him irrevocably and irreducibly "different." He may resent his being "different," he may desire to get rid of it; he may even make a strenuous effort to come to terms with his world and conform to its totalistic pattern—but so long as he remains a Jew, so long as he remains known as a Jew, he cannot possibly succeed. The Christian and the secular democrat have it within their power to cease to be Christians or democrats; but can the Jew ever "un-Jew" himself? Can he, by anything he may do, rid himself of that in him which makes him so intolerable to a Hitler or a Stalin? History gives its own answer, and that answer is unequivocally in the negative.

It would seem, then, as though the Jew were "chosen," through his very Jewishness, to be a witness against totalitarianism. If we define the conviction that nothing of this world, no idea, institution, or individual, no man, or nation, or "ism," may be divinized and worshiped as something ultimate, if we define this conviction as the "principle of anti-idolatry," then we can state it as the inescapable lesson of history that the Jew is the living embodiment of this principle. He is that not only because the principle stems directly from his religious tradition, but also and more fundamentally because any violation of it—any tendency to absolutize a man, a nation, a culture, a system, or an "ism"—sooner or later brings with it a threat to his very existence as a Jew, no matter how otherwise well established in society he may be. The Jew, it has been said with considerable insight, is a kind of living litmus paper by which the spiritual health of a society of culture may be judged.

This fact, so clearly evidenced in recent history, is not peculiar to our time. The tendency of ideas, institutions, and systems to absolutize themselves is perennial in human affairs; man is always prone to make absolute, idolatrous claims for himself and his works, and to strive to comprehend all life in their terms. Whenever that happens, and to the degree that it happens, the Jew falls into trouble: his merely *being a Jew* is felt to be an intolerable challenge and affront. Whether it is the Hellenistic effort to establish a divinized world culture, or the medieval attempt to exalt Christendom as indeed the very City of God, or the Nazi and Communist efforts to erect a divinized total state: it is always the Jew who is the enemy to be singled out and destroyed.

In the face of such facts, it would seem hard to avoid the conclusion that somehow, in some way, the Jew has, through the centuries, been made to serve a certain very distinctive function in history—the function of calling into question, *by his very Jewishness,* the self-idolizing, self-absolutizing tendencies in men and society. The fact may be variously interpreted and explained, but it remains a fact, a hard, undeniable fact, a fact that would seem, on the face of it, to give real contemporaneous content to the traditional Jewish conviction of "chosenness." For after all, as Buber has pointed out, the important thing "is not whether we feel or do not feel that we are chosen . . . [The important thing is rather] that our role in history actually has been unique." It is history in the first place that speaks to the modern Jew about the meaning of his "chosenness."

II

But history is not something that comes upon the individual from the outside; it is really the interior life of man externalized. Does not the testimony that history gives of the "chosenness" of Israel reflect, and is it not reflected by, the sense of "chosenness" that permeates the life and behavior of the individual Jew, however much he may repudiate the doctrine?

It is a mere commonplace, yet an important truth, nevertheless, that the Jew, whatever his position in society or his field of activity, is aware not only that he is "different," but that something different is expected of him—in the first place, by himself. The Jewish businessman will acknowledge a special ethical obligation ("There are certain things a Jew doesn't do!"), even as he violates it and tries to make up for his shortcomings by philanthropy. The Zionist may vehemently asseverate, and perhaps even believe, that he is just another "nationalist" striving to regain his "national homeland," but he betrays himself in his every word and thought which breathes the passion of the age-old Messianic idea. The Jewish socialist, too, reveals the Messianic origins of the impulse that animates him, and, indeed, often relates his "idealism" to "Jewish ethics," just as the Jewish scholar or scientist will find his intellectual concern quite natural in view of the "Jewish tradition of learning" and the "Jewish zeal for truth." I have myself heard Jewish labor leaders, men remote indeed from the faith and practice of Judaism, explain confidentially that their "progressivism" was somehow the consequence of their being Jewish. These things are matters of common experience, and I have yet to find a Jew who does not in some manner or form exhibit this profound sense of "difference" and special vocation. It is simply a fact that "consciously or not, the Jew moves in the context of a long and special history and religio-ethical tradition that lays upon him, whether as a burden or as a badge of pride, the sense of being 'chosen' . . ." (Elliot E. Cohen, ed., *Commentary on the American Scene*). Let the Jew who rejects the doctrine of "chosenness" examine his conscience and see whether these words do not ring true to the inmost reality of his being.

A phenomenology of Jewish character as affected by the hidden conviction of "chosenness" still remains to be written. It would have to include cases like Disraeli, about whom a recent critic remarks acutely that his "awareness of being 'different' gave him self-confidence and an abiding detachment," and it would have to include others with whom the consciousness of difference has made for anxiety and self-rejection. It would have to show how the Jew's recalcitrance to becoming totally absorbed in his environment and in the claims of success and power has given him a keener social vision and a greater sensitivity to social evil, but also how at the same time it has made him more susceptible to Utopian schemes and to entrapment in false Messianic movements like Communism. It would have to indicate how the consciousness of being a Jew often operates to create a high sense of *noblesse oblige,* but also how it can degenerate into the senseless arrogance that makes the word "Jewish" stand for everything right and proper and its antonym *"goy"* for everything gross and brutish. It would have to show how the Jew, in his Jewishness, acquires his "intellectual pre-eminence," but often at the price of becoming, for good or bad, a "disturber of the intellectual peace," "an alien of uneasy feet," "an intellectual wayfaring man, a wanderer in the intellectual No Man's Land, . . . seeking another place to rest, further along the road, somewhere over the horizon . . ." (Thorstein Veblen). Everywhere the hidden effects of the sense of "chosenness" would reveal themselves, and testify that through this sense of being "chosen," an extra dimension has, indeed, been added to Jewish life and personality.

The reference to Thorstein Veblen may serve to remind us that in recent years it has been the sociologists, psychologists, and historians, rather than the theologians, who have, in however indirect a manner, called attention to the Jew's hidden sense of "chosenness" and to its wide ramifications in individual and social life. A considerable documentation could be compiled from the writings of these specialists, but such documentation would, after all, be not nearly so impressive as the everyday testimony that the Jew himself gives in his thinking, feeling, and behavior, in his very life as a Jew in a non-Jewish world.

The events of the past two decades have strikingly reversed the earlier trend toward "assimilation" on the part of American Jews; a new urge to self-identification as Jews is to be noted among all sections of American Jewry, particularly perhaps among the younger people. But this has raised in a new form an old problem of profound significance: *What does it mean to be a Jew?* It cannot be simply by virtue of belonging to a particular race, or to a particular nation, or to a particular culture, or even to a particular religious denomination, that one is a Jew. Many and diverse racial strains are to be found among Jews; Jews have, and have long had, the most varied national origins, allegiances, and cultures; and even those Jews who renounce the Jewish religion, or religion in general, somehow remain Jews. The answer to the question "What does it mean to be a Jew?" is not an easy one; perhaps no final or complete answer can be given. But is it not true that when the Jew of today, whether he is "religious" or "nonreligious"—perhaps even sooner in the latter case than in the former—comes to examine himself in order to make sense of his Jewishness, some inkling of "difference," of "chosenness," necessarily enters into his own understanding of himself as a Jew?

III

Sociologists, psychologists, and historians not blinded by doctrinaire formulas have, as I have suggested, long noted and documented these facts of Jewish existence as they manifest themselves in individual life and society. They have their interpretations and explanations, of course. There is no occasion whatever for quarreling with them, for there is a great deal of truth in what they say as far as it goes. The anomalous position of the Jew in the non-Jewish world, his marginality, his apparently ineradicable minority status, do indeed make him an "outsider," somehow *in,* but never entirely *of,* the world in which he finds himself. Thus he can hardly avoid putting a note of interrogation to every established dogma or institution; his very being a Jew does that, whether he desires it or not. His very Jewish "particularism," because it transcends every national and cultural boundary, becomes strangely enough a vehicle and witness to universalism. The distinctiveness of the Jew, his sense of "difference" and "chosenness," as well as his special role in history are thus understood as functions of his anomalous position in society.

This may be granted, but the question always arises: *Why* this unique and anomalous position in which the Jew is forever barred from losing himself in the mass and becoming "like everyone else"? Other groups there are which had been marginal and "unadjusted" in this or that society, under such and such circumstances—but the Jew is marginal and "unadjusted" everywhere, at all times, under all circumstances. However genuinely at home he may feel in his society, he remains the "eternal outsider," and neither he nor his society can ever really lose awareness of this fact.

Explaining it all in terms of anti-Semitism merely begs the question. What is this anti-Semitism that has accompanied the Jew from the beginning of his historical career till this very day, despite all changes in social, economic, political, and cultural conditions? Is it not, after all, really the obverse of the problem of Jewishness? The sociologists, psychologists, and historians can teach us a great deal, but when they have had their say, the fundamental fact still remains a fact, neither "explained" nor explained away: Jewish existence, individual and collective, bears witness to a sense of "difference" that is immediately recognizable as the substance of the traditional belief in "chosenness."

It is at this point that the modern Jew, who shies away from the explicit doctrine of "chosenness," ought to begin to question himself. Is it not true that his own sense of being "different" and standing under a special responsibility points beyond itself? Does not the sense of "chosenness" raise the question of *"chosen" by whom?* The question may be phrased in various ways, employing or avoiding the traditional vocabulary, but posed in some manner it must be by the Jew who is not afraid to pursue the logic of his Jewishness. Most modern-minded Jews, if they can get themselves to face the question at all, tend to answer it in terms of "history" or "destiny"; not so long ago, quasi-racialist theories of "innate gifts" and a special *Volksgeist* of Hegelian provenance were quite popular. But do not all such answers, welcome as they are in testifying to the ineradicable conviction of "chosenness," tend to turn history, or destiny, or the alleged *Volksgeist* into a kind of god before which we must bow as the ultimate law of life? And somehow this kind of god we cannot swallow. There is something in us that responds to the warning, "There is no god but God," and drives us beyond all premature and arbitrary absolutes to the transcendent.

Dostoievsky, who cannot be accused of too great a fondness for Jews, once affirmed his conviction that no Jew, whatever he might say, could really be an atheist. We can now see what he meant. The Jewish "atheist," if he is a Jew at all, in effect proclaims: "There is no God, but we are His people!" He may vehemently, and quite sincerely, assert that he does not "believe in God," but does not his very being as a Jew testify to the *existential* belief still alive within him that "there is no god but God" and that the Jews are His people?

What I am contending, in short, is that the Jew's sense of his "chosenness"—and this sense would seem to be operative in all Jews who hold themselves to be Jews, and perhaps even in those who reject their Jewishness—is an implicit *religious* affirmation which inevitably points beyond itself to the God who acts to "choose." Jewish existence, as Dostoievsky saw, is intrinsically religious and God-oriented. Jews may be led to deny, repudiate, and reject their "chosenness" and its responsibilities, but then their own Jewishness rises to confront them as refutation and condemnation. "God, Torah, and Israel" do, indeed, form the indivisible unity of tradition, each member of the triad implying, and being implied by, the others.

IV

This approach to the question may seem rather devious to those accustomed to think of religion as a system of abstract metaphysical propositions about God and morality. From such a point of view, "belief in God" comes first as the foundation of "ethical monotheism," and only afterward, if at all, comes the corollary of the "chosenness" of Israel. But such is not the way of Jewish religious tradition, Biblical and rabbinic. In Jewish religious tradition, it is the conviction of "chosenness," of Israel's being the covenanted people of God, that is the central fact. The God of Jewish faith is not an abstract "Supreme Being," but the God of Abraham, Isaac, and Jacob, the God of Israel, the God of the Covenant, who redeemed His people from the darkness of Egypt and "chose" them to be His witnesses forever. This is the primordial confession of Jewish faith: the conviction of "chosenness" lies at its very heart.

In Jewish tradition, the People Israel is conceived of as neither a nation nor a religious group in the ordinary sense; in Jewish tradition, Israel is understood as a people "called" into being by God to serve His purposes in the world. It is understood as a community created by God's special act of covenant, first with Abraham, whom He "called" out of the heathen world, and then, supremely, with Israel collectively at Sinai. The "chosing" is also a *calling*, a vocation, "a summons and a sending"; what Israel is called to is best expressed in the rabbinic formula, *kiddush ha-Shem*, the "sanctification of the Name." Stripped of its mystical and metaphysical overtones, this rabbinic formula means to bear witness to the God of Israel amidst the idolatries of the world, to proclaim in word and deed, in life and thought, that "there is no god but God," and to "give the world no rest so long as it has no God" (Jacques Maritain). The late Judah Magnes was speaking true to the Biblical-rabbinic teaching when he declared: "It is the Jew's historical function to question, to challenge, to deny every idolatry which the world in its self-delusion comes to worship, whether this idolatry be of nature, of science, or of state and society—and beyond these, to point to God. This is his real reason for existence."

The vocation of Israel as witness against idolatry emerges with particular force in the relations between Jew and Christian, Israel and the Church. "It is important that there always be Judaism," Paul Tillich, the distinguished Protestant theologian, has testified. "It is the corrective against the paganism that goes along with Christianity. . . ." No one who recalls the experience of the churches in Germany during the days of Nazism will fail to see the relevance of Tillich's words; their truth is a truth evidenced by the whole history of Christendom. The Chrisitian who is tempted to bow the knee to the idolatrous gods of his society and culture will always find in the Jew an accusing witness against him, for in the Jew he will see the victim of the idols he is prone to worship.

Anti-Semitism is the "natural" consequence of this witness to God in a world beset with idolatry; however it may express itself, at bottom anti-Semitism reflects the revolt of man and society against the God of Israel and His absolute demand. This was obvious in pre-Christian anti-Semitism, but it is also true of anti-Semitism in the Christian world, where "hatred of Judaism is at bottom hatred of Christianity" (Maritain). For, as Franz Rosenzweig so clearly saw, "whenever the pagan within the Christian soul rises in revolt against the yoke of the Cross, he vents his fury on the Jew." Very much the same view has been set forth by a number of recent psychologists and sociologists, who see the Jew as representing the "bad conscience of Christian civilization" and anti-Semitism as a kind of revolt against the "spiritual collective super-ego" (Ernst Simmel). We recall what the Rabbis say of the Mountain of the Covenant: "It is called Sinai because *sinah,* hatred [toward Israel] came down to the nations because of it" (B. Shab. 89b).

Although it converts Jewry into an "exposed signal station flashing a warning of the wandering of Satan upon the earth" (Magnes), the "chosenness" of Israel has always been the bulwark of its existence. It was the conviction of "chosenness" that enabled the Jew to defy the powers of destruction and to reverse the normal patterns of history. Military defeat and the annihilation of nation and state did not mean the end of Jewry or the extinction of its hopes; on the contrary, it inspired the emergence of Israel in a new form and with a more profound consciousness of its destiny. Precisely because his Jewishness has never been completely tied to state or territory, to culture or nation, but has always been defined in terms of the suprahistorical reality of his "chosenness," the Jew has been able to survive all the disasters of history. The Jew has always found a home in the Covenant whenever he has been at odds with the world, for it is the Covenant that is his true "fatherland," and the world that confronts him with the need for redemption.

Within the corporate vocation of Israel, the individual Jew, according to Biblical-rabbinic teaching, finds his own "calling," and therewith also the meaning and power of his life. He sees himself a "son of the Covenant," upon whom has been laid a great and special responsibility of "sanctifying the Name." He understands that the fateful question for him is not, as religious "liberalism" would have it, "Shall I or shall I not be a Jew? Have I or have I not been 'chosen'?" The real question he finds on an altogether different level; it is: "Shall I recognize my 'chosenness,' my special 'calling, and live an *authentic* life; or shall I deny it, and as a consequence, live an *inauthentic* one?" Judaism, in sum, means living out the affirmative decision.

It will thus be seen that in the tradition of Jewish faith, Judaism, Jewishness, being-a-Jew, is not primarily or essentially a doctrine, a moral code, or a system of observances, although it does in some way include all of these. Judaism, Jewishness, being-a-Jew, in the tradition of faith, is primarily and essentially a *vocation*, a "calling" under God, which defines the Jew's position and responsibilities in the world. The Jewish religious tradition, on its human side, may best be understood as the Jew's attempt through the ages to discern, define, and implement his vocation under God.

V

To the believing Jew of tradition, the "chosenness" of Israel was a central fact, a basic reality, illuminating every aspect of his existence as a Jew. Yet for most Jews today, even for those who hold themselves to be religious, the doctrine of "chosenness" is a scandal and an offense. We have a vague distaste for it; it somehow runs counter to our modernity and to too many of our intellectual and moral presuppositions. Even though, as I have been insisting, the Jew cannot help but exemplify the hidden conviction of "chosenness" in his life and thought, the modern Jew, at least, feels very uncomfortable with the doctrine and is moved to reject it whenever he comes face to face with it.

Why is this doctrine of "chosenness" so hard for the modern Jew to accept, even when he still lives in its light? The reasons, I think, are of various orders. There are, first, the intellectual, or philosophical, objections, frequently held by people who profess a religious view of life. A truly rational and universal God, it is maintained, could not do anything so arbitrary as to "choose" one particular group out of mankind as a whole. It is, indeed, "odd of God to choose the Jews" because it is odd of God to "choose" anybody. God is the God of all alike, and, therefore, cannot make distinctions between nations and peoples. To this is added the moral argument that the doctrine of "chosenness" is little better than crude ethnocentrism, in which a particular group regards itself as the center of the universe and develops doctrines that will flatter its pride and minister to its glory. Such notions are held to be primitive and unworthy of being embodied in a "mature" religion.

These arguments are, in fact, far from modern. They were all advanced, almost two thousand years ago, by pagan philosophers like Celsus, who made them the basis of a powerful polemic against Judaism and Christianity. What can we say to these arguments, whether ancient or modern? Well, in the first place, it may be pointed out that to be scandalized by the universal God acting in and through the particularities of time, place, and history, is to conceive the divine in essentially impersonal, intellectual terms. Universal ideas are impersonal and timeless, and if religion is simply the apprehension of universal ideas, then of course the particularistic claims of Jewish faith are absurd on the face of it. But if religion is a matter of personal relation and action, as both Judaism and Christianity affirm, the matter takes on an altogether different aspect. Truly personal relations are never universal; they are always concrete and particular. And while an idea or a doctrine may be made available to all men universally and timelessly, action must necessarily be particular in the sense that it is action here and now, in reference to this particular group or person rather than to another. The insistence on historical particularity contained in the notion of "chosenness" is thus seen to be part of the Biblical-rabbinic affirmation of a *"living"* God, who meets man in personal encounter in the context of life and history. Within the framework of Jewish faith, therefore, the doctrine of "chosenness" constitutes no incongruity; it is only to abstract and self-sufficient human reason that it constitutes a scandal and offense. But then to abstract and self-sufficient human reason, all history, in its inexpugnable particularity, must constitute the same kind of scandal and offense.

Nor does the moral argument hold up any better. The most superficial reading of Scripture is enough to indicate that the teaching about the "chosenness" of Israel is as far as possible from being an ethnocentric device of self-flattery and self-glorification. The covenant by which Israel is "chosen" is never held to mean that Israel is better, or wiser, or more deserving than the "nations of the world"; on the contrary, the fickleness, obduracy, and disobedience of the people is constantly emphasized to highlight the miracle of God's love and steadfastness. Nor is the "chosenness" interpreted as implying special privilege for Israel; just the reverse, the "choosing" is a demand and a summons upon Israel; involving greater obligation, heavier responsibility, a harder destiny, and a sterner judgment: "You only have I known among all the families of the earth; *therefore* will I visit upon you all your iniquities" (Amos 3:2). Finally, though the "choosing" of Israel is the "choosing" of a particular group to act in the particularities of time and history, its purpose is universal, to promote the supreme welfare of all mankind: "In you [Abraham] shall all the families of the earth be

blessed" (Gen. 12:3), "I the Lord have called you in righteousness
. . . and have made you a light for the nations" (Is. 42:6). Whatever may be the corruptions which the doctrine of "chosenness" has
suffered at various times in the long history of the Jews, the doctrine itself, as it appears in normative Jewish faith, is anything but
the crude ethnocentrism its critics accuse it of being.

But, of course, neither the philosophical nor the moral argument
really gets to the heart of the difficulty. The fundamental objection
of the Jew, today as ever, is not that the doctrine of "chosenness"
offends rational or ethical principles, but rather that it places an
altogether unbearable burden upon him and condemns him to be
"different," the "eternal stranger," the "marginal man," the "suffering servant." Throughout the centuries, the Jew, being human, all
too human, has rebelled against the "yoke of the Covenant," and
has demanded the right to be "like unto the nations." The Bible is
full of the protests of the "natural" man in the Israelite against the
demand of God and the destiny of Israel, and current discussions
about the "normalization" of Jewish life reecho these protests in a
hundred different ways. "Chosenness" is a *calling*, "a summons and
a sending," a "summons" to obedience and a "sending" to service,
sometimes even to suffering and death, and those who do not find it
in their hearts to be able to obey and serve and suffer—and how
many of us can truly say that we do?—are only too prone to deny
the calling and reject the doctrine in which it is embodied.

It is, however, part of the force of divine providence (or of historical factuality) that the protests of the recalcitrant Jew against
the unwanted distinction have rarely been more than a vain cry of
outrage and embitterment. Life and history—the man of faith
would say God—have somehow refused to free him of the burden of
his uniqueness, and he has gone through the ages an often unwilling witness to the God he is tempted to deny.

VI

To the traditional Jew, the "chosenness" of Israel was a central
fact, ever present in his consciousness. The *kiddush* he repeated on
Sabbaths and festivals was a constant proclamation of it; in the
Alenu, the climax of the daily liturgy, he thanked God for it; in
every prayer, he was reminded of it. Indeed, no phase of his life was
without some acknowledgment of the "chosenness" of Israel. It was

the cornerstone of his personal existence as a Jew, as it was of the corporate existence of Jewry.

For the Jew of today, everything has become problematic. Yet ultimately, the Jew of today too must come face to face with the fact of his Jewishness, and every attempt to do so almost at once raises the question of "chosenness" and demands an answer. The "chosenness" of Israel, whether believed in or not, is an inescapable fact for the Jew. He cannot think or live as a Jew without in some way implying it. For better or for worse, it confronts him as a destiny which he cannot escape because he cannot escape himself and his history.

INTRODUCTION TO

MAN'S MORALS AND GOD'S WILL

David Baumgardt

It is not my intention, in offering David Baumgardt's moving essay on Abraham's choice at Mount Moriah, to cut one more limb from the already dying tree of traditional morality. In order of succession in this Reader it is appropriate, at this point, that we move our consideration from the grounds of faith, its philosophic and existential difficulty for the modern Jew, to the actual predicament of faith: what must a man do that he may believe and *still* act? The use of "still" may alarm you, but it is correctly the "still" which is at issue. Of course, many readers will regard Judaism as reducible to ethics, and for such readers (if you have read systematically and to this point, and remain unshaken by the arguments so far undertaken in defence of a fideist interpretation of Jewish existence) David Baumgardt's essay and my gloss upon it will be unavailing. But for others the issue is perplexing. It is not simply that the Biblical text develops with miraculous simplicity and brevity the most profound religious dilemma, a man's decision to obey the unrationalized will of God who orders the commission of an act which, not only God, but the unaided natural reason of man, makes unlawful and criminal. How shall Abraham choose between obedience to God and the explicit prohibition of murder?

It is no surprise that Baumgardt's essay does not seek a neat and satisfactory resolution of the problem. He points out, quite tellingly, that both rabbinic and postrabbinic sources as well as Christian and philosophic interpreters of the *akedah,* have often missed the point, either shading the narration in such a way as to exculpate Abraham and rationalize God or else to compel such a radical polarization as to remove both Abraham and God, the knight of faith and his Lord, from the bounds of the ethical. But even Kierkegaard, radical of radicals though he was, misses the point in so far as Judaism is concerned. Jewish religion will not incorporate as theological *docta* "the teleological suspension of the ethical," whereunder Abraham's action is removed from the domain of the ethical, from the dialectic of means and ends, and seen under the absolute obligation of the Holy. Baumgardt interprets differently then Kierkegaard, no less absolutely, but no less in the spirit of Judaism.

If it is the case that God *really* asked of Abraham that he sacrifice Isaac, Abraham has no choice but to assent or to renounce God. He may not temporize nor remonstrate: he must do the deed or refuse to do the deed. He elected to sacrifice Isaac, to obey the divine request, and in doing so he took a position which extends the rule of obedience wider than the rule of law. Abraham obeyed an injunction to do what is otherwise evil. Absolute ethics, that is, a decision which is validated by the *person* of the lawgiver in contradiction to the law which he gave, is higher than the law itself. The law gives over to the kingdom of men the administration of the ethical, but God reserves Himself to Himself. He makes alive and kills, as Isaiah says; and in this instance he orders to kill and can restore to life, ransoming Isaac at the penultimate moment before the knife descends.

Baumgardt notes in his conclusion that the imperative to joy is a greater obligation of Jewish service than resignation to suffering. The joy which comes out of transfiguration (the transfiguration of Abraham before the trusting passivity of Isaac), although linked to suffering, is not equal to it nor measured by it. It is in this sense, pointing toward an "unnatural" ethics, an ethics at variance with nature and law, that the understanding of the *akedah* must be defined. The moral commandments are commandments which address fixed situations where clear directives may be defined. But as the situation shades and darkens in complexity, as the alternatives become vastly more difficult and oppository, the moral commandments become harder to apply and he who would exhort one or the other is legitimately castigated by us as a moral windbag, useless to our deliberation.

The issue put to modern man by the *akedah* is that our moral judgments are not able to be defined either by rational exposition of right action or by appeal to the instruction of moral principles. Abraham's choice may well have been more simple than ours would be, for at least Abraham believed in God, heard God address him, and elected to obey *him* rather than the prohibition against murder. Abraham believed and acted. But we, rather less than Abraham, do not hear God clearly, do not ascertain his will with sureness and mighty resolution and yet we, too, must make moral decisions—to fight in wars, to defend our homes, to support him who might become our enemy because his cause is just however much his enmity may be erroneous, and so forth. We have confused authority addressing us, confused choices to unravel, and unclear alternatives to action. We cannot imitate Abraham, but at least we can know that Abraham struggled, chose, endured, and was vindicated. In measure our survival is a vindication of Abraham, for we, like Isaac, are his children.

MAN'S MORALS
AND
GOD'S WILL

The Meaning of Abraham's Sacrifice

DAVID BAUMGARDT

And it came to pass after these things, that God did prove Abraham, and said unto him: "Abraham"; and he said: "Here am I."

And He said: "Take now thy son, thine only son, whom thou lovest, even Isaac, and get thee into the land of Moriah; and offer him there for a burnt-offering upon one of the mountains which I will tell thee of."

And Abraham rose early in the morning, and saddled his ass, and took two of his young men with him, and Isaac his son; and he cleaved the wood for the burnt-offering, and rose up, and went unto the place of which God had told him.

On the third day Abraham lifted up his eyes, and saw the place afar off.

And Abraham said unto his young men: "Abide ye here with the ass, and I and the lad will go yonder; and we will worship, and come back to you."

And Abraham took the wood of the burnt-offering, and laid it upon Isaac his son; and he took in his hand the fire and the knife; and they went both of them together.

And Isaac spoke unto Abraham his father, and said: "My father." And he said: "Here am I, my son." And he said: "Behold the fire and the wood; but where is the lamb for a burnt-offering?"

And Abraham said: "God will provide himself the lamb for a burnt-offering, my son." So they went both of them together.

And they came to the place which God had told him of; and Abraham built the altar there, and laid the wood in order, and bound Isaac his son, and laid him on the altar, upon the wood.

And Abraham stretched forth his hand, and took the knife to slay his son.

And the angel of the Lord called unto him out of heaven, and said: "Abraham, Abraham." And he said: "Here am I."

And he said: "Lay not thy hand upon the lad, neither do thou anything unto him; for now I know that thou art a God-fearing man, seeing thou hast not withheld thy son, thine only son, from Me."

And Abraham lifted up his eyes, and looked, and behold behind him a ram caught in the thicket by his horns. And Abraham went and took the ram, and offered him up for a burnt-offering in the stead of his son.

And Abraham called the name of that place Adonai-jireh; as it is said to this day: "In the mount where the Lord is seen."

And the angel of the Lord called unto Abraham a second time out of heaven,

And said: "By Myself have I sworn, saith the Lord, because thou hast done this thing, and hast not withheld thy son, thine only son,

"That in blessing I will bless thee, and in multiplying I will multiply thy seed as the stars of the heaven, and as the sand which is upon the seashore; and thy seed shall possess the gate of his enemies;

"And in thy seed shall all the nations of the earth be blessed; because thou hast hearkened to My voice."

—Gen. 22

Goethe credited himself with having put a good deal of mystery into his *Faust*. How much more merit then must be given to the author of the *akedah*—the story of Abraham's near sacrifice of Isaac—for the more than one hundred thousand interpretations (literally) elicited by the few sentences of his story! The fundamental distinctions between religion and ethics, laws of aesthetics, the nature of all moral and legal obligations, whole modern philosophies, have come into being and have matured through an interpretation of these few lines of the Old Testament.

Philologists and historians have again and again tried to ascertain the "true," the literal sense, "the correct and only meaning" of this Biblical story. There is no doubt that such a critical analysis of texts and the contriving of hypotheses as to the genesis and final composition of the Scriptures are interesting and valuable. But when historians and philologists claim that they can establish a *single* exclusively valid interpretation of the meaning of any great Biblical myth, they are floundering in deep waters. Some levels of interpretation are only relevant to men as scholars, while others, directed to men as men, present truths wrested from life and preserved in the religious and poetical documents of mankind.

Indeed, it may be said that a poetical or religious document remains alive only in so far as it gives rise to new and changing

288

interpretations according to the needs and insights of later generations. As soon as it becomes a mere topic of historical research and no longer an occasion for personal concern and personal meaning, it ceases to be living religion, living art, or living poetry, because it ceases to be experienced "subjectively," as personal emotion and insight.

Countless efforts have been made to spell out the true moral of the Abraham and Isaac story, sometimes in a rather cheap and even theatrical way. As early as about the end of the first century CE, the so-called *Antiquities* of Philo—which was certainly not written by that great Jewish thinker himself—added a number of touches to the original Biblical account designed to make the blind obedience of the two main actors even more conspicuous. The Bible says only that Abraham "rose early in the morning" after he had received the divine call. The *Antiquities,* however, says that after Abraham had heard the harsh divine command he "immediately . . . set forth . . . and . . . did not gainsay" Isaac. And Isaac proudly shows his firm resolve to offer himself up joyfully by delivering a long and bombastic speech to his father. For, contrary to the report of the Bible and the *Book of Jubilees,* the *Antiquities* says that Abraham had not told Isaac evasively that God would provide a lamb in time for the offering; Abraham was barbarous enough to tell his son "the whole truth," that he would be sacrificed "for a burnt offering." There is certainly a little too much easy bravura in the *Antiquities'* version of the story. Heroes who feel so little difficulty in sacrificing their sons or in being sacrificed themselves are the fancies of bookish minds.

In a similarly unconvincing way, the fearlessness of Isaac is emphasized in the *Fourth Book of the Maccabees;* here we are assured that "seeing his father's hand lifting the knife against him, Isaac did not shrink"—although the Bible does not say one word about such doubtful bravery on Isaac's part. The *Sefer Hayashar* (which even as late as the early nineteenth century was sometimes thought to be the book quoted in Joshua 10:13 and II Samuel 1:18, but could hardly have been written before 1100 CE) tries to "improve" on the Biblical account in the same way. It, too, frees Abraham from the reproach of having told Isaac that a lamb would be provided for the offering. And here—no less demonstratively than in the Pseudo-Philo or in the Christian *First Epistle of Clement to the Corinthians* and numerous other post-Biblical writings

—Abraham and Isaac are said to be especially cheerful, and even gay, as they go to slaughter and be slaughtered. The *Sefer Hayashar*, however, compensates for this improbable heroism by inserting at least a touchingly naive motif of filial tenderness. As he lies bound on the altar Isaac asks his father to bring his ashes, the "smell of Isaac," to his mother Sarah; but not to announce his death to her when she is sitting on a high place or a well "lest she should cast her soul after me" in the shock of her sorrow.

It is also true that in some *selihot* (prayers for forgiveness), such as the "Akedah" written by Benjamin ben Serah in Germany in the eleventh century, we read that at the sacrifice Abraham felt as if Isaac were being married and that Isaac felt as if united with a bride in wedlock. But in Benjamin's "Akedah" this sort of forced beatitude is certainly outweighed by the profound feelings of contrition and anxiety that dominate the prayer.

The most detailed, though often rather tearful, glorifications of Abraham's and Isaac's heroism are perhaps to be found in old French *mystères*, in old Italian, Spanish, Dutch, German, and English mystery plays, and in Theodore de Bèze's *Abraham Sacrifiant* (1550). Theodorus Beza, the ardent follower, biographer, and successor of Calvin, devoted so many sentimental verses to the self-sacrificing spirit of the two patriarchs in his *tragédie françoise* that even Satan is moved by their dialogue and feels pity for them.

It seems to me that a far deeper layer of the meaning of the *akedah* is probed by those Christian interpreters who stress primarily the suffering of Abraham and Isaac rather than their unswerving courage and the rich reward their fortitude brought in the end. The Church Fathers, Irenaeus, Augustine, and especially Tertullian, already indicated that the firewood carried by Isaac on his way to Mount Moriah was the "cross" of human passion. And even the Jewish *Bereshith Rabba* compares the wood with a "cross that someone carries on his shoulder." How profoundly, however, this theme has been elaborated in Christian thought may probably best be seen in the speculations of Jakob Böhme and Sören Kierkegaard.

Böhme dedicated a whole chapter to the *akedah* in his *Mysterium Magnum* of 1623. As the Zohar had done several centuries earlier, Böhme argues that it was only in this trial that Abraham came face to face with God's rigor, and it is important that he himself was forced to exercise rigor against Isaac; for without exercising this rigor, by living only in the spirit of love, no one can "perfect himself."

Isaac is, according to Böhme, a symbol of Adam and all humanity. Humanity is tried in the fire and wrath of God. In this trial, in the fire of God, humanity must mortify its own will in order to be reborn. As all the impure substances of metal "evaporate" in fire and only pure gold or silver "subsides," so the fire of sacrifice morally purifies man; and as Abraham rose up "early in the morning" to follow the voice commanding him to sacrifice his son, so must man never postpone or evade the call to sacrifice and to repentance.

Since the days of Adam, the original union of "God's love and anger" has been "rent asunder," and this fracture has to be healed. Sin and weakness must be bound to the wood, as Isaac was bound to the wood and Jesus was nailed to a wooden cross. Only if this binding of blind self-love and vanity is carried out "in very real sincere earnestness," will it mean anything. For it would seem nothing if we did not give ourselves "wholly into the process" with all our "thoughts and mind"—if only words were said and if sins were confessed only with our lips in our coming "before the altar."

But if the true purification of self-will is carried out, then the divine spirit cries out in us: do "nothing to thy nature! For now I know" that by thy nature "feareth God." In the end *das Reich der Natur,* the sphere of nature and its needs, cannot be rejected and thrown away. The ultimate will of God is not to impose endless self-punishment on man, eternal martyrdom and self-flagellation; the ultimate aim is the rebirth, the greater wholeness and perfection of human nature. It is in this way that trial and reward are connected in Böhme's searching comments on the story of the Old Testament.

Kierkegaard's Christian asceticism, however, pays almost no regard to the reward promised to Abraham. In *Fear and Trembling,* it is the cruelty of Abraham's trial to which our attention is primarily drawn; the glory of the reward is practically ignored. Kierkegaard relentlessly stresses that the divine command, "Sacrifice thy son," enjoins the gravest immorality. Here the divine command means the command to murder and, moreover, to commit the vilest kind of murder: infanticide, and, at the same time, the most paradoxical murder: that of one's own innocent and infinitely beloved child.

Kierkegaard writes: "What ordinarily tempts a man is that which would keep him from doing his duty. But in this case," paradoxically, "the ethical, the doing of one's duty, is itself the temptation." The seeming absurdity of Abraham's case is this: if he had insisted on doing his moral duty and had refused to kill his son, he would *not* have passed the trial; fulfillment of his ethical duty would have meant disobedience to God.

Kierkegaard carefully distinguishes the conflict that is won by the moral hero from that mastered by Abraham, the "knight of faith" and the "father of faith." The moral hero has to sacrifice only his personal inclinations for the sake of something that is evidently of higher universal value. This sacrifice of personal happiness may often be very difficult and even tragic, yet it is negligible in comparison with the "fear and trembling" that must be endured in those diabolic conflicts of life in which the moral choice is not that between a clear-cut, universally acknowledged right, and an evident wrong, but a choice between two kinds of right—or the "moral" alternative between wrong and wrong. Abraham knew that it was wrong to disobey God and wrong to kill his son.

No references to universal moral laws can guide us in these dilemmas. In Abraham's case, obviously, a "suspension" of all moral imperatives takes place, since here the will to murder is explicitly praised as true obedience to God. In other words, if the story of Abraham's trial means anything, it means that when it comes to the hardest decisions of life no other human being can advise us. No longer free to wander on the broad highway of "universally valid" morality, we are confronted as solitary individuals with God alone; and no one can accompany us on our climb "outside the universal" on the "narrow . . . steep and solitary path" of faith.

It has been rightly said that Judaism—in contradistinction to Kierkegaard's Christian teaching—cannot tolerate any ultimate suspension of morality. It is certainly justifiable to say that "if the separation of religious faith from ethical conduct is not essential to Christianity, it at least finds a much more favorable theological climate there than in Judaism."[1] After all, even in the *akedah,* God does not accept the sacrifice of a child in the end. But this does not mean that he did not even demand the sacrifice, as Jewish apolo-

---

1. Joseph H. Gumbiner: "Existentialism and Father Abraham," *Commentary,* February 1948.

getics—somewhat precipitately and far too assiduously—have often assured us.

If the many modern attempts to harmonize the differences between Judaism and Christianity are so unsatisfactory, too many of the attempts to celebrate them are, alas, equally so—on both sides. If Kierkegaard's interpretation of the *akedah* is unsatisfactory because he almost neglects the final restoration of morality after its "suspension," it seems to me even less pardonable to lose sight of the truly paradoxical nature of the divine command in the Abraham and Isaac story, to overlook the "absurdity" of the moral conflict involved, and the torment, the fear and trembling endured. To explain all this away and celebrate a far too easy triumph over the amorality, the nonrationalism, the "polytheism" of Christian belief has made many a Jewish apologetic as pointless and flat as the Christian distortions of the meaning of Jewish Law.

Kierkegaard answers beforehand certain modern Jewish ways of ironing out the difficulties in the *akedah.* "A trial!" he exclaims ironically—alas, it means far too little if the whole thing is got over as quickly as the word "trial" is pronounced. "One mounts a winged horse, the same instant one is at Mount Moriah, the same instant one sees the ram; one forgets that Abraham rode only upon an ass which walks slowly along the road, that he had a journey of three days, that he needed even time to cleave the wood, to bind Isaac, and to sharpen the knife." All of us know that what Abraham had to go through on his way to Mount Moriah was "just a trial," merely a trial; but *he* certainly did not know that. The farcical element in all the popular "cheap editions" of the Abraham story is, according to Kierkegaard, that they blot out the most important point in it—the "dread"—and make the happy ending intervene just as handily, just as "unexpectedly" and "easily as a prize in the lottery."

Kierkegaard also protests strongly against any confusion of this "suspension of ethics" with easygoing immorality. Jewish criticism of Kierkegaard has insisted that by the "teleological suspension of the ethical," by "the divorce of religious faith from the practice of ethical works, the content of religious life is emptied out. Each subjective thinker may replenish the cisterns from the vagaries of his own mind. There is no check on the quality of the inflow beyond the intensity of the individual's appropriation" (Gumbiner). But to this criticism Kierkegaard has retorted: "He who

believes that it is easy enough to be an individual can always be
sure that he is not a knight of faith, for vagabonds and roving
geniuses are not the men of faith." The true knight of faith knows
only too well how "glorious" and beatifying it is "to belong to the
universal," to be the individual who acts according to the universal
moral law in a way morally "intelligible to all." But he also knows
that now and then fate or the will of God confronts us with
dilemmas in which universal moral law in the generally accepted
sense of the word ceases to be a guide.

If, as Jewish apologetics say far too often, Torah means nothing
but "sound correctives for man's propensity towards sin," then the
Torah does not teach us anything about the conflict in the *akedah*,
the conflict of that solitary individual who had to choose between
two sins, the sin of disobedience to God and the sin of murder. And
Kierkegaard would not be wrong then in replying to his Jewish
critics by saying that it is not he who has emptied religious life by
the "elimination" of the ethical (he had spoken only of a "teleological suspension" of common morality), but his critics who let
God become merely "an invisible vanishing point, an impotent
idea," thus "emptying" basic realms of life and filling the whole of
reality with the ethical—that is, the ethical in the grossly over-
simplified sense of an absolute protection from sin.

But are not, perhaps, the Torah and the greatest leaders of
Jewish tradition better guides through the depths of human suffering and moral conflict than the modern moralistic defenders of the
Torah, better even than the greatest representatives of mere asceticism? As ancient a Jewish interpreter of the Bible as Philo can show
us how to combine the emphasis on the anguished "narrative" of
the *akedah* with the "purpose" of the narrative and its happy
ending. In his "On Abraham," Philo explains, in the best tradition
of the Jewish midrash, that "Isaac" means literally "laughter." "But
the laughter here understood is not the laughter which amusement
arouses in the body." It is "eupathy" of the mind. This joy the Sage
is said to sacrifice as part of his duty to God, thus showing in a
parable that rejoicing is most closely associated with God alone,
mankind being subject to grief. God, however, "fitly rewards by
returning the gift [of joy] in so far as the recipient's capacity
allows." Thus sacrifice and the return of joy for sacrifice are coupled
in Philo.

This will to sacrifice Isaac, to sacrifice the highest joy, ranks—for

Philo just as for Kierkegaard—higher than all the heroism of the great Greek patriots and even higher than Abraham's other achievements. For no pressure of custom cleared the way for Isaac's sacrifice, nor was any promise of fame and "universal" recognition held out to Abraham; the hero of this conflict had even to experience the fear of ignominy. Yet, as Philo adds far more emphatically than Kierkegaard, just because this hero was willing to bear this loneliest kind of fear and pain did he receive back his highest joy.

The Talmud, too, emphasizes that to understand Abraham one must take into account his fear of God as much as his love. His fear is attested by the text of the *akedah;* his love must—in fact, somewhat forcibly—be inferred from Isaiah 41:8. Abraham's fear and despair, his "crying aloud," is—contrary to modern moralizing interpretations—further stressed in numerous Jewish *midrashim.*

The most dramatic specification of the reality of Abraham's conflict is perhaps to be found in *Midrash Bereshith Rabba,* where Samael, the Devil, indicates in a veritable climax the different degrees of the gravity of Abraham's temptation. With the telling wit and realistic causticity of the tempter, Samael first turns against what is possibly the weakest point in Abraham's personal moral armor, his old age, his presumptive senility. "Old man," says the Devil to Abraham, "are you out of your senses already? Are you going to slaughter a son born to you at the age of a hundred?" This argument failing, he ridicules the pious obedience of the patriarch in another way by saying to him: Would you do, perhaps, even more for God than murder your son? "Canst thou stand even more?" And only after this argument fails does the Devil advance his most devastating piece of skepticism and his most dangerous temptation by asking Abraham: "Will not God say to thee tomorrow that thou art a bloodshedder? Thou hast murdered thy son! Thou art guilty!"

The *Midrash Bereshith Rabba* adds that this trial—the conflict between "self-evident" moral law, the universally valid law forbidding murder, and God's command, in which the alternative was between two wrongs—weighed as much on Abraham as all the previous trials put together. "If Abraham had not stood this test, all he had done before would have been in vain."

Even Maimonides, who generally shuns any discussion endangering the strength of purely rational argument in his metaphysics and ethics, does not omit to indicate in his *Moreh Nebuchim* that to ask the sacrifice of one's own life or one's possessions would have been a morally rational demand on God's part; but that the divine command issued to Abraham at his trial was something surpassing all that is thought morally possible and rationally comprehensible, something that seemingly goes against the very emotional as well as moral nature of man.

Small wonder that an earlier Jewish thinker of the Middle Ages, Abraham ibn Daud—though he, too, was a great rationalist in many respects—went even further than Maimonides in this direction. It has been frequently said that the Bible is not afraid on certain occasions to show man engaged in a rational moral dispute with God; there is the case of Job, for instance, and there is also Abraham arguing about the number of the righteous and the wicked in Sodom and Gomorrah. But as Abraham ibn Daud emphatically says in the very last sentences of his *Emunah Ramah*, in the *akedah* Abraham does not argue with God but silently obeys him, realizing that "there is no common standard by which to compare his insight with divine wisdom."

It appears to me to be most significant that Abraham behaves so silently and passively in the *akedah*. Granted, that the primitiveness of the narrator may provide some "excuse" for his having said so little about the intellectual and emotional stirrings inside Abraham. But if this is the reason, then primitiveness may here express great profundity. When such a "visitation" comes over us as came over Abraham, only charlatans can feel that they are being called on to do "great things." The true hero, when placed in a situation like that of the *akedah*, thinks only of "saddling his ass" and of going on without being in any way sure of where the road leads.

The only sign of Abraham's inner reaction, as mentioned in the Biblical story, is, grossly expressed, that he tells a white lie when he says to his son that God *will* choose the lamb for the burnt offering, although it had been made quite clear to him that God had already chosen a definite sacrifice—namely Isaac, his son. Kierkegaard, Rashi, and the *Pirke Rabbi Eliezer* try hard to exculpate Abraham on this point, but in my opinion they fail completely. It seems to me far more true to the text to admit what is clearly stated there: that Abraham did not tell the truth to his son.

But this certainly does not demonstrate that the Pentateuch regards the telling of a lie lightly. The Old Testament takes the most serious view possible of lying and cheating. Yet it obviously thinks that the telling of a white lie is not only justifiable but even morally required, if it can spare a human being the feeling of doom for even a short time. The Old Testament leaves to St. Augustine, Kant, and Fichte the task of teaching that a lie is immoral under any circumstances. The moral hero of the *akedah* was evidently not capable of such a spectacular suppression of his paternal feelings. He could not even for a few hours inflict inner torture on his son for the sake of an ephemeral confession of truth. He was prepared to slaughter him on the ground of an irrevocable command, but he was not willing to inflict gratuitous, avoidable torment on him.

The *akedah* conveys more than anything else the impression that Abraham silently, and under pain hardly grasped to its full extent, bore the brunt of a hardly bearable destiny. He goes ahead silently and tries to do his task without the slightest sign of self-assuredness, as sincere men in the most difficult moments of their lives always have had to tread their paths alone—without knowing where the journey to Moriah would lead, with a heavy heart and even with a gnashing of teeth.

Isaac is, of course, even more in the dark and totally unaware of what is going on when he asks: where is the lamb for the burnt offering? This question becomes even more pathetic in that it reveals the gulf between his familiarity with the technicalities of sacrifice and his utter ignorance of the real meaning of the one that stands before him. With all the practical interests characteristic of his age, the lad is well acquainted with the usual routine of the service but totally unaware of the diabolic meaning that the very word "offering" takes on in his mouth when he asks his father his innocent question! Thus, too, Isaac's fate is characteristic of a situation laden with symbolic significance: that in which one is crushed as a blameless victim in a great moral conflict whose nature is entirely beyond one's grasp.

Finally, the happy ending, the great award! The angel's first announcement does not make Abraham's reward appear so magnificent. The angel says only that Abraham has sufficiently documented his obedience to the divine command. The angel's second announcement may be taken as a mere variant on this from the viewpoint of critical text-analysis. But the two pronouncements do seem to me of great symbolic expressiveness.

In the moments when great moral deeds are to be performed they do not appear so dazzling. And even immediately after they have been done, fate simply states that the test was met, the examination passed with a satisfactory grade; the right moral decision was made in a conflict in which no fixed moral code could provide a ready-made, self-evident rule. Only the ultimate evaluation and clarification of world-history—like the second announcement of the angel—reveals the full impact of these great and lonely moral decisions. That man who once, in the throes of his most difficult inner struggle, could not find the heart to tell the truth to his own son but had to bear his blackest grief alone, silently riding on his ass into the unknown—this man has become for all times one of the shining incarnations of a great life. And in his seed all the nations of the earth shall take heart.

Once more, what does all this amount to? Can it ever mean that, in the end, Judaism advocates the complete surrender of ethics to faith, to a philosophy of life in which a nonrational "fear and trembling" is the highest value and has the final word? By no means. What Judaism, in my opinion, stands for and what we need more than anything else today is a revision of our narrow, pseudo-rationalistic notions of ethics, and a considerably revised interpretation of what ethics means in its relation to faith.

One may, I believe, say with Rabbi Gumbiner that Judaism on the whole keeps itself aligned with the best traditions of hedonism from Democritus to Bentham. That an *epikores* is an atheist in the Talmud is not counter-evidence. The Jews, the people who have in the past two millennia gone through more suffering than any others, have not idolized suffering as the highest value. Not suffering as such and in itself, but joy is for them the highest legitimate aim of man. True joy is for them more profound than pain—in this world and any world to come.

But Judaism also teaches that there are highest joys that, in the nature of things and according to the unfathomable will of God, are linked up with suffering. These joys can be bought only at the price of pain; and the only comfort religion can give is to establish that they are worth that price.

Judaism has laid down a considerable body of strict moral principles—the Ten Commandments and others. These do not demand national honor and national aggrandizement, but they do demand that one tell the truth and love one's fellow men. It might be said that Judaism considers certain moral principles self-evident and obligatory under all ordinary circumstances. But beyond even the best fixed moral rules, there is what Judaism calls the will of God. If this word is not a mere conventional phrase or a superstitious belief, then the will of God must mean something like fate, as fate is experienced by the purest energies of morally wrestling men. This will of God confronts us with situations like that of the *akedah,* where the fixed moral commandments do not become wrong, but remain silent.

But even then our ultimate moral and religious aim must remain the increase, the maximization, of joy. This aim must never become irrational or subjectively capricious. But, as in the case of the *akedah,* there are instances of the will of God that permits us to rely no longer on simple strict adherence to the Ten Commandments; we are forced to choose between two moral commandments, and the breach of either of them spells guilt. In these extreme conflicts of life, the supreme rational command to work ceaselessly for the maximization of happiness leaves to us the risk and responsibility of applying the command properly. This is certainly no elimination of ethics and even no "suspension of the ethical," if the term ethics is taken in its true and most vital sense.

I feel that I cannot kill. But I cannot dare to condemn morally him who may hate the spilling of blood as much as I do but who, nevertheless, fights and kills because, while considering all the possible consequences, he sees no other way to avoid the endless slaughter of far more innocent victims. And who can say, without wishful thinking, that peaceful methods always achieve a good greater than that which can be achieved by even the limited use of force? I may be mistaken in thinking and feeling this way. Perhaps they are much wiser who restrict the "unfathomable character of God" to his regulation of the cosmos and insist that no unfathomable sign of God can intrude upon or suspend the rigid, abstract rationality of those moral commandments that ordinarily govern our lives. The teaching of the *akedah* is, as it seems to me, incompatible with such a view of Judaism. Why in any case does the contemporary boasting about the rigor of Jewish morality and the purity of Jewish monotheism sound so strangely hollow when it tries to explain away the concrete features of that great old stirring myth of the *akedah?*

TRADITION AND COMMENTARY AS RELIGIOUS CATEGORIES IN JUDAISM

Gershom G. Scholem

Scrupulous readers will doubtless observe that there is lacking thus far in this Reader any discussion of Jewish *tradition,* or the *halachah.* This is certainly an omission, but like most conspicuous omissions, no less apparent to the offender than to the offended.

Please recall: we have set out to explore the response of the Jewish thinkers to the last three decades of Jewish experience. Three decades is a short time, but we should have no hesitation in regarding these recent times as perhaps the most critical in Jewish history since the Exodus from Egypt, the giving of the Torah, and the destruction of the Jewish state by Rome. Our time has witnessed the thorough decimation of the Jew in the most significant cultural and religious center of the Dispersion and the even more remarkable restoration of the Jewish people in its ancestral homeland. Our times are seismic. We have old origins and continuous history, but we have as well unprecedented conclusions and new beginnings. No fossil, this people Israel!

What is critical in the essay of Gershom G. Scholem, the greatest scholar and interpreter of Jewish mysticism, is that in addressing himself to the nature of tradition and commentary he has given us the opportunity of seeing the substratum of *halachah* in a new dimension; and since it is new (or at least unfamiliar) dimensions of Jewish thought that interest us, we are obliged to pay him heed.

Tradition and commentary present theological problems—not only the obvious theological problems, those which affect the character of individual observance and the directives which the Torah addresses to the conscience of the individual Jewish believer, but problems that involve our very understanding of God and revelation. It will be readily recalled that *Sayings of the Fathers* opens with a recitation of the continuity of transmission of the tradition, the *Masorah,* from God and Moses to the generations of the Talmudic Sages. We may add the beyond—from the Sages to the Geonim and the Academies, to the tosafists, the legists and codifiers, the respondents and interpreters to our own day. There is a continuity which wrests from the obedient generation of those who heard at Sinai (and needed fewer proscriptions to action for they knew what was demanded of them) to our own time when, as temptation increases and disaffection mounts, it becomes apparently necessary to make the law more strict that we be kept farther from the possibility of transgression.

All this assumes, however, that the Law was given to Israel once and for all and that the generations of faithful receivers took those instructions and from them elaborated meanings and significances which they contained but had not expressed explicitly. The Word is divine, but the commentator mediates divinity to historical circumstance and requirement. Such a view succeeds in defining linear continuity of the *halachah.* The *halachah* is given over by God to the custodial keeping of man; it is in the hands of the Sages to describe the ambit of the Law and the faithful in Israel to fulfill its requirements. Ours, however, is not a faithful generation in any way recognizable by historical Judaism. This is not to deny that there are millions of believing and observant Jews; it is, however, to characterize the whole of Israel. If the criterion of faithfulness is obedience to *halachah,* it could not be denied that this is an unobservant and, hence, faithless generation.

The power of Scholem's essay—understated, cool, reasoned as it is—lies in the suggestion that there is another way of regarding the continuity of tradition. The *Kabbalah,* which quite literally means the receiving of the Torah, suggests a rather different approach. Its approach depends, however, upon regarding God as not only the origin of Torah, but as its continuous, ever-productive source. God did not give over the Torah into the hands of man once and for all. The paradox is that a Living God does not live but once and complete himself on revelation, emptying himself out, pouring out Torah and ceasing for eternity. This is to deny to life continual vitality; and if it is incorrect to imagine that human life is progenitive but once and thereafter is quiescent, so, by analogy, and how much more so, is this the situation of God. God is that being who is in continuous motion and productivity. Having added to the reality of God the existential element of presentness to history, the God of the pure act is, not simply an intellectual essence, but a reality. The *Kabbalah* insists, then, upon the metaphysical contemporaneity of God, the immediate continuity which binds the God who speaks to man to every man, in the particularity of his here and now.

There is no easy way to bring together the historical continuity of the tradition with the wisdom of the *Kabbalah*. The one is a real continuity that has been employed to underscore a doctrine of revelation. The *Kabbalah* begins the other way around—with the nature of the creative God, the God whose existence is the totality of meanings of creation, from whose creativity meanings proceed, accumulate, and are sifted by man. To the former, tradition is a fixity, beginning at one moment and carrying Israel to the end of days; for the latter, tradition is an organism whose validity and endurance lies, not in its horizontal continuity and the wisdom of authority, but in the productive vitality of the center from whom, not only all wisdom, but All proceeds.

TRADITION AND COMMENTARY
AS RELIGIOUS CATEGORIES
IN JUDAISM

GERSHOM G. SCHOLEM

I

In considering the problem of tradition, we must distinguish between two questions. The first is historical: How did a tradition
endowed with religious dignity come to be formed? The other
question is: How was this tradition understood once it had been
accepted as a religious phenomenon? For the faithful promptly
discard the historical question once they have accepted a tradition;
this is the usual process in the establishment of religious systems.
Yet for the historian the historical question remains fundamental:
in order to understand the meaning of what the faithful simply
accept, the historian is not bound to accept fictions that veil more
than they reveal concerning the origins of the accepted faith. Thus,
tradition as a special aspect of revelation is historically a product of
the process that formed rabbinic Judaism between the fourth or
third pre-Christian centuries and the second century of the Common Era.

In all religions, the acceptance of a Divine revelation originally
referred to the concrete communication of positive, substantive,
and expressible content. It never occurred to the bearers of such a
revelation to question or to limit the specific quality and closely
delineated content of the communication they had received. Where,
as in Judaism, such revelation is set down in holy writings and is
accepted in that form, it initially constitutes concrete communication, factual content, and nothing else. But inasmuch as such

revelation, once set down in holy scriptures, takes on authoritative character, an essential change takes place. For one thing, new historical circumstances require that the communication, whose authoritativeness has been granted, be applied to ever-changing conditions. Furthermore, the spontaneous force of human productivity seizes this communication and expands it beyond its original scope. "Tradition" thus comes into being. It embodies the realization of the effectiveness of the Word in every concrete state and relationship entered into by a society.

At this point begins the process in which two questions gain importance: How can revelation be preserved as a concrete communication, i.e., how can it be passed on from generation to generation? (This is a virtually impossible undertaking by itself.) And, with ever-greater urgency: Can this revelation be applied at all, and, if so, how? With this second question, spontaneity has burst into the nascent tradition. In the process of this renewed productivity, holy scriptures themselves are sometimes enlarged; new written communications take their place alongside the old ones. A sort of no man's land is created between the original revelation and the tradition. Precisely this happened in Judaism, for example, as the Torah, to which the quality of revelation was originally confined, was "expanded" to include other writings of the Biblical canon that had at first been subsumed, completely and emphatically, under the heading of tradition and considered merely repositories of this. Later, the boundaries often shifted: the canon, as Holy Writ, confronted tradition and, within the tradition itself, similar processes of differentiation between written and oral elements were repeated.

From now on tradition asserts itself ever more emphatically as a new religious value and as a category of religious thinking. It becomes the medium through which creative forces express themselves. By the side of the Written Torah tradition arraigns itself, and it is called Oral Torah from approximately the first Christian century on. Tradition is not simply the totality of that which the community possesses as its cultural patrimony and which it bequeathes to its posterity; it is a specific selection from this patrimony, which is elevated and garbed with religious authority. It proclaims certain things, sentences, or insights to be Torah, and thus connects them with the revelation. In the process, the original meaning of revelation as a unique, positively established, and clearly delineated realm of propositions is put in doubt—and thus a development as fruitful as it is unpredictable begins which is highly instructive for the religious problematic of the concept of tradition.

The unfolding of the truths, statements, and circumstances that are given in or accompany revelation becomes the function of the Oral Torah, which creates in the process a new type of religious person. In the history of religion, this type has evoked admiration as much as rejection and derision, and not without reason. The Biblical scholar perceives revelation, not as a unique and clearly delineated occurrence, but rather as a phenomenon of eternal fruitfulness to be unearthed and examined: "Turn it and turn it again, for everything is in it." Thus the achievement of these scholars, who established a tradition rooted in the Torah and growing out of it, is a prime example of spontaneity in receptivity. They are leaders because they know themselves to be led. Out of the religious tradition they bring forth something entirely new, something that itself commands religious dignity: commentary. Revelation needs commentary in order to be rightly understood and applied—this is the far from self-evident religious doctrine out of which grew both the phenomenon of Biblical exegesis and the Jewish tradition which it created.

This inner law of development of the concept of revelation is also traceable in other religions which accept the authority of revelation. The process under discussion here is, therefore, of general significance for the phenomenology of religion. Judaism experienced this process in a peculiarly vigorous and consequential form, and its agents examined it with great thoroughness. This will make our consideration of the present complex of problems especially illuminating and far-reaching.

A creative process begins to operate which will permeate and alter tradition—the Midrash: the more regulated Halachic and the somewhat freer Aggadic exegesis of scriptures, and the views of the Biblical scholars in their various schools, are regarded as implicitly contained in the Written Torah. No longer only old and carefully guarded sentences but now also the analyses of scriptures by the scholars themselves lay claim to being tradition. The desire for historical continuity which is of the very essence of tradition is translated into a historical construction whose fictitious character cannot be doubted but which serves the believing mind as a crutch of external authentication. Especially peculiar in this historical construction is the metamorphosis of the prophets into bearers of tradition—a very characteristic, albeit to our minds a very paradoxical, transformation. Originally only the last of the prophets, Haggai, Zechariah, and Malachi, had been meant by this proposition, for they possess special importance in the doctrine of the uninterrupted chain of tradition[1]: the last of the prophets are, not without all justification, regarded as the first of the scribes and "men of the Great Assembly." Subsequently, also the older prophets are designated as links in the chain, which would otherwise have had to be invisible.

This leads to the viewpoint expressed daringly in Talmudic writings, namely, that the total substance of the Oral Torah, which had in fact been the achievement of the scholars, comes from the same source as the Written Torah, and that it was, therefore, basically always known. The saying "turn it . . ." reflects this viewpoint. But underneath this fiction, the details of which do not concern us here, there lies a religious attitude which is interesting and which had significant results. I refer to the distinctive notion of revelation including within itself as sacred tradition the later commentary concerning its own meaning. This was the beginning of a road which, with a full measure of inherent logic, was to lead to the establishment of mystical theses concerning the character of revelation as well as the character of tradition.

Here we immediately encounter a significant tension in the religious consciousness of the scholars themselves, between the process by which the tradition actually developed and the interpretation of that process. On the one hand, there was the blossoming productivity of the academies where the Scriptures were explored and examined in ever greater detail—the spontaneous achievement of the generations upon whom, in turn, was bestowed such authority as was transmitted by the great teachers and the tradition. On the other hand, there arose the claim apparently flowing from the dogma of the revealed nature of the Oral Law. What this claim amounted to was that all this was somehow part of revelation itself—and more: not only was it given along with revelation, but it was given in a special, timeless sphere of revelation in which all generations were, as it were, gathered together; everything really had been made explicit to Moses, the first and most comprehensive

---

1. Comp. Bacher, *Tradition und Tradenten*, pp. 27–31.

recipient of Torah. The achievement of every generation, its contribution to tradition, was projected back into the eternal present of the revelation at Sinai. This, of course, is something which no longer has anything in common with the notion of revelation with which we began, namely, revelation as unequivocal, clear, and understandable communication. According to this new doctrine, revelation comprises within it everything that will ever be legitimately offered to interpret its meaning.

The patent absurdity of this claim reveals a religious assumption that must be taken all the more seriously. The Rabbis did not hesitate to express this assumption in rather extravagant formulations. In the forty days that Moses spent on Mount Sinai (*Ex.* 34:28), he learned the Torah with all its implications.[2] Rabbi Joshua ben Levi (a third-century Palestinian teacher) said: "Torah, Mishna, Talmud, and Aggadah—indeed even the comments some bright student will one day make to his teacher—were already given to Moses on Mount Sinai"—and even the questions that such a bright student will some day ask his teacher![3] In our context, statements such as these are highly suggestive. They make absolute the concept of tradition in which the meaning of revelation unfolds in the course of historical time—but only because everything that can come to be known has already been deposited in a timeless substratum. In other words, we have arrived at an assumption concerning the nature of truth which is characteristic of rabbinic Judaism (and probably of every traditional religious establishment) : Truth is given once and for all, and it is laid down with precision. Fundamentally, truth merely needs to be transmitted. The originality of the exploring scholar has two aspects. In his spontaneity, he develops and explains that which was transmitted at Sinai, no matter whether it was always known or whether it was forgotten and had to be rediscovered. The effort of the seeker after truth consists not in having new ideas but rather in subordinating himself to the continuity of the tradition of the Divine word and in laying open what he receives from it in the context of his own time. In other words: not system but *commentary* is the legitimate form through which truth is approached.

This is a most important principle indeed for the kind of produc-

---

2. *Midrash Tanhuma*, ed. Buber, II, p. 60a.
3. Ibid., p. 58b.

tivity we encounter in Jewish literature. Truth must be laid bare in a text in which it already pre-exists. We shall deal later with the nature of this pre-existent givenness. In any case, truth must be brought forth from the text. Commentary thus became the characteristic expression of Jewish thinking about truth, which is another way of describing the rabbinic genius. Under the influence of Greek thought, there were also explications and attempts at system-construction within Judaism. But its innermost life is to be found where holy texts received commentary, no matter how remote from the text itself these commentaries and their ideas may appear to the present-day critical reader. There is, of course, a striking contrast between the awe of the text, founded on the assumption that everything already exists in it, and the presumptuousness of imposing the truth upon ancient texts. The commentator, who is truly the Biblical scholar, always combines both attitudes.

Tradition as a living force produces in its unfolding another problem. What had originally been believed to be consistent, unified, and self-enclosed now becomes diversified, multifold, and full of contradictions. It is precisely the wealth of contradictions, of differing views, which is encompassed and unqualifiedly affirmed by tradition. There were many possibilities of interpreting the Torah, and tradition claimed to comprise them all.[4] It maintains the contradictory views with astounding seriousness and intrepidity, as if to say that one can never know whether a view at one time rejected may not one day become the cornerstone of an entirely new edifice. In Jewish tradition the views of the schools of Hillel and Shammai, two teachers who lived shortly before Jesus, play an important part. Their mutually contradictory attitudes toward theoretical and practical problems are codified by the Talmud with great thoroughness, although the rule is that in the application of the law the views of Hillel's school are decisive. But the rejected views are stated no less carefully than the accepted ones. The

---

4. Of R. Meir it is said in *Erubin* 13b: "He pronounces the impure pure and proves it and the pure impure and proves this" (in order to force the scholars to think through the problems most conscientiously before arriving at a decision). Of his disciple Symmachos it is there reported that he adduced 48 reasons for the impurity of each impure object and 48 reasons for the purity of each pure object. In the same place the Talmud reports very soberly the tradition, which must be particularly disquieting to a pious mind, that in Jabneh there was even an acute student who was able to adduce 150 reasons why a crawling animal is pure—whereas in fact the Torah explicitly and unambiguously prohibits it.

Talmudists formulated no ultimate thesis concerning the unity of these contradictions, concerning dialectical relationships within the tradition. It was only one of the latest Kabbalists who formulated the daring and, at first blush, surprising thesis, which has since been often reiterated, that the *Halachah* would be decided according to the now rejected view of the school of Shammai in the Messianic era. That is to say, the conception of the meaning and of the applicability of the Torah which is unacceptable at any given time within history in reality anticipates a Messianic condition in which it will have its legitimate function—and thereby the unity of the Torah, which embraces all of this, is fully sealed.[5]

Thus, tradition is concerned with the realization, the enactment of the Divine task which is set in the revelation. It demands application, execution, and decision, and at the same time it is, indeed, "true growth and unfolding from within." It constitutes a living organism, whose religious authority was asserted with as much emphasis as is at all possible within this system of thought.

The question remains: Does tradition keep its freshness in such a view, or does it freeze into Alexandrianism and lose its organic ability to grow when too much is demanded of it? At what point does deadly decay lurk? The question is as important as it is hard to answer. As long as there is a living relationship between religious consciousness and revelation there is no danger to the tradition from within. But when this relationship dies, tradition ceases to be a living force. To be sure, this looks very different to an outside observer. Everyone who studies the tradition of any religious community is aware of this antinomy. For example: For the Church Fathers the rabbinical students of Scripture were still guardians of a valuable tradition; to later Christendom, they appeared incomprehensible and rather terrifying—and this at a time when the tradition enjoyed a very active inner life. For tradition, omnipotence and impotence dwell closely together; all is in the eye of the beholder.

In Judaism, tradition becomes the reflective impulse that intervenes between the absoluteness of the Divine word—revelation—and its receiver. Tradition thus raises a question about the possibility of immediacy in man's relationship to the Divine, even

---

5. This thesis seems first to have been stated by Moses Graf of Prague; see his *Vayakhel Moshe,* Dessau 1699, pp. 45b and 54a.

though it has been incorporated in revelation. To put it another way: Can the Divine word confront us without mediation? And, can it be fulfilled without mediation? Or, given the assumption of the Jewish tradition which we have formulated, does the Divine word rather not require just such mediation by tradition in order to be apprehensible and therefore fulfillable? For rabbinic Judaism, the answer is in the affirmative. Every religious experience after revelation is a mediated one. It is the experience of the voice of God rather than the experience of God. But all reference to the "voice of God" is highly anthropomorphic—a fact from which theologians have always carefully tried to escape. And here we face questions which, in Judaism, have been thought through only in the mystic doctrines of the Kabbalists.

II

The Kabbalists were in no sense of the word heretics. Rather they strove to penetrate, more deeply than their predecessors, into the meaning of Jewish concepts. They took the step from the tradition of the Talmudists to mystical tradition. In order to understand the mystical concepts of tradition, we must take a step backward and try to visualize the Kabbalists' concept of Torah as revelation and as the word of God. The Kabbalists sought to unlock the innermost core of the Torah, to decode the text, so to speak. (Here we have a new concept of tradition: after all, the Hebrew word *kabbalah* means "the receiving of the tradition".) This goes far beyond what had been thought about these questions in esoteric Judaism, and yet the Kabbalists' thinking remains specifically Jewish. In a way, they have merely drawn the final consequence from the assumption of the Talmudists concerning revelation and tradition as religious categories.

The first question which presented itself to the Kabbalists in this connection concerned the nature of that Torah which is known as the "Written Torah." What is it that God can actually reveal, and of what does the so-called word of God consist that is given to the recipients of revelation? The answer is: God reveals nothing but Himself as He becomes speech and voice. The expression through which the Divine power presents itself to man in manifestation, no matter how concealed and how inward, is the name of God. It is this that is expressed and given voice in scripture and revelation, no matter how hieroglyphically. It is encoded in every so-called communication that revelation makes to man. "For the Holy Scriptures, the great mysterium of the revelation of God, containing all within all, is a hieroglyph of unending hieroglyphs, an eternal spring of mysteries, inexhaustible, pouring forth without end, ever new and glorious."[6] To be sure, those secret signatures (*rishumim*) that God had placed upon things are as much concealments of His revelation as revelation of His concealment. The script of these signatures differs from what we view as Torah, as revealed Scripture, only in the unconditional, undistracted concentration in which these are here collected. The language, which lives in things as their creative principle, is the same; but here, concentrated upon its own essence, it is not (or at most thinly) concealed by the creaturely existence in which it appears. Thus, revelation is revelation of the name or names of God, which are perhaps the different modes of His active being. God's language has no grammar; it consists only of names. The oldest Kabbalists—Nachmanides, for example—profess to have received as tradition this understanding of the structure of the Torah. It is clear, however, that this was originally a tradition of magical character, now transposed into a mystical tradition.

The creative force thus concentrated in the name of God, which is the essential word that God sends forth from Himself, is far greater than any human expression, than any creaturely word can grasp. It is never exhausted by the finite, human word. It represents an absolute which, resting in itself—one might as well say: self-moved—sends its rays through everything that seeks expression and form in all worlds and through all languages. Thus, the Torah is a texture (Hebrew: *ariga*) fashioned out of the names of God and, as the earliest Spanish Kabbalists already put it, out of the great, absolute name of God, which is the final signature of all things. It constitutes a mysterious whole, whose primary purpose is not to transmit a specific sense, to "mean" something, but rather to express the force of the Divinity itself which is concentrated in this "name." This conception has nothing to do with any rational understanding of the possible social function of a name; this Name cannot, after all, even be pronounced. The Torah is built up out of this Name, just as a tree grows out of its root, or, to use another favorite image of the Kabbalists, just as a building is erected out of an artistic interweaving of bricks that ultimately also consist of one basic

6. Molitor, F. J., *Philosophie der Geschichte oder Ueber die Tradition,* vol. I (1857), p. 47.

material. This is the thesis repeated in every possible form in the classical writings of the Kabbalah: "The whole Torah is no more than the great name of God." As Joseph Gikatilla has set forth in great detail, in the Torah the living texture constructed out of the tetragrammaton is seen as an infinitely subtle braiding of the permutations and combination of its consonants; these in turn were subjected to more such processes of combination, and so on ad infinitum, until they finally appear to us in the form of the Hebrew sentences of the Torah. Thus, the very words that we read in the written Torah and that constitute the audible "word of God" and communicate a comprehensible message, are in reality mediations through which the absolute word, incomprehensible to us, is offered. This absolute word is originally communicated in its limitless fullness, but—and that is the key point—this communication is incomprehensible! It is not a communication which provides comprehension; being basically nothing but the expression of essence, it becomes a comprehensible communication only when it is mediated.

This strict, mystical view of the nature of revelation is basic to any analysis of tradition. It has significant consequences. One of them is so radical that it was taught only in veiled, symbolical terminology. It amounted to the assertion that there was no such thing as a written Torah in the sense of an immediate revelation of the Divine word. For such a revelation is contained in the Wisdom of God, where it forms an "Ur-Torah" in which the "word" rests as yet completely undeveloped in a mode of being in which no differentiation of the individual elements into sounds and letters takes place. The sphere in which this "Ur-Torah" (*Torah kelula*) comes to articulate itself into the so-called Written Torah, where signs (the forms of the consonants) or sounds and expressions exist—that sphere itself is already interpretation. An old dictum of the Midrash, according to which the pre-existent Torah was written before God with black fire upon white fire, was given the esoteric interpretation that the white fire is the Written Torah in which the letters are not yet formed; only by means of the black fire, which is the Oral Torah, do the letters acquire form. The black fire is likened to the ink on the parchment of the Torah scroll. This would imply that what we on earth call the Written Torah has already gone through the medium of the Oral Torah and has taken on a perceptible form in that process. The Written Torah is not really the blackness of the inked writing (already a specification), but the mystic whiteness of the letters on the parchment of the scroll on which we see nothing at all. According to this, the Written Torah is a purely mystical concept, understood only by prophets who can penetrate to this level. As for us, we can perceive revelation only as unfolding oral tradition.

While this notion was only rarely hinted at, there was general acceptance of another conclusion drawn from the principle of the Torah as the name of God, and this one is central to our discussion. It is the thesis that the word of God carries infinite meanings, however it may be defined. Even that which has already become a sign in the strict sense, and is already a mediated word, retains the character of the absolute. But if there is such a thing as God's word, it must, of course, be totally different from the human word. It is far-reaching, all-embracing, and, unlike a human word, cannot be applied to a specific context of meaning. In other words: God's word is infinitely interpretable; indeed, it is *the* object of interpretation par excellence. Saying that, we have, indeed, moved far away from the origin of our consideration, i.e., from the original historical notions of revelation as a specific and positive communication. In this new perspective, the old notions are but the exoteric garments of an insight that probes far deeper. Here revelation, which has yet no specific meaning, is that in the word which gives an infinite wealth of meaning. Itself without meaning, it is yet quintessential interpretability. For mystical theology, this is a decisive criterion of revelation. In every word there now shines an infinite multitude of lights. The primeval light of the Torah that shines in the holy letters refracts on the unending facets of "meaning." In this connection, the Kabbalists always speak of the "seventy faces of the Torah"; the number seventy simply represents the inexhaustible totality and meaning of the Divine word.

We now face the problem of tradition as it presented itself to the Kabbalists. If the conception of revelation as absolute and meaning-giving but in itself meaningless is correct, then it must also be true that revelation will come to unfold its infinite meaning (which cannot be confined to the unique event of revelation) only in its constant relationship to history, the arena in which tradition unfolds. Theologians have described the word of God as the "absolutely concrete." But the absolutely concrete is, at the same time, the simply unfulfillable—it is that which in no way can be put into practice. The Kabbalistic idea of tradition is founded upon the dialectic tension of precisely this paradox: it is precisely the absoluteness that effects the unending reflections in the contingencies of fulfillment. Only in the mirrorings in which it reflects itself does revelation become practicable and accessible to human action as something concrete. There is no immediate, undialectic application of the Divine word. If there were it would be destructive. From this point of view, so-called concreteness—which has so many admirers these days and whose glorification is the labor of a whole philosophical school—is something mediated and reflected, something that has gone through many refractions. It is the tradition of the word of God—for the Kabbalists the basis of any possible action that deserves the name of action—that permits its application in history. Tradition undergoes changes with the times, new facets of its meaning shining forth and lighting its way. Tradition, according to its mystical sense, is Oral Torah, precisely because every stabilization in the text would hinder and destroy the infinitely moving, the constantly progressing and unfolding element within it, which would otherwise become petrified. The writing down and codification of the Oral Torah, undertaken in order to save it from being forgotten, was, therefore, as much a protective as (in the deeper sense) a pernicious act. Demanded by the historical circumstance of exile, it was profoundly problematic for the living growth and continuance of the tradition in its original sense. It is, therefore, not surprising that, according to Talmudic report,[7] it was originally prohibited to write down the Oral Torah; and it is not surprising that great Kabbalists (Nathan Adler in Frankfurt, for example) are said not to have committed their learning to writing because, since he and his students were keeping tradition from being forgotten, the prohibition against writing it down continued to be valid for him.

The understanding of tradition as a process that creates productivity through receptivity can now be seen clearly. Talmudic literature recognizes two types of men who preserve the tradition. One is the man who was useful in the Houses of Study, who could recite from memory the texts of all the old traditions of the schools—mere receptacles who preserved tradition without augmenting it in the slightest by their own inquiry. But this man, a conduit for tradi-

---

7. *Gittin* 6ob.

tion, is at best an expedient, virtually an oral book. The truly learned man is the one who is bound to tradition through his inquiries. So far as the consciousness of future generations is concerned, only the men of the second type are the true carriers of tradition, for tradition is living creativity in the context of revelation. Precisely because tradition perceives, receives, and unfolds that which lives in the word, it is the force within which contradictions and tensions are not destructive but rather stimulating and creative. For those who stand within the tradition it is easy to see the organic unity of these contradictions, precisely because it presents a dialectic relationship in which the word of revelation is developed. Without contradictions it would not perform this function.

The scholar and commentator, therefore, fulfills a set task: to make the Torah concrete at the point where he stands, to make it applicable *hic et nunc,* and, moreover, to fashion his specific form of concretization in such a manner that it may be transmitted. The latter Kabbalah formulated a widely accepted dictum: that the Torah turns a special face to every single Jew, meant only for him and apprehensible only by him, and that a Jew therefore fulfills his true purpose only when he comes to see this face and is able to incorporate it into the tradition. The "chain of tradition" is never broken; it is the translation of the inexhaustible word of God into the human and attainable sphere; it is the transcription of the voice sounding from Sinai in an unending richness of sound. The musician who plays a symphony has not composed it; still, he participates in significant measure in its production. This, of course, is valid only for those who assume a metaphysical contemporaneity for all tradition. For those, on the other hand, who see tradition as the creature of history, in whose course revelation is reflected, tradition legitimately represents the greatest creation of Judaism, which when properly understood is constituted only within this tradition.

For the Kabbalists the voice from Sinai was the constant medium, the foundation for the continuing existence of tradition. The unique event called revelation—in just the sense analyzed here—is juxtaposed to the continuity of the voice. Every carrier of tradition refers back to it, as is emphasized by the texts I shall now examine. These texts attempt to unify the exoteric concept of tradition as developed by the Talmudists with the mystical concept that was conditioned by the assumptions of the Kabbalists concerning the nature of revelation. They are extracts from two of the most important works of later kabbalistic literature and to me seem highly important for our considerations.

In this literature, the most extensive discussion concerning the nature of tradition is found in the work *Avodat ha-Kodesh,* written in 1531 in Turkey by Meir ben Gabbai.[8] He set out to prove that tradition is not a profane achievement of human thought and deliberation, but that it is precisely "Oral Torah" and a re-sounding of the voice (in the sense adduced earlier). At the same time, Meir ben Gabbai tried to answer the question of how it was possible, even necessary, for the tradition to offer such differing conceptions concerning the observance of the Torah, since the Torah, perfect within itself, is after all the revelation of the Divine Will. I quote here one of his very detailed explications:

"The highest wisdom [the *sophia* of God, which is the second *Sefira*] contains as the foundation of all emanations pouring forth out of the hidden Eden the true fountain from which the Written and the Oral Torah emanate and are impressed [upon the forms of the celestial letters and signatures]. This fountain is never interrupted; it gushes forth in constant production. Were it to be interrupted for even a moment, all creatures would sink back into their nonbeing; for the gushing forth is the cause of God's great name appearing in its oneness and in its glory [as depicted by this emanation]. On this fountain rests the continued existence of all creatures; it is said of it *(Ps. 36:10)* : 'For with Thee is the fountain of life.' And this is a life that has no measure and no end, no death or dissolution. Now, since the nature of the original source is also preserved in what was formed from it, it neccessarily follows that the Torah, arising out of this source, also never has an interruption within itself. Rather, its fountain always gushes forth, to indicate the source whence it was formed [literally: 'hewed out']. We learn this from the prayer which designates God as The One Who 'gives the Torah' [present tense]. For that great voice with which He gave it has not ceased. After He gave us His holy words and caused us to hear them as the very essence of the whole Torah, He did not cease to let us hear its details through His prophet, the trusted one of His house [i.e., Moses]. This is what Onkelos meant when he

---

8. *Avodat ha-Kodesh,* Lemberg 1857, part I, chapters 21 and 22, as well as part III, chapters 20–24.

interpreted the Hebrew text of *Deuteronomy* 5:19 on the voice of God at the revelation [which, if taken literally, can more readily have the opposite interpretation] as 'a great voice that did not cease speaking.' That great voice sounds forth without interruption; it calls with that eternal duration that is its nature; whatever the prophets and scholars of all generations have taught, proclaimed, and produced they have received precisely out of that voice which never ceases, in which all regulations, determinations, and decisions are implicitly contained, as well as everything new that may ever be said in any future. In all generations, these men stand in the same relationship to that voice as the trumpet to the mouth of a man who blows into it and brings forth a sound. In that process, there is no production from their own sense and understanding. Instead, they bring out of potentiality into actuality that which they received from that voice when they stood at Sinai. And when the Scriptures say: 'All these words God spoke to your congregation, a great voice that does not cease speaking, everything is thus contained in it . . .' Not only did all the prophets receive their prophecy [out of this voice] at Sinai, but also all the sages who arose in every generation. Everyone received that which is his from Sinai, from that continuous voice, and certainly not according to his human understandinig and reckoning. And this is so because the completion of the unity has been entrusted into the hands of man, as the Scriptural verse says (*Is.* 43:10) : 'If ye are my witnesses, says the Eternal One, I am God.' All words that can ever be said in a new way have thus been placed into this fundament which is the Divine voice; the Master of the world desired that they receive actuality through men of this earth who form and fulfil God's name. That great voice is the gate and the portal for all other voices, and that is [the meaning of] 'fence of unity,' and the reference of the verse in the *Psalms:* 'This is the gate of the Lord,' the gate representing the Oral Law which leads to God, Who is the Written Torah, guarded by the Oral Torah. This is the reason for the fences and limitations with which the scholars enclose the Torah. But since that voice is never interrupted and that fountain always gushes forth, the deliberations of the scholars in the Talmud were necessary; Rabina and Rab Ashi, its redactors, refrained from interrupting that stream [which flows and becomes visible in those deliberations]. And this is also the path walked by scholars of all generations, and there is no fulfillment of the Torah except on that path. If new teachings [regarding the understanding of the Torah] are produced daily, this proves that the fountain ever gushes and that the great voice sounds forth without interruption. For that reason, the deliberations upon the Torah may not suffer any interruptions, nor the production of new teachings and laws and incisive discussion. But the authority of the prophets and scholars who know the secret is nothing but the authority of that voice from which they have received all they have produced and taught, which in no way arose out of their own mind and out of their rational investigations" (III, chapter 23).

Later on in this disquisition, we discover how Meir ben Gabbai explains the conflicts of opinion that appear in the tradition from this kabbalistic point of view. He holds them to be facets of revelation:

"That ever-flowing fountain [of emanation from which the Torah originates] has different sides, a front and a back; from this stem the differences and the conflicts and the varying conceptions regarding the clean and the unclean, the prohibited and the permitted, the usable and the unusable, as it is known to the mystics. The great, continuing voice contains all these diverse ways of interpretation, for in that voice there can be nothing missing. According to the size and strength of that voice the opposing interpretations appear within it and confront one another. For the one has seen the face of that voice as it was turned toward him and made his decision for purity, the other one for impurity, each according to the place where he stood and where he received it. But all originates from one place and goes [despite all apparent contradictions] to the one place, as is explained in the *Zohar* (III, 6b). For the differences and contradictions do not originate out of different realms, but out of the one place in which no difference and no contradiction is possible. The implicit meaning of this secret is that it lets every scholar insist on his own opinion and cite proofs for it from the Torah; for only in this manner and in no other way is the unity [of the various aspects of the one stream of revelation] achieved. Therefore, it is incumbent upon us to hear the different opinions, and this is the sense of 'these and those are the words of the living God.' For all depend ultimately upon the Divine wisdom that unites them in their origin, even though this is incomprehensible for us and the last portal remained closed to Moses. For that reason, these things appear contradictory and different to us, but only as seen from our own standpoint—for we are unable to penetrate to those points where the contradictions are resolved. And it is only because we are unable to maintain two contradictory teachings at the same time that the *halachah* is established according to one of these two teachings; for all is one from the side of the Giver. But from our side it appears as manifold and different opinions, and the *halachah* is established according to the teaching of the school of Hillel."

This interpretation achieved its widest dissemination above all through the authority of Isaiah Horowitz (*ca.* 1565–1630), who presented an unexcelled synopsis of rabbinic and kabbalistic Judaism in his great work, *The Two Tables of the Covenant.* Drawing upon the disquisition just quoted, he develops the religious dignity of the creative tradition by proceeding from the explanation of a particularly pointed Talmudic saying which states: "The Holy One blessed be He, speaks Torah out of the mouths of all rabbis."[9] Horowitz comments:

"Some interpret this saying in reference to the petition which we express in the prayer 'Give us our share in Thy Torah,' which is taken to mean: Give us a share in the Torah which God Himself studies; or else: May we become worthy of having Him say a teaching in our name. And this is the situation: the scholars produce new words [in the understanding of the Torah] or derive them through the power of their insight. But all of it was contained in the power of that voice that was heard at the revelation; and now the time has come for them to bring it from potentiality into actuality through the efforts of their meditation. But God is great and mighty in power, and there is no limit to His understanding. His potentiality permits no interruption [in this voice]; rather, it is boundless and endless, and all this [that the sages hear in the voice] is guided by the measure of renewal and the origin of souls in every generation as well as the ability of man to arouse the higher power. It thus follows that while we say of God that 'He has given the Torah' [in the past], He can also be designated at the same time [in every present time] as 'the One Who gives the Torah.' At every hour and time the fountain gushes forth without interruption, and what He gives at any time was potentially contained in what He gave [at Sinai]. Let me explain the essence of

---

9. *Chagiga* 15b.

this matter further. We know that the domain of what is made more stringent [in the law by the rabbis] becomes enlarged in every generation. In the days of our teacher Moses the only prohibitions were those which he had expressly received at Sinai. Nevertheless, he added ordinances here and there for special purposes as they arose; and so did the prophets after him, and the scribes, and every generation with its scholars. For the more the snake's poison spreads, the more is the protecting fence needed, as is said (*Ecc.* 10:8) : 'He who breaks the fence is bitten by the snake.' The Holy One, blessed be He, gave us 365 prohibitions [in the Torah] in order to prevent the snake's poison from taking effect. The more this poison spreads within a generation, the larger must the realm of prohibition become. If this had been so at the time when the Torah was given, then all these prohibitions would have been written into the Torah. As it is, all this is contained by implication in the Torah's prohibitions; for in all this, there is only one point [namely, fighting the snake's poison]. Therefore, God commanded: Set a watch upon the watch,[10] which means: act according to the prevailing conditions. Thus, all the additional stringencies [in fulfilling the Torah] that had to be added in every generation derive from the authority of the Torah. As the snake's poison spreads, and more of its potential becomes actual, the statement[11] that God created the evil inclination as well as the antidote to it becomes valid. Then we need stimulation from above in order to translate the [additional] prohibitions from potentiality into actuality as well, until [at the time of redemption] we shall again be reunited with the highest fountain of all fountains [which will then nullify the prohibitions]."

"I must reveal further secrets which are related to this matter in order to make plain that all the words of the wise men are words of the living God [and thus have religious dignity]. The words of the Talmud in Tractate '*Erubin* (f. 13b) will thereby become understandable: 'Rabbi Akiba said in the name of Rabbi Samuel: For three years the school of Shammai and the school of Hillel engaged in argument. The one said the *halachah* is according to us, and the other one said the *halachah* is according to us. A Divine voice then sounded forth and said: Both these and those are the words of the

---

10. *Yebamoth* 21a, as an interpretation of *Leviticus* 18:30.
11. *Baba Bathra* 16a.

living God, but the *halachah* is to be decided according to the school of Hillel.' Rabbi Yomtov ben Abraham of Seville reported in his commentary that the rabbis of France had raised the question: How is it possible that both are the words of the living God when one prohibits what the other one permits? Their answer was that when Moses ascended the heights in order to receive the Torah he was shown forty-nine reasons for a prohibition and forty-nine reasons for a permission for every problem. He asked God about this and was told that this would be left to the sages of Israel of every generation, and that the decision was theirs to make. And this—so says the scholar from Seville—is correct according to the Talmud; but according to the Kabbalah there is a special reason for this. It appears to me that the expression of the Talmud 'These and those are the words of the living God' is justified *prima facie* only where it is possible to hold that the words of both parties are valid at the same time. This applies, for example, to the place in the Talmud (*Gittin*, f. 6b) which refers to the unfaithfulness of the concubine in Gibea (*Judges* 19:2) : 'Once when R. Ebiathar met the prophet Elijah and asked him what the Holy One, blessed be He, was thinking about, Elijah answered: "About the story of the concubine in Gibea" [about which Ebiathar and his colleagues Jonathan had expressed different opinions]. "What did he say about it?" [asked the rabbi]. "My son Ebiathar says thus, and my son Jonathan says thus." The rabbi said: "Is it possible for God to have doubt?" Elijah answered: "These and those are the words of the living God." For it is possible to consider the sayings of both valid. But in a situation where one prohibits something which the other permits, it is clearly impossible to consider both of their sayings valid. For the decision supports the one, and we do not accept the validity of the words of the other. But if these words are also considered words of the living God, how can one word of His be invalid?' The full import, therefore, cannot rest with the words of the French rabbis, since they are insufficient in this case. But it can rest with the reason and the secret that apply here according to the kabbalistic tradition, as indicated by the rabbi from Seville. The verse in *Ecclesiastes* 12:11: The words of the wise are as goads, and as nails well fastened are those that are composed in collections, they are given from one shepherd' is interpreted in the Tractate *Chagiga* (f. 3b) as follows: "Composed in collections, this refers to the Biblical scholars who sit in assemblies and occupy themselves with the

Torah; some declare a matter unclean, and others declare it clean; some prohibit, others permit; some declare it unusable, and others declare it usable. Someone might say: If this is so, how can I study the Law? Therefore Scripture continues: 'They are given by *one* shepherd; One God gave them, one spokesman [Moses] said them out of the mouth of the Lord of all actions, praised be He, as is said' (*Ex.* 20:1) : 'And God spoke all these words.' You, too, turn your ear into a funnel and fashion for yourself an understanding heart in order to understand the words of those who declare as unclean and the words of those who declare as clean, the words of those who prohibit and the words of those who permit, the words of those who declare as unusable and the words of those who declare as usable. We have here the affirmation that all differences of opinion and viewpoint that contradict one another were given by one God and said by one spokesman. This seems to be very alien to human understanding, and man's nature would be unable to grasp it were it not for the help given to him by the prepared way of God, the pathway upon which dwells the light of the Kabbalah."[12]

In the Jewish conception, therefore, genuine tradition, like everything that is creative, is not the achievement of human productivity alone. It derives from a bedrock foundation. Vegh's quotation of Max Scheler is relevant here: "The artist is merely the mother of the work of art; God is the father." The tradition is one of the great achievements in which relationship of human life to its foundations is realized. It is the living contact in which man takes hold of ancient truth and is bound to it, across all generations, in the dialogue of giving and taking. The poet's word applies to it:

> The truth that long ago was found,
> Has all noble spirits bound,
> The ancient truth, take hold of it.

> (Das Wahre war schon laengst gefunden,
> Hat edle Geisterschaft verbunden,
> Das alte Wahre, fass es an.)

---

12. Cf. Isaiah Horowitz, *Shne Luchot ha-Brith,* Amsterdam 1698, pp. 25b–26a.

JOB AND THE POSSIBILITY OF BIBLICAL TRAGEDY

Baruch Kurzweil

There is no Biblical tragedy because the relationship between man and God is absolute. There is no question but that man may suffer pains of guilt and remorse and wither from the punishments laid upon him by an angered or disappointed God, but tragedy as the West knows this dramatic form is never Biblical. The exploration of this theme, undertaken by an Israeli literary critic regarded by Hebraists as the most exacting critical intellect in modern Hebrew literature, is devastating and persuasive. Kurzweil, ranging the philosophic interpreters of tragedy from Aristotle and Hegel to Max Scheler, Karl Jaspers, Georg Lukacs, and Erich Heller as well as the canon of dramatic literature from Greek drama, the medieval miracle and mystery cycles to Dante, Goethe, Shakespeare, and the modern dramatic literature, is in search of a differentiating principle.

Tragedy occurs only when the tragic hero is blind to the sacral, hieratic organization of reality. Biblical tragedy is always impossible because God is present as the primal source of human action. The fact that man is at odds with God, that he fails to understand His requirements, that he trespasses upon divine sancta, that he is obstinate, blind, or ignorant of God's ways is essentially untragic since the conflict is unequal.

The Bible is intended to describe the history of the events whereby a specific people undertook to seek and to find God, to live in covenant with him and, failing in obedience, to be chastised and returned to fealty, and, in reward of faith and right action, to receive into its midst the hope and expectation of vindication. Indeed, individuals such as Abraham, Moses, Saul, David frequently misunderstood the divine intention and, in the absence of clear knowledge or right action, suffered. It may well be that to our minds—relatively unbelieving as those minds may now be when contrasted with the minds of faith with which the Bible deals— their suffering is tragic. We may say in commiseration that "they tried to obey, but they were only human," and temporizing our sympathies we may wish to rebuke God for the punishments he laid upon them. True enough, but for that they are not "heroes," nor is their condition become "tragic." Rather it is the case that the Bible is a didactic vehicle, intended by the example of the destinies of the Patriarchs, Kings, Prophets, and Sages of Israel to demonstrate to us the kind and quality of obedience expected from us. That we insist upon desacralizing the Biblical terrain and making of it an open field where the play of passions and the concealments of knowledge which confound heroes of classic tragedy may be enacted, reflects more upon our own secularization of the Bible than it does the elevation of anguished Saul or remorseful David into tragic heroes.

Job is the epitome of the Biblical tragedy, but even he fails. In the end he, too, is constrained to confess his sin and to acknowledge that what he had wanted to believe and believed inconstantly he now sees with his own eye. God lives and speaks to Job. Job, abashed, abhors his words, repents, and mourns his unbelief. The essence of Biblical drama is the reluctance of man to believe and the insistence of God that man be forced to see and hear. In this there is no tragedy, only the loving constraints which any moral education entails.

JOB AND THE POSSIBILITY
OF BIBLICAL TRAGEDY

BARUCH KURZWEIL

> . . . *I know that Thou canst do everything,*
> *And that no purpose can be withholden from Thee.*
> *Who is this that hideth counsel without knowledge?*
> *Therefore have I uttered that which I understood not,*
> *Things too wonderful for me, which I knew not . . .*
> *I had heard of Thee by the hearing of the ear;*
> *But now mine eye seeth Thee;*
> *Wherefore I abhor my words and repent,*
> *Seeing I am dust and ashes.*
>
> —Job 42: 2–6
>
> *Das tragische Leben ist das am ausschliesslichsten*
> *diesseitige aller Leben.*
> —Georg V. Lukacs, *Metaphysik der Tragödie*[1]

I

Despite contemporary efforts to differentiate between considerations of a "purely" literary nature and the ideational analysis of a literary work, there is no escaping the fact that the very choice of one literary form or another tacitly assumes the existence of a mutual relationship between the decision to choose that specific form and the specific idea or concept that underlies and overlaps it. Moreover, the very choice of the form determines somewhat its idea-content, knowingly or unknowingly. Granted that one cannot judge a literary work, be it the most profound, as a speculative, philosophic statement, concretely conveyed, since its method is not at all

---

1. *Logos*, 1911, p. 88.

that of methodical deliberation; nevertheless, belles lettres undoubtedly reflect an overall Weltanschauung. Any depth study of the problems of literary morphology introduces perforce questions of a speculative nature, and one may certainly inquire into the essence of a mode of thought whose characteristic embodiment is the epic, the novel, or tragedy.

The student of literature meets with a surprising phenomenon: while theater exists in medieval Christendom, it seems utterly devoid of tragedy. The era of the mystery play appears to have lost a sense of the tragic drama of the Greeks. The Roman tragedies of Seneca and the comedies of both Plautus and Terence were accepted by the Christian world after undergoing editing that appears arbitrary and artificial to us. This approach to tragedy surely does not reflect a dulled aesthetic sensibility. The Christian chivalric epic and that awesome "cosmic epic," Dante's panorama of the Christian universe, *The Divine Comedy,* refute such an assumption no less than do the Gothic cathedrals or the paintings of Giotto. The fundamentally different outlook of Christianity and its sacral art engendered a new perspective on the tragic world view. "A style that presents sacral figures is not the inevitable outcome of a unique way of looking at non-sacral figures. The sacral artist's eye stands in the service of the sacral, not the reverse."[2]

The sacral poet's eye serves the sacral, and the moment the holy Mass, and later the performance of the mystery plays on church grounds, became the theatrical vehicle of the sacral artist, the voice of Greek tragedy fell silent for him. Its spiritual realm seemed foreign and strange to him: man no longer saw himself—nor the ancient gods—as a bedrock certainty compared with which all else appeared uncertain; rather, that which could not be comprehended was the sole reality. "No longer does man question that which is not given him to comprehend (such was the case in Greece) ; to the contrary, that which cannot be comprehended, all that is beyond him, all that is transcendental, above him, containing him—that makes an uncertainty of man."[3]

The Christian world was incapable of responding to the challenge of tragedy, for the spirit of tragedy was fundamentally alien to the Christian universe. However, the difference between the two

---

2. A. Malraux, *Les Voix de Silence.*
3. Ibid.

world views rules out the preference or belittling of either. The difference must not be blurred. It demands recognition.

II

The history of drama and tragedy is essentially an unceasing confrontation with the *Poetics* of Aristotle. This history comprises closed and open battles. The open battles conducted by writers who view Aristotle as an authority attempt an exhaustive reinterpretation of the famous passages on tragedy in the *Poetics*. For the sacral poet, however, the strictures of the *Poetics* were no longer authoritative. Sacral theater left no room for tragedy in the full sense of the word. In Christianity "there is no longer tragedy. The splendor of bliss and salvation, the glow of love pierces through terror and blazons forth. Seen from this viewpoint, Christian redemption counterposes itself to tragic knowledge. The sure possibility of redemption, private salvation, inescapably dooms the tragic predicament. Consequently there is no such thing as Christian tragedy in the full sense of the word."[4]

What has been said of Christianity applies as well to Judaism. As we shall explain at greater length, the value system of Judaism is not particularly compatible with the prerequisites for tragedy. Moreover, ancient Judaism did not produce any theater which would enable us to examine the degree of its affinity to tragedy and the tragic. Medieval Christianity, however, has left a great deal of theatrical material that permits us to draw conclusions that are also applicable to the attitude of Judaism toward tragedy. That is to say, it is likely that one of the most important conclusions to be drawn by anyone who studies the medieval mystery plays is that there exists a sharp irreconcilable cleavage between positive and negative characters within the play. These figures are the epitome of perfection, wholly saints or the Devil incarnate. Relative valuations have no place within the medieval scheme. In this regard there is no difference between German, Czech, French, English, or Spanish mystery plays. In contrast to national-linguistic differences, the monotony and uniformity of characterization along saintly and wicked lines is astounding. This fact is of crucial significance and must be taken into account in any consideration of the possibilities of Biblical tragedy. It is, of course, well known that this kind of

---

4. K. Jaspers, *Uber das Tragische*, Piper Vorlag, Munich, 1958, p. 16.

sharp differentiation is foreign to Greek tragedy. More importantly, it contraverts the very essence of tragedy, as an analysis of *Oedipus Rex, Prometheus Bound,* or *Antigone* will reveal. Neither Creon nor Antigone are completely virtuous. On the other hand, they are not wholly evil. Their actions are the necessary consequences of disparate sets of values, and what appears to them to be absolute values are gradually revealed to the spectator or reader as merely relative. The same holds true for the relationship between Prometheus and Zeus. Zeus, too, does not represent absolute justice and Aeschylus does not tire of indicating to us that brute force provides the basis for Zeus's "justice." The "law" and "justice" on whose behalf Prometheus speaks differ from the "law" and "justice" imposed by Zeus. Likewise, in *Antigone* much of the dialogue is given over to a clarification of the relativity of the opposing claims made on behalf of "law" and "justice."

Any deliberation on the essence of tragedy from Aristotle's time to our own turns on this central point: the relativism in our evaluation perspective of appreciation and a disclosure of the dialectic between rescue and salvation, on the one hand, and ruin, on the other. "Since the structure of the finest tragedy must not be simple but complex, and since it must imitate things that arouse fear and pity . . . it is clear, firstly, that good men should not be shown moving from good to ill fortune, since this does not arouse pity or fear but only appalls us. Nor, secondly should bad men be shown changing from ill fortune to good fortune; there is nothing more untragic than this . . . The only possibility left, then, is for tragedy to be about the man who is in an intermediate position. Such a man is not outstanding for virtue or justice. . . ."[5]

It is my opinion that any aesthetic-metaphysical theory of the tragic and tragedy, to the extent that it does not aspire to an anti-Aristotelian posture, is essentially an interpretation, expansion, or limitation of Aristotle's thesis. In this regard there is no difference in principle between Schopenhauer and Hegel. Even the most modern theories (to the extent that they are not out-and-out Marxist), such as that of Lukacs, prior to his Marxist period, or those of Max Scheler, Karl Jaspers, or P. Zondi, all assume that the

---

5. From Aristotle's *Poetics* in *The Philosophy of Aristotle,* edited by Renford Bambrough and translated by A. E. Wardman and J. L. Creed (New York, Mentor Books), 1963, p. 421.

values or truths in tragedy are relative and expressive of a multiplicity of meaning. In so far as this fundamental viewpoint of the essence of tragedy is concerned, it makes no difference whether the fear and pity aroused by the tragedy is meant to exalt the idea and the objective ethical forces, according to Hegel, or whether they are a means of demonstrating the ethical fortitude of the hero doomed to destruction, as Scheler thought. The idea, stressed most interestingly by Scheler—who holds that the tragic is a universal phenomenon, not restricted to the human sphere, and that this phenomenon is grasped only when one sees its affinity to the domain of values—this idea, too, in effect, is only an amplification of what is contained in Aristotle's *Poetics*. Scheler treats the tragic phenomenon (and not only tragedy) primarily in two places—in his book, *Vom Ewigen in Menschen*,[6] and in his essay, "Zum Phänomen des Tragischen."[7]

In his book, *On the Eternal in Man*, he clearly demurs from Schopenhauer and the theories of metaphysical pessimism or pantheism which he originated. "The phenomenon of the tragic itself constitutes a proof that not only pantheism . . . but even assignment of the origin of evil to the basis of the world is fallacious. It is the *tragic* necessity lying in the bond of good and evil, good and wickedness, in the world we know, which precludes us from seeking the origin of evil only in human wickedness. This tragic bond is itself the *greatest evil*."[8]

The tragic phenomenon, however, according to Scheler, is not revealed in the struggle between absolute good and absolute evil. Relative values clash in our world, and, in so far as the human is the locus of tragedy, longing for the perfect and the absolute is in vain. Scheler bases his interpretation on Kant's assertion that "man is made of wood too twisted to allow for anything straight to be plowed with it."[9] In conformity with Christian belief, Scheler rejects all attempts at "self-redemption." He accepts Cardinal Newman's opinion that " 'the world has fallen away from its Creator: it is not constitutively in accord with him. This is a truth *as certain as my own and God's existence.*' "[10]

---

6. M. Schler, *Vom Ewigen in Menschen*, Francke, Bern, V., p. 229 (*On the Eternal in Man*, trans. by Bernard Noble).
7. Ibid., p. 235.
8. Ibid.
9. Ibid.
10. Ibid.

While Scheler's remarks on tragedy exhibit a clear Christian bias, they are not different in essence from the principle found in Aristotle's *Poetics* or Hegel's aesthetics; that is, we are here concerned with a struggle between bearers of values. This thesis is set forth explicitly in an essay, "Toward the Tragic Phenomenon": "The tragic phenomenon is dependent on this—that the forces destroying the positive value of a higher plane derive from the upholders of positive values. Consequently the tragic phenomenon is revealed in its most naked and pure state when those who bear values of equal worth seem condemned to undermine and destroy each other." This, however, is not merely a variation of the Hegelian theory that "tragedy lies in the clash of ethical forces each of which has justification, and each of which achieves its end by injuring the other."[11] Therefore, tragic guilt is only relative. It is actually guilt that contains within itself its own vindication. Or in Hegel's words, "It is the distinction of great personalities to be guilty."[12] Consequently Hegel calls tragic heroes at once guilty and blameless.

The ultimate source of this relativism, however, is found in Aristotle's remarks on tragedy. Following Aristotle and Hegel, Lukacs asserts: ". . . there is no place for relativism, for crossing boundaries, for degrees of guilt in defining the religious personality. . . ."[13]

After making this differentiation between the religious and tragic personalities, Lukacs contrasts the mystic with the tragic man. The tragic personality is an entity sealed up within itself, whereas emphasis of the self within an entity higher than itself characterizes the mystic personality. "Utter devotion is the way of the mystic; battle, that of the tragic man." And he concludes that "the tragic life is the most extreme in its 'here-ness' of all the possible ways of life."[14]

All modern theories on tragedy in one way or another hinge on the thesis that the focus of tragic action is the conflict between values and that each upholder of values embodies their relativism. The degree to which studies of the essence of tragedy are merely a renewed clash with the heart of Aristotle's argument in the *Poetics* can be seen most clearly in Hegel. But Hegel influenced almost all

---

11. J. Vokelt, *Asthetik des Tragischen,* Munich, 1906, p. 151.
12. Hegel, *Vorlesungen über die Ästhetik,* Berlin, 1843.
13. Lukacs, *Metaphysik der Tragödie,* p. 81.
14. Ibid.

who wrote on tragedy after him: "Herein lies the origin of the essentially tragic situation—that within a confrontation of this nature the opposing sides both have separate justifications, while they are so constituted as to represent and emphasize the true positive meaning of their cause and character only as they negate and combat another force that is equally justified. Thus, in and through their ethics they arrive at guilt in equal measure."[15] Hegel speaks of each of the upholders of values as *gleichberichtigte Macht* (equally powerful). However, it is precisely this balanced representation of the relative value that allows us to inquire into the nature of a world view that admits of the possibility of the existence of this balance.

In a passage close to the above Hegel offers a profound interpretation of Aristotle's demand that tragedy arouse fear and pity. Again, it is not the emotional aspect of "fear and pity" that is the determining factor in the Aristotelian demand, according to Hegel, but the value, the content: "As regards this statement of Aristotle's, too, we must not think simply of experiencing the emotion of fear and pity but of the principle of content . . . that which man must truly fear is not external brute force and the oppression [it gives rise to] but ethical force . . . *true pity is . . . empathizing with the moral absolution of the sufferer* [my emphasis] . . . and in order for the tragic character to . . . arouse within us tragic empathy, he himself, inwardly, must be valuable and worthy of respect."[16]

It seems to me that the main thrust of Scheler's critique is contained in this Hegelian interpretation of Aristotle's *Poetics*. Is there any need to go to great lengths to prove how vast is the distance between a world that acknowledges the equal validity of relative values and the Judeo-Christian world of faith? Is there any place in the Christian or Jewish world for setting up such a balance of relative values? It seems to me that medieval Christian theater gave its answer to the question. It did not allow for the emergence of such a conflict between upholders of principles of equal value because it did not acknowledge their existence. Good was absolute good and evil was absolute evil. Franz Rosenzweig well defined the essence of the tragic hero as "an exclusive turning into the core of

---

15. Hegel, *Vorlesungen über die Ästhetik*, p. 529.
16. Ibid.

one's self [*dies nur nach innen Gekehrstein des Selbst*]."[17] This self, however, is utterly closed off to the outside, to God and men at once. The dialogues of the tragic heroes are imagined dialogues. At times they comprise a desperate effort to break through the walls of selfhood, whose "stamp of greatness and weakness is silence. The tragic hero has only one language that suits him perfectly: silence."[18] There is much truth in this paradoxical, extreme definition of Rosenzweig. It is clear in the case of Aeschylus, for his Prometheus speaks, in effect, to himself. However, the dialogues between Sophocles' Creon and Antigone only serve to heighten the absence of any real dialogic situation. The stubborn self abandons its lonely state only to outward appearances. The imaginary dialogue, the hopeless groping beyond the sphere of self, pushes the hero all the more forcefully into its magic circle. The "arguments" of the heroes form only the illusion of a dialogic situation. The tragic self is its own prisoner. This truth is implicit in Shakespeare's heroes and is realized in its purest state in Richard III, a radical exemplification of the cutting off of the tragic hero from all bridges that lead beyond the self. Eros is the strongest force by which a man maintains bridges beyond the self. Eros, not sex. The tragic hero either closes himself off from eros in all its manifestations or drowns in its depths. Either way, however, it overpowers him. Richard lives in a meta-erotic world.

> I have no brother, I am like no brother;
> And this word "love" which greybeards call divine,
> Be resident in men like one another
> And not in me: I am myself alone.
>
> (*Henry VI,* Third Part, V, 6)

The tragic hero is bent on destruction. "He yearns for the loneliness of his destruction for there is no loneliness greater . . . the congealed character of the heroic self is immortality. Eternity is just good enough to give back the echo of his silence. (*Die Ewigkeit ist ihm gerade gut genug, sein Schweigen wiederzutönen.*) "[19]

As has been said, Shakespeare's Richard is a borderline case. Here, too, however, Shakespeare undoubtedly arouses tragic empathy in us because something of Richard's satanic self lies buried in the soul of every man. Moreover, his self is not completely

---

17. F. Rosenzweig, *Der Stern der Erlösung,* I, p. 103.
18. Ibid., p. 101.
19. Ibid., pp. 103–4.

divorced from the realm of values that are stirred, even in the innermost recesses of his soul, in nightmares. And the point of departure for the tragedy of Richard III, discloses to us other landscapes of the soul. Richard loves his father, his brothers. His self has not yet wrecked what remains of those bridges that might still ensure an existence beyond the self. Shakespeare brings even this hero close to the realm of values and the realm of humanity because the self turns in upon itself. Not only has it swallowed the entire world, all that exists outside of it, but it threatens itself.

> Have mercy Jesu! Soft I did but dream.
> What! do I fear myself? *there's none else by:*
> Richard loves Richard; *that is, I am I.*
> Is there a murderer here? No, Yes, I am:
> Then fly: what! from myself? (V, 8)

This is to say, the self has left no room for anything outside it: "There's none else by." But now it stands alone. It endangers itself. If there be no brother, there can be no self. Identification with one's self is cast in doubt. Where there is no "thou" there is also no "I." The Torah knew this: "And the Lord said to Cain, 'Where is Abel thy brother?' And he said, 'I know not. . . .'" Cain is all self. But he is a wanderer. Richard reaches the limits of selfhood when the self faces itself. The statement "I am I" in the midst of the wilderness is a vain consolation that immediately gives rise to the question, "Is there a murderer here? No, Yes, I am." But then the "I" has to flee itself, become a wanderer, for the "I" stripped of all links to that which lies beyond itself turns against itself. This is Richard's decisive realization, one that nullifies the absolute imperative of the self and for a brief instant opens a window onto the sphere of human values. The decided relativism of what purports to be an absolute demand reveals itself even in the depths of the tragic hero's soul which subsists at the border of human possibility. No, there is no room in any tragedy and in any tragic hero for an absolute value. The chorus of the Greek tragedy reminds us of this important truth time and again. Thus it is in *Prometheus* and thus it is in *Oedipus Rex* and *Antigone*. This theme passes like a scarlet thread from Aristotle through the most recent theoreticians of tragedy: ". . . The choral imagery in *Antigone* carries the idea that neither Antigone nor Creon is wholly right nor wholly wrong."[20]

---

20. W. G. McCollom, *Tragedy*, Macmillan, New York, 1957, p. 164.

Since relativism is the indubitable sign of the tragic situation, it follows that disunity is an additional characteristic of the tragic realm: it does not recognize one, sole truth. Indeed, one can even maintain that the absence of one sole truth from the sphere of tragic incident seals the fate of its protagonists. "The fragmentation is a fragmentation into discrete truths. One truth confronts another and by virtue of its right is commanded to battle not only against evil, but also against other rights and other truths."[21]

III

"Job's questions on guilt and fate are of the kind that are likely to be raised by great writers. The characters, themselves, in contrast to Job, do not even think of raising them. To do so they would have to break their silence."[22]

What seems more appropriate or closer to the world of tragedy than so lofty a theme as that of the book of Job? Those who speak of Job as a tragedy, and of Biblical tragedy in general, no doubt will find support and encouragement for their arguments in the very fact that one of the greatest artists of all time, Goethe, followed in the footsteps of this Biblical work in his "Prologue in Heaven" in *Faust*. The plot of *Faust* hinges upon the wager between "the master" and Mephistopheles, a wager framed along the lines of the Biblical story. We know of other writers, of greater or lesser stature, Jewish and non-Jewish, who have undertaken Biblical tragedies. However, the adoption of a Biblical theme does not in itself attest to a writer's desire or capacity to grasp the Biblical spirit. It sometimes happens that the writer consciously blinds himself to it, sometimes is utterly incapable of comprehending it. There is a third possibility, too: that precisely the selection of a Biblical subject testifies more eloquently than a hundred witnesses to the writer's avoidance of the depths of tragedy. Goethe, for example, wrote that the very attempt to write a tragedy would destroy him. His opposition to the greatest dramatist of his day, Heinrich von Kleist, is well known. The *Iphigenia, Tasso,* and *Faust* are not tragedies. "*Iphigenia* is lyrically, but not dramatically, true. . . ."[23] As far as *Faust* is concerned, the "Prologue in Heaven," which is based on the Job story, denies *Faust* a tragic conclusion, since the mercies of a liberal

---

21. K. Jaspers, *Über das Tragische,* p. 57.
22. F. Rosenzweig, op. cit., p. 103.
23. Erich Heller, *The Disinherited Mind,* p. 41.

God assure the hero a positive resolution, something which was foreign to the plan of the play in its original version. Goethe made this turning point about 1796–97, that is, twenty-five years after the composition of the original *Faust*. Enlisting the mysteries of the Divine love of the Catholic church at the end of *Faust* (Part II) utterly contraverts the principles of tragedy. "In the spiritual climate of the 18th and the beginning of the 19th centuries the terror of man's exposure to the need for ultimate moral or religious decisions could not be creatively grasped either on the level of Greeek tragedy or on that of undiluted Christianity, or indeed even on the level of that unique encounter of both which took place in the Elizabethan drama."[24] That is to say, Goethe's turning to the book of Job to provide a key for the non-tragic ending of *Faust* is an indication of his avoidance of the tragic sphere. His use of the Biblical source removes the hero, Faust, from the tragic realm, replacing him there with the weak, wretched and mediocre figure of Gretchen. Compared to the tragedy of *Hamlet, Faust* represents what *Hamlet* would have been "if Ophelia and not the Prince of Denmark were to be its protagonist."[25]

Faust's dependence upon the first chapter of Job removes it from the world of tragedy, but does not bring it into the Biblical world. Faust is an unrepentant and faithless miscreant, devoid of the fear of sin and any yearning to attain a dialogue with God. How far removed Faust is from the reconciliation of Job at the end of the book: "I had heard of Thee by the hearing of the ear, but now mine eye seeth Thee. Wherefore, I abhor my words and repent, seeing, I am dust and ashes" (Job 42: 5–6). Job's true goal is to arrive at a dialogue with God, something which is beyond Faust. "Here-ness" is for Faust the exclusive, the sole reality:

> Nach drüben ist die Aussicht uns verrannt;
> Tor, wer dorthin die Augen blinzelnd richtet,
> Sich über Wolken seinesgleichen dichtet.

> The view beyond is barred to mortal ken;
> A fool! who thither turns his blinking eyes
> And dreams he'll find his like above the skies.
> Faust II, Act V, 11442–44, G. Priest, ed.

---

24. Ibid., pp. 53–54.
25. Ibid., p. 56.

Hence we see that the use of the machinery of Divine salvation is external, fictitious, and is not truly rooted in Faust's world. Only a few moments before his death he denies the existence of that Divine authority which outwardly is his last resort. Sacral truth becomes here merely artistic fiction. The retreat to the myth of both the Jewish and Christian faiths destroys the play's inner truth. Here we have, as is so often the case in modern art, merely an aesthetic game that takes no account of the mythic truth in which the believer is rooted; for the believer, there is no reality above and beyond it. This holds for the tragedies of Aeschylus and Sophocles. This holds for Biblical narrative, which for its writer was the most certain of all facts. "The Divine in which man finds refuge . . . is that which encompasses us, that which we live and breathe, that which takes hold of us and is realized in the alertness and lucidity of our senses and spirits. It is found in everything . . . from this point of view the religious experience has a different character; more than that, it alone has a character, in contrast with the opinion that 'feeling is all' while 'God is merely an echo, a voice, smoke' as Faust says to Gretchen."[26]

True myth comprises a reality that brooks no comparison. Its dynamism shapes life. It is no aesthetic or intellectual game, as it is for modern artists or scholars, for whom the sacral sphere constitutes only a source of "subjects" for artistic or historical fictions. Even mysticism, as opposed to myth, is a phenomenon that testifies to a deterioration of certainty in God's existence. Actually mysticism appears only in a period where nearness to God is becoming a thing of the past and insecurity is on the upsurge. Nietzsche expressed this in bitter words: "The moment when doubt and longing couple, mysticism comes into being."[27]

It is proper to ask: what is the nature of the truth emerging from the meeting of the modern artist with myth, be it the myth of tragedy or that of Biblical narrative? The degree of legitimacy in using Biblical subjects depends upon the answer to this question. Jean Anouilh has shown us how disbelief in the myth of Antigone turns the tragedy into a comedy. For comedy and the grotesque are the sole legitimate vehicles for an era of no faith—this is the central awareness of the drama of Dürrenmatt. "Tragic depiction based on

26. Walter F. Otto, *Theophania*, Rohwolt, p. 58.
27. Ibid., p. 59.

knowledge of the existence of gods and demons as crucial powers is meaningful only for one whose life is rooted in belief in these gods."[28] One can say, following Jasper's definition, that the dramatic depiction of Biblical subjects is legitimate only for one who believes in the sacral reality depicted in the Bible. Any other type of depiction is fictitious. Hence we see that in judging the possibilities of Biblical tragedy we must first and foremost examine three points:

1) Does Biblical narrative accord at all with the elements of the tragic world?

2) Is it legitimate to deal with a Biblical subject without believing in the assumptions underlying Biblical narrative?

3) What happens to a sacral text when it is cut off from the faith it is grounded in and is transferred to the realm of "fiction"?

From all that has been said thus far it is clear that the answer to our problems in their totality is dependent upon the morphological fact that the writers of Scripture chose a literary form that suited their spiritual and ethical world. But this morphological fact teaches us that Biblical narrative, be it the story of Job, Joseph, Saul, David, or Abraham, has no notion of the existence of the hero in the tragic sense. There are occasions when a Biblical figure senses the possibility of tragedy, but he does not surrender himself to it. Certainly there is room in Abraham's mind for tragic knowledge in the account of the binding of Isaac. Here, too, one value confronts another. But the final choice is clear, for the uppermost value, the Absolute Value, is known; that is, the Divine command, despite all the terror it contains. Tragic knowledge does nest in Job's heart. He does not understand how the Absolute Value has destroyed his relative, happy world, the warm, protective world of human values. Again and again his statements revolve about this incomprehensible and inconceivable state of affairs. He also knows, though, "You are all powerful and I know that Thou canst do everything and that no purpose can be withholden from Thee." He capitulates to the superiority of the omnipotent God: ". . . I understood not, things too wonderful for me which I knew not." Capitulation of this sort is antitragic, it is the antithesis of the self of the tragic hero. Let us conjure for a moment the possibility of Prometheus' capitulating to Zeus or let us picture for ourselves Macbeth as a penitent. Instantly

---

28. K. Jaspers, *Über das Tragische*, p. 54.

we sense the collapse of the entire artistic structure. Even the mighty, dark Biblical figure of Saul capitulates before the emissary of the Absolute Value. In that same scene so saturated with tragic knowledge (I Samuel 15) there is no evolution into tragedy. "The Lord hath rent the kingdom of Israel from thee this day, and hath given it to a neighbor of thine, that is better than thou. . . . Then he said, 'I have sinned. . . .' "

Even in chapter 28, which describes King Saul in the full glory of his aloneness and soul's despair, all he passionately desires to do is break out of the magic circle of self. He fears it. ". . . He was afraid and his heart trembled greatly. And when Saul inquired of the Lord, the Lord answered him neither by dreams, nor by Urim, nor by prophets." And what he was seeking was a dialogue with Samuel: "And Saul answered: 'I am sore distressed . . . and God is departed from me, and answereth me no more, neither by prophets, nor by dreams; therefore I have called thee, that thou mayest make known unto me what I shall do.' " This, however, is a surrender of self. It is a-tragic. Following this passage we learn of the destruction of the "hero."

Cain, too, voices surrender to the Absolute: "And Cain said unto the Lord, 'My sin is more than I can bear.' " Similarly, the confrontation of David and Nathan over the affair of Bathsheba, wife of Uriah, does not attain to tragedy but to a recognition of sin. "Then David said unto Nathan, 'I have sinned unto the Lord.' " We must, moreover, bear in mind that this scene is, for the narrator, the key to the whole "tragic" chain of events in David's house—the episodes with Amnon and Tamar and the rebellion of Absalom.

In answer then to the first question raised, we can say that Biblical narrative by itself, if its essence remain unchanged and if it is not taken out of the sphere peculiarly suited to it—that is, the sacral sphere—lacks all the elements requisite to the tragic realm. The hero does not remain the captive of his self. Biblical narrative has no place for value relativism and no place for different truths equal in worth and importance. Biblical narrative defines what is good and what is evil in absolutely unambiguous terms, and that is something we do not find in tragedy.

From what has been demonstrated thus far—and here we enter upon a consideration of the second question—it becomes clear that any artistic treatment of a Biblical subject that has as its object the portrayal of Biblical figures as tragic heroes is made possible only by the abandonment of the artistic and sacral foundation on which Biblical narrative rests. That is to say, only a rejection of the truth that is the life breath of Biblical narrative makes possible the transformation of a Biblical figure into a tragic hero. Desacralization, in other words, is the cornerstone of tragic interpretation. However, the desacralization of a sacral text is an illegitimate, arbitrary act, turning sacral reality—the document of sacral faith—into "fiction."

"All works of fiction begin with: 'Let us suppose that. . . .' The Monreale *Christ* had not been a supposition but an affirmation. Neither the Chartres *David* nor Giotto's *Meeting at the Golden Gate* had been suppositions. A *Virgin* by Lippi or by Botticelli had aspects of fiction; Leonardo's *Virgin of the Rocks* and *Last Supper* were sublime tales."[29]

Only after the Biblical text ceases to be a document of faith and only when the internal truth of the Biblical narration no longer exists for the writer can he convert it into a "subject" for tragedy. The book of Job is not a tragedy, even as the stories of Saul or Abraham or Moses are not tragedies. More than that, the immanent truth to which these sacral writings give testimony is utterly opposed to the truth of tragedy. Only the negation of sacral truth can lead to a transformation of Biblical narrative into tragedy and pave the way for the emergence of secular, subjective "fiction." Here, however, we see clearly and unambiguously what happens to a sacral text after it is cut off from the ground of its faith and is transplanted into the realm of "fiction." It becomes a "subject" for secular literature.

IV

In our consideration of the possibility of tragedy in the Bible we have discussed the transition from sacral literature to secular "fiction." Only a period that has ceased to understand the peculiar spiritual elements of sacral literature can give rise to the attempt to see Biblical figures as tragic figures who could serve as heroes in modern tragedy. Biblical narrative by itself, without any arbitrary secular interpretation that distorts its truth, limits itself vis-à-vis the

---

29. A. Malraux, *Museum Without Walls*, trans. by Stuart Gilbert and Francis Price, p. 15.

ancient tragic world and vis-à-vis the possibilities of modern drama and modern literature in general.

Biblical literature is fundamentally distinguished from ancient tragedy in that it is founded upon a structure of values that leaves no room for relativism. Similarly, Biblical narrative does not contain the concept of the hero enclosed within his own self. The existence of differing and contrary truths, more or less equal in value, opposes the spirit of Biblical narrative. On the other hand, a situation in Biblical narrative bereft of any hope of salvation, of God's mercies, is unthinkable. Salvation always awaits Biblical man and repentance is the road which leads to it, even in the most extreme case of Cain, who confessed his guilt: "My sin is greater than I can bear." And Job submits after the possibility of dialogue is opened to him: "I had heard of Thee by the hearing of the ear, But now mine eye seeth Thee. Wherefore I abhor my words, and repent, Seeing I am dust and ashes." (Job 42: 5–6) Something of this sort is inconceivable in the world of Greek or postsixteenth-century European tragedy. The redemption of man through God's grace does not allow tragic knowledge to overcome man, for such redemption does not admit of true tragedy. True tragedy has no way out. Where there is faith in redemption, however, there is a way out.

Furthermore, Greek tragedy stands under the sign of myth. Although Biblical narrative, too, is saturated with mythic elements, these have been subdued by the overall concept of one God, lone and absolute. His omnipotence and truth rule out variant and relative truths. The independence of myths is shattered in the Biblical world: "Such is the nature of myth—an existence that does acknowledge nothing above it nor beneath it. This is a life with no lordship over objects (*ohne beherrschte Dinge*), without gods imposing their rule (*ohne herrschende Götter*). And it makes no humans or objects. This life is naked in itself."[30] This type of myth is the absolute antithesis of Biblical narrative. Again, it is fruitful to consider Aeschylus' *Prometheus* to understand how great is the distance between the world of Greek myth (to the extent that it still figures in tragedy) and Biblical narrative. Prometheus' accusation expresses his anguish over the relativism that purports to appear as the highest value. This is the meaning of Prometheus' cry

30. F. Rosenzweig, op. cit., I, p. 47.

against Zeus. Zeus is "a new ruler on his throne. . . . The son of Cronos has become a ruler without law. . . . He lusted after this mortal maiden and became a curse to her. . . . When this tyrant falls, the curse of his father Cronos will come upon him. . . . I am consumed without judgment." Clearly then, the book of Job, and Biblical writing in general, stand apart from tragedy to the same degree that the God of the Bible stands apart from Greek myth or neomodern myth. Biblical narrative is separated from modern tragedy, and modern literature and art in general, by the chasm gaping between sacral art and the art of secular fiction.

What value, then, is there to those studies that seek to draw comparisons between literatures which cannot be compared? What meaning is there to judgments such as "Reflections on Tragedies from Jewish Tradition"?[31] Such studies can only stem from an apologetic approach that fails to see the difference in essence between the two realms, a difference that is to be accepted respectfully, not blurred over.

Any attempt to blind oneself to the tremendously fundamental difference between sacral art and the art of secular fiction wretchedly dooms to failure the primary enterprise of the literary critic: the attaining of an understanding of the truth inherent in a literary work.

One can approach Biblical narrative, like any sacral art, from two polar, primary assumptions: from that of the believer in the sacral reality of the story; or from the skeptical, artistic viewpoint that makes sacral evidence a matter of fiction. As we shall see further, the second approach allows for a differentiation that does not change much as regards the basic distinction. One can state the major difference between sacral art and secular fiction paradoxically. Sacral art knows no religious theme, for its entire realm is holy. The religious theme, as one theme among many, is the incontrovertible sign of secular art, the art of fiction that rises from an autonomous world. In the "imaginary museum" of autonomous secular art (following Malraux' phraseology, "Le musée imaginaire"), there is also an honorable place for religious art. However, what was once the ultimate, truest of all realities, holy witness, becomes fiction, a small detail amid the endless mosaic of secular art.

---

31. A. Kaminka, *An Introduction to Greek Tragedy*, p. 31.

The secular approach to sacral art can give rise to still two more variations in its confrontation with sacral art. Biblical narrative has served as the theme for both these variations. By this I mean mythic art not underpinned by mythic faith, and meeting the Biblical theme beyond fiction.

Regarding the first possibility, I have in mind works such as *Joseph and His Brothers* by Thomas Mann. As opposed to the approach of Enlightenment, which preserves the body of the fiction but does not take seriously its mythic elements, Mann's books evidence the will to see in Biblical myth an awesome reality—but a reality that does not compel the narrator to accept its truth. Mann's correspondence with K. Kerenyi attests to the seriousness of Mann's effort to confront anew the truth of Biblical myth. The neomythic perspective, it is true, is more objective than the rationalistic approach to Biblical themes. However, as regards the immanent truth of sacral literature, it might well be more dangerous.

Another tack in the desacralization of Scripture is provided most interestingly in modern Hebrew poetry. Biblical themes stand out prominently in the poems of Jonathan Ratosh and Amir Gilboa, but their very modern formulation no longer retains the external fiction. That is to say, the modern Hebrew poet does not wish even to create the illusion of "historic fidelity." This illusion still exists in the poems of Michal, for example ("The Death of Samson," "Jael and Sisera," "Solomon and Koheleth") or in the poems of Y. L. Gordon ("David and Barzilai" and "Zedekiah in Prison"). Clearly the approach there, too, is secular and subjective and serves ideational and didactic ends. The poets of the Enlightenment, however, were still concerned with the fiction of "historic fidelity." Such is not the case in contemporary writing. Amir Gilboa writes a series of Biblical poems whose common denominator is their disregard of the fiction, as though the poet's intent were to raise up a historical figure from the past. What Gilboa has attempted is a new integration of a Biblical figure in a reality beyond the sacral sphere. Poems like "Isaac," "Moses," "Rahab," "Saul," "Under Siege," "By the Rivers of Babylon"[32] show us the new reality of the Biblical figure in the new inner landscape of a child living in the secular world.

32. Amir Gilboa, *Shirim Baboker Baboker*, Hakibbutz Hame'uchad, 1952, pp. 23–28.

The sacral world does not exist, but the Biblical figure is an inner reality in the soul of the child. This inner reality becomes bound up progressively with the landscape of daily secular life. In the following manner, for example, a boy who has heard of the binding of Isaac dreams, putting one of his acquaintances, Isaac, into the story:

> Early in the morning the sun took a walk in the forest
> Together with me and Father
> And my right hand in his left.
> Like lightning a knife flamed between the trees.
> And I so fear the terror of my eyes facing blood on the leaves.
> Father, Father hurry and save Isaac
> And no one will be missing at lunchtime.
> It is I who am being slaughtered, my son,
> And my blood is already on the leaves.
> And Father's voice was stifled.
> And his face pale.
> And I wanted to cry out, writhing not believe
> And tearing open the eyes.
> And I woke up.
> And bloodless was the right hand.[33]

The central words from the account of the binding of Isaac rise up from a new world beyond any pretensions to "historical truth," beyond "historic fiction": "together," "knife," "wood," "blood," the father and son, the sacrifice. The Biblical figure is beyond the sacral realm and beyond the fiction of "historic truth." The Biblical figure is a new presence! Analysis of Gilboa's other Biblical poems, or those of Ratosh, would lead us to the same conclusion. This artistic representation is legitimate precisely because it contains not the least trace of a demand to identify itself with the original Biblical story.

However, attempts to look upon Biblical narrative as "tragedy" are an entirely different matter. Only a confusion of bounds can lead to such a perspective. It is possible to take a Biblical story out of its context, out of its world, and force upon it the subjectivity of the autonomous secular artist. This rendering of a Biblical figure into a modern tragic hero, however, is possible only after a complete

---

33. Arieh Sachs' translation in *The Modern Hebrew Poem Itself*, edited by Stanley Burnshaw, T. Carmi, and Ezra Spicehandler (New York, Schocken), 1966, p. 137.

divorcing of the Biblical story from its world. Job or any other Biblical figure attains to the level of tragic hero only when one willingly or unwillingly blinds oneself to the sacral reality of the story; and these attempts originate from a turning to the various branches of secular fiction.

PART THREE
CHALLENGES TO JEWISH BELIEF

GOD AND THE PSYCHOANALYSTS

Irving Kristol

The psychoanalytic description of human nature appears to demythologize that which has been historically postulated by religion. But is that really so? Let us assume the correctness of Irving Kristol's lucid exposition of the conflict of *Weltanschauungen* between classic, unrevised Freudian theory and classic Judaism's vision of the world. For the one, the myths of religion (of which the benign and tyrannical God is primary) arise out of the requirements of the unreconciled ego, struggling with the stern guidance of the superego to subdue the aggressive libido. Religion, in such a view, is a systematic myth intended to provide a structure which supports, validates, and redeems the ego in its contest with its history, its unconscious impulses, and its objective situation. Religion is false to psychoanalysis because irrational projection—even if functional—is no substitute for truth about human nature, even if it be truth unto despair.

At the time of Kristol's writing, the responses of Judaism to the assault of psychoanalysis reflected more a spirit of capitulation, an attitude akin to that of those who, failing to subdue the opposition, join it; a mood characterized by all manner of anti-intellectual vulgarity ranging from those who would employ psychoanalytic insight as a means of restoring and perfecting the harmony between God and man (which harmony hardly exists) to those who simply understood Freud as a sex-obsessed renegade Jew.

The psychoanalytic fashion has waned considerably. No longer does one hear either religion polarized to Freudianism or religion proudly espousing its psychoanalytic knowledge-ability. This is not to say that the number of Jews seeking psychoanalytic help nor the number of Jews who are the psychoanalysts has diminished; nor does it mean that religion is any the less embarrassed by those of its teachings which incorporate so explicitly those primal myths which Freud discerned to lie at the heart of religious commitment and expectation. The problem is no different now than it was nearly twenty years ago when Kristol wrote his essay.

Let us try, however, to begin afresh. Viktor Frankl, the Viennese psychoanalyst, whose concept of logotherapy, unfolded to him out of the dynamics of survival in the concentration camps, points a direction. It is not an unprecedented direction, since the existential analysis which he defined has clear antecedents in Karl Jaspers, Martin Buber, and others. But for our purposes there are suggestions implicit in Frankl's methods which may help to alleviate the ironic despair which underlies Kristol's discussion. Psychoanalysis is the science of objectifying the unconscious: first, discovering its nature, principles, and operation; second, discerning its universal structure individuated in each psyche; third, assessing the distortions and dislocations of its functioning which occasion both adaptational neurosis and severe psychological dysfunctionalism. The purpose of the therapy elaborated by psychoanalysis is to provide the subject-psyche with more efficient adaptations than those defined as neurotic and to relieve the symptoms or reconstruct the organization of character where psychosis is diagnosed. The patient is obliged ultimately to deal with the truth about himself. The truth is not universal truth, however much the truth appropriate to the self of the patient participates in those dynamics and processes of the unconscious and the conscious self which are true and valuable. The question to be put to psychoanalysis by religion, more specifically by theologians who are concerned with truth arrived at rather than with truth received, is this: Is the ground of the self identical with the self; that is, can we ever say that the self is exhausted by the denotation of its constitutive elements—the Freudian tripartite structure of ego, superego, and id? In one sense, the answer is affirmative, for the self is defined by the specific arrangement and tension between its elements. In another sense, psychoanalysis recognizes that what is given to the self, the environment of the self, will weigh the balance of self-awareness and identity. The self has an *eschaton*. It is never finished; it is always respondent, therefore, to its history and open to its future. If the self is never closed, then the Freudian dream of the id subdued by the lucidity of rational consciousness is no less a chiliasm than the religious vision of the apocalypse. But this is no argument by itself. The fact that psychoanalysis dreams utopian dreams is no less damning than that Judaism attends to signs and wonders and seeks the Kingdom of God. All it establishes is that there is one dream which is founded upon a true understanding of human nature (the view of psychoanalysis) and another which projects a dream founded upon the unanalysed confusions of the unconscious seeking authority, direction, and redemption outside itself.

Once, however, it can be recognized that the self cares to transcend its conditions toward meaning, a fruitful dimension is opened. There is no assurance that self-transcendence will end in God, even less in the God of traditional theology, but there is at least a piercing of the self-contained circle of the psyche. The psyche is no longer the arbiter of the world; the world is no longer incorporated into the solitary psyche. Given the desire of man, not merely to endure in community with others—that is, simply to minimize conflict and maximize compatibility—but to achieve a "good" society or a "just," a "peaceful," or a "loving" fraternity among men, the goal ceases to be coterminal with the resolution of psychological conflict. Indeed, it is quite possible to conceive that a man will achieve a viable, "healthy" integration of the self, one not beset by debilitating conflict (what one might loosely call "the happy self") and still be in despair—despair for the truth unknown, for the wisdom unrealized, for the meaning withheld. Such a human being can be brought to the recognition of the limit situations of life of which Jaspers speaks so eloquently—anguish, finitude, mortality—while all the while maintaining a fruitful and productive involvement with the immediacies of his environment.

Shall it be denied then that man is the creature who can elect to be more than his limits, who can recognize his limits—the scope and possibility of clarity and understanding—and yet wish to transcend them? The theological question to psychoanalysis is then neither the fanatic refusal of its doctrine of human nature nor the wholehearted and frequently demeaning demythologizing of theology in the interests of "mental health," but rather the willingness to join with psychoanalysis in asking questions of the eschatology implicit in psychoanalytic utopianism. The theologian must make the analyst aware of his secular Messianism, while at the same time learning from psychoanalysis the means of stating more truly the vision of Biblical faith in man's perfecting himself toward and with God.

GOD AND THE
PSYCHOANALYSTS

Can Freud and Religion Be Reconciled?

IRVING KRISTOL

*My courage fails me, therefore, at the thought of rising up as a prophet
before my fellow-men, and I bow to the reproach that I have no consolation to offer them; for at bottom that is what they all demand—the frenzied
revolutionary as passionately as the most pious believer.*

—Sigmund Freud

Psychoanalysis was from its very beginnings disrespectful, when not
positively hostile, toward all existing religious creeds and institutions. Naturally, the religious rhetoricians replied with heat,
though, it must be said, with unequal light. The contest was not
exactly an exciting one, if only because few people could get
enthusiastic about God, one way or the other. The psychoanalysts
found it sufficient to explain with supreme objectivity just how it
was that this mountain of nonsense and error came to rest on
human shoulders. The preachers retorted with anathemas or plaints
of misrepresentation. The general conviction of the century was
that the analysts were going to unnecessary extremes of detail to
dissect a patient ripe for the grave, and that the patient was
showing a lack of taste in hanging on so grimly to a life that held no
future for him.

But then the contest was transplanted to the melting pot of
America, with astonishing consequences. In America all races and
creeds live and work peacefully side by side—why should not ideas
do likewise? For the ancient habit of supposing that an idea was

351

true or false, there was substituted the more "democratic" way of regarding all ideas as aspects of a universal Truth which, if all of it were known, would offend no one and satisfy all. It is under such favorable circumstances, and in such a benign climate of opinion, that the current love affair between psychoanalysis and religion has been, time and again, consummated. There have been bickerings and quarrels, of course, and the Catholic Church has shown itself to be a rather frigid partner. But, all in all, things have gone well, and the occasional Catholic reserve has been more than made up for by Protestant acquiescence and Jewish ardor.

Where once a Judaism liberated from the ghetto fled into the arms of a universal Pure Reason (which did, after all, proclaim honorable intentions), now a Judaism liberated from just about everything religious embraces psychoanalysis without a first thought as to the propriety of the liaison. So we read of a speech by the dean of Hebrew Union Schools, calling for a re-examination of religious teachings to determine whether "they strengthen or weaken the mental and emotional health of the common man"—the assumption obviously being that God is a fiction anyhow and He may as well make Himself useful. Another distinguished professor at Hebrew Union College is on record with this "tip" for alert investors: "The person who will contribute money for religio-psychoanalytic inquiry will have entered upon the way of all ways in which religion can be furthered by money." And two bright young rabbis have proposed to a conference of Jewish chaplains that the prayer books for hospitalized Jewish veterans be "screened" by psychiatrists to eliminate "many mystic elements from religion." Everyone knows how toxic mysticism is.

The monument to this tendency is, of course, the late Joshua Loth Liebman's *Peace of Mind*. This book informs us quite simply that "psychological discoveries about conduct and motive are really the most recent syllables of the divine"; that "men who are inwardly tormented and emotionally unhappy can never be good partners of God"; that the Decalogue was, for its time, rather sensible: "in the stages of human development from infancy to adolescence, it is quite proper to present rules of moral behavior as categorical commandments"; that atheism is the result of a child's being rejected by its parents; that "businessmen attacking the administration, grumbling about taxes, or worrying about our relations with Russia" ignore the fact that "the true root of their anxiety lies deep within themselves"; that "a wise religion" [no mention is made of a true one] "is indispensable to peace of mind"; that self-confident Americans who regard themselves as "responsible coworkers with God" can have no use for all those religious notions which arose out of the "helpless, poverty-stricken, powerless motifs in European culture." The book closes with a list of "commandments of a new morality," the first of which is: "Thou shalt not be afraid of thy hidden impulses."

In an attempt to dispel the impression that *Peace of Mind* made upon many—that today no one is so sick as our spiritual healers—Fulton J. Sheen wrote a Catholic *Peace of Soul*. Archbishop (then Monsignor) Sheen makes it clear that it is only with the greatest of distaste that he has written this book, and that it is to be taken as a concession to modern man's moral disorder. He is repelled by the "scum and sediment" of the unconscious and feels sure that ecclesiastical dogma would prefer that the unconscious not exist. But since it reputedly does, Archbishop Sheen sets out to purge psychoanalysis of its impurities, absorb it into the Catholic intellectual hierarchy, and leave it to perish there of boredom. These impurities are attributed to a mis-emphasis on "sex analysis" (Freudianism), which Archbishop Sheen accuses of undermining the moral order and defying the prerogatives of religion and church. Specifically, he dislikes the fact that psychoanalytical patients spend so much time on their backs, a posture which invites the devil; he wishes to save "sin" as a reality born of a defective will and not let it be dismissed as a neurotic fancy; and he would like to mark out the boundaries between the confessional and psychoanalysis, leaving for the latter only those situations where the emotional derangement could have had no moral (or immoral) antecedents—which would leave it with very little at all. He is especially friendly to self-analysis because the intimacy between patient and analyst is a sore temptation as well as a trespass on the clerical province.

All this indicates that Archbishop Sheen is considerably more zealous than was Rabbi Liebman in asserting the priority of morality and the church over psychoanalysis. Yet they have more in common than would appear at first sight, even more than their literary ties to the fraternity of vulgar journalism (Archbishop Sheen writes: "Nine months later the Eternal established its beachhead in Bethlehem. . . ."). Both would like to be of assistance to those modern psychoanalysts who would "revise" or emasculate

Freud to make him palatable, or even useful, to the *ecclesia*. Though Archbishop Sheen, unlike Rabbi Liebman, gives a positive religious status to anxiety—as a necessary quality of man who is a fallen creature, and as a spur to seeking God—he is just as eager for this anxiety not to be taken too much to heart: Archbishop Sheen promises peace of soul inside the Catholic Church as glibly as Rabbi Liebman promises peace of mind outside it. Where for Rabbi Liebman an excess of anxiety is "unhealthy," for Archbishop Sheen it is—unless it is quickly dissolved into Catholic "peace of soul"—a possible prelude to heresy and a certain sign of deficient faith. For neither of these two clerics is the existence of God, and man's relation with Him, a problem which should worry men to morbid excess. And both join their voices in eagerly quoting from psychiatrists' testimonials concerning the beneficent influence of religion on mental health.

But, most of all, what Archbishop Sheen and Rabbi Liebman and their numerous Protestant counterparts share is a disinclination, or inability, to take Freud seriously, to take his challenge to religion seriously, and in the end, to take religion itself seriously.

What is remarkable in all current demonstrations of how well religion and psychoanalysis supplement each other, is that the question of truth—whether we live under God or entirely in the realm of nature—is ignored. Most clerics and analysts blithely agree that religion and psychoanalysis have at heart the same intention: to help men "adjust," to cure them of their vexatious and wasteful psychic habits (lasting despair and anxiety), to make them happy or virtuous or productive. In so far as religion and psychoanalysis succeed in this aim, they are "true." But against this stands the overwhelming objection of Nietzsche: "Nobody will very readily regard a doctrine as true merely because it makes people happy or virtuous. . . . A thing could be *true,* although it were in the highest degree injurious and dangerous; indeed the fundamental constitution of existence might be such that one succumbed by a full knowledge of it."

And Moses and Freud are in agreement with at least the first part of Nietzsche's statement; they came to speak the truth about the fundamental constitution of existence and not to sow propaganda which would lead men to feel themselves happy or virtuous. Moses did not promise the Jews "happiness," nor did he say they should walk in the path of the Law because he thought it a virtuous law.

The Law was true because it was divine—it was God's Law, a revelation of man's place in the fundamental constitution of existence. Though men suffer and die in the following of it, yet it is the truth, and men's true happiness and virtue are in adhering to this truth—because it is true; any other kind of pretended happiness is but mere euphoria. Freud, in turn, did not assert that religion made men "unhappy,"[1] but that it was based on an illusion about the fundamental constitution of existence. Freud, like Moses, could not conceive of authentic happiness as something separate from truth. In his eyes, religion was a mass obsessional neurosis, and all attempts to enlist psychoanalysis in its support were dementedly clever stratagems whereby the neurotic incorporated a new experience into a larger obsessional pattern. Even if it could be proved that men could not live without religion, that "they succumbed by a full knowledge" of reality, this showed only that man was a creature who could not live in the truth.

The truths of religion and psychoanalysis, it should be clear, lay mutually exclusive claims upon the individual; their understanding of "the fundamental constitution of existence" is antithetical.

For religion, we live under the jurisdiction of the past. The truth is in the revelation on Sinai, and in Scripture, which fully comprehends us while we are powerless to fully comprehend it. God's word, spoken in the remote past and now hardly audible, is ever more true than the persistent chatter of men. Religion informs us that our ancestors were wiser and holier than we; that they were therefore more normal because they lived by divine Law, while our laws are driftwood in the stream of time; that no matter how mightily we strive we shall probably never see with their clarity into the fundamental constitution of existence and shall always be of little worth compared with them; and that, indeed, the virtue we inherit by reason of being descendants of Abraham, Isaac, and Jacob is far greater than any we can hope to claim to have merited. "What are we? What is our life? What is our piety? . . . Nevertheless we are Thy people, the children of Thy covenant, the children of Abraham. . . ."

---

1. That religion could claim a "therapeutic" value, Freud understood very well in his own way: "The true believer is in a high degree protected against the danger of certain neurotic afflictions; by accepting the universal neurosis he is spared the task of forming a personal neurosis"; and further: "At such a cost— by the forcible imposition of mental infantilism and inducing a mass delusion— religion succeeds in saving many people from individual neuroses."

Psychoanalysis, on the other hand, must repeat Freud's words: "But these ancestors of ours were far more ignorant than we." Psychoanalysis insists that it understands the past better than the past understood itself. Since all men have been driven by unconscious motivations which only we moderns really understand, and of which past generations were for the most part ignorant, a Freud of the twentieth century, or, presumably, one of his competent pupils, equipped with the tools of psychoanalysis, can know Moses, Da Vinci, Michelangelo, and Dostoevsky better than they knew themselves. At most we can say of certain great minds of the past that they had an intuitive and premature inkling of the true constitution of human nature and existence which is now known (or will soon be known) in its fullness. The history of the human race is a tale of growth from primitive times—when men were as children—to the present age of adulthood, when man finally understands himself and his history.

There is a crucial disagreement here, which can never be mediated, as to what is the true and the real. Psychoanalysis explains religion; it describes how and why religion came into being, how and why what we clearly see to be irrational was accepted as superrationally true, and how and why that which we know to be a product of the human fancy came to be regarded as an existing, supernatural being.[2] To this, religion answers that the understanding of psychoanalysis is only a dismal, sophisticated misunderstanding, that human reason is inferior to divine reason, that the very existence of psychoanalysis is a symptom of gross spiritual distress, and that religion understands the psychoanalyst better than the psychoanalyst understands himself.

In this dialogue between psychoanalysis and religion, it is to be expected that psychoanalysis would try to establish its position behind the starched apron of science. What is surprising is that the religionists should be so eager to assist it—until we remember that in the long, grueling warfare between science and organized religion, the latter received valuable instruction in tactics. Abandoning the frontal attack, the pastors were successfully able to persuade the scientists that science was not at all atheistic, as some brash people

---

2. The psychoanalytical theories of Jung, which accept the subjective religious experience as something ultimate, are an interesting deviation from this line. But Jung never commits himself as to whether God *is*, and therefore cannot genuinely decide whether the religious experience is normal or abnormal.

claimed, but that its sphere of activity was quite a different one from that of religion, that it dealt with an "abstract" reality and not the "real" reality, that its arid language was inadeqaute to religious statement, that it operated on another "level of meaning," and so on. In the same way today, pacific priests and analysts are eager that psychoanalysis should renounce its wild and Freudian past and become a medical science; for the more medicinal it is, the smaller is the danger that it will seem to say anything about the fundamental constitution of existence, the less does it encroach upon religion, and the greater is the mutual security of religious and psychoanalytic institutions; psychoanalysis would deal only with "health" and never with "truth." The result is a revision and "correction" of Freud—especially in America—which tends to make of psychoanalysts mental counselors, in no necessary conflict with religion, "adjusting" patients to their infirmities, their limitations of talent, their jobs (or else the analyst serves as a vocational guide), their bad luck, their wives, their children, and, in the armed forces, to their officers. Some analysts even send their patients to church, as a therapy.

Psychoanalysis, then, would seem to be on its way to becoming simply the medical treatment of the psyche, cohabiting with religion in all amiability. But on this way it stumbles and falls. For if psychoanalysis is disloyal to the implications of its method—to what this method assumes as the fundamental constitution of existence, as enunciated by Freud—it sinks into a realm of relativism in which the human intellect circles upon itself like a dog chasing its tail.

Psychoanalysis is unlike traditional medicine in that nature does not so readily supply us with a working definition of the psychically "normal." Our definition of physical normality ("health") is not something we have strenuously to imagine or blindly to postulate, and there are obvious and sharp limits to possible disagreement; it is simply given to us because we are what we are. But psychoanalysis is in a more ambiguous position. Its definition of mental health has to be in good measure "thought up," and it must be done by men whose ideas are influenced by their lives and times. Psychoanalysis is always open to the accusation that its criteria of "neurosis" and "mental health" and "adjustment" have a cultural bias, and are influenced by political ideologies, national prejudices, and personal whims. To take the accusation in its most general form: any psychoanalytical approach which, out of diplomatic cordiality toward religion, renounces its claim to an objective knowledge of human nature or to a lasting, true insight into the fundamental constitution of existence, must admit that it is historically and socially conditioned. And once there is no objectively *true* human nature which is taken as the norm, there is no possibility of general agreement on what it means to be "sick" and what it means to be "cured." We can then have Communist analysts, Nazi analysts, democratic analysts, anarchist analysts, all with irreconcilible criteria of mental health.

Actually, the dilemma of the "revisionist" schools of psychoanalysis arises from their reluctance to abandon—at the same time that they drop all Freudian "metaphysics"—either of the two branches of psychoanalysis joined by Freud: the pathological and the general psychological. (This distinction is very lucidly made by Theodore Reik in *Listening with the Third Ear.*) Pathological psychology seems to have some intimate relation with the organic, intimate enough, in any case, for it to be a (still largely unexplored) subbranch of medicine. But in this field, psychoanalysis has to compete with formal psychiatry and neurology, both of which are closer to what is universally deemed medical science: psychoanalysis can "explain" more than psychiatry only because it is less rigorously scientific. To be sure, psychoanalysis has effected cures of pathological cases. But cures have also been reached by treatments which have nothing to do with psychoanalysis, nor can psychoanalysis claim greater efficiency, greater rapidity, or any other advantage. Moreover, psychoanalysis is splintered into various schools, all of which claim to cure, and no way exists of deciding for or against any one of them, or of finding out whether they may work for reasons quite different from those given by all of them. In pathology, psychoanalysis stands to the ideal of medical science as the herbdoctor (whose herbs work too sometimes, and not entirely by chance) to a diagnostician.

Yet when psychoanalysis turns to nonpathological cases, and tries to fall back upon general psychology, upon its theory of human nature, for a warrant of competence, then it has to say what human nature rightfully *is;* it has to be explicit as to whether man prays to God or is trapped in an obsessional neurosis, it has to decide the question of truth before it dares raise the question of therapy. And this would involve it in those discussions about man and his place in the universe which would be fatal to its ambitions to live at peace with religion.

Freud, too, was faced with the problem that before one could aim at healing human nature it was necessary to decide what human nature in its undamaged state is, and in his analysis of dreams he stepped unhesitatingly from pathology to depth (general) psychology. The pathological and the abnormal were points of departure for the determination of the "really" normal, and Freud ceased to be a doctor and became a thinker. Truth precedes healing—Freud's own italicized definition of the task of psychoanalysis was *"education to reality."* Where in all of his past history man had achieved only a self-deceptive self-consciousness, riddled with mythical projections of the unconscious, now man has acquired the ability to see the human situation as it really is.

Perhaps because of the verbal resonance of such terms as the "unconscious" and the "libido," and certainly because of his own harsh comments on various facile and optimistic beliefs, Freud is often viewed as a reaction to the nineteenth century's certainty that man was master of his fate and to its adoration of the goddess Reason. Freud himself, in certain passages, seemed to encourage this interpretation, as when he noted the three wounds inflicted by science on humanity's self-love: the cosmological blow of the Copernican revolution, the biological blow of Darwinian evolution, and the psychological blow of Freudianism. But such an interpretation of Freud would be erroneous, and Freud's remarks seeming to support it must be understood mainly as a not unflattering explanation of the hostility which his contemporaries directed at him.

Copernicus, Darwin, and Freud did not attack *man's* self-love, but only the *religious man's* self-respect. They diminished God (though, except for Freud, without intention) and aggrandized man as the rational animal. They did not undermine man's reason, but enthroned it, at the expense of the religious authority. Freud did not come to proclaim the law of Reason at an end—he came to fulfil it, at the same time explaining how previous efforts at fulfilment had been overly glib and superficial. Man, by virtue of Freud's work, was not less than he had been; he was infinitely more, facing for the first time the prospect of an authentic self-consciousness and self-control which would make him the true measure of all things. Though Freud, in comparison with his contemporaries, complicated human nature, it was the kind of theoretical complication (like Einsteinian physics) which makes possible the lucid solution of hitherto baffling problems; it is a gain for Reason, not a loss.

Freudianism was a legitimate son of nineteenth-century philosophy (Marxism was another) which declared that in all previous world history the human mind had not been free but had been enslaved to nature or society, and that now life according to true Reason (not ideological or neurotic rationalization) was within men's reach. The epoch of human history in which man's mind had been "alienated" from reality was approaching its end. And Freud was supremely a man of the nineteenth century in his idea of history as the development of the human race from infancy to adulthood, in his conceiving of the biography of humanity as entirely analogous to the biography of the individual, with religion as a childlike obsessional neurosis which the child had failed to outgrow and which the doctor was now hurrying to cure, so as to secure, in his own words, "the psychological ideal, the primacy of the intelligence."

Freud is of one mind with Spinoza, that to have a rational understanding of what our instincts (Spinoza called them passions) are up to, is to make us master of them. The purpose of psychoanalysis is to redeem the ego from compulsive irrationality (neurosis) and to place the instinctual libido in the service of a rational ego, for it is not the instinctual unconscious itself which resists psychoanalytical treatment—its goal is to be discharged, into consciousness or action—but the irrational ego, the ego that has "solved" its problems by a nonrational adjustment (neurosis) and that desperately defends its precarious "solution." This redemption of the rational ego is achieved in the three steps of the psychoanalytical treatment: (1) the "recall" of the repressed—a conscious awareness of what is behind the particular neurosis; (2) transference, or redirection of the libidinal force to the analyst, which gives the ego a chance to wrestle openly, through a transference-neurosis, with the material raised from the unconscious; (3) mastery of the instinctual urges by the rational ego.

It is clear from this how absurd is the charge against Freud of being the high priest of the irrational, goading the instincts, especially the sexual instincts, into a *coup d'état*. (Archbishop Sheen seems to be of this opinion.) It would be more accurate to say that Freud was a supreme puritan. The tenor of Freud's writings is that the present sexual standards of respectability are maliciously provocative of nervous disorder. His plea for greater sexual freedom is the plea of a wise and experienced statesman, not the appeal of an irresponsible radical. For Freud, sex is the blind, powerful, and eternally rebellious subject of the legitimate despot Reason. Revolt means calamity: at the least, the established order is forced to share power with new tribunes, in an uneasy compromise; at the most, sheer anarchy prevails. It is because of his fear of the herd of sexual instincts that Freud would concede so much to them, would abrogate the existing sexual morality in favor of a less provocative one, would assure a free genital sexuality in order to provide protection to all those other zones threatened with erotic invasion. The localization in the genitals of the sexual urge is the necessary condition for the natural reign of Reason. The greater the liberty of the genitalia in satisfying this urge, the greater the security of the Rational state.

There are two fairly distinct trends in Freud's analysis of religion, both of them hostile, but corresponding, respectively, to his earlier mood of moderate hope and his later mood of only faintly relieved gloom. The second is more important in what it tells us about the ultimate destiny of psychoanalysis. The first is important too, however, in that it provided a crucial supplement to the rationalist refutation of religion. Though rationalists of the eighteenth and nineteenth centuries spoke of the slow education of human reason from superstition upwards, from credulousness and helplessness to manly independence of spirit, it was Freud who came to show the psychological necessity of this evolutionary process. Freud's attack on religion cut more deeply than even that of Voltaire or Marx, for while Voltaire could expose the unreasonableness of religious dogmas, and Marx could show how religion mirrored the inauthenticity of man in the pre-Communist era, neither could satisfactorily explain the psychological mechanisim by which human beings came to be so duped in the first place and why it lasted as long as it did.

According to Freud, religion is the price paid for the *blind* renunciation of inherent instincts. Religious prohibitions deprive sexuality of its due at the same time that religious creeds leave reason defenseless and feeble, so that sexuality is able to reappear in the disguise of neurotic behavior such as prayer, pilgrimage, theological speculation, and the like. Religions owe their obsessive character to "important happenings in the primeval history of the human family" and "derive their effect on mankind from the historical truth they contain"—a truth imprinted on the racial memory of every newborn child. The "happening" from which religion grew was the slaying and communal eating, in the primal horde, of the primal father by his sons, who had joined together in order to share the father's sexual prerogatives—the original Oedipean revolt, and one which each individual recapitulates in his own mental experience. But the victorious sons were tormented by anxiety about their portentous deed, and by fear of continual, bloody sexual rivalry. So there came into being, in these "ages of ignorance and intellectual weakness," the sense of guilt and sin, as well as moral codes and religious catechisms, to repress all sexual rivalry with the fathers, to appease the memory of the primal father who had been transformed into God, and to guarantee the existence of an orderly community. And each individual not only "remembers" the historic past, but in his own lifetime has to make some sort of adjustment to his own Oedipus complex, his impotence as a child to challenge the father for the mother's favors, his jealousy, and the anxious repression of it.

The history of religion is analogical to the history of neurosis in the growing child, its strength gathered from childhood anxieties and frustrations, and this strength dissipated with natural growth into adult rationality. The history of humanity, like the life-history of every one of its members, is a process of maturation in which the instinctual renunciations necessary for the stability of the community are rationally comprehended and lose their malevolent potential. Freud writes:

"We know that the human child cannot well complete its development towards culture without passing through a more or less distinct phase of neurosis. This is because the child is unable to suppress by rational mental effort so many of those instinctual impulsions which cannot later be turned into account, but has to check them by acts of repression, behind which there stands as a rule an anxiety motive. Most of these child neuroses are overcome spontaneously as one grows up, and especially is this the fate of the obsessional neuroses of childhood. The remainder can be cleared up later by psychoanalytical treatment." And in the same volume (*The Future of an Illusion*): "One might prophesy that the abandoning of religion must take place with the fateful inexorability of growth, and that we are just now in the middle of this phase of development."

By virtue of science and psychoanalysis, mankind begins to see the approaches to the Kingdom of Reason. The false knowledge of a supernatural Other, which was only an evasion of true self-knowledge, will be sloughed off like an outworn garment, and God, together with bibles, saints, and churches, will be consigned to the museum of human infancy.

What can religion reply to this? It is impossible to ask: what *does* religion reply to this, for religion in our time for the most part does not reply at all. It either gives up the ghost and tries to show its social and psychological utility in an imperfect world where the triumph of Reason is not yet complete; or it utters grave twaddle about incorporating "the enduring insights" of psychoanalysis in a "larger perspective," as if its perspective were infinitely elastic. Religion is uncertain, does not know whether we were really on Sinai or whether it was only a dream.

Yet there are certain lines of argument, it seems to me, which religious thought, because it is religious, must take. Religion must agree with psychoanalysis that the world in which we live is sick, but where psychoanalysis asserts that religion is a symptom of this illness, religion must cling to its own diagnosis and see psychoanalysis itself as a symptom of a mind diseased. Religion has to deny the thesis of progressive human evolution, and must explain psychoanalysis, must explain it away, by tracing its genesis and showing that the error in which it is involved points to the truth which it denies.

Psychoanalysis, in the eyes of religion, is a historical passion of men obsessed with the death of God. Nietzsche proclaimed that God was dead, Freud followed with the news that we had eaten and devoured His human archetype, and that His spiritual existence had always been an illusion. Both were right, for the nineteenth and twentieth centuries have regarded God as a corpse whose essence has been appropriated by man—the so-called divine attributes have been made over into human possibilities. Yet in this era of humanism and godlessness, man found himself more than ever alienated: his flight from God has also been a flight from his true self, which had been made in His image. So it was that Freud could build a theory of human nature on the basis of his experience with hysterics and neurotics, a unique and strange achievement which testifies to our modern psychic equilibrium, whose fulcrum is at the edge of an abyss.

Religion cannot deny that psychoanalysis has discovered the unconscious. It can only say that the unconscious as such is a new phenomenon, the toll paid to God and nature for the presumptive effort to have man's conscious rationality prevail over all of existing reality—including divine reality; in the days when God's face was turned to man, the unconscious was integrated with consciousness and did not whirl madly free thorough psychic space. The age of Reason, through a series of strenuous introjections, has attempted to press all of religious reality into the rational intellect and to imprison God, cowering and sullen, behind the forehead. The reward of this effort is psychic fragmentation, for divine reality is not within the rational mind of man but outside it, and the mind which would encompass it bursts. Instead of a divine reality that was a great chain of being, there is now, for each man, only a hall of mirrors. Since man has cut all ties with divine reality, has indeed denied to it reality, his psyche has been sentenced to follow upon itself in a dark and unending maze.

Psychoanalysis, religion might say, comes not to remove insanity, but to inaugurate it.

It would seem that this debate between psychoanalysis and religion can continue indefinitely, until it is terminated by God speaking unequivocally or the Kingdom of Reason being attained. And since God is silent and the Kingdom of Reason unborn, the debate goes on, important but nonetheless wearisome. But it is not a debate without end—for that we have Freud's word. Freud's final and tragic message is that the truth is with Reason and against God, but it is a truth in which man probably cannot live. Rational self-consciousness is the avenue to perfect wisdom, which leads in most men to perfect despair. Though Reason still has the task of "reconciling men to civilization," it is an authority entirely vitiated by the fact that "man is a creature of weak intelligence who is governed by his instinctual needs."

This message is found in Freud's later "metapsychological" works, such as *Beyond the Pleasure Principle* and *Civilization and Its Discontents*. Many contemporary psychoanalysts, exercising the privilege of little minds to "revise" greater ones, casually dismiss these writings as deviations from the pure principles of science. But

Freud was no eccentric, and if he went beyond the conventional limits of psychological science in his later works (just as he did, incidentally, in his earlier ones), he must have been of the serious opinion that the limits were too confining for the truth as he then saw it. In a letter to Einstein in 1932, in which he outlined his theory of the death instinct as the cause of war, Freud wrote: "All this may give you the impression that our theories amount to a species of mythology, and a gloomy one at that! But does not every natural science lead ultimately to this—a sort of mythology?"

Freud's final "mythology" involves a modification of the earlier postulated contradiction between sexual instincts and ego instincts into one between Eros and Thanatos, the life instinct and the death instinct. The concept of instinct is redefined as "a tendency innate in living organic matter impelling it toward the reinstatement of an earlier condition." What is this earlier condition? "It must be an ancient starting point, which the living being left long ago, and to which it harks back again by all the circuitous paths of development. If we may assume as an experience admitting of no exception that everything living dies from causes within itself, and returns to the inorganic, we can only say 'The goal of all life is death.' . . ." This drive toward extinction is countered by the sexual and reproductive instincts, which are the only ones which do not have as their aim the reinstatement of a previous condition, and which push to life, its extension and unificaiton.[3]

Instead of being the evolution of Reason and its eventual enthronement, history is blind and its contradictions unresolvable: "And now, it seems to me, the meaning of the evolution of culture is no longer a riddle to us. It must present to us the struggle between Eros and Death, between the instincts of life and the instincts of destruction, as it works itself out in the human species." The death instinct, under the influence of Eros, is extraverted and becomes aggression. Civilization is a huge detour constructed by Eros so as to make the death instinct take the long way home.

Civilization tries to disarm the aggressive instinct by directing it

---

3. There are important variations in Freud's formulations of his metapsychology. Thus, he seems to say at times that the sexual instinct too is conservative, and that it too aims at death. In *Beyond the Pleasure Principle* he makes use of the myth in Plato's *Symposium* of an original hermaphroditic nature which split into male and female, so that living matter, through sex, seeks a primordial unity.

against the ego, by making it over into the "super-ego" whose aggression against the ego takes the form of "conscience." This tension between the ego and the super-ego results in the sense of guilt, which while possibly neurotic by the absolute standard of Rational Man, is a normal quality of the human animal in the state of civilization. "The price of progress in civilization is paid in forfeiting happiness through the heightening of the sense of guilt."

Men who are loyal to the truths of Reason are doomed by their very natures to unhappiness. Happiness (but not *true* happiness, not happiness in the *truth*) is available only to those—the immense majority—who cannot face the truth of man's condition, who live with and by illusions, illusions of God, salvation, and the world to come. Freud's metapsychology concedes no more truth to religion than did his psychology. His "mythology" is a rational one. It is a mythology of rational despair.

The present attempts to wed a vulgarized psychoanalysis to a vulgarized religiosity are certain to fail: between the two parties is stretched the sword of truth, and both are pledged to keep their backs to it. Sooner or later, the world will perceive the lineaments of frustration and will know that the union was never fully consummated. But this marital catastrophe is not inevitable—all the mates have to do is, acting together in full consciousness, stealthily to remove the sword of truth and hide it under the bed.

Oddly enough, it is only on the late-Freudian foundation of rational despair that psychoanalysis can be "reconciled" with religion—but at a price, a price that Freud, with his intense personal loyalty to the truth, could never pay. For there are a few men, very few, who are willing to look at life boldly as a bleak prelude to death, and at civilization as an enormous distraction from self-extinction. These men submit to the truths of Reason, because in them Reason is the master of the instincts and not its slave. But in the great mass of men, it is the opposite: Reason is the toy of instinct and happiness in untruth is preferred to truth.

If God does not exist, and if religion is an illusion that the majority of men cannot live without, then psychoanalysis and religion can be "reconciled"—if that is what one wishes—by the simple expedient of a double standard of truth. Let men believe in the lies of religion since they cannot do without them, and let the handful of sages, who know the truth and can live with it, keep it among themselves. Men are then divided into the wise and the foolish, the philosophers and the common men, and atheism becomes a guarded, esoteric doctrine—for if the illusions of religion were to be discredited, there is no telling with what madness men would be seized, with what uncontrollable anguish. It would indeed become the duty of the wise publicly to defend and support religion, even to call the police power to its aid, while reserving the truth for themselves and their chosen disciples.

Psychoanalysis itself, which assumes religion to be an illusion, would become a form of esoteric wisdom, and the psychoanalyst would, with regard to dreams, agree with Maimonides: "Persons whose mental capacity is not fully developed, and who have not attained intellectual perfection, must not take any notice of them."

Such a program is bound to sound unpleasant in the ears of twentieth-century Americans, though it does have the advantage of enabling many to do what they seem to want to do: to drive in two directions at once, in pursuit of peace-of-mind at any cost and in pursuit of rational truth. But, of course, there is always the further possibility that the truth is not with Freud and Reason, but with God, and that men *can* live in this truth and find their happiness— simply living in it, though it be a scandal to Reason. "Because the foolishness of God is wiser than men."

APOLOGIA CONTRA RABBINES

Ben Halpern

and

ARE WE ISRAELIS STILL JEWS?

Ernst Simon

These two essays define an almost choral antiphon, for the persuasion of the one is the anguish of the other; the certitudes of Ernst Simon are the very substance of Ben Halpern's ironic dismay. On the one hand there are secular Jewish culturalists (and without rigorous attention to the in-group categorizing of the factions, one may number Ben Halpern with these) who are able from within the American Jewish community to deny to American Judaism a capability for self-redemption, much less the redemption of the whole of the Exile; on the other hand, there are religious Israelis, like Ernst Simon, who question the adopted postures of Israeli religiosity and can in all seriousness raise the question of the authenticity of the Jewishness of Israelis. Where Ben Halpern can employ Israel as the actual as well as critical norm for the assessment of the varieties of American Jewish adaptation, Ernst Simon will put that very norm into question.

Both are right, for both speak out of different situations and the very rightness of their predicament should give pause to those who would have either a Judaism so mechanistically self-sanctifying as to lose all connection with the profane (which it is its task to redeem) or so totally committed to the mysticism of the profane as to rationalize all its manifestations on the ground of its being Jewish, not Gentile, secularity.

The existential wrench for Ben Halpern is that he is still a Jew of

America. His argument, however, is not compromised by his continued sojourning in this land, but it does weaken the existential force with which he brings his unique kind of low-key critical acumen to the problems of American Judaism. Quite rightly his observation that within the American environment attempts to define a "Catholic" Israel in the terms which Solomon Schechter made meaningful rings somewhat hollow. What results from such attempts is not that integration of the holy with the realities of the world, but rather a ringing of the psyche with girds and defenses against encroachment which makes of Jewish existence an island in a hostile sea (or at least a neutral and indifferent one). It is from this predicament that Halpern correctly, I think, sees the emergence of Jewish cultism in America. Since America is not a Jewish nation, it cannot be imagined that Jews can create a total Jewish environment. They can hold to certain beliefs, they can practice certain customs, they can observe certain *halachot,* but they cannot—by the very nature of their situation—bring Judaism to bear upon the whole of their existence. They could if they were *totally* Orthodox. However, that entails the forcible exclusion of the American ambience in order to allow one thoroughly Jewish to obtain (of course, this is finally nothing more than creating a Jewish society within American society—a society which enjoys all but the juridical and police powers of the general society, and in certain respects is not even lacking in these). They are obliged finally to settle for a cult, and not even a cult enjoying *pari passu* equality with the regnant pluralism of the culture, for that pluralism was a Protestant Christian gift to the ideology of the nation and is founded upon principles which derive from the theology of the Christian conscience as surely as it does from the enlightenment philosophy of John Locke.

Halpern states the predicament of the religious well, but is somewhat less candid in his own self-estimation. He does not exclude God or the mysteries of belief from the ambit of his concern, but as an avowed secular Socialist Zionist encamped on American soil, he has difficulty making clear what such a God, much less a God of the Jews, might really mean. Given his seriousness, he is confident of God's leniency to his disengagement from Jewish religious cult. His is a truthful honesty in that he recognizes that Jewish secularism is certainly "a detour, if not a total departure, from the roads upon which the Jewish people historically have sought God." This is so, Halpern acknowledges, because the Jewish seeking of God was always, from the beginning, the seeking of the Jewish collective, the people. But where his argument descends into rhetorical flourish is at his insistence that however much Jewish secularism may be a freeing of the Jew from religious forms and from the bonds of tradition, the Jew still avails himself of religious experience whenever, wherever, if ever it can be found, and even if he never acquires a clear image of God he is still an unquestionably authentic Jew. The latter is a fist-pounding for authenticity. It may be well to have done with those religious ideologists who wish to use God as an umbrella to keep the rain of reality from inundating the American Jew, but it is quite another to hope that the Jews in America can be much of anything that is lucid, organic, and integrated unless its wholeness be essentially religious.

Halpern has it easy enjoying as he does the psychological displacement which is involved in being an American of Israeli intent, while the rest of us are simply Jews of American descent. The American Jew is doing *galut* here, but *galut* unlike diaspora is, not only a physical dislocation which entails social and ethnic confusion, but a category for the understanding of all history. *Galut* is the historical coefficient for the unredeemedness of the world.

Ernst Simon speaks of Israel in the way in which Ben Halpern might wish he could speak of American Judaism, if America were somehow not a Christian nation and Jews were somehow not in *galut*. Saadia Gaon could say in the tenth century that "our people is a people only by virtue of its religion," but such a statement can no longer be made. The universality of "Catholic" Judaism, which united Jews wherever they might reside in common fidelity to Torah and its instructions, has certainly vanished. The "Protestant" phase of Judaism, which was a by-product of European nationalism, was undercut by the accrescent virulence of anti-Semitism, for it was implausible for Jews to accept the premise that any and all religion would enjoy the toleration of the state as long as its adherents were loyal subjects of secular power. Clearly such a Protestant subjectivity was doomed. With the founding of the State of Israel and the consummation of Zionist aspiration, the predicament of Jewish religion became all the more severe. No longer was Catholic Judaism possible without clericalism or theocracy, while Protestant Judaism had neither a base of operations nor a viable ideological translation to make it efficacious to Israel. What remains is either a muddy Messianism which consecrates Israeli secularity, because it is enlisted in the work of redeeming holy soil, or an Orthodox clericalism which can only polarize to Kulturkampf the religious and the secular.

What Simon offers as the alternative to these is the spirit of prophetic criticsm. The prophet does not take fright at freedom. His concern is to enlist life in the service of the Kingdom of God; not to repress life, but to evoke the sanctity it contains. Almost as though Simon were alluding to the Kabbalistic doctrine of the sparks which are hidden in the secret recesses of nature and man, ransomed by the *hasid,* and brought to flame by his passion that all life declare the presence of the Living God, so the task of the prophet is to provide the possibility of contact between the sacred and the profane, that redemption may grow, that the Kingdom of God (whose form is always unknown) emerge from the chrysallis of small works and deeds. There is a kind of vagueness in Simon. There is always vagueness as vision exceeds sight; but the vision is undiminished by the vagueness of the delineation.

It is not unfair to think that the conclusion of Ernst Simon's essay—"the faith of the hopers, of those who desire to remain Jews . . . their faith remains strong and unshaken in Him who placed the true redemption of man *in the future.* . . . This is the faith in Him who made the distinction between sacred and profane"— would be shared by Ben Halpern. It is the task of the future of the Jew to work out the way in which both hopes may become one.

APOLOGIA CONTRA RABBINES

BEN HALPERN

I keep having the strange experience these days of finding myself talked at when I open a journal of Jewish discussion. Not talked to—talked *at;* I might even say scolded. Somehow I can't believe I deserve it.

I am not speaking as an individual now, of course, but as a representative type: as a "secularist," socialist, Zionist Jew. The triply qualified Jew that I represent has, I find, become a favorite target for sermons, expostulations, and reproofs ever since the establishment of the State of Israel caused American Jews, or their rabbis and ideologists, to reopen the discussion of the Jewish problem.

As a secularist, I find myself apostrophized by Will Herberg, Jacob B. Agus, and a host of others who warn me that I am headed straight for paganism, for Nazi or Communist totalitarianism, for the idolatrous absolutization and deification of man, or society, or science. It does no good to protest that I don't feel like an idolater at all. This only leads to being told that I am in a transitional stage, that my so-called nonidolatrous secularism, inherently unstable and untenable, can be maintained only because of what I owe to inherited religious culture, that if not I, then my children or children's children, educated on secularist lines, will inevitably become idolaters—and that the only refuge is in the leap of faith to God. Even Mordecai M. Kaplan, who is considered by some to be almost a secularist himself, has this to tell me:

. . . faith in the highest potentialities of human nature and persistence
in activating them cannot be sustained without a religious feeling for
history and the time process or without a sense of destiny which transcends the life of individuals and societies.

This is not a line of argument that could inspire discussion. The
answer to it is too ready; it takes the form of a rejoinder rather than
a rebuttal. For the first, automatic reaction of a secularist is to retort
that *religion* inherently tends to dogmatism, hence to intolerance,
persecution, and theocratic totalitarianism—and that if some "religionists" manage nevertheless, to preserve a liberal tolerance, it is
thanks only to the secular cultural tradition of the society they live
in, for if religion were to succeed in overcoming secularism it would
inevitably lead to the antihumanist reaction that is the natural
tendency of a religiously governed society. To this, no doubt, some
"religionists" would hotly reply that absolutism is only a degeneration of and a departure from true religion; at which I should then
cry out that totalitarianism, as the deification of secular values, is
only a perversion of true secularism. And the argument would have
degenerated into a quarrel.

Accordingly, I have not the remotest intention of discussing the
general problem of secularism versus religiosity.

But the argument is brought much closer to home and, moreover,
based on more or less controllable sociological and historical premises when the religious exhorters apply themselves to the contemporary Jewish problem in America. American Jewry, they contend, is
basically defined as a religious community. This is the way Jews are
regarded by the Gentiles, and the way, too, in which they regard
themselves; taking into account, of course, that a "religious community" under American conditions represents the socially accepted
legitimate form for the segregation of groups that differ from the
older, settled, "Anglo-Saxon," Protestant community in ethnic origin and folkways as well as in creed. But in no other form than in a
religious community, they insist, can ethnic differences be maintained in America. What, then, is demanded by our "existential"
situation, ask these new ideologists. Since we Jews exist in America,
and can only exist in America as a religious community under the
established form of religious diversity through the division of
church and state, and since this is so owing to the irresistible pressure of sociological laws, it is up to us to make our "existential"

status "authentic": to realize our religious calling as individuals and collectively to accept our religious mission.

The argument goes on to this further conclusion: the chief antagonist who must be overcome so that American Jewry may live up to its mission is none other than myself—the secularist socialist Zionist. I am he who stands in the way, and I must go. To be more precise, I have two options. I am challenged to see the error of my ways and join a synagogue, or else I may consider myself to all intents and purposes excommunicated.

Mordecai M. Kaplan chastises me with the whips of kindness, Jacob B. Agus with the scorpions of wrath. "From the standpoint of ethical influence, which should be the true measure of religion," says Dr. Kaplan, "there is incomparably more of the truly religious spirit in the basic princples by which members of the *Histadrut* are expected to regulate their daily lives than in the most devout worship and ritual practices. But in failing to recognize this, in the inability to see those transcendental or cosmic meanings which give point to its own ethical striving, the *Histadrut* is missing its opportunity to make Zionism the kind of humanist religious movement that it must become, if Zionism is to survive." Consequently, if I reform and recognize, first, that what the secular socialist Zionists in Israel are building is, in fact, a religion and, secondly, that American Jews can and should share in that religion while permanently established in America—then I am helping the Jews individually to achieve salvation and collectively to survive. If not, then "failing a Zionist philosophy that could make a difference in the personal and communal life of Diaspora Jewry, the steadily widening cultural and spiritual gap between the Jews in Israel and the rest of world Jewry is leading both groups from frustration to frustration."

Dr. Agus, on the other hand, neither wants nor expects anything from me. When one leading Zionist, Dr. Samuel Margoshes, recently showed an inclination to take Dr. Kaplan's advice, Dr. Agus reacted with a polite letter making, in substance, the rude suggestion that such a Zionist, now that he had come to his senses, should go the whole hog and stop calling himself a Zionist. To me (that is, to Zionists who show no desire to redefine themselves as suggested by Dr. Kaplan) he says this: *"Those who have no faith in America obviously cannot be trusted with the task of building the future of Jewry in America."* And, again: "[The community] need repudiate only such groups as negate the value of our continued existence in the Diaspora—whether in the name of a totalitarian Zionism or in the name of totalitarian Americanism."[1]

If I may now, for a moment, revert to my individual self, the reason I find these views require discussion is that I accept in all essentials the sociological and historical premises upon which they are based. I think it is correct that a "naturalized" Jewish community in America must tend more and more to define itself as a religious community, and that its right to remain permanently distinct from the Gentile Americans is most easily recognized as legitimate under the principle of freedom of worship. That is precisely why I have so little "faith in America" as the home of a creative Jewish community and a vital Jewish culture.

It is by no means *impossible,* of course, that a secular Jewish culture, such as our parental generation knew, should continue to be maintained in America. Yiddish, among other minority cultures, has flourished particularly in this country and still sustains a literary and social vitality deserving the utmost respect. The Hebrew-speaking and Hebrew-writing circles active in America are bent upon reproducing themselves, and one cannot safely predict their demise. America is large and free, and if any group is sufficiently devoted to a cult to contribute the necessary time and energy for its preservation, there is room for it to thrive.

To be sure, what we have in this instance is not a culture but only a cult: it is an artificial growth, and it can only complete its life cycle, run to seed, and sprout new growth if a loving hand supplies both fertilizer and topsoil, with no consideration of cost. Far from arising from the natural social conditions of our country, it requires special social conditions such as favor the segregation of a group of cultists. Such social conditions existed in the America of our parents' days because, as immigrants, their first habitat in America was the ethnically diverse immigrant ghetto. In our own largely native-born generation, which has emerged into America-at-large, religion alone establishes a natural and legitimate segregation of Jews from other Americans. Still, there is no reason why devotees of Yiddish and Hebrew culture should not by voluntary exertions

---

1. Everything italicized in the above quotations, by the way, was italicized in the sources, as though conveying instructions that here the sermon is to be read in a raised voice and more deliberate tempo, for emphasis.

maintain both the schooling and the type of segregation required to foster Yiddishism and/or Hebraism as one among America's many exotic cults.

Yet while not impossible such an effort is hardly likely to continue over a long stretch or on any significant scale. A secular cult, unable to exist by its own natural appeal, depends on ideological justification. There is ultimately only one justification for the survival of a secular cult. It can only command the enthusiasm and devotion required to foster it artificially if its adherents can believe that the time will come when their faith will prevail organically, as a natural culture. In short, a myth is required that envisions the ultimate triumphant enthronement of the cultists' exotic beliefs over historical society. In our specific case, the cult of Yiddishism in America, which once found a kind of natural habitat in the immigrant ghetto, could now thrive over the long stretch and on a significant scale among our own largely native-born generation only if it could successfully propagate the myth of an America-of-the-future based on a federalism of autonomous, secular, ethnic cultures. But we are unable to believe in such a myth for America; and the more we recognize the manifest destiny of America to be culturally federalistic on religious lines only, the less likelihood there is of working up popular enthusiasm for the cult of secular Jewish culture in America.

Religion stands superior to these difficulties. The very reason why religion is inherently cultist is that it is somehow above history. The religious myth is a transhistorical myth, and to have faith in it does not in any important degree require that history furnish some corroborative evidences of its probable, let alone imminent, materialization. The ideologists of a religious faith have, accordingly, a justification relatively easy to validate and popularize, and the creative devotees of the cult, while not really dependent on popular response at all, can also appeal to a response not essentially dependent on favorable conditions of immediate history and habitat. Thus, it is a fairly safe prediction that (barring catastrophes) there will "always" be something in the nature of Jewish traditional religion.

Moreover, Jewish religion does not have to rely on this exemption from the chances of history in order to survive in America. It is warranted as a legitimate American form of social diversity, and it stands in the direct line of the probable trends of contemporary history. I need not labor the point of the much-touted religious revival in this country. It is clear and accepted that for every real enthusiast and devotee of Judaism as a cult we have a far larger actual and potential throng of "religionists" simply conforming to current conventions.

Well, then, here am I (on behalf of all the secularists, socialists, Zionists among the Jews in America), confessing that I stand opposed to this wave of the future. I do not really think that what I represent offers so serious a threat to achieving the promise of this future that it should call for the kind of hectoring tone used in the current phillipics against me. But I can well understand that there may be some nuisance value to *any* nonconformity in these days. And I admit my obligation to offer some reason for persisting as a public nuisance.

The idea that I, the secularist socialist Zionist with "no faith in the *galut*," am a threat to American Jewry is not a new complaint first uttered by the religious ideologists. The same logic and the same tone of embittered anger are quite familiar from the old polemics of the Yiddishist-Hebraist *Shprachenkampf* and I find myself responding in the same weary and exasperated way. "Why is Yiddish having such a hard row to hoe in America?" we so often heard the Yiddishists moan. "Because the Zionists persecute Yiddish in Israel and leave it no hope for survival there, that is why it is impossible to win over the youth in America for Yiddish." When Yiddishists resorted to this argument in their anguish at the inexorable decline of the cult in which their whole lives had been invested, even our understanding the psychological sources of those futile recriminations could hardly make us suffer the foolishness gladly. *We* were responsible for thwarting the Yiddishists in their campaign to capture the hearts of American youth? Never were we aware of such influence over young America. But now the religious ideologists, riding their wave of the future, come too and complain that the pessimism of us here, the American secularist socialist Zionist *galut* negators, and of Ben Gurion in Israel, this is what is destroying the confidence upon which rests the whole future of American Jewry. Isn't this really too much? With the whole institutional setup of America guaranteeing the viability and prevalence of their point of view, why do they still have to have us as their scapegoats? What are *they* afraid of?

But if I look closer at some of these writings, I see that the authors really are afraid, just as I am, and for just the same reasons. If they are angry at me, it is because I coldly entertain the very fears they are so hotly trying to overcome or repress. "Jews at present resemble a demobilized army," says Dr. Kaplan. ". . . With the decay of supernaturalistic religion as a uniting bond, no other inner cohesive force has thus far been generated. Jewish unity, whatever of it still exists, is buttressed from *without* by the Christian tradition and by its offspring Anti-Semitism, but its *inner* supports are crumbling." In order to escape from their "spiritual isolation and moral anomie," Jews "desperately" build synagogues and religious schools. They face "inevitable frustrations" in their flight to religion, because "though their spiritual leaders have long abandoned supernaturalism they have not replaced it with any other dedicated faith." As for the schools, "the number of men and women . . . *qualified* to teach Jewish subject matter is shockingly small," and so low do American parents rate the degree of Jewish culture they need to transmit to their children that attendance is low, brief, and perfunctory: "The Jewish religious schools are like the subway trains, always full, with people constantly getting on and getting off at every station." What wonder then that the most gifted spirits among American Jews cannot "be associated with any type of normative Judaism," that "few of our bright young Jews are really interested in Judaism or Jewish culture," and that even among the "synagogued Jews there are few who really live the Judaism that they profess to believe in." In other words, Dr. Kaplan does not feel comfortable sitting on the wave of the future; he is all too painfully aware that it is just so much froth and water. He is not content with having so many Jews come to roost under the wing of the synagogue, for what he earnestly wishes is that he could feel them to be real Jews.

How familiar is this melancholy outlook; so like our own—and yet so different! The secularist socialist Zionist in America has long been riding an ebbing rather than a rising tide. What we see flowing away from us is all that water upon which the new religious ideology floats; but what we are left with, and what we have always had, are, as we intensely feel, real and authentic Jews.

Why do we, the secularist socialist Zionists, have the sense of being real and authentic Jews, why have the Yiddishist groups always had it, and why, for that matter, do the Orthodox in their tight ghetto have it, while the Jews who accept most unreservedly the standard of American institutions have lost that feeling? Dr. Kaplan does not ask this question, but what his answer might be is obvious enough. It emerges quite clearly from the demands he makes upon us, as well as from the proposals he makes for the reconstruction of the American Jewish community. Israel must help save American Jews, according to Kaplan, by not only living a full ethical, Jewishly inspired life-in-this-world, as it has begun to do, but by formulating its practices as principles and expressing these as ceremonies which could be adopted by the Jewish cult in America: in other words, he asks the Israelis to create that *culture* that could give body and substance and vitality to Judaism as a *cult*. The same tendency is apparent in Dr. Kaplan's proposals for an "organic" Jewish community in America. He cannot be satisfied with a synagogue Judaism alone, even though (since Jewishness must be defined mainly as a cult in America) he defends the centrality of the synagogue. But, clustered around the synagogue, he demands that there be maintained in organic relationship—that is to say, in some sort of organized, democratically responsible unity—a whole array of "legislative" and administrative, social, economic, educational, welfare and civic defense activities. In other words, he wishes to give even American Jewry, as far as possible, the scope and aspect of a culture, not only a cult.

That is the crux of the question. To become a mere cult would make of American Jewry a collection of something less than real Jews; this is a truth that all these religious ideologists themselves cannot help but feel. The most consistent and ruthlessly logical partisan of the new ideological anti-Zionism, the one who is just about ready to call it by that very name, Dr. Jacob B. Agus, defines his position in these words:

> In any synthesis of national sentiments with religious values it is the latter that must be raised to the supreme level of importance; the former may be allowed but a subsidiary role, and encouraged only as they remain in accord with the standards and ideals of ethics and religion. . . . But when subordinated to higher considerations Jewish nationalism may continue to be a powerful creative force, serving the ends of Jewish religion, as it did in the past, by bringing to the aid of piety additional motivation, and by supplying foci of sentimental loyalty within the Jewish community.

These are strange and discordant notes in the otherwise almost monotonously harmonic logic of Dr. Agus' essays. But what they express is the irrepressible sense that the price of Judaism as a pure cult is the inability of Jews to be real Jews.

A signal characteristic of the new cultist ideologies is that they are all bothered by a serious problem of definition. At least, what is characteristic is that *they* consider the question of defining "Jew" and "Judaism" to be of critical and fundamental importance—as one well may if he is dealing no longer with real Jews but with Jews who still have to be converted into the real thing. Thus Dr. Agus realizes that "the most telling objection raised against the conception of a religious status for American Jewry is the indubitable fact of its limited inclusiveness." He suggests that one could adopt "two complementary definitions" demarcating "nuclear and protoplasmic sections" of Jewry, the former consisting of strict observers, the latter distinguished from Gentiles only by the "inexorable hairline of conversion." Still, this would leave in the outer darkness of the protoplasmic section "many spiritually sensitive people unaffiliated with the syngogue, yet . . . profoundly stirred by Jewish associations"; and it would include in the inner circle of the nucleus "masses of indifferent materialists . . . cold and unmoved by any appeal to spiritual values." Nevertheless, when facts fail to accord with the definition, all Dr. Agus can suggest is that we are obliged to bring them into conformity. So seriously does he take the definition! Dr. Kaplan's view is well known. He has always felt that one could almost reduce the entire Jewish problem to one cardinal difficulty: we have lost a defined status as a community.

This is a difficulty that never really bothered the Orthodox Jews, the Yiddishists and ethnic autonomists, and the old-line Zionists, for all of these never doubted that they constituted groups of real Jews. As a result, whatever the disapproval and outright hostility each may have felt toward the other at times, or in general to other kinds of Jews outside their own party, they never viewed them with that peculiar troubled irritability of the religious ideologists towards Jews who escape their definitions; they never doubted the validity of other Jews' credentials or the reality behind their own. There was an underlying sense of easy brotherhood towards all Jews, precisely because it was so obvious the Jews were a real thing. The Orthodox knew beyond question that all the seed of Abraham were included in the Covenant, and if they rebelled against God, they were simply bad Jews—*poshei Yisrael*—but as real as any other. The Yiddishists and ethnic autonomists were, perhaps, somewhat limited in their Jewish perception, effectively feeling as their fellow Jews mainly the Yiddish-speaking community, but though the historic bond that bound them to Sephardim or to the "assimilated" Jews of the West may have grown thin, it was of such a kind that by extension it could include them, too: if *history* made one a Jew, all who shared it were indubitably real Jews. We, lastly, the Zionists, felt most keenly the critical and problematic state of Jewish existence. We arose out of a sense of the disintegration and collapse of the Jewish people. But by our very rise, by our assertion and drive toward a common destiny, we overcame the problem in the moment of grasping it, we gave body to the Jewish people in the moment of evoking its national will—and in that moment, too, we (together with the Yiddishists) gave freedom and creative *élan* to Jewish culture.

This, too, is a source of great perplexity to the new religious ideologists, for it is not only "Jew" but "Judaism" which appears to them to be seriously in need of redefinition. They are afflicted here, too, by severe doubt that what really exists as Jewish religious culture is valid, and driven to anxious efforts to conjure into reality that which by their definition Judaism ideally is. I need not quote from Dr. Kaplan, since it is well known that his whole life has been given over to the passion of reconstructing Judaism in order to shape it into something that would fit his definition of a contemporary "salvational" system.

Dr. Agus is in the so-called right wing of American Conservative Judaism, yet he, too, is unable to accept Jewish tradition simply as it has been handed down to us by what Solomon Schechter called Catholic Israel—namely the consensus of generations upon generations of pious Jews. While accepting the Law as given—at least to start with—Dr. Agus refuses to accept the methods of reasoning through which the rabbis formerly derived the laws. He is very actively concerned with *rethinking* the body of law, just as is Dr. Kaplan, and he applies the same methods of thought, namely the universal logic of all men and not the traditional logic of the Talmud; he differs from Dr. Kaplan in that the aim he ultimately accepts is not "this-worldly" but (superficially, at least) "otherworldly." To be recognized by him as valid for Judaism today, any traditional practice (or proposed departure from it) must be shown to conduce toward making contemporary American Jews more pious.

Thus Catholic Israel has in effect been reduced to contemporary American Jewry—or rather, to a small committee of rabbis in the Conservative movement who undertake to revise Jewish religious culture in line with what they think is likely to make their congregations (given their temperaments, distractions, level of knowledge and commitment, and other circumstances) more pious. That there has indeed been a major shrinkage of Solomon Schechter's original (undoubtedly rather vague) conception of Catholic Israel is stated quite explicitly by Robert Gordis: ". . . Catholic Israel must be conceived of differently from hitherto accepted views. Catholic Israel embraces all those who observe Jewish law in general, although they may violate one or another segment of it, and who are sensitive to the problem of their nonobservance because they wish to respect the authority of Jewish law." What better description could one ask of Conservative Judaism in America—or, even more particularly, of the "group mind" emerging from the collective cogitations of the Law Committee of the Rabbinical Assembly? And Catholic Israel, so defined, has only one function, that of reducing the traditional religious culture of Judaism to the dimensions of a contemporary American cult.

It may be asked why I, the self-confessed secularist, am apparently so exercised over the matter. The question is certainly a fair and pertinent one. Just to make it even more pointed, let me make this further confession: I find far more *sympathiques* those ideologists of neo-Orthodoxy, like Will Herberg or Abraham J. Heschel, who try to persuade me to leap to God and land in the age-old net of *halachah* than I do the ideologists of the new Catholic Israel. For I find in the former, who seem hardly concerned with rewinding the springs of our run-down *halachic* system so that it may tell time for the new era, a breadth and freedom of culture that are, to my mind, notably lacking in the latter, absorbed as they are in tinkering with the works to make *halachah* run in a new tempo.

I say this in spite of the fact that it has been a major achievement of secularist *Yiddishkeit,* and above all of Zionism, to break the mold within which religious tradition had frozen Jewish culture, and to let the creative stream flow freely once more. We have given even to Orthodoxy a future, for the history that Zionism has made can go unmarked by no Jewish doctrine that experiences as its core the great Jewish theme of Exile and Redemption. But it was Orthodoxy that gave us a past. This past we wished to expand, to open up, to unfold, to expose to the light, to explore and find in it colors suppressed, rebellions forgotten, nuances denied by Catholic Israel in the course of its massive flow. Upon this past we still stand and reach out to new, it may be extravagant, it may even be illusory perspectives. And they who would bring us back to it, regarding us as straying children, they, too, know that we belong together however opposed, just as we feel akin to them. For the old Jewish values were the values of a *people,* they constituted a culture—a religious culture, to be sure, but not the bare bones of a cult. The attempt to redefine Judaism as a cult, to make it over into an intelligently engineered curriculum for training in piety, to reduce it to the scale of experience of no more than the contemporary synagogue, not only in principle excludes us secularists; it constitutes an assault upon our past. Much could be said on this point, but I will only add that to a secularist socialist Zionist *galut* negator like myself, any version of Judaism which tries to dispense with the concept of Exile and Redemption from Exile is attempting nothing less than a divorce from our central historic experience as a people. Such a Judaism (if it could ever exist) would have cut itself off from its memory, and could have no Jewish future. To be sure, the awareness of Exile is today merely repressed, not effectively expunged, but even this much success of the American ideology can hardly fail to estrange us.

The Neo-Orthodox offer me *halachah* as a mystery which they themselves do not pretend to understand, and they ask me to take it on faith, as I should God. But they offer me my Jewish past whole and complete[2]—and they would have me accept it with all of me, just as I am, with my sense of Exile and my will to Redemption. Orthodox Judaism is, of course, "normative," like any religious doctrine, which means that there are always some spontaneous cultural expressions that it would suppress as heretical. Moreover, in Eastern Europe the "Orthodox"[3] Jews lived in a community which, because of the sluggish pulse of all history in that part of the world

---

2. I would make this assertion even of such neo-Orthodox apologists as Will Herberg who, coming back to Judaism from estrangement, must themselves slowly acquire the whole of Jewish culture, and may, at first, fail to appreciate some of its central themes.

3. I use quotation marks around this expression because it is really a misnomer. It is my impression that it never occurred to anyone to call a particular version of Judaism "Orthodox" until Reform Judaism arose and its opponents in Central Europe adopted this name in contradistinction.

and because of the high degree of Jewish isolation, allowed its religious culture, intense as it was, to become hemmed in and crabbed by conventions. It was precisely this constriction against which Zionism and Jewish secularism revolted. But, however strait-jacketed "Orthodox" Judaism was in Eastern Europe, it still functioned as an expression of a people, not of a union of congregations. It had in it the inherent freedom and responsiveness of a culture, not the automatism of a cult. It is not surprising, then, if after the emergence of Orthodox Jewry into the Western world, its intellectual adherents, even while taking up the old ritual life unaltered, live in free communication with all of Western culture, just as had Jews before them in Spain, Italy, the Moslem countries, and wherever the Gentiles around them had a significant culture.

It may seem a paradox to charge Conservative Judaism and its new ideologists even by implication with being anything but completely open to all the winds of contemporary culture. Is it not, after all, their major preoccupation to pull in the slack of that cultural lag with which Jewish tradition seems to be afflicted? But precisely this seems to me to be a basic error, an atrocious lapse of the instinct for culture. The Jewish religious folkways may or may not be out of tune with contemporary social conditions—if they are, rely on it that the Orthodox Jews will eventually alter them both here and in Israel by a movement almost glacial in its massiveness and imperceptibility, or, when they are good and ready, by some more abrupt transition acceptable to themselves. But what is quite clear is that these folkways cannot be incompatible with any true culture, whether contemporary or futurist. Such products of a massive cultural experience can be out of fashion culturally, just as they can be "out of adjustment" socially; but these are two distinct and separate phenomena. That a cultural expression may have gone out of fashion means that men have lost a capacity to appreciate its intrinsic merit—a merit it nevertheless still possesses, as it always has, if it were indeed ever anything more than a fashionable novelty. The time may come when new men with new capacities will appreciate it in new ways. But even when, in the autonomous development of culture itself, men turn from the old to the unexplored new—if this is a process of authentic culture, not of sociocultural engineering—they leave intact what they reject and they simply burst beyond its bounds along a line of flight contained potentially within the parent mass.

The real root of my objections may be, of course, that the new religious ideologists cannot accept such an "aberration" as myself—at least, they cannot if they adhere rigorously to their doctrine. It may seem as though I am putting too much emphasis on what is, after all, a merely academic question, for in spite of polemics the new ideologists have always been closely connected, in actuality, with us secularist socialist Zionists; so closely, indeed, that Dr. Kaplan, for one, wishes to call his doctrine the "New Zionism." If there have been occasions when this group viewed some cultural development in American Jewry with a censorious eye, it was usually a development with which we, too, had scant sympathy. But the point is not only that this group occasionally did show censorious tendencies, but that censoriousness is far more characteristic of them in principle than it has ever been (or, let us hope, ever will be) in practice. For the new doctrine is normative in a much more serious sense than Orthodox Judaism ever was, regardless of the incomparably worse actual record of the Orthodox as an obscurantist force. The Orthodox normative technique used a logic and method so "unscientific" that almost anything could in theory be justified by it, no matter how much was in fact, and on non-cultural grounds, excluded. But the new ideology operates with a precisely defined objective and a rigorous method: to cut and trim Jewish religious culture to a cult whose doctrines and practices can be shown by experimental evidence and logical inference to conduce to the attachment of the average American Jew to his synagogue.

As for God Himself, in whose name all the religious ideologists of whatever coloration join in chiding us, I have no doubt, on the strength of our acquaintanceship with Him through the medium of the vast, many-sided Jewish tradition, that He will be indulgent enough to let us make our way to Him through whatever detours we may each chance to find on our several routes. For it is clear enough that, in terms of normative Jewish tradition, Jewish secularism represents at least a detour, if not a total departure, from the roads upon which the Jewish people historically have sought God. What was characteristic of the Jews was that they sought God collectively, as a people, and incorporated their joint findings in a canonical literature and a normative set of folkways. The individual God-seeker, of course, always had his place in Judaism, whether as a prophet, Kabbalist, or ethical and ritual rigorist. But the "religious virtuoso" among Jews not only guarded himself to an unusual degree from a break with the community; the community went with him an extraordinarily long way on the road of devotion. Jewish culture, accordinigly, was a religious culture, a form of collective prayer in fact.

Contemporary Jewish secularism means a twofold break with this background. It means not only freeing Jewish culture from religious forms which we felt had become hidebound; it also means freeing religion from the bonds of tradition. By the latter, however, are implied not only the bonds of the tradition formed in Eastern Europe and corresponding to conditions there. Whatever religious impulse secularists experience feels itself quite as free from all those new traditions that are being reconstructed for us with scissors and paste in America. For better or worse, the Jewish secularist must find God out of his own, free individual experience. He may not even find Him as easily in the forms of Jewish tradition (and this can be true of men by whom the values of Jewish culture are profoundly experienced) as in quite unrelated forms. He may never find Him in any clear and distinct vision—but he cannot on that account abandon his Jewishness or his concern with Jewish culture!

Nothing the religious ideologists may say can affect one hard fact with which we secularists in the Jewish community—that is, we committed but extra-synagogue Jews—are continually confronted. Both by will and by force of circumstances, we are Jews, real, unquestionable Jews. In America, in the exile generally, our Jewishness has become a problem ever since its tie with God became evanescent. We find ourselves, moreover, in the self-defeating position of turning our secular Jewishness into a cult. Only in the movement to concentrate the Jewish people in Israel do we sense a real possibility that our Jewishness may strike roots as a natural culture. But there, too, we realize that the lost tie with God stands as a challenge to Jewish culture.

What, then, is our quarrel with the American religious ideologists? Paradoxically enough (if they will only believe us) it is that they offer us God too cheaply. We do not want Him as a solution for the problem of the Jewish Diaspora in America, nor as a least common denominator to reduce the differences between Israel and the Diaspora, or between contemporary and traditional Jewish culture. To make such a use of God seems to us respectful neither to

Him nor to our problems. The latter we wish to solve in their own terms. As to God, again I say, we have faith that He will be indulgent enough to let us, individually and collectively, make our way to Him by whatever detours we chance to meet on the road that we must travel.

ARE WE ISRAELIS
STILL JEWS?

The Search for Judaism in the New Society

ERNST SIMON

The late Jan Huizinga, famous Dutch cultural historian, characterized the latter part of the Middle Ages in this way: "Life was so
infused with religion that, at any given moment, the separation
between sacred and profane could have ceased to be meaningful."
This kind of religious situation may be called "Catholic," where
religion seeks to sanctify and control the life of the individual and
the community on every level—eating, drinking, work, rest, the
principles of community and state; love and war. History has shown
us many such "Catholic" religions. But it has also shown us that
they are likely to produce from within themselves the seeds of their
own destruction. For the time comes when various spheres of life
throw off the yoke of religion, assert themselves as autonomous
forces, and absorb religion as they previously had been absorbed in
it. In such critical periods, a new kind of religion emerges, the
"Protestant" type.

The protest at the root of this new religion is twofold, being
directed, first, against the decay of the "Catholic" religion, and
second, against the attempts of extreme heretics to deny that religion—already lost to the community as a whole—is of any value
even to the individual. The "Protestant" religion seeks to compensate for the loss of the "Catholic" religion by special emphasis on
the individual, his direct relation to God, and his personal salvation
by faith—essentially an individual act—rather than by good works,
which are always social acts. In a thoroughgoing and typically

"Protestant" religion, good works cease to bear the sanctified character of "sacrament" or "commandment" and become part of a sphere of cultural life called "ethics" that is wholly or partially detached from religion.

The contemporary crisis of the Jewish religion is reflected in three crucial phenomena: the collapse of the ancient "Catholic" Judaism; the weakening of the new "Protestant" Judaism; and the futile attempt to achieve a new spiritual vitality by attributing a Messianic purpose to the creation of the State of Israel in our own day.

"Catholic" Judaism came into being in the first centuries of the Common Era, in the period of the Mishnah and the Talmud; but its roots were already to be found in the Bible, particularly in the legal portions of the Pentateuch. Its inherent nature became most clearly articulated during its two greatest crises; the first crisis, the *Haskalah* ("Enlightenment") of the eighteenth and nineteenth centuries, shook the foundations of the absolute role of "Catholic" Judaism; the second crisis, the nationalism of the twentieth century, put an end to it for all practical purposes. In both cases phenomena appeared that had been developing slowly, but in concealment, over centuries.

The breakdown of "Catholic" Judaism was reflected in its inability to dominate all the spheres of life. In theory, it never relinquished this total claim. But it had lost the power to translate it into practical activity. Orthodoxy today rules only in certain homes, schools, and synagogues. It has been forced to give up, for all practical purposes, its sway over commerce, technology, society, the army, and the state; for modern economics, technology, *et al.*, are the products of a secular spirit. In modern times, religion generally, and the Jewish religion in particular, comes after the fact.

I

The central concept of every "Protestant" approach is that of "culture." It is no accident that this word (Hebrew: *tarbut*) —so current among Israel's intellectuals, and endowed by them with the very highest spiritual values—does not at all have such a positive and elevated connotation anywhere in the Bible or Talmud. When the founders of the secular Hebrew schools of East Europe sought a term to distinguish their school system from the traditional *yeshivot*, they adopted the word *tarbut*. The new positive meaning of this term, which had been neutral or even negative before, was a function of its being a translation of the German *Kultur,* for which there is no real equivalent in Hebrew.

While the concept *Torah* testifies to a suprahuman, revealed source, the concept *culture* refers back to a human one; and it is precisely here that we touch upon the unique weakness of "Protestant" Judaism as against Christian Protestantism. The latter, it is true, likewise ran the risk, often, of having its teaching transformed into merely an aspect of secular culture, but the Protestant faithful knew how to distinguish in the teachings of their first Reformers and of the best of those who succeeded them, between religion and worldly wisdom—this, despite their appreciation of the latter. The chief historical reason for the ability of the Protestants to make this distinction lay in the fact that they still clung to the Bible as revelation, while rejecting the traditional interpretation of Scripture given by the Roman Catholic Church. They could, and did, base this attitude on the authority of the dogmas of primitive Christianity itself. Thus the Reformation could appear as a restoration of Christianity in its original evangelical form. Luther made Scripture the possession of all Christians when he broke the priestly monopoly on sacred and secular studies, and this constituted a religious "expansion" that compensated—at least in theory—for the Protestant transfer of universal temporal authority from the Church to territorial princes, and of the totality of worldly wisdom from priests to humanist university professors.

The modern liberal Reform movement in Judaism, coming as it did three centuries later, was unable to do likewise. It did draw secular and religious conclusions from the breakdown of "Catholic" Judaism, but these conclusions were, in the main and at bottom, only negative ones. While the Lutheran or Calvinist could claim that he was a better Christian than the Catholic, the liberal Jew of today generally knows that he is a less faithful Jew than his Orthodox coreligionist. The success of Reform Judaism brought a loss of faith in the authority and revealed nature, not only of the tradition, but of the Torah itself. And while Reform's stress on prophetic morality was certainly on a high level, it failed to provide a substitute for that unique Jewish content given to everyday life by Orthodoxy. So the Torah became, for Liberal Judaism, only one of the many aspects of knowledge that were subsumed under the general heading of "culture"; indeed, it became the relic of a foreign culture in a foreign tongue.

A second reason for the failure of "Protestant" Judaism, in contrast to the success of Protestant Christianity, is directly related to one of the fundamental characteristics of "Catholic" Judaism: in contradistinction to Roman Catholicism, Judaism has no central institution that fixes the articles of faith obligatory for every Jew. As a colleague of mine once phrased it, there are Jewish *dogmas,* but there is no Jewish *dogmatics.* The reasons for this are extremely complicated and need not be gone into here. Religious philosophy, the philosophical interpretation and defense of Jewish religion, we have had aplenty. But systematic theology—the interpretation of God, the world, and man on the basis of the Jewish religion—that is almost completely lacking in the older Hebrew literature.

Now, a "Protestant" religion absolutely requires a theology. In so far as it is a religion, it neither desires nor is able to content itself with a "cultural" *Weltanschauung* alone. Despite all its concessions to culture, it seeks a vantage point of its own from which to approach the world, and it can find this only in a theology. Christian Protestantism was able to draw upon the great tradition of Catholic theology, even when it attacked and differed with it. Not so Jewish "Protestantism." The Jewish reformers who sought a Jewish theology were like children just learning to count. There was no one and nothing to assist them. Often enough, their attempts, in all their daring, looked to their traditional brethren like the behavior of a *"goy* studying Torah."

A third factor that militated against the success of "Protestant" Judaism was the national character of the Jewish people. Saadia Gaon, when "Catholic" Judaism was in full bloom, could say, "Our people is a people only by virtue of its religion." By the time of the rise of "Protestant" Judaism, the sentiment had become: "Our religion is a religion only within the framework of the nation." But what of the individuals whose tie with the "nation" was on the verge of being broken, yet sought to guard their bond with the Jewish *religion* and even to strengthen it? These Jews knew, indeed, that Jews—unlike Christians—are born before they are made, but this plain fact no longer told them what it had told their ancestors. As they sought their individual paths to Judaism they became consumed by doubts as to whether the objective essence of being a Jew was capable of being attained in this subjective way. Yet they had no other.

They were rescued from this dilemma by Zionism—not all of them, but some, and even these only for a time, and superficially. For a while everything became clear: a great national movement had arisen that strove to "renew our days as of old" in the ancestral home, resuscitating the scriptural tongue, glorifying all the "sanctities of the nation," and assuring every adherent a full Jewish life. But difficult questions, particularly religious ones, began to appear as the national movement neared its goal: what would be the character of the new Jewish society? And if a state were created, what would it look like? The internal conflicts within Zionism, held so far in abeyance, now became sharper and clearer.

II

These questions now require immediate and practical solutions in Israel, but only "Catholic" Judaism has as yet found an official platform in that country. "Protestant" Judaism, though it has many adherents, has acquired no general religious voice, either organized or individual; it is thwarted by the alliance between official Orthodoxy, with its recognized institutions, and the indifference of the nonreligious.[1] On the other hand, responsible and dynamic "Catholic" Judaism in Israel is represented by two groups: the stubborn purists of the ultra-Orthodox Neturai Karta, and the circle around Dr. Isaiah Leibowitz, a lecturer in chemistry at the Hebrew University and one of the intellectual leaders of Israeli youth.

The Neturai Karta have lost all practical effectiveness by separating themselves from the state, which will not knuckle under to their demands. Dr. Leibowitz, like them, aspires to the "Catholic" ideal of a fully lived Jewish religious life. In his view Halachah, the prescribed practice, will cease being Halachah if it goes on relinquishing one area of life after another, and he demands that it reconquer all of them that it has lost. But to this end—and here he differs with the Neturai Karta as well as the Chief Rabbinate—it is incumbent on the Halachah to adapt itself to new circumstances and needs of which its ancient masters were ignorant: the needs of an independent state, a national economy, a complex technology,

---

1. This situation has somewhat moderated during the past decade and a half, although Simon's point remains essentially correct. [Editor]

and military security. Jewish religion, according to Dr. Leibowitz, must produce new ways of life that the bulk of the community can live by—instead of demanding for itself and its Torah a sanctuary guaranteed by the secular and profaning work of *Shabbos goyim*.

The result of all this is paradoxical in the extreme: only "Protestant" Judaism, satisfied to save its own individual soul or that of its limited group, can allow itself today to remain conservative with regard to traditional Law, which may serve as a personal or social style, but no longer as the nation's way of life as a whole. Meanwhile, that "Catholic" Judaism which feels responsible toward the whole community is driven to revolutionary withdrawal—like the Neturai Karta—or to revolutionary reform. The principal difference between the withdrawers and the reformers lies in their attitudes toward the State of Israel: the former deny it but the latter affirm it religiously.

The late Chief Rabbi of Palestine, Abraham Isaac HaCohen Kook, went even further and viewed the Return to Zion in his own days as a Messianic event. In his yeshiva at Jerusalem, so we are told, he established a small group of *kohanim* (descendants of the priestly caste) whose sole function was to study the Priestly Code, the laws of the Holy Temple and of the sacrifices—in order to be prepared for the great day when the Messiah himself would appear and the Temple service be reinstituted.

The full-bodied Messianism in Rabbi Kook's system was connected with his highly original understanding of the problem of the relation between sacred and profane. As he saw it, the religious deterioration of the Chosen People in their exile could be accounted for by the shriveling of the secular seed that served as the source of life for the Holy. The economic, political, and communal abnormality of the Jewish situation in *galut* resulted in a surplus of holiness, so to speak, that remained untranslated into effective activity and creation. The great merit of the Zionist movement was to activate this fund of holiness. In this way, secular activity fulfilled, and continues to fulfill, a completely religious function. Said Rabbi Kook: "Worldly holiness which sanctifies the profane is the holiness that is in nature and it reveals itself in the Holy Land."

Rabbi Kook was the sole rabbinical representative of "Catholic" Judaism to deal seriously with the fact of secularization in the life of the people, and to seek to restore the crown of the Torah to its ancient glory without turning his back upon the historical process of secularization. "Heavenly holiness is blessed according as the lower, secular foundation is informed with a pure spirit." For "the holy must be built on a secular foundation." Also, the realm of holiness expands as does the realm of the profane: "Spirituality cannot be achieved in our generation except through the fulfillment of the physical." Thus sacred and secular do not conflict, but nourish each other, even though there is a clear distinction betweeen them, as between foundation and higher level. The people and its land—they are the concrete basis for the true life of holiness.

The peculiarly problematic nature of this conception of "Messianism in process" was illustrated in the way it was received by the Jews of Palestine. Rabbi Kook's approach led him to take an exceedingly tolerant attitude toward the *halutzim,* who had discarded the yoke of the traditional *mitzvot.* He saw them as *tsadikim* ("righteous ones") despite themselves, and compared them to the workers in the Temple who had been exempt from certain injunctions. This attitude was, of course, readily accepted in Palestine, especially by the workers. But it was not understood in that quarter that this same attitude led Rabbi Kook to come out strongly in defense of individuals involved in alleged or real acts of terrorism, because of his profound conviction that no Jew was capable of such deeds—just as he refused to admit that the *mitzvah* of the redemption of the land by the *halutzim* could be performed by sinners. For him the Jewish nation was a *corpus mysticum* and all its members were sanctified.

Great as the Rabbi was, a grave danger inhered in such a political Messianism as his. Under the cover of a teaching whose intention is wholly beneficent, good and evil can mingle promiscuously. As Rabbi Kook himself said: "Just as the praise of the Lord rises from the righteous, so too it rises from evil men; just as it rises from Paradise, so too it rises from Gehenna." The tragic conclusion of this doctrine of Messianism in process is evidenced in its most recent secular devolution: the coronation of the epoch of the new State of Israel as the "Days of the Messiah."

The principal change to be effected by the Days of the Messiah, according to Jewish tradition, is the achievement of political independence as a *means* to moral and religious wholeness. To drain the concept "Days of the Messiah" of its ethical content and religious form, and equate it with strictly political achievement, would open the door wide to a danger that threatens every human action: the greatest of all such dangers—the stilling of conscience. After all, the freedom and urge to criticize assume that the state and its leaders can make mistakes—but Messiahs never do.

A completely different type of stricture must be brought against the position of Dr. Isaiah Leibowitz, who asserts that the religious crisis in Judaism requires "religious solutions" and "a new religious legislation." In other words—reform. He demands the kind of "program that will both require and make possible its being acted upon by the whole of Israel, not a program restricted to a sect of Sabbath-observers within a framework of a Sabbath-profaning people."

These words appeared in an article in *B'terem,* a staunchly Mapai fortnightly. One wonders whether the editors really grasped the basic intention of their guest contributor. For his program, while it would *permit* work on the Sabbath in necessary government and community services, in certain technological installations, and in economic, financial, and military activities, would *require* the state to enforce the observance of the Sabbath by all Jews, religious and nonreligious alike. Dr. Leibowitz's article does more to outline the basis for a clerical regime than does all the activity, or lack of it, of the Chief Rabbinate in Israel. A clerical regime means a kingdom of priests *without* a holy people, as opposed to a theocratic state, which means a kingdom of priests *with* a holy people. A theocracy implies the wholehearted agreement of the bulk of the people in a great communal act such as the "we will obey and we will hearken" at Sinai, or the "pact" in the time of Ezra—an agreement to accept the Lord's Torah and fulfill it willingly. A true theocracy is not based on force, whereas a clerical regime cannot survive without it. Dr. Leibowitz's program is indeed a minimal program for the Orthodox minority, but if it were realized it would become, for the secular majority, a maximal program.

The only positive argument Dr. Leibowitz uses—this, to convince a secular audience—is his religious affirmation of the State of Israel. This supplies him with the Halachic principle by which to justify the reform he suggests, and with the link without which his program could not in any sense be considered "Catholic" Judaism. He writes: "The rabbinic prohibition of work on the Sabbath did not apply, as we know, to the service in the Temple—since it was the service of Israel, and not the work of any individual Jew for his personal needs or pleasure. We ought to consider, in all seriousness, whether the necessary services of a modern state should not occupy the same place in Halachah as did the sacrifices in the Temple."

Dr. Leibowitz holds that the need to preserve a religious order in Jewish society is sufficient to justify a systematic reform of Halachah. But, granting that, is there not a grave danger that, in reconciling Halachah *toto caelo* with the needs of a modern state, Halachah itself may lose its character as a religious category by having its social role simply identified with its religious and moral ground? The requirements of security are quite legitimately defined by the statesman, but the man of Halachah must find the spiritual strength to reject decisions of state if and when they conflict with his religious principles. Thus it is not enough, by far, to undertake a revision of Halachah merely because it is required by the needs of a new polity: these very needs must themselves be founded on explicit moral premises. Dr. Leibowitz's thoroughgoing legal formalism threatens to deprive Halachah of its religious burden. Anyone who undertakes to reform Halachah must assure himself above all that the firm and *immediate* ground of faith is not shifted away from under him.

III

On the first anniversary of the death of Julius Guttman, late professor of Jewish philosophy at the Hebrew University, a group of intellectual, communal, and youth leaders took part in Jerusalem in a symposium on the prospects for a contemporary Jewish religious philosophy. Of the many views aired there, those on the pessimistic side made the greatest impression. The chief speaker was Gershom Scholem, whose negative argument ran as follows: Yesterday we had religious philosophy; tomorrow, perhaps, we may actually have theology; today we have neither. The state tore away the false mask that covered the crisis of Jewish religion. That crisis was laid bare. But there is hope that this nothingness may some day give birth to a new reality. Meanwhile, we must wait, think, and learn.

But neither educational philosophy nor practical pedagogics can rest content with this abstract hope. While care must be taken to avoid the characteristic tendency of practical pedagogics to jump to premature and half-baked conclusions simply because immediate, practical decisions are required, this cannot justify passivity.

The philosopher can wait. Perhaps he is compelled to wait and to hope in order to be able to think and study. But children and their education cannot wait. "Meanwhile" they grow up and decide their own future and that of the state. While philosophers and pedagogues have been groping, a new generation has grown up in Israel whose contact with the Torah and with religion has come, not from original sources of piety and faith, but through a variety of one-sided interpreters, the bearers of wholesale secularization. A nine-year-old in a kibbutz who was asked, "What do you think? Who created the world?" answered with assurance, "The workers created the world." A Palestine-born high school student expressed himself in this way: "Religion is a matter for fools and wise men, but not for us, the in-between."

What we see here is the feeling of ease in being "in-between," and the transformation of in-betweenness into an end in itself. The abstention implied by the notion of "we, the in-between," seems to be characteristic of much of the youth of Israel, and is the result of the recent escape from the social and psychological conditions of a life led as a minority in exile. These conditions compelled the Jewish people to make special exertions, and by these exertions even mediocre minds rose to a higher level. But in the absence of such special effort in the realm of spirituality, religion is threatened, and while the "mediocre" now perform acts of heroism and pioneering sacrifice, action cannot compensate for a lack or weakness of thought, or for a want of individuality.

Recently, a sixteen-year-old sabra asked me: "What must I read in order to determine whether I am still a Jew?" Had a *galut* Jew, in the late nineteenth century or at the beginning of the twentieth, posed the question of his Jewishness in this way, he would have been understood, in most cases correctly, to be raising a sociological or a nationalistic, but not a religious question. Zionism and the State of Israel, having secured the social and national conditions for an independent Jewish existence, have also made it possible to study the principles and commandments of the Jewish religion for their own sake—independently, that is to say, theologically—it being no longer either necessary or possible to base them on national needs alone. In the State of Israel the birth of a human being, as a son to his people, does not by itself make him a Jew. And so the history of Jewish religion has arrived at a new point of departure.

The sharp break with the heritage of the past, expressed programmatically in a scorn of the *galut* image of the Jew that verges on Zionist anti-Semitism, has reduced the role of tradition. As a very popular song among Israeli young people has it: "In place of yesterday we have a tomorrow."

IV

Even for those who hope to see a "Catholic" Jewish faith renewed, the Jewish religion in all its many forms has now become a deeply personal rather than communal question. The Torah, this "Catholic" Torah, this Torah of life that seeks to sanctify all of life, is known to us and yet lost to us; it is no longer "given," it has become a thing to be chosen.

This paradoxical situation calls for paradoxical undertakings: Judaism is, indeed, a "Catholic" religion when viewed objectively; but in the present crisis we can approach it only subjectively, from a "Protestant" point of view. The difference between the latter approach and that "Protestant" Judaism whose deterioration I analyzed above consists in the clear realization that this individualistic approach is not an end in itself, not a legitimate construction of Judaism as such, but merely a not dishonorable means whose use is forced upon us by necessity.

So long as we remain in a situation of beginning and of transition, we have neither the possibility nor the right to link religion to the state. On the contrary, it is necessary to keep them as far apart as possible. Not merely to guarantee the secular character of a democratic state, but especially to secure a completely free approach to the problems of religion. But even the secular State of Israel must provide the Torah full scope for development and influence, by assuring it freedom of action. The religious home, the religious school, religious life as it is expressed rhythmically during the week, on Sabbaths and holidays, and especially the social experiments of the religious labor movements—all these merit a positive attitude on the part of the state. Their existence must be based on legal right and not on sufferance. Those who act upon this right will realize fully that the secular majority of Israel is not with them, but they are still entitled, nay obligated, to act upon it as a necessary condition for the strengthening of their faith. Once it was the faith of all Israel, and "there is hope" still that it will some day regain that status.

Toward this end there must be a renewal of the spirit of

prophetic criticism. That spirit was not the special property of the era of the prophets: it belongs to all of us who are heirs to their words and students of their message. The prophets of Irael sought to enlist all of life, beginning with social relations and ending with foreign policy, under the banner of holiness. In the Diaspora this "Catholic" demand could not be implemented on the highest level, that of social law, because the Jews lived under foreign rule and were not responsible for the whole of public existence. So the prophetic call became only a matter of conscience, naked and shaky. With, and after, the first Return to Zion from the Babylonian Exile, Pharisaic Judaism, arising out of its prophetic predecessor, succeeded in translating the demands of conscience—which had formerly been addressed to the people through the mediation of individuals—into life forms that were addressed to the individual through the mediation of the people as a whole. It is in the light of this development that we can understand the rabbinic dictum: "The Man of Torah is superior to the Prophet."

But in view of the destruction of those ways and forms of life, we must return, above all, to their original foundation stone: to the spirit of criticism by the prophetic conscience. Our aim must be, not the isolating of that spirit, as was the case with many "Protestant" Jews, but the evocation of the "catholicity" hidden in it, so that it may once more stamp itself on our whole life. Here there is no fundamental disagreement between such men as Martin Buber, for instance, and Rabbi Kook: both of them deny that Judaism is an isolated religious province standing separate within a larger secular life; it is, rather, a mighty experiment in the transformation of all of human life into one great sanctified whole. So long as the experiment goes on—that is, until *final* redemption—whoever truly yearns for redemption, in Rabbi Kook's words, "will be able more keenly to discern the difference between sacred and profane."

In the land of Israel, we have been given the chance to sanctify certain areas of existence that had become secularized in exile. There lies, in this opportunity, a great hope—and a no less great danger. The hope is the sanctification of the profane, including the state; the danger is the profanation of the holy, including religion, through politicalization.

The only way to pursue such a course of hope is to adopt moral and religious criteria with which to evaluate what is done and what is left undone in our midst. Our positive attitude toward the State

399

of Israel cannot be a "Messianic" one that obscures evils; it must be a critical one that reveals evils in order to correct them. We need men who will constantly ask disturbing questions about every aspect of our life as a people.

Frederick the Great in 1752, writing in his political testament on the instruction of the young princes, his sons, commands their teachers "to speak of the army in the same hallowed phrases as priests use in reference to Divine Revelation. . . ." Jews have always rejected this attitude and still reject it when they encounter it in another people. Shall we accept it now when a leading educator compares the "Kingdom of Priests," which is the heritage of the past, with the "Kingdom of Soldiers" that has taken its place, and when he asserts that the future belongs to this latter?

It is here that we are called upon to utter our "Nay" with complete clarity. We can draw an *a fortiori* argument from Maimonides, who declared that no man can know the form of the Messianic Era. But we can all envisage what the form of those Days will *not* be and from this negation we can infer its converse. Judaism's miraculous force of life lay in the "Nay" that it knew how to utter in the face of every call to redemption that did not fit the image of the true Redemption: Christianity, Islam, Sabbatianism, Communism. And by the strength of that negation, the People of Israel remained *the* People of Redemption and guarded the hope of redemption in an unredeemed world. To attribute a Messianic character to the State of Israel is equivalent to losing the criteria of true Redemption.

Above all, the individual Jew must begin with himself. In his last novel, *Die Schuldlosen,* the late Jewish poet and philosopher Hermann Broch uttered this indictment of those who, at ease with themselves, ignore the evil that is done before their eyes: "This indifference toward the suffering outside you is but the consequence of your indifference to the man within you." The hope of the hopers is that we may be freed from this indifference to the man within us and outside us. And this hope is based on faith.

Not a few see in the history of Israel, and especially in the events of the last few years, the revelation of Him who "records the generations" and "orders the cycles of time." These people who sense the approach of the Days of the Messiah can no longer discern the difference between holiness and profanation, or even between good and evil. By contrast, the faith of the hopers, of those who desire to remain Jews—or better still, who desire to become Jews once again—their faith remains strong and unshaken in Him who placed the true redemption of man *in the future,* in the Days of the Messiah and the World to Come. This is the faith in Him who made the distinction between sacred and profane.

INTRODUCTION TO

THE ISSUE BETWEEN JUDAISM AND CHRISTIANITY

Jacob Taubes

It is a post-Christian era. This is only to say that the secularization of the West is nearly complete. Secularization is not necessarily a defect, for the neutrality of the public domain and the indifference of institutions to their historically inherited religious presuppositions make it possible for non-Christians and un-Christians to endure. But what must happen if, despite the fact of post-Christianity, the major contestant to Christianity continues to define its opposition by the tacit acceptance of Christian terms of argument. Such an opponent is doubly oppressed: it not only suffers from the indifference of a neutral public order which no longer grants privilege to the natural law of belief, but as well it continues to define its identity by contrast to a Christianity that is already ineffectual and disused. Such a religion is twice beset, and if one listens to the argument of Jacob Taubes's essay Judaism is *that* religion.

Martin Buber, Franz Rosenzweig, Hans Joachim Schoeps, any and all Jewish theological apologists (and I suspect myself included) have all defined the Jewish stance vis-à-vis Christianity in terms which all but concede the force of the Christian argument. The early Jewish respondents to Christianity, those, that is, who took cognizance of her existence prior to the emancipation and enlightenment, did so while conceding nothing. Christianity was simply irrelevant. Not even a Jewish heresy, Christianity was a nullification of

Judaism and consequently either quite simply the enemy or beside the point.

The rabbis of the Talmudic Age down to the close of the Middle Ages were disciples of Paul when he was still Saul, for the reign of Torah was complete and definitive and the task of Messianic redemption was left to God. The Paul of the Epistles, however, defined a position exactly the reverse of him who claimed to be an obedient Pharisee and disciple of Gamaliel, for where Saul accepted the reign of the Law, Paul denies it, substituting in its place the suasions of love; where Saul believed that doing the Law obeyed God, Paul would argue that believing in the dispensation of Jesus as the Christ, believing *on him* rather than obeying a Law which fulfilled him was sufficient to salvation. It is Taubes's argument that by accepting the validity of the Christian dispensation—even if only for the Gentiles—Buber, Rosenzweig, *et al.*, concede what no Jew can ever concede, namely that the Torah is a parochial dispensation, that Jews are an arcanum (a vestige might be more accurate) compelled by history to function alongside Christianity, neither true nor false, but historically relativized.

The real issue is that Jews no longer begin theology from the Law. Rather they begin theology, as Christians begin theology, from principles of belief. To the extent that they depass the Law, they permit Paul a victory by default. The force of Taubes's argument is immense, but perhaps there is a possible response, not a response which exculpates those of us who argue against Christianity by the employment of Christian method, but one which takes the issue in an entirely different direction. The fact that this is described as a post-Christian era carries with it the equally compelling recognition that it is also a post-Jewish era. That is to say, "confessional religion" is over and the man of today is no longer willing to take his stand upon ground tilled and tended by any institutional establishment. But the fact that this is a postreligious time does not mean that men no longer ask questions of the universe. If we cannot begin any longer from antinomian salvation in Jesus as Christ nor in the just reign of law which awaits a salvation to come, we are no less obliged to ask first questions. It may be true that a Jewish theology which defines itself only by opposition to Christianity is involved in a double death, but this does not mean that a Jewish theology cannot begin by asking questions of God, man, and world.

The historical progeneration of the theology of Franz Rosenzweig, for example, was his near conversion to Christianity and his ultimate commitment to the Law. His seminal work, *The Star of Redemption,* however, does not begin with an autobiographical crisis, but with a description of the threefold interrelation of God, man, and world. We may no longer be able to begin the Jewish argument from the announcement of Torah, but that does not mean that we cannot end there.

THE ISSUE BETWEEN
JUDAISM
AND CHRISTIANITY

Facing Up to the Unresolvable Difference

JACOB TAUBES

For all the current popularity of the term "Judeo-Christian" tradition, the differences between the Jewish and Christian religions are not at all resolved. They are basic, and their consequences still influence every moment of our lives. True, the immediate and more pressing issues in Jewish-Christian relations are social and political, but this does not justify postponing an examination of the fundamental issue, which is theological—and from which all the social and political questions spring originally.

As long as a clear awareness existed of the basic theological differences between Judaism and Christianity there was no great need to argue the matter explicitly. But in the last twenty years it has become fashionable to gloss over and distort these differences. Now we need to restate them. Nor need we be afraid to. There is warrant for believing that, even in the sphere of the "practical," we have more to gain by defining and understanding the issues involved than by obscuring them and pretending they do not exist.

For centuries the controversy between Jewish religion and Christian dogma had for its frame the historical victory of the Christian church. All that the church required of the synagogue was that she admit her defeat. If necessary, the church could always appeal to the secular arm of the state to end the argument.

The magic spell of Christianity's historical success remains, though the church no longer uses the sword to decide her dispute with the synagogue, and this spell still constrains the Jewish-Christian dialogues of our time. Its influence can be seen in the exchange of letters between Franz Rosenzweig and Eugen Rosenstock, in the dialogue between the Protestant theologian Karl Ludwig Schmidt and Martin Buber, and in the dispute between the Christian ideologue of anti-Semitism, Hans Blüher, and the Prussian Jew Hans Joachim Schoeps. The fact that the history of the nations unfolded under the triumph of the cross (though only in the West) has for Franz Rosenzweig and Hans Joachim Schoeps, as to lesser degree for Martin Buber, a weight and relevance that seem to me to be fatal to any claim that might be made for their thought as *Jewish* theology.

A sober analysis of the Jewish-Christian controversy must set aside the argument from history, which embodies a dangerous temptation to take what *is* for what *ought to be*. After all, how can history "decide" in matters of theology? And, especially, what can historical success prove for a religion like Christianity that claims to be not of this world and heralds the end of history?

Nor is *this* a time for the Christian church to use the argument from history. From the viewpoint of worldly success, do we not stand on the threshold of a post-Christian era, when Christian symbols and dogmas have begun to look as antiquated as the Old Testament seemed in the Christian era? And indeed, looking at the present spiritual situation, it is most probable that the age to come will shape its religious forms in a way equally remote from both Jewish and Christian patterns. Be that as it may, the historical argument is certainly two-edged. There is a good deal of irony in the fact that, whereas Christian theologians today steer clear of the "proof" from history (warned off by such a critic as Nietzsche's friend, Franz Overbeck), Jewish thinkers like Hans Joachim Schoeps and Will Herberg have become so spellbound by Christianity's historical success that they try to give it a "theological" justification.

The issue between the Christian and Jewish religions starts from the Christian side. According to Christian doctrine, the Jewish people are an integral part of the Christian history of salvation. The synagogue is, in the eyes of the early church fathers, the shadow of the body of the church. Christian theology views the history of mankind as a progressive covenant between God and man. The covenant begins with Adam and manifests itself in different stages: from Noah to Abraham, from Abraham to Moses, from Moses to

David, from David to the son of David "who is the Christ." In the ultimate sacrifice of Jesus of Nazareth who is the Christ, the covenant is made final. The last step in the covenant between God and man, according to Christian theology, is the incarnation of God in the Son of Man. The history of Israel prefigures the story of redemption; the events recorded in the Old Testament do not contain their ultimate meaning in themselves, but point beyond themselves: the death of Abel, the sacrifice of Isaac, the kingdom of David, the Temple in Jerusalem prefigure the life and death of Jesus the Christ, as well as the history of the church.

The Jewish people, however, not only "prefigure" the story of redemption, but are an active "figure" in the drama of salvation. The fundamental statement in the Gospel according to St. John—"for salvation is of the Jews"—does not, according to Christian theology, refer to past history or to the mere "racial" fact that Jesus the Christ and his first disciples were of Jewish origin; it points rather to the essential role of Israel in that drama of salvation which the first theologian of the Christian community described in his Epistle to the Romans: Has Israel stumbled that it should fall? Paul denies this, interpreting the refusal of the Jewish community to accept Jesus as the Christ as part of the universal drama of redemption: Israel's rejection of Jesus made it possible for salvation to come to the Gentile nations. Israel became an enemy of Jesus Christ, writes Paul to the Christian community in Rome, *"for your sakes—."*

In other words, Paul can call the Jewish destiny a mystery because the role of the Jewish people is mysteriously interwoven with the role of the redeemer in the Christian drama of redemption. The Jewish synagogue refuses Jesus as the Christ, but this refusal is essential to universal redemption. The dark and mysterious "necessity," according to Paul, of the Jewish people in the drama of redemption affords no reason for Gentile self-gratulation or for condemnation of Israel. The Gentile nations should remember that the Jewish people are the natural branches of the tree of redemption, whose "root" is Israel's history. The Gentile nations were grafted onto the tree of redemption "contrary to nature," and shall be cut off if they fail in their faith in Christ. Let the Jews only not persist in their refusal of Jesus as the Christ, and how much more shall they, who are the natural branches of the tree of redemption, adorn and make part of it.

However, the key sentence, "for salvaton is of the Jews," must be read in the context of the Johannine Gospel's violent attack on the synagogue. (Some serious writers on the Johannine Gospel, such as Rudolf Bultmann, the German theologian, think the clause is a gloss, since it does not accord with that dominant tendency of the Gospel which has led some Protestant commentators to call it the most anti-Jewish pamphlet ever to have appeared.) The Johannine Christ denies that Jews and Christians have one Father in God; the Jews, in refusing to acknowledge Jesus as the Christ, serve the "Devil." They do not know God the Father since they do not acknowledge the divine Son in Jesus.

But *from the Jewish point of view,* the division of the divinity into "Father" and "Son" splits the divine essence; it was, and is, regarded by the synagogue quite simply as blasphemy. The doctrine of the synagogue and the Gospel according to St. John both "agree" as to what they regard as the basic point at issue, the heart of the argument, even if they arrive at opposite conclusions.

To sum up the Christian argument then: the Jewish people have a definite role in the Christian drama of salvation. Israel's history is the "root" of the tree of redemption, Israel serving in its denial of Jesus as the Christ as a negative but necessary element in the process of salvation.

If one accepts my description of the Christian "economy of salvation," I think that my statement of the basic Jewish premise can be readily understood: the Christian religion in general, and the body of the Christian church in particular, is of no *religious* relevance to the Jewish faith. There is a Jewish "mystery" for the church, but there is no Christian "mystery" for the synagogue. Christian history can have no religious significance of any kind for the Jewish creed; nor can the division of historical time into "B.C." and "A.D." be recognized by the synagogue. More than that, it cannot even be recognized as something which, though meaningless for the Jewish people, represents truth for the rest of the world.

This basic Jewish premise was obscured when Franz Rosenzweig, introducing a new "theological" notion into Jewish thought, interpreted the coming of Jesus as having a Messianic significance for the Gentile nations, but not for the Jewish people. Rosenzweig based his theological *tour de force* on a bold reading of a fundamental *logion* of the Johannine Christ: "I am the way . . . no man cometh unto the Father, but by me" (14:6). The history of the nations is, according to Rosenzweig, the "way" to the divine fulfillment, and this "way" to the Father leads for the Gentiles through Jesus the Christ. No man "cometh," as Rosenzweig emphasized, into the divine covenant but through the Son of God—except the Jewish nation whom God "elected" from its very beginning to make a covenant with.

The election of Israel—which is a Christian article of faith, too—implies that Israel does not march along the eternal way of history, but stands in the eternal presence of the covenant with God. The life of Israel in the divine covenant is the eternal life. Till the end of history, so argues Rosenzweig, the "eternal life" (the transhistorical destiny of Israel) and the "eternal way" (the historical destiny of the Gentile nations in Jesus Christ) are divided. Only at the end of days, when the Son of God shall deliver up the "Kingdom" to God and lay aside all his power and authority, shall the eternal life and the eternal way come together; Israel shall cease to be the holy nation living in the eternal divine presence only when Christ shall cease to rule over the eternal way of the nations.

The Christian church, says Rosenzweig, must understand that it is the essence of the mystery of salvation that the Jews shall remain separate so long as Christ does not deliver up his authority to God the Father. Through Paul, the church became the church of the nations. According to Rosenzweig, it is both anachronistic and contradictory for the church to wish to see the Jews converted: anachronistic, because it implies a return to the pre-Pauline situation; contradictory, because Christian eschatology places the conversion of the Jews at the end of time, beyond history.

I do not deny the grandeur of Rosenzweig's interpretation. Yet it seems to me a dubious thing to make Rosenzweig's highly doubtful reading of a *Christian* text the basis for the doctrine of the synagogue. What Rosenzweig is expressing here is his own spiritual biography: *his* return to Judaism started from a point on the borderline between the two faiths, when he was just about to cross over to the church. However much personal validity Rosenzweig's interpretation may have, it is theologically irrelevant. It is only too obvious that his "theological" arguments do violence to the spirit of the Gospel according to St. John, and that Jesus of the Fourth Gospel offers the weakest possible basis for the view he advances.

Rosenzweig's dichotomy between nations that are on the "way" through Jesus the Christ and "come" into the divine covenant, and a Jewish people that "are" already in the divine covenant, contradicts the whole Johannine scheme of salvation. John denies the Jewish people any knowledge of God, insisting that only through the Son could the Jews have known the Father (8:19). Moreover, the same sentence that calls Jesus Christ the "way" (which is the basis of Rosenzweig's speculation about the division between the "eternal way" and the "eternal life") also calls Christ the life: "Jesus saith unto him, I am the way, and the truth, and the life. . . ." I do not understand how Jesus can be conceded to be the Christ in Rosenzweig's halfway fashion: how can Jesus be the Messiah come to redeem the nations, but not the Jewish people? Rosenzweig categorically denies that Jesus has any Messianic significance for the Jewish people, and denies even the significance for the Jewish people of Messianic redemption in general (since Israel exists outside the Messianic dialectic of history); but under the spell of the success of the church in the Western World, he raises Christianity's mundane history, in the fashion of his master Hegel, to the level of the divine.

Even as speculation, Rosenzweig's argument has a glaring weakness: Islam. He treats Islam, which made its appearance centuries after the advent of Christianity, in exactly the same way as such Protestant scholars of the New Testament era as Schuerer and Weber treated the period of "late Judaism" in the time of Jesus—that is, as an irritating supererogation. A thorough analysis would show that Rosenzweig was a captive of the Protestant vocabulary, the only difference being that where the Protestant scholars say "rabbinic theology," he says the Islamic religion. Since Islam hardly counts as a social factor in the West, and there was no group to take up the cudgels on its behalf, Rosenzweig's caricature of Islam could pass. Will Herberg, accepting Rosenzweig's view of Islam, calls it a "kind of Jewish-Christian heresy." This summary disposal of a world religion follows readily enough from Mr. Herberg's (highly private) conception of a Jewish-Christian "orthodoxy." Yet Islam, because it claims only the title of *prophet* for Mohammed, is much more the complement (less heretical!) of Judaism than is Christianity.

I shouldn't have criticized Rosenzweig on this point if his example had not given the lead to other Jewish writers. Hans Joachim Schoeps states that, from a Jewish point of view, "perhaps [?] no Gentile can come to God the Father otherwise than through Jesus

Christ." Will Herberg is convinced that it is sound Jewish doctrine to assert that Israel can bring the world to God only (!) through Christianity. I cannot help asking: who informed Mr. Schoeps and Mr. Herberg that the Gentile nations have no way but the Christian one to salvation? Israel can acknowledge *prophets* to the nations and of the nations. But to posit an event that has Messianic significance for the Gentiles yet does not touch Israel is absurd, and "arranges" a *rapprochement* between Christians and Jews somewhat too neatly.

On the Christian side again, I cannot see what justifies Rosenzweig's and Schoeps's assumption that Paul's Epistle to the Romans —especially chapters 9 to 11, which are the basis for my description of the Christian attitude to the Jews—constitutes no Christian dogma, but is rather Paul's subjective opinion. Karl Barth bases his remarkable description of the Jews in the light of Christian dogma entirely on these chapters of the Epistle to the Romans, and the Catholic church declared as early as 1236 that even though she held her arms affectionately out to every convert, yet she embraced Jewish converts "with even greater affection"—basing this attitude on Paul's likening of the Jews to the natural branches of the tree of redemption.

It remains a puzzle that Franz Rosenzweig, who more than anyone before him appreciated the theological relevance of the realm of liturgy, should have overlooked the special place assigned in it to Israel. On Good Friday the Catholic church prays that all mankind may receive the fruit of redemption. The church prays for the church, the Pope, the bishops, and the holy nation of the church; she prays for the government (of the medieval empire), for the pagans, and for all heretics and schismatics. The church also prays for the Jews—but how? "We pray also for the perfidious[1] Jews [*pro perfidis Judaeis*], that the Lord our God may lift the veil from their heart so that they may acknowledge Jesus Christ our Lord."[2] More significant than the prayer itself (which already applies the ominous theological adjective, "perfidious," to the Jews) is the

---

1. The meaning of the Latin *perfidus*—"faithless" or "infidel"—is not quite the same as the English "perfidious," which necessarily includes the meaning "treacherous."

2. As of 1967, following the Ecumenical Council's instruction, this passage of the Good Friday liturgy was amended to remove any suggestion of conversionary petition. The practice of "No Amen" referred to subsequently is not used in American churches. [Editor]

ritual accompanying—or rather not accompanying—it. In all other prayers the deacon exhorts the community: *Oremus. Flectamus genua* (let us kneel and pray). But when the prayer for the Jews is reached, a gloss remarks: "No Amen. At this point the deacon omits calling the community to their knees lest the memory of the shameful genuflections with which the Jews mocked the Savior at this hour be renewed."

Eugen Rosenstock, in his discussion with Franz Rosenzweig, declared that it was no longer a Christian dogma that the Jewish people were "obdurate." But this mut be regarded as a personal opinion, since the church continues to pray for an end to Jewish obduracy and for the redemption of the Jews from their darkness (*a suis tenebris*).

In their exchange of letters both Rosenzweig and Rosenstock presented marginal attitudes rather than the classic positions of church and synagogue; nor did they express theologicial doctrine. Both were preparing the way to a post-Christian existence for themselves, since the era of the Christian church, Catholic and Protestant, had come to an end for them in Hegel's philosophy and Nietzsche's prophecy.

The dispute between Karl Ludwig Schmidt and Martin Buber is more central. The Protestant theologian insists that the "only relevant question" is Israel's obdurate rejection of Jesus as the Christ, and he asks whether the destruction of the Temple was not its consequence—a consequence that deprived the Jewish people of a spiritual center. Schmidt, in accordance with the whole Christian tradition, establishes a "theological" relation of crime and punishment between the Crucifixion and the destruction of the Temple. The nearly forty years that elapsed between the Crucifixion (33 C.E.) and the destruction of the Second Temple (70 C.E.) are "symbolically" seen as years of trial, similar to the forty years' wanderings in the wilderness.

Martin Buber, answering from "inside" the Jewish consciousness, states that the Jewish people do not feel themselves to be "rejected" by God. In an enigmatic phrase he admits that for Israel the Christology of Christianity is "surely a relevant event between above and below," but insists that Israel experiences the earthly reality as unredeemed by a Messiah, and cannot admit such a cesura in history as Jesus, as the Christ, represents. Moreover, since no divine revelation can exhaust the divine essence, Israel cannot allow that there should ever have been an ultimate incarnation of the divine in human flesh.

Buber's description of Jewish experience and doctrine is excellent; but it seems to me that he is vague when it comes to dealing with the concrete question asked by the Protestant theologian: did the Jewry of the Diaspora lose its spiritual center after the destruction of the Temple? The answer to this question is simple but fundamental: not the Temple but the Torah was, and is, the spiritual center of Jewry. The Jewish people did not come to life with the laying of the first stone of the Temple, but with the giving of the Law to Israel in the Covenant of Sinai. It is clear, however, that Martin Buber was not at all prepared to give this answer, since he has always emphasized the Agadic or mythical element of the Jewish tradition, as against the tradition of the Law.

It is perhaps no paradox that Paul, a Pharisee and son of a Pharisee, who claimed to have studied under Gamaliel and to have excelled in his zeal for the Law and tradition—that this same Paul was better prepared than modern Jewish apologists to define the basic issue dividing Judaism and Christianity. That issue is the Law. All the premises of Paul's theology were "Jewish" and even "Pharisaic," but from these he drew heretical conclusions: thus from the possibly legitimate Jewish premise that the Messiah would usher in the end of the Law, he drew the heretical conclusions of Christianity, holding that the Messiah had already come and that the Law was superseded: "For Christ is the end of the law for righteousness to every one that believeth" (Rom. 10:4). But the basis of the Jewish religion since Ezra has been the Torah, the Law, or better still—Halachah, the "way" of the Law in a man's life. All theological speculations are secondary to this.

The recent insistence on a rigid monotheism as the defining characteristic of Jewish religious life is contradicted by a fact that contemporary Jewish thinkers tend to overlook: the centuries-long predominance of the Lurianic Cabala in Judaism. The Cabala developed theogonic speculations that can only be compared to the Gnostic (and pagan) mythologies. The mythical union of the divine King and Queen, the Adam-Kadmon speculation, the mythology of the Ten Sefirot, which are not attributes but essentially different manifestations of the divine, challenge every historian of religion who presumes to judge what is Jewish and not Jewish by the criterion of a "rigid monotheism." The Jewish religion could not have withstood the outburst of Cabalistic mythologizing if its fundamental and defining characteristic were a rigid monotheism. As it was, it was able to absorb the Cabala's insights, and draw added power from them.

The Cabalistic mythologies did not shatter the structure of Jewish life; on the contrary, they strengthened it in time of crisis by their enhancing of the prestige of Halachah. Halachah, which is the conduct of life according to the *mitzvot,* they did not understand as a pedagogical system (as in the period of medieval enlightenment), but as a way to achieve sacramental union with the divine. The bulk of the *mitzvot* became a *corpus mysticum* reflecting the divine and cosmic order in the human realm; in this way they attained an importance they had never had before in Jewish history—and in any case, the Jewish vision of God is far too rich and various to be reduced to an abstract monotheism. Challenges not to Judaism's monotheism, but to the validity and interpretation of the Law, shake the Jewish religion and community to their foundations. Any Messianic claim represents such a challenge because it claims to have ushered in an age in which the Law is superseded.

It is hasty to conclude, as so many do, that because Halachah shapes the classical pattern of Jewish life, Judaism is purely "legalistic." Halachah is a structure in which a considerable variety of religious experience is integrated. The language of Halachah is capable of expressing such contraries as rationalist philosophy (Saadia and Maimonides) and mystical mythology (Moses de Leon and Isaac Luria), ecstatic prophetism (Abulafia) and magical ritualism (Jacob Halevi of Marvege). Yet Halachah is not an empty vessel into which any sort of contents can be poured. It has its limit in the divine law, and Messianism in any form must necessarily transgress that limit. It is true that Christian orthodoxy in interpreting itself tries to set up limits against heresies that would discard the Decalogue. But Judaism is bound to insist that Paulinian doctrine still remains destructive of the Law, and therefore at this point, too, Judaism must reject Christianity's interpretation of itself. Paul, when he was Saul, would have been the first to admit this, and indeed he persecuted the early Christian community on the very ground that it was setting aside the Law. Judaism never traveled the road to Damascus; and it cannot, without committing suicide, change Saul's judgment.

Christian history, Jesus' claim to the title of Messiah, and Paul's theology of Christ as the end of the Law, are not at all "unique events" for Judaism, but things that have recurred in the Jewish pattern of religious existence. Christian history, as I have said, constitutes no "mystery" for the Jewish religion. Christianity represents a crisis that is "typical" in Jewish history and expresses a typical Jewish "heresy": antinomian Messianism—the belief that with the coming of the Messiah, not observance of the Law, but faith in him is required for salvation.

So far as we can judge, rabbinic tradition has always regarded Jesus' Messianic claim and Paul's theology as heretical antinomianism. Maimonides, in his Code, specifically lists Jesus with other heretics who sought to persuade Israel to abandon the Law. No statement as to the Messianic significance of Jesus for the Gentile nations can be got from any Jewish Halachah.

Gershom Scholem, in his study of Sabbatian Messianism, makes an arresting comparison that enables us to see the beginnings of Christianity in a new light. Sabbatai Zevi's appearance, quickening all the latent hopes of the seventeenth-century Jewish ghetto, precipitated the most tragic Messianic episode in modern Jewish history. The fact is that the new Messianic community of the Sabbatians, like that of the early Christians, centered around a catastrophic event which, like the death of Jesus, could only be overcome and transcended by the "paradox of faith." For the Sabbatians, this paradox was Sabbatai Zevi's conversion to Islam. His apostasy shook the community of his followers to its foundations, yet became the motor of the Sabbatian "paradox of faith."

The tragic paradox of a dying Messiah in the one case, and of an apostate savior in the other, was interpreted in the light of the prophetic vision of the "suffering servant." "In both cases," writes Scholem, "a certain mystical attitude of belief crystalized round a historical event that drew its strength, in turn, from the very fact of its paradoxicality. Both movements began by adopting an attitude of intense expectation toward the *Parousia,* the advent or return of the savior, be it from Heaven or fom the realm of impurity. In both cases the destruction of the old values in the cataclysm of redemption led to an outburst of antinomian tendencies, partly moderate and veiled, partly radical and violent; in both cases you get a new conception of belief as the realization of the new message of salvation . . . in both cases, finally, you get in the end a theology with some kind of Trinity and with God incarnated in the person of the savior." These striking parallels between Sabbatianism and early Christianity cannot be attributed to the influence or imitation of Christian prototypes, since the Sabbatian heresy arose in the Islamic ghetto. Both Sabbatianism and early Christianity were independent expressions of crises into which the Jewish community was plunged when believers in an arrived Messiah were summoned by their theologians to strike off the shackles of the Law, that harsh schoolmaster whom the redemption was to render obsolete.

If, then, the issue between the Christian religion and the Jewish community revolves around the Law, I would hold that the Jewish argument cannot ultimately be given in Midrashic—or rather pseudo-Midrashic—terms. The counterpart to Christian dogma is not a Jewish dogma affirming certain articles of faith concerning the nature of the Divinity and its manifestations. Christiain theology is based on Christology, which means that all things, human and divine, achieve relevance only as they relate to Jesus the Christ. Judaism, based on the Law, grants relevance to all things, human and divine, only as they relate to Halachah. It is the weakness of all modern—and not only modern—Jewish theology that it fails to name Halachah, the Law, as its alpha and omega. The Jewish religion has been in a crisis since the time of the Emancipation because it lost its center when Halachah lost its central place and cogency for Jewish thought and conduct.

The moment Halachah ceases to be the determining force in Jewish life, the door is opened to all the disguised anti-Halachic (antinomian) and Christian assumptions current in modern secularized Christian society. Judaism ceases to be a matter of principle and remains only one of tradition. Religious revivals that do not reckon with Halachah as the vital essence of Judaism degenerate into so much romantic nostalgia and only hasten the end of Judaism. A few months ago I attended services at an Orthodox *shul*. The rabbi, product of a modern yeshiva, gave me a cordial greeting and "explained" (during the reading of the Torah!) that "ceremonies" and "rituals" are only "external" and not "so important" as would seem at first sight. He surely did not realize that by translating *mitzvot* by "ceremonies" and "ritual" he had surrendered to the Paulinian criticism of the Law.

Halachah is inevitably eclipsed in an age that can envisage religion only in terms of man's "private" experience, as a (poetic) dialogue between man's lonely soul and the lone God. But such a religion of the heart, even of the "pure" heart, remains disembodied—and who but the elect can lay claim to purity of heart? Halachah is based essentially on the principle of representation: the intention of man's heart and soul has to be presented and represented in his daily life. Consequently, Halachah must become "external" and "juridical," it must deal with the minutiae of life, for only in the detail of life is a presentation of the covenant between God and man possible. Halachah is the "path" of man's life on which he can "walk" before God. Against the ecstasy and delirium of man's soul, Halachah emphasizes the rational and everyday sobriety of justice. Halachah is the law because justice is the ultimate principle. Ecstatic or pseudo-ecstatic religiosity, however, sees only dead legalism and external ceremonialism in the sobriety of justice, just as anarchy can conceive of law and order only as tyranny and oppression.

Emancipation opened the doors of Western civilization to the Jewish community. But that civilization rests on Christian presuppositions and is shaped by Christian symbols. The civil calendar is the same as the Christian calendar; the initials "B.C." and "A.D." express a fundamental Christian article of faith. I am aware that the civil calendar is losing its Christian character, that its Christian initials are being transformed into mere technical signs. But though the Christian meaning of the calendar may be suppressed, it can never become obsolete. The Christian calendar has withstood a number of attempts to replace it with a secular calendar; the French Revolution in the eighteenth century and the Italian Fascists and the Russian Communists in our own century tried to do so, and failed. We, therefore, do right to keep in mind the Christian foundation upon which our civil society rests.

This is not all. By the very language we use decisions are made that limit and define our spiritual horizons. The Jewish Holy Scriptures are called the "Old Testament" in English. The term "Old Testament," however, implies the basic Christian claim that the "old" covenant has been superseded by the "new." But it is a Jewish article of faith that the Law never becomes antiquated, that the Covenant of Sinai is as valid today as it has always been. Even to call the Torah "law" already implies that pejorative meaning which Paul ascribed to the Mosaic law in his violent critique of it.

The antinomian critique made by a secular society that is nevertheless Christian in its presuppositions is reinforced by the critique of the Law that was made within the Jewish community; the modern Jewish stress on redemption through belief, rather than through a way of life conforming to divinely ordained law, reached its peak in Abraham Geiger's criticism of rabbinic Law. It is an established fact that the last stage of the Sabbatian heresy ushered in the first stage of Jewish Reform. Is it at all surprising that, in these circumstances, the Jewish side in the Jewish-Christian controversy cannot argue today from the center of Jewish faith and experience? The inner crisis of the Jewish religion determines the character of its controversy with the Christian one. If Halachah is no longer valid as the divine and human way of life, if Halachah, in a caricature of "reconstruction," is reduced to a mere bundle of customs and folkways, where shall the Jewish argument get the strength to stand up against the Pauline rejection of the Law?

Modern Jewish thinking is in large part a prisoner of this antinomianism, which pervades modern thought in general; in the world today the principle of law is reduced to a juridical device and the "pathological inclination of love" (Kant) is exalted over against the "blind principle" of justice. The pseudo-Agadic stress in modern Jewish religious thinking on the "romance" of Hasidism, or the romance of a mythologized East European Jewry in general, is in the end no obstacle to the Christianizing of the Jewish people. For what greater "romance" can there be than the incarnation of God in flesh? Only the principle of Halachah offers a check to "romance" between God and man by making the sobriety of justice the foundation of man's life. The controversy between the Jewish and Christian religions points to the perennial conflict between the principle of law and the principle of love. The "yoke of the Law" is challenged by the enthusiasm of love. But the "justice of the Law" may, in the end, be the only challenge to the arbitrariness of love.

INTRODUCTION TO

RELIGION AND STATE

Aharon Lichtenstein

The relevance of a religion is determined as much by its ability to address itself to the broadest possible kind of human question as by its ability to provide the means for interpreting and ordering man's relations with God. The breadth of relevance which a religion enjoys will make it no more true than if its purview remained theologically narrow, but it will enable it to be flexible in times of adversity, for the very comprehensiveness which relevance entails suggests that no dilemma of man is beyond its reach. Aharon Lichtenstein bears out this logic for in the present essay (to my view one of the most closely reasoned and penetrating essays on the assumptions of a *Jewish* politics), quite clearly, Torah and tradition supply the foundations for a doctrine of the relations between religion and state.

In recent years theocentric Jews have been hard-pressed to elicit from Judaism the principles which may instruct, if not guide, political behavior. How many Jews—unnecessarily, it would now seem—have been obliged to turn to neutral sources of ethical instruction, if not to traditions theologically alien to Judaism, to define the grounds for their political conduct, whether that involved dissent from the regnant establishment or justification of its actions. Lichtenstein has not solved the problems; that is to say, he has not provided Jews with a natural law doctrine which enables them (as it enables other religionists) to ground their pacifism, their civil disobedience, their contingent anarchism, or their obedience, their patriotism, their assent to civil authority upon *halakhah*. What he has succeeded in doing in the present essay is to define the centrality of the *halakhah* as a religious system which provides not only for the doing of explicitly religious *mitzvot* but for interpreting the relationship between *mitzvot* and the whole of human experience, between *mitzvot* and the incursions of the ostensibly neutral public domain.

The decisive point which he makes is that the *halakhah* is not (and in this he echoes the argumentation of Jacob Taubes) contingent mediation of the divine word. *Halakhah,* in so far as it is the decretal of special revelation, addresses the whole life of the Jew, not only as the Jew seeks to be Holy, but as the Jew avoids being profane. The *halakhah* is not in itself an *aide-mémoire* of revelation, not merely a system of mnemonics (and thereby only symbolic and contingent upon interpretation), but a vertical elaboration of revelation and a horizontal historical continuum of deliberative, objective judgment and decision.

It does not interest me particularly (although it will interest, indeed, annoy and arouse many readers) that Lichtenstein's cool-headed centralization of the *halakhah* leads in the direction of a theocratic polity (cf. Ernst Simon's essay, pp. 388–401), for the real thrust of his argument is that the *halakhah* is vital, adjustable, a tension of stasis and challenge, and not, as deniers of revelation would have it, a system of subjective and contingent laws or, as unreasoning defenders would have it, a system of laws which, since given by God, is therefore timeless, eternal, and unsusceptible of yielding accommodation to the intellectual and moral dilemmas thrown up by history. Lichtenstein's is a passionate, learned, trenchantly argued interpretation of the relation of Torah to politics, and, as such, should give pause to those who would construe a libertarian doctrine as though it were itself Torah.

RELIGION AND STATE

The Case for Interaction

AHARON LICHTENSTEIN

Seen from a Jewish perspective, the question of religion and state[1] is both very old and very new. It goes back, on the one hand, to the "desert generation" which constituted the first independent Jewish political community. This is so in a double sense: Textually and conceptually, the problem is rooted in sections of the Torah, Written or Oral, concerning the appointment of various governmental bodies; while, historically, it finds its first concrete manifestation in the charismatic figure of Moses—at once king and prophet, judge and priest,[2] legislator and teacher. On the other hand, the problem is, in a very real sense, barely twenty years old. Having lain dormant for centuries, upon the advent of the State of Israel it suddenly burst upon the scene with a vengeance, confronting us existentially with what had previously been purely theoretical issues—and largely quiescent issues at that.

A hiatus of fifteen or twenty centuries in the application of any Halachic area would pose severe difficulties, even if the practical situation in that area had remained relatively stable. How much greater the difficulty when that area has radically altered.

The nature of the change is twofold. First, the religious fabric of Jewry has changed fundamentally. Our last previous political ex-

---

1. Throughout this essay I assume that the concept of a state in the modern sense of the term, distinct from either a city or a kingdom, is Halachically valid. I have no doubt that this is so, but I should point out that its precise Halachic character and status require careful formulation. This is not my present purpose, however.

2. See *Zebahim* 101b and *Shebuoth* 15a.

perience, be it in the Land of Israel or the Diaspora, occurred within a context of basic allegiance to Torah. Whatever his personal behavior, the Second Commonwealth or Babylonian Jew essentially subscribed to the idea of normative Judaism.[3] Needless to say, a substantial segment of contemporary Jewry, within or without the State of Israel, has rejected this concept in favor of some secular orientation. Second, the general Western political climate has been thoroughly transformed. The ancient world assumed not only co-operation and liaison between political and religious authorities but, at least to a limited extent, their actual identity. In the Graeco-Roman world, who but a smattering of philosophers could even have imagined otherwise? The modern Western temperament, by contrast, considers separation the norm and, at most, tolerates some *pro forma* Established Church. Moreover, whereas the ancient world thought primarily in terms of the group, be it tribe, race, *polis*, or *civitas*, modern man instinctively thinks in terms of the individual. Regardless of what philosophers may hold, popular social thought is presently atomic rather than organic.

This change bears directly upon the current question of religion and the state. For, in the intervening centuries, the question has taken two distinct forms. In its medieval phase, it revolved around the relation of church and state as two centers of power. The major issues concerned the demarcation of their respective provinces and the resolution of recurrent conflicts. Since the seventeenth century, however, these themes, while still relevant, have gradually faded into the background. The emphasis has shifted to the consideration of personal liberty, its rights and its limits. In its modern formulation, therefore, the problem tends to pit both church and state against the individual citizen—public power *vs.* private conscience. In this sense, it is reduced—not without some distortion—to one aspect of the broader question of authority *vs.* the individual.

No doubt, any truly comprehensive exposition of the problem must come to grips with both its medieval and its modern aspects. Indeed, it must maintain a threefold perspective, viewing each issue with an eye to preserving the integrity of religion, of the state, and

---

3. Historians have disagreed on the degree of actual observance in this period. But, apart from the fact that I am inclined to assume that it was reasonably widespread, the mere general profession or assumption of commitment is in itself crucial.

of the individual. Yet, one can hardly overlook the fact that the question of religion and the state today is primarily one of the individual and his relation to authority. It is with this aspect, therefore, that the present analysis will be principally concerned.

II

The quest for a sound Jewish position concerning the basic issues of religion and state can only be undertaken by reference to fundamental principles—principles not only social and political, but moral and religious as well. Given the secularist's premises—and, hence, his priorities—many of his contentions appear almost irrefutable. However, within a different axiological framework, from a religious and Halachic rather than secular and nationalistic perspective, we may—nay, we must—reach quite different conclusions.

What is this religious framework? Its basic components—each of which may, in turn, consist of a number of elements—are four:

1) Man was created by God as a spiritual being, a singular and unique personality, endowed with freedom and vouchsafed a personal relation to God. Metaphysically, he is, therefore, a responsible moral and religious agent, capable of responding to an ethical norm or to a divine imperative.

2) The individual realizes himself and fulfills the purpose of his life only in so far as he adheres to God—whether this be understood in conative or contemplative terms—and freely gives himself to Him. Society attains its end to the extent that it becomes a vehicle for, and a manifestation of, personal and collective beatitude.

3) Although He is, in essence, wholly transcendent, God has chosen to reveal Himself to created beings and to relate to them—through the very act of their creation, through the indirect expression of His will as manifested in nature and in history, through direct communication with man, and through an ongoing dialectical encounter with him.

4) Through the interaction of divine will and human aspiration, a single people, Israel, entered into a covenant with God and thus assumed a unique position in history. As a result of both grace and merit, it became a holy nation, a community committed, individually and collectively, to God and His Torah, and hence invested with a special character and unique responsibilities.

These principles do not, in and of themselves, dictate a single political theory. Nor do they prescribe a specific solution to the problem of religion and state. They do, however, provide a basis and a frame of reference which serve, paradoxically, both to intensify the scope and difficulty of the problem and to point a direction for its resolution.

On the one hand, the opposition of personal liberty and social control assumes for the religious thinker a far more complex character than it may have for the secularist. Confronted with the dichotomy of the individual and the community, the secularist can opt for either. He can, with Mill and his followers, champion the absolute rights of the individual and relegate society and its rights to the role of a qualifying factor, a limit imposed upon one individual in the interest of collective preservation. Or he can, with totalitarian theorists, wholly subordinate the individual to the needs of the state, even sacrificing him, if need be, to satisfy the ravenous appetite of Leviathan. The religious thinker, on the other hand, specifically, the Jew committed to Halachic values and a Torah *Weltanschauung*, has no such latitude. He cannot abandon personal liberty or communal commitment; he cannot regard either the individual Jew or *knesset Israel* as simply a limit of the other; neither can he be reduced to a merely negative factor preventing anarchy or automatism, restraining the excesses of either license or tyranny. To the Halachah, both poles in the antinomy—the individual and the community, the moral freedom of the Jew and the historic destiny of Israel—are indispensable positive elements. At the practical level, their interests may no doubt clash, and some quasi-Hegelian synthesis or a transcendent *modus operandi* must be developed to harmonize them. As a value, however, each is self-validating, worthy of being preserved for its own sake. They exist in dialectical tension, and their reconciliation or integration must revolve around coordinate foci.

III

The traditional importance of both elements is quite clear. The *mishna* in *Sanhedrin* testifies adequately of one: "For this reason man was created alone . . . to proclaim the greatness of the Holy One, blessed be He. For when a man strikes many coins from one mold, they all resemble each other, but the King of the kings of kings, the Holy One, blessed be He, fashioned every man in the stamp of the first man, and yet not one of them resembles his fellow. Therefore, every individual is obligated to say: 'The world was created for my sake.' "[4] And innumerable texts, both Biblical and Rabbinic, concerning Israel's collective covenant and its spiritual nationality, speak eloquently of the other.

It should be emphasized, however, that Judaism does not regard the destinies and development of the individual and the community as merely independent desiderata. It sees them as inextricably intertwined, not only supplementary, but complementary. A spiritually oriented society is not only necessary *per se* as a realization of divine purpose and collective destiny. It is an indispensable condition for the fulfillment of the individual Jew—not only in the obvious pragmatic sense that his total personality cannot properly mature in isolation, or that perhaps, as some would have it, the very notion of a wholly nonsocial human existence is inconceivable, but rather in the far deeper sense that his identification with *knesset Israel* is an integral aspect of the Jew's personal identity. His community is not only a context within which the Jew thrives and from which he derives sustenance; it is the vehicle through which his personal experience transcends the bounds of his own existence. It transmutes an isolated act into an aspect of a divinely ordered plan. It relates the Jew to history and to metahistory. The Rambam's strictures with respect to the *poresh midarchei tzibur,* "he who diverges from communal paths," speaks for themselves: "One who diverges from the communal paths, even though he has committed no transgressions but only separates himself from the congregation of Israel and does not do *mitzvot* as one of them, does not participate in their trouble, and does not fast with them, but goes his own way like one of the Gentiles, and as if he were not one of them (i.e., the Jews) —such a person has no portion in the world to come."[5]

This conception of the relation of the Jew to *knesset Israel* is persistently reflected in the Halachic emphasis upon their practical interaction. Both as a fact—"either fellowship or death"[6]—and as a value, the social emphasis is writ large throughout the Halachah. Not only political or economic activity but even the Jew's spiritual existence are cast within a social mold. There is little yearning for the nomadic or the monastic. We encounter no idealization of the spiritual hermit, the *schöne Seele* which cannot or will not come to

---

4. *Sanhedrin* 37a. See also, ibid., 38a, and *Tosefta, Berakhoth* 6:2.
5. *MT, Teshuva,* 3:11.
6. *Taanith* 23a.

grips with the world and resigns itself to becoming, in Byron's phrase, a "pilgrim of eternity." Indeed, the *talmid chacham* is enjoined from living in a place which lacks basic social institutions.[7] Moreover, innumerable *mitzvot*, ranging from charity to the observance of holydays, and including both those "between man and God" as well as those "between man and his fellow" require a social framework for their optimum fulfillment. Even prayer, "worship of the heart" though it be, has a prominent public aspect. No doubt, in its essence religion is ultimately, in Plotinus' phrase, "the flight of the alone to the Alone." Nevertheless, for the Jew, the purpose and direction of his religious existence is defined by his membership in *knesset Israel*.

In one sense, then, the principles outlined above sharpen our problem, for they compel us to consider the relation of religion and the state with reference to not one ultimate goal but two. In another sense, however, they attenuate it, or rather, they indicate a direction for its resolution. In moving from a homocentric to a theocentric context, they shift the focus from rights to duties, from privileges to responsibilities, from endowments to obligations. The question of religion and the state is thus largely shorn of its quasi-juridical character. At the public level, the issue is no longer one of defining the respective rights and provinces of civil or ecclesiastical authority. It is rather a matter of discovering the social structure which, at any given time, will best enable the community to attain its collective spiritual ends. The accent is upon destiny rather than hegemony. At the individual level, likewise, both the role and the character of personal liberty are radically transformed. Personal liberty retains its immense significance—not, however, as an inalienable civil or natural right but rather as an essential factor, both an instrument and a condition, in the quest for beatitude. From a religious perspective, neither the concept nor the content of liberty resembles the secularist's *jus naturalis*. It is not a lack of restraint but a capacity for self-realization; not a freedom *from* but a freedom *to*.[8] For the Jew, liberty is the power to realize his spiri-

---

7. See *Sanhedrin* 17b.

8. Of course, while this view of freedom is deeply Jewish, it is by no means exclusively so; and while, in a certain sense, it implies a more restricted freedom than the eighteenth-century Enlightenment had envisioned, it has been espoused by some liberal, as well as by conservative thinkers. A prime example would be T. H. Green, for whom the concept of what he called "positive freedom" was

tual potential as an individual—as a being existing in special relation to God—and as a member of a community endowed with a unique historical destiny and charged with a singular commitment. Its ultimate point of reference lies beyond the order of rights or goods, on a plane where freedom and servitude are no longer polar opposites as man realizes himself in service to God. "They are My slaves, for I have taken them out of the land of Egypt;"[9] and yet, "there is no free man but he who engages in Torah."[10]

To be sure, such a transcendent harmony is not ordinarily attained on the social and political level. However, even on that plane the positive conception of a teleological freedom changes the problem of religion and the state from a theoretical and juridical issue of rights into a pragmatic issue of means. There is only one question to be asked: What, at any given time, is the social and political structure which will best preserve the spiritual integrity and identity of both the individual Jew and of *knesset Israel,* and which will best promote the fulfillment of their historic destiny?

IV

In addressing ourselves to the question of separation in its contemporary setting, we encounter formidable claims—I speak, of course, of religiously valid claims—on both sides. To begin with the arguments for separation, these are of two types—theological and practical. It may be contended, first, that there should be no link between religion and the state because they relate to wholly diverse areas of human experience, the sacred and the profane, and between the two there can be no real relation. As a citizen, man lies within the order of nature; as a communicant, within the order of grace; and between the two there lies an unabridgeable chasm.

If one adopts this dichotomy, holding that nature and grace are not only distinct but disjunct, then, of course, there is little basis, if any, for the interaction of the political and the religious. The counsel of rendering unto God and Caesar their respective dues is

---

central. See Guido de Ruggiero, *The History of European Liberalism,* tr. R. G. Collingwood (Oxford, 1927), *passim,* and especially pp. 347–57.

9. *Lev.* 25:42.

10. *Aboth,* 6:2. Cf. *Erubin* 54a, where the same idea is developed with reference to the collective, national scope. The conflict between organic and democratic theory, so irreconcilable in secular terms (see T. D. Weldon, *State and Morals,* London 1946, pp. 26–61) assumes an entirely different character within a religious framework.

very much in place. Indeed, it then matters little who Caesar may be. The radical separation of nature and grace is generally rooted in the conviction that the order of nature is a *massa perditionis,* inherently corrupt and lacking in ultimate spiritual relevance. So long, therefore, as there is no direct interference with the citizens' religious life—no ordinances, for instance, commanding the transgression of divine norms—does it really matter by whom and how this doomed carnal province is superintended? Thus, Calvin could, on the one hand, demand absolute fealty and obedience to Francis I, holding that even martyrdom at the hands of the most tyrannous monarch was preferable to any resistance;[11] while, on the other hand, English Puritans could argue for democracy on the ground that in the secular political sphere their own will could reign supreme.[12]

If we should reject this position, we are still confronted by a number of options. One is to assume the virtual identity of the sacred and the profane—or, at least, to assume it sufficiently so as to have both ruled by a single power. This is the basis of the institution of the king-priest prevalent in so many primitive societies.[13] A second is to assume that the sacred and the profane are neither identical nor disjunct but distinct on the one hand and integrated on the other. Within Christianity, the political consequence of this position is the famous doctrine—dating from the patristic period and given modern formulation in Leo XIII's *Immortale Dei*[14]—of "two powers" which rule separate realms independently but which, in theory at least, sustain and assist each other, so that their relations are governed by perfect concord.

From a Jewish point of view, none of these solutions is truly adequate. Judaism certainly has not espoused either the renuncia-

---

11. See the selections from his writings published under the title, *On God and Political Duty,* ed. John T. McNeill (New York: Liberal Arts Press, 1950). It should be pointed out, however, that Calvin's acceptance of even the most tyrannous civil authority and his insistence that martyrdom was preferable to resistance was due, in large measure, to his acknowledgment of the former's existence as providentially ordained. The bifurcation of nature and grace was not the only factor.

12. This position was not adopted by all Puritans. One should beware of oversimplifying generalization. See A. S. P. Woodhouse's introduction to *Puritanism and Liberty,* 2nd ed. (London, 1950), especially pp. 35–60.

13. See Christopher Dawson, *Religion and Culture* (London, 1949), ch. 6.

14. See *The Church Speaks to the Modern World: The Social Teachings of Leo XIII,* ed. E. Gilson (Garden City, N.Y.: Image Books, 1954), pp. 167–68.

tion of the secular or its severance from the religious. On the contrary, the whole thrust of the Halachah lies in its demand that all of life be redeemed and sanctified. Nor has it identified the sacred and the profane. *Havdalah* (Separation) is no less a *mitzvah* than *kiddush* (Sanctification). Indeed, according to Maimonides they are both part of a single *mitzvah*.[15] And, as regards our area specifically, we might recall the strictures of Maimonides against the Hasmoneans' attempted union of royal and priestly authority.[16] Nor yet can we be genuinely satisfied with the traditional Roman Catholic position. The Halachah is not content with the integration of the secular and the religious into a single harmonious scheme. It demands their interpenetration. The sacred must not only relate to the profane but—even as the two remain distinct—impregnate it. Halachah proclaims the central truth that while religion is, in one sense, an area of experience, in another sense it frames all of experience, inasmuch as it concerns man's relation to God, the ground and goal of life itself. It is not only a quantitative but also a qualitative aspect of existence, and, as such, it impinges upon every area. "All human activity," the Rambam insisted, "is subsumed under 'the fear of God,' and every human act ultimately results in either a *mitzvah* or a transgression."[17] Every act, therefore, does not merely lead *to*, but is itself, in the broader sense of the term, a part *of*, the religious life. Both the strength and the problematic of Halachah derive precisely from its attempt to relate these two senses of religion and to grasp their often dialectical tension. Hence, the concept of "the two realms," suggesting, as it does, the parceling out of spheres of influence to political and religious authority respectively, does not satisfy the radical demands of the Halachah. The Halachic ideal would seem to call for a more organic relation.[18]

From a Jewish standpoint, therefore, the interaction of religion

---

15. See *MT, Shabbath,* 29:1.

16. See his comment on *Gen.* 49:10.

17. *Teshuvot Ha-Rambam,* ed. J. Blau (Jerusalem, 1960), p. 715.

18. The scope of the Halachah could conceivably assign a far-reaching social role to a religious court (*beth din*). However, the definition of the proper role of a *beth din* and of its practical relations to civil government requires fuller and more precise Halachic formulation than can here be undertaken. I might just refer to the radically different definitions of the *mitzvah* of appointing a *beth din,* formulated by Maimonides, *Sefer Hamitzvoth, mitzvoth assei,* 176, and Maimonides, *Deut.* 16:18; and to the eleventh of *Rabbenu Nissim's Twelve Drushim,* which deals specifically with the delineation of civil and religious authority.

and state is theologically not only possible but desirable. But there remain formidable practical (I do not mean simply pragmatic) objections grounded upon the potential danger posed by such interaction. To the committed Jew, genuinely concerned with the maximal preservation of both religious values and moral freedom, the danger is twofold. It threatens Judaisim, on the one hand, and the Jew, on the other. We are confronted first by the prospect of Erastianism, the facile system all too readily accepted by (to paraphrase C. D. Broad's description of Bacon) "sincere if unenthusiastic Jews of that sensible school which regards the Sanhedrin as a branch of the Civil Service, and the Chief Rabbi as the Israeli Minister for Divine Affairs." The Erastian danger is itself two-edged. There is, first, the external threat. The state may seek to impose its authority and values upon religion in order to advance its own secular, perhaps even antireligious ends. Medieval and modern European history is replete with instances of such interference, occuring in both Catholic and Protestant countries; and, if we go back somewhat in time, our own Second Commonwealth polity offers a glaring example of the deleterious effects of political meddling in religious life. Erastianism poses, secondly, an internal threat, the danger that the spiritual quintessence of religion will be diluted, if not perverted, by its official status. Quite apart from the threat of overt or covert state interference, an Establishment religion lives under a Damocles' sword of worldliness, the perennial possibility that its public investiture will corrode the fiber of its principles and purpose, that it will fall prey to spiritual pride writ large.

As its marriage to the state thus endangers organized religion, on the one hand, so it threatens the individual citizen spiritually, on the other. The loss of religious liberty diminishes man's spiritual stature. It fractures the *tzelem elohim,* the "human face divine" within him. Man most fully realizes his potential when he acts and exists as a subject and person rather than as an object; and to live as personality means to live freely, in consonance with conscience and on the basis of moral choice. Consequently, the danger of tyranny is not merely political or social. It is religious.

V

These dangers posed by the interrelation of religion and state are no doubt very real. A spiritual religion ignores them at its peril, and secularists are quite right—indeed, perform a genuine service to religion—in calling attention to them. From the perspective of Jewish history, they are only half the story, however. Probing the problem in its entirety, I think we shall find that the practical inferences secularism draws from these points are both unwarranted and subversive.

The secularist prescription would avert some diseases but kill the patient. It would preserve Jews—or rather, some of their civil liberties—and destroy Jewry; not only Judaism, but Jewry. For *knesset Israel* is not just a social and political entity. It is not merely what James Baldwin says he found in Israel, a collection of individuals bound by the Hebrew language and memories of the European Holocaust. *Knesset Israel* is, in its essence, a spiritual community, or, more specifically, a religious community. It does not simply consist of brothers bound by a common past—important as that may be—but of comrades committed to a common future. We are, by definition and constitution, a people of spiritual destiny and commitment. As Rav Saadya Gaon put it, "our nation is a nation only by virtue of its *Torot*."[19]

Advocates of a secular State of Israel are, therefore, trying to put a square peg in a round hole. It is not only that the approach is wrong, but that it will produce deplorable results. Secularization *ought* not take place, and it *cannot* take place—unless, that is, we are ready to dismantle the community of Israel as it has historically evolved and as it presently exists. For we must not underestimate the scope of the secularist's position. He does not simply argue for a secular state. He advocates a secular society—a society in which individuals could practice religion freely and within which religious institutions could exist, but which, in character and structure, would be essentially secular. If the issue were solely one of church and state, if it involved only the relations of organized government and organized religion, one could give the case for separation a sympathetic hearing. It might be argued that, from a tactical point of view, disestablishment is now in the interests of both religion and state. Indeed, some genuine advocates of Halachah have at times inclined to this position, if not subscribed to it. The modern secularist plays for much higher stakes, however. Not only the organs of government but the fabric of Israeli society, ultimately the

---

19. *Ha-emunot veha-deot*, III, 7.

very fiber of the Jew himself, are to be gradually secularized. Of course, even within the political sphere the type of separation which would be motivated by religious considerations would perhaps be fundamentally different from that envisioned by a secularist. But this is hardly the main point. The crux of the current Israeli *Kulturkampf* is clear and simple: Are we to adhere to our historic commitment and retain our identity as a spiritual community? Or are we to abjure our heritage and undergo, in Keble's famous phrase, "national apostasy?"

The danger that the total separation of religion and state will increasingly secularize society as a whole does not derive solely from secularists' demands. It is inherently rooted in the structure of modern society. So long as democratic theory and practice were dominated by the laissez-faire approach of classical Liberalism, the effects of disestablishment were relatively minor. The church lost its privileged position, but the field was left fully open for its operation as a purely voluntary force. The French or the American Revolutions ended government's patronage of religion, but they did not posit it as a rival. However, the century-old abandonment of laissez-faire has changed the situation drastically. The erosion of the private sector attendant upon the intrusion of the state into all walks of life has directly and materially affected church-state relations. The primary threat to religion posed by a secular state is no longer suppression but competition. The danger is not persecution but displacement. It is not the threat of being uprooted but rather of becoming desiccated that is paramount.[20]

This is true in three ways: First, in so far as a sense of comfortable security—shallow as it may be—and the loss of private initiative and personal responsibility have deadened the individual's spiritual élan generally and his religious verve specifically. Such torpor is by no means wholly due to the modern state *per se*. As De Tocqueville and Mill emphasized, the sheer weight and breadth of a democratic society are likely to lead to conformist mediocrity, especially in an age of mass communications. Welfare state paternalism has been of crucial importance, however. The Grand Inquisitor knew whereof he spoke. Not the bang but the whimper, not dissipation but ennui have become the spiritual dragons of the Beveridge age.

---

20. See Christopher Dawson, *Religion and the Modern State* (New York, 1935), chap. 3.

Second, the expansion of the state's activity has enabled it to make inroads upon the emotional attachment to religion. In one area after another—education, philanthropy, family counseling, and so on—government has preempted the former social role of religion. In so doing, it has not only reduced the church's hegemony; it has alienated the affections of its adherents. The modern state engages the emotions of its constituents in spheres undreamt of by Talleyrand and Palmerston. It is no mere accident that the notion of treason as a major crime—popularly regarded with an abhorrence reserved for few transgressions—is so relatively recent.[21]

Third, the omnivorous state competes with organized religion at a more pedestrian level—for money, for energy, above all, for time. The individual or nation with limited human and economic resources is confronted by government and religion with conflicting claims, claims which are theoretically reconcilable but, practically speaking, mutually exclusive. To be sure, religion demands much more than material elements, and when it ossifies into demanding nothing else a period of retrenchment and disengagement from the world is perhaps in order. As a viable institution, however, it does require material elements, too, in order to fulfill its distinctly spiritual function; and at this level, it is in direct competition with the state. Needless to say, within a separatist structure in which the claims of government are binding and those of religion purely voluntary, the competition is rather unequal.

Such being the rivalry, conscious or unconscious, between government and religion, a purely "neutral" disestablished state is no more than a pipe dream. In theory, there is a fine ring about it. The power of the state is to be exerted neither *pro* nor *con* religion, with reference to which a wholly voluntary approach is to prevail. In practice, however, things shape up somewhat differently. Religious education is voluntary—but only after a student has spent the lion's share of his time in state schools in which nary a prayerful syllable may be uttered. To be sure, there is an alternative. An American parent can forego the free education his tax dollars have bought for his children and spend up to a few thousand dollars a year on tuition.[22] But just how voluntary is such a choice? Again, financial

---

21. See Margaret Boveri, *Treason in the Twentieth Century*, tr. Jonathan Steinberg (London, 1961), pp. 13–18, 33–44.

22. The situation is somewhat different in Israel where, as in early Victorian England, the government supports a number of educational channels. But this pluralism is precisely part of what advocates of separation are attacking.

support for religious institutions is voluntary—but, of course, only with funds left over after the state has extracted its own sizable share!

Such a state is not neutral at all. A government which is deeply enmeshed in all spheres of life and yet operates in a purely secular manner is not just religiously inert. Beyond a certain point, omission is commission. To exercise significant control over society while remaining aloof from religion is, in effect, to oppose it. In a pluralistic democracy, this problem is aggravated by government's own tendency to become progressively more secular. Initially, assuming a generally religious society, even an avowedly disestablished state is likely to be involved in some aspects of religion. But in a religiously pluralistic society, a state committed to full separation will, at most, support only those aspects of religious life for which there is generally universal approval. In time, therefore, as any new form of dissent, however radical, crops up, the area of full consensus gradually contracts, and the state disengages itself more and more from religious involvement. With government directing so much of civic life, the public role of religion is gradually neutralized in one area after another, until it is whittled down to a private enclave within the overall social structure.

American experience, especially in its recent phases, illustrates this pattern clearly,[23] and its possible Israeli counterpart can only be projected with trepidation. I am far from suggesting that the separation of religion and state in Israel would immediately produce such a secular society. Certainly, religion is too potent a force at every level of Israeli life to disintegrate overnight. Yet, before we set out on the path recommended to us by the advocates of separation, we would do well to scrutinize its direction and terminus.

---

23. For a lucid and compact account of the legal history of this area—prior, however, to the ban on prayer in public schools—see Harry W. Jones, "Church-State Relations: Our Constitutional Heritage," in *Religion and Contemporary Society*, ed. Harold Stahmer (New York, 1963), pp. 156–214. We should not be misled here by the apparent strength of the churches as reflected in recent social and political struggles. By and large, the churches have been able to exercise this power only where they have, in effect, whether consciously (as with Harvey Cox and his confrères) or unconsciously, worked on the terms of the secular gospel. One must entertain strong reservations as to whether they could muster widespread support over an issue which was purely religious and lacked secular sanction. It may not even be amiss to wonder whether, once their present social desiderata are attained, some church leaders will not find themselves somewhat adrift, groping—like many post-Depression liberals—for direction and purpose.

Moreover, separation would have greater repercussions in Israel than it has had in America. The specific practical demands of Christianity are, after all, relatively few, so that the secular character of the state might not have so direct and extensive an impact upon the nature of society. Judaism, by contrast, imposes numerous practical demands in virtually all walks of life. Its distinctive quality is best characterized by its scope. Hence, the adverse religious effect of a purely secular government would be correspondingly more serious within a Jewish than within a Christian state. The withdrawal of the state from a number of crucial areas—which, practically speaking, is no withdrawal at all but a positive thrust in a secular direction—would directly undermine the Jewish character of Israeli society as a whole.

VI

It is against this background that the problem of state religious coercion[24] needs to be seen. The problem proper has two aspects, for coercion may be opposed on two distinct grounds. The first is the general notion that the state has no business interfering in the personal affairs of private citizens. Each man's home is his castle, and so long as he tends his vineyard and does not disturb his neighbor no one else has the right to disturb him. This individualistic credo, which constituted the core of eighteenth- and nineteenth-century liberalism, once seemed almost irresistible. However, its contemporary force has been considerably blunted. The transition from laissez-faire to a welfare state has been attended by extensive governmental encroachment upon the so-called private sector. Even in the democracies, once inviolable property rights have been ignominiously trampled in the name of transcendent human rights; and once untouchable private enclaves have been subjected to extensive legislation and regulation. The century since *On Liberty* has eroded liberty in the interests of equality. Hence, if the argument against religious coercion rested solely on this general individualistic ground, it would have relatively little contemporary

---

24. It should be emphasized that the question of coercion should not be identified with the problem of separation. A state can be involved in religion in a noncoercive manner (even though there is ultimately an indirect coercive element, since taxes are used to finance all state endeavors), and coercion can be exercised by a voluntary society, such as a union or, in an indirect manner, by society at large. This fact is added reason for proceeding carefully in defining the concepts of consent or coercion.

force. We could then indulge ourselves in the well-founded suspicion that modern latitudinarianism is more the result of religious indifference than of libertarian conviction.

There is, however, a second and more powerful argument against specifically religious coercion. Its contention is not so much that government *ought* not compel moral and religious action as that it *cannot.* Morality and religion depend upon inner conviction, and this lies beyond external control. Hence, T. H. Green insisted, "the question sometimes put, whether moral duties should be enforced by law, is really an unmeaning one; for they simply cannot be enforced. They are duties to act, it is true, and an act can be enforced: but they are duties to act from certain dispositions and with certain motives, and these cannot be enforced. Nay, the enforcement of an outward act, the moral character of which depends on a certain motive and disposition, may often contribute to render that motive and disposition impossible."[25] At best, the state can try to develop an environment within which morality can flourish.

On the whole, this argument is not directly relevant to the religious legislation now being attacked by Israeli secularists. The laws presently on the books have not sought solely or even primarily to impose a degree of religiosity upon all private citizens but rather to safeguard certain public areas. While the act of betrothal, *kiddushin,* constitutes a *mitzvah,*[26] no one imagines that the purpose of the *chok ha-ishut* (the Marriage Act) was to insure that every eligible Jew should perform this one additional *mitzvah.* Nor do the local Sabbath's ordinances aim so much at compelling personal observance as at preserving the Sabbath's public character. Regardless of its lack of immediate relevance, however, no discussion of religion and state can ignore this problem, and at least a summary attempt to deal with it is, therefore, in order.

From a Halachic perspective, this argument should be considered on three levels—the ideal, the normative, and, what, for lack of a better term, I shall call the tactical. Ideally, of course, religion should be spiritual in character. Religious acts should be motivated by profoundest inner commitment and religious existence should be permeated by the pervasive devotion of mind and will. "God desires

25. *Lectures on the Principles of Political Obligation* (London, 1895), p. 34 (sec. 10).
26. See *Kiddushin* 41a, where it is stated that one should betroth in person rather than through an agent because the *mitzvah* is thus greater.

the heart,"[27] said the Rabbis. Anyone with even a nodding acquaintance with Halachah and endowed with any sensitivity to its values is fully aware of this; and he hardly needs to be told that "religion should be a force by virtue of being a norm, not a norm by virtue of being a force." This is so self-evident, however, as to be almost tautological. The real question is entirely different. In the absence of such ideal motivation, does an act become morally and religiously worthless?

From a purist or from a Kantian perspective, this question should probably be answered in the affirmative. But the Halachah has thought otherwise. While it has always emphasized the need for striving toward an ideal motivation, it has never denigrated lower levels of commitment. It demands that the Jew engage in Torah and *mitzvot lishma,* out of a pure love of God. But it acknowledges the value of inferior motivation as well. "Let a man always engage in Torah and *mitzvot,* though it be not for their own sake, for out of [doing them with] an ulterior motive he comes to [do them for] their own sakes."[28] On the one hand, it defines the *mitzvah* of loving God as precluding not only serving Him for the sake of earthly rewards but even for theological hedonism as well: "Lest you shall say," explains the *Sifre,* " 'I shall study Torah, in order that I shall become wealthy, in order that I shall be called "rabbi," or in order that I shall receive reward in the world to come'—therefore the text says, 'to love God, your Lord'—all that you do, you should do solely out of love."[29] And yet, on the other hand, it can state that "Whoever says, 'let this selah [coin] go to charity in order that I shall be a member of the world to come'—he is considered wholly virtuous."[30] However we resolve the apparent contradiction,[31] it should be clear that the Halachah has acknowledged both

---

27. *Sanhedrin* 106b.

28. *Pesahim* 50b. As the Netziv pointed out, this should be understood to mean that the involvement has present intrinsic merit, even if *lishma* is never attained, and not just as an advisable ploy because it can lead to greater heights; see *Meshiv Davar,* I, 44.

29. *Parshat 'Eikev,* 41, in commenting on *Deut.* 11:13; cf. *Nedarim* 62a.

30. *Pesahim* 8a.

31. Various solutions have been propounded for reconciling the citation from *Pesahim* with other texts which clearly demand that the individual purge himself of ulterior motivations; see commentaries, *ad locum,* and in parallel texts. I might only mention that R. Hananel (*Rosh Hashana* 4a) reads *tzedaka gemura* rather than *tzadik gamur*—suggesting that the act is valid or meritorious even though the agent may be spiritually deficient.

the ideal of selfless spirituality—"His *mitzvot* he [i.e., the virtuous man] desires very much; but not the reward of His *mitzvot*"[32]— and the inferior but yet valid externally motivated virtue.

Hence, even actions which might otherwise not have been undertaken spontaneously, but are performed in response to promises or threats, may have some merit. Conceived simply as present actions, they may derive some value from their objective—one might almost say, their metaphysical—character. A *mitzvah* performance—or contrarily, a transgression—has intrinsic significance. This is a notion which the Greeks would have understood readily, but which the modern mind—since Descartes so subjectively and introspectively oriented—no doubt finds difficult to grasp. It seems more mystical than Halachic. And yet it ought not be so inconceivable that objects, times, places, or actions, which have been singled out by divine command should be endowed—on a legal, and not just on a mystical, plane—with a certain character; and that acts which conform to certain external specifications could be described as objective religious acts even when their motivation is not impeccable. Second, such acts may have some value with reference to the future—as part of an educative process which can eventually lead the sluggish or recalcitrant Jew to a higher level of religious devotion. Under certain conditions, actual engagement in religious performances may turn initial reluctance into ultimate enthusiasm. It is altogether too easy to be a rigorous purist in this area. To contend, in Ernest Barker's words, "that true religion is a matter of the mind, to be sought and found in voluntary co-operation with others of like mind, and therefore to be sought and found in the area of Society,"[33] so that the state is, on the whole, effectively excluded, is to take far too simple a view of the complex interaction of the physical and spiritual aspects of human experience. In one sense, no doubt, opponents of civil rights legislation were right in arguing that morality cannot be legislated. Yet, quite apart from any objective attainments, we ought not underestimate the impact of external action and habit upon inner conviction. It is precisely because it avoided this pitfall that the Halachah defined moral or religious acts in relatively liberal terms.

There is, however, a crucial proviso. The Halachah, like Kant,

---

32. *Avodah Zarah* 19a.
33. *Principles of Social and Political Theory* (Oxford, 1951), p. 46.

does demand motivation, though not to the same total extent. In order to constitute a valid religious performance, a *mitzvah* action must be accompanied by *kavvanah*, by an awareness on the part of the agent that he is acting in response to a divine imperative and by a desire that the action constitute a proper fulfillment of his duty.[34] Such *kavvanah* obviously involves moral and theological presuppositions of no little import; and the need for it reduces drastically the scope of any possible coercion. We are, therefore, inevitably led, first, to accept R. Meir Simcha's[35] position that any religious coercion mentioned in the *Gemara* is limited to situations in which it can be reasonably assumed that the application of external pressure will lead to an inner change of heart. Second, we are led to ponder the conditions under which such a situation obtains. They do not admit of easy and precise definition, but at least their general outline may be indicated. The crucial principle, I believe, rests upon a distinction between two types of will—a specific and immediate will which resists a command or bridles at a restriction, and a more general and settled moral will which may acknowledge in principle the very authority which, on a different level, is then resented.[36] Broadly speaking, I know that I oughtn't double park, and, fundamentally, I recognize the state's right to prevent me from so doing. But when I return from the dentist to find that my car has

---

34. These remarks assume the view of the *tannaim* and *amoraim* who held that *mitzvot* are invalid if performed without *kavvanah;* see especially *Pesahim* 114b–115a and *Rosh Hashana* 28a–29a. This is the view which was accepted in the *Shulchan Aruch, Orach Chaim,* 60:4. However, not all *rishonim* accepted this view. My basic position here would not be severely affected in any event, as many *rishonim* stressed that all would agree that acts done with rebellious or resistant intention could certainly not be considered fulfillment of the *mitzvah.* The whole problem of objective and subjective elements in Judaism, the role of "inwardness," and especially the crucial relation of law and morality, require, of course, much fuller treatment. I hope to be able to present it in a future paper. It should be added that these remarks deal with coercion as a stimulus to positive religious behavior. Punishments for transgressions and their use as a deterrent would pose a somewhat different problem. The argument with reference to them would, therefore, follow a different—albeit, in some respects, parallel —course. The conclusion at the tactical level would be pretty much the same, however.

35. *Or Sameach, Hilchot Gerushin,* 2:20.

36. The distinction is by no means my own discovery. It has classical origins; it was prominent in Burke (see Charles Parkin, *The Moral Basis of Burke's Political Thought* [Cambridge, Eng., 1956]) , and was especially developed and applied in Bernard Bosanquet, *The Philosophical Theory of the State,* 3d ed. (London, 1920) , chaps. 3, 5–6.

been towed away, I am genuinely, if temporarily, resentful. If we reject the notion that all sin or vice is simply error, and if we recognize the clear fact that we are regularly derelict in performing duties of whose essential value and normative character we are fundamentally convinced—then we shall grasp the essence of paradoxically convincing coercion. When agent and patient share a basic recognition of the law and of its authority to impose upon the individual, coercion, even in the moral and religious sphere, becomes possible. Where such recognition is lacking, it is wholly unworkable—and then, of course, as R. Meir Simcha emphasized, it becomes immoral. There is no middle ground here. Coercion either effects inner conviction—and then it may be justified, or else it is not simply neutral but Halachically forbidden.

On the ideal level, then, the Halachah strives for maximal spirituality. On another level, it asserts that in principle external pressure may sometimes be morally justified. What are we to assume, however, on a third level—the tactical? Even if the power and the authority to impose Halachah exist or did exist, would it now be wise and moral to exercise them?

The answer must be sought in the light of the principles outlined above and with an eye to contemporary conditions.[37] Quite obviously, with respect to many, if not most, Halachic demands, fundamental acceptance by nonobservant Israelis simply does not exist. This is not solely due to the fact that nonobservant Jews are now so much more numerous than they were before the Enlightenment, although this is a factor. It is due, in large measure, to the fact that the recalcitrant Jew is now differently motivated. Whereas derelic-

---

37. I have omitted any discussion of the most obvious tactical argument for pluralism—namely, that, if generally pursued, the insistence on spreading one's truth leads to conflict and instability, resulting finally in the situation commended by Dr. Johnson to Boswell: "Every man has the right to speak his mind, and every other man has the right to knock him down for it." On the assumption that one has the truth, however, this is primarily a pragmatic rather than a moral argument; and the possibility that a system may be false (one of Mill's arguments) cannot itself be part of the meaning of that system. Of course, from the perspective of Kant's categorical imperative, this *is* a moral argument, and a most persuasive one—but only within a philosophic framework which rejects the concept of particular revelation. To say that the argument is pragmatic rather than moral is not to dismiss it, and the various factors in any given situation—e.g., what would be the effect of religious legislation in Israel upon Jews potentially subject to equivalent legislation in non-Jewish countries—need to be weighed. Such calculation occurs at a different level, however, and it lies outside the purview of this essay.

tion in fulfilling religious duties would previously have been probably due to frailty and backsliding—a volitional failing—it is now generally the result of unbelief—an intellectual failing. The type of resistance encountered is, therefore, entirely different, and it is not amenable to formerly effective modes of response. Moreover, within the generally libertarian climate of modern Western society, attempted coercion is usually not only ineffectual but destructive. Inasmuch as it generates resentment, it does not simply fall short but backfires. Within the present context, therefore, coercion, as a technique of stimulating positive religious observance, cannot generally succeed.

VII

Lest I be misunderstood, let me emphasize that I am not suggesting that all religious legislation is now *ipso facto* out of court. Some laws may aid in preserving our public national character even if they do not materially promote individual observance. And for others there may be general basic acceptance. I simply point out that, by and large, coercion is no longer a feasible and justifiable *modus operandi;* and that now, more than ever, our main thrust must be educational. This does not mean that we should introduce total separation of religion and state—a step which could entail the gravest consequences. The modern state has many other means at its disposal besides coercion. The schools are no less a part of its apparatus than the courts. I think it would be a great mistake to sever the state from religion totally. From both a moral and pragmatic point of view, however, we need to be most careful about the stress and scope of its involvement.

It should be clear that such reservations about the present value of much specific legislation are radically different from the total opposition in principle espoused by secularists. Before a Jewish State institutes religious ordinances, it must evaluate empirically the overall impact of a given law upon the quality of national and individual religious life. It must ascertain whether the game is worth the candle. The possibility that resistance engendered will outweigh any gain in observance or commitment; that individual personality will be impaired by the impingement upon civil liberties; that the spirituality and the independence of organized religion will be diluted by its increased affiliation with the state—all must be carefully considered, spiritual gain in one sector being balanced against possible loss in another. However, the right of legislation *per se* does exist. We cannot ignore valid objections to religious legislation; but if we are to maintain a viable Jewish society, neither can we assume that they must always be decisive.

The realities of life will not let us have our cake and eat it, too. We cannot be both wholly free and truly committed. No society can be fully open unless it is genuinely open-ended. Most modern Western readers are no doubt revolted by the middle books of Plato's *Republic*. Even while sharing in this revulsion, however, we need to realize what drove the greatest of classical thinkers to such extremes. It was, of course, commitment—commitment to the true, the beautiful, and the good, to the idea of virtue, the ideal of a *polisi* saturated with *arete*. We must realize further that, unless it wishes to rely upon Pollyannish hopes, any society committed to any ideal will have to take some step down this Platonic road. It will have to encourage—perhaps even compel—action it deems necessary to preserve that ideal and maintain its character; and to this end, it will almost inevitably involve its political arm, the state. If we agree with Aristotle that the state does not exist solely for the sake of life but for the sake of the good life—taking "good" to be in some sense ideal rather than utilitarian—then we must recognize that at some point the state will have to act in order to promote that life. In so doing, it will employ its two principal weapons: the carrot and the stick. The only question is how much use will be made of one or the other. To us the question is crucial, but from the point of view of those who would divorce a state's political activity from its ultimate commitment it is thoroughly irrelevant. The principle of separation is breached by blandishment or education no less than by threat.

Hence, the only truly neutral state is one governed by a relativist ethic. If no absolute values are assumed, then, of course, a fully open society is quite feasible. However, if a society wishes to lead its members and, therefore, itself in a certain direction, it must be prepared at some point to act to this end politically. No doubt, the main thrust should always be educational, the basic language always spiritual, the primary appeal always to minds and hearts rather than to bodies or pockets. Nevertheless, we cannot *a priori* eschew a political approach entirely. Let us make no mistake: ultimately, we are not only confronted with the problem of religion and state but with the broader question of morality and state.

Philosophically, the same arguments which militate against the state's involvement in the one apply likewise to the other.

These remarks have a particular relevance for a Jewish society—by definition, to use Rav Soloveitchik's phrase, "the community of the committed." Ours is, moreover, a specific commitment, rooted in our history and revolving around an apocalyptic experience. We are not just committed to some abstract Platonic idea but to the God of Abraham, Isaac, and Jacob. Indeed, our moral claim to the very possession of the Land or the State of Israel rests solely on the historic destiny growing out of that historical commitment. The commitment and the experience must be created anew in every generation—"let them [the words and commands of the Torah] be treasured by you as if you had received them this very day from Sinai; and let them be as regularly upon your tongue as if you had heard them this very day."[38] But at the same time they must be transmitted and inculcated, and to this end we cannot *a priori* reject governmental assistance entirely. Even if we should be sufficiently optimistic to imagine that such assistance need never be extended in the interests of natural religion or morality (and one need hardly be a Hobbesian to reject such a judgment), we cannot assume the same with reference to Judaism. Without external guidance and with no knowledge of tradition whatsoever, a spiritually minded person may perhaps become a devotee of Bahai; but a Jew—hardly. He must somehow learn that God has spoken to Israel and receive the content of the divine message; and to this end, he needs some guidance. To establish a purely secular State of Israel at present would mean to preclude such guidance from the vast areas of life influenced, if not controlled, by government. This could not be countenanced by the *knesset Israel* out of whose past we have evolved and in whose future we have devout faith. It was not for this that our forefathers lived and died, and it is not through this that our children can hope to survive. Ours is a unique destiny: to serve as a vehicle of God's purpose in history, and this entails not just glory but responsibility.

VIII

Midway through his essay, "Secularism and Religion in Israel,"[39] Professor Nathan Rotenstreich quietly executes a remarkable *volte-*

---

38. *Sifre, Parshat Re'ei*, 58, commenting on *Deut.* 11:32.
39. *Judaism*, Summer, 1966, vol. 15, no. 3.

face. Whereas he had previously appeared to champion not only a secular state but the secularist gospel *in toto,* he now proceeds to advise religionists how they ought best to promote their cause. We are no longer told that a state should be secular *per se* but that it must be secular because this is in the best interest of religion; and we are told further how religion—or more specifically, Halachah— must reform or transform itself if it is to survive in the modern world. This section, therefore, goes far beyond political problems, and its challenge to traditional Judaism is very different from what we have hitherto encountered. Precisely for this reason, however, the issues it raises, serious and fundamental as they are, require much fuller treatment, both intensive and extensive, than can be presented if the present essay is to remain within reasonable bounds. Nevertheless, the issues cannot and ought not be ignored entirely; and I shall attempt, if only in brief summary, to come to grips with the heart of the argument.

Professor Rotenstreich's critique of Halachic Judaism opens with the observation, borrowed from Solomon Schiller, "that the development of Orthodox Judaism is governed by the law of inertia." If I remember my physics correctly, the classical law of inertia simply reads: "Every body continues in its state of rest or uniform motion in a straight line except in so far as it is compelled by external forces to change that state." Secularists, observing Halachic Judaism from without, apparently assume it to be in a state of continuous rest; hence, the intended criticism. Traditional Jews, however, who have known and live Halachah from within, and who experience it as a vibrant and dynamic force, see it as being constantly in motion—or perhaps (shades of Zeno!) as being, paradoxically, both at rest and in motion. They might, therefore, find Schiller's remark not quite so damning. Indeed, if we can disregard the mechanical overtones of the metaphor, it is downright flattering.

These remarks are not made in jest. They cut to the root of Professor Rotenstreich's argument, for he fails to appreciate properly what to the traditional Jew is the most pulsating reality of all, Divine Revelation. What the Halachist finds succulent and vital is for him arid and sterile; and the failure to grasp both the vibrancy and the significance of revelation lies at the heart of his critique. Professor Rotenstreich advances two contentions, one historical and the other normative. He claims, on the one hand, that Jewish thought has always been isolationist in character, and that this is

444

due, primarily, to the intrinsic nature of Halachah and secondarily, in recent times, to the dominance of Eastern European (i.e., Halachah-saturated) Jewry. On the other hand, he argues that Judaism should abandon the traditional limited objective framework of Halachah in favor of a more general approach.

Underlying both statements is the failure to regard seriously either Halachah or the Revelation upon which it is grounded. As a matter of bare fact, it is no doubt true that "throughout its history, the primary concern of Jewish thought has been self-interpretation, interpretation of the heritage of Judaism, interpretation of the relation between Judaism and other religious or philosophical world-outlooks and traditions." But why? Partly, no doubt, because of the inherently separatist nature of the Jew—"the whole world is on one side and he [i.e., Abraham] is on the other;"[40] and, partly, because of the lengthy sojourn in a Diaspora whose alien environment drew Jewry inward upon itself and assigned top priority to the sheer preservation of distinctive identity and values. Primarily, however, this concern derived from the utter and genuine earnestness with which both the idea and the content of Revelation were taken. Can those who are convinced that the heritage of Judaism is grounded in the Divine Word make anything but that their primary concern? Such concentration does not constitute a flight from reality. On the contrary, it is rooted in the quest for a higher reality to which the Jew can relate both himself and his world. It is, however, admittedly confining. In the very process of revelation, God limited Israel, closing some options even as He opened others; and to the extent that he has sought to respond to that Revelation and to interpret it, the Jew *has* limited himself somewhat. To be sure, the degree of confinement has varied. Medieval Ashkenazic Jewry was more intense and narrow than its Sephardic counterpart. In some measure, however, confinement has persisted throughout.

Nevertheless, it would be wrong to assume that traditional Jewry cannot or ought not come to grips with contemporary problems. The primary concern with the heritage of Judaism has not constituted a deliberate aversion from the world but rather a yearning for the Word and for the Divine presence revealed through it. The possibility, indeed the obligation, of dealing with general contemporary issues within a Halachic framework is very much alive,

---

40. *Bereshith Rabba,* 13:42.

however. Inasmuch as we are enjoined not only to understand Halachah but to experience it, and not only to experience but apply it, we shall—even as the interpretation of our heritage remains our primary concern—strive to understand the modern world, to grapple with its problems, and to cope with its inexorably increasing impingement upon Jewry and its values. And we shall not assume, *a priori*, that these tasks cannot be performed.

Professor Rotenstreich's second contention, that Judaism and Halachah should be less objective in character, likewise ignores the full implications of our commitment to Revelation. He laments the rigidity of Halachah and contends that "only a view which transcends the Halachah can constitute a foundation for suggested innovation"; and he goes on to complain that even critics of the "current interpretation of the Halachah in Israel generally base their criticism upon the Halachah itself rather than upon a more comprehensive view which transcends it. If, accordingly, the Halachah is a realm in which Jewish thought is confined, how can the Halachah itself make available to its dwellers the means of breaking through its walls?" Well, why not go a step further? Since Judaism is a realm within which Jewish thought is confined, how can Judaism itself make available to its dwellers the means of breaking through those walls? And ought we not, therefore, opt for a universal religion?

This is not merely an exercise in one-upmanship but an attempt to point out the obvious. If we take the idea of Revelation—and of Halachah as its explication—seriously, we cannot look for ways of transcending it. We *can* properly speak of values which are both the basis and the *telos* of Halachah and which transcend specific normative sections; and we can validly attempt—on the practical plane and in accordance with Halachic processes—to harmonize the values and the norms, the spirit and the letter, of Halachah when changed conditions tend to rend them asunder. But this is hardly the same as transcending the Halachah in its entirety.

This is not to deny the possibility of a certain type of development or change within Halachah. Change does take place, and anyone who doubts this should try to decide Halachic questions by referring solely to the *Gemara*. However, the change grows out of creative insight, disciplined interpretation, occasional legislation, and perceptive application to contemporary conditions—all operating in accordance with valid Halachic procedure. It cannot result from random tampering. We can hardly tinker with a system grounded in Divine Revelation.

To be sure, Halachah does contain a human element, and the Rabbis not only acknowledged it but, in a sense, glorified it.[41] But this element cannot take the form of casuistic engineering or self-willed revision. It rather consists, on the one hand, of an honest attempt to explicate and apply the Divine Word and the legal corpus grounded upon it in accordance with one's best human lights, and, on the other hand, within certain limits and in the spirit of Halachah, of the promulgation of new laws by recognized authorities endowed with sound scholarship and developed Halachic intuition. It may be argued that in certain areas the authority for change properly available within Halachah itself has been insufficiently exercised. But this is hardly the same as to criticize its essential objective character. To make subjectivism its conscious operative principle is not so much to transcend Halachah as to abandon it.[42]

The very nature of the human element in Halachah demands that definitive interpretation be left to acknowledged authorities, *talmidei chachamim* whose informed scholarly judgment and profound commitment to Tradition can qualify them for competent decision. Since this element is not a matter of sheer fiat but of insight and interpretation, it must meet a certain standard of knowledge and responsibility vis-à-vis the Tradition. While the obligation to study Torah and to attempt to interpret it is universal, the right to make definitive decisions is not. Luther's principle, short-lived even within the more limited domain of Scriptural explication, hardly applies to more complex Halachic interpretation. In the final analysis, undemocratic as it may sound, Halachic decision does indeed rest with Halachists. With whom else?

IX

At this point, we are confronted by the spectre of ecclesiasticism, with all its attendant overtones of overcentralization and worldliness. Professor Rotenstreich is perfectly right to call attention to

---

41. See *Makkoth* 22b and *Chiddushei Ha-Ritva, Erubin* 13b.

42. Within certain limits, there is some leeway for deciding objectively and legally questionable matters on the basis of one's subjective ethical inclinations. But while this point is important, it constitutes a nuance within an objective framework rather than a general denial of that framework.

these dangers, although I think he errs in asserting that the Israeli rabbinate's current status has no Jewish precedent. The ancient Sanhedrin is one, the structure of Babylonian Jewish society is a second, and the more recent *Va'ad Arba Ha'aratzot* is a third. Whether or not there are precedents, however, the dangers inherent in ecclesiasticism are ever present and very real, and proponents of spiritual religion must be constantly ready to detect and denounce any onset of ossification or creeping worldliness. It does not, therefore, follow, however, that the abrogation of Rabbinic authority is the proper alternative. At most, we have here an argument—not necessarily decisive—against *centralized* Halachic authority—the transposition to another milieu, as it were, of the struggle between the Congregationalists and the Presbyterians. This position can be argued, but let us recognize the argument for what it is worth. It hardly militates for taking Halachic authority out of the hands of those who, by knowledge and commitment, are best qualified to exercise it.

The failure to appreciate the significance of Revelation also underlies Professor Rotenstreich's comments concerning the Orthodox attitude toward the secular segment of the community. Rotenstreich lays great stress on the secularist's voluntary renunciation and demands that it be acknowledged. In one sense, I agree with him wholeheartedly. As a Jew committed to the Halachic tradition, I naturally make it the basis of my action; and its truth, values, and interest serve as a point of departure for my thinking. However, I know full well that many Jews—very often, through no fault of their own—lack this commitment, and that any concession which they make to its normative demands is, more likely than not, purely voluntary. To the extent that such renunciation is ethically motivated—say, by a desire for national unity or out of deference to one's fellow—I not only acknowledge this voluntary element but salute it. However, if Professor Rotenstreich means not only that, given his rejection of Tradition, the secularist's renunciation is to be lauded but that we should recognize his right to reject the Tradition in the first place—an Orthodox Jew cannot but demur. We must no doubt be charitable in evaluating the subjective reasons for such rejection, but we can hardly assume, given our acceptance of Revelation, that a Jew has the right to renounce it. We recognize, of course, that secularism is one approach, and that secularists are not all profligate libertines. But is it a Jewish approach? Something more was demanded and committed at Sinai. I am perfectly willing, again, to consider Professor Rotenstreich's statement that it is tactically and psychologically wiser—and hence, morally and religiously purer—to ask him to renounce voluntarily rather than to attempt to impose upon him. However, I cannot do so without holding that he ought to be bound by Halachah even while I know he is not. The basic principle that normative Judaism, as a divinely ordained order, is binding upon *knesset Israel* is not my personal possession to renounce.

A similar flaw pervades Rotenstreich's comments concerning the Halachic attitude toward "the problem of non-Orthodox piety." Of course, Orthodox Jews recognize that heterodox piety does exist, just as they realize that secularists may lead genuinely ethical lives (albeit only because they are unwittingly inconsistent with their own principles). I hope Professor Rotenstreich does not seriously believe that the attitude he ascribes to Orthodox Jews—"better an atheist than a non-Orthodox Jew"—is a genuinely Halachic position.[43] Particularly in an age when belief is so largely conditioned by environmental influences and prevalent intellectual currents, it would be both unwise and immoral to deny the genuine reality of heterodox religious experience. It does not, therefore, follow, however, that the distinction between Orthodox and non-Orthodox Judaism can be safely ignored. Viewed as a subjective phenomenon, heterodox piety may constitute invaluable religious experience, and this consideration is crucial for any intelligent assessment of the

---

43. In one sense, of course, one might think that atheism *is* "better" than heterodoxy inasmuch as it poses a clear alternative to Orthodoxy rather than an adulteration or dilution of it, so that it does not threaten it in quite the same way. It is precisely for this reason that personal and institutional relations between Orthodox and non-Orthodox Jews are often more strained than the relations of either with atheists. In this sense, however, the term "better" has political (I use the term in a good sense), rather than moral and theological, overtones. As to whether anyone ought rather be an atheist than a non-Orthodox Jew, it is inconceivable that any advocate of Halachah would assume the position ascribed to him by Rotenstreich. One should not be misled by R. Tarfon's statement "that if someone were pursuing me I would rather escape into houses of *avodah zarah* (idolatry) than into houses of *minim* (heretics). For worshippers of *avodah zarah* reject Him without knowing Him, but the *minim* know Him and yet reject Him" (*Yerushalmi, Shabbat,* 16:2). As the text specifies, the distinction is not between two degrees of remoteness from God but two types of motivation, one conscious rebellion and the other unwitting rejection. Wherever, because of different circumstances than R. Tarfon's, the distinction in motivation does not exist, the statement would not apply.

individual involved. However, as interpretations of Revelation and the Tradition which explicates it, heterodox versions are quite invalid. If we take the idea of an objective revealed divine will seriously, then, no matter how charitably or tolerantly we may wish to regard our fellow Jews, we cannot treat all readings of it equally. Beyond a certain point, sincerity and good will are not enough. We have a responsibility not only to preserve our own moral integrity but also to see that the revealed will of God prevail. That the existence of an objective element within Halachah may occasionally produce apparent anomalies (whether or not the case of Brother Daniel be one) is unquestionable. This is inherent in the nature of law. But Professor Rotenstreich's alternative to the Halachic dialectic between subjective and objective poles poses far graver problems than it resolves. He would, as Sterling said of Carlyle, take us into the desert and leave us there. In any event, however, the believer in objective revelation has no real choice here. If we scratch Rotenstreich's essay enough, I think we encounter not only opposition to Halachah but universalistic repugnance to the notion of Special Revelation.

Yet Special Revelation, paradoxical a doctrine though it may seem, is the core of Judaism. It assisted at our birth, it defined our essence, and it molds our destiny. To constitute, in some particular sense, a "dwelling" for the suffusive Presence of the *shechinah,* to testify to a singular divine message, received, on the one hand, and to be borne, on the other—this is the essence of Jewish history. Covenants ago, in a land by rivers bounded, two roads diverged in a wood. We took the one as yet untraveled—and that has made all the difference.

INTRODUCTION TO

HOW LIVE BY JEWISH LAW TODAY?

Hans Joachim Schoeps

Every religion is marked by a distinctive differentia, which defines, not only its internal uniqueness and claim, but sets it off from other historical religions. The curiosity of Judaism is that it remains a remarkably ancient religion, but one which has survived unchanged in all essential characteristics from the time of the Bible. Indeed in the world in which Judaism grew up, the religions of the civilized (and uncivilized) worlds, if not pagan, were assuredly polytheistic.

The distinction between paganism and polytheism I take to reflect not simply a degree of passion in opposition but a more fundamental difference in attitude. This is perhaps incorrect, paganism reflecting *only* the hostility of the true believer to the heathen; polytheism *only* a technical indication of the theological mistake of the pagan. But if one presses further to the underlying Dionysiac excess involved in classic paganism, an attitude which defines the dependency of the gods upon the pacifications, attentions, and services of man, it is not false to regard paganism as the achievement of human apotheosis and polytheism as the consequent fragmentation of theologoumenon, impossible to preserve in integrated wholeness, if the gods are to be fashioned in the image of man.

Ancient Judaism was at war with the paganism within its own psyche and the polytheism around it. The pagan is, however, an ongoing temptation and polytheism is a relief to the insupportability of pagan hubris. It is taken then as an assumption that man seeks unity and reconciliation, but that he is often unable to achieve it, lacking both the insight and the sophistication of feeling to put himself under the rule of a single God. His impulse to disorder and chaos is the essential motif of the paganic psyche. He wishes the confusion of sex and sexuality, the overlapping of the moral and the aesthetic; he cannot support clarity. It is at these moments—both ancient and modern—that his paganism overflows; and it is only in fear and anguish, still attentive to his confusion, that he makes his idols of sticks and stones, fabricates his gods out of nature, and worships them that they might release in him some clarity amid confusion. Ancient Judaism repudiated this, militantly, harshly, without compassion. It was fighting for its own vision, when it destroyed the backsliders within, those who would go whoring after the gods of the neighbors. It paid a price, for what Judaism has come to enjoy in measure and balance, in a doctrine of the equity of needs and the control of passions, it has tended to lose (in all but its mystic traditions) in exuberance and visceral passion.

This is all by way of preface to observing that the core of Hans Joachim Schoeps's essay (an exhortative elaboration of the position taken earlier by Franz Rosenzweig) is the restoration of an unavoidably paganic need, a paganic need, however, which does not result in polytheism, but in a return to classic Judaism. The Law is a given, a *factum brutum*, whole, self-consistent, and self-perpetuating. It has no referent beyond itself, no simple, immediate mechanism of adaptation to changing circumstance (*vide* the observations of Aharon Lichtenstein on this point). It changes, but only against the background of precedent within the Law, rather than exigencies without. The predicament of the Law today is, however, that it is inadequately observed or for the most part ignored. The contemporary era is not even one that backslides from the Law, for it has not known the Law as a demand. Given this situation, but, even more, given the focal centrality of the Law as the institution which differentiates Judaism from the religions that once surrounded it, and now, from Christian, Muslim, and Oriental, it is decisive that a strategy be devised to return Jews, at least, to the recognition of the Law as a demand made upon them.

The paganic impulse is recognized in the insistence of Buber, Rosenzweig, and now Schoeps, that the Law is not imposed and that God is not primarily a Lawgiver. God is Lord and it is his person (beheld by man as Lord) that obliges that he impart order to those he rules. God creates Law, but is not Law; Judaism is not Law, but being a Jew. Given this crucial distinction, it is improper to regard the *halakhah* as a juridical instrumentality of accounting Jews good or bad, faithful or unfaithful. It is, indeed, logically possible that a Jew may be drawn closer to God, intent upon serving his immanent history in the world, faithful to his person, longing for the wholeness of Israel, striving for the Kingdom of God, and yet unable to observe the Law. Correctly Schoeps would insist that such a Jew cannot claim ignorance of the Law, regarding natural virtue and morality as sufficient means of reconciling himself to God, for the institutions of the Law were institutions created *for* Israel. To be ignorant is no excuse. However, to be unable to obey is. The Jew who says that he will observe *this* wholly but *that* he cannot observe, is a Jew who begins to do *some* thing, knowing full well that he has turned himself in the direction of doing *every* thing.

The underlying power of this view is that it is recognized that now, as never before, man is a creature suffering, not only from the excess of pride (with which he is traditionally berated), but with an equally profound (and often humbly sensitive) disorder. He is a creature beset by heteronomy. No longer ruled by traditional institutions, no longer able to obey single doctrines or exclusivist ideas, his is a world of competitive demands and requirements. And his is no paganic joy, but a paganic confusion. Not Dionysian (although surely there is no less a revival of the Dionysian) and not yet Apollonian, not the victim of frenzied passion and sensuality nor yet the exemplar of measured rationality, the contemporary Jew must be led back to the Law by the compassion of the Law. His pagan condition, if not his pagan nature, must be acknowledged.

The Schoepsian position, however much it may not return Jews to the 613 commandments, may well return them to a body of practice not so much selected to convenience, as authentically believed.

HOW LIVE
BY JEWISH LAW
TODAY?

A Proposal for Those Who Have Fallen Away

HANS JOACHIM SCHOEPS

We Jews of the mid-twentieth-century live today in what might be called a post-Jewish situation. That is to say, the reality of each day's living is such that it is no longer possible for most of us to experience our Jewishness simply and directly. This is true for both America and Europe—it may even apply to the secular State of Israel—and must be fully appreciated by anyone who hopes to say something about the present situation of Judaism that will be to the point.

It is time for us to renounce all fictions of the "as if" kind. We can not act *as if* we were still living in the ghetto and *as if* it were possible artificially to keep alive the way of life that flourished there; we can not act *as if* the laws of the Torah still signified for most of us the rules of conduct; *as if* fear of God and not self-aggrandizement were the common fact; *as if* the sermon's conventional opening words, "Worshipful congregation," really applied to those seated beneath the pulpit, who may be ready to listen to their rabbi's opinions only if he is a "good speaker." There is no point in deceiving ourselves: the Jew of today may be the grandson or great-grandson of a pious man, but he himself is completely a man of his age. The newspaper has more interest for him than the Bible, and he prefers the movies to an edifying Midrashic (not to say Halachic) discourse.

And, really, there is a question as to whether he is not perhaps right, after all, in his preference; for the events enacted on the

454

movie screen probably have more meaning for him in the concrete circumstances of his life than an exposition of a problem in the Law or in the ritual regulations of cleanliness. Law and ritual are often something he no longer even understands, or at least can no longer regard as meaningful and apposite to the problems of his daily living. It is of little help to the Jew of today to ponder the problems his fathers racked their brains about, for the circumstances out of which the problems sprang have disappeared or grown incomprehensible. What a friend of mine wrote in connection with the Maimonides memorial year has a general validity: "On the whole it is impossible to make an alien existence one's own; the best one can do is . . . to *co*exist with it. But there are already great stretches of time for which this is no longer possible. The eight hundred years that separate the Jews of today from Maimonides are not to be rolled back. There is only the hope that—if we genuinely inquire in our own time as to the meaning of Judaism—we shall somewhere, sometime, light upon Maimonides. . . . True studying, however, means first of all not Maimonides, *it means ourselves.*"

The question, then, is: how shall a modern man reconcile the Judaism that was with the Jew that he is?

As the Jew of all previous centuries understood it, the great turning point in Jewish history, the real breach of the historical tradition, was the destruction of the Temple by the Romans under Titus in the year 70 c.e. It is generally agreed that we have the Pharisaic theologians of the time to thank for the fact that this rupture of the historical tradition did not prove fatal and put an end to Jewish history altogether. It was the sages of Jabneh, of Lydda, of Caesarea, and BeneBrak who were the first to develop the concept of the "as if" into an enduring principle of Jewish history. The theocracy no longer existed, but its constitution remained in force as if it did. The Temple no longer existed, but Jews the world over bowed in prayer in its direction as if it did. The High Priest no longer made his expiatory sacrifice on the Day of Atonement, but the ritual formula was learned and recited on that day as if he did. Meanwhile, other things took the place of the actual sacrifice: study of Torah, good works, prayer—the fulfilling of these commandments counted as much as the animal sacrifice of ancient times.

This disregard of the actual facts, this abstracting of Judaism from every reality of the here and now, was a huge accomplishment. It did indeed "save" Judaism—that is to say, by means of the "as

455

if," Judaism was adapted to exile and was removed to the plane of the timeless. The faith of the Jews proved more real than reality and overcame it. The sages of Jabneh assumed, as the most self-evident thing in the world, that the royal decrees of God the King as set forth in the constitution of the Covenant (the Torah) were as valid in their day as before. Hence they strove, by putting up "a fence around the Torah," to preserve Judaism in isolation from time and space. From Johanan ben Zakkai to Joseph Caro, law was heaped on law, and in defiance of all reasonable expectation Judaism was successfully translated to the timeless, the Jews learning to live their lives more or less alongside time.

This was a greater feat than Alexander's conquests or the empire of the Caesars. For it effected a paradoxical retroactive annulment of historical fact: the Jewish state turned out not to have fallen at all in the year 70, but was preserved in its laws and lived on, metamorphosed, in the ghetto. It was Johanan ben Zakkai, the betrayer of his country to the Romans, who became its savior, and not the nationalist Bar Kochba, whose reaction to his country's disgrace was only—a patriot's. The sages of Jabneh proved more farsighted than the Zealots, with a farsightedness that reached seventeen hundred years into the future. During this time they reigned supreme—because the laws they had clung to did not remain mere fictions but *became a reality through faith*. It was only in an age of disbelief that they became fictions—that is, about the beginning of the period of Western European emancipation.

It is, therefore, the Emancipation that is the most fateful breach in the continuity of Jewish history, for this time there was no bridge improvised to span the abyss. Where the Tannaim of the second century had succeeded in making over the Law to suit the new historical epoch, the Reform rabbis of the nineteenth century signally failed. Now the thread was really broken, and the great question that had lain hidden, all these years, in the heart of the year 70 first revealed itself for what it really was: the question of Judaism's destiny. The Emancipation for the first time shattered the inner historical coherence of Judaism and put an end to the legislative power of the Jewish state, which thanks to Johanan ben Zakkai had maintained a fictitious existence-through-faith seventeen hundred years beyond its actual end. With the disappearance of the ghetto, faith as a collective phenomenon and the all-inclusive regulation of life according to the Mosaic law ceased to exist.

Moses Mendelssohn's generation was the last to hold completely with the sages of Jabneh, regulating their lives according to the unabridged Mosaic law as fixed by Moses Isserles and Joseph Caro. Since then the number of families remaining faithful to the Law—of whom Samson Raphael Hirsch was a representative spokesman in the nineteenth century—has steadily declined. For a host of others, whose numbers increased generation after generation as the observance of the Law fell off (until only a pure distillation of the ethical element—little more than the Ten Commandments—remained), the ancient Law was but a fiction, because faith was lacking.

Once the fence was torn down, and once the Jews had established themselves in the new reality of the modern world, all further need of the "as if" became superfluous. However, from Michael Creizenach and S. L. Steinheim to Leo Baeck, Jewish thinkers have been sensible of the void that had arisen within, and now began to pose more and more urgently the question of the "essence of Judaism." Their question, in short, was: what now was left of Judaism?

What is it, in a Law suffering a gradual loss of all authority, that is worthy of surviving? What is the Jewish faith today? Wherein is it to be found and how can it be established?

There is nothing in the Jewish tradition to countenance the asking of such questions; and because such questions were never asked before, no earlier answers exist to guide us today. All those who have not perceived the belated manifestation, commencing about 1800, of the fatality concealed in the year 70, who have not perceived the growing untenability of the "as if" set down by the sages of Jabneh, will never recognize the right to ask these questions. But it is vital for us that we ask them, for it has ceased to be apparent why the body of the Jewish people should still maintain its separate identity if the individual Jew is going to know as little as he does about the origin (election) and end (God's supremacy) of the Covenant, and its constitutional obligations (Law).

It is, therefore, legitimate to ask what are the basic tenets of the Jewish faith—on this question the further existence of Judaism depends. If one has a deep enough understanding of the question, deeper at any rate than the nineteenth century's, one must ask oneself if it is possible for men today to realize the Covenant in their lives. The man of today, no longer feeling any need to justify himself before God, answerable only to himself for his observance or nonobservance of the Law, will no longer countenance God, faith, Law, and the Covenant of Israel as the *a priori* of his consciousness or the whole content of his life. Jewish Orthodoxy has nothing to say to him. For it to speak to modern man, it would have to be able to divorce itself from its presuppositions, and its very inability to do so is what constitutes its greatness; if it could really make itself comprehensible to him, it would cease being Jewish Orthodoxy. The Levitical laws of purification, or the concept underlying the application of most of Jewish law—that man, by the correct fulfillment of these laws, from time to time becomes *yotseh* (perfect) before God—are now as incomprehensible as the well-reasoned Halachic belief that the turning on of an electric light or talking over the telephone on the Sabbath is against the will of God. The direct and unbroken connection of civilized life in the twentieth century with the will of God manifested four thousand years ago can no longer be perceived.

The *factum brutum* confronting us today is just this apparently ineradicable disharmony which has arisen between life under the Law and the modern secular scientific and technological understanding of reality.

Yet to almost every living Jew for whom the Bible is not an entirely closed book, the answer that men had once made with their lives to God's summonses can never be lost. Even in periods most distant from the primal source, these constitutive events of Judaism will be understood, and Jews must willy-nilly hear the words by which Scripture declares their eternal election and preservation. For Jewishness—which is not merely the experience of anti-Semitism but also the sense of an eternal pattern and recurrence—is an ineluctable destiny, as we in the mid-twentieth century are coming to recognize. Events have prompted us once again to discover ourselves as Jews. *It is no longer the case today that the Jewish teachings instruct us in our destiny, but rather that our Jewish destiny recalls us to the forgotten Jewish teachings.* Thus our way to Judaism lies in a direction clean contrary to tradition's: our way is that of a modern, historically conscious Jewish theology.

If a modern Jew who has blithely accepted the life he leads as a citizen of contemporary America or Europe or the State of Israel comes to question the meaning of his Jewish origin, which even in the twentieth century causes him to suffer the fate of the Jew, then

Jewish theology has a real answer to give to this question. The answer goes something like this: our sufferings have their origin in the denial or forgetting of something that goes back three and a half millennia and which has nothing at all to do with our being "for" or "against" it, an event that befell our fathers, was reported in the Bible, and so has been handed down through all history. God elected Israel to receive His Covenant, out of His free will He chose one people among the many on earth. To understand the essence and the destiny of the Jewish people, one must understand its origin as being spiritual yet real: God took one people for His own, calling it to represent His royal will. ". . . ye shall be Mine own treasure from among all peoples; for all the earth is Mine; and ye shall be unto Me a kingdom of priests, and a holy nation" (Ex. 19: 5–6). Or as Buber has translated it, giving a sharper accent to its meaning: "And ye shall become unto Me a realm of priests, a nation singled out from amongst all the others." Israel, by the unfathomable will of God, was chosen as the object of His intention to conclude a compact with His creation. The terms of this Covenant, ever since the event on Sinai, is the Law of the Torah, by which the Jews shall be placed under God's will. Taken, therefore, in the legitimate Jewish sense, the Covenant is an objective matter that has nothing to do with the will, wish, or allegiance of the individual Jew and thus is not dependent on whether a modern Jew can comprehend it or not. At Moriah, and in the promise made to Abraham, all the seed of Israel were chosen—everyone born of a Jewish mother since that time has a share in Abraham's election, becomes with Isaac a son of the Promise, and by his birth acquires membership in the Covenant. The external symbol of this is circumcision, marking the Jew as a sharer in the Covenant of Abraham. This is circumcision's "sacramental" meaning—it is not a hygienic measure, but a means to annihilate the historical distance dividing the Jewish child from the primal father Abraham; through circumcision a Jewish child becomes contemporaneous with Abraham.

Today we see how this sacrament has lost its efficacy, how it seems no longer possible to achieve this contemporaneity, because our *being,* as determined for us by Jewish destiny, and our *consciousness,* as modern men, gape apart. This schism of being and consciousness is the crisis in which we find ourselves today. The modern-minded Jew no longer acknowledges his original Jewish destiny, abandons that law of his origins which separated him from the world, and tries to dwell in the world a man like other men. But the destiny of his being, that being which his membership in the Jewish collectivity willy-nilly gives him, does not change because his consciousness has changed; the schism between the two is the Jewish fate as we know it today. There is no variety of assimilation that permanently succeeds, neither the assimilation of individuals nor that other assimilation which wants to place the Jewish nation under the laws of other nations. It has never failed, in all the centuries that lie behind us, that an Israel wanting to free itself, to throw off the yoke of its separateness, has been compelled to resume its life apart, its "sanctification." "And they shall be upon thee for a sign and for a wonder, and upon thy seed for ever. . . . And the Lord shall scatter thee among all peoples, from one end of the earth even unto the other end of the earth. . . . And among these nations shalt thou have no repose, and there shall be no rest for the sole of thy foot; but the Lord shall give thee there a trembling heart, and failing of eyes, and languishing of soul" (Deut. 28: 46, 64, 65).

Now these are all things which a modern man without faith can very well see for himself, for they are part of a history that continually repeats itself, and which those generations, in particular, upon whom the punishment is visited learn to understand. In every case this is what we are left with: the responsibility of reflecting on the underlying causes of our Jewish destiny in order to arrive at a true understanding of it. This indeed is not yet Jewish faith, but taking thought in this way may lead to it. By this historical-theological approach, by coming to know the continuity of Jewish history, we catch sight of a part of the Jewish reality which otherwise would be concealed from us. It can, indeed, inspire a man with a truer adherence to the Jewish reality than all the so-called positive approaches, which in the last analysis are for the most part merely unreal and anachronistic attempts artificially to reconstruct the past.

But the historical-theological approach by itself can do no more than teach the modern Jew a historical lesson; it cannot make a believer out of him, change the reader of a "sacred hieroglyph" (Ranke) into one who beholds the revelation of the living God. It can only lead him to the threshold, confront him with the Jewish reality; all the learned study in the world cannot do more than this.

To go further—for the person who has been led to acknowledge the spiritual truths of Jewish history to become a believer—he must turn from the general and abstract to the personal and concrete; the historical truth of the election of Israel that he has perceived must pass out of his abstract understanding and be realized in his personal existence. And this brings us to the last possibility of contemporary man. The laws recorded in the Bible must be felt not only as commandments to the generation of the wilderness, but to oneself, God's word spoken to oneself, to which one makes answer with one's life. *How* this happens it is impossible to say, because it is one of the secrets between God and man. One can and must, however, speak of what it leads to, for everything leading to the reality of the Covenant leads to the charter of this Covenant—the Law.

When a modern Jew thinks of the Law, it is of a series of "fine old customs" whose practice was an important part of the life of his parents or grandparents. A Jewish theology which simply insisted that these "fine old customs" were the "real" Judaism he was seeking, would be a deception. It is of course possible in every age to experience God's will in forms and customs too; yet one must first have felt it at a deeper level of one's being.

A man who has grown aware of Judaism's importance to him is not helped appreciably by a theology that sends him to the ritual precepts of the book of Leviticus without at the same time telling him that he will only understand their meaning after he has read the books of Genesis and Exodus. He will not then, as he reads, pass lightly over the account, at the beginning of the Bible, of Adam's disobedience to God. He will not fail to see the exemplary character of this first man's disobedience (sin), endlessly repeated in the lives of all the sons of Adam (particularly of the great ones of this earth). God, however, it is shown to him, keeps faith with the faithless, and in mercy makes his Covenant with one people whom he has called from among the peoples of mankind. This Covenant is based upon the promise and the Law. The Law points out to each man, and each generation, who are forever backsliding anew, the right path to what is "good" in the eyes of God. The generation that was vouchsafed the revelation, the generation of the wanderings in the wilderness, handed down as Law what for them had been their answer to the divine summons. However, each subsequent generation faces the task of distinguishing, amid the precepts and prohibitions recorded for the most part in Leviticus, God's commandment to *it*—that is, *through the Law it must come to understand the revelation.*

Martin Buber once wrote as follows to Franz Rosenzweig on this point: "I don't believe that revelation is ever lawgiving; and in the fact that lawgiving is always its result I see the fact of human contradiction, the human factor." God's pure word is changed in Moses' mouth into human words and dogma, God's pronouncement veils itself in the Law of Torah, the Word vanishes behind the word. But this insight of Buber's does not lead to a flat rejection of Law. He does not doubt that the generation receiving the revelation perceived truly the will of God; there is only the doubt that God's will as handed down—the Law as fixed in the Torah—can be taken over wholesale in later times by generations not vouchsafed the revelation. To make it truly one's own, to "believe," it must first have been experienced as *commandment;* it must first have been heard as the answer to the questions of one's own life—or as Buber puts it, "only so much of it (the Law) must be acknowledged as I can acknowledge as having been said to me." In this way, to be sure, the universal validity of the Law is lost; but this loss of the unchanging and universal Law is precisely what defines the modern situation.

Despite this loss of a universal and timelessly valid Law, I feel certain things can be asserted with confidence. The first and foremost religious possibility for the individual is and will always be through the ethical. Though in the Bible the moral commandments go hand in hand with the ritual, sacrificial, dietary, and marriage laws, they are nevertheless separable from them. Tradition was well aware of this, but had no reason to attribute any great importance to the matter. Today, however, the pre-eminence of the ethical is plain, for the moral law is an elementary demand whose insistence every human being can feel (hence the primacy of the Decalogue for all men), whereas this is not at all the case with the dietary laws or the sacrificial regulations.

Thus, for example, the force of the commandment, "Thou shalt love thy neighbor as thyself," can be felt by everyone in every age for the very reason that man does not love his neighbor, does not keep his neighbor's good in mind. But here it can happen that one feels one's offence, and in the distress of this feeling can come to see one's behavior for what it is, a falling away from the will of God. In the moment that a man acknowledges his guilt the word of God has found its way to him. In discovering that God's will and man's wish are not the same, the primal wound of life is opened in him, and he is driven by the pain he feels to seek that help which human hands can no longer give him. In this divergence of the human and the divine, God's sovereign claim upon mankind is recognized and man's faith in his supposed self-sufficiency dwindles to nothing. For in the claim that God asserts upon us by His commandments we feel our helplessness, we realize that everything we are and have is held in fee from Him, is a sign of the creature whom his creator has summoned to do His will. Where this original disparity between the Almighty God and creature man is made to live again, there is always the possibility of God's drawing near to us out of His remoteness, His will coming to guide our life, His commandment passing into our life as "Law."

Life is not a pursuing of necessarily brief and infrequent encounters with the Divine, but a continual living and doing of what in these encounters we have been called upon by the Divine to do—a living of the Law. Yet it is also true that the Torah can never become the law of man's life today without his discovering it for himself in this encounter with the Divine, for modern skepticism forbids his accepting his forefathers' laws save if he has learned them with his own life. Today the realization of the Law is only possible to a postskeptical attitude of faith that has weathered every doubt.

At this point, to be sure, a host of questions confronts us. How many and which of the laws is it possible to realize today? Will it be possible eventually to realize all the Torah laws, or is it not the very nature of this modern religious attitude to bar us from realizing the majority of them? At what point will a halt be called, or will the modern man of the Torah go on to make the law of the red cow a constituent part of his life? What implications are there in this approach for adult religious education?

Merely to ask these questions, however, shows how impossible it is to fix a new objective standard of the law. No new Shulchan Aruch can be truly derived from the modern sensibility—to try to do so, as many Reform and Conservative Jews would like, would merely bring on a schism. The way of all those who, in our time, have seen the Star of the Covenant and have gone forth to make the Law once again an effective reality in their lives, lies through the same

463

old countryside but no longer along the same road. For, Franz Rosenzweig once wrote, "there has been no road there these one hundred and fifty years. Its prolongation into modern times, to be sure, 'is still there,' but under the best of circumstances this is only one among innumerable roads, no longer *the* road. So we shall have to content ourselves with the unity of the countryside. Let us hope that the day will come when there will be a main road running through it once again. And I believe that that day will come. Or rather not some *one* road surely, but a *system* of roads perhaps. But this can only be guesswork today. It isn't time yet for systems. Building our individual roads, however, is the right way to go about it."

Franz Rosenzweig himself found such a way, a way to recapture and reintegrate Jewish law with one's personal life; he returned to the observance of *kashrut,* to respect for the Sabbath, and to daily prayers. He achieved all this step by step, and by himself. He championed "something," *his* "something," against Orthodox Jews who wanted "everything" and atheist Jews who wanted "nothing." In a letter to Rudolf Hallo, dated November 27, 1922, he wrote:

"Here, as everywhere else, I reject this Everything-or-Nothing politics. Neither the Everything nor the Nothing belongs to us; the Something does. The Something is given to us. We have to settle ourselves down in the Something. I don't say that my particular Something is an example for anyone else. What may be taken as an example is that I have the courage—just as much against the idealists of the Nothing as against those of the Everything—to live in my Something. This cannot be exemplary as regards detail. I'm really only beginning. I don't know what will come out of it, and don't want to know. I hope and know that others are beginning, too. Something exemplary will develop out of the whole. I, we, all those who don't say 'Everything or Nothing,' are today trying once more to do what Jewish liberalism tried to do a hundred years ago and failed in. It failed because it tried to set up principles first and then act according to them. These principles remained, like the ones they opposed, officers without soldiers, hence fathers without children. We begin with the act. Let the principle for it be formed in time to come, by ourselves or by others. I silently hope that, some day, in decades, I shall know the principles, the laws, 'the Law,' at last, and that I shall once again be able to open my mouth and teach. But it doesn't matter whether it's I or others—the best would be: I and others."

A deep insight into the nature of the Law is at the bottom of this: Judaism is *not* Law. It *creates* Law, but is not Law itself. It *"is"* being a Jew.

What Rosenzweig again and again came back to was living experience, not the dead appropriation of stores of knowledge, forms of tradition, or even the imitation of lives lived by others, but the realization of Biblical law in one's own life out of inner necessity. The Law, which was written in the Bible stands for everyone, should in this hour become a living command precisely for *me*. And anyone who studies Torah in the right frame of mind can, like me, come upon this retransformation of Law into commandment. Rosenzweig experienced what had been experienced in ages past: the priority of revelation over Law, the priority of God as Lord over God as Lawgiver. "Only man in his sluggishness changes the commands into Law—by the way in which he carries them out—changes them into something systematized, capable of being obeyed without fear and trembling."

Franz Rosenzweig's way has been an example for many people of our era; but neither his way nor another's can serve us all in common. All of us today must go our several ways—ultimately, we feel sure, to arrive at the one goal where all our ways shall meet. That goal lies beyond all our individual lives. We have no authoritative Judaism of our own to set over against that of earlier times or against the Judaism of those among us who still represent that earlier time in their lives, and we may look ashamed on all our miserable efforts bespeaking, it would seem, no more than the weakness of our faith. Yet such as it is, we must stand by it as our life's reality, and seek to realize so much of the Torah as we individually can, according to our living faith. We may feel ashamed and self-conscious at setting aside Friday evenings for quiet conversation with friends, instead of going to the synagogue and lighting candles at home. But if that is all we *can* do—that is what we *must* do.

So long as every one of us today strives to make real the possibility that is his, we can be certain that our contemporary Jewish faith, for all its inability to realize the Law in full, has not yet ceased to be part of the tradition.

And should we meet up, as we go our way, with those figures standing at the beginning of post-Biblical history, I am confident that the great rabbis will indeed smile in astonishment at the appearance of their descendants, but they will surely never despise us. They, who have handed down sayings that all our ponderings shall never exhaust, will surely stand in awe before the mystery of God's ways. Ben Azzai said: "Despise no man and deem nothing impossible for there is not a man that has not his hour, and there is not a thing that has not its place" (Aboth, IV, 3).

PART FOUR

THE EXPECTATION AND THE TRUST

THE PANGS OF REDEMPTION

Yehezkel Kaufmann

"The Pangs of Redemption," the concluding section of Yehezkel
Kaufmann's polemical history of the idea and reality of *galut*, was
written in 1930 (and as such the only essay in this Reader written
prior to the Holocaust), at a mid-point between the Kishinev po-
grom and the extermination of Europe's Jewry. The former event
symbolized for him as it did for all sectors of world Jewry a crystallization of the hopelessness of the Diaspora; the latter event, though
it could not be anticipated, was always anticipated. The Holocaust
overwhelms, not by its concept, but by its magnitude—the sheer scale
and efficiency of the enterprise suggests patience and planning. In
the past the fury of peasant mobs was relatively spontaneous and
unpremeditated, the only magnitude being that of Pope or folk
leader, whether Innocent III or hetman Bogdan Chmielnicki. Hitler introduced deliberative, orderly magnitude. Kaufmann could
not have known this and, indeed, it is remarkable that he anticipated so much, knowing something of how history leaps to implausible conclusions from obscure causes. He is first and foremost a
historian, and as in the case of Dubnow—with whose views he is at
odds—it is the knowledge of history that gives to his ideological
polemic its intensity and passion.

Exile and Alienage (Golah v'Nechar), from which this selection
has been chosen, is a historical interpretation of the concept of the
Jewish People. For Kaufmann, the beginnings of the tragic dilemma of Jewish Exile, may be traced to those early theoreticians of

emancipation and enlightenment, Moses Mendelssohn and the epigones he inspirited, who sundered, Kaufmann argues, the living connection between faith and the people in order thereby to return the people to that pristine and uncomplicated quasi-mythic state which preceded their entrance into world history. The enlightenment doctrine of transconfessional fraternity, binding men of culture and reason together in a community that exceeds the exclusivism of religious dogma, promised to inaugurate an era of democratic civility and egalitarianism. In the future, faith would be private, a matter for the home and the heart, while the public domain would be the sphere of moral and political compatability. This view left out of account both the specific character of Judaism —that it is a religion of the public order, not easily restricted to home—and the specific character of Christianity—that it is a religion laying claim to all mankind and, therefore, incapable of regarding antagonistic views as having equal right and privilege as itself. The process of spiritual and intellectual attrition, combined with the overwhelming poverty of the masses of Europe's Jews and the consistent hostility of the Gentile world, produced by the end of the nineteenth century an attenuation of the Jewish will to endure meaningfully.

Kaufmann's analysis in *Exile and Alienage* is directed to the demonstration of the continuity in the reality and idea of Exile, to its permanence as a feature of Jewish life. It has, however, the significant intention of transforming the reality of Exile and the meaning of redemption from the spiritual plane to the domain of action and achievement. The ideology of the spiritual Zionists is, for Kaufmann, essentially conservatory, having little or no vital political significance but serving primarily to preserve the pride of the people until its will is inspired to dedicated action. The autonomism of Simon Dubnow, the intellectual Zionism of Ahad Ha'am, the utopianism of Herzl are so many postures of unrealism, for what they conserve they run the risk of destroying, the passion of the people to will its own redemption.

The importance of *Exile and Alienage*—aside from its prophetic awareness of the conflict between the claims of Jew and Arab and Kaufmann's awareness of Arab national concerns—is the hardheaded statement of the need for national self-redemption and the total secularization of religious concepts which is the basis of his argumentation. It is difficult to fault Kaufmann, the historian. But it is questionable whether the antitheological bias of Kaufmann's argument must be equally respected. It is true that Kaufmann wrote in 1930, after Kishinev, after the Russian Revolution, after the Balfour Declaration, after the Arab massacres of Jewish settlements in 1929, and before the tyranny of Hitler and Stalin; but it remains the case that although Kaufmann's ostensible solution of the Jewish problem has been realized, the Jewish People—in the Diaspora and in Israel—are, religiously speaking, still in *galut*.

The concern of Kaufmann is the regeneration of pride, the reestablishment of the nexus between land, territoriality, and the desire of the people to foster its own culture on its own terms. The People Israel is in alienage because it is obliged by the circumstance of its environmental inheritance to regard all foreign societies as inhospitable and, by response, ghetto territoriality as the only social enclave in which to achieve marginal security. The Land of Israel is not for Kaufmann a myth to be dreamed of in fantasy and appealed to in prayer, but a positive reality through which the ancient pride will be restored.

Since 1930, however, much has happened. Even though Kaufmann recognizes that imperialism and colonialism are over, he regards nationalism—whether it be the nationalism of the Arabs, the countries of Asia, or the Jews—as still viable. The socialist impulse of the postwar era (despite its sympathies for the national movements of liberation in Cuba, South America, Africa, Asia, and the Middle East) cannot help but regard Israel as the creation of the Big Powers, redressing their guilt and restoring an equable conscience, and not as an achievement of the Jewish will. It is, of course, of no particular interest to counter the ideological hostility of socialism to Israel, for so much of the socialist confusion about Israel arises from the Jewish solvent in socialist doctrine which can regard the Jews only as a vestigial symbol of a corrupt bourgeois capitalism (cf. Isaac Deutscher's volume, *The Non-Jewish Jew and Other Essays*, 1968) and can view assimilation as the only solution of the Jewish problem. Kaufmann correctly, to my view, considers assimilation to be a contemptible (and unworkable) solution.

But if the socialist critique of Jewish nationalism is irrelevant (except in so far as it points to the capacity of any nationalism to become jingoist, imperialist, and immoral), the critique of the religious visionary is legitimate. Kaufmann acknowledges that Jews will remain in the Diaspora, that all Israel will not be ingathered, that the condition of Jewry will resemble Alexandrian times, and not the times before the destruction of the First Temple. Jews will focus upon the Land, but may not elect to live there. The question will then remain: To those Jews who do not live on the Land, who cannot feel (or do not feel, as I do not feel) the need to be re-generated by the Land, is a measure of pride in being Jews denied? In other words, is the bondage of Exile and the psychological dis-placement of alienage a condition which affects us only in the flesh? Is it because our bodies are wracked by pain, our flesh dissipated by poverty, our substance depredated by persecution that we wish the pride of our own Land? It may well have been a half-truth once, back in 1930, but it cannot be the basis of any viable appeal of Israel to the Diaspora today. It cannot be, because the ultimate destruction has been wrought and there is no part of the Jewish body which does not have its scars, nor is the concern of the State of Israel (and it is no longer a simple territorialism of which we speak) simply to contain its existence, for the containment of its security demands more and more in order that it be genuinely safe (and what is the limit to "more," and where can it find a safety and security so palpable and sure as to overcome the new scars it now displays from three wars with the Arab world?).

Above the pride of the People Israel there remains the vision of the People Israel, which, given the rebuke of the prophets, is not solely the pride of its territory, its language, or its institutions. Even if it is not for the sins of the People that the Jews were sent into *galut,* it may be that what it forgot is more important than what it feels obliged by historical circumstance and fatality to remember.

THE PANGS OF REDEMPTION

YEHEZKEL KAUFMANN

When we contemplate the past fate of the Jewish people and attempt to penetrate the veil of the future, a natural question arises: was it fate, a consequence of the Exile, an inevitability etched by a moving finger on history's "iron tablets," so that we need only to decipher that original script to understand it?

Men of faith, theological historians or pseudohistorians of the materialist school will undoubtedly respond in the affirmative. For them, past and future alike are engraved on heavenly tablets or immutably fixed in the logic of history's Lord or history's canon. Calculators of history's denouement need only find the key, decipher the secret code of these eternal, irrevocable laws.

The answer of the empirical historian will be more complex and conditional. The fate of the Jewish people, like any other historic phenomenon, contained the element of necessity. First of all, however, this was not the iron necessity of "history" but the internal necessity of elements, which in combination, defined the fabric of Jewish history. Moreover, these included the ideational factor, one which encompasses history's latitude—to the degree that history is a human enterprise. There *was* something inexorable about Jewish history. However, to the extent that it was also influenced by ideas, one can speak of the various options its course afforded. This is especially true when one looks to the future. The future is not delineated by a moving finger. Ideational consciousness, the root of man's empirical freedom, is vital here. This consciousness can push the will in one direction or another. The future is not "in heaven" or at least not solely there; the human spirit has a decisive influence on its course. . . .

Was the *galut*, the Exile, inevitable? Is it today? And if it be so, what hope is there of our freeing ourselves from it?

The question of the Exile's inevitability has many facets. First, was the religio-ethnic separatism of the Jewish people inevitable? Second, was their state of alienation inevitable? Third, was the penury of the Exile inevitable? Fourth, could the people have freed itself from its state of alienation and the Exile?

The Exile was unavoidable in the same sense that any reality, natural or historical, is unavoidable. It is unavoidable to the extent that its phenomena are attributable to causes, even though these never derive from a proven "primus causus," an absolute determinant that would explain everything and leave no room for the question of "why?" We do not know the ultimate cause of Jewish history. However, once we are given the specific reality, the rest flows from it inevitably.

The peculiar course of Jewish history can be explained by two primary factors: the character of the unique religious concept that was born and took root among the tribes of Israel in ancient times, and the ethnopolitical strength of these tribes. Ultimately we cannot adequately explain the existence of these two factors. However, given their existence, attested to by historical experience, we can explain the first phenomena of Jewish exilic history: the destruction and the dispersion, the religious singularity of the Judean and Israelite exiles and their ethnic distinctiveness. This holds for what follows as well. National-territorial consciousness and recognition of the natural corporate right of a national group dwelling on its land necessarily resulted in the state of alienation in which the Jewish exiles found themselves. The nature of the relationship usually evolving between rival peoples, on the one hand, and religious zeal, on the other, gave rise to a near universal hatred of the Jewish people, scattered throughout the world and, in the bargain, everywhere regarded as a stranger. The Exile, then, did not flow from "historic law" but was the outcome of a combination of factors, the result of laws governing various spheres of societal life, on the one hand; and, on the other, the result of a given social circumstance whose ultimate roots cannot be uncovered. These factors that forged and perpetuated the Exile also included, however, another,

474

unique one—the national will, coupled with the life of those same ideas that reigned supreme among the Jewish people.

The exilic fate did have an objective determinant, a combination of external forces that lay outside the bounds of the people's will. However, of crucial significance was the character of the Jewish battle for existence in exile, the paths taken by the people in their war on the blight of exile. Here the people's disposition, its view of the Exile and the concept of the redemption it yearned for, are also critically important. Here was no objective, external governance of necessity. In the war of survival in the Exile there was room for invention, for a redemptive idea, one that would point the way to new methods of waging the battle. The Exile was necessarily bound up with Jewish settlement in ghettos. However, was settlement in ghettos itself an objective, externally imposed necessity? Had the Jewish people no other alternatives? We know that other peoples did not follow this path. Other peoples founded independently based cities and villages and established national communities in various lands. The Jews, too, tried to found communities of this sort outside the land of Israel, as in Babylonia. However, what is decisive is the fact that the people did not look upon such national settlement as a means of redemption. They did not attribute vital significance to the mode of settlement. They swam with the currents of dispersal and migration. They did not hold ghetto dwelling to be the source of the Exile nor did they pin their hopes of deliverance on national settlement. The people awaited the kingdom of God and that stamped, in large measure, their attitude toward the Exile. They awaited the messiah, the kingdom of heaven, the end of days or waged political struggles from Messianic impulses, but never imagined they could reverse the deprivations of the Exile through a program of national colonization.

To the degree that the specific Jewish image of the Exile and the redemption was of decisive importance, one cannot regard the Exile as it developed as absolutely inevitable, the result of history's decree or an immutable reality. There was an element of latitude here, the same afforded the working of any idea in many social circumstances. Drought inevitably leads to famine at a certain stage of development of work tools, under given social conditions, but man can free himself from this inevitability through his culture and his social will. A society that recognizes slavery as a just institution and whose slaves recognize their masters' right to rule over them, as in Asiatic society, can know no redemption from slavery. However, there is deliverance in a society in which the idea of freedom grows stronger and the slaves seek to throw off their masters' yokes.

The same holds true of Israel's Exile. So long as the people did not wish to free themselves from it through natural means, so long as they saw the Exile as a Divine judgment and so long as they linked the Exile's termination to the inception of God's kingdom, exile was "inevitable." However, a different conception of the Exile could have delivered the Jews from exile. Here, too, there was room for the action of a commanding personality, a "creative" act that would have put the people in a different frame of mind. It is difficult to imagine what Jewry's fate would have been had there appeared among the "messiahs" that arose throughout the ages a folk hero who could have drawn the people to a new land, founding there a new Jewish settlement, a haven for his scattered brothers. It is difficult to imagine what Jewry's fate would have been had the people devoted at least a portion of the vast energy they spent on political-Messianic rebellion to founding new ethnic settlements, had they not gone out to found neighborhoods of foreigners alongside non-Jewish settlements in all the nations of the world, had they put their minds to the conquest of a new land for themselves. This, after all, was within their power. Here, an "idea" was of vital consequence. The disposition of the people played a decisive role.

In this sense one can speak of both the inevitability and the contingency of Jewry's fate today.

The ethnic distinctiveness of the Jewish people and the state of alienation deriving therefrom are inevitable. The war of survival in the Exile is inevitable. The people cannot obliterate these factors. In this respect, the lot of the Exile imposed upon the Jews possesses a measure of inexorability. However, to the extent that the Exile exists on the strength of the Jewish people's attitude toward it, on the strength of the traditional concept of the Exile, it should not be looked upon as absolutely determined. In this respect it is "willed" and therein lies the hope of redemption.

However, national deliverance, too, is not "ordained." Neither national deliverance as a general prospect nor its specific moment have been incised by the moving finger on the tablets of the universe. It is not destined to come "of itself" through the working of irreversible laws. National redemption is ineluctable only in the sense that Jewry, in the foreseeable future, has no solution to the problem of the Exile except through national deliverance. Israel's release from exile, however, can only take place through an act of will. In this respect it resembles any correction of a social evil, whether such be linked to class or nation, or to economic or political realities. The correction of a social ill is, of course, dependent upon a number of factors, foremost among which are the resolve of the oppressed to be rid of oppression and that attitude or disposition which Marxism labels "consciousness." Without "consciousness" of the social evil and with no hunger to be freed from it there can be no social liberation, even when there is a decidedly objective need for the same. Consciousness and aspiration are also prerequisite to the redemption of Israel from the Exile—the consciousness that the Jewish people has no escape from the Exile except through national redemption and the aspiration toward that redemption.

The extrication of the Jewish people from the Exile is a vast and arduous social undertaking thwarted by many real impediments. Undoubtedly the monumental stumbling block in this unique enterprise is the fact that the people have sought temporary rescue variously and have not focused their energies on the longing for national redemption. However, here, too, unawareness of the need for national redemption undoubtedly constituted a primary factor or even the decisive factor in the failure of the movement for deliverance. In this regard there is a decided similarity between ancient and modern times. The horrible suffering endured by the Jewish people in pagan and Christian exile did not lead to any attempt to break free of the ghetto through nationalistic colonization because the Jews firmly believed that release would come from heaven, that it would be political-Messianic.

In our time the old Messianic belief is no longer all-powerful. It has been replaced by other theories of emancipation that deflect the people from the path of national redemption. From the time of the Enlightenment to our own day fringe elements of Jewry have been drawn after various illusions that clouded the true character of the Jews' exile predicament and the one means of escaping from it. The age of Enlightenment believed that emancipation would come as justice and humanism engulfed the world. Then there arose a belief that emancipation would issue from the national and political assimilation of the Jewish people in their nations of domicile and

477

the limiting of Judaism to a "religious community." Later, the hope arose that socialism and the proletarian revolution would put an end to the Exile. Justice, human rights, equality, assimilation, socialism, the new humanity, national "minority" rights, conversion, mixed marriages—these were the proffered solutions to the woes of the Exile.

Modern times have imposed harsh and grievous suffering upon the Jewish people. However, Jews have tended to look upon all these incidents as terminal phenomena. Every catastrophe—including the gruesome butchery in the Ukraine at the dawn of the Russian Revolution—has been proclaimed as the "dying gasp" of the forces of reaction pouring out its venom upon the Jewish people. Young Jews have fought on all fronts against the old order in the belief that the new society—democratic-bourgeois or socialistic—would put an end to the Jewish exile, either by affording Jews the option of assimilating into surrounding civilizations, or autonomous rights. These new illusions parallel the ancient religious Messianic faith and, like it, restrain the people from focusing their will upon the effort of national redemption.

We have already defined a critique of these illusions.[1] The Exile will be abolished only through national redemption or by the utter annihilation of the Jewish people. This has been our essential purpose in this book: to make clear that *nechar,* the state of alienation, and *galut,* exile, are not rooted in a special frame of mind of a particular society or class, but are bound up with elemental concepts and feelings ever dominant in the human soul. We find "exile" and "a state of alienation" in all times and places in varying forms. With respect to Jewish history, however, these crystalized and received a unique configuration that led perforce to unique results. Nowhere does the Jewish people have any national territory. This is a fact, a hard, social reality of tremendous import, not a fabrication of anti-Semites or a triviality concerning outmoded theoretizing of the old "nationalistic" group. The alien state of the Jewish people is felt deeply in the folk soul. Moreover, this feeling of alienation will not be rooted out by any revolution in the workings of state or society, so long as the Jewish people continues to exist as a distinct group and so long as it remains in its ghetto condition. Belief in

1. The earlier sections of *Golah v'Nechar* define Kaufmann's critique of the concepts of exile, redemption, and the Jewish people proposed by the major religious and philosophic interpreters of Jewish thought. [Editor]

redemption that will come about through political-national assimilation, belief in "minority rights," in liberation effected through social revolution—all assume the abolition of primary instincts, ethnic certainties that generate the felt right of national suzerainty over a given territory and the feeling of alienation that is the mother of the exile. To hope for the eradication of these instincts is Utopian. Utopian, too, is the belief in the assimilation of the entire people. Utopian, again, is the belief in the abolition of religion throughout the world in the future day. In any case, these beliefs are "end of days" visions not to be regarded as historic solutions to the problem of the Exile. Furthermore, it is inconceivable that the Jewish masses, still bound to their "Jewishness" with all the fibres of their being, and in many countries separated by a gulf from their surrounding cultures, would purposely set out to solve the problem of their existence by pinning their hopes on complete self-effacement at some future time or on the hope of "nirvana" in the age of "new humanism." The Jewish masses passionately hunger for redemption, but not the redemption of destruction, neither through the ignominy of national suicide or the sanctity of nirvana. For the multitude of Jews there is but one path to deliverance—the path of national redemption.

This objective Jewish need for national redemption is the motive power of the national movement in all its manifestations; and imbuing the people with an awareness of this need is the principal task of the national movement in our time. Zionism should have tirelessly struggled to root out the illusions that the last generations have strayed after. Only by implanting within the people cognizance of the necessity for national redemption can the movement hope to succeed in fulfilling its historic task.

The national movement, however, itself discontinued the development of the ideal of liberating the people from the Exile. The national movement wandered off on byroads, compacted with the affirmers of the Exile, set itself a spiritual goal, and itself strengthened the dominance of illusions. This perverse logic prevented the movement from even fulfilling its prior, primary mission—heightening the consciousness of the need for national redemption from the Exile. The national movement itself turned its eyes from this need, denied it; for even as the people began to feel the need for redemption they began to experience bitter misgivings as to the possibility of bringing it about.

Redemption is Utopian—such was the contention of the opponents of the movement for national redemption from the outset, a contention that poisoned the thinking of the very bearers of the national idea. From the very day of its birth, the national movement was thrust between the felt need for redemption and doubt in its possibility. The people greeted Mordecai Emanuel Noah's proclamation, the first glimmer of the new concept of redemption, by shaking their heads. "Utopia!" proclaimed assimilationists and affirmers of the Diaspora in the eighties, and later during the era of Herzlian political Zionism. "Utopia!" cried spiritual nationalists and spiritual Zionists alike.

The accusation of Utopianism was the first leveled by Ahad Ha'am against political Zionism. He proved by a simple calculation that "the ingathering of the exiles was beyond nature." The Jewish problem in the Diaspora could be solved only by a mass exodus. However, a mass migration to "the Jewish State" was unthinkable. Even after the founding of "the State" the Jews would be able to settle there only very gradually, in accordance with the people's vigor and the country's level of economic development. Economic enterprises that could support immigrants in the land of the Jews could evolve only very gradually; if Jews arrived en masse, they would be forced to flee the country for want of food, being unable to find a means of sustenance there. Consequently, settlement would have to proceed at a snail's pace. Moreover, the natural increase of the colonists as well as that of Jews remaining in the Diaspora would, on the one hand, glut the land so that new settlers could not be absorbed; and, on the other hand, would lead to no significant decrease in the number of Jews remaining in the Diaspora. Therefore, there could be no hope of gathering the dispersed of Israel, by any natural means, from "the four corners of the earth" and putting an end to the Jewish exile.[2] However, if we examine the Jewish people's condition today, we will see that they are so trapped in a dead end of "Utopias" that redemption—ingathering of the exiles—is ultimately less "Utopian" than them all.

---

2. Herzl, "The Jewish State and the Jewish Question," *Altneuland*. "The Hour Has Come" (First Letter), and other essays by Ahad Ha'am. Dubnow makes the same point and added one of his own: "Letters on the Old and New Jewry," (Letter VI). See also Dr. J. Klausner's article, "A Ratified Lie," *Luah Ahiasaf*, 1894.

A doubly Utopian approach is, first of all, spiritual nationalism in all its varieties. Spiritual nationalism does not realize how, in attempting to repudiate the movement for redemption, it is negating itself as well; for if the people are won over to this attitude—that they ought not seek deliverance from the Exile through nationalism and that the lands of the Diaspora are their true future homes—then of necessity the desire to thoroughly assimilate will grow stronger and reach the same large proportions it attained prior to the rise of the nationalist movement. The pressure of the Exile is the true underpinning of the thrust for "autonomy," labors for a national "center" or "refuge" in the land of Israel and all other manifestations of the national movement. The aspiration underlying Zionism as a social movement is, in any event, the aspiration for redemption. The people have not yet grasped the teaching of spiritual Zionism with all that that theory implies; they still link the old muddled hope for "an end of the Exile" to the name "Zion"; they still have not made peace, at bottom, with the decree of eternal exile. For one finds that all that has been done in the land of Israel of late is due only to the awesome afflictions laid upon the Jews recently by the Exile. It is by no means inconsequential that spiritual Zionism, when it comes to address the people, threatens placid Jewry with "a day of darkness." It is aware of its life source. The people have not yet grasped the failure of the concept of redemption and have not yet adopted the new "penitence"—the penitence of assimilation. This penance, however, will come of necessity if they despair finally of the hope of redemption.

Utopias, in what follows, refer to all the various beliefs in redemption with which recent generations have deluded themselves: faith in utter assimilation, progress, minority rights, socialism, and the like. Decidedly Utopian is the theory that the Jewish people will be rescued from the Exile and their alien state without taking possession of a land through primal national colonization. Furthermore, these theories assume, as has been said, the extirpation of primary instincts that cannot be obliterated, whereas realization of the ideal of national redemption is ultimately dependent upon the national will and the marshaling of national energies. We cannot determine how strong this will is in the absence of historic experience. The people have done almost nothing thus far to achieve this goal and we cannot say how effective they would be when the "national decision" would arise from the agony of the "end" moment.

Once we recognize that there can be no historic solution to the problem of the Exile except national liberation and that all attempts to solve the problem will not put an end to the Jews' alien status, will not root the Jews firmly in their present lands of settlement, will not rid them of the ills stemming from their exilic situation, it will become clear to us that the social energy latent in exilic Jewry is incalculable. The great error of Herzl, who sought to calculate the denouement of Jewish history, did much to cover over the idea of redemption. Spiritual Zionism opposed its own reckoning to that of Herzl's and rightly so. Still, this reckoning cannot be considered valid by anyone who views the movement for deliverance, not from the vantage point of one generation's need, but from the vantage point of the fate of a people who must choose between national redemption or the agonies of eternal exile.

After all, despite this "reckoning," it is a historic fact that Jews have more than once migrated collectively from one country to another. Not only were Jews widely dispersed, they also left various countries and entered others en masse. "Natural increase" did not prevent the emptying of Palestine, Babylonia, and southern Europe of Jews. Of course, these migrations were the result of awesome and shattering events. Still, the termination of the Exile, too, will certainly come about through shattering social events—"the pangs of the Messiah," as stated in the folk faith. The war of the Exile is tribal warfare. An exodus from the Exile would be a national migration similar to national migrations that occur from time to time in the wake of clashes between national groups. Such an evacuation is a "catastrophe." The Exile is by definition an existence pregnant with cataclysm and for this reason it contains energies that do not enter into a reckoning of peaceful times. The "normality" of the Exile—that is, its daily abnormality—always constituted the crucial underpinning of the Messianic hope. Ever growing bondage and the agonized fear of imminent catastrophe were the life breath of the Messianic movement.

There were, however, real disasters that did in fact initiate "national migrations." Therefore, we can say that the hour of redemption has visited the Jews more than once but that the people were not "ripe." They moved from one exile to another and paid no attention to rebuilding themselves as a people. The social energies generated by exilic terrors bore no fruit whatever. The "migrations" did not lead to the winning of a national territory but to a mere change of ghettos. The people did not envision a "redemption" that could be ushered in through national colonization. Messianic-political efforts swallowed up all the travail of redemption and brought it to nothing.

Yet the new goal of redemption, despite its fundamental divergence from the old Messianic dream is itself "Messianic" in that its real base, too, is flawed exilic existence and its realization is contingent upon suffering and cataclysm. "The ingathering of the exiles" is not the goal of the movement for redemption in so far as it would involve gathering scattered Jewry through an organized pre-arranged scheme of colonization. The ingathering of the exiles is the movement's historic outer limit, the last historic opportunity toward which it aspires and labors, materially and spiritually. The movement for redemption can only lay the groundwork for what must follow. The concept of redemption can be the germ of an idea, a logos that will create a universe from the inchoate forces latent in the endlessly calamitous exile. The confidence of adherents of this idea is rooted in the realization that no matter to what degree redemption comes about peacably, it is destined to spring from suffering and horror—when the people will be ready and the work of preparation will have been done. Jewish nationalism, however, can fulfill its function only after it disowns the inner fraud that holds it back; when it stops nurturing the "spiritual revival" casually as a trivial offshoot of troubles and "happenstance" but understands that a spiritual revival, too, can only serve as the groundwork of redemption, redemption from the source of those very troubles and "happenstance"—from the alien state of the Jew.

Events of the last war and the Russian Revolution have proven that mass migration, even the transfer of peoples, is still possible in our day. The Jews themselves have undergone great "expulsions" during the war, albeit "internal" expulsions. The Communist revolution in Russia later uprooted great masses of people and forced them to leave the country. Such migrations also took place in the Balkans and the Near East. Of signal importance was the example of the return of the Greeks to their homeland from their lands of dispersion. In May of 1914, three hundred thousand Greeks returned to Greece from East Turkey and Asia Minor. Incredibly larger, however, was the number of returnees after the downfall of

Greek forces in Asia Minor after the World War. Commencing with the autumn of 1922 about one and a half million Greek refugees, primarily from Asia Minor and Turkey, but also from the Caucusus and Bulgaria, returned within a brief period. Furthermore, the entire population of tiny Greece is only five million! Finally, Greece, at that time, was impoverished and downtrodden after ten years of internal conflict, and the returnees were overwhelmingly destitute. Through loans effected with the help of the League of Nations the Greeks managed to solve the problem of the economic integration of the refugees into their country. By Ahad Ha'am's calculation one could have proven that this ingathering of Greek exiles was "beyond nature." Yet it happened! The mighty enterprise of Greece puts all Jewry, with its many "calculations," to shame.

The largest objective impediment to the redemption of the Jewish people today is its ethnic character. Thousands of years of ghetto life have all but eradicated every one of the traits essential to a national colonization program. It was an ill omen indeed for the Jewish people that it did not bestir itself to stake out territory in the New World discovered by Columbus and in whose conquest Jews took part. Great nations that dwelt in safety on their soil sent their sons to the forests of America to claim an inheritance for them. Jewry, however, scurried from ghetto to ghetto, never considering the possibility of acquiring a place for itself under the sun. Mordecai Manuel Noah's proclamation at a later date aroused mockery or anger. This man who called upon Jews to leave the lands where they enjoyed the protection of "benevolent monarchs" the Jews regarded as a madman. Only after America provided a firm base for ghetto settlement did Jews start streaming there. The first awakening of this people to the effort of redemption was ghettoish—redemption through assimilation. In the ghetto they suffered exile, in the ghetto they sought to be redeemed. The emancipation was an attempt to link redemption with the ghetto. The Jew wished to disguise himself as a *goy* of Mosaic persuasion on foreign soil, so that he might be redeemed.

The socioeconomic character of the Jews is only part of the difficulty and not the decisive element. Many have spoken of the extremely problematic economic changeover that Jews would have to undergo to sink roots in a land and acquire it as national territory. Jews are urbanites, and national colonization demands that at least some of them settle in villages. Such a transition from city to countryside is unnatural. Likewise it is claimed that Jews are a nation of "peddlers and middlemen," a nation unused to manual labor and consequently incapable of readying territory for settlement.

Undoubtedly these misgivings have some basis in fact, and we certainly cannot expect Jews to become farmers after the manner of age-old tillers of the soil such as exist in most countries today. In civilized nations, however, villagers aspire to urban modes of life and country folk have increasingly abandoned the status of "slaves of the soil," boorish and conservative in outlook and in their work methods, as was once the case. Industrialization and the appurtenances of modern technology have penetrated the village more and more, utterly transforming it. Jewish human material would undoubtedly succeed in village settlement of this sort, for the widespread accusation that Jews despise work is rooted in a weird distortion of fact. A large sector of Jewry does, indeed, toil laboriously to maintain itself. Beyond this, the migration to America proved that the Jewish masses can adjust to a change of this sort. Tens of thousands, upon arriving in the New World, completely changed their way of life and turned proletarians from "peddlers and middlemen." Furthermore, the experiment in Palestine is of singular consequence. The Jewish endeavor in that country in recent years demonstrates the great dimensions of the untapped energies of the Jewish people. Palestine shows that the national redemption of the Jewish people is possible beyond the shadow of a doubt. Here the Jews have converted sandy soil and swampland to rich and abundant fields. Here the Jews have built and are building new and handsome neighborhoods and cities, something they have not done since they became a nation. A drive for cultural and material creativity has surfaced among the people, a drive they never exhibited heretofore. Everyone who regards the Jewish effort in Palestine—if he has a soul—must be dumbfounded and fired with enthusiasm, and, if he is a Jewish nationalist, with hope and faith in the future of the Jewish people. The Jew can found a new, national community.

National migrations that have come about during the war and after, on the one hand, and the Jewish endeavor in Palestine, on the other, clearly demonstrate that the charge of Utopianism is ungrounded, in so far as it focuses on objective conditions.

The problem is, at bottom, a question of will and inclination; for what is almost utterly lacking to the Jewish masses is this—a real inclination for primary creation, for laying foundations, a real will to colonize. The notion of settlement that has dominated its thinking through the ages remains that of ghetto settlement. Varying elements have combined to set this stamp upon the character of the Jewish people, and disdain for work or pursuit of easy occupations have not been among them. Even when the vast majority of Jews engaged in manual labor, they were not a colonizing people, they did not set sail for far-off lands to fell virgin forests and introduce settlements in the wilderness. Residential enclaves alongside foreign communities—such was the people's picture of settlement. And this idea has remained regnant among the Jewish masses to this very day. Anti-Semitism, persecution, harsh decrees, cruel torments have been unable to dislodge this aspiration. At any rate the people never sensed or recognized that ghetto settlement was the source of the Exile and only national colonization could bring about redemption. The new concept of redemption, therefore, demands a thoroughgoing revolution. It can be realized only through a deep-seated national change of heart, a complete redirecting of inner energies, a new ideal of redemption. The old goal of ghetto settlement must be demolished. Colonization *ab initio*—this is the new ideal. The national movement must replace the old political-religious dream embedded in the people's heart or supplement it with the new scheme of redemption through colonization *ab initio*. Only this vision can break a new path for the massive national energies pent up by the pressures and cataclysms of the Exile. The fate of the Jewish Diaspora depends upon the fate of this idea.

The ethnic devastation of the Jewish people underlies the focusing of the new national idea on the old symbol of redemption—the land of Israel, the land of the past. The people, faltering, lacked the strength to conquer a new territory through cultural creativity and so staked out a corner for themselves in the ancient fatherland. Here they hoped to find their redemption, not through primary creation alone, but also on the strength of the past. Here they had an inheritance; here they did not have to begin, lay foundations; of sovereignty over this land remained fixed in the people's heart;

the merit of the Patriarchs would aid the descendants. The feeling here there was no need of acquiring rights of ownership through cultural, colonizing creativity. The movement of redemption undoubtedly turned to Palestine as a consequence of this feeling of ownership sustained and nurtured by Judaism through the generations and not as a result of some "metaphysical" or "cosmic" link between the people and a certain tract of land. No nation is eternally tied to a given territory, nor does a land have the same crucial significance that a language does in the life of a people. The migration of peoples from one land to another is commonplace in world history. However, civilized nations who have attained to a certain level of development do not leave their land. The reason for this, however, is that they dwell there and there have struck their life roots with all their national heritage. Nonetheless, even these nations spread out into other lands, making their homes on new soil so that "their land" is not something to be experienced within established, well-defined borders. Everywhere that the people strikes roots it can develop its national way of life. Of course the land is a partner in the creation of national character. The "land," however, in this sense, is not a given plot of earth defined by borders to which the people is indissolubly linked. Once the people is born, it creates its own "land" through wandering, conquest, and expansion. Thus we find that there are locales that exerted a decisive influence on a people's life and character without having become incorporated into the national domain. Mount Sinai and the Sinai Peninsula, for example, are sites inextricably bound up with the very beginnings of Jewish history, but the Jewish people never felt any need, "metaphysical" or "cosmic," to incorporate them into its territory. At any rate, a people that has left its land is not required to return there for the sake of rounding out its national character. And if the movement for Jewish redemption turned precisely to the land of the past, what was operative here was not any metaphysical link to this ground but (in addition to the religious link, a connection apart) the residual feeling of ownership. This feeling is without doubt an awesome social force bestowing upon Palestine incalculable value.

However, may we still pin the Jewish people's entire future on the future of Palestine?

The Jewish people demands, in the land of Israel, the sole national rights of a poor and oppressed folk on a portion of its ancestral land. Opponents of Zionism claim that the movement is doing the work of British imperialism in Palestine, but they make this claim either through obtuseness or willful, slanderous distortion. Except for this tract of land, the Jewish people nowhere has a national foothold and is everywhere a foreigner. Only on this territory does it have historic rights; it cannot abandon this land. However, can colonization of Palestine solve the dilemma of the Jewish people? Spiritual Zionism can pin all its hopes on this land, but if the national movement resumes its historic identity and aspires to a national solution to the problem of the Exile, it cannot narrowly limit itself to the confines of the ancient fatherland. The problem of the Exile will not be solved without a migration of masses of Jews from the Diaspora. Palestine, however, is too tiny to constitute a haven for a migration large enough to make an appreciable impact upon the situation of Diaspora Jewry. Furthermore, if the colonization effort in Palestine spreads into adjacent lands, what would the results be? Even if we disregard the question of political and economic conditions, we cannot disregard the crucial and complex problem of the Arabs. This question, incomparably difficult even in the tiny, historic land of Israel, will become doubly perplexing in an enlarged "land of Israel" spilling over into sections of the adjoining countries.

Palestine, it seems to me, is the only land in the world over which two peoples have rights of ownership; for no one doubts that not only the Jewish people has an historic right to the land, but the Arabs too. At any rate the Arabs have a claim to a national right to the land, and the nations acknowledge the justice of this claim. Moreover, the Arabs have this advantage over the Jews: they inhabit the land, whereas the Jews only intend to return to it. At its outset the Zionist movement scarcely was aware of the existence of an "Arab question." In folk imaginings, Palestine was desolate and mournful, waiting for "the ingathering of its children within it." Not only was this outlook typical of popular Zionism, but the political Zionism of Herzl and his colleagues, too, took almost no account of the people dwelling on the land. Herzlian political Zionism was governed by the old political concepts that passed over the people in favor of the state. The power taken into account by political Zionism was Turkey, not the Arab people. A "charter" from the Sultan was to decide the fate of Zionism. The movement put out of mind the question of the Arabs to such a degree that it pinned its hope on the downfall of the old aristocratic Turkish regime or even the breakup of the Turkish Empire, giving no thought to the fact that the Arabs would demand their place among the natural heirs of that empire. However, all these theories, whether of the folk or political Zionists, are outdated, unfounded in reality. Blinding ourselves to reality and relying upon our imaginations will avail us nothing. Ethnographic changes have transformed the face of nations and have also overtaken the ancient borders of Palestine. It is not only that members of another people have settled the land and have struck deep roots there, but they comprise only one tribe of many that make up a large nation dwelling to the north, to the east, and to the south. From the ethnographic viewpoint, Palestine has constituted part of the "land of Arabia" for about one thousand years, even though Arabia does not constitute one political body nor even a "geographic entity." The old political tradition has not allowed the Arab-settled lands to coalesce. However, can we regard this situation as permanent?

It is difficult to doubt that the twentieth century will be for Asia what the nineteenth was for Europe—a period of the entrenchment of popular and national sovereignty. The democratic idea and the national idea are making advance and spreading, albeit slowly, through the nations of Asia. The democratic idea draws nationalism in its train, and vice versa, as was the case in Europe. The nations are awakening from slumber. The old order is crumbling. Peoples are shucking off the yoke of the benevolent monarchs. Along with this, nationalistic movements are throwing the nations of Asia into a tumult. The movement at times takes on "Asiatic" garb, but it is hard to mistake its essential character. Enlightenment, democracy, nationalism, religious romanticism—all these are operative in one large tangle. The nationalistic movement here merges with the "enlightened" war against tradition and with the mania for imitation of Europe as well as "fascistic" despotism, as in Turkey following the war and to a lesser degree in Persia. It merges with religious and nationalistic romanticism and with opposition to Europe, as in India. It sometimes makes common cause wth religious fanatacism, as in Arab nations. Old and new mingle confusedly, they clash and seek to compact together. However, we find analogous phenomena in the democratic and nationalistic movement in Europe. There, too, the nationalistic movement was democratic and revolutionary at root, and it waged war upon atavism. Yet from time to time it made common cause with forces diametrically opposed to it. At its outset the Spanish nationalist movement had a Catholic religious base; the war against Napoleon was also a war for the Catholic faith, a nationalistic war in which priests bore arms. German nationalism at the outset of the last century merged with Christian romanticism. In the latter half of the nineteenth century even the standard bearers of the old regime compacted with basically democratic-revolutionary nationalism. Yet despite nationalism's disgressions and setbacks in Europe, it still fixed its imprint upon European history from the nineteenth century up to our own day. We see a like development in Asia, in spite of the great, natural discrepancies between democracy and nationalism in Asia and Europe.

Pan-Islamic religious universalism and pan-Arab secular nationalism are clashing within Arab nations as well as within the Arabic-speaking, Mohammedan population of Palestine. Nationalism, however, does not hesitate to seek an alliance with religion. Arab nationalism loves to flaunt its opposition to Europe. In truth, however, nationalism was introduced here from Europe, and to the extent that European influence increases within the Arab world, the influence of nationalism will also rise. Also, nationalism in the Arab world does not enjoy the same democratic base it had in Europe. Yet the wind from the West blows in with nationalism the idea of democratic rule. The people are opening their eyes, if very slowly. The development of the democratic idea is naturally bound to strengthen nationalism. Will nationalism lead to the formation of one Arab state that will unify all the Arab nations? At this time we are very far from such a state. The thrust of tribal separatism is still strong within the Arab fold. The feeling of tribal (and even clan) distinctiveness is still extremely potent, certainly capable of overriding any general, nationalistic impulses. However, even while tribal sentiment can impair a shared feeling of nationhood, it can constitute an expression of strengthened national identity. The thrust toward national unity and the propulsion toward tribal distinctiveness can both merge in nationalism. We see both these forms of nationalism in Germany—on the one hand, democratic nationalism's aspiration to form a unified German state, but on the other hand reactionary nationalism's demand for the preservation of the cultural and political distinctiveness of the separate German groups. The fostering of the common German language, on the one hand, and the fostering of regional dialects, on the other, both express German nationalism. Ultimately nationalism will no doubt merge with tribalism in the Arab world. This, however, will not hold back the evolution and strengthening of a general consciousness of nationhood. What the relationship between tribal and national sentiment will be is difficult to estimate.

In any event, the seeds of nationalism have already been sewn on Asian soil. The nationalistic movement is on the upsurge, flinging up waves in India, China, Turkey, Persia, Egypt, Syria, and other lands. Involuted are the paths of this nationalistic movement, and at times its forms are strange and unfamiliar to Western eyes. Not all that is bound up in this movement stems from a genuine national revival. Many "nationalistic" acts flow from corrupt sources, for this movement is, after all, Asian, despite its European genesis. Nonetheless, one cannot doubt the existence of a genuine nationalistic movement among the peoples of Asia. This movement, too, as in the West, aspires to the cultural and political freedom of the people and their unification; and even if Asian nationalism strikes out on new paths, different than those of European nationalism, it is still destined to make national consciousness an important and even decisive factor in the history of the peoples of Asia.

Noting these circumstances, one cannot consider East Asian lands as allowing for primary ethnic settlement. The existent ethnographic situation, at any rate, sets a fixed limit to any such colonization. Even the Arab lands do not afford space for new primary ethnic colonization in the true meaning of the term. The Jewish people cannot abrogate their sole historic national right to Palestine, but heaven forbid that it abrogate or denigrate the importance of the fact that Palestine is also part of a region of Arab settlement which has seen the inception of a movement of nationalistic resurgence. The Jewish people cannot—even if the question of justice be set aside—wrest their land from the Arabs and settle it alone. At best they can live in the midst of the Arabs. The Arabs, though, view the land as their national property and the Jews as an alien people who have come to make their home upon it. The entrenchment of national consciousness among the Arabs as well as their rise to democratic political rule will increasingly intensify their opposition to Jewish colonization; and if Jewish settlement extends beyond certain limits and proportions, it might touch off contention and hatred whose outcome it is difficult to foresee. A population mixed ethnically and internally divided spells danger anywhere, all the more so under conditions such as these. The Jewish community will find itself surrounded by Arab settlement on all sides. The history of other nations of whatever era or locale one chooses gives no basis to believe that the Arabs will look favorably upon this Jewish enclave in their midst. The ethnographic status of the land of Israel and the neighboring countries consequently fixes a narrowly defined area for Jewish residence. We cannot imagine that this colonization could perceptibly contribute to the solution of Jewish exilic dilemma.

What, then will become of the problem of the Exile?

Anyone who throws up his hands in despair over the matter has despaired of the Jewish people. Whoever says, "The Jewish people has no redemption," is saying, in effect, "Assimilate, convert, or devote your energies to destroying the world, so that you can die 'with the Philistines.' Try it—perhaps God will have mercy upon you"; but whoever does not despair of the Jewish people cannot escape this solution to the problem of the Exile: a land is required for the Jewish people, a new land. Let Jews settle Palestine to the best of their ability, but to solve the problem of the Exile they will have to seek out another land, perhaps even other lands. The conundrum of the Exile can be solved only in a land that will allow for settlement *ab initio,* primary ethnic colonization. Indeed, not only Jews stand in need of a land in our time. Great masses of people dwelling on their own soil are setting their hearts and hopes on far-off shores, on unsettled tracts, virgin forests untouched as yet by civilization. However, only in the case of the Jewish people does the need for a land have national roots. Still the Jews do share this need with broad masses of humanity. Can endless exile divert Jewish resolve from this sole path to the solution of the problem of the Exile?

Territorialism, a theory that has drawn to it outspoken proponents of national redemption, is presently in the process of being abandoned as an antiquated theory. In effect, the idea of redemption has been locked up with it. Even spokesmen for the Workers' Party of the Land of Israel (Mapai), who pride themselves on hardheaded realism, love to vaunt their opposition to territorialism and proudly recall their war upon "Uganda." Today the idea of territorialism arouses astonishment and head-shaking. Colonization

efforts in North America and Argentina have demonstrated that
there is no hope for national settlement in any land other than the
land of Israel. All the dreams of the territorialists have been exploded as things of naught. If one speaks of "a land"—where is the
land which Jews can make their home? There is none such. There
are those who acknowledge this to a degree and say, in despair, "We
are too late!"

The idea of territorialism has not, however, truly died. It is
almost impossible to imagine what would occur were a new Baron
Hirsch to arise in this generation with a scheme like that of the
"Argentina plan" of the nineties of the last century. Can one doubt
that tens of thousands of young people would stream to that
"Argentina" from their wretched domiciles in the Diaspora? The
idea of territorialism has even sprung up among Jewish Communists in Russia, despite their unbridgeable distance from any kind
of "Zionism" or "nationalism." Even in Communist Russia there is
"Herzlism"—"Soviet Herzlism" that arouses the wrath of old-line
Communists. It is an indication of the depth of the Jewish people's
felt need, today, for land beneath their feet.

Granted that the attempts at settling North America and Argentina did not succeed; what did the national movement do for
the support and success of this endeavor? Individuals devoted themselves to it seflessly, but Zionism allowed the venture to whither
away. Not one ray of encouraging light was beamed by the national
movement to those pioneers. Here was a failure of the people, not
territorial theory. For lack of ethnic forces, for lack of healthy
national impulses and for lack of clear thinking on the people's
part, Jews treated lightly or disparaged all the efforts of the upholders of territorialism, beginning with Mordecai Manuel Noah's
Ararat and ending with Herzl's Uganda. Was this expressive of
their loyalty to Palestine? Surely other peoples dwelling on their
native soil have not refrained from settling new lands. The British,
uncontestably faithful to their motherland, did not hold back their
sons from America and Australia. The Spaniards did not refrain
from settling Mexico, or the French, Canada, and so on. Loyalty to
Palestine did not prevent the Jewish people from taking up residence in all the nations of the world; are we to believe that this
loyalty prevented Jews from conquering territory for themselves?
Not loyalty to the land of the past is to blame, in the final analysis,
but an ethnic failing, the people's internal rot. Still there has been

some change since the Flood to the present. The idea of nationhood has struck roots. The will toward redemption has been awakened. Young Jews are disgusted with Diaspora life, in the shadow of the "benevolent monarchs" to whom "enlightened" Jews lifted their eyes in the time of Mordecai Manuel Noah. The national effort in Palestine attests to the stir of new forces in the Jewish people. A generation has arisen that feels the need for a land, that has set its mind on a land, that has shown a talent and a capacity for conquering a land culturally. Such a generation will succeed in its undertaking; but the great magic of the ancient land of redemption sheds its light on this generation as it did upon its ancestors. Indeed the magic is mighty and sweet, and laden with blessing. The people's confrontation with the land of their fathers is no light matter. Still it would be disastrous were this magic to blind the people to its obligation to redeem itself from the Exile and find a national inheritance in "the land of the Jews."

Where is this land?

Surely the Jewish people itself cannot find it. Yet there is hope that the land will be found when the question of redemption becomes once more international. For the question of the Exile is not truly a private Jewish concern, but an international issue in the full meaning of the term, as Herzl discerned. The question of the continuation of Judaism is solely an internal Jewish affair. The enigma of the Exile, however, the Jewish question, is a general problem touching the nations also. For two thousand years now, Jews of the Dispersion have been inhabiting special quarters alongside non-Jews. Immeasurable jealousy and detestation, rivalry and hatred, rapine and murder have sprung up from this ill-matched cohabitation. The "eternal Jew" wanders among the nations endlessly like a gloomy, grizzly ghost. The interminable alien status of the Jews not only poisoned their own lives but that of the nations as well. The new Europe sincerely sought to end this bloody tragedy, end the affliction of the Jewish people and thereby stop one of the sources of the poison infecting its own system. The new Europe sought to give the Jews an inheritance in her midst and imagined that success would come through the "national" assimilation of the Jews among their neighbors. Europe believed that emancipation would bring redemption in its wake and so believed Jewry during that pre-nationalist period. However, one hundred and fifty years of emancipation have sufficed to prove that this is not the route to Jewish

494

redemption. Recognition of this fact, this baring of the illusion of redemption through emancipation, marked the beginning of the nationalistic movement, and the movement's first task was to strengthen this awareness both in the midst of Jewry and the international community as well. The Jews have the right to seek their emancipation; that, of course, cannot be forgone. This struggle, however, need not prevent us from realizing that emancipation will not solve the problem of the Exile. Emancipation is the due of the individual Jew, whereas the problem of the Exile is the problem of the Jewish group, one which emancipation cannot solve. Early and late the national movement should have driven home this truth to the nations of Europe. It should have constantly reminded the new Europe that the Exile, with its attendant curses, would not come to an end in the absence of Jewish settlement of a national territory and that Europe, whose self-interest dictated the solution of the problem of the Exile, was obligated to come to the Jews' aid in this effort toward redemption. Jewish nationalism, however, did not fulfill its obligation.

It did not. It could not have, for in the meantime Jewish nationalism itself abandoned the dream of redemption, despaired of the "ingathering of the exiles," restricting itself to the domain of national spiritual goals. To solve the problem of the Exile, the Jewish question, the only goal it could advance was—emancipation. Thus Jewish nationalism joined hands with assimilationist Jewry in the solution of the fundamental problem, only asking, in addition, national rights. Not national redemption, but a "national home" in Palestine and the rights of national minorities for Diaspora Jewry— this was the demand presented by the emissaries of Jewish nationalism to the International Congress of Versailles.[3] Jewish nationalism took its stand on faith in Diaspora redemption. It did not unroll before the nations the scroll of Jewish agonies in our time, did not present its own viewpoint on Jewish existence, did not reveal the chicanery of emancipation and the need for a new, nationalistic solution to the Jewish problem. It did not strip bare the illusion of emancipation. To the contrary, it bolstered it and thereby swallowed the root concept of Jewish nationalism. It con-

---

3. See "The Copenhagen Manifesto" of the Zionist Federation, October 25, 1918, and the memorandum of the "Committee of Jewish Delegates" to the Paris Peace Conference: Georg Landauer, *Das geltende Jüdische Minderheitenrecht*, 1924, pp. 101–4.

founded the Jewish question with that of national minorities, became an accomplice to the giant deception that the Jewish question is not a matter of exile but one of a "national minority" demanding its rights with all other minorities. The movement did not raise a hue and cry over the catastrophe of the Jewish people, the tragedy of residing in perpetual exile, landless. It did not shriek out in the hearing of the nations, "A land!"—but worried only about the rounding out of the national image, the nation's peace of mind and "the realization of its talents and energies for the good of mankind," imagining that it would win its goal through a spiritual center in Palestine and national rights in Diaspora lands. So it was that Jewish nationalists themselves masked the mortal wound of the Jewish people, the tragedy of endless exile. The Jewish question, as grasped fundamentally by the Jewish nationalist movement, was in no way set before the nations. Jewish nationalism helped blur and cloud it over. And had it been raised, could there have been any avoiding the one possible solution—a solution in a land capable of sustaining initial ethnic settlement?

Assuredly the nations are capable of feeling and comprehending the Jewish dilemma, which is also their own problem, but not the question of the fate of Jewish civilization. Even the ceding of a "national home" constituted a sincere effort to aid the redemption of the Jews. Of course, they were not aware of the change that had taken place in the mood of the nationalist movement, to wit, the triumph of spiritual nationalism. Exemplary non-Jews can, it is true, be fired by the goals of spiritual Zionism. Spiritual Zionism, however, cannot ever be grasped or felt by the general public as a real social issue. The astonishing reaction of the Gentile public— even in England, itself the guardian of the Mandate and the "national home"—to the bloody events of August 1929 in Palestine is explained thereby. Zionism, in turning its back on the question of the Exile, cut the ground from beneath its very feet. The Zionist movement became a romantic fantasy, not regarded by the world as necessary or indispensable.

Consequently, if the very effort in Palestine is not bringing about the endeavor of redemption, if it itself does not constitute the beginning of the end of exilic tragedy—it, too, will fade away. However, the boundaries of the redemptive movement are necessarily broader than the borders of Palestine. Zionism, which limited itself to Palestine, had to abandon the idea of redemption. If, however, the nationalist movement returns to its roots, to the aspiration for redemption, it will return of necessity to the territorial concept.

Does this concept constitute some kind of "betrayal" of Palestine?

Palestine, the land of Israel, will remain engraved forever upon the people's soul, and the community arising there will undoubtedly constitute the heart of the Jewish people wherever they may be. The sacrifices the people have made for its sake have not been in vain. However, the solution to the problem of the Exile is not to be found here. Another dream was always bound up with the age-old golden vision of a return to the land of Israel—a silver dream of a wondrous Jewish kingdom, the kingdom of the "ten tribes" or a kingdom of the "red Jews" beyond "the Sambation." This hidden "land of the Jews" also occupied a place in the Messianic vision. It was a second "land of Israel" for the people, a land of longed-for, imagined redemption. The territorial idea is, therefore, not completely new; only the religiously oriented concept of redemption never allowed it to take real shape. This is not the case with the movement for redemption. History has imposed this attempt upon the Jewish people—finding a new national estate after two thousand years of wandering. No romanticism can free it of this decree.

The idea of redemption is at root neither religious nor political, but a social-national concept. Politics is only the means, and one means, toward attaining the end, but is not itself the end. Not a "Jewish State" but a "Jewish land" a national territory for the Jews, is the goal. Political independence or autonomy as the natural desideratum of any ethnic group can be a complementary aspiration of the redemptive movement, one that rounds out the idea of redemption; but it is not itself the primary, vital goal. The concept of redemption does not come to belittle "spiritual" endeavors or preach to the nation a new ideal of "manual" labor, as Ahad Ha'am claimed in opposing Herzl. One cannot level the well-known accusation that at best the Jews will establish a small state along the lines of Bulgaria or Serbia, one not worth the effort expended. It is not the state that is the fundamental, popular goal of the aspiration for redemption, but—deliverance from the state of alienation, from this poison infecting the Jewish people alone. Does "so meagre a redemption as this" comprise "payment" or "compensation" to the Jews for the torment they have undergone in Exile? This world does not render to any nation or individual "payment" for his suffering and labors. Who will give the farmers "payment" for all the generations of slavery and degradation? Who will render "payment" to the proletariat for its misery and poverty? What "payment" can be rendered all the poor of the earth, all the oppressed with their tears? Man is compelled to redeem himself from the evil confronting him in all its manifestations. The war of the Exile is warfare between national groups. Such wars have existed from the day man first appeared on the face of the earth, and its victims have been beyond number. The Exile is one of the most corrupt sources of this evil, and it is incumbent upon the nation of the exile to redeem itself and the world from this evil without any special payment or reward. What is to be done, though, seeing that there can be no redemption from the exile without national migration? Such a migration has no ultimate "end" at all. Its purpose is to save a nation or group from the straits in which it finds itself, whether through natural disasters or pressures of another people. National migrations are commonplace in human history and in themselves do not constitute tragedies. Of course, a people does not turn wayfarer unless it feels the heavy hand of necessity upon it. However, if it has hope in its heart, its migration has something of a creative act in it. The *Mayflower* pilgrims, the fathers of North American settlement, were forced to leave their homelands, but created a whole new world. The Jewish tragedy does not lie in the necessity of wandering, but the lack of willpower and inner strength for a redemptive enterprise. We cannot imagine, however, that the national will, can only be aroused through the influence of the "historic strength" of the land of the past. The hammer blows of the Exile will forge that will. The new exile of the age of nationalism has imposed upon the people the obligation of acquiring a "homeland." This new reality calls for us to assimilate completely, forbids us to wander forever in alien lands. For one hundred and fifty years our people has been writhing in agony struggling to free itself from the curse of its alien state. This is a new drive in Jewish history. Heretofore, the people considered foreign domicile as an incontestable decree, operative until history's end. The search for a "homeland," the desire to acquire a "homeland" through assimilation is the hallmark of the era. However, the people cannot pay the price for a "homeland" in alien lands: they cannot assimilate to the point of losing their identity. Whether from will or of necessity they will labor strenuously for national redemption. However, this path to redemption is a new one, and no one knows what the Jewish people will yet endure until it finds its way to salvation.

The concept of the permanence of the Exile, the recognition that the exile of Jewry cannot be ended through assimilation, contains the most decisive, the most forceful repudiation of the Exile, a repudiation flowing from the national will as an absolute imperative to the people to free themselves from the perverseness of alien life through a national undertaking. This repudiation differs from that negation of exilic life that undercuts the foundations of the national redemptive movement and proclaims assimilation as the ultimate solution to the Jewish question. This repudiation, while encompassing the absolute imperative to combat the Exile, also obliges the nation to work for national revival in the Diaspora; for this viewpoint does not hold that redemption is the frantic work of a few individuals racing to save their souls or the people's "soul" from national destruction decreed upon the Diaspora. This viewpoint asserts that redemption is the need of the nation, of its every component whether they acknowledge that need as yet or not. Consequently, the work of redemption necessitates national endeavor in the Diaspora, for Jewry in its masses will remain there indefinitely. The task is not a temporary duty of guarding ruins, but a generations-long labor of building and renewal whose goal is the rebirth of a civilization and the national unity of all Diaspora Jewry wherever they may be for the purpose of redemption. Repudiation of the Exile as an absolute national imperative does not look to an end of the Exile through assimilation nor does it want to save the people from the Exile's termination. It envisions the endurance of the Exile and wishes to save Jewry from their eternally alien status. This movement does not believe in the dream of the "Messianic ghetto" but aspires to building a spiritual "ghetto" to underlie the aspiration toward redemption. This movement combats assimilation first of all from an awareness that assimilation is a vain effort that cannot bestow upon the Jewish group a territory, a "homeland"; and that Jewry can fulfill the task laid upon it in our time, finding a "homeland," only through a national undertaking. Therefore, it is not via assimilation that the Jewish people will be saved but through national revival, whose beginnings lie in a cultural revival and an awakening to the idea of redemption. The nationalist movement is thereby set on its true historic foundation and is confronted with the awesome depth and gravity of its mission. It has not been generated through passing travail or the death throes of a people, but through the oppression of an ancient fate. It has not arisen to solve vain fantasies of daydreamers but to find a solution to an evil and ancient problem, one of blood and fire and shame and slavery and an endlessly abysmal existence—the problem of the eternal Jew.

JUDAISM FOR THE NATIONS

Erich Isaac

The Messianic dimensions of Judaism cause embarrassment, most frequently, to Jews. The embarrassment does not imply any diminution of enthusiasm for the implications latent within the doctrine, but as often as not Jewish Messianism is confined either to private theological fantasy or released in secular disguises—social activism or revolutionary politics.

The considerable value of Erich Isaac's suggestive essay, "Judaism for the Nations," is that he raises the issue of Messianic obligation in a context at once wholly relevant to the predicament of modern Judaism and accurate to the situation of peoples throughout the world who may be disposed to receive it. The essay is neither programmatic nor polemical and in so far as it eschews these inflammatory alternatives it is both harmless and insidious—harmless because it permits the reader to ignore its significance if he chooses, and insidious because its argument is so quietly persuasive.

What I particularly admire about his thesis is that it commands that the reader adopt a thoughtful theological position: he must either view the Jewish mission to the nations as one of passive witness and even support for the outgoing expansiveness of other daughter religions—Christianity and Islam, leaving to them (and even more specifically only to Christianity) the task of diffusing the teaching of One God and his moral imperatives (following Franz Rosenzweig's view of Judaism as a religion in ontological stasis *with* God and Christianity as a religion in constant process *toward* God);

or else, if denying the passive-witness function of Judaism, recognizing that Judaism has an obligation to move out amid the nations, to bring its light to them, and to actively seek and convert.

Of course, the crucial question which Isaac poses is that of the willingness of the Jewish people to assume the burden of proselytization. The traditional foundations for a conversionary posture are clear, nor does the unavoidable hostility of opposition communities raise more than pragmatic objections (indeed, Isaac rightly assumes the possibility of martyrdom befalling missionary Jews). The decisive question is whether Jews any longer believe enough in the meritorious truth of their religion to regard it as relevant to the nations in particular and the eschatological fulfillment of prophetic expectation in general.

There are several considerations which may be raised: the rabbis of the first century, those against whom the Gospels and Pauline Epistles direct their charges of proselytic zealotry, confronted a wholly pagan world, a world in which the promises of God were but dimly mediated and moral corruption widespread. In such a time the wisdom vouchsafed to Israel was salvific—the anguished in the pagan world found surcease in the clarity, precision, and directness of Jewish moral and religious practice. The pagan was genuinely "edified." The triumph of temporal Christianity and subsequently the missionary enterprise of Islam obliged even Jewish halachists to acknowledge that, however compromised and inadequate their doctrine, both Christianity and Islam served the interests of the true God. Judaism ceased to claim for itself the exclusive *obligation* of missionizing. History has freed the Jews from the necessity of insisting upon its unique and exclusive possession of saving truth. This did not free it from the conviction that the daughter religions were but copies and imitations—badly conceived and executed—of the original model of truth, but such rationalization, well-motivated by persecution and economic and political instability, missed the critical issue. Truth is truth; partial truth saves not at all. There is then a kind of moral revenge against the non-Jewish world for its failure to accede to Judaism and, implicit in such an interpretation, a view which may be described as *épater les goyim*.

What confronts the Jew today, if he wishes to take Isaac's thesis seriously, is that he rethink the question of his truth. If his truth is relative and complementary to the truths of others, if all theological truth is relative, it is obviously irrelevant—except in so far as one

would be interested in extending Jewish power through membership expansion—to proselytize. If the claim of Judaism to be *primus*
(whether *inter pares* or not doesn't matter) not only in the order of
history but in the order of truth, it seems incumbent upon us to
take up Isaac's challenge.

JUDAISM FOR THE NATIONS

ERICH ISAAC

In doing geographic fieldwork in Central Africa some years ago, I was struck, as so many others have been, by the variety of independent, nativist, secessionist churches—whatever the term preferred. I was also struck by the inappropriateness of the explanation which has so readily been offered to cover the proliferation of these groups: political protest. No doubt the element of political protest is strong, but it seems to me one makes an error by tagging as "political" or "religious" what in its nature is complex and partakes of many things.

While many of these churches are ostensibly Christian, students of these movements have noted that there is a strong "Judaistic" trend in some of them and indeed a few call themselves Jewish. Similar phenomena, of course, have occurred outside Africa. There are many signs that Christianity is now on the defensive and the question may be posed whether Judaism, untrammelled by a colonial image and perhaps helped by its own long history of persecution by Christianity, should pursue an active role especially in relation to those groups which spontaneously have declared themselves to be Jewish whether in this country or elsewhere.

Of course, not all students of the present moment in history subscribe to the view that Christianity has been steadily losing ground. Kenneth Scott Latourette has declared: "We live in one of the great days of the Church. Thanks to the inherent power of the Gospel and the labors of our predecessors, the Church is now represented in almost every land and among nearly every tribe and people." This triumphant statement is hedged and qualified by Latourette in his subsequent work, but it represents a widespread view of the achievement of Christianity and the attainment of its self-imposed task, formulated in the exuberant fashion of the nineteenth century as "the evangelization of the world in this generation." Certainly Christianity, a missionary faith from its earliest stages, has achieved a farther reach than any other religion has ever enjoyed. In our own generation Afghanistan, Nepal, and the Mongolian People's Republic are the only countries without organized and visible Christianity. Again, in the words of Latourette: "In our generation, for the first time in history, the church can be called global."

In contrast, Judaism, viewed in a spatial perspective, has an incomparably less impressive territorial hold and for a variety of reasons has been barely able to hold its own. Jewish communities in new areas have generally been established by a process of refugee colonization. Although the attempt to convert to Judaism is not contrary to Jewish law, it has been so uncharacteristic in the last fifteen hundred years that Judaism has come to be considered in the mind of Jew and Gentile alike as a nonproselytizing religion.

There is, however, another light in which Christianity and its achievement can be regarded: as a religion pagan in its fundamental conception, reinforcing the ancient paganisms which it ostensibly replaced, having very limited success outside what became its European home and even there severely threatened today by secular ideologies and attitudes, and always harboring within it a Judaic impulse—potentially perhaps, for some Christians at least, capable of becoming actively Jewish.

Despite the high ethical and moral systems of the Christian teachers and in spite of millennia of Christian thought regarding the mystery of the event which brought about Christian salvation, that event is a mystery of the pagan world from which Judaism removed itself. In its narrative the mystery recapitulates the ancient "truth" of the agricultural hearth of the Near East—the death and resurrection of the God. In centuries of sometimes staunch and occasionally wavering opposition, Judaism managed to distance itself from cults celebrating the resurrected deity, whether as Marduk, Tammuz, Osiris, Baal, etc. Certainly the war was joined: "After the doings of the land of Egypt wherein ye dwelt, ye shall not do; and after the doings of the land of Canaan, whither I bring you, ye shall not do" (*Levit.* 18:3).

In the early centuries of Christianity, by a peculiar irony a Jew served as the vehicle for the triumph of the very myth against which the Jews had fought so long. Kyrios Christos was ascendant over Serapis, Mithras, Dionysus, Sabazios, etc. Students of the religious history of the Greco-Roman period such as Bousset and Gunkel err when they confine their analysis of Christian roots to that period, for the roots are very ancient. But they are probably right in judging Christianity "further removed from Jesus than Jesus himself is removed from the most noble figures of Jewish piety." It was the discoveries of the historical school that led Overbeck to observe: "Only madness can allow Christianity to begin with Jesus as an historical person."

Christianity triumphed over its rival versions by a combination of political accidents, the subversion of long-established Jewish channels of propaganda, the immediacy achieved by the attachment of the myth to a recent historical figure, and the ease with which the new religion could accommodate itself to similar pagan mythologies in the areas which it rapidly colonized. Pagan festivals were continually being incorporated into Christianity. Purification, Annunciation and Assumption were introduced in the sixth century, All Saints and Nativity in the ninth, Conception and probably Trinity in the tenth, and All Souls in the thirteenth century. Bede himself reports that the pagan lustrations around the fields which took place in February in England before the adoption of Christianity to ward off spirits were in his time, the earlier part of the eighth century, celebrated by "processions in which lighted candles are borne in memory of that divine light which has illuminated the world."

All religions carry within them survivals and remnants of the past and borrow from other religions. But while Judaism, like Christianity, has its pagan elements, what is important about Christianity is that the attempted reinterpretation of pagan rite and myth was handicapped by the fact that these were incorporated into a religion whose hard core was a pagan mystery. In this lay the hazard of such tactical maneuvers as the conversion of temples into churches recommended by Gregory the Great to Bishop Mellitus and the error of theologians, such as Karl Adam, who have assumed that the worship of saints became permissible only because Christianity was so firmly rooted that there was no danger that the saints, themselves often in their origin gods, would be worshiped as such. Actually, of course, the reasons why saints are unknown in early Christianity is that the early Christians were Jews or lived in the immediacy of a faith that had not yet distanced itself from Judaism. Saints became absorbed not because Christian faith had become so strong that allowances could be made without danger to faith but because the new Christians were pagan. But in some ways the church did shatter pagan world views. The process of Christianization led to a de-deification of the world in so far as gods with strict territorial attachments were banned or reinterpreted. Pagan food prohibitions were at least in principle abandoned as were holy days and weeks. In regard to all these, "Christian freedom" was proclaimed and the world and God were separated in a polar relationship. Yet at the same time that the Church defined itself as the body of Christ—in other words from the divine rather than the worldly pole—it remained tied to the Jewish idea that the kingdom of God is for this world ("Thy will be done on Earth as it is in Heaven"). In order to free the world from the Christian secularization the Church itself bestowed, the Church sets out to conquer it. Thus the Church itself becomes secularized and acquires the paraphernalia of a political institution *in imitatio imperii per sacerdotium,* availing itself in its territorial expansion of the devices of empire. Christianity thus fell into the dual traps of paganization and secularization.

As to its territorial expansion, Christianity has had negligible impact upon areas occupied by older universal religions. This is true in the Buddhist as well as in the Hindu world. No amount of dwelling on the truly heroic sacrifices involved in the planting and maintaining of Christian communities in these lands can obviate the fact that the efforts were largely in vain. Further, where Christendom confronted in open conflict one major religion, Islam, it lost more than half of the territory it held. It is also noteworthy that in Islamic areas that fell under European imperialist control in the last centuries, as for example French North Africa or Russian Central Asia, Christian missionary success was notable for its absence. Islam was able to take advantage of European pacification of pagan tribal territories in Africa and Asia to effect its own conversion among primitive pagan groups.

Successful establishment of Christianity outside Europe took place mainly in the Western Hemisphere, Australia and New Zealand. This achievement was facilitated by the total or partial eradication of native peoples, either by planned campaigns of liquidation or sporadic unplanned warfare or simply by European settlement with its introduction of disease, destruction of native economic resources, and the totality of effects generally enumerated in discussions of cultural breakdown in culture-contact situations. While it was not Christianity that was responsible for the evils of colonization, many a missionary thought of the words of Paul, "the good that I would I do not, but the evil which I would not I do." Generally speaking, in the Indo-Iberian culture-region of the Western Hemisphere, because of restrictive emigration policies of Spain and Portugal, native survival rates were comparatively high. The introduction of Negroes and biological interchange between the major population groups changed the racial physiognomy of Indo-Iberia and its cultures as well. The societies of the area are statistically largely Christian; in reality their religions range from West African cults through more or less intact Indian religious to various syncretic cults.

The peoples of Africa, unlike other populations that came in contact with Europeans, proved resistant to biological annihilation. Christian missions made some of their finest efforts in the attempt to convert Negro Africans, but again, in spite of heroic effort, even the non-Islamic part of Africa cannot be claimed for Christianity. Notable successes were achieved in Sierra Leone and Uganda, which added its share of martyrs to Christianity, but on the whole, outside of areas of substantial European settlement, in spite of the profusion of mission stations, the impact remains minimal. There is an African Christianity, but with the exception of the native ministry (and not always excepting that) the congregants have not been severed from their tribal religions. The backbone of Christianity, at least as Christianity is more commonly recognized, remain Christians of European origin.

Finally, in the areas in which Christianity was substantially formulated, Mediterranean, Central and Western Europe (I am ignoring here the old North African and west-southwest Asian centers which have been lost through medieval and more recent events or, where surviving politically, are theologically dormant), widespread and open defections from Christianity have occurred. In Eastern Europe and the U.S.S.R. the successor churches of Latin and Byzantine Christianity share more or less the fate of all religious bodies and doctrines in the Communist world. Byzantine successor churches outside of the Communist realm may well be called "the sick man of Christendom."

Perhaps in summary it can be said that outside of Christian Europe, though the Christian missionary is everywhere that he is not excluded by law, successful establishment of Christianity has, with minor exceptions, taken place in areas of important European settlement. In this Christianity differs from Islam, whose realm was vastly expanded by Turks, Malays, Chinese, etc. without the presence of large colonies from the older Arab world of Islam.

Within Christianity there have of course always been Judaistic impulses. These impulses manifested themselves in Anabaptism and the Hussite uprising, with politically greater success in Protestantism, and perhaps even earlier in the Gnostic and Manichaean movements. It is also very possible that the social revolutions of the eighteenth, nineteenth, and early twentieth centuries derived in a cultural-historical sense from the Jewish Bible with its demands for recognition of the sanctity of life and the God-given rights of the individual and a view of the nature of man of great revolutionary potential. While every uprising or *Jacquerie* that occurred in Europe cannot be derived from ancient Israel, the principle of overturn to rectify a world gone astray has as one important origin the Biblical promise, "and the crooked shall be straight and the ridges shall become valleys" (*Isa.* 40:4).

Within the areas to which Christianity has spread and where there are no Jewish communities, movements have developed within Christianity some of which have specifically identified themselves as Judaic, or have been identified, sometimes with derision by Christian students of these phenomena, as "Judaistic." The proliferation of sects is today nowhere more evident than in Africa, where in South Africa alone there are more than seventeen hundred functioning "prophetic movements" estimated to include about a million members. To some extent the reason for this development is sectarianism within "older" Christianity: in 1938 there were no less than forty mission societies—excluding Catholic orders—at work in southern Africa alone.

The independent churches of South Africa today have been grouped into Ethiopian, Zion, and Bethesda types. The Ethiopian churches seceded from their parents bodies on racial grounds as well as on doctrinal and ritual issues. The Zion churches are primarily healing churches with much stress on purification rites, glossolalia, and cures for disease. The Bethesda churches are a "Zionist" variant centered mainly on baptismal-pond purification rites. The Ethiopian movement has no connection with the Ethiopian Christianity of Abyssinia but derives its name from *Psalms* 68, especially verse 32: "Ethiopia shall hasten to stretch out her hands unto God." The Zion churches take their name from Zion City, Illinois, where the American Negro churches of this type were founded, but in the present mythology of these churches the name signifies a claim that they are the original possessors of the Bible. This claim, indeed, is nearly universal in the African churches. Of course, there are political motives in the appearances of these churches. There was a marked increase in membership in South Africa after the Native Lands Act of 1913. There are personal elements too, for in a society doomed to political inactivity the road open to personal ambition and sometimes wealth was religious leadership.

That these movements are nativist has often been stressed in detailed studies. In Africa and elsewhere such religious organizations appear as precursor phenomena of native nationalism—a fact recognized as early as 1904 in South Africa in the worried discussion about the Ethiopian program, when signs of a political underground were suspected in the formation of separatist African churches. Nativist is the stress on one's own cultural identity and contribution even where the content and form of the movement are clearly foreign: the rejection of Christian injunctions as corruption of Biblical revelation where the Christian doctrine interferes with old tribal institutions (e.g., polygamy, circumcision, etc.) ; the creation of elaborate rituals and taboos construed from Biblical texts and far more comprehensive than the Sunday and holy day rituals of the churches; and the reinterpretation of old tribal social structures in terms of Biblical social structure.

The self-identification with old Israel flows partly from the circumstances in which the African of southern Africa finds himself today. The Exodus narrative inspires the native church leaders to become a "Moses for these Israelites," to call themselves Israelites and observe the Sabbath instead of Sunday (e.g., "The Church of God and Saints of Christ" in Natal) . It has inspired self-emancipatory proclamations like those by John Masowe (d. 1932) , head of the Apostolic Sabbath Church of God (the "Korsten Basketweavers") of Port Elizabeth, who refused to accept unskilled laborers in his movement, for "You are Israelites and should not work as slaves for non-Israelites." Another leader, Enoch Mgijima, after the Native Land Act (1913) called his dispossessed flock Israelites and their enemies Midianites (English) and Philistines (Boers). The struggles against these archenemies of God's people had revealed one thing to Mgijima—their Jesus was clearly not the God of the displaced: the Lord of Hosts was. Isaiah Shembe (1870–1935), the founder of the *nazirites* (*ama nazaretha*), imposed all the Biblical restraints of *nezirim* on his flock and in 1920 abjured Christ and Sunday observance, choosing instead Israel's God, and the Sabbath, "For there is no other name/by which we can be saved./ Only the name of Jehovah/ by which we can be saved."

While a variety of forces have gone into the making of the separatist independent or prophetic churches, to interpret them as strictly political protests, or, even as Katesa Schlosser does, as an outgrowth also of economic distress or personal ambition and only "religious in the rarest cases," is to ignore the Messianic character and the idea of judgment as well as religious ideas concerning the nature of man manifest in such movements. The prophets are often driven men who set forth on their mission according to an inward vision or dream which is not in fact generally related to prevailing external conditions. Even where overt conflict with the European results, one cannot willy-nilly attribute it to anticolonial sentiment. The clash of the Bensu sect's adherents with the British police in 1932 was the result of a march on Accra to liberate the prisoners of Ussher Fort prison because of the sect's reading of *Isaiah* (58:6): "Let the oppressed go free." It was this more than anti-British sentiment which sparked the action. One must agree with C. G. Baeta's judgment on much of the literature concerning "separatism": "It must be remembered that those who assembled the data at present available have been, for the most part, persons primarily interested in, and on the lookout for, any happenings which might have political import. Personalities and groups in whose activities no such significance is discernible would tend to be ignored, or only smiled at indulgently." Baeta's description of Ghana's sects as engaged in "an all-out effort to probe the reality of spiritual things" is applicable to many of the churches of southern Africa as well, where the political situation has masked the genuine religiosity of leadership and followers to outsiders. All the same objections and more hold true for views of these movements as solely the product of cultural tensions, conflicts and psychological upheavals. True, the churches provide a home for the detribalized and uprooted, but the leadership is apparently quite self-confident and practical, taking in hand what they consider to be their job of leading and healing. It further must be remembered that "prophetism" is a perennial phenomenon in Africa and not a product of present-day conditions alone. What is unique to the present situation is the merging of a perennial African phenomenon with Messianic and eschatological traditions that originated in ancient Israel.

I have dwelt on Africa at length even though there are similar, if less numerous, prophetic movements, separatist sects, and independent indigenous churches among the peoples of the Pacific, the West Indies, South America, and the Indians of North America. While in general clear self-identification with the Jews is not found, there are examples of this too, as in the repudiation of Christianity by the Maoris in 1864 and the emergence of the Hau-hau movement which bitterly fought the British troops and settlers of New Zealand. The prophet Te-Ua regarded himself as a new Moses and was also called Tiu—or Jew. Jehovah was the name of the Supreme deity of the cult, and Te-Ua asserted that Maoris and Jews were children of the same father. The identification of Maoris with Jews was accepted as fact. When the Hau-hau assaulted a British ship (1865), an Anglican priest aboard was hanged and the crew was imprisoned, while Captain Levy was set free. "The God of the Hau-hau protects his Chosen People," and while whites were regarded as enemies "unlimited haven and hospitality were offered to a Jew."

Jews have thus far failed to take an attitude toward such movements as Jews. This is all the more remarkable in view of the general eminence of Jews in anthropology and sociology, although perhaps not so surprising in that many of these authorities chose these fields because of their own Messianic—if secular—promptings. But traditional Jewry also has taken very little interest in Judaizing movements, although there are clearly reasons why it might have done more. The Jew, who has suffered so much under the Christian heel and thus shares to some extent the historical experience of all those who feel themselves crushed by the European-Christian world, might have seized the opportunity of trying to make those "Judaic impulses" that developed independently of Jewish instigation explicitly Jewish.

Of course, in the last fifteen hundred years Judaism has become almost completely defined as a nonmissionizing religion. Yet this was not always so. The preoccupation of the Torah with proselytes is intense and presumably reflects efforts at conversion in ancient Israel. With hammering persistence and but little variation, the refrain of "the one law that applies to the home-born and to the proselyte" is repeated in the Hebrew Bible. The Tannaitic Halachic *midrashim* stress that the rule holds even for commandments and ordinances which do not explicitly refer to the proselyte, and that the words of the covenant made on the steppes of Moab: "Neither with you only but with him that is not here with us this day" (*Deut.* 29:14–15) refer to future proselytes who by virtue of this formulation can regard themselves as if they had stood among the covenanting congregation. The Tannaim also sought to give a wider meaning to statements which might be taken in a restrictive sense as pertaining only to blood descendants of the Patriarchs. Thus the confession of the first-fruit offering, *Deut.* 26:3–15, in which the Jew refers to the land which "the Lord swore unto our fathers to give us" is also incumbent upon the proselyte. For, as R. Yehuda stated: "He [the proselyte] offers [the first fruit] and confessed. For it was said to Abraham, 'father of a multitude of nations have I made thee' (*Gen.* 17:5); formerly you were the father of Aram, and henceforth you will be a father to all the nations that shelter under the wings of the *Shechina*." As children of Abraham, the proselytes are entitled to their share in the land, which had been given, as Ezekiel had earlier said: "For an inheritance unto you and to the proselytes that sojourn among you, who shall beget children among you; and they shall be unto you as the home-born among the children of Israel; they shall have inheritance with you among the tribes of Israel. And it shall come to pass that in the tribe in which the proselyte sojourneth, there shall ye give him his inheritance, saith the Lord God" (*Ezek.* 47:21–23).

The evidence points not only to the existence of large numbers of proselytes but also to the active pursuit of missionary activities. There is Matthew's incharitable observation: "Woe unto you, scribes and Pharisees, hypocrites! for ye compass sea and land to make one proselyte" (23:15). Also well known is the statement of

R. Eleazar b. Pedat and R. Johanan (*Pesachim* 87b) that the children of Israel had been scattered to make converts, a view they based on *Hosea* 2:25 and the irascible remarks of R. Judah (d.299) and R. Ashi (d. 427) concerning Jewish communities that made no converts (*Berakhot* 17b). Indirect evidence comes from prohibition of church council after council against Jewish proselytizing. In spite of the penalties, converts continued to come and were accepted, although active pursuit of proselytes had probably ceased in Christendom. Conclusive evidence as to whether active missionary efforts ceased completely early or later in the Middle Ages is lacking. When converts did come, their path to Judaism was made easier, as Rabbi Halevi of Regensburg observed, on the ground that "when the time has come to act for the Lord, they have violated The law" (*Ps.* 119:126). This same principle, deduced from the same text, was used much earlier in the Talmud, in the decision to allow writing down of the Oral Torah, which was perhaps also permitted with an eye to proselytizing and not just the Oral Torah.

That there have been ambiguities in the attitude to proselytes is perhaps to be expected. There is natural resistance to newcomers who are invested with the full rights of the old-timers. There are also ambiguous expressions regarding the proselyte, e.g., "Proselytes are hard on Israel like the scab." This may be an early example of Jewish humor which later humorless Jews have misinterpreted. The most likely explanation of the saying was offered by R. Abraham Ha-Ger, himself a thirteenth-century Hungarian proselyte, who commented: "Because the proselytes have studied the commandments."

The question then is not whether there is a proselytizing tradition in Judaism but whether that tradition should be revived. An argument against such a revival is that, although no serious doctrinal objections exist and although the expectation is clear that eventually all men will form one bond before God, there is no real sense of urgency that it is a task incumbent upon the Jews to save man. Indeed, the Written Law nowhere explicitly imposes an obligation to propagate it among the nations but rather records the setting apart of Israel as a holy nation. And although Jews have viewed their historical existence from different points of view, those views which attribute an active role to Jewry in the divine plan to achieve all men's salvation have been submerged. Jewry increasingly regarded itself as a witness to God's plan, or as His suffering servant. The Exile became theodicy. Anti-Jewish measures by Moslems as well as Christians have only given a certain inevitability to the triumph of this view. It is this viewpoint which is most deeply entrenched today in the circles from which Jewish missionaries would otherwise most logically be drawn. More serious is the almost unquestioning certainty of most Jews, even those who have merely a tenuous connection with Judaism, that theirs is not a proselytizing religion. A social-psychological attitude, itself the product of historical circumstance, receives a kind of secular sanctification. Exclusiveness and homogeneity are deemed desirable in themselves and a secular ethnicism is identified with the ontologic structure of Judaism. Yet Jews today carry the imprint of many racial types, a fact perhaps more visually obvious in Israel, but basically no less true in Europe or the United States.

But even if the obstacle of current Jewish attitudes were overcome, the problem would remain of the content of a Jewish mission. Would such a mission seek full-scale Halachic conversion (*Gerei Zedek*)? The problem is a real one, for sectarian Jewish missions could be a potential source of conflict within the Jewish community, and the present realms of mutual accommodation between Jewish groups, always shaky, would be threatened not less by missionary than by convert zeal. The experience with one Jewish sectarian mission to the Gentiles, Christianity, has been anything but happy. Any attempt to teach merely "Jewish ethics" would be bound to fail or be transformed, for ritual and ceremonial are essential to man as religious expressions. One of the chief characteristics of nativist churches is not the rebellion against ritual but against its scantiness.

Again, there is the problem of deciding whether a Jewish mission would be universal or confined to non-Occidental lands. The Roman Catholic Church, having now rejected the notion that Jews were or are deicides, reveals a liberalizing spirit which might receive a severe jolt if within a short period substantial numbers of Italians, for example, were to follow the path of San Nicandro. The fear of a sharp reaction would certainly act to deter Jews from pressing a mission in Catholic lands. For psychological and other reasons, Germany might be a fruitful ground for a Jewish mission. The Soviet Union might also yield an unsuspected harvest of converts—and Jewish martyrs. Although the Arab world would be a very desirable realm in which to pursue a Jewish mission, at this historical moment Judaism, even more than Christianity, cannot expect success there. Nevertheless, contact with Islam should be possible at its outposts, such as Malaya, Indonesia, Iran, or even Turkey.

The lack of missionary traditions would impose severe difficulties. Jews have nothing comparable to the missionary families from which recruits have come often for generations in Christianity. Funds for such work might be forthcoming, but seminaries would have to be created greatly superior to the present institutions of higher Jewish learning. What would be needed is really dedicated persons who would combine excellent religious training with thorough geographic, historical, and ethnological knowledge of a region and with a profession—whether medicine or carpentry. The movement would also have to be strong enough to withstand setbacks such as death of its emissaries in Soviet prisons or Congolese cooking pots.

Even more serious than any of these objections is the historical one: the experience of both Christianity and Judaism in Africa, for example, which would inevitably become a major arena for a Jewish mission, has been an unhappy one. Paganization has been rife, aided by the similarity of Christian rites and symbols to native African practices which are after all derived from the same prehistoric cultural substratum. The wealth of undigested symbolism, rites, and concepts already flooding Africa would make the absorption of any related Jewish contribution to an existing pagan structure all the more likely.

Finally, there is the very serious question whether Jews believe in Judaism sufficiently to convert anyone else to it, and whether secularism is not everywhere so strong that genuine conversion to religious beliefs is impossible or perhaps confined to one generation. The predicament of modern man is that, even where he is one of the large religious communities, he has not been touched by religious experience but is guided by habit and tradition. To the extent that faith influences action, it is part magic and part technolatry. Thus we have to do with true primitives, for as Ortega y Gasset would have it, we deal with "a primitive man, a barbarian appearing on the stage through the trap door, a 'vertical invader.'" Indeed, there is a difference, but the difference is in favor of the primitive. The primitive magician knows that there are limits to his ability, while modern man believes himself capable of everything, and what he cannot *yet* he will one day do. Is conversion possible in an age when neither the converter nor the converted really takes religion seriously? Of those who stride on Gasset's stage, some will wear the garb of religion, for they assume this role, but the individual does not really participate in it. He is not an individual, he is a wearer of hats. Of course, we have religious individuals, but they live in a society that, paying lip service to their beliefs, barely tolerates those who really believe.

Despite the hazards and problems for any Jewish mission, there remain crucial advantages. Six million Jews have died in the European furnace. Many thousands of others have chosen to give up Judaism actively or simply by ceasing to identify as Jews. Israel stands exposed, tiny as nations go even in this era of the explosion of nation-states, in a hostile region. There would be a political value in bringing about an identification of Africans and Asians, for example, with the Jews of Israel. Israel as a state is obviously under serious restraints in its contacts with these nations, but a Jewish mission would be able to work more freely. There is nothing wrong with a political motive for proselytizing; the forces that have determined whether Jews proselytized or not in the past have always been essentially political. Judaism makes no sharp distinction between political and religious realms. Politics in the ancient sense was religious, and the Kingdom of Heaven was for this earth. Josephus writes about the Jews of the early Roman period in Palestine who worked towards its coming, pleading to be freed from "the royal and other forms of [human] government, and to be allowed to serve God alone" (*Antt.* xvii. 11.2,304 ff.). The Kingdom of God in the Gospels carries the same idea, although the emphasis in Christianity came to rest upon the other-worldly kingdom.

Despite the triumph of secularism, or perhaps because of it, there is a search for religious identification, and there are areas today where the problem of what the identification should be seems strong. This is true in Africa and in Asia, and there in Japan perhaps especially. The motive for acceptance of Judaism might not necessarily be primarily religious but a desire to take on the historical experience of the Jews as a relevant one for the experience of many nationalities and many individuals who are in exile in their homeland. On a small scale there have been spontaneous expressions of this feeling without any Jewish promptings, e.g., the Black Jews in the United States. When it is taken to connote more than a political philosophy, secularism covers a variety of humanist, antihumanist, nihilistic, atheistic, etc. systems and doctrines which cannot be understood except as an outgrowth of the Occident's Christian and Jewish past. Secularism is quite uncharacteristic of most of mankind, and there is a question whether even in a post-Christian world a conscious secularism would take the place of the churches. The process of secularization may itself reach a limit characterized by noncommital notions of a "Supreme Being," vague toyings with East Asian religions and lapses into astrology and magic. Society, as Friedrich Delekat notes, becomes endangered by a series of what he calls subterranean movements. Even assuming secularism is totally triumphant, what then? It would be naive to believe that new forms of society will emerge without a new ethos and belief, and such ethos may well be religious.

From a theological point of view objections might well be raised to a large-scale Jewish missionary effort undertaken essentially for political reasons and directed to peoples who would accept Judaism not because they believe in the theonomic origin of the *mitzvot* but because they wish to identify with the Jewish historical experience. The only answer that could be made is that, for whatever reason converts should observe whatever Halachah would be given to them, the observance itself might be of value. Though with us pure formalism in the observance of custom is the rule and sentiment is usually aroused only by the violation of the custom, in itself indifferent, customs given as external norms may, and often by their observance do, give rise to conviction.

INTRODUCTION TO

THE PERSONAL MESSIAH

Steven S. Schwarzschild

Fittingly this anthology should close with Steven S. Schwarzschild's impassioned argument for the restoration to centrality of the doctrine of the personal Messiah. The issue is not Messianism, nor is it redemption, nor is it the Kingdom of God, but Messiah, Redeemer, and King—persons, not essences.

It is, of course, a convenience of the emancipated intellect to imagine that by transforming felt realities into concepts experience is made more objective, dispassionate, and scientific. The reluctance with which we confess to having feeling and the concomitant insistence that feeling, to be validated, must be construed as the outcome of sustained ratiocination is but one among many psychological self-deceptions that are commonplace to modern men. That the Messiah has suffered from our optimism, our historicism, and our scientism there can be no doubt.

Let me confess therefore, in this preface, that I believe in the coming of the Messiah, that I believe in the resurrection of the flesh and that I haven't the vaguest notion of precisely how God intends to accomplish these miraculous undertakings. Having confessed this, let me push further to explain something of my feeling. In part I base this conviction upon historical reflection: the extremity of history compels me either to affirm God as redeemer and justifier of his behavior or to completely disown him. I must believe that the silence of God—for reasons I cannot fathom, but which I am obliged to honor in dismay—is not gratuitous. Were I to believe that God's hiddenness, his distance and silence in the hours of this and other centuries when we have needed him, were either the result of God's anger and punishment of Israel (in which case I would loathe him as a tyrant and would willingly perish rather than be obedient to him) or else that he is indifferent (in which case his cruelty would undermine all my love for him), I should have no choice but to deny him or to declare him dead. Since I have no reason to accept the classical doctrine of retributive justice, nor can I believe his goodness compatible with indifference, I must conclude that his silence is maintained in the face of an awesome future, that God, like we who believe in his promises, is turned toward the future, toward the *eschaton*. The *eschaton* cannot be less magnificent than the brutalities that anticipate its achievement. What we await cannot be less than what we have endured. In the order of feeling I await what God has promised and believe what he has revealed.

This argument is from feeling, but it is theological argument. It stands within the circle of faith, not outside it. It says that God is my God and I believe in him, however much we disappoint each other.

THE PERSONAL MESSIAH

Toward the Restoration of a Discarded Doctrine

STEVEN S. SCHWARZSCHILD

Into the first blessing of the prayer, *Shmoneh Esreh,* liberal Judaism has introduced one change which is linguistically minor but doctrinally major. The traditional formulation—He "brings a Redeemer"—now reads, He "brings redemption." This changed liturgical formula persists in practically all authorized liberal prayer books to this day (including the "Conservative" version of Reconstructionism), although the theological reasons which induced the change were among the very earliest issues raised against Orthodoxy at the beginning of the nineteenth century.

Much, if not most, of the liberal Jewish platform has been modified in these one hundred fifty years, and the trend of such modifications has almost unexceptionally been in the direction of a gradual and limited return to the original, traditional position of Judaism. The doctrine of the peoplehood of Israel and the concomitant significance of the earthly Jerusalem for Jewish hopes have long been restored to non-Orthodox religious thinking; the meaningfulness of ritual and ceremonial has been emphatically reasserted; even the validity of the continuous authoritativeness of Jewish law, if not actually re-established, is certainly increasingly becoming a matter of major concern to Reform Jews. It is, therefore, a little surprising that almost the only basic claim of pristine Jewish liberalism which has not been subjected to this process of re-evaluation in the course of time, should be the doctrine of the Messiah.[1]

---

1. The only theologian who seems to have concerned himself with the problem, and he with his customary perspicacity and ardor, is the much neglected

The reason for this comparative neglect may well be that the doctrine of the Messiah superficially appears to be merely a matter of theory. The question whether the Messianic fulfillment is to be brought about by the instrumentality of a single, individual person or through the collective progress of mankind seems of little moment when put side by side with such pressing, concrete problems as Zionism, the homogeneity of the Jewish community, the observance of Jewish practice and obedience to Jewish law. If this assumption were correct, it would be perfectly proper to relegate so theoretical a question to the background. And yet, it is very easy to demonstrate that the Messianic doctrine is not academic at all but, on the contrary, exceedingly "practical"; perhaps it can even be proved that it, too, requires reinvestigation within the framework of contemporary, non-Orthodox Jewish thinking and life.

There were basically three reasons why liberal Judaism in the first half of the nineteenth century was moved to transform the doctrine of the personal Messiah into the doctrine of the Messianic age—or, to use the phraseology of the *Shmoneh Esreh* prayer, the doctrine of the Redeemer into the doctrine of redemption. These three reasons can be described respectively as antinationalistic, antimiraculous, and optimistic.

In the minds of the early reformers, lay as well as rabbinical, the foremost consideration in favor of the depersonalization of the Messiah certainly seems to have been the fact that they regarded the personal Messiah as inextricably interwoven with the hope of the eventual restoration of the people of Israel from the lands of the Diaspora to Palestine, the re-establishment of the Temple and the sacrificial cult. For the present, it implied the foreign character of Jews in the countries of their domicile. These promises, or implications, of the belief in the personal Messiah they rejected most strenuously. They had begun to receive civil rights in Germany and throughout Western Europe, where Reform had its origin; together with nonJewish liberals, they continued to agitate for expansion and completion of their citizenship rights; and they confidently looked forward to an early consummation of these aspirations. To declare, at this juncture of history, that they were still awaiting a person who would lead them from their present homes and reconsti-

---

Max Wiener, *Der Messiasgedanke in der Tradition und seine Umbiegung im modernen Liberalismus,* in *Festgabe für Claude G. Montefiore,* pp. 151–56.

tute them as a separate nation in a distant land struck them as aiding and abetting their antagonists who insisted on refusing them their civil rights on the grounds that they neither were nor wished to be members of their host-nations. Thus, in his report of the pertinent discussions at the Rabbinical Conferences of 1844–46, Philipson relates that Dr. Mendel Hess identified the personal with the "political" Messiah.[2] Even earlier, the Frankfort Society of the Friends of Reform, in the single substantive statement of its beliefs, had announced: "A Messiah who is to lead back the Israelites to the land of Palestine is neither expected nor desired by us. The nonexpectation is understandable and, in this context, logical; the undesirability evokes the ironical picture of the Messiah appearing in Frankfort and being received at the city gates by a delegation of respectable Jewish citizens with the urgent request kindly to remove himself since his presence was likely to obstruct current attempts at the complete emancipation of German Jews. We know no fatherland except that to which we belong by birth or citizenship." And, in another hemisphere as well, many years later, K. Kohler still says: "A complete change in the religious aspiration of the Jew was brought about by the transformation of his political status and hopes in the nineteenth century. The new era witnessed his admission in many lands to full citizenship on an equality with his fellow citizens of other faiths. . . . He therefore necessarily identified himself completely with the nation whose language and literature had nurtured his mind, and whose political and social destinies he shared with true patriotic fervor. He stood apart from the rest only by virtue of his religion. . . . Consequently the hope voiced in the Synagogal liturgy for a return to Palestine, the formation of a Jewish State under a king of the house of David, and the restoration of the sacrificial cult, no longer expressed the views of the Jew in Western civilization. The prayer for the rebuilding of Jerulsalem and the restoration of the Temple with its priestly cult could no longer voice his religious hope. Thus the leaders of Reform Judaism in the middle of the nineteenth century declared themselves unanimously opposed to retaining the belief in a personal messiah. . . . They accentuated all the more strongly Israel's hope for a Messianic age, a time of universal knowledge of God and love of man, so

---

2. *The Reform Movement in Judaism*, pp. 5, 122, 173–80.

intimately interwoven with the religious mission of the Jewish people. . . ."[3]

It may be taken for granted that this particular reason for the abolition of the doctrine of the personal Messiah in liberal Judaism need no longer be taken seriously in the middle of the twentieth century. In the further pursuit of the argument quoted above, Kohler explains that Eastern European Jewry, still subject to disenfranchisement and persecution, continues to adhere to the Orthodox longing for a Jewish political restoration—that for this reason Zionism was born there as an answer to anti-Semitism—and that both of these situations are inapplicable to Western Europe in the first place, and must, in the second place, be made superfluous everywhere else by social progress. The irreconcilability of Zionism with liberal Judaism has long been given the lie in theory as well as in practice and need no longer be argued. But one additional observation must still be made in this connection before we proceed to the next point. It is surely an ironical paradox that Reform Judaism eliminated the personal Messiah because it was held that belief in him was inevitably accompanied by Jewish nationalism, while extreme right-wing orthodoxy of the *Aggudat Yisrael* brand rejected Jewish nationalism because it awaited the advent of this very Messiah! The *Aggudah* argued exactly the other way around: the personal Messiah will redeem the Jewish people; therefore, we must not attempt to anticipate by human action what he will do on divine instruction. Reform remained aloof from Zionism because it did not believe in the personal Messiah, the *Aggudah* remained aloof because it did.

This ironical paradox conclusively illustrates the essential *non sequitur* of Reform reasoning on this point: whether one believes in the personal Messiah or not has nothing whatever to do with Jewish nationalism. Theoretically, there is no reason why the personal Messiah must mean Jewish nationalism and the Messianic age must mean "universalism." It is just as possible, logically, to believe that the Messianic person will bring universal redemption rather than the ingathering of the Jewish people, and that the Messianic stage in human history will bring with it the national restoration of Israel rather than its complete absorption among the converted

---

3. *Jewish Theology*, pp. 388f.

nations of the world.[4] Practically speaking, the outstanding Reform Jews who, during the last half century, were also Zionist leaders do not seem to have been inhibited in their Jewish nationalism by their rejection of the belief in the personal Messiah.

In short, not only has the antinationalistic argument against the doctrine of the personal Messiah been refuted in theory and in fact, but it can be shown never to have been a cogent argument in the first place.

A logically more tenable argument against the personal Messiah was the belief that to await him implied in fact expectation of a miracle. Traditionally, in Bible, Talmud, and post-Talmudic Jewish literature, the functions which the Messiah would fulfill were regarded as being indeed miraculous: nature itself would be transformed to accord with moral requirements, human life would be rid of all natural or moral deficiencies, Israel and Judaism would be established in their proper place of spiritual primacy.[5] But such a doctrine ran counter, of course, to the positivistic, scientific outlook of nineteenth-century liberals. As Kohler put it straight-forwardly: "Our entire mode of thinking demands the complete recognition of the empire of law throughout the universe, manifesting the all-pervasive will of God. The whole cosmic order is one miracle. No room is left for single or exceptional miracles. Only a primitive age could think of God as altering the order of nature which He had fixed, so as to let iron float on water like wood to please one person. . . ."[6]

On closer analysis, however, even on its own premises, this objection to the doctrine of the personal Messiah on "scientific" antimiraculous grounds cannot long be maintained. In the first place, it is very difficult to understand why the achievement of the Messianic aims by many ordinary men—which is, after all, what the concept of the Messianic age boils down to—is any less miraculous than their achievement by one extraordinary person. Even if it be granted that the state of the world in Messianic times must be considered a miracle from our perspective, a notion which, as we

---

4. The identification of the personal Messiah with nationalism was based on the traditional identity of the Messiah as a descendant of David the King. Thus, the Jewish monarchy was believed to be involved and with it all the features of a reconstituted state.

5. Cf. J. Klausner, *The Messianic Concept in Israel*, Jerusalem, 5710, p. 138f.

6. Op. cit., p. 165.

shall see immediately, is not necessary to the doctrine as such, it presumably will be miraculous regardless of the agency through which it is brought about. In one sense, therefore, the transformation of the doctrine does not accomplish this declared aim of rationalization. In the second place, however, it is not at all certain that miraculousness is necessarily one of the ingredients of the Messianic state. Long before the nineteenth-century reformers came along, the medieval Jewish scholastic rationalists, at their head, Maimonides himself, on occasion objected to a supernatural interpretation of this tenet: "Let it not occur to anyone that in the days of the Messiah a single thing will be changed in the natural course of the world or that there will be any kind of innovation in nature. Rather, the world will continue to exist as it always has. . . . The Messiah will come exclusively in order to bring peace to the world. . . . How all these things will come about none can know until they have actually come about."[7] And yet they certainly anticipated the arrival of the person of the Messiah "though he may tarry, at any time." Therefore, as in the case of the antinationalistic objection to the doctrine of the personal Messiah, here, too, a complete *non sequitur* in the liberal argumentation must be noted: in fact, people, and often "better people than we," have believed in him without subscribing to his miraculous advent. In theory, Messianism is bound up with miraculousness either in both of its variants, the personal and the collective, or in neither. Thus, miraculousness cannot decide the issue between them.

We have stated that miraculousness is inherent in the Messianic doctrine even when it is reformulated in liberalistic, collective terms. Apart from the common-sensical argument already adduced to that effect, no better evidence can perhaps be added than that of Hermann Cohen, the man who was rightly described by Klatzkin as "a spiritual giant who guarded the inheritance of an impoverished generation,"[8]—the liberal generation. In him, liberal theology, including the depersonalization of the Messiah, reached its grand consummation—and if it failed here it must be regarded as having failed *in toto*.

History was for Cohen the infinite human process of striving for the ideal, and Messianism is the term designating the completion of

7. *Mishneh Torah,* Laws of the Kings, 12.1.
8. *Hermann Cohen,* Berlin, 1921, p. 11.

this infinite process. But how can infinity be completed? If, to use an analogy of which Cohen was fond, the ideal state of the future lies on an axis which the curve of human history approaches ever more closely but cannot actually touch, like an asymptote, then perfection is not an ideal whose reality is guaranteed at some point however far removed but a mathematical impossibility—and there is no guarantee of success at all; to the contrary, there is only a guarantee of relative failure.[9] The conception of the Messiah as an age leaves man swimming desperately in the ocean of history without a shore where he might eventually reach safety. Julius Guttman had pointed out that Cohen's depersonalization of the concept of God had deprived it of the ability to perform the real, historical, and ontological function which Cohen himself had ascribed to it.[10] The same must be said of his view of messianism.[11] In fact, the rational picture presents itself in this manner: that there may be such a thing as history at all, progress must be possible; for progress to be possible there must be a logical guarantee of the eventual attainability of the goal of progress; by Cohen's own admission the goal of progress, perfection, is unattainable through human endeavor. If, therefore, the goal is to be reached at all, it can be reached only by a divine intercession at the end-point of history. And once the theological, even the philosophical necessity of divine, i.e., miraculous intercession is established, it becomes absurd and arrogant to declare the concept of the miraculous, personal Messiah out-of-bounds. To say that the Messianic state must be miraculously brought about, if at all, but not through the miraculous agency of a person, is clearly a purely arbitrary assertion.

Another, usually unexpressed, reason may have contributed to the hostility which the reformers of the last century felt toward the concept of the individual Messiah. Maimonides had stipulated the belief in the bodily Messiah as a fundamental doctrine of Judaism and declared the denyer thereof to be a heretic.[12] Taenzer has convincingly demonstrated that the medieval philosopher, Joseph

---

9. Cf. *Rosenzweig*, Glatzer, p. 358: "According to the words of a philosopher whom I regard as an authority even greater than Hermann Cohen, what is not to come save in eternity will not come in all eternity."

10. *Die Philosophie des Judentums*, p. 351.

11. Cf. Cohen, *Religion der Vernunft*, pp. 276–313. I have discussed this point somewhat more lengthily in "The Democratic Socialism of Hermann Cohen," *Hebrew Union College Annual*, vol. XXVII, "Conclusion."

12. Cf. Thirteen Principles, last no.; *Mishneh Torah*, Laws of Repentance, 3:6.

Albo, relegated this doctrine to a very much lower level of Jewish obligatoriness. On this level, belief or disbelief in the personal Messiah by the individual Jew would be without effect on his full religious status.[13] In effect, Albo proclaimed not only that a Jew need not necessarily believe in the Messiah but actually, by implication, recommended against such belief. The historical conditions under which he lived explain his attitude. By his time, the doctrine had become a serious obstacle to Jewish theological self-assertion, for it was used to good effect by Christians in formal as well as informal religious disputations. "Also the others (!) make out of it [the messianic doctrine] a basic principle with which to refute the Torah of Moses."[14] Once the principle of an individual Messiah was accepted, and with the narratives of the New Testament difficult to refute in an age bereft of historical or literary criticism, the crucial issue between Jews and Christians seemed to become one of picking the right person to fit the messianic prerequisites—an unproductive quarrel at best. By eliminating the Messianic doctrine, Albo hoped to prevent further unconstructive controversies and even to strengthen the Jewish position which could then actually turn the argument around: the Messiah having been declared to be irrelevant to true religion, a religion which made him the central test of faith demonstrated its own unauthenticity.

From the Jewish point of view, the phenomenon of Christological Christianity is, of course, only one of many pseudo-Messianisms. By the nineteenth century there had been many such movements in Jewish history; some of them extremely unsettling. If enlightened, rationalistic, liberal Christians of that era were embarrassed by the traditional claims of Christianity regarding the historical Jesus, as indeed they were, how much more eager must liberal Jews have been to rid themselves of all the theological preconditions which might again lead, as they had done so often in the past, to the recurrence of enthusiastic messianic claims. One recalls Graetz's immoderate observations on the subject.[15] How much easier to answer the claims of traditional Christianity, than to dissociate oneself from Jewish pseudo-Messianisms and the entire Jewish

---

13. *Die Religionsphilosophie Josef Albo's,* pp. 34–37.
14. Albo, *Ikarim,* 1, 4.
15. Cf. *History,* vol. 10, pp. 190f., 312f., 387f. The Zohar, the source of much late Jewish messianism he never refers to other than as "the book of lies."

Messianic doctrine, and thus prove the rationality of Judaism. In short, this was Joseph Albo in nineteenth century disguise.

Perhaps it is no longer necessary to show both the uselessness and the invalidity of this procedure. It is truly a case of throwing out the true gods together with the false ones. If a doctrine is to be rejected because it can be or even has been abused, the very belief in God must be dispensed with, since men have also often represented themselves as God and created havoc by the falsehoods announced in his name. Furthermore, Buber quotes the pointed Chassidic story which compares the pseudo-Messianic movements to wet compresses that keep the patient awake until the doctor comes: "When God saw that the soul of Israel had fallen sick, he covered it with the painful shawl of the *Galut*. So that it could bear the pains, however, He bestowed upon it the sleep of numbness. Again, so that it would not be destroyed, He awakens it each hour with a false Messianic hope and then lulls it to sleep again until the night will have passed and the real Messiah will appear. For the sake of this work, the eyes of the wise are occasionally blinded."[16] Franz Rosenzweig made the same point in a less anecdotal, more theological and poetic fashion: "The expectation of the coming of the Messiah, by which and because of which Judaism lives, would be a meaningless theologumenon, a mere 'idea' in the philosophical sense, empty babble, if the appearance again and again of a 'false Messiah' did not render it reality and unreality, illusion and disillusion. The false Messiah is as old as the hope for the true Messiah. He is the changing form of this changeless hope. He separates every Jewish generation into those whose faith is strong enough to give themselves up to an illusion, and those whose hope is so strong that they do not allow themselves to be deluded. The former are the better, the latter the stronger. The former bleed as victims on the altar of the eternity of the people, the latter are the priests who perform the service at this altar. And this goes on until the day when all will be reversed, when the belief of the believers will become truth, and the hope of the hoping a lie. Then—and no one knows whether this "then" will not be this very day—the task of the hoping will come to an end and, when the morning of that day breaks, everyone who still belongs among those who hope and not among those who believe will run the risk of being rejected. This

---

16. Quoted in *Israel-Volk und Land,* p. 31.

danger hovers over the apparently less endangered life of the hopeful."[17] Herein also lies the answer to those who will always worry: if the belief in the personal Messiah as such is granted, why not Jesus?

Underlying all these motivations for the depersonalization of the Messiah-concept lay an optimism about the future of the Jewish people and of mankind as a whole. This optimism resulted in the belief that, as already indicated, the redeemer had become not only impossible and undesirable, but also unnecessary. After all, the Messiah was logically and historically a product of need. In the former sense, the anticipation of his coming implied consciously and unconsciously that man by himself could not master his destiny or reach his goal. Instead, a divine agent would either have to bring about or at least complete the messianic, i.e., perfect human society. And historically it is true that, as Israel's historic situation became increasingly hopeless, the concept of the Messiah became increasingly supernatural, for the greater the need the more powerful had to be the person who would triumph over it. "The burden of exile narrowed their horizon. They could see no other way of redemption from their abject position than by supernatural events.[18] Or as Baeck put it impressively: "It was especially true in the centuries of despair: only by seeing before him a mirage was many a man able to procure the strength with which to keep on marching through the desert which life had become for him.[19] Now, in the nineteenth century, it was believed that such pessimism about the nature of man and the prospects of history had once and for all been refuted.

Certainly, the political development of the times seemed to indicate that the Jewish despair which had so largely formed the concept of the Messiah had become a thing of the past. Everywhere and increasingly Jews were being enfranchised and at least promised, often also given, equal rights with their fellow citizens. Physical persecution, except in some God-forsaken corners of Russia, had almost completely ceased. Liberal democracy was making headway everywhere in the West; material and technological developments

17. Glatzer, *Rosenzweig—His Life and Thought,* p. 350f.; cf. Rosenzweig, *Jehudah Halevi,* p. 239.

18. Greenstone, *The Messiah Idea in Jewish History,* p. 264f.

19. *The Essence of Judaism,* 4th ed., p. 273f.

were fast progressing. And even culturally, the mellowing of Christianity as evidenced by the new liberal theology, Unitarianism, ethical humanism and similar phenomena, persuaded the usually sober I. M. Wise that America would be Jewish within the foreseeable future. Thus Samuel Hirsch declared: "Everywhere the emancipation of mankind is being striven for so that a morally pure and holy life may be possible of being lived by man on this earth."[20] Auerbach agreed with him: "In our days the ideals of justice and the brotherhood of men have been so strengthened through the laws and institutions of modern states that they can never again be shattered; we are witnessing an ever nearer approach of the establishment of the Kingdom of God on earth through the strivings of mankind."[21] Herzfeld chimed in: "The conference must declare what it means by redemption; yes, it should state that we are now entering upon the period of redemption. Freedom and virtue are spreading, the world is growing better."[22] And, of course, the famous Pittsburgh Platform announced: "We recognize, in the modern era of universal culture of heart and intellect, the approaching of the realization of Israel's greatest Messianic hope for the establishment of the kingdom of truth, justice, and peace among all men."[23] In this respect, Wiener summarizes the spirit of the time trenchantly and convincingly: "The new generation was dominated by an almost too gay optimism. . . . Transcendent, eschatological ideas receded in the face of the confidence that this world would soon be the scene of divine justice within the moral life of humanity. By the latter was meant above all the completion of equality of civil rights in all countries—which was an understandable preoccupation, though it became embarrassing by being constantly overemphasized." He recalls that for Moritz Lazarus the outcome of the Dreyfus Affair was positively "a Messianic event." Wiener indicts this entire generation of shallowly optimistic, self-centered and self-deceiving leaders when he states: "If it is ever true that religious beliefs are the ideological superstructure of the economic-political conditions of society, then it was certainly true of this class. It interpreted and accommodated religious doctrines in

---

20. Ibid., p. 178.
21. Ibid.
22. Ibid.
23. Ibid., p. 356.

conformity with its enthusiastic attitude toward civil society which it regarded as final, eternal, and divine."[24]

This outlook no longer deserves a reply. The neoexistentialists, Jewish, Christian, and nonreligious, have effectively knocked down this straw man to build up a case for themselves. Rosenzweig, for example, reports the famous incident in which Hermann Cohen is supposed to have pleaded with him that he must expect the Messiah within no more than fifty years.[25] Thus, he wanted to reveal this vapid optimism for the self-deceiving hallucination that it was— and as a symbol his story serves well enough; although we must add that as a truthful report of Cohen's mind it is a thoroughly incredible tale. It belies everything that Cohen stood for in his affirmation of the infinite Messianic process, his violent rejection of all forms of eudaemonism, and even his definition of the Messiah itself. Nonetheless, that the contemporary pessimists have completely and justifiably deflated this hallucination cannot be disputed. We have learned for a fact that the nineteenth century was profoundly wrong in its vast overestimation of the social abilities of man. If persecution, pogroms and oppression are indeed the rationale for Messianism, then our age is, and by rights ought to be, the most Messianic age of all in the history of Israel.

If, then, we must discard the third main reason which the liberals of the nineteenth century proffered for the abolition of the concept of the personal Messiah, literally not one of their arguments has been found to withstand critical examination. Their antinationalism has been repudiated by Jewish history; their antimiraculousness has been refuted by the necessities of their own position, not to speak of the views of others; their optimism has been repudiated by general history. Furthermore, it turns out that at least two of their reasons were not logically constructed in the first place. In short but brutal fact, their case against the personal Messiah crumbles at the first touch.

We could end the argument at this point. Religious tradition must always be regarded as valid until, and unless, invincible reasons are brought forth against it. The reasons militating against the traditional doctrine under consideration have been shown to be

---

24. *Juedische Religion in Zeitalter der Emancipation*, p. 172f.; *Der Messiasgedanke*, op. cit., p. 153.
25. Glatzer, loc. cit.; *Jehudah HaLevy*, loc. cit.

anything but invincible, and we may, therefore, with good and calm consciences return to the original position. Ours is not necessarily the task to prove the doctrine positively; to refute its refutation ought to suffice. Nevertheless, without venturing to prove its tenability, there are a few hints which may be given toward the construction of the positive case.

The first is a mere technicality. The liberal prayer books of the last century have abounded, and still abound, with phrases which must, if they are to be intellectually acceptable, be interpreted very broadly by the Jews who use them. "The Torah of Moses" is as clear-cut an example as any, although there are many others. Do liberal Jews believe that "the" Torah was given to, by, or from Moses? As a matter of fact, the very ritual reading from the Torah has become a metaphoric act for most of them. A very high percentage, certainly well over half, of everything read from it, if it is to be acceptable at all, must be homiletically decontaminated of its original historical, theological, moral, or social intent. And nonetheless these things are retained—reinterpreted but retained. Yet the phrase "Who brings a redeemer" cannot be so treated; it must be changed!? All that was required to bring the traditional text into conformity with liberal belief was the interchange of a single letter of the Hebrew alphabet, an *Heh* at the end for a *Vav* in the middle of the word. But this had to be done through a surgical operation on the prayer book, when much more serious problems were solved with exegetical palliatives. We may assuredly draw two conclusions from this observation: (1) There was more to this than meets the eye; more fundamental interests were involved than those that were expressed; (2) A return to the original phrase is justified if only because it will violate no one's conscience; completely free exegesis will still be offered to anyone who wishes to take advantage of it.

In analyzing the views of Hermann Cohen, we pointed out the intimate connection between the belief in the personality of the Messiah and the belief in the personality of God. For him, as for the liberal mentality in general, the entire concept of personality as such was a terrible stumbling block. As Kierkegaard and existentialism never tire of pointing out, the existence of the individual personality defies all the universal and theoretical laws of science as well as of idealism. They, therefore, try to dissolve it into general propositions. God as an idea, the Messiah as an age—these are entities with which theoretical reason can deal. The persons of God and of the Messiah, on the other hand, are hard, stubborn, even—as it were—empiric realities that defy classification. But then, so does every individual. And thus, the depersonalization process does not stop with God or the Messiah so far as liberalism was concerned.

A change was likewise introduced into the second benediction of the *Amidah*. "Praised be Thou, O Lord, who bringest to life the dead" seemed to be a liturgical formulation of the doctrine of resurrection, and this doctrine was regarded as outmoded as the reference to the personal Messiah. Do we not know that the body decomposes in the grave? Where would physical resurrection take place in the spiritual world of God? Does not the belief in the eternity of the body imply a vast overemphasis on the material aspect of life? And so the modernistic arguments ran. Therefore, again the liturgical formulation was changed, and so remains to this day: "Praised be Thou, who hast implanted within us eternal life." In this manner, belief in the immortality of the soul was substituted for the concept of resurrection of the body.

The rejection of the belief in resurrection is closely connected with the rejection of the personal Messiah—not only because they both found expression at the very beginning of the *Amidah*. Ever since Ezekiel pictured the messianic rebirth of Israel in terms of the famous revived bones, one of the traditional marks of the advent of the Messiah in Jewish thought has been the resurrection of the dead.[26] "May the All-merciful make us worthy of the days of the Messiah and of the life of the world-to-come."[27] And at the Conference of American Reform rabbis in Philadelphia in 1869, the rejection of the one doctrine was immediately and logically followed up with the rejection of the other.[28] Thus, the depersonalization process has gone one step further: God is not a person but an idea or a force; the Messiah is not a person but an age; and man is not a person but a universal reason confined in an individualizing and debasing body—a state of affairs fortunately remedied in the hereafter!

Herein also lies the most important reason for our time for a return to the personalism of the Messiah. Not only have we reacknowledged the unitary character of the human person: if scien-

---

26. Cf. Greenstone, op. cit., pp. 57–60. Elbogen, *Judaica, Cohen Eestschrift,* p. 671 indicates that resurrection precedes the advent of the Messiah.

27. Grace after the meal.

28. Phillipsohn, op. cit., p. 263.

tific conclusions have any bearing on this discussion, they tend to assert the indivisibility, even the indistinguishability of "body" and "soul." Martin Buber's philosophy of dialogue is premised on the recognition of persons, human and divine, as the carriers of life. The outlook of the Bible which deals with "the whole man" is reasserting itself in the form of what is called "personalism." Baeck[29] describes this outlook in these words: "It is particularly true of prophetic thinking that it is far removed from abstract descriptions and instead envisages the figure of a real human being with its views and deeds. The prophets speak less of a future time than of a future person. The ideal of the future becomes for them an ideal personality. . . . The son of David is the future man. As a man of flesh and blood he makes real and vivid what the ideal man ought to be and will be." As Tillich puts it: "Ontology generalizes, while Biblical religion individualizes."[30] And specifically with regard to the Messiah, the "liberal" Wiener puts the case clearly: "It is always the great miracle, the emergence into overpowering visibility of the deeds of God Himself, which characterize the days of the Messiah— the expression of the personal shaping of world-history by the personal God. For this reason so much emphasis is put on the personality of the Messiah. . . . It is precisely in the belief in the Messiah that one can recognize the full vitality of a religiosity for which God is personality and His revelation the tangible guidance by means of miracle. One is inclined to say that at this point piety is most distantly removed from everything abstract, from conceptual ideology—and that it rather becomes faith in the true sense of the word, believing confidence in the revelation of concrete facts."[31] We have learned from religious as well as nonreligious existentialism, that all moral reality, as distinguished from nature or mathematics, is the reality of persons. Man, the person, is the *locus* of ethics, not ages, ideas, or forces. The Messianic age is a Utopia; the Messiah is a concrete, though future, reality.

Let us consider one last objection which will be raised against this view. It will be said again, as it has often been said in the past, that reliance on the Messianic fulfillment will lead to moral quietism and passivism. If men expect a divine agent to bring about

29. Op. cit., pp. 269f.
30. *Biblical Religion and the Search for Ultimate Reality*, p. 39.
31. *Der Messiasgedanke*, op. cit., p. 154f.

perfection, they will sit back, relax their own efforts toward the good, and leave to him the work they themselves ought to do. This has, indeed, often happened. Was it not a delegation of Orthodox rabbis of the *Aggudah* type who requested the British mandatory governor not to withdraw his troops since Zionism was human superorogation anyway, and the Messiah was to come in 1999? But the drawing of an improper conclusion does not mean that the doctrine ought be abolished. It ought rather be protected against false interpreters.

"Perish all those who calculate the end,"[32] was the motto of the Talmudic rabbis who opposed the view that the Messianic time was fixed mechanically without regard to the human contribution to its hastening. They taught emphatically that the arrival of the Messiah was dependent upon man's actions: if they were good it would be sooner, if evil—later. "God said: everything depends on you. Just as the rose grows with its heart toward heaven, so do you repent before Me and turn your hearts heavenward, and I will thereupon cause your redeemer to appear."[33] There is even the view, which commends itself on ethical grounds, that the Messiah will appear after the Messianic state has been established, leaving its attainment to humanity but guaranteeing its maintenance thereafter. Even Mendelsohn seems to have held this view.[34] The nineteenth-century proto-Zionist, R. Hirsch Kalischer stipulated the return to Zion as a prerequisite, not consequence, of the Messianic advent.[35] And even the man who was later to become one of the foremost and most radical leaders of American Reform, Samuel Hirsch, in the days before he went to greater extremes, advanced this same thought. "It is up to us to turn to God, for the Messiah cannot come before we have become completely good. . . . No, it is not the duty of the Messiah but that of the entire household of the vanguard against evil, the entire house of Jacob, to wage this battle on behalf of all the inhabitants of the world, and the root of Jesse cannot shoot forth out of its midst until it has fulfilled this duty and carried out its task."[36]

---

32. *Sanh.* 97b.
33. *Midr. Tehillim* 45:3; cf. generally, A. H. Silver, *Messianic Speculation in Israel,* "Opposition to Messianic Speculation," pp. 195–206.
34. Cf. Wiener, op. cit., p. 170.
35. Cf. Greenstone, op. cit., p. 267.
36. *Die Messiaslehre der Juden,* pp. 402, 404.

Therefore, not only is it untrue that the doctrine of the personal Messiah must necessarily lead to quietism. On the contrary, it can help in suppressing the peculiar modern variant of pseudo-Messianism. One of the most horrible and disastrous illusions to which modern men have fallen prey is that they have actually achieved the Messianic state. It is on the basis of this self-deception that our contemporary dictatorships have ruthlessly eliminated all dissent, for they maintain that dissent from perfection is, by definition, falsehood. Whereas in the Middle Ages pseudo-Messianisms operated around a central, individual pseudo-Messianic person, in our time it is characteristic of our collectivist and societally minded frame of references that pseudo-Messianisms take the form of national movements. More than ever, therefore, the absence of the person of the redeemer should constitute a constant warning against such blasphemous exaggerations. This warning is, furthermore, not without its applicability to the present Jewish world-situation. The Messianic undercurrent in the history of modern Zionism has in turn led to the far-reaching secularization of "the Messianic thought in Israel," as a result of which, as Leon Roth has pointed out, we no longer ask in the words of the Bible: "Who will recount the mighty deeds of God?" but rather in the words of the Israeli song: "Who will recount the mighty deeds of Israel?" What is even much more dangerous is the hazy notion floating through the minds of a not inconsiderable number of super-Zionists that the establishment of the State itself constitutes the Messianic fulfillment. Here lies the road to certain disaster! When Rabbi Kurt Wilhelm, formerly of Jerusalem and now chief rabbi of Sweden, and this writer dared point out in a series of articles that Jewishly there is a vast difference between *yeshuah,* historical salvaging, and *ge'ulah,* redemption, an Israeli newspaper attacked us vehemently as new *retestrabbiner!*"[37] If this journalist had only been waiting for the Messiah!

37. *Yedi'ot Chadashot,* October 3, 1950.

AFTERWORD

In the preparation and selection of the essays included in this reader, literally hundreds of essays were reviewed and complete runs of the major Jewish periodicals published in this country and abroad were consulted. I did not imagine that in making this selection I was doing more than providing a medium for constructing a theological dialogue, an antiphon of statement and editorial gloss, intended to exhibit to the reader something of the dynamics and vitality of contemporary, post-Holocaust Jewish thought. Obviously, this reader could have been expanded two or three times and issues passed over or only slightly (sometimes slightingly) discussed could have been presented. But there is a center to this reader and from that center I did not wish to depart into byways and thickets, however engaging or demanding. I have by and large ignored problems of the Jewish community as such, of liturgy and the arts (material is somewhat scant and thin here), of the theology of "the Death of God" (which I confess does not much interest me), although I refer several times to this movement in its psychopathological dimension; moreover, on many subjects it would have been possible to include a number of essays, each with varying strengths and differing contentions. This apologia is not designed to apologize, however, at all, but rather to underscore. What interested me in this selection was not objectivity, comprehensiveness, or dispassion. My whole view of the enterprise of Jewish belief is nonobjective (although certainly not subjective), specific (and hence not all-embracing), and quite passionate. Those authors whose essays I have selected for inclusion may well object to being present here as those whom I have omitted. The fault (as well as the strength) is my own responsibility.

NOTES ON CONTRIBUTORS

HAROLD ROSENBERG, art critic of *The New Yorker,* is the author of *The Tradition of the New* and *The Anxious Object.*

HANNAH ARENDT is the author of *The Origins of Totalitarianism, Eichmann in Jerusalem, On Violence* and many other works on politics and intellectual history.

LESLIE FIEDLER, literary historian and novelist, is the author of *The Image of the Jew in American Fiction, Love and Death in the American Novel* and *The Last Jew in America.*

HANS MEYERHOFF, until his death, was Professor of Philosophy at the University of California and editor of an anthology, *The Philosophy of History in Our Time.*

NAHUM N. GLATZER, Professor of Judaic Studies at Brandeis University, is the author of numerous works and is primarily responsible for the introduction and dissemination of the writings of Franz Rosenzweig in the English-speaking world.

WILL HERBERG, Graduate Professor of Philosophy and Culture, Drew University, is the author of *Judaism and Modern Man* and *Protestant–Catholic–Jew.*

J. L. TALMON, Professor of Modern History at the Hebrew University in Jerusalem, is the author of numerous works, the first in a series of which was *The Origins of Totalitarian Democracy.*

ERICH UNGAR, until his death in 1950, lived in England to which he had emigrated in 1933. Among his books, which frequently express a Judaic interpretation of ethics, were *Politik und Metaphysik, Gegen die Dichtung, Wirklichkeit, Mythos, Erkenntnis,* and *The Imaginaton of Reason.*

ARTHUR A. COHEN is the editor of *Arguments and Doctrines.*

STEVEN S. SCHWARZSCHILD, Professor of Judaic Studies in the Department of Philosophy, Washington University in St. Louis, is the author of *Franz Rosenzweig: A Guide for Reversioners.*

MONFORD HARRIS is Professor and Chairman of the Department of Jewish Studies at Rosary College, River Forest, Illinois.

LOU H. SILBERMAN is Hillel Professor of Jewish Literature and Thought at Vanderbilt University.

S. H. BERGMAN, Professor Emeritus of Philosophy at the Hebrew University, Jerusalem, is the author of numerous essays and monographs on philosophy in both Hebrew and German. His essay in *Arguments and Doctrines* was translated by Judah Hanegbi.

EMIL FACKENHEIM, Professor of Philosophy at the University of Toronto, is the author of *Metaphysics and Historicity* and *Paths to Jewish Belief.* His recent book, *Quest for Past and Future,* contains the two essays presented in this book.

DAVID BAUMGARDT is consultant in philosophy to the Library of Congress and is the author of many philosophical works, most of them in German. He was born in Erfurt, Germany, in 1890.

GERSHOM SCHOLEM is Professor of Jewish Mysticism at the Hebrew University. Among his works are the classic *Major Trends in Jewish Mysticism* and *On the Kabbalah and Its Symbolism.* His essay in *Arguments and Doctrines* was translated by Henry Schwarzschild from the *Eranos Jahrbuch* (XXXI, 1962) where it first appeared in German.

BARUCH KURZWEIL is the foremost Israeli literary critic and historian. The essay in *Arguments and Doctrines* has been translated from the Hebrew by David S. Segal.

IRVING KRISTOL, until recently an executive of a major New York publishing house, is coeditor with Daniel Bell of *The Public Interest.*

BEN HALPERN is Research Associate in Israelia Studies at Harvard University and is the author of *The American Jew* and *The Idea of the Jewish State.*

Notes on Contributors

ERNST SIMON, Israeli philosopher and educator, was born in Berlin in 1899. He was coeditor of *Der Jude* with Martin Buber and taught at Rosenzweig's *Freies Judisches Lehrhaus* in Frankfurt until his emigration to Israel in 1928. His essay in *Arguments and Doctrines* was translated by Moshe Decter from a much longer Hebrew version originally published in *Luach Ha-aretz,* an Israeli almanac.

JACOB TAUBES, who presently teaches in Berlin, has taught at Columbia, Harvard and Princeton. He is the author of *Abendländische Eschatologie.*

AHARON LICHTENSTEIN is a Professor of Talmud at Yeshiva University.

HANS JOACHIM SCHOEPS is Professor of the History of Religion at Erlangen University, Germany. Among his numerous books *Paul* and *The Jewish-Christian Argument* have been translated into English. His essay in *Arguments and Doctrines* was translated by Martin Greenberg.

YEHEZKEL KAUFMANN was until his death professor of Bible at the Hebrew University. In addition to his major work, *History of Israelite Religion,* abridged in translation as *The Religion of Israel,* he is the author of a two volume work, *Exile and Alienage,* from which the concluding chapter has been translated from the Hebrew by David S. Segal for *Arguments and Doctrines.*

ERICH ISAAC is professor of geography at the City College of the City of New York, with special emphasis on the geography of religion.

70 71 72 73 10 9 8 7 6 5 4 3 2 1